Excel® 2007 Formulas

John Walkenbach

Wiley Publishing, Inc.

Excel® 2007 Formulas

Published by
Wiley Publishing, Inc.
10475 Crosspoint Boulevard
Indianapolis, IN 46256
www.wiley.com

For general information on our other products and services or to obtain technical support, please contact our Customer Care Department within the U.S. at (800) 762-2974, outside the U.S. at (317) 572-3993 or fax (317) 572-4002.

Wiley also publishes its books in a variety of electronic formats. Some content that appears in print may not be available in electronic books.

Library of Congress Control Number: 2007920006

ISBN: 978-0-470-04402-5

Manufactured in the United States of America

10 9 8 7 6 5 4 3 2 1

WILEY

This one's for Pamn, who pretty much left me alone while I was writing it.

About the Author

John Walkenbach is a leading authority on spreadsheet software, and principal of J-Walk and Associates Inc., a one-person consulting firm based in southern Arizona. John has received a Microsoft MVP award every year since 2000. He's the author of about 50 spreadsheet books, and has written more than 300 articles and reviews for a variety of publications, including *PC World*, *InfoWorld*, *PC Magazine*, *Windows*, and *PC/Computing*. John also maintains a popular Web site (*The Spreadsheet Page*, www.j-walk.com/ss), and is the developer of several Excel utilities, including the Power Utility Pak, an award-winning add-in for Excel. John graduated from the University of Missouri, and earned a Masters and PhD from the University of Montana.

Credits

Acquisitions Manager: Gregory S. Croy

Project Editor: Pat O'Brien

Senior Copy Editor: Teresa Artman

Technical Editor: Bill Moorehead

Editorial Manager: Kevin Kirschner

Vice President & Executive Group Publisher: Richard Swadley

Vice President and Publisher:
Andy Cummings

Editorial Director: Mary C. Corder

Project Coordinator: Patrick Redmond

Graphics and Production Specialists:
Denny Hager
Joyce Haughey
Jennifer Mayberry
Barbara Moore
Melanee Prendergast

Quality Control Technicians:
Jessica Kramer
Brian H. Walls

Media Development Project Supervisor:
Laura Moss

Media Development Specialist:
Steve Kudirka

Proofreading: Techbooks

Indexing:
Broccoli Information Management

Anniversary Logo Design:
Richard Pacifico

Contents at a Glance

Part VI: Developing Custom Worksheet Functions

Part VII: Appendixes

Table of Contents

Part II: Using Functions in Your Formulas

Part V: Miscellaneous Formula Techniques

Acknowledgments

Thanks to everyone who purchased previous editions of this book. I'm especially grateful to those who took the time to provide me with feedback and suggestions. I've incorporated many of the reader suggestions into this new edition.

I am also grateful to Dick Kusleika, fellow Microsoft MVP and Excel wizard. Dick made valuable contributions to many chapters in this book, and without his help it would have been delayed by several months.

Finally, I wish to thank the folks at Wiley for publishing this book, especially Greg Croy, acquisitions editor. This certainly isn't your "typical" Excel book, and publishing it was a risky venture. The risk paid off, however, as evidenced by the fact that it's now in its fourth edition. Special thanks to Pat O'Brien, my project editor. He made my job much easier.

Thanks for buying my book. If you want to develop killer formulas and take Excel to a new level, you've purchased the right book. I'm confident that you'll agree that your money was invested wisely.

Why I Wrote This Book

I approached this project with one goal in mind: To write the ultimate Excel book that would appeal to a broad base of users. That's a fairly ambitious goal. But based on the feedback I received from the first three editions, I think I've accomplished it.

Excel is the spreadsheet market leader, by a long shot. This is the case not only because of Microsoft's enormous marketing clout, but because it is truly the best spreadsheet available. One area in which Excel's superiority is most apparent is formulas. Excel has some special tricks up its sleeve in the formulas department. As you'll see, Excel lets you do things with formulas that are impossible with other spreadsheets.

It's a safe bet that only about ten percent of Excel users really understand how to get the most out of worksheet formulas. In this book, I attempt to nudge you into that elite group. Are you up to it?

What You Should Know

This is *not* a book for beginning Excel users. If you have absolutely no experience with Excel, this is probably not the best book for you — unless you're one of a rare breed who can learn a new software product almost instantaneously.

To get the most out of this book, you should have some background using Excel. Specifically, I assume that you know how to

- Create workbooks, insert sheets, save files, and other basic tasks
- Navigate through a workbook
- Use the Excel 2007 ribbon and dialog boxes
- Use basic Windows features, such as file management and copy and paste techniques

What You Should Have

I wrote this book for Excel 2007. If you're using an older version of Excel, I suggest that you put down this book immediately and pick up a previous edition. The changes in Excel 2007 are so extensive that you might be hopelessly confused if you try to follow along using an earlier version of Excel.

To use the examples on the companion CD-ROM, you'll need a CD-ROM drive. The examples on the CD-ROM are discussed further in the "About the Companion CD-ROM" section, later in this preface.

NOTE

I use Excel for Windows exclusively, and I do not own a Macintosh. Therefore, I can't guarantee that all of the examples will work with Excel for Macintosh. Excel's cross-platform compatibility is pretty good, but it's definitely not perfect.

As far as hardware goes, the faster the better. And, of course, the more memory in your system, the happier you'll be. And, I strongly recommend using a high-resolution video mode: at least 1024 x 768, preferably higher.

Conventions in This Book

Take a minute to skim this section and learn some of the typographic conventions used throughout this book.

Keyboard Conventions

You need to use the keyboard to enter formulas. In addition, you can work with menus and dialog boxes directly from the keyboard — a method you may find easier if your hands are already positioned over the keys.

FORMULA LISTINGS

Formulas usually appear on a separate line in `monospace font`. For example, I may list the following formula:

```
=VLOOKUP(StockNumber,PriceList,2,False)
```

Excel supports a special type of formula known as an *array formula*. When you enter an array formula, press Ctrl+Shift+Enter (not just Enter). Excel encloses an array formula in brackets in order to remind you that it's an array formula. When I list an array formula, I include the brackets to make it clear that it is, in fact, an array formula. For example:

```
{=SUM(LEN(A1:A10))}
```

NOTE

Do not type the brackets for an array formula. Excel will put them in automatically.

VBA CODE LISTINGS

This book also contains examples of VBA code. Each listing appears in a `monospace font`; each line of code occupies a separate line. To make the code easier to read, I usually use one or more tabs to create indentations. Indentation is optional, but it does help to delineate statements that go together.

If a line of code doesn't fit on a single line in this book, I use the standard VBA line continuation sequence: a space followed by an underscore character. This indicates that the line of code extends to the next line. For example, the following two lines comprise a single VBA statement:

```
If Right(cell.Value, 1) = "!" Then cell.Value _
   = Left(cell.Value, Len(cell.Value) - 1)
```

You can enter this code either exactly as shown on two lines, or on a single line without the trailing underscore character.

KEY NAMES

Names of keys on the keyboard appear in normal type, for example Alt, Home, PgDn, and Ctrl. When you should press two keys simultaneously, the keys are connected with a plus sign: "Press Ctrl+G to display the Go To dialog box."

FUNCTIONS, PROCEDURES, AND NAMED RANGES

Excel's worksheet functions appear in all uppercase, like so: "Use the SUM function to add the values in column A."

Macro and procedure names appear in normal type: "Execute the InsertTotals procedure." I often use mixed upper- and lowercase to make these names easier to read. Named ranges appear in italic: "Select the *InputArea* range."

Unless you're dealing with text inside of quotation marks, Excel is not sensitive to case. In other words, both of the following formulas produce the same result:

```
=SUM(A1:A50)
=sum(a1:a50)
```

Excel, however, will convert the characters in the second formula to uppercase.

Mouse Conventions

The mouse terminology in this book is all standard fare: "pointing," "clicking," "right-clicking," "dragging," and so on. You know the drill.

What the Icons Mean

Throughout the book, icons appear to call your attention to points that are particularly important.

NEW

This icon indicates a feature new to Excel 2007.

NOTE

I use Note icons to tell you that something is important — perhaps a concept that may help you master the task at hand or something fundamental for understanding subsequent material.

TIP

Tip icons indicate a more efficient way of doing something, or a technique that may not be obvious. These will often impress your officemates.

ON THE CD

These icons indicate that an example file is on the companion CD-ROM. (See the upcoming "About the Companion CD-ROM" section.)

CAUTION

I use Caution icons when the operation that I'm describing can cause problems if you're not careful.

CROSS REF

I use the Cross Reference icon to refer you to other chapters that have more to say on a particular topic.

How This Book Is Organized

There are hundreds of ways to organize this material, but I settled on a scheme that divides the book into six main parts. In addition, I've included a few appendixes that provide supplemental information that you may find helpful.

Part I: Basic Information

This part is introductory in nature, and consists of Chapters 1 through 3. Chapter 1 sets the stage with a quick and dirty overview of Excel. This chapter is designed for readers who are new to Excel, but who have used other spreadsheet products. In Chapter 2, I cover the basics of formulas. This chapter is absolutely essential reading in order to get the most out of this book. Chapter 3 deals with names. If you thought names were just for cells and ranges, you'll see that you're missing out on quite a bit.

Part II: Using Functions in Your Formulas

This part consists of Chapters 4 through 10. Chapter 4 covers the basics of using worksheet functions in your formulas. I get more specific in subsequent chapters. Chapter 5 deals with manipulating text, Chapter 6 covers dates and times, and Chapter 7 explores various counting techniques. In Chapter 8, I discuss various types of lookup formulas. Chapter 9 deals with databases and lists, and Chapter 10 covers a variety of miscellaneous calculations such as unit conversions and rounding.

Part III: Financial Formulas

Part III consists of three chapters (Chapters 11 through 13) that deal with creating financial formulas. You'll find lots of useful formulas that you can adapt to your needs.

Part IV: Array Formulas

This part consists of Chapters 14 and 15. The majority of Excel users know little or nothing about array formulas — a topic that happens to be dear to me. Therefore I devote an entire part to this little-used yet extremely powerful feature.

Part V: Miscellaneous Formula Techniques

This part consists of Chapters 16 through 21. They cover a variety of topics — some of which, on the surface, may appear to have nothing to do with formulas. Chapter 16 demonstrates that a circular reference can be a good thing. In Chapter 17, you'll see why formulas can be important when you work with charts, and Chapter 18 covers formulas as they relate to pivot tables. Chapter 19 contains some very interesting (and useful) formulas that you can use in conjunction with Excel's conditional formatting and data validation features. Chapter 20 covers a topic that I call "megaformulas." A *megaformula* is a huge formula that takes the place of several intermediary formulas. And what do you do when your formulas don't work correctly? Consult Chapter 21 for some debugging techniques.

Part VI: Developing Custom Worksheet Functions

This part consists of Chapters 22 through 25. This is the part that explores Visual Basic for Applications (VBA), the key to creating custom worksheet functions. Chapter 22 introduces VBA and the VB Editor, and Chapter 23 provides some necessary background on custom worksheet functions. Chapter 24 covers programming concepts, and Chapter 25 provides a slew of worksheet function examples that you can use as-is, or customize for your own needs.

Part VII: Appendixes

What's a computer book without appendixes? This book has four appendixes. In the appendixes, you'll find a quick reference guide to Excel's worksheet functions, tips on using custom number formats, and a handy guide to Excel resources on the Internet. The final appendix describes all the files on the CD-ROM.

How to Use This Book

You can use this book any way you please. If you choose to read it cover to cover while lounging on a sunny beach in Kauai, that's fine with me. More likely, you'll want to keep it within arm's reach while you toil away in your dimly-lit cubicle.

Due to the nature of the subject matter, the chapter order is often immaterial. Most readers will probably skip around, picking up useful tidbits here and there. The material contains many examples, designed to help you identify a relevant formula quickly. If you're faced with a challenging task, you may want to check the index first to see whether the book specifically addresses your problem.

About the Companion CD-ROM

This book contains many examples, and the workbooks for those examples are available on the companion CD-ROM, arranged in directories that correspond to the chapters.

The example workbook files on the companion CD-ROM are not compressed, so you can access them directly from the CD (installation not required). These files are all Excel 2007 files. Files that have an *.xlsm extension contain VBA macros. In order to use the macros, you must enable the macros.

In addition, the CD-ROM contains an electronic version of this book. It's a searchable PDF file that's a perfect companion for your notebook computer when you take your next cross-country flight.

CROSS REF

Refer to Appendix D for more information about the example files on the CD-ROM.

About the Power Utility Pak Offer

Toward the back of the book, you'll find a coupon that you can redeem for a discounted copy of my award-winning Power Utility Pak — a collection of useful Excel utilities, plus many new worksheet functions. I developed this package using VBA exclusively.

You can also use this coupon to purchase the complete VBA source code for a nominal fee. Studying the code is an excellent way to pick up some useful programming techniques. You can take the product for a test drive by installing the shareware version from the companion CD-ROM.

NOTE

Power Utility Pak requires Excel 2000 for Windows or later.

You can download a 30-day trial version of the most recent version of the Power Utility Pak from my Web site:

www.j-walk.com/ss

If you find it useful, use the coupon to purchase a licensed copy at a discount.

Reach Out

I'm always interested in getting feedback on my books. The best way to provide this feedback is via email. Send your comments and suggestions to:

author@j-walk.com

Unfortunately, I'm not able to reply to specific questions. Posting your question to one of the Excel newsgroups is, by far, the best way to get such assistance. See Appendix C for more information about the newsgroups.

Also, when you're out surfing the Web, don't overlook my Web site ("The Spreadsheet Page"):

www.j-walk.com/ss/

Now, without further ado, it's time to turn the page and expand your horizons.

Part I

Basic Information

Chapter 1

Excel in a Nutshell

IN THIS CHAPTER

- ◆ A brief history of Excel
- ◆ The object model concept in Excel
- ◆ The workings of workbooks
- ◆ The user interface
- ◆ The two types of cell formatting
- ◆ Worksheet formulas and functions
- ◆ Objects on the worksheet's invisible drawing layer
- ◆ Macros, toolbars, and add-ins for Excel customization
- ◆ Internet features
- ◆ Analysis tools
- ◆ Protection options

Microsoft Excel has been referred to as "the best application ever written for Windows." You may or may not agree with that statement, but you can't deny that Excel is one of the *oldest* Windows products and has undergone many reincarnations and face-lifts over the years. Cosmetically, the current version — Excel 2007 — barely even resembles the original version. However, many of Excel's key elements have remained intact over the years, with significant enhancements, of course.

This chapter presents a concise overview of the features available in the more recent versions of Excel, with specific emphasis on Excel 2007. It sets the stage for the subsequent chapters and provides an overview for those who may have let their Excel skill get rusty.

 NOTE

If you're an old hand at Excel, you may want to read only the section on the Excel user interface and ignore or briefly skim the rest of the chapter.

The History of Excel

You probably weren't expecting a history lesson when you bought this book, but you may find this information interesting. At the very least, this section provides fodder for the next office trivia match.

Spreadsheets comprise a huge business, but most of us tend to take this software for granted. In the pre-spreadsheet days, people relied on clumsy mainframes or calculators and spent hours doing what now takes minutes.

It Started with VisiCalc

Dan Bricklin and Bob Frankston conjured up VisiCalc, the world's first electronic spreadsheet, back in the late 1970s when personal computers were unheard of in the office environment. They wrote VisiCalc for the Apple II computer, an interesting machine that seems like a toy by today's standards. VisiCalc caught on quickly, and many forward-looking companies purchased the Apple II for the sole purpose of developing their budgets with VisiCalc. Consequently, VisiCalc is often credited for much of Apple II's initial success.

Then Came Lotus

When the IBM PC arrived on the scene in 1982, thus legitimizing personal computers, VisiCorp wasted no time porting VisiCalc to this new hardware environment. Envious of VisiCalc's success, a small group of computer enthusiasts at a start-up company in Cambridge, Massachusetts, refined the spreadsheet concept. Headed by Mitch Kapor and Jonathon Sachs, the company designed a new product and launched the software industry's first full-fledged marketing blitz. Released in January 1983, Lotus Development Corporation's 1-2-3 proved an instant success. Despite its $495 price tag (yes, people really paid that much for a single program), it quickly outsold VisiCalc and rocketed to the top of the sales charts, where it remained for many years. Lotus 1-2-3 was, perhaps, the most popular application ever.

Microsoft Enters the Picture

Most people don't realize that Microsoft's experience with spreadsheets extends back to the early 1980s. In 1982, Microsoft released its first spreadsheet — MultiPlan. Designed for computers running the CP/M operating system, the product was subsequently ported to several other platforms, including Apple II, Apple III, XENIX, and MS-DOS. MultiPlan essentially ignored existing software user-interface standards. Difficult to learn and use, it never earned much of a following in the United States. Not surprisingly, Lotus 1-2-3 pretty much left MultiPlan in the dust.

Excel partly evolved from MultiPlan, first surfacing in 1985 on the Macintosh. Like all Mac applications, Excel was a graphics-based program (unlike the character-based MultiPlan). In November 1987, Microsoft released the first version of Excel for Windows (labeled Excel 2 to correspond with the Macintosh version). Excel didn't catch on right away, but as Windows gained popularity, so did Excel. Lotus eventually released a Windows version of 1-2-3, and Excel had additional competition from Quattro Pro — originally a DOS program developed by Borland International, then sold to Novell, and then sold again to Corel (its current owner).

Excel Versions

Excel 2007 is actually Excel 12 in disguise. You may think that this name represents the twelfth version of Excel. Think again. Microsoft may be a successful company, but its version-naming techniques can prove quite confusing. As you'll see, Excel 2007 actually represents the tenth Windows version of Excel. In the following sections, I briefly describe the major Windows versions of Excel.

Excel 2

The original version of Excel for Windows, Excel 2 first appeared in late 1987. It was labeled Version 2 to correspond to the Macintosh version (the original Excel). Because Windows wasn't in widespread use at the time, this version included a *runtime* version of Windows — a special version with just enough features to run Excel and nothing else. This version appears quite crude by today's standards, as shown in Figure 1-1.

Excel 3

At the end of 1990, Microsoft released Excel 3 for Windows. This version offered a significant improvement in both appearance and features. It included toolbars, drawing capabilities, worksheet outlining, add-in support, 3-D charts, workgroup editing, and lots more.

Excel 4

Excel 4 hit the streets in the spring of 1992. This version made quite an impact on the marketplace as Windows increased in popularity. It boasted lots of new features and usability enhancements that made it easier for beginners to get up to speed quickly.

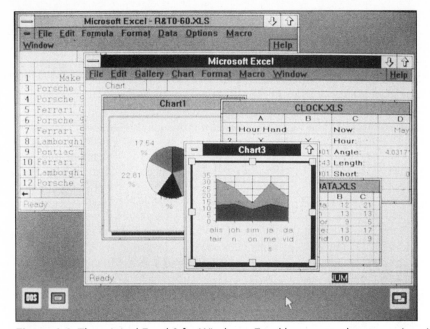

Figure 1-1: The original Excel 2 for Windows. Excel has come a long way since its original version. (Photo courtesy of Microsoft Corporation)

EXCEL 5

In early 1994, Excel 5 appeared on the scene. This version introduced tons of new features, including multisheet workbooks and the new Visual Basic for Applications (VBA) macro language. Like its predecessor, Excel 5 took top honors in just about every spreadsheet comparison published in the trade magazines.

EXCEL 95

Excel 95 (also known as Excel 7) shipped in the summer of 1995. On the surface, it resembled Excel 5 (this version included only a few major new features). However, Excel 95 proved to be significant because it presented the first version to use more advanced 32-bit code. Excel 95 and Excel 5 use the same file format.

EXCEL 97

Excel 97 (also known as Excel 8) probably offered the most significant upgrade ever. The toolbars and menus took on a great new look, online help moved a dramatic step forward, and the number of rows available in a worksheet quadrupled. And if you're a macro developer, you may have noticed that Excel's programming environment (VBA) moved up several notches on the scale. Excel 97 also introduced a new file format.

EXCEL 2000

Excel 2000 (also known as Excel 9) was released in June of 1999. Excel 2000 offered several minor enhancements, but the most significant advancement was the ability to use HTML as an alternative file format. Excel 2000 still supported the standard binary file format, of course, which is compatible with Excel 97.

EXCEL 2002

Excel 2002 (also known as Excel 10) was released in June of 2001 and is part of Microsoft Office XP. This version offered several new features, most of which are fairly minor and were designed to appeal to novice users. Perhaps the most significant new feature was the capability to save your work when Excel crashes and also recover corrupt workbook files that you may have abandoned long ago. Excel 2002 also added background formula error checking and a new formula-debugging tool.

EXCEL 2003

Excel 2003 (also known as Excel 11) was released in the fall of 2003. This version had very few new features. Perhaps the most significant new feature was the ability to import and export XML files and map the data to specific cells in a worksheet. It also introduced the concept of the List, a specially designated range of cells. Both of these features would prove to be precursors to future enhancements.

EXCEL 2007

Excel 2007 (also known as Excel 12) was released in early 2007. Its official name is Microsoft Office Excel 2007. This latest Excel release represents the most significant change since Excel 97, including a change to Excel's default file format. The new format is XML based although a binary format is still available. Another major change is the Ribbon, a new type of user interface that replaces the Excel menu and toolbar system. In addition to these two major changes, Microsoft has enhanced the List concept introduced in Excel 2003 (a List is now known as a Table), improved the look of charts, significantly increased the number of rows and columns, and added some new worksheet functions. For more, see the sidebar, "What's New in Excel 2007?".

NOTE

XML (eXtensible Markup Language) stores data in a structured text format. The new file formats are actually compressed folders that contain several different XML files. The default format's file extension is `.xlsx`. There's also a macro-enabled format with the extension `.xlsm`, a new binary format with the extension `.xlsb`, and all the legacy formats that you're used to.

The Object Model Concept

If you've dealt with computers for any length of time, you've undoubtedly heard the term object-oriented programming. An object essentially represents a software element that a programmer can manipulate. When using Excel, you may find it useful to think in terms of objects, even if you have no intention of becoming a programmer. An object-oriented approach can often help you keep the various elements in perspective.

Excel objects include the following:

- Excel itself
- An Excel workbook
- A worksheet in a workbook
- A range in a worksheet
- A button on a worksheet
- A ListBox control on a UserForm (a custom dialog box)
- A chart sheet
- A chart on a chart sheet
- A chart series in a chart

Notice the existence of an *object hierarchy*: The Excel object contains workbook objects, which contain worksheet objects, which contain range objects. This hierarchy is called Excel's *object model*. Other Microsoft Office products have their own object model. The object model concept proves to be vitally important when developing VBA macros. Even if you don't create macros, you may find it helpful to think in terms of objects.

The Workings of Workbooks

The core document of Excel is a workbook. Everything that you do in Excel takes place in a workbook.

Beginning with Excel 2007, workbook "files" are actually compressed folders. You may be familiar with compressed folders if you've ever opened a file with a .zip extension. Inside the compressed folders are a number of files that hold all the information about your workbook, including charts, macros, formatting, and the data in its cells.

An Excel workbook can hold any number of sheets (limited only by memory). The four types of sheets are

- Worksheets
- Chart sheets

- MS Excel 4.0 macro sheets (obsolete, but still supported)
- MS Excel 5.0 dialog sheets (obsolete, but still supported)

You can open or create as many workbooks as you want (each in its own window), but only one workbook is the active workbook at any given time. Similarly, only one sheet in a workbook is the active sheet. To activate a different sheet, click its corresponding tab at the bottom of the window, or press Ctrl+PgUp (for the previous sheet) or Ctrl+PgDn (for the next sheet). To change a sheet's name, double-click its Sheet tab and enter the new text for the name. Right-clicking a tab brings up a shortcut menu with some additional sheet-manipulation options.

You can also hide the window that contains a workbook by using the View⇨Window⇨ Hide command. A hidden workbook window remains open but not visible. Use the View⇨ Window⇨Unhide command to make the window visible again. A single workbook can display in multiple windows (choose View⇨Window⇨New Window). Each window can display a different sheet or a different area of the same sheet.

Worksheets

The most common type of sheet is a worksheet — which you normally think of when you think of a spreadsheet. Every Excel 2007 worksheet has 16,384 columns and 1,048,576 rows. After years of requests from users, Microsoft finally increased the number of rows and columns in a worksheet.

How Big Is a Worksheet?

It's interesting to stop and think about the actual size of a worksheet. Do the arithmetic (16,384 × 1,048,576), and you'll see that a worksheet has 17,179,869,184 cells. Remember that this is in just one worksheet. A single workbook can hold more than one worksheet.

If you're using a 1024 x 768 video mode with the default row heights and column widths, you can see 15 columns and 25 rows (or 375 cells) at a time — which is about .000002 percent of the entire worksheet. In other words, more than 45 million screens of information reside within a single worksheet.

If you entered a single digit into each cell at the relatively rapid clip of one cell per second, it would take you over 500 years, nonstop, to fill up a worksheet. To print the results of your efforts would require more than 36 million sheets of paper — a stack about 12,000 feet high (that's ten Empire State Buildings stacked on top of each other).

NOTE

Versions prior to Excel 2007 support only 256 columns and 65,536 rows. If you open such a file, Excel 2007 enters compatibility mode to work with the smaller worksheet grid. In order to work with the larger grid, you must save the file in one of the Excel 2007 formats. Then close the workbook and reopen it.

Having access to more cells isn't the *real* value of using multiple worksheets in a workbook. Rather, multiple worksheets are valuable because they enable you to organize your work better. Back in the old days, when a spreadsheet file consisted of a single worksheet, developers wasted a lot of time trying to organize the worksheet to hold their information efficiently. Now, you can store information on any number of worksheets and still access it instantly.

You have complete control over the column widths and row heights, and you can even hide rows and columns (as well as entire worksheets). You can display the contents of a cell vertically (or at an angle) and even wrap around to occupy multiple lines.

NOTE

By default, every new workbook starts out with three worksheets. You can easily add a new sheet when necessary, so you really don't need to start with three sheets. You may want to change this default to a single sheet. To change this option, use the Office⇨ Excel Options command, click the Popular tab, and change the setting for the option labeled Include This Many Sheets.

Chart Sheets

A chart sheet holds a single chart. Many users ignore chart sheets, preferring to use embedded charts, which are stored on the worksheet's drawing layer. Using chart sheets is optional, but they make it a bit easier to locate a particular chart, and they prove especially useful for presentations. I discuss embedded charts (or floating charts on a worksheet) later in this chapter.

Macro Sheets and Dialog Sheets

An Excel 4.0 macro sheet is a worksheet that has some different defaults. Its purpose is to hold XLM macros. XLM is the macro system used in Excel version 4.0 and previous versions. This macro system was replaced by VBA in Excel 5.0 and is not discussed in this book.

An Excel 5.0 dialog sheet is a drawing grid that can hold text and controls. In Excel 5.0 and Excel 95, they were used to make custom dialog boxes. UserForms were introduced in Excel 97 to replace these sheets.

What's New in Excel 2007?

Here's a quick and dirty overview of the new features in Excel 2007:

- A new tab/Ribbon user interface
- New XML file formats
- Worksheet tables
- Significantly larger worksheet grid (1,048,576 rows x 16,384 columns)
- Ability to use more memory
- Unlimited conditional formats per cell
- 100 levels of undo
- Maximum formula length increased to 8,000 characters
- Support for 64 levels of nesting in a formula
- Formula autocomplete
- Better-looking charts
- Workbook themes
- Skins
- Page Layout view
- New conditional formatting options
- Less confusing Excel Options dialog box
- New collaboration features (requires SharePoint)
- SmartArt and Improved WordArt
- Compatibility checker
- Easier pivot tables
- Twelve new worksheet functions, plus integration of the Analysis ToolPak functions
- PDF output (via a downloadable add-in)
- Resizable formula bar
- Many new templates
- More control over the status bar

The Excel User Interface

A *user interface* (UI) is the means by which an end user communicates with a computer program. A UI includes elements such as menus, dialog boxes, toolbars, and keystroke combinations, as well as features such as drag and drop.

A New User Interface

Almost every Windows program you use employs the menu and toolbar approach. That is, at the top of the screen is a menu bar that contains virtually every command that's available in the application and below that, one or more toolbars, which provide shortcuts to some of the more frequently used commands. For Excel, and most of the other Microsoft Office applications, the days of menus and toolbars are over.

The new UI for Excel consists of components like the Ribbon, the Office Button, the Mini Toolbar, and the Quick Access toolbar. The Quick Access toolbar is the only UI element that can be customized by end users.

The Ribbon

The Ribbon is the primary UI component in Excel. It replaces the menu and most of the toolbars that were common in previous versions, and is a very significant departure from the interfaces of most Windows-based applications.

ONE-STOP SHOPPING

Microsoft felt that the commands contained in the old menu and toolbar system were becoming so numerous that a new paradigm was necessary. One of the main goals for developing the Ribbon was to provide the user with a single place to look for a particular feature. Every commonly used command available in Excel would be contained in the Ribbon (or in a dialog box accessed via the Ribbon). Although Microsoft succeeded in putting most of the available commands on the Ribbon, it's still a pretty big place. Long-time Excel users will have to endure a certain amount of frustration while they get used to the new layout.

 NOTE

A few commands failed to make the cut, but they are still available if you know where to look for them. Right-click the Quick Access toolbar and choose Customize Quick Access Toolbar. Excel displays a dialog box with a list of commands that you can add to your Quick Access toolbar (QAT). Some of these commands aren't available elsewhere in the UI.

TABS, GROUPS, AND TOOLS

The Ribbon is a band of tools that stretches across the top of the Excel window. About the vertical size of three of the old style toolbars, the Ribbon sports a number of tabs including Home, Insert, Page Layout, and others. On each tab are groups that contain related tools.

On the Home tab, for example, you find the Clipboard group, the Font group, and the Alignment group.

After you get past the Ribbon, the tabs, and the groups, you get to the tools, which are similar to the tools that existed on the old style toolbars with one major difference: their different sizes. Tools that are used most often are larger than less-frequently used tools. Half of the Clipboard group is consumed by the large Paste tool; the Cut, Copy, and Format Painter tools are much smaller. Microsoft determined that the Paste tool is the most used tool and thus sized it accordingly.

The Ribbon and all its components resize dynamically as the Excel window is resized horizontally. Smaller Excel windows collapse the tools on compressed tabs and groups, and maximized Excel windows on large monitors show everything that's available. Even in a small window, all Ribbon commands remain available. You just may need to click a few extra times to access them.

Figure 1-2 shows three sizes of the Ribbon when the Home tab is displayed using an increasingly smaller horizontal window size.

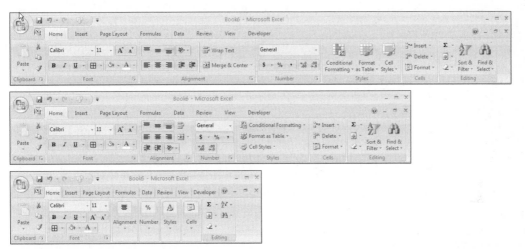

Figure 1-2: The Ribbon sizes dynamically, depending on the horizontal size of Excel's window.

NAVIGATION

Navigation of the Ribbon is fairly easy with the mouse. You click a tab and then click a tool. If you prefer to use the keyboard, Microsoft has added a feature just for you. Pressing Alt displays tiny squares with shortcut letters in them that hover over their respective tab or tool. Each shortcut letter that you press either executes its command or drills down to another level of shortcut letters. Pressing Esc cancels the letters or moves up to the previous level. For example, a keystroke sequence of Alt+H+B+B adds a double border to the bottom of the selection. The Alt key activates the shortcut letters, the H shortcut activates the Home tab, the B shortcut activates the Borders tool menu, and the second B shortcut executes the Bottom Double Border command. Note that it's not necessary to keep the Alt key depressed while you press the other keys.

CONTEXTUAL TABS

The Ribbon contains tabs that are visible only when they are needed. Generally, when a previously hidden tab appears, it's because you selected an object or a range with special characteristics (like a chart or a pivot table). A typical example is the Drawing Tools contextual tab. When you select a shape or WordArt object, the Drawing Tools tab is made visible and active. It contains many tools that are only applicable to shapes, such as shape-formatting tools.

SCREENTIPS AND DIALOG ICONS

Hovering over a tool on the Ribbon displays a ScreenTip that explains the command the tool will execute. ScreenTips are larger and, in most cases, wordier than the ToolTips from previous versions. They range in helpfulness from one word to long paragraphs and even pictures.

At the bottom of many of the groups is a small box icon (a *dialog box launcher*) that opens a dialog box related to that group. Users of previous versions of Excel will recognize these dialog boxes, many of which are unchanged. Some of the icons open the same dialog boxes but to different areas. For instance, the Font group icon opens the Format Cells dialog box with the Font tab activated. The Alignment group opens the same dialog box but activates the Alignment tab. The Ribbon makes using dialog boxes a far less-frequent activity than in the past because most of what can be done in a dialog box can be done directly on the Ribbon.

GALLERIES AND LIVE PREVIEW

A gallery is a large collection of tools that look like the choice they represent. If you've used previous versions of Excel, you may have noticed that the font names in the drop-down box on the Formatting toolbar were in their own font. Galleries are an extension of that feature. The Styles gallery, for example, does not just list the name of the style but lists it in the same formatting that will be applied the cell.

Although galleries help to give you an idea of what your object will look like when an option is selected, Live Preview takes it to the next level. Live Preview displays your object or data as it will look right on the worksheet when you hover over the gallery tool. By hovering over the various tools in the Format Table gallery, you can see exactly what your table will look like before you commit to a format.

The Office Button Menu

Although menus are a thing of the past in Excel 2007, one holdout remains: the Office Button menu. In the upper-left corner of the Excel window is a round Microsoft Office logo that is known as the Office Button. Click it, and you see a traditional menu with menu commands (see Figure 1-3). Saving workbooks, opening workbooks, and printing are a few of the commands available.

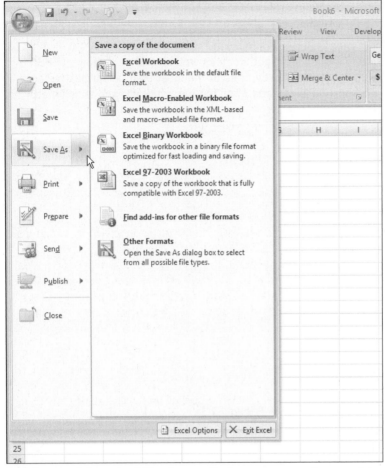

Figure 1-3: Clicking the Office Button displays a menu, and some of the menu items have submenus.

The Office Button menu also contains the list of recent documents, just as it had in previous versions. The recent documents list has undergone a major overhaul, however; the maximum number of documents on the list is now 50 from the previous of 9, with push-pin icons next to each entry that can be used to hold that document in its place on the list regardless of how many files you open and close.

At the bottom of the Office Button menu is the Excel Options button. This button opens the Excel Options dialog box, which contains dozens of settings for customizing Excel.

Shortcut Menus and the Mini Toolbar

Excel also features dozens of shortcut menus. These menus appear when you right-click after selecting one or more objects. The shortcut menus are context sensitive. In other words, the menu that appears depends on the location of the mouse pointer when you right-click. You can right-click just about anything — a cell, a row or column border, a workbook title bar, and so on.

Right-clicking many items displays the shortcut menu as well as a Mini Toolbar. The *Mini Toolbar* is floating toolbar that contains a dozen or so of the most popular formatting commands. Figure 1-4 shows the shortcut menu and Mini Toolbar when a range is selected.

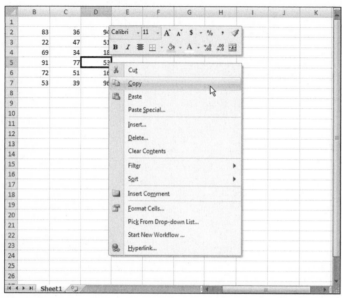

Figure 1-4: The shortcut menu and Mini Toolbar appears when you right-click a range.

The Quick Access Toolbar

The Quick Access toolbar (or QAT) is a set of tools that the user can customize. By default, the QAT contains three tools: Save, Undo, and Redo. If you find that you use a particular Ribbon command frequently, right-click the command and choose Add to Quick Access Toolbar. You can make other changes to the QAT from the Customization tab of the Excel Options dialog box. To access this dialog box, right-click the QAT and choose Customize Quick Access Toolbar.

Smart Tags

A Smart Tag is a small icon that appears automatically in your worksheet after you complete certain actions. Clicking a Smart Tag reveals several clickable options.

For example, if you copy and paste a range of cells, Excel generates a Smart Tag that appears below the pasted range (see Figure 1-5). Excel features several other Smart Tags, and additional Smart Tags can be provided by third-party providers.

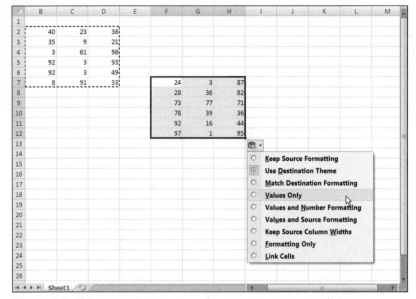

Figure 1-5: This Smart Tag appears when you paste a copied range.

Task Pane

Excel 2002 introduced the task pane. This is a multipurpose user interface element that is normally docked on the right side of Excel's window (but you can drag it anywhere you like). The task pane is used for a variety of purposes, including displaying the Office Clipboard, providing research assistance, displaying pivot table fields, and mapping XML data. Figure 1-6 shows the task pane that appears when you insert clip art.

Drag and Drop

Excel's drag-and-drop UI feature enables you to freely drag objects that reside on the drawing layer to change their position. Pressing Ctrl while dragging duplicates the selected objects. These objects include shapes, embedded charts, and SmartArt.

Excel also permits drag-and-drop actions on cells and ranges. You can easily drag a cell or range to a different position. And pressing Ctrl while dragging copies the selected range.

NOTE

You can disable the ability to drag and drop cells. To change this setting, choose Office⇨Excel Options to display the Excel Options dialog box. Click the Advanced tab and clear the Enable Fill Handle and Cell Drag-And-Drop check box (located in the Editing Options section).

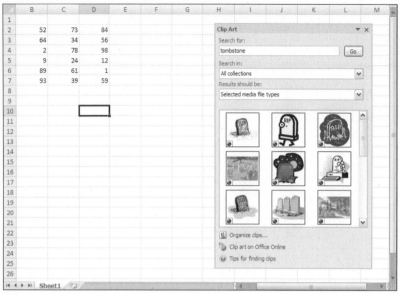

Figure 1-6: The Clip Art task pane allows you to search for and insert an image.

Keyboard Shortcuts

In addition to the keyboard shortcuts for navigating the Ribbon, Excel has many other keyboard shortcuts that execute commands directly. For example, you can press Ctrl+C to copy a selection. If you're a newcomer to Excel or if you just want to improve your efficiency, do yourself a favor and check out the shortcuts listed in Excel's Help system. (Search for Excel Shortcut and Function Keys using the Search box or locate the topic under the Accessibility chapter of Help's table of contents.) The Help system contains tables that summarize useful keyboard commands and shortcuts.

To ease the transition from previous versions to Excel 2007, Microsoft includes the Office 2003 Access Keys feature. Many Excel users are accustomed to navigating the old menu system with their keyboard, and they would become much more inefficient if they had to rely on the new Ribbon. If you type an Alt+*letter* sequence that isn't a part of the Ribbon but that did exist in Excel 2003, you get a ScreenTip near the top of the Excel window, like the one shown in Figure 1-7.

Customized Onscreen Display

Excel offers some flexibility regarding onscreen display (status bar, formula bar, the Ribbon, and so on). For example, by choosing View⇨Workbook Views⇨Full Screen, you can get rid of everything except the title bar, thereby maximizing the amount of visible information. To get out of full-screen mode, right-click and choose Exit Fullscreen from the shortcut menu (or press Esc). A little less drastic is pressing the Ctrl+F1 shortcut key to hide (and restore) the Ribbon.

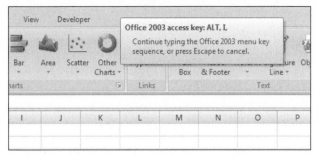

Figure 1-7: Using a keyboard sequence like Alt+I+R (for Insert⇨Row) can still be used to insert a row and will display this ScreenTip during the process.

The status bar has also been enhanced in Excel 2007. Right-click the status bar, and you see lots of options that allow you to control what information is displayed in the status bar.

Many other customizations can be made by choosing Office⇨Excel Options and clicking the Advanced tab. On this tab are several sections that deal with what displays onscreen.

Data Entry

Data entry in Excel is quite straightforward. Excel interprets each cell entry as one of the following:

- A value (including a date or a time)
- Text
- A Boolean value (TRUE or FALSE)
- A formula

NOTE
Formulas always begin with an equal sign (=).

Object and Cell Selecting

Generally, selecting objects in Excel conforms to standard Windows practices. You can select a range of cells by using the keyboard (using the Shift key, along with the arrow keys) or by clicking and dragging the mouse. To select a large range, click a cell at any corner of the range, scroll to the opposite corner of the range, and press Shift while you click the opposite corner cell.

You can use Ctrl+* (asterisk) to select an entire table. And when a large range is selected, you can use Ctrl+. (period) to move among the four corners of the range.

Data-Entry Tips

The following list of data-entry tips can help those moving up to Excel from another spreadsheet:

- To enter data without pressing the arrow keys, enable the After Pressing Enter, Move Selection option on the Advanced tab of the Excel Options dialog box (which you access from the Office➪Excel Options command). You can also choose the direction that you want to go.

- You may find it helpful to select a range of cells before entering data. If you do so, you can use the Tab key or Enter key to move only within the selected cells.

- To enter the same data in all cells within a range, select the range, enter the information into the active cell, and then press Ctrl+Enter.

- To copy the contents of the active cell to all other cells in a selected range, press F2 and then Ctrl+Enter.

- To fill a range with increments of a single value, press Ctrl while you drag the fill handle at the lower-right corner of the cell.

- To create a custom AutoFill list, select the Edit Custom Lists button on the Popular tab of the Excel Options dialog box.

- To copy a cell without incrementing, drag the fill handle at the lower-right corner of the selection; or, press Ctrl+D to copy down or Ctrl+R to copy to the right.

- To make text easier to read, you can enter line breaks in a cell. To enter a line break, press Alt+Enter. Line breaks cause a cell's contents to wrap within the cell.

- To enter a fraction, enter **0**, a space, and then the fraction (using a slash). Excel formats the cell using the Fraction number format.

- To automatically format a cell with the currency format, type your currency symbol before the value.

- To enter a value in percent format, type a percent sign after the value. You can also include your local thousand separator symbol to separate thousands (for example, 123,434).

- To insert the current date, press Ctrl+; (semicolon). To enter the current time into a cell, press Ctrl+Shift+;.

- To set up a cell or range so that it accepts entries only of a certain type (or within a certain value range), use the Data➪Data Tools➪Data Validation command.

If you're working in a table (created with the Insert➪Tables➪Table command), you'll find that Ctrl+A works in a new way. Press it once to select the table cells only. Press Ctrl+A a second time, and it select the entire table (including the header and totals row). Press it a third time, and it selects all cells on the worksheet.

Clicking an object placed on the drawing layer selects the object. An exception occurs if the object has a macro assigned to it. In such a case, clicking the object executes the macro. To select multiple objects or noncontiguous cells, press Ctrl while you select the objects or cells.

The Excel Help System

One of Excel's most important features is its Help system. The Help icon, a blue circle with a question mark in it, is located near the upper-right corner of the Excel window. Clicking the Help icon or pressing the F1 function key displays the help window, as shown in Figure 1-8.

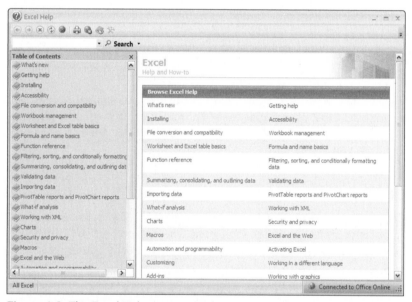

Figure 1-8: The Excel Help system window.

The two primary methods for navigating help are the Search box and the Table of Contents. Typing keywords into the Search box and clicking the Search button displays a list of relevant help articles in the main window. The Table of Contents lists many related help articles in chapters. The Table of Contents window can be hidden when not in use. Note that the Search button is actually a drop-down control. Click the small arrow, and you can choose the general type of Help you need.

By default, the content shown is downloaded from the Microsoft Office Online Web site. If you do not have Internet access or you prefer to limit Help to articles on your computer, click the Connection status bar in the lower-right corner of the Help window. A small menu appears that allows you to specify which help system to use and also includes a Help icon — help for the Help system.

Cell Formatting

Excel provides two types of cell formatting — numeric formatting and stylistic formatting.

Numeric Formatting

Numeric formatting refers to how a value appears in the cell. In addition to choosing from an extensive list of predefined formats, you can create your own custom number formats in the Number tab of the Format Cells dialog box . (Choose the dialog box launcher at the bottom of the Home⇨Number group.)

Excel applies some numeric formatting automatically, based on the entry. For example, if you precede a value with your local currency symbol (such as a dollar sign), Excel applies Currency number formatting.

 CROSS REF

Refer to Appendix B for additional information about creating custom number formats.

The number format doesn't affect the actual value stored in the cell. For example, suppose that a cell contains the value 3.14159. If you apply a format to display two decimal places, the number appears as 3.14. When you use the cell in a formula, however, the actual value (3.14159) — not the displayed value — is used.

Stylistic Formatting

Stylistic formatting refers to the cosmetic formatting (colors, shading, fonts, borders, and so on) that you apply in order to make your work look good. The Home⇨Font and Home⇨ Styles groups contain all the commands that you need to format your cells and ranges.

A new formatting concept in Excel 2007 is *document themes.* Basically, themes allow you to set many formatting options at once, such as font, colors, and cell styles. The formatting options contained in a theme are designed to work well together. If you're not feeling particularly artistic, you can apply a theme and know the colors won't clash. All the commands for themes are in the Themes group of the Page Layout tab.

Don't overlook Excel's conditional formatting feature. This handy tool enables you to specify formatting that appears only when certain conditions are met. For example, you can make the cell's interior red if the cell contains a negative number. Excel 2007 includes many new conditional formatting options, and the feature is much easier to use than in previous versions.

 CROSS REF

See Chapter 19 for more information on conditional formatting.

Tables

A Table is a specially designated range in an Excel 2007 worksheet. If you used Lists in Excel 2003, you will already be familiar with some of what the Table object has to offer. If not, don't worry. Excel 2007 makes it easy to designate a range as a Table and makes it even easier to perform many functions on that data.

The data in a table is related in a specific way. The rows represent related objects, and the columns represent specific pieces of information about each of those objects. If, for instance, you have a table of library books, each row would hold the information for one book. Columns might include title, author, publisher, date, and so on. In database terminology, the rows are records, and the columns are fields.

If your data is arranged in this fashion, you can designate it as a table by selecting the range and then choosing Insert⇨Tables⇨Table. Excel inserts generic column headings if none exist, color banding, and heading drop-down arrows into the data. These arrows, as well as the Table Tools context tab on the Ribbon, provide quick access to many table-related functions like sorting, filtering, and formatting. In addition, using formulas within a table offers some clear advantages.

CROSS REF

See Chapter 9 for more information about the new Table feature in Excel 2007.

Worksheet Formulas and Functions

Formulas, of course, make a spreadsheet a spreadsheet. Excel's formula-building capability is as good as it gets. You will discover this as you explore subsequent chapters in this book.

Worksheet functions allow you to perform calculations or operations that would otherwise be impossible. Excel provides a huge number of built-in functions, and Excel 2007 includes a few new functions. In addition, worksheet functions that formerly required the Analysis ToolPak add-in are now incorporated into Excel.

CROSS REF

See Chapter 4 for more information about worksheet functions.

Most spreadsheets allow you to define names for cells and ranges, but Excel handles names in some unique ways. A *name* represents an identifier that enables you to refer to a cell, range, value, or formula. Using names makes your formulas easier to create and read.

CROSS REF
I devote Chapter 3 entirely to names.

Objects on the Drawing Layer

As I mention earlier in this chapter, each worksheet has an invisible drawing layer, which holds shapes, SmartArt, charts, pictures, and controls (such as buttons and list boxes). I discuss some of these items in the following sections.

Shapes

You can insert a wide variety of shapes from Insert⇨Shapes. After you place a shape on your worksheet, you can modify the shape by selecting it and dragging its handles. In addition, you can apply built-in shape styles, fill effects, or 3-D effects to the shape. Also, you can group multiple shapes into a single drawing object, which you'll find easier to size or position.

Illustrations

Pictures, clip art, and SmartArt can be inserted from the Insert⇨Illustrations group. SmartArt replaces Diagrams from previous versions and have been expanded to include dozens of choices. Figure 1-9 shows some objects on the drawing layer of a worksheet.

Figure 1-9: Objects on a worksheet drawing layer. Excel makes a great doodle pad.

Part I

Linked Picture Objects

A linked picture is a shape object that shows a range. When the range is changed, the shape object changes along with it. To use this object, copy a range and then choose Home⇨Clipboard⇨Paste⇨Paste As Picture⇨Paste Picture Link. This command is useful if you want to print a noncontiguous selection of ranges. You can "take pictures" of the ranges and then paste the pictures together in a single area, which you can then print.

Controls

You can insert a number of different controls on a worksheet. These controls come in two flavors — Form controls and ActiveX controls. Using controls on a worksheet and can greatly enhance the worksheet's usability — often, without using macros. To insert a control, choose Developer⇨Controls⇨Insert. Figure 1-10 shows a worksheet with various controls added to the drawing layer.

NOTE

The Ribbon's Developer tab is not visible by default. To show the Developer tab, choose Office⇨Excel Options, navigate to the Popular tab, and check Show Developer Tab in the Ribbon.

ON THE CD

If you'd like to see how these controls work, the workbook shown in Figure 1-10 is available on the companion CD-ROM. The file is named `worksheet controls.xlsx`.

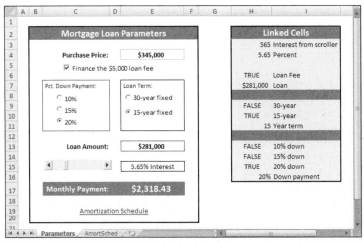

Figure 1-10: Excel enables you to add many controls directly to the drawing layer of a worksheet.

Charts

Excel, of course, has excellent charting capabilities. As I mention earlier in this chapter, you can store charts on a chart sheet or you can float them on a worksheet.

Excel offers extensive chart customization options. Selecting a chart displays the Chart Tools contextual tab, which contain all the tools necessary to customize your chart. Right-clicking a chart element displays a shortcut menu.

You can easily create a free-floating chart by selecting the data to be charted and selecting one of the chart types from the Insert⇨Charts group.

CROSS REF

Chapter 17 contains additional information about charts.

Customization in Excel

This section describes two features that enable you to customize Excel — macros and add-ins.

Macros

Excel's VBA programming language is a powerful tool that can make Excel perform otherwise impossible feats. You can classify the procedures that you create with VBA into two general types:

- Macros that automate various aspects of Excel

- Macros that serve as custom functions that you can use in worksheet formulas

CROSS REF

Part VI of this book describes how to use and create custom worksheet functions using VBA.

Add-in Programs

An add-in is a program attached to Excel that gives it additional functionality. For example, you can store custom worksheet functions in an add-in. To attach an add-in, use the Add-Ins tab in the Excel Options dialog box.

Excel ships with quite a few add-ins, and you can purchase or download many third-party add-ins from online services. My Power Utility Pak is an example of an add-in.

CROSS REF

Chapter 23 describes how to create your own add-ins that contain custom worksheet functions.

Internet Features

Excel includes a number of features that relate to the Internet. For example, you can save a worksheet or an entire workbook in HTML format, accessible in a Web browser. In addition, you can insert clickable hyperlinks (including e-mail addresses) directly into cells.

CAUTION

In Excel 2003, HTML was a round-trip file format. In other words, you could save a workbook in HTML format, reopen it in Excel, and nothing would be lost. That's no longer the case with Excel 2007. HTML is now considered an export-only format.

You can also create Web queries to bring in data stored in a corporate intranet or on the Internet.

Analysis Tools

Excel is certainly no slouch when it comes to analysis. After all, most people use a spreadsheet for analysis. Many analytical tasks can be handled with formulas, but Excel offers many other options, which I discuss in the following sections.

Database Access

Over the years, most spreadsheets have enabled users to work with simple flat database tables (even the original version of 1-2-3 contained this feature). Excel's database features fall into two main categories:

- **Worksheet databases:** The entire database is stored in a worksheet. In Excel, a worksheet database can have no more than 1,048,575 records (because the top row holds the field names) and 16,384 fields (one per column).

- **External databases:** The data is stored outside Excel, such as in an Access MDB file or in SQL Server.

Generally, when the cell pointer resides within a worksheet database, Excel recognizes it and displays the field names whenever possible. For example, if you move the cell pointer within a worksheet database and choose the Data⇨Sort & Filter⇨Sort command, Excel allows you to select the sort keys by choosing field names from a drop-down list.

A particularly useful feature, filtering, enables you to display only the records that you want to see. When Filter mode is on, you can filter the data by selecting values from pull-down lists (which appear in place of the field names when you choose the Data⇨Sort & Filter⇨Filter command). Rows that don't meet the filter criteria are hidden. See Figure 1-11 for an example.

If you convert a worksheet database into a table (by using Insert⇨Tables⇨Table), filtering is turned on automatically.

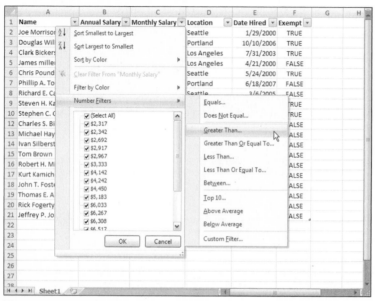

Figure 1-11: Excel's Filter feature makes it easy to view only the database records that meet your criteria.

If you prefer, you can use the traditional spreadsheet database techniques that involve criteria ranges. To do so, choose the Data⇨Sort & Filter⇨Advanced command.

 CROSS REF

Chapter 9 provides additional details regarding worksheet lists and databases.

Excel can automatically insert (or remove) subtotal formulas in a table that is set up as a database. It also creates an outline from the data so that you can view only the subtotals or any level of detail that you desire.

Outlines

A worksheet outline often serves as an excellent way to work with hierarchical data, such as budgets. Excel can create an outline automatically by examining the formulas in your worksheet (use the Data⇨Outline⇨Subtotal command). After you've created an outline, you can collapse or expand the outline to display various levels of details. Figure 1-12 shows an example of a worksheet outline.

	A	B	C	D	E	F	G	H	I	J
1	State	Jan	Feb	Mar	Qtr-1	Apr	May	Jun	Qtr-2	Total
2	California	1,118	1,960	1,252	4,330	1,271	1,557	1,679	4,507	8,837
3	Washington	1,247	1,238	1,028	3,513	1,345	1,784	1,574	4,703	8,216
4	Oregon	1,460	1,954	1,726	5,140	1,461	1,764	1,144	4,369	9,509
5	Arizona	1,345	1,375	1,075	3,795	1,736	1,555	1,372	4,663	8,458
6	West Total	5,170	6,527	5,081	16,778	5,813	6,660	5,769	18,242	35,020
7	New York	1,429	1,316	1,993	4,738	1,832	1,740	1,191	4,763	9,501
8	New Jersey	1,735	1,406	1,224	4,365	1,706	1,320	1,290	4,316	8,681
9	Massachusetts	1,099	1,233	1,110	3,442	1,637	1,512	1,006	4,155	7,597
10	Florida	1,705	1,792	1,225	4,722	1,946	1,327	1,357	4,630	9,352
11	East Total	5,968	5,747	5,552	17,267	7,121	5,899	4,844	17,864	35,131
12	Kentucky	1,109	1,078	1,155	3,342	1,993	1,082	1,551	4,626	7,968
13	Oklahoma	1,309	1,045	1,641	3,995	1,924	1,499	1,941	5,364	9,359
14	Missouri	1,511	1,744	1,414	4,669	1,243	1,493	1,820	4,556	9,225
15	Illinois	1,539	1,493	1,211	4,243	1,165	1,013	1,445	3,623	7,866
16	Kansas	1,973	1,560	1,243	4,776	1,495	1,125	1,387	4,007	8,783
17	Central Total	7,441	6,920	6,664	21,025	7,820	6,212	8,144	22,176	43,201
18	Grand Total	18,579	19,194	17,297	55,070	20,754	18,771	18,757	58,282	113,352
19										

Figure 1-12: Excel can automatically insert subtotal formulas and create outlines.

Scenario Management

Scenario management is storing input values that drive a model. For example, if you have a sales forecast, you may create scenarios such as best case, worst case, and most likely case.

Excel's Scenario Manager can handle only simple scenario-management tasks, but most users find it adequate. However, it is definitely easier than trying to keep track of different scenarios manually.

Pivot Tables

One of Excel's most powerful tools is the *pivot table,* which enables you to display summarized data in just about any way possible. Data for a pivot table comes from a worksheet database (or table) or an external database, and is stored in a special cache, which enables Excel to recalculate data rapidly after a pivot table is altered.

CROSS REF

Chapter 18 contains additional information about pivot tables.

As a companion to a pivot table, Excel also supports the pivot chart feature. Pivot charts enable you to link a chart to a pivot table. In Excel 2007, pivot charts have improved significantly.

Auditing Capabilities

Excel also offers useful auditing capabilities that help you identify errors or track the logic in an unfamiliar spreadsheet. To access this feature, choose commands in the Formulas⇨ Formula Auditing group.

 CROSS REF

Refer to Chapter 21 for more information about Excel's auditing features.

Solver Add-in

For specialized linear and nonlinear problems, Excel's Solver add-in calculates solutions to what-if scenarios based on adjustable cells, constraint cells, and, optionally, cells that must be maximized or minimized.

Protection Options

Excel offers a number of different protection options. For example, you can protect formulas from being overwritten or modified, protect a workbook's structure, and protect your VBA code.

Protecting Formulas from Being Overwritten

In many cases, you may want to protect your formulas from being overwritten or modified. To do so, you must unlock the cells that you will allow to be overwritten and then protect the sheet. First select the cells that may be overwritten and choose Home⇨Cells⇨ Format⇨Lock to unlock those cells. (The command toggles the Locked status.) Next, choose Home⇨Cells⇨Format⇨Protect Sheet to show the Protect Sheet dialog. Here you can specify a password if desired.

 NOTE

By default, all cells are locked. Locking and unlocking cells has no effect, however, unless you have a protected worksheet.

Beginning with Excel 2002, Excel's protection options have become much more flexible. When you protect a worksheet, the Protect Sheet dialog box (see Figure 1-13) lets you choose which elements won't be protected. For example, you can allow users to sort data or use autofiltering on a protected sheet (tasks that weren't possible with earlier versions).

Figure 1-13: Choose which elements to protect in the Protect Sheet dialog box.

You can also hide your formulas so they won't appear in the Excel formula bar when the cell is activated. To do so, select the formula cells and press Ctrl+1 to display the Format Cells dialog box. Click the Protection tab and make sure that the Hidden check box is selected.

Protecting a Workbook's Structure

When you protect a workbook's structure, you can't add or delete sheets. Use the Review⇨Changes⇨Protect Workbook command to display the Protect Structure and Windows dialog box, as shown in Figure 1-14. Make sure that you enable the Structure check box. If you also mark the Windows check box, the window can't be moved or resized.

Figure 1-14: The Protect Structure and Windows dialog box.

CAUTION

Keep in mind that Excel is not really a secure application. The protection features, even when used with a password, are intended to prevent casual users from accessing various components of your workbook. Anyone who really wants to defeat your protection can probably do so by using readily available password-cracking utilities.

Password-protecting a Workbook

In addition to protecting individual sheets and the structure of the workbook, you can require a password to open the workbook. To set a password, choose Office⇨Prepare⇨ Encrypt Document to display the Encrypt Document dialog box (see Figure 1-15). In this dialog box, you can specify a password to open the workbook.

Figure 1-15: Use the Encrypt Document dialog box to specify a password for a workbook.

Chapter 2

Basic Facts about Formulas

IN THIS CHAPTER

◆ How to enter, edit, and paste names into formulas

◆ The various operators used in formulas

◆ How Excel calculates formulas

◆ Cell and range references used in formulas

◆ How to make an exact copy of a formula

◆ How to convert formulas to values

◆ How to prevent formulas from being viewed

◆ The types of formula errors

◆ Circular reference messages and correction techniques

◆ Excel's goal-seeking feature

This chapter serves as a basic introduction to using formulas in Excel. Although I direct its focus on newcomers to Excel, even veteran Excel users may find some new information here.

Entering and Editing Formulas

This section describes the basic elements of a formula. It also explains various ways of entering and editing your formulas.

Formula Elements

A formula entered into a cell can consist of five element types:

- **Operators:** These include symbols such as + (for addition) and * (for multiplication).
- **Cell references:** These include named cells and ranges and can refer to cells in the current worksheet, cells in another worksheet in the same workbook, or even cells in a worksheet in another workbook.
- **Values or strings:** Examples include 7.5 or *"Year-End Results."*
- **Worksheet functions and their arguments:** These include functions such as SUM or AVERAGE and their arguments.
- **Parentheses:** These control the order in which expressions within a formula are evaluated.

Entering a Formula

When you type an equal sign into an empty cell, Excel assumes that you are entering a formula because a formula always begins with an equal sign. Excel's accommodating nature also permits you to begin your formula with a minus sign or a plus sign. However, Excel always inserts the leading equal sign after you enter the formula.

As a concession to former 1-2-3 users, Excel also allows you to use an "at" symbol (@) to begin a formula that starts with a function. For example, Excel accepts either of the following formulas:

```
=SUM(A1:A200)
@SUM(A1:A200)
```

However, after you enter the second formula, Excel replaces the @ symbol with an equal sign.

You can enter a formula into a cell in one of two ways: Enter it manually, or enter it by pointing to cell references. I discuss each of these methods in the following sections.

ENTERING FORMULAS MANUALLY

Entering a formula manually involves, well, entering a formula manually. You simply activate a cell and type an equal sign (=) followed by the formula. As you type, the characters appear in the cell as well as in the formula bar. You can, of course, use all the normal editing keys when entering a formula. After you insert the formula, press Enter.

NOTE

When you enter an array formula, you must press Ctrl+Shift+Enter rather than just Enter. I discuss array formulas in Part IV.

After you press Enter, the cell displays the result of the formula. The formula itself appears in the formula bar when the cell is activated.

ENTERING FORMULAS BY POINTING

The other method of entering a formula still involves some manual typing, but you can simply point to the cell references instead of entering them manually. For example, to enter the formula =A1+A2 into cell A3, follow these steps:

1. Move the cell pointer to cell A3.

2. Type an equal sign (=) to begin the formula. Notice that Excel displays Enter in the left side of the status bar.

3. Press the up arrow twice. As you press this key, notice that Excel displays a moving border around the cell and that the cell reference (A1) appears in cell A3 and in the formula bar. Also notice that Excel displays Point in the status bar.

   If you prefer, you can use your mouse and click cell A1.

4. Type a plus sign (+). The moving border becomes a solid blue border around A1, and Enter reappears in the status bar. The cell cursor also returns to the original cell (A3).

5. Press the up arrow one more time. A2 adds to the formula.

   If you prefer, you can use your mouse and click cell A2.

6. Press Enter to end the formula. Like with entering the formula manually, the cell displays the result of the formula, and the formula appears in the formula bar when the cell is activated.

   If you prefer, you can use your mouse and click the check mark icon next to the formula bar.

Pointing to cell addresses rather than entering them manually is usually less tedious and is almost always more accurate.

Pasting Names

As I discuss in Chapter 3, you can assign a name to a cell or range. If your formula uses named cells or ranges, you can type the name in place of the address or choose the name from a list and have Excel insert the name for you automatically.

To insert a name into a formula, position your cursor in the formula where you want the name entered and use one of these three methods:

- Press F3 to display the Paste Name dialog box. Select the name and click OK.

- Choose Formula⇨Use in Formula to display a drop-down list of names. Choose the name from the list, and it is inserted into the formula.

- Take advantage of the formula autocomplete feature. When you type a letter while constructing a formula, Excel displays a list of matching options. These options include functions and names. Use the down-arrow key to select the name and then press Tab to insert the name in your formula.

Spaces and Line Breaks

Normally, you enter a formula without using any spaces. However, you can use spaces (and even line breaks) within your formulas. Doing so has no effect on the formula's result but can make the formula easier to read. To enter a line break in a formula, press Alt+Enter. Figure 2-1 shows a formula that contains spaces and line breaks.

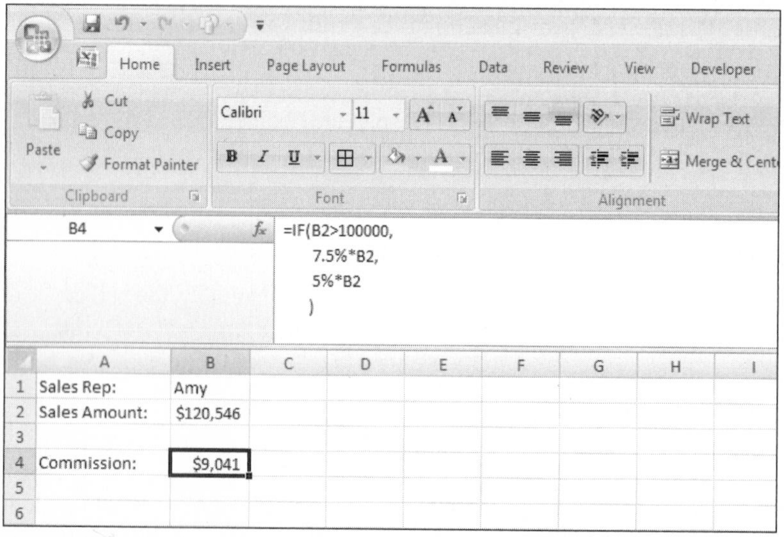

Figure 2-1: This formula contains spaces and line breaks.

TIP

To make the formula bar display more than one line, drag the border below the formula bar downward.

Formula Limits

A formula can consist of up to about 8,000 characters. In the unlikely event that you need to create a formula that exceeds this limit, you must break the formula up into multiple formulas. You also can opt to create a custom function by using VBA.

CROSS REF

Part VI focuses on creating custom functions.

Sample Formulas

If you follow the above instructions for entering formulas, you can create a variety of formulas. This section provides a look at some sample formulas.

- The following formula multiplies 150 × .01, returning 1.5. This formula uses only literal values, so it doesn't seem very useful. However, it may be useful to "show your work" when you review your spreadsheet later.

  `=150*.01`

- This formula adds the values in cells A1 and A2:

  `=A1+A2`

- The next formula subtracts the value in the cell named Expenses from the value in the cell named *Income:*

  `=Income-Expenses`

- The following formula uses the SUM function to add the values in the range A1:A12.

  `=SUM(A1:A12)`

- The next formula compares cell A1 with cell C12 by using the = operator. If the values in the two cells are identical, the formula returns TRUE; otherwise, it returns FALSE.

  `=A1=C12`

- This final formula subtracts the value in cell B3 from the value in cell B2 and then multiplies the result by the value in cell B4:

  `=(B2-B3)*B4`

Editing Formulas

If you make changes to your worksheet, you may need to edit formulas. Or if a formula returns one of the error values described later in this chapter, you need to edit the formula to correct the error. You can edit your formulas just as you edit any other cell.

Here are several ways to get into cell edit mode:

- **Double-click the cell.** This enables you to edit the cell contents directly in the cell. This technique works only if the Double-click Allows Editing Directly in Cell check box is enabled on the Advanced tab of the Excel Options dialog box.

- **Press F2.** This enables you to edit the cell contents directly in the cell. If the Double-click Allows Editing Directly in Cell check box is not enabled, the editing will occur in the formula bar.

- **Select the formula cell that you want to edit and then click in the formula bar.** This enables you to edit the cell contents in the formula bar.

When you edit a formula, you can select multiple characters by dragging the mouse over them or by holding down Shift while you use the arrow keys. You can also press Home or End to select from the cursor position to the beginning or end of the current line of the formula.

Using the Formula Bar as a Calculator

If you simply need to perform a calculation, you can use the formula bar as a calculator. For example, enter the following formula into any cell:

```
=(145*1.05)/12
```

Because this formula always returns the same result, you may prefer to store the formula's result rather than the formula. To do so, press F2 to edit the cell. Then press F9, followed by Enter. Excel stores the formula's result (12.6875), rather than the formula. This technique also works if the formula uses cell references.

This technique is most useful when you use worksheet functions. For example, to enter the square root of 221 into a cell, enter **=SQRT(221)**, press F9, and press Enter. Excel enters the result: 14.8660687473185. You also can use this technique to evaluate just part of a formula. Consider this formula:

```
=(145*1.05)/A1
```

If you want to convert just the expression within the parentheses to a value, get into cell edit mode and select the part that you want to evaluate. In this example, select 145*1.05. Then press F9 followed by Enter. Excel converts the formula to the following:

```
=(152.25)/A1
```

TIP

Suppose you have a lengthy formula that contains an error, and Excel won't let you enter it because of the error. In this case, you can convert the formula to text and tackle it again later. To convert a formula to text, just remove the initial equal sign (=). When you're ready to return to editing the formula, insert the initial equal sign to convert the cell contents back to a formula.

Using Operators in Formulas

As previously discussed, an operator is the basic element of a formula. An *operator* is a symbol that represents an operation. Table 2-1 shows the Excel-supported operators.

TABLE 2-1   EXCEL-SUPPORTED OPERATORS

Symbol	Operator
+	Addition
–	Subtraction
/	Division
*	Multiplication
%	Percent*
&	Text concatenation
^	Exponentiation
=	Logical comparison (equal to)
>	Logical comparison (greater than)
<	Logical comparison (less than)
>=	Logical comparison (greater than or equal to)
<=	Logical comparison (less than or equal to)
<>	Logical comparison (not equal to)

Percent isn't really an operator, but it functions similarly to one in Excel. Entering a percent sign after a number divides the number by 100 and formats the cell as percent.

Reference Operators

Excel supports another class of operators known as *reference operators;* see Table 2-2. Reference operators, described in the following list, work with cell references.

TABLE 2-2   REFERENCE OPERATORS

Symbol	Operator
: (colon)	Range. Produces one reference to all the cells between two references.
, (comma)	Union. Combines multiple cell or range references into one reference.
(single space)	Intersection. Produces one reference to cells common to two references.

Sample Formulas That Use Operators

These examples of formulas use various operators:

- The following formula joins *(concatenates)* the two literal text strings (each enclosed in quotes) to produce a new text string: *Part-23A:*

  ```
  ="Part-"&"23A"
  ```

- The next formula concatenates the contents of cell A1 with cell A2:

  ```
  =A1&A2
  ```

  Usually, concatenation is used with text, but concatenation works with values as well. For example, if cell A1 contains 123 and cell A2 contains 456, the preceding formula would return the value 123456. Note that, technically, the result is a text string. However, if you used this string in a mathematical formula, Excel will treat it as a number. Many Excel functions will ignore this "number" because they are designed to ignore text.

- The following formula uses the exponentiation operator to raise 6 to the third power, to produce a result of 216:

  ```
  =6^3
  ```

- A more useful form of the preceding formula uses a cell reference instead of the literal value. Note this example that raises the value in cell A1 to the third power:

  ```
  =A1^3
  ```

Part I

- This formula returns the cube root of 216 (which is 6):

  `=216^(1/3)`

- The next formula returns TRUE if the value in cell A1 is less than the value in cell A2. Otherwise, it returns FALSE:

  `=A1<A2`

  Logical comparison operators also work with text. If A1 contains Alpha and A2 contains Gamma, the formula returns TRUE because Alpha comes before Gamma in alphabetical order:

- The following formula returns TRUE if the value in cell A1 is less than or equal to the value in cell A2. Otherwise, it returns FALSE:

  `=A1<=A2`

- The next formula returns TRUE if the value in cell A1 does not equal the value in cell A2. Otherwise, it returns FALSE:

  `=A1<>A2`

- Unlike some other spreadsheets (such as 1-2-3), Excel doesn't have logical AND or OR operators. Rather, you use functions to specify these types of logical operators. For example, this formula returns TRUE if cell A1 contains either 100 or 1000:

  `=OR(A1=100,A1=1000)`

  This last formula returns TRUE only if both cell A1 and cell A2 contain values less than 100:

  `=AND(A1<100,A2<100)`

Operator Precedence

You can (and should) use parentheses in your formulas to control the order in which the calculations occur. As an example, consider the following formula that uses references to named cells.

`=Income-Expenses*TaxRate`

The goal is to subtract expenses from income and then multiply the result by the tax rate. If you enter the preceding formula, you discover that Excel computes the wrong answer. Rather, the formula multiplies expenses by the tax rate and then subtracts the result from the income. In other words, Excel does not necessarily perform calculations from left to right (as you might expect).

The correct way to write this formula is

`=(Income-Expenses)*TaxRate`

To understand how this works, you need to be familiar with *operator precedence* — the set of rules that Excel uses to perform its calculations. Table 2-3 lists Excel's operator precedence. Operations are performed in the order listed in the table. For example, multiplication is performed before subtraction.

Use parentheses to override Excel's built-in order of precedence. Returning to the previous example, the formula without parentheses is evaluated using Excel's standard operator precedence. Because multiplication has a higher precedence, the *Expense* cell multiplies by the *TaxRate* cell. Then, this result is subtracted from *Income* — producing an incorrect calculation.

The correct formula uses parentheses to control the order of operations. Expressions within parentheses always get evaluated first. In this case, *Expenses* is subtracted from *Income,* and the result multiplies by *TaxRate.*

TABLE 2-3   OPERATOR PRECEDENCE IN EXCEL FORMULAS

Symbol	Operator
Colon (:), comma (,), space( )	Reference operators
–	Negation
%	Percent
^	Exponentiation
* and /	Multiplication and division
+ and –	Addition and subtraction
&	Text concatenation
=, <, >, <=, >=, and <>	Comparison

Nested Parentheses

You can also *nest* parentheses in formulas — that is, put parentheses inside of parentheses. When a formula contains nested parentheses, Excel evaluates the most deeply nested expressions first and works its way out. The following example of a formula uses nested parentheses.

```
=((B2*C2)+(B3*C3)+(B4*C4))*B6
```

This formula has four sets of parentheses. Three sets are nested inside the fourth set. Excel evaluates each nested set of parentheses and then sums the three results. This sum is then multiplied by the value in B6.

It's a good idea to make liberal use of parentheses in your formulas even when they aren't necessary. Using parentheses clarifies the order of operations and makes the formula easier to read. For example, if you want to add 1 to the product of two cells, the following formula will do the job:

```
=A1*A2+1
```

Because of Excel's operator precedence rules, the multiplication will be performed before the addition. Therefore, parentheses are not necessary. You may find it much clearer, however, to use the following formula even though it contains superfluous parentheses:

```
=(A1*A2)+1
```

TIP

Every left parenthesis, of course, must have a matching right parenthesis. If you have many levels of nested parentheses, you might find it difficult to keep them straight. Fortunately, Excel lends a hand in helping you match parentheses. Matching parentheses are colored the same although the colors can be difficult to distinguish if you have a lot of parentheses. Also, when the cursor moves over a parenthesis, Excel momentarily displays the parenthesis and its matching parenthesis in bold. This lasts for less than a second, so watch carefully.

In some cases, if your formula contains mismatched parentheses, Excel may propose a correction to your formula. Figure 2-2 shows an example of Excel's AutoCorrect feature in action.

CAUTION

Simply accepting the correction proposed in the dialog box is tempting, but be careful. In many cases, the proposed formula, although syntactically correct, isn't the formula that you want. I omitted the closing parentheses after January. In Figure 2-2, Excel proposed this correction:

```
=SUM(January/SUM(Total))
```

In fact, the correct formula is

```
=SUM(January)/SUM(Total)
```

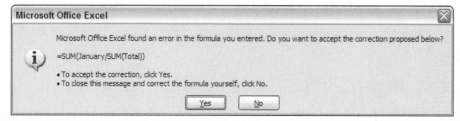

Figure 2-2: Excel's Formula AutoCorrect feature often suggests a correction to an erroneous formula.

Don't Hard-Code Values

When you create a formula, think twice before using a literal value in the formula. For example, if your formula calculates 7.5 percent sales tax, you may be tempted to enter a formula such as

```
=A1*.075
```

A better approach is to insert the sales tax rate into a cell and use the cell reference in place of the literal value. This makes it easier to modify and maintain your worksheet. For example, if the sales tax range changes to 7.75 percent, you need to modify every formula that uses the old value. If the tax rate is stored in a cell, you simply change one cell and all the formulas automatically get updated.

Calculating Formulas

You've probably noticed that the formulas in your worksheet get calculated immediately. If you change any cells that the formula uses, the formula displays a new result with no effort on your part. This occurs when Excel's Calculation mode is set to Automatic. In this mode (the default mode), Excel follows certain rules when calculating your worksheet:

- When you make a change (enter or edit data or formulas, for example), Excel calculates immediately those formulas that depend on new or edited data.

- If working on a lengthy calculation, Excel temporarily suspends calculation when you need to perform other worksheet tasks; it resumes when you finish.

- Formulas are evaluated in a natural sequence. For instance, if a formula in cell D12 depends on the result of a formula in cell D11, cell D11 is calculated before D12.

Sometimes, however, you may want to control when Excel calculates formulas. For example, if you create a worksheet with thousands of complex formulas, you may find that things can slow to a snail's pace while Excel does its thing. In this case, you can set Excel's calculation mode to Manual. Do this by choosing Formulas⇔Calculation⇔ Calculation Options⇔Manual.

When you work in Manual calculation mode, Excel displays `Calculate` in the status bar when you have any uncalculated formulas. The Formulas⇔Calculation group contains two controls that when clicked, perform a calculation: Calculate Now and Calculate Sheet control. In addition to these controls, you can use the following shortcut keys to recalculate the formulas:

- **F9:** Calculates the formulas in all open workbooks (same as Calculate Now control).

- **Shift+F9:** Calculates only the formulas in the active worksheet. It does not calculate other worksheets in the same workbook (same as Calculate Sheet control).

- **Ctrl+Alt+F9:** Forces a complete recalculation of all open workbooks. Use it if Excel (for some reason) doesn't seem to return correct calculations.

- **Ctrl+Shift+Alt+F9:** Rechecks all the dependent formulas and then forces a recalculation of all open workbooks.

CAUTION

Contrary to what you might expect, Excel's Calculation mode isn't specific to a particular worksheet. When you change Excel's Calculation mode, it affects all open workbooks— not just the active workbook. Also, the initial Calculation mode is set by the Calculation mode saved with the first workbook you open.

Cell and Range References

Most formulas reference one or more cells by using the cell or range address (or name if it has one). Cell references come in four styles; the dollar sign differentiates them:

- **Relative:** The reference is fully relative. When the formula is copied, the cell reference adjusts to its new location.

  Example: A1

- **Absolute:** The reference is fully absolute. When the formula is copied, the cell reference does not change.

  Example: $A$1

- **Row Absolute:** The reference is partially absolute. When the formula is copied, the column part adjusts, but the row part does not change.

  Example: A$1

- **Column Absolute:** The reference is partially absolute. When the formula is copied, the row part adjusts, but the column part does not change.

  Example: $A1

Creating an Absolute or a Mixed Reference

When you create a formula by pointing to cells, all cell and range references are relative. To change a reference to an absolute reference or a mixed reference, you must do so manually by adding the dollar signs. Or when you enter a cell or range address, you can use the F4 key to cycle among all possible reference modes.

If you think about it, you may realize that the only reason you would ever need to change a reference is if you plan to copy the formula.

Figure 2-3 demonstrates an absolute reference in a formula. Cell D2 contains a formula that multiples the quantity (cell B2) by the price (cell C2) by the sales tax (cell B7):

```
=B2*C2*$B$7
```

	A	B	C	D	E	F
1	Item	Quantity	Price	Sales Tax	Total	
2	Chair	4	$125.00	$37.50	$162.50	
3	Desk	4	$695.00	$208.50	$903.50	
4	Lamp	3	$39.95	$8.99	$48.94	
5						
6						
7	Sales Tax:	7.50%				
8						
9						
10						

Sheet1 Sheet2 Sheet3

Figure 2-3: This worksheet demonstrates the use of an absolute reference.

The reference to cell B7 is an absolute reference. When the formula in cell D2 is copied to the cells below, the $B$7 reference always points to the sales tax cell. Using a relative reference (B7) results in incorrect results in the copied formulas.

Figure 2-4 demonstrates the use of mixed references. Note the formula in cell C4:

```
=$B3*C$2
```

This formula calculates the area for various lengths (listed in column B) and widths (listed in row 2). After you enter the formula, it can then be copied down and across. Because the formula uses absolute references to row 2 and column B, each copied formula produces the correct result. If the formula uses relative references, copying the formula causes the references to adjust and produce the wrong results.

	A	B	C	D	E	F	G	H
1				Width				
2			1.0	1.5	2.0	2.5		
3		1.0	1.0	1.5	2.0	2.5		
4		1.5	1.5	2.3	3.0	3.8		
5		2.0	2.0	3.0	4.0	5.0		
6		2.5	2.5	3.8	5.0	6.3		
7		3.0	3.0	4.5	6.0	7.5		
8								
9								

Length

Sheet1 Sheet2 Sheet3

Figure 2-4: An example of using mixed references in a formula.

A1 versus R1C1 Notation

Normally, Excel uses *A1 notation.* Each cell address consists of a column letter and a row number. However, Excel also supports *R1C1 notation.* In this system, cell A1 is referred to as cell R1C1, cell A2 as R2C1, and so on.

To change to R1C1 notation, choose File⇨Excel Options to open the Excel Options dialog box, click the Formulas tab, and place a check mark next to the R1C1 Reference Style option. Now, notice that the column letters all change to numbers. And all the cell and range references in your formulas also adjust.

Look at the following examples of formulas using standard notation and R1C1 notation. The formula is assumed to be in cell B1 (also known as R1C2).

Standard	*R1C1*
=A1+1	=RC[-1]+1
=$A$1+1	=R1C1+1
=$A1+1	=RC1+1
=A$1+1	=R1C[-1]+1
=SUM(A1:A10)	=SUM(RC[-1]:R[9]C[-1])
=SUM($A$1:$A$10)	=SUM(R1C1:R10C1)

If you find R1C1 notation confusing, you're not alone. R1C1 notation isn't too bad when you're dealing with absolute references. When relative references are involved, though, the brackets can drive you nuts.

The numbers in brackets refer to the relative position of the references. For example, R[-5]C[-3] specifies the cell that appears five rows above and three columns to the left. Conversely, R[5]C[3] references the cell that appears five rows below and three columns to the right. If you omit the brackets, it specifies the same row or column. For example, R[5]C refers to the cell five rows below in the same column.

Although you probably won't use R1C1 notation as your standard system, it *does* have at least one good use. R1C1 notation makes it very easy to spot an erroneous formula. When you copy a formula, every copied formula is exactly the same in R1C1 notation. This remains true regardless of the types of cell references you use (relative, absolute, or mixed). Therefore, you can switch to R1C1 notation and check your copied formulas. If one looks different from its surrounding formulas, it's probably incorrect.

However, you can take advantage of the background formula auditing feature, which can flag potentially incorrect formulas. I discuss this feature in Chapter 21.

Referencing Other Sheets or Workbooks

A formula can use references to cells and ranges that are in a different worksheet. To refer to a cell in a different worksheet, precede the cell reference with the sheet name followed by an exclamation point. Note this example of a formula that uses a cell reference in a different worksheet (Sheet2):

```
=Sheet2!A1+1
```

You can also create link formulas that refer to a cell in a different workbook. To do so, precede the cell reference with the workbook name (in square brackets), the worksheet name, and an exclamation point, like this:

```
=[Budget.xlsx]Sheet1!A1+1
```

If the workbook name or sheet name in the reference includes one or more spaces, you must enclose it (and the sheet name) in single quotation marks. For example

```
='[Budget Analysis.xlsx]Sheet1'!A1+A1
```

If the linked workbook is closed, you must add the complete path to the workbook reference. For example

```
='C:\MSOffice\Excel\[Budget Analysis.xlsx]Sheet1'!A1+A1
```

Although you can enter link formulas directly, you also can create the reference by using normal pointing methods discussed earlier. To do so, make sure that the source file is open. Normally, you can create a formula by pointing to results in relative cell references. But, when you create a reference to another workbook by pointing, Excel creates *absolute* cell references. If you plan to copy the formula to other cells, you must edit the formula to make the references relative.

 CAUTION
Working with links can be tricky and may cause some unexpected problems. For example, if you use the Office Button⇨Save As command to make a backup copy of the source workbook, you automatically change the link formulas to refer to the new file (not usually what you want). You also can mess up your links by renaming the source workbook file.

Making an Exact Copy of a Formula

When you copy a formula, Excel adjusts the formula's cell references when you paste it to a different location. Usually, adjusting the cell references is exactly what you want. Sometimes, however, you may want to make an exact copy of the formula. You can do this by converting the cell references to absolute values, as discussed earlier — but this isn't always desirable.

A better approach is to select the formula while in edit mode and then copy it to the Clipboard as text. There are several ways to do this. Here I present a step-by-step example of how to make an exact copy of the formula in A1 and copy it to A2:

1. Select cell A1 and press F2 to activate edit mode.

2. Press Ctrl+Home to move the cursor to the start of the formula, followed by Ctrl+ Shift+End to select all the formula text. Or you can drag the mouse to select the entire formula. Note that holding down the Ctrl key is necessary when the formula is more than one line long but optional for formulas that are a single line.

3. Choose Home⇨Clipboard⇨Copy (or press Ctrl+C). This copies the selected text to the Clipboard.

4. Press Esc to end edit mode.

5. Activate cell A2.

6. Choose Home⇨Clipboard⇨Paste (or press Ctrl+V). This operation pastes an exact copy of the formula text into cell A2.

You also can use this technique to copy just part of a formula to use in another formula. Just select the part of the formula that you want to copy by dragging the mouse or by using the Shift+arrow keys. Then use any of the available techniques to copy the selection to the Clipboard. You can then paste the text to another cell.

Formulas (or parts of formulas) copied in this manner won't have their cell references adjusted when you paste them to a new cell. This is because you copy the formulas as text, not as actual formulas.

Another technique for making an exact copy of a formula is to edit the formula and remove its initial equal sign. This converts the formula to text. Then, copy the "non-formula" to a new location. Finally, edit both the original and the copied formula by inserting the initial equal sign.

Converting Formulas to Values

If you have a range of formulas that always produce the same result (that is, dead formulas), you may want to convert them to values. You can use the Home⇨Clipboard⇨Paste⇨ Paste Values command to do this.

Suppose that range A1:A10 contains formulas that calculate a result that never changes. To convert these formulas to values:

1. Select A1:A10.

2. Choose Home⇨Clipboard⇨Copy (or press Ctrl+C).

3. Choose Home⇨Clipboard⇨Paste⇨Paste Values.

4. Press Enter or Esc to cancel paste mode.

You can also take advantage of a Smart Tag. In Step 3 in the preceding list, press Ctrl+V to paste. A Smart Tag will appear at the lower-right corner of the range. Click the Smart Tag and choose Values Only (see Figure 2-5).

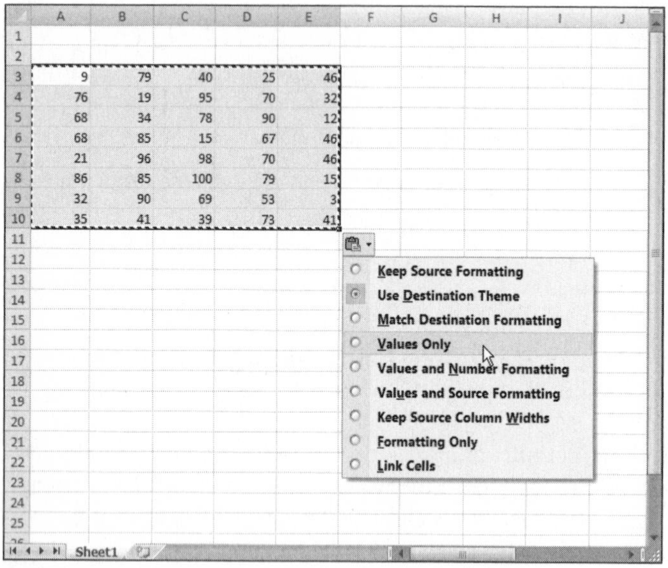

Figure 2-5: A Smart Tag appears after pasting data.

This technique is very useful when you use formulas as a means to convert cells. For example, assume you have a list of names (in uppercase) in column A. You want to convert these names to proper case. In order to do so, you need to create formulas in a separate column; then convert the formulas to values and replace the original values in column A. The following steps illustrate how to do this.

1. Insert a new column after column A.

2. Insert the following formula into cell B1:

```
=PROPER(A1)
```

3. Copy the formula down column B, to accommodate the number of entries in column A. Column B then displays the values in column A, but in proper case.

4. Select all the names in column B.

5. Choose Home⇨Clipboard⇨Copy.

6. Select cell A1.

7. Choose Home⇨Clipboard⇨Paste⇨Paste Values.

When to Use AutoFill Rather Than Formulas

Excel's AutoFill feature provides a quick way to copy a cell to adjacent cells. AutoFill also has some other uses that may even substitute for formulas in some cases. I'm surprised to find that many experienced Excel users don't take advantage of the AutoFill feature, which can save a lot of time.

For example, if you need a list of values from 1 to 100 to appear in A1:A100, you can do it with formulas. You enter **1** in cell A1, enter the formula **=A1+1** into cell A2, and then copy the formula to the 98 cells below.

You also can use AutoFill to create the series for you without using a formula. To do so, enter **1** into cell A1 and **2** into cell A2. Select A1:A2 and drag the fill handle down to cell A100. (The *fill handle* is the small square at the lower-right corner of the active cell.) When you use AutoFill in this manner, Excel analyzes the selected cells and uses this information to complete the series. If cell A1 contains 1 and cell A2 contains 3, Excel recognizes this pattern and fills in 5, 7, 9, and so on. This also works with decreasing series (10, 9, 8, and so on) and dates. If there is no discernible pattern in the selected cells, Excel performs a linear regression and fills in values on the calculated trend line.

Excel also recognizes common series names such as months and days of the week. If you enter Monday into a cell and then drag its fill handle, Excel fills in the successive days of the week. You also can create custom AutoFill lists using the Custom Lists panel of the Options dialog box. Finally, if you drag the fill handle with the right mouse button, Excel displays a shortcut menu to enable you to select an AutoFill option.

8. Press Enter or Esc to cancel paste mode.

9. Delete column B.

Hiding Formulas

In some cases, you may not want others to see your formulas. For example, you may have a special formula you developed that performs a calculation proprietary to your company. You can use the Format Cells dialog box to hide the formulas contained in these cells.

To prevent one or more formulas from being viewed

1. Select the formula or formulas.

2. Right-click and choose Format Cells to show the Format Cells dialog box (or Press Ctrl+1). In the Format Cells dialog box, click the Protection tab.

3. Place a check mark in the Hidden check box, as shown in Figure 2-6.

Figure 2-6: Use the Format Cells dialog box to change the Hidden and Locked status of a cell or range.

4. Use the Review⇨Protect command to protect the worksheet. To prevent others from unprotecting the sheet, make sure you specify a password in the Protect Sheet dialog box.

By default, all cells are locked. Protecting a sheet prevents any locked cells from being changed. Therefore, you should unlock any cells that require user input before protecting your sheet.

 CAUTION

Be aware that it's very easy to crack the password for a worksheet. Therefore, this technique of hiding your formulas does not ensure that no one can view your formulas.

Errors in Formulas

It's not uncommon to enter a formula only to find that the formula returns an error. Table 2-4 lists the types of error values that may appear in a cell that has a formula.

Formulas may return an error value if a cell that they refer to has an error value. This is known as the ripple effect: A single error value can make its way to lots of other cells that contain formulas that depend on that cell.

TABLE 2-4   EXCEL ERROR VALUES

Error Value	Explanation
#DIV/0!	The formula attempts to divide by zero (an operation not allowed on this planet). This also occurs when the formula attempts to divide by an empty cell.
#NAME?	The formula uses a name that Excel doesn't recognize. This can happen if you delete a name used in the formula or if you misspell a function.
#N/A	The formula refers (directly or indirectly) to a cell that uses the NA function to signal unavailable data. This error also occurs if a lookup function does not find a match.
#NULL!	The formula uses an intersection of two ranges that don't intersect. (I describe this concept later in this chapter.)
#NUM!	A problem occurs with a value; for example, you specify a negative number where a positive number is expected.
#REF!	The formula refers to an invalid cell. This happens if the cell has been deleted from the worksheet.
#VALUE!	The formula includes an argument or operand of the wrong type. An *operand* refers to a value or cell reference that a formula uses to calculate a result.

NOTE

If the entire cell fills with hash marks (#########), this usually means that the column isn't wide enough to display the value. You can either widen the column or change the number format of the cell. The cell will also fill with hash marks if it contains a formula that returns an invalid date or time.

Depending on your settings, formulas that return an error may display a Smart Icon. You can click this Smart Icon to get more information about the error or to trace the calculation steps that led to the error. Refer to Chapter 21 for more information about this feature.

Dealing with Circular References

When you enter formulas, you may occasionally see a message from Excel like the one shown in Figure 2-7. This indicates that the formula you just entered will result in a *circular reference*.

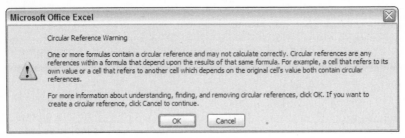

Figure 2-7: Excel's way of telling you that your formula contains a circular reference.

A circular reference occurs when a formula refers to its own value, either directly or indirectly. For example, if you enter =**A1** into cell A3, =**A3** into cell B3, and =**B3** into cell A1, this produces a circular reference because the formulas create a circle where each formula depends on the one before it. Every time the formula in A3 is calculated, it affects the formula in B3, which in turn affects the formula in A1. The result of the formula in A1 then causes A3 to recalculate, and the calculation circle starts all over again. The calculation of these formulas continues in a circle forever, never resolving to any value.

When you enter a formula that contains a circular reference, Excel displays a dialog box with two options: OK and Cancel.

Normally, you'll want to correct any circular references, so you should click OK. When you do so, Excel inserts tracing arrows and displays the Help topic for circular references. The status bar will display *Circular References: A3,* in this case. To resolve the circular reference, choose Formulas⇨Formula Auditing⇨Error Checking⇨Circular References to see a list of cells involved in the circular reference. Click each cell in turn and try to locate the error. If you cannot determine whether the cell is the cause of the circular reference, navigate to the next cell on the Circular References submenu. Continue reviewing each cell on the Circular References submenu until the status bar no longer reads *Circular References.*

CROSS REF

In a few situations, you may want to use a circular reference intentionally. Refer to Chapter 16 for some examples.

TIP

Instead of navigating to each cell using the Circular References submenu, you can click on the tracer arrows to quickly jump between cells.

If you ignore the circular reference message (by clicking Cancel), Excel enables you to enter the formula and displays a message in the status bar reminding you that a circular reference exists. In this case, the message reads *Circular References: A3.* If you activate a different worksheet or workbook, the message simply displays *Circular References* (without the cell reference).

CAUTION

Excel doesn't warn you about a circular reference if you have the Enable Iterative Calculation setting turned on. You can check this in the Excel Options dialog box (in the Calculation section of the Formulas tab). If this option is checked, Excel performs the circular calculation the number of times specified in the Maximum Iterations field (or until the value changes by less than .001 — or whatever other value appears in the Maximum Change field). You should, however, keep the Enable Iterative Calculation setting off so that you'll be warned of circular references. Generally, a circular reference indicates an error that you must correct.

When the formula in a cell refers to that cell, the cause of the circular reference is quite obvious and is, therefore, easy to identify and correct. For this type of circular reference, Excel does not show tracer arrows. For indirect circular reference, like in the preceding example, the tracer arrows can help you identify the problem.

Goal Seeking

Many spreadsheets contain formulas that enable you to ask questions, such as, "What would be the total profit if sales increase by 20 percent?" If you set up your worksheet properly, you can change the value in one cell to see what happens to the profit cell.

Goal seeking serves as a useful feature that works in conjunction with your formulas. If you know what a formula result should be, Excel can tell you which values of one or more input cells you need to produce that result. In other words, you can ask a question such as, "What sales increase is needed to produce a profit of $1.2 million?"

Single-cell goal seeking (also known as *backsolving*) represents a rather simple concept. Excel determines what value in an input cell produces a desired result in a formula cell. You can best understand how this works by walking through an example.

A Goal Seeking Example

Figure 2-8 shows a mortgage loan worksheet that has four input cells (C4:C7) and four formula cells (C10:C13). The formulas calculate various values using the input cell. The formulas are

C10: =(1-C5)*C4

C11: =PMT(C7/12,C6,-C10)

C12: =C11*C6

C13: =C12-C10

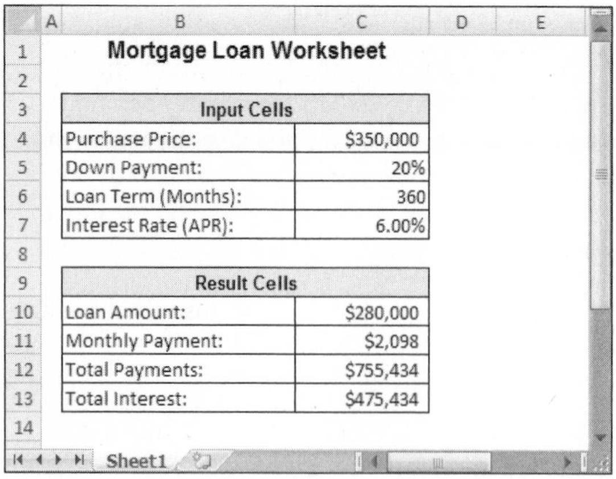

Figure 2-8: This worksheet presents a simple demonstration of goal seeking.

Imagine that you're in the market for a new home and you know that you can afford $1,200 per month in mortgage payments. You also know that a lender can issue a fixed-rate mortgage loan for 6.00 percent, based on an 80 percent loan-to-value (a 20 percent down payment). The question is, "What is the maximum purchase price you can handle?" In other words, what value in cell C4 causes the formula in cell C11 to result in $1,200? You can plug values into cell C4 until C11 displays $1,200. A more efficient approach lets Excel determine the answer.

To answer this question, choose Data⇨Data Tools⇨What-If Analysis⇨Goal Seek. Excel displays the Goal Seek dialog box, as shown in Figure 2-9. Completing this dialog box resembles forming the following sentence: Set cell C11 to 1200 by changing cell C4. Enter this information in the dialog box by either typing the cell references or by pointing with the mouse. Click OK to begin the goal seeking process.

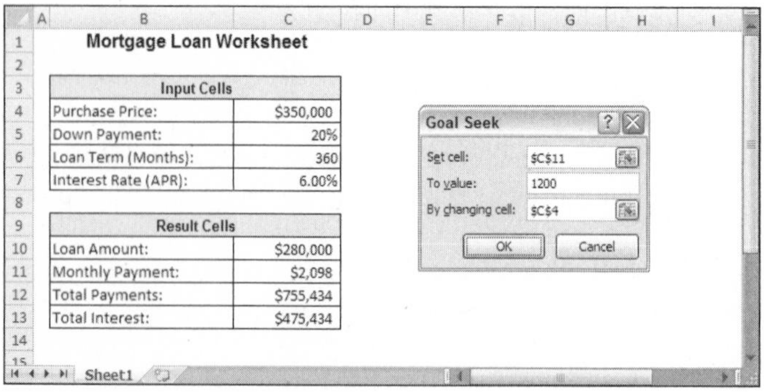

Figure 2-9: The Goal Seek dialog box.

Almost immediately, Excel announces that it has found the solution and displays the Goal Seek Status box. This box tells you the target value and what Excel came up with. In this case, Excel found an exact value. The worksheet now displays the found value in cell C4 $200,150). As a result of this value, the monthly payment amount is $1,200. Now, you have two options:

- Click OK to replace the original value with the found value.

- Click Cancel to restore your worksheet to its original form before you chose Goal Seek.

More about Goal Seeking

If you think about it, you may realize that Excel can't always find a value that produces the result you're looking for — sometimes a solution doesn't exist. In such a case, the Goal Seek Status box informs you of that fact. Other times, however, Excel may report that it can't find a solution even though you believe one exists. In this case, you can adjust the current value of the changing cell to a value closer to the solution, and then reissue the command. If that fails, double-check your logic and make sure that the formula cell does indeed depend on the specified changing cell.

Like all computer programs, Excel has limited precision. To demonstrate this, enter **=A1^2** into cell A2. Then, choose Data⇨Data Tools⇨What-If Analysis⇨Goal Seek to find the value in cell A1 that causes the formula to return 16. Excel returns a value of 4.00002269 — close to the square root of 16, but certainly not exact. You can adjust the precision in the Calculation section of the Formulas tab of the Excel Options dialog box (make the Maximum change value smaller).

In some cases, multiple values of the input cell produce the same desired result. For example, the formula =A1^2 returns 16 if cell A1 contains either −4 or +4. If you use goal seeking when two solutions exist, Excel gives you the solution that is nearest to the current value in the cell.

Perhaps the main limitation of the Goal Seek command is that it can find the value for only one input cell. For example, it can't tell you what purchase price *and* what down payment percent result in a particular monthly payment. If you want to change more than one variable at a time, use the Solver add-in.

Chapter 3

Working with Names

IN THIS CHAPTER

◆ An overview and the advantages of using names in Excel

◆ The difference between workbook- and worksheet-level names

◆ Working with the new Name Manager dialog box

◆ Shortcuts for creating cell and range names

◆ How to create names that extend across multiple worksheets

◆ How to perform common operations with range and cell names

◆ How Excel maintains cell and range names

◆ Potential problems that may crop up when you use names

◆ The secret behind names, and examples of named constants and named formulas

◆ Examples of advanced techniques that use names

Most intermediate and advanced Excel users are familiar with the concept of named cells or ranges. Naming cells and ranges is an excellent practice and offers several important advantages. As you'll see in this chapter, Excel supports other types of names — and the power of this concept may surprise you.

What's in a Name?

You can think of a *name* as an identifier for something in a workbook. This "something" can consist of a cell, a range, a chart, a shape, and so on. If you provide a name for a range, you can then use that name in your formulas. For example, suppose your worksheet contains daily sales information stored in the range B2:B200. Further, assume that cell C1 contains a sales commission rate. The following formula returns the sum of the sales, multiplied by the commission rate:

```
=SUM(B2:B200)*C1
```

This formula works fine, but its purpose is not at all clear. To help clarify the formula, you can define one descriptive name for the daily sales range and another descriptive name for cell C1. Assume, for this example, that the range B2:B200 is named *DailySales* and cell C1 is named *CommissionRate*. You can then rewrite the formula to use the names instead of the actual range addresses:

```
=SUM(DailySales)*CommissionRate
```

As you can see, using names instead of cell references makes the formula self-documenting and much easier to understand.

Using named cells and ranges offers a number of advantages:

- Names make your formulas more understandable and easier to use, especially for people who didn't create the worksheet. Obviously, a formula such as =Income–Taxes is more intuitive than =D20–D40.

- When entering formulas, a descriptive range name (such as *Total_Income*) is easier to remember than a cell address (such as AC21). And typing a name is less likely to result in an error than entering a cell or range address.

- You can quickly move to areas of your worksheet either by using the Name box, located at the left side of the formula bar (click the arrow for a drop-down list of defined names) or by choosing Home⇨Editing⇨Find & Select⇨Go To (or F5) and specifying the range name.

- When you select a named cell or range, its name appears in the Name box. This is a good way to verify that your names refer to the correct cells.

- You may find that creating formulas is easier if you use named cells. You can easily insert a name into a formula by using the Formulas⇨Defined Names⇨Use in Formula command.

- Macros are easier to create and maintain when you use range names rather than cell addresses.

A Name's Scope

Before I get into creating and working with names, it's important to understand that all names have a scope. A name's *scope* defines where you can use the name. Names are scoped either at the workbook level or at the worksheet level for a particular sheet.

Referencing Names

You can refer to a workbook level name just by using its name from any sheet in the workbook. For worksheet level names, you must precede the name with the name of the worksheet unless you're using it on its own worksheet.

For example, assume you have a workbook with two sheets, Sheet1 and Sheet2. In this workbook, you have *Total_Sales* (a workbook level name), *North_Sales* (a worksheet level name on Sheet1), and *South_Sales* (a worksheet level name on Sheet2). On Sheet1 or Sheet2, you can refer to *Total_Sales* by simply using the name:

```
=Total_Sales
```

If you're on Sheet1 and you want to refer to *North_Sales,* you can use a similar formula because *North_Sales* is defined on Sheet1:

```
=North_Sales
```

However, if you want to refer to *South_Sales* on Sheet1, you'll need to do a little more work. Sheet1 can't "see" the name *South_Sales* because it's defined on another sheet. Sheet1 can only see workbook level names and worksheet level names defined on Sheet1. To refer to *South_Sales* on Sheet1, prefix the name with the worksheet name and an exclamation point:

```
=Sheet2!South_Sales
```

TIP

If your worksheet name contains a space, enclose the worksheet name in single quotes when referring to a name defined on that sheet:

```
='My Sheet'!My_Name
```

Generally, it's a good practice to scope your names as narrowly as possible. If you will be using a name on only one worksheet, set that name's scope at the worksheet level. For names that you want to use throughout your workbook, a workbook level scope is more appropriate.

NOTE

Only the worksheet-level names on the current sheet appear in the Name box. Similarly, only worksheet-level names on the current sheet appear in the list under Formulas⇨ Defined Names⇨Use in Formulas.

Referencing Names from Another Workbook

Chapter 2 described how to use links to reference cells or ranges in other workbooks. The same rules apply when using names defined in another workbook.

For example, the following formula uses a range named *MonthlySales*, defined in a workbook named `Budget.xlsx` (which is assumed to be open):

```
=AVERAGE(Budget.xlsx!MonthlySales)
```

If the name *MonthlySales* is a worksheet level name on Sheet1, the formula looks like this:

```
=AVERAGE([Budget.xlsx]Sheet1!MonthlySales)
```

Conflicting Names

Using worksheet-level names can be a bit confusing because Excel lets you define worksheet-level names even if the workbook contains the same name as a workbook-level name. In such a case, the worksheet-level name takes precedence over the workbook-level name but only in the worksheet in which you defined the sheet-level name.

For example, you can define a workbook-level name of *Total* for a cell on Sheet1. You can also define a worksheet-level name of *Sheet2!Total*. When Sheet2 is active, *Total* refers to the worksheet-level name. When any other sheet is active, *Total* refers to the workbook-level name. Confusing? Probably. To make your life easier, I recommend that you simply avoid using the same name at the workbook level and worksheet level.

One way you can avoid this type of conflict is to adopt a naming convention when you create names. By using a naming convention, your names will tell you more about themselves. For instance, you could prefix all your workbook level names with *wb* and your worksheet level names with *ws*. With this method, you'll never confuse *wbTotal* with *wsTotal*.

The Name Manager

Now that you understand the concept of scope, you can start creating and using names. Excel 2007 provides a new way for maintaining names called the Name Manager, as shown in Figure 3-1.

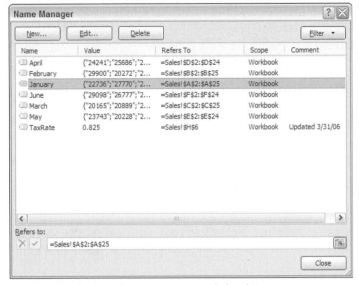

Figure 3-1: The Excel Name Manager dialog box.

To display the Name Manager, choose Formulas⇨Defined Names⇨Name Manger. Within this dialog box, you can view, create, edit, and delete names. In the Name Manager main window, you can see the current value of the name, what the name refers to, the scope of the name, and any comments you've written. The names are sortable, and the columns are resizable, allowing you to see your names in many different ways. If you use a lot of names, you can also apply some predefined filters to view only the names that interest you.

Note that the Name Manager dialog box is resizable. Drag the lower-right corner to make it wider or taller.

Creating Names

The Name Manager contains a New button for creating new names. The New button displays the New Name dialog box, as shown in Figure 3-2.

Figure 3-2: The New Name dialog box.

In the New Name dialog box, you name the name, define its scope and what it refers to, and make any comments about the name to help yourself and others understand its purpose. The Refers To field is a standard RefEdit control, meaning you can select cells or type a cell reference or formula similar to how you would do it in the formula bar.

TIP

The keyboard shortcut for displaying the Name Manager is Ctrl+F3.

Editing Names

Clicking the Edit button displays the Edit Name dialog box, which looks strikingly similar to the New Name dialog box. You can change any property of your name except the scope. If you change the name's name, all the formulas in your workbook that use that name will be updated.

TIP

To change the scope of a name, you must delete the name and re-create it. If you're careful to use the same name, your formulas that use that name will still work.

The Edit Name dialog isn't the only way to edit a name. If the only property you want to change is the Refers To property, you can do it right in the Name Manager dialog box. At the bottom of the dialog box is the field labeled Refers To. Simply select the name you'd like to edit in the main window and change the reference in the Refers To box.

TIP

If you edit the contents of the Refers To field manually, the status bar displays `Point`, indicating that you're in point mode. If you try to use keys such as the arrows, Home, or End, you'll find that you're navigating around the worksheet rather than editing the Refers To text. To switch from point mode to edit mode, press F2 and note that the status bar changes to show `Edit`.

Deleting Names

Clicking the Delete button permanently removes the selected name from your workbook. Of course, Excel warns you first because this action cannot be undone. Unfortunately, Excel isn't smart enough to replace deleted names with cell references. Any formulas that use a name that you delete will display the #NAME? error.

Shortcuts for Creating Cell and Range Names

Excel provides several ways to create names for cells and ranges other than the Name Manager. I discuss these methods in this section, along with some other relevant information that pertains to names.

The New Name Dialog Box

You can access the New Name dialog box by choosing Formulas⇨Defined Names⇨Define Name. The New Name dialog box displayed is identical in form and function to the one from the New button on the Name Manager dialog.

Rules for Naming Names

Although Excel is quite flexible about the names that you can define, it does have some rules:

- **Names can't contain any spaces.** You might want to use an underscore or a period character to simulate a space (such as *Annual_Total* or *Annual.Total*).

- **You can use any combination of letters and numbers, but the name must begin with a letter or underscore.** A name can't begin with a number (such as *3rdQuarter*) or look like a cell reference (such as *Q3*).

- **You cannot use symbols, except for underscores and periods.** Although not documented, I've found that Excel also permits a backslash (\) and question mark (?) as long as they don't appear as the first character in a name.

- **Names are limited to 255 characters.** Trust me — you should not use a name anywhere near this length. In fact, doing so defeats the purpose of naming ranges.

- **You can use single letters (except for R or C).** However, generally I don't recommend this because it also defeats the purpose of using meaningful names.

- **Names are not case sensitive.** The name *AnnualTotal* is the same as *annualtotal*. Excel stores the name exactly as you type it when you define it, but it doesn't matter how you capitalize the name when you use it in a formula.

Excel also uses a few names internally for its own use. Although you can create names that override Excel's internal names, you should avoid doing so unless you know what you're doing. Generally, avoid using the following names: *Print_Area, Print_Titles, Consolidate_Area, Database, Criteria, Extract, FilterDatabase,* and *Sheet_Title*.

NOTE

A single cell or range can have any number of names. I can't think of a good reason to use more than one name, but Excel does permit it. If a cell or range has multiple names, the Name box always displays the name that's first alphabetically when you select the cell or range.

A name can also refer to a noncontiguous range of cells. You can select a noncontiguous range by pressing Ctrl while you select various cells or ranges with the mouse.

Creating Names Using the Name Box

A faster way to create a name for a cell or range uses the Name box. The Name box is the drop-down list box to the left of the formula bar. Select the cell or range to name, click the Name box, type the name, and then press Enter to create the name. If a name already exists, you can't use the Name box to change the range to which that name refers. Attempting to do so simply selects the original range. You must use the Name Manager dialog box to change the reference for a name.

CAUTION

When you type a name in the Name box, you *must* press Enter to actually record the name. If you type a name and then click in the worksheet, Excel won't create the name.

The Name box serves double-duty by also providing a quick way to activate a named cell or range. To select a named cell or range, click the Name box and choose the name, as shown in Figure 3-3. This selects the named cell or range. Oddly, the Name box does not have a keyboard shortcut. In other words, you can't access the Name box by using the keyboard; you must use the mouse. After you click the Name box, however, you can use the direction keys and Enter to choose a name.

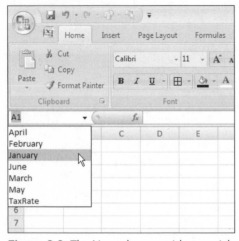

Figure 3-3: The Name box provides a quick way to activate a named cell or range.

TIP

Names created using the Name box are workbook-level in scope by default. If you want to create a worksheet-level name, you can type the worksheet's name and an exclamation point before the name (for example, Sheet2!Total). Because the Name box works only on the currently selected range, typing a worksheet name other than the active worksheet results in an error.

Creating Names Automatically

You may have a worksheet containing text that you want to use for names of adjacent cells or ranges. Figure 3-4 shows an example of such a worksheet. In this case, you might want to use the text in column A to create names for the corresponding values in column B. Excel makes this very easy to do.

	A	B	C	D
1				
2				
3	**Month**	**Sales**		
4	January	60,983		
5	February	61,960		
6	March	62,913		
7	April	63,557		
8	May	64,130		
9	June	65,285		
10	July	66,449		
11	August	67,302		
12	September	68,064		
13	October	68,728		
14	November	69,763		
15	December	70,785		
16				

Sheet1 Sales

Figure 3-4: Excel makes it easy to create names by using text in adjacent cells.

To create names by using adjacent text, start by selecting the name text and the cells that you want to name. (These can consist of individual cells or ranges of cells.) The names must be adjacent to the cells that you're naming. (A multiple selection is allowed.) Then choose Formulas⇨Defined Names⇨Create from Selection (or Ctrl+Shift+F3). Excel displays the Create Names From Selection dialog box, as shown in Figure 3-5.

The check marks in this dialog box are based on Excel's analysis of the selected range. For example, if Excel finds text in the first row of the selection, it proposes that you create names based on the top row. If Excel doesn't guess correctly, you can change the check boxes. Click OK, and Excel creates the names. Note that when Excel creates names using text in cells, it does not include those text cells in the named range.

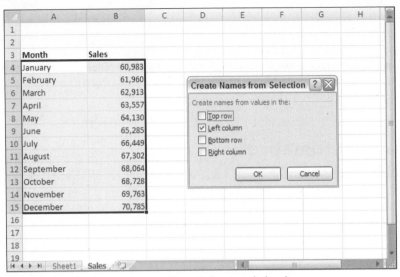

Figure 3-5: The Create Names From Selection dialog box.

If the text in a cell would result in an invalid name, Excel modifies the name to make it valid. For example, if a cell contains the text Net Income (which is invalid for a name because it contains a space), Excel converts the space to an underscore character and creates the name *Net_Income.* If Excel encounters a value or a formula instead of text, however, it doesn't convert it to a valid name. It simply doesn't create a name.

CAUTION

Double-check the names that Excel creates. Sometimes, the Create Names From Selection dialog box works counterintuitively. Figure 3-6 shows a small table of text and values. Now imagine that you select the entire table, choose Formulas⇨Defined Names⇨Create From Selection, and then accept Excel's suggestions (Top row and Left column options). You'll find that the name Products doesn't refer to A2:A6, as you may expect, but instead refers to B2:C6. If the upper-left cell of the selection contains text and you choose the Top row and Left column options, Excel uses that text for the name of the entire set of data—excluding the top row and left column. So, before you accept the names that Excel creates, take a minute to make sure that they refer to the correct ranges.

Naming Entire Rows and Columns

Sometimes it makes sense to name an entire row or column. Often, a worksheet is used to store information that you enter over a period of time. The sheet in Figure 3-7 is an example of such a worksheet. If you create a name for the data in column B, you need to modify the name's reference each day you add new data. The solution is to name the entire column.

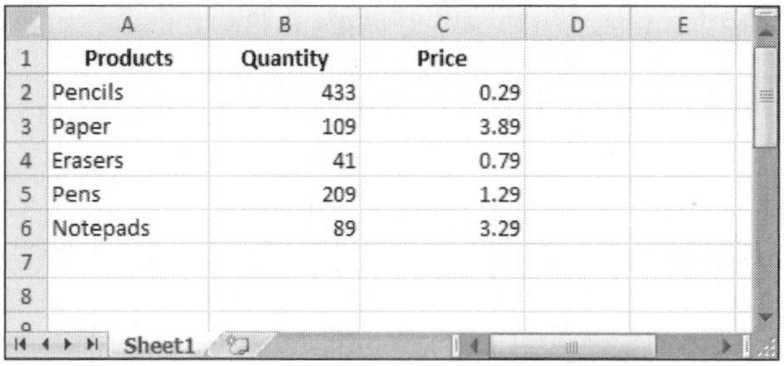

	A	B	C	D	E
1	Products	Quantity	Price		
2	Pencils	433	0.29		
3	Paper	109	3.89		
4	Erasers	41	0.79		
5	Pens	209	1.29		
6	Notepads	89	3.29		
7					
8					

Figure 3-6: Using the Create From Selection command to create names from the data in this table may produce unexpected results.

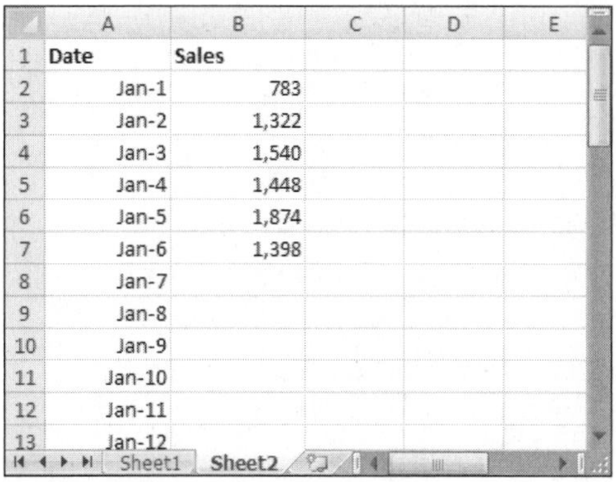

	A	B	C	D	E
1	Date	Sales			
2	Jan-1	783			
3	Jan-2	1,322			
4	Jan-3	1,540			
5	Jan-4	1,448			
6	Jan-5	1,874			
7	Jan-6	1,398			
8	Jan-7				
9	Jan-8				
10	Jan-9				
11	Jan-10				
12	Jan-11				
13	Jan-12				

Figure 3-7: This worksheet, which tracks daily sales, uses a named range that consists of an entire column.

For example, you might name column B as *DailySales.* If this range were on Sheet2, its reference would appear like this:

```
=Sheet2!$B:$B
```

To define a name for an entire column, start by selecting the column by clicking the column letter. Then, type the name in the Name box and press Enter (or use the New Name dialog box to create the name).

After defining the name, you can use it in a formula. The following formula, for example, returns the sum of all values in column B:

```
=SUM(DailySales)
```

Names Created by Excel

Excel creates some names on its own. For example, if you set a print area for a sheet, Excel creates the name *Print_Area.* If you set repeating rows or columns for printing, you also have a worksheet-level name called *Print_Titles*. When you execute a query that returns data to a worksheet, Excel assigns a name to the data that is returned. Also, many of the add-ins that ship with Excel create hidden names. (See the "Hidden Names" sidebar.)

You can modify the reference for any of the names that Excel creates automatically, but make sure that you understand the consequences.

Hidden Names

Some Excel macros and add-ins create hidden names. These names exist in a workbook but don't appear in the Name Manager dialog box or the Name box. For example, the Solver add-in creates a number of hidden names. Normally, you can just ignore these hidden names. However, sometimes these hidden names create problems. If you copy a sheet to another workbook, the hidden names are also copied, and they may create a link that is very difficult to track down.

Unfortunately, Excel doesn't make it very easy to work with names. For example, you have no way of viewing a complete list of names defined in a workbook. When you use the Name Manager dialog box, it lists only the worksheet-level names in the active worksheet. And it never displays hidden names.

If you'd like a better tool to help you work with names, you can use the Name Lister utility, which is part of the Power Utility Pak (see the accompanying figure). This utility displays a list of all names, and you can filter the list in a number of ways — for example, you can show only sheet-level names or only linked names. The utility is also useful for identifying and deleting *bad* names — names that refer to an invalid range. You can download a trial version of Power Utility Pak from `http://j-walk.com/ss`.

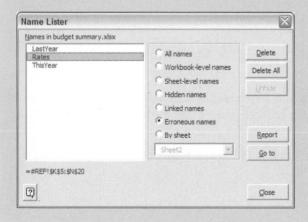

Creating Multisheet Names

Names can extend into the third dimension; in other words, they can extend across multiple worksheets in a workbook. You can't simply select the multisheet range and enter a name in the Name box, however. You must use the New Name dialog box to create a multisheet name. The format for a multisheet reference looks like this:

```
FirstSheet:LastSheet!RangeReference
```

In Figure 3-8, a multisheet name (DataCube), defined for A1:C3, extends across Sheet1, Sheet2, and Sheet3.

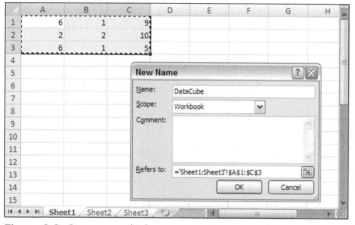

Figure 3-8: Create a multisheet name.

You can, of course, simply type the multisheet range reference into the Refers To field. If you want to create the name by pointing to the range, though, you'll find it a bit tricky. Even if you begin by selecting a multisheet range, Excel does not use this selected range address in the New Name dialog box.

Follow this step-by-step procedure to create a name called *DataCube* that refers to the range A1:C3 across three worksheets (Sheet1, Sheet2, and Sheet3):

1. Activate Sheet1.

2. Choose Formulas⇨Defined Names⇨Define Name to display the New Name dialog box.

3. Type **DataCube** in the Name field.

4. Highlight the range reference in the Refers To field, and press Delete to delete the range reference.

5. Select the range A1:C3 in Sheet1. The following appears in the Refers To field:

   ```
   =Sheet1!$A$1:$C$3
   ```

6. Press Shift and then click the Sheet tab for Sheet3. You'll find that Excel inexplicably changes the range reference to a single cell. At this point, the following appears in the Refers To field:

```
='Sheet1:Sheet3'!$A$1
```

7. Reselect the range A1:C3 in Sheet1 (which is still the active sheet). The following appears in the Refers To field:

```
='Sheet1:Sheet3'!$A$1:$C$3
```

8. Because the Refers To field now has the correct multisheet range address, click OK to close the Define Name dialog box.

After you define the name, you can use it in your formulas. For example, the following formula returns the sum of the values in the range named *DataCube*.

```
=SUM(DataCube)
```

 NOTE

Multisheet names do not appear in the Name box or in the Go To dialog box (which appears when you choose Home⇨Editing⇨Find & Select & Go To). In other words, Excel enables you to define the name, but it doesn't give you a way to automatically select the cells to which the name refers.

If you insert a new worksheet into a workbook that uses multisheet names, the multisheet names will include the new worksheet — as long as the sheet resides between the first and last sheet in the name's definition. In the preceding example, a worksheet inserted between Sheet1 and Sheet2 will be included in the *DataCube* range. However, a worksheet inserted before Sheet1 or after Sheet 3 will not be included.

If you delete the first or last sheet included in a multisheet name, Excel changes the name's range in the Refers To field automatically. In the preceding example, deleting Sheet1 causes the Refers To range of *DataCube* to change to

```
='Sheet2:Sheet3'!$A$1:$C$3
```

Multisheet names should always be workbook-level in scope. Multisheet names that are worksheet-level will work properly but will display an error in the Name Manager dialog.

Working with Range and Cell Names

After you create range or cell names, you can work with them in a variety of ways. This section describes how to perform common operations with range and cell names.

Creating a List of Names

If you create a large number of names, you may need to know the ranges that each name refers to, particularly if you're trying to track down errors or document your work.

You might want to create a list of all names (and their corresponding addresses) in the workbook. To create a list of names, first move the cell pointer to an empty area of your worksheet. (The two-column name list, created at the active cell position, overwrites any information at that location.) Use the Formulas⇨Defined Names⇨Use in Formula⇨ Paste command (or press F3). Excel displays the Paste Name dialog box (see Figure 3-9) that lists all the defined names. To paste a list of names, click the Paste List button.

Figure 3-9: The Paste Name dialog box.

CAUTION

The list of names does not include worksheet-level names that appear in sheets other than the active sheet.

The list of names pasted to your worksheet occupies two columns. The first column contains the names, and the second column contains the corresponding range addresses. The range addresses in the second column consist of text strings that look like formulas. You can convert such a string to an actual formula by editing the cell by pressing F2 and then pressing Enter. The string then converts to a formula. If the name refers to a single cell, the formula displays the cell's current value. If the name refers to a range, the formula returns a #VALUE! error; or, in the case of multisheet names, a #REF! error.

Using Names in Formulas

After you define a name for a cell or range, you can use it in a formula. For example, the following formula calculates the sum of the values in the range named *UnitsSold:*

```
=SUM(UnitsSold)
```

Recall from the section on scope that when you write a formula that uses a worksheet-level name on the sheet in which it's defined, you don't need to include the worksheet name in the range name. If you use the name in a formula on a different worksheet, however, you must use the entire name (sheet name, exclamation point, and name). For example, if the name *UnitsSold* represents a worksheet-level name defined on Sheet1, the following formula (on a sheet other than Sheet1) calculates the total of the *UnitsSold* range:

```
=SUM(Sheet1!UnitsSold)
```

As you type a formula, you can select the name from the list at Formula⇨Defined Names⇨ Use in Formula to inserts that name into your formula. At the bottom of the list is the Paste command, which displays the Past Name dialog (or by pressing F3). Displaying the Paste Name dialog box and selecting a name has the same effect as selecting the name from the list. As I previously mention, the Paste Name dialog box lists all workbook-level names, plus worksheet-level names for the active sheet only.

NEW

Typing an equal sign in Excel 2007 activates the Formula AutoComplete feature, as does typing the open parenthesis of a worksheet function. Formula AutoComplete is a list of worksheet functions and defined names that appears below the active cell. To use Formula AutoComplete, begin typing the defined name until it is highlighted on the list and then press Tab to complete the entry.

If you use a nonexistent name in a formula, Excel displays a #NAME? error, indicating that it cannot find the name you are trying to use. Often, this means that you misspelled the name.

Using the Intersection Operators with Names

Excel's range intersection operator is a single space character. The following formula, for example, displays the sum of the cells at the intersection of two ranges: B1:C20 and A8:D8:

```
=SUM(B1:C20 A8:D8)
```

The intersection of these two ranges consists of two cells: B8 and C8.

The intersection operator also works with named ranges. Figure 3-10 shows a worksheet containing named ranges that correspond to the row and column labels. For example, *January* refers to B2:E2, and *North* refers to B2:B13. The following formula returns the contents of the cell at the intersection of the *January* range and the *North* range:

```
=January North
```

	A	B	C	D	E	F
1		North	South	West	East	
2	January	2,260	1,668	1,218	2,226	
3	February	2,946	2,635	2,873	1,298	
4	March	1,352	2,388	1,219	1,085	
5	April	2,773	2,354	1,413	2,158	
6	May	1,951	1,136	2,278	2,527	
7	June	1,752	1,762	1,770	2,095	
8	July	1,967	1,187	1,092	1,996	
9	August	3,000	2,429	2,484	1,498	
10	September	2,442	1,044	1,468	2,133	
11	October	2,597	1,146	1,446	1,724	
12	November	1,818	1,765	1,965	1,098	
13	December	1,914	2,131	1,330	1,933	
14						

Sheet1

Figure 3-10: This worksheet contains named ranges that correspond to row and column labels.

Using a space character to separate two range references or names is known as *explicit intersection* because you explicitly tell Excel to determine the intersection of the ranges. Excel, however, can also perform *implicit intersections,* which occur when Excel chooses a value from a multicell range based on the row or column of the formula that contains the reference. An example should clear this up. Figure 3-11 shows a worksheet that contains a range (B3:B8) named *MyData.* Cell D5 contains the simple formula shown here:

```
=MyData
```

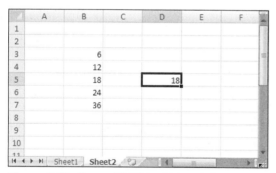

	A	B	C	D	E	F
1						
2						
3		6				
4		12				
5		18		18		
6		24				
7		36				
8						
9						
10						
11						

Sheet1   Sheet2

Figure 3-11: Range B3:B8 in this worksheet is named *MyData.* Cell D5 demonstrates an implicit intersection.

Notice that cell D5 displays the value from *MyData* that corresponds to the formula's row. Similarly, if you enter the same formula into any other cell in rows 3 through 8, the formula displays the corresponding value from *MyData.* Excel performs an implicit intersection using the *MyData* range and the row that contains the formula. It's as if the following formula is being evaluated:

```
=MyData 5:5
```

If you enter the formula in a row not occupied by *MyData,* the formula returns an error because the implicit intersection returns nothing.

By the way, implicit intersections are not limited to named ranges. In the preceding example, you get the same result if cell D5 contains the following formula (which doesn't use a named range):

```
=$B$2:$B$8
```

Using the Range Operator with Names

You can also use the range operator, which is a colon (:), to work with named ranges. Refer to Figure 3-10. For example, this formula returns the sum of the values for North through West for January through March (nine cells):

```
=SUM((North January):(West March))
```

Referencing a Single Cell in a Multicell Named Range

You can use Excel's INDEX function to return a single value from a multicell range. Assume that range A1:A50 is named *DataRange.* The following formula displays the second value (the value in A2) in *DataRange:*

```
=INDEX(DataRange,2)
```

The second and third arguments for the INDEX function are optional although at least one of them must always be specified. The second argument (used in the preceding formula) is used to specify the row offset within the *DataRange* range.

If *DataRange* consists of multiple cells in a single row, use a formula like the following one. This formula omits the second argument for the INDEX function, but uses the third argument that specifies the column offset with the *DataRange* range:

```
=INDEX(DataRange,,2)
```

If the range consists of multiple rows and columns, use both the second and third arguments for the INDEX function. For example, this formula returns the value in the fourth row and fifth column of a range named *DataRange:*

```
=INDEX(DataRange,4,5)
```

Applying Names to Existing Formulas

When you create a name for a cell or range, Excel does not scan your formulas automatically and replace the cell references with your new name. You can, however, tell Excel to "apply" names to a range of formulas.

Select the range that contains the formulas that you want to convert. Then choose Formulas⇨Defined Names⇨Define Name⇨Apply Names. The Apply Names dialog box appears, as shown in Figure 3-12. In the Apply Names dialog box, select which names you want applied to the formulas. Only those names that you select will be applied to the formulas.

Figure 3-12: The Apply Names dialog box.

TIP
To apply names to all the formulas in the worksheet, select a single cell before you display the Apply Names dialog.

The Ignore Relative/Absolute check box controls how Excel substitutes the range name for the actual address. A cell or range name is usually defined as an absolute reference. If the Ignore Relative/Absolute check box is enabled, Excel applies the name only if the reference in the formula matches exactly. In most cases, you will want to ignore the type of cell reference when applying names.

If the Use Row and Column Names check box is selected, Excel takes advantage of the intersection operator when applying names. Excel uses the names of row and column ranges that refer to the cells if it cannot find the exact names for the cells. Excel uses the intersection operator to join the names. Clicking the Options button displays some additional options that are available only when you have the Use Row and Column Names check box enabled.

Applying Names Automatically When Creating a Formula

When you insert a cell or range reference into a formula by pointing, Excel automatically substitutes the cell or range name if it has one.

In some cases, this feature can be very useful. In other cases, it can be annoying; you may prefer to use an actual cell or range reference instead of the name. Unfortunately, you cannot turn off this feature. If you prefer to use a regular cell or range address, you need to type the cell or range reference manually (don't use the pointing technique).

Unapplying Names

Excel does not provide a direct method for unapplying names. In other words, you cannot replace a name in a formula with the name's actual cell reference automatically. However, you can take advantage of a trick described here. You need to change Excel's Transition Formula Entry option so it emulates 1-2-3. Choose File⇨Excel Options and then click the Advanced tab in the Excel Options dialog box. Under the Lotus Compatibility Settings section, place a check mark next to Transition Formula Entry and then click OK.

Next, press F2 to edit a formula that contains one or more cell or range names. Press Enter to end cell editing. Next, go back to the Options dialog box and remove the check mark from the Transition Formula Entry check box. You'll find that the edited cell uses relative range references rather than names.

NOTE

This trick is not documented, and it might not work in all cases, so make sure that you check the results carefully.

Names with Errors

If you delete the rows or columns that contain named cells or ranges, the names will not be deleted (as you might expect). Rather, each name will contain an invalid reference. For example, if cell A1 on Sheet1 is named Interest and you delete row 1 or column A, *Interest* then refers to =Sheet1!#REF! (that is, an erroneous reference). If you use *Interest* in a formula, the formula displays #REF.

In order to get rid of this erroneous name, you must delete the name manually using the Delete button in the Name Manager dialog box. Or, you can redefine the name so it refers to a valid cell or range.

NEW

Excel 2007's new Name Manager allows you to filter the names displayed using predefined filters. One of the filters provided, Names with Errors, shows only those names that contain errors, which enables you to quickly locate problem names.

Viewing Named Ranges

When you zoom a worksheet to 39 percent or lower, you see a border around the named ranges with the name displayed in blue letters, as shown in Figure 3-13. The border and name do not print; they simply help you visualize the named ranges on your sheet.

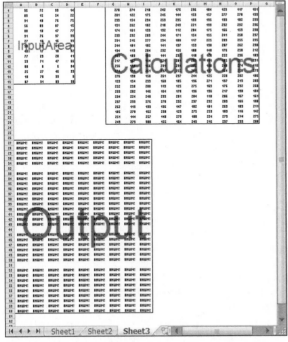

Figure 3-13: Excel displays range names when you zoom a sheet to 39 percent or less.

Using Names in Charts

When you create a chart, each data series has an associated SERIES formula. The SERIES formula contains references to the ranges used in the chart. If you have a defined range name, you can edit a SERIES formula and replace the range reference with the name. After doing so, the chart series will adjust if you change the definition for the name.

CROSS REF

See Chapter 17 for additional information about charts.

How Excel Maintains Cell and Range Names

After you create a name for a cell or range, Excel automatically maintains the name as you edit or modify the worksheet. The following examples assume that Sheet1 contains a workbook-level name *(MyRange)* that refers to the following nine-cell range:

```
=Sheet1!$C$3:$E$5
```

Inserting a Row or Column

When you insert a row above the named range or insert a column to the left of the named range, Excel changes the range reference to reflect its new address. For example, if you insert a new row 1, *MyRange* then refers to =Sheet1!$C$4:$E$6.

If you insert a new row or column within the named range, the named range expands to include the new row or column. For example, if you insert a new column to the left of column E, *MyRange* then refers to =Sheet1!$C$3:$F$5.

Deleting a Row or Column

When you delete a row above the named range or delete a column to the left of the named range, Excel adjusts the range reference to reflect its new address. For example, if you delete row 1, *MyRange* refers to =Sheet1!$B$3:$D$5.

If you delete a row or column within the named range, the name range adjusts accordingly. For example, if you delete column D, *MyRange* then refers to =Sheet1!$C$3:$D$5.

If you delete all rows or all columns that make up a named range, the named range continues to exist, but it contains an error reference. For example, if you delete columns C, D, and E, *MyRange* then refers to =Sheet1!#REF!. Any formulas that use the name also return errors.

Cutting and Pasting

When you cut and paste an entire named range, Excel changes the reference accordingly. For example, if you move *MyRange* to a new location beginning at cell A1, *MyRange* then refers to =Sheet1!$A$1:$C$3. Cutting and pasting only a part of a named range does not affect the name's reference.

Potential Problems with Names

Names are great, but they can also cause some problems. This section contains information that you should remember when you use names in a workbook.

Name Problems When Copying Sheets

Excel lets you copy a worksheet within the same workbook or to a different workbook. Focus first on copying a sheet within the same workbook. If the copied sheet contains worksheet-level names, those names will also be present on the copy of the sheet, adjusted to use the new sheet name. Usually, this is exactly what you want to happen. However, if the workbook contains a workbook-level name that refers to a cell or range on the sheet that's copied, that name will also be present on the copied sheet. However, it will be converted to a worksheet-level name! That is usually *not* what you want to happen.

Consider a workbook that contains one sheet (Sheet1). This workbook has a workbook-level name *(BookName)* for cell A1, and a worksheet-level name *(Sheet1!LocalName)* for cell A2. If you make a copy of Sheet1 within the workbook, the new sheet is named Sheet1 (2). You'll find that, after copying the sheet, the workbook contains four names, as shown in Figure 3-14.

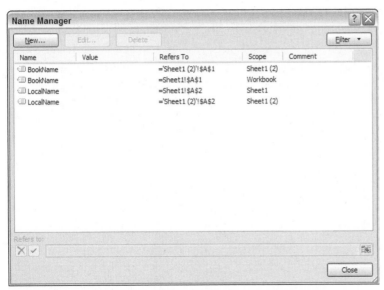

Figure 3-14: Copying a worksheet creates duplicated names.

This proliferation of names when copying a sheet is not only confusing, but it can result in errors that can be very difficult to identify. In this case, typing the following formula on the copied sheet displays the contents of cell A1 in the copied sheet:

```
=BookName
```

In other words, the newly created worksheet-level name (not the original workbook-level name) is being used.

If you copy the worksheet from a workbook containing a name that refers to a multisheet range, you also copy this name. A #REF! error appears in its Refers To definition.

When you copy a sheet to a new workbook, all the names in the original workbook that refer to cells on the copied sheet are also copied to the new workbook. This includes both workbook-level and worksheet-level names.

NOTE

Copying and pasting cells from one sheet to another does not copy names, even if the copied range contains named cells.

Bottom line? You must use caution when copying sheets from a workbook that uses names. After copying the sheet, check the names and delete those that you didn't intend to be copied.

Name Problems When Deleting Sheets

When you delete a worksheet that contains cells used in a workbook-level name, you'll find that the name is not deleted. The name remains with the workbook, but it contains an erroneous reference in its Refers To definition.

Figure 3-15 shows the Name Manager dialog box that displays an erroneous name. The workbook originally contained a sheet named Sheet1, which had a named range (a workbook-level name, *MyRange*) for A1:F12. After deleting Sheet1, the name *MyRange* still exists in the workbook, but the Refers To field displays the following:

```
=#REF!$A$1:$F$12
```

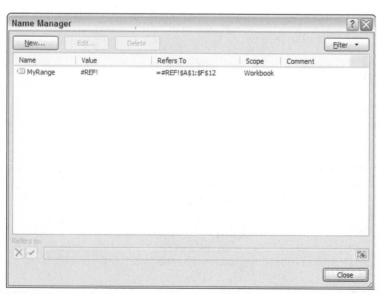

Figure 3-15: Deleting the sheet that contains the cell for *MyRange* causes an erroneous reference.

Naming Objects

When you add an object to a worksheet (such as a shape, or clip art), the object has a default name that reflects the type of object (for example, *Rectangle 3* or *Text Box 1*).

To change the name of an object, select it, type the new name in the Name box, and press Enter. Naming charts is an exception. To rename a chart, use the Chart Tools⇨ Layout⇨Properties⇨Chart Name control.

Excel is a bit inconsistent with regard to the Name box. Although you can use the Name box to rename an object, the Name box does not display a list of objects. Excel also allows you to define a name with the same name as an object, and two or more objects can even have the same name. The Name Manager dialog box does not list the names of objects.

As far as I can tell, keeping erroneous names in a workbook doesn't cause any harm, but it's still a good practice to delete or correct all names that contain an erroneous reference.

The Secret to Understanding Names

Excel users often refer to *named ranges* and *named cells.* In fact, I've used these terms frequently throughout this chapter. Actually, this terminology is not quite accurate.

Here's the secret to understanding names: When you create a name, you're actually creating a named formula. Unlike a normal formula, a named formula doesn't exist in a cell. Rather, it exists in Excel's memory.

This is not exactly an earth-shaking revelation, but keeping this "secret" in mind will help you understand the advanced naming techniques that follow.

When you work with the Name Manager dialog box, the Refers To field contains the formula, and the Name field contains the formula's name. You'll find that the contents of the Refers To field always begin with an equal sign, which makes it a formula.

As you can see in Figure 3-16, the workbook contains a name *(InterestRate)* for cell B1 on Sheet1. The Refers To field lists the following formula:

```
=Sheet1!$B$1
```

Whenever you use the name *InterestRate,* Excel actually evaluates the formula with that name and returns the result. For example, you might type this formula into a cell:

```
=InterestRate*1.05
```

Figure 3-16: Technically, the name *InterestRate* is a named formula, not a named cell.

When Excel evaluates this formula, it first evaluates the formula named *InterestRate* (which exists only in memory, not in a cell). It then multiplies the result of this named formula by 1.05 and displays the result. This cell formula, of course, is equivalent to the following formula, which uses the actual cell reference instead of the name:

```
=Sheet1!$B$1*1.05
```

At this point, you may be wondering whether it's possible to create a named formula that doesn't contain any cell references. The answer comes in the next section.

Naming Constants

Consider a worksheet that generates an invoice and calculates sales tax for a sales amount. The common approach is to insert the sales tax rate value into a cell and then use this cell reference in your formulas. To make things easier, you probably would name this cell something like *SalesTax*.

You can handle this situation another way. Figure 3-17 demonstrates the following steps:

1. Choose Formulas⇨Defined Names⇨Define Name to bring up the New Name dialog box.
2. Enter the name (in this case, **SalesTax**) into the Name field.
3. Click the Refers To box, delete its contents and replace it with a simple formula, such as =**.075**.
4. Click OK to close the dialog box.

The preceding steps create a named formula that doesn't use any cell references. To try it out, enter the following formula into any cell:

```
=SalesTax
```

Figure 3-17: Defining a name that refers to a constant.

This simple formula returns .075, the result of the formula named *SalesTax*. Because this named formula always returns the same result, you can think of it as a named constant. And you can use this constant in a more complex formula, such as the following:

```
=A1*SalesTax
```

If you didn't change the scope from the default of Workbook, you can use SalesTax in any worksheet in the workbook.

Naming Text Constants

In the preceding example, the constant consisted of a numeric value. A constant can also consist of text. For example, you can define a constant for a company's name. You can use the New Name dialog box to create the following formula named *MS:*

```
="Microsoft Corporation"
```

Then you can use a cell formula such as

```
="Annual Report: "&MS
```

This formula returns the text, *Annual Report: Microsoft Corporation.*

NOTE

Names that do not refer to ranges do not appear in the Name box or in the Go To dialog box (which appears when you press F5). This makes sense because these constants don't reside anywhere tangible. They *do* appear in the Paste Names dialog box and in Formula AutoComplete, however, which *does* make sense because you'll use these names in formulas.

As you might expect, you can change the value of the constant at any time by accessing the Name Manager dialog box and simply changing the formula in the Refers To field. When you close the dialog box, Excel uses the new value to recalculate the formulas that use this name.

Although this technique is useful in many situations, changing the value takes some time. Having a constant located in a cell makes it much easier to modify. If the value is truly a "constant," however, you won't need to change it.

Using Worksheet Functions in Named Formulas

Figure 3-18 shows another example of a named formula. In this case, the formula is named *ThisMonth,* and the actual formula is

```
=MONTH(TODAY())
```

Figure 3-18: Defining a named formula that uses worksheet functions.

The formula in Figure 3-18 uses two worksheet functions. The TODAY function returns the current date, and the MONTH function returns the month number of its date argument. Therefore, you can enter a formula such as the following into a cell and it will return the number of the current month. For example, if the current month is April, the formula returns 4.

```
=ThisMonth
```

A more useful named formula would return the actual month name as text. To do so, create a formula named *MonthName,* defined as

```
=TEXT(TODAY(),"mmmm")
```

 CROSS REF
See Chapter 5 for more information about Excel's TEXT function.

Now enter the following formula into a cell and it returns the current month name as text. In the month of April, the formula returns the text, *April.*

```
=MonthName
```

Using Cell and Range References in Named Formulas

Figure 3-19 shows yet another example of creating a named formula, this time with a cell reference. This formula, named *FirstChar,* returns the first character of the contents of cell A1 on Sheet1. This formula uses the LEFT function, which returns characters from the left part of a text string. The named formula is

```
=LEFT(Sheet1!$A$1,1)
```

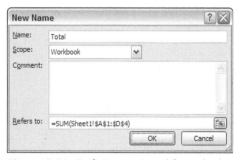

Figure 3-19: Defining a named formula that uses a cell reference.

After creating this named formula, you can enter the following formula into a cell. The formula always returns the first character of cell A1 on Sheet1.

```
=FirstChar
```

The next example uses a range reference in a named formula. Figure 3-20 shows the New Name dialog box when defining the following named formula (named *Total*).

```
=SUM(Sheet1!$A$1:$D$4)
```

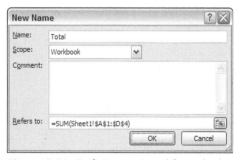

Figure 3-20: Defining a named formula that uses a range reference.

After creating this named formula, you can enter the following formula into any cell on any sheet. The formula returns the sum of the values in A1:D4 on Sheet1.

```
=Total
```

Notice that the cell references in the two preceding named formulas are absolute references. By default, all cell and range references in named formulas use an absolute reference, with the worksheet qualifier. But, as you can see in the next section, overriding this default behavior by using a relative cell reference can result in some very interesting named formulas.

Using Named Formulas with Relative References

As I noted previously, when you use the New Name dialog box to create a named formula that refers to cells or ranges, the Refers To field always uses absolute cell references and the references include the sheet name qualifier. In this section, I describe how to use relative cell and range references in named formulas.

USING A RELATIVE CELL REFERENCE

Begin with a simple example by following these steps to create a named formula that uses a relative reference:

1. Start with an empty worksheet.
2. Select cell A1 (this step is very important).
3. Choose Formulas➪Defined Names➪Define Name to bring up the New Name dialog box.
4. Enter **CellToRight** in the Name field.
5. Delete the contents of the Refers To field and type the following formula (don't point to the cell in the sheet):

   ```
   =Sheet1!B1
   ```
6. Click OK to close the New Name dialog box.
7. Type something (anything) into cell B1.
8. Enter this formula into cell A1:

   ```
   =CellToRight
   ```

   You'll find that the formula in A1 simply returns the contents of cell B1.

Next, copy the formula in cell A1 down a few rows. Then enter some values in column B. You'll find that the formula in column A returns the contents of the cell to the right. In other words, the named formula *(CellToRight)* acts in a relative manner.

You can use the *CellToRight* name in any cell (not just cells in column A). For example, if you enter **=CellToRight** into cell D12, it returns the contents of cell E12.

Part I

To demonstrate that the formula named *CellToRight* truly uses a relative cell reference, activate any cell other than cell A1 and display the New Name dialog box (see Figure 3-21). You'll see that the Refers To field contains a formula that points one cell to the right of the active cell, not A1. For example, if cell E5 is selected when the New Name dialog box is displayed, the formula for *CellToRight* appears as

```
=Sheet1!F5
```

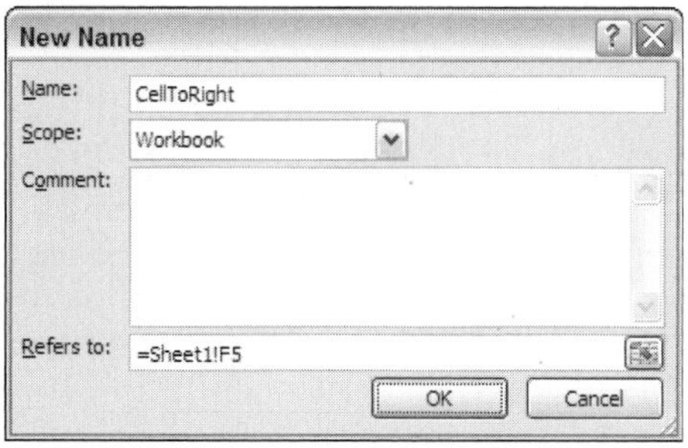

Figure 3-21: The *CellToRight* named formula varies, depending on the active cell.

If you use the *CellToRight* name on a different worksheet, you'll find that it continues to reference the cell to the right — but it's the cell with the same address on Sheet1. This happens because the named formula includes a sheet reference. To modify the named formula so it works on any sheet, follow these steps:

1. Activate cell A1 on Sheet1.

2. Choose Formulas⇨Defined Names⇨Name Manager to bring up the Name Manager dialog box.

3. In the Name Manager dialog box, select the CellToRight item in the list box.

4. Delete the contents of the Refers To field and type this formula:

   ```
   =!B1
   ```

5. Click OK to close the Define Name dialog box.

After making this change, you'll find that the *CellToRight* named formula works correctly on any worksheet in the workbook.

NOTE

The named formula does not work if you use it in a formula in column XFD because the formula attempts to reference a nonexistent cell. (There is no column to the right of column XFD.)

USING A RELATIVE RANGE REFERENCE

This example expands upon the previous example and demonstrates how to create a named formula that sums the values in ten cells directly to the right of a particular cell. To create this named formula, follow these steps:

1. Activate cell A1.

2. Choose Formulas⇨Defined Names⇨Define Name to bring up the New Name dialog box.

3. Enter **Sum10Cells** in the Name field.

4. Enter this formula in the Refers To field:

```
=SUM(!B1:!K1)
```

After creating this named formula, you can insert the following formula into any cell in any sheet, and it will display the sum of the ten cells directly to the right:

```
=Sum10Cells
```

For example, if you enter this formula into cell D12, it returns the sum of the values in the ten-cell range E12:N12.

Note that because cell A1 was the active cell when you defined the named formula, the relative references used in the formula definition are relative to cell A1. Also note that the sheet name was not used in the formula. Omitting the sheet name (but including the exclamation point) causes the named formula to work in any sheet.

If you select cell D12 and then bring up the Name Manager dialog box, you'll see that the Refers To field for the *Sum10Cells* name displays the following:

```
=SUM(!E12:!N12)
```

 NOTE

The Sum10Cells named formula does not work if you use it in a cell that resides in a column beyond column XET. That's because the formula becomes invalid as it tries to reference a nonexistent cell beyond column XFD.

USING A MIXED RANGE REFERENCE

As I discuss in Chapter 2, a cell reference can be absolute, relative, or mixed. A mixed cell reference consists of either of the following:

- An absolute column reference and a relative row reference (for example, $A1)
- A relative column reference and an absolute row reference (for example, A$1)

As you might expect, a named formula can use mixed cell references. To demonstrate, activate cell B1. Use the New Name dialog box to create a formula named *FirstInRow,* using this formula definition:

```
=!$A1
```

This formula uses an absolute column reference and a relative row reference. Therefore, it always returns a value in column A. The row depends on the row in which you use the formula. For example, if you enter the following formula into cell F12, it displays the contents of cell A12:

```
=FirstInRow
```

NOTE

You cannot use the *FirstInRow* formula in column A because it generates a circular reference—a formula that refers to itself.

Advanced Techniques That Use Names

This section presents several examples of advanced techniques that use names. The examples assume that you're familiar with the naming techniques described earlier in this chapter.

Using the INDIRECT Function with a Named Range

Excel's INDIRECT function lets you specify a cell address indirectly. For example, if cell A1 contains the text C45, this formula returns the contents of cell C45:

```
=INDIRECT(A1)
```

The INDIRECT function also works with named ranges. Figure 3-22 shows a worksheet with 12 range names that correspond to the month names. For example, *January* refers to the range B2:E2. Cell B16 contains the following formula:

```
=SUM(INDIRECT(A16))
```

This formula essentially returns the sum of the named range entered as text in cell A16.

TIP

You can use the Data⇨Data Tools⇨Data Validation command to insert a drop-down box in cell A16. (Use the List option in the Data Validation dialog box, and specify A2:A13 as the list source.) This allows the user to select a month name from a list; the total for the selected month then displays in B16.

	A	B	C	D	E	F
1		North	South	West	East	
2	January	2,260	1,668	1,218	2,226	
3	February	2,946	2,635	2,873	1,298	
4	March	1,352	2,388	1,219	1,085	
5	April	2,773	2,354	1,413	2,158	
6	May	1,951	1,136	2,278	2,527	
7	June	1,752	1,762	1,770	2,095	
8	July	1,967	1,187	1,092	1,996	
9	August	3,000	2,429	2,484	1,498	
10	September	2,442	1,044	1,468	2,133	
11	October	2,597	1,146	1,446	1,724	
12	November	1,818	1,765	1,965	1,098	
13	December	1,914	2,131	1,330	1,933	
14						
15						
16	March	6,044				
17						

Sheet1 / Sheet2 / Sheet3

Figure 3-22: Using the INDIRECT function with a named range.

You can also reference worksheet-level names with the INDIRECT function. For example, suppose you have a number of worksheets named Region1, Region2, and so on. Each sheet contains a worksheet-level name called *TotalSales.* This formula retrieves the value from the appropriate sheet, using the sheet name typed in cell A1:

```
=INDIRECT(A1&"!TotalSales")
```

Using the INDIRECT Function to Create a Named Range with a Fixed Address

It's possible to create a name that always refers to a specific cell or range, even if you insert new rows or columns. For example, suppose you want a range named *UpperLeft* to always refer to the range A1. If you create the name using standard procedures, you'll find that inserting a new row 1 causes the *UpperLeft* range to change to A2. Or inserting a new column causes the *UpperLeft* range to change to B1. To create a named range that uses a fixed address that never changes, create a named formula using the following Refers To definition:

```
=INDIRECT("$A$1")
```

After creating this named formula, *UpperLeft* will always refer to cell A1, even if you insert new rows or columns. The INDIRECT function, in the preceding formula, lets you specify a cell address indirectly by using a text argument. Because the argument appears in quotation marks, it never changes.

NOTE

Because this named formula uses a function, it does not appear in the Go To dialog box or in the Name box.

Using Arrays in Named Formulas

An array is a collection of items. You can visualize an array as a single-column vertical collection, a single-row horizontal collection, or a multirow and multicolumn collection.

CROSS REF

Part IV of this book discusses arrays and array formulas, but this topic is also relevant when discussing names.

You specify an array by using brackets. A comma or semicolon separates each item in the array. Use a comma to separate items arranged horizontally and use a semicolon to separate items arranged vertically.

Use the New Name dialog box to create a formula named *MonthNames* that consists of the following formula definition:

```
={"Jan","Feb","Mar","Apr","May","Jun","Jul","Aug","Sep","Oct","Nov","Dec"}
```

This formula defines a 12-item array of text strings, arranged horizontally.

NOTE

When you type this formula, make sure that you include the brackets. Entering a formula into the New Name dialog box is different from entering an array formula into a cell.

After you define the *MonthNames* formula, you can use it in a formula. However, your formula needs to specify which array item to use. The INDEX function is perfect for this. For example, the following formula returns *Aug:*

```
=INDEX(MonthNames,8)
```

You can also display the entire 12-item array, but it requires 12 adjacent cells to do so. For example, to enter the 12 items of the array into A1:L1, follow these steps:

1. Use the New Name dialog box to create the formula named *MonthNames*.

2. Select the range A1:L1.

3. Type **=MonthNames** in the formula bar.

4. Press Ctrl+Shift+Enter.

Using Ctrl+Shift+Enter tells Excel to insert an array formula into the selected cells. In this case, the single formula is entered into 12 adjacent cells in Figure 3-23. Excel places brackets around an array formula to remind you that it's a special type of formula. If you examine any cell in A1:L1, you'll see its formula listed as

`{=MonthNames}`

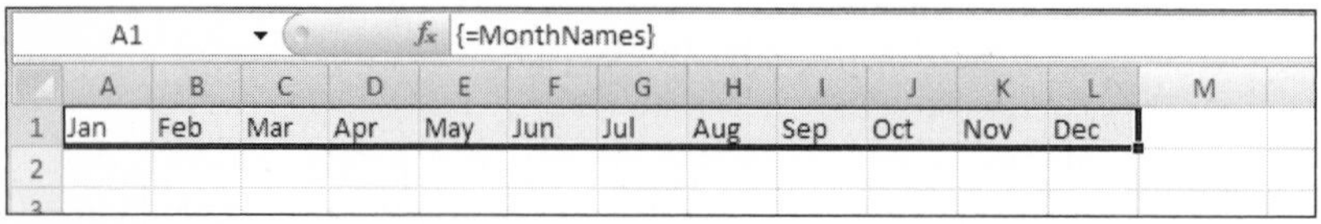

Figure 3-23: You can enter a named formula that contains a 12-item array into 12 adjacent cells.

Creating a Dynamic Named Formula

A *dynamic* named formula is a named formula that refers to a range not fixed in size. You may find this concept difficult to grasp, so a quick example is in order.

Examine the worksheet shown in Figure 3-24. This sheet contains a listing of sales by month, through the month of May.

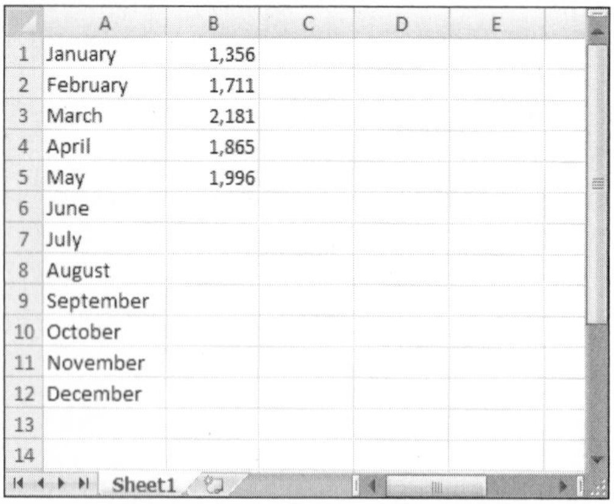

Figure 3-24: You can use a dynamic named formula to represent the sales data in column B.

Suppose you want to create a name *(SalesData)* for the data in column B, and you don't want this name to refer to empty cells. In other words, the reference for the *SalesData* range would change each month as you add a new sales figure. You could, of course, use the Name Manager dialog box to change the range name definition each month. Or, you could create a dynamic named formula that changes automatically as you enter new data.

To create a dynamic named formula, start by re-creating the worksheet shown in Figure 3-24. Then follow these steps:

1. Bring up the New Name dialog box.

2. Enter **SalesData** in the Name field.

3. Enter the following formula in the Refers To field:

   ```
   =OFFSET(Sheet1!$B$1,0,0,COUNTA(Sheet1!$B:$B),1)
   ```

4. Click OK to close the New Name dialog box.

The preceding steps create a named formula that uses Excel's OFFSET and COUNTA functions to return a range that changes, based on the number of non-empty cells in column B. To try out this formula, enter the following formula into any cell not in column B:

```
=SUM(SalesData)
```

This formula returns the sum of the values in column B. Note that *SalesData* does not display in the Name box and does not appear in the Go To dialog box. You can, however, type **SalesData** into the Name box to select the range. Or, bring up the Go To dialog box and type **SalesData** to select the range.

At this point, you may be wondering about the value of this exercise. After all, a simple formula such as the following does the same job, without the need to define a formula:

```
=SUM(B:B)
```

The value of using dynamic named formulas becomes apparent when creating a chart. You can use this technique to create a chart with a data series that adjusts automatically as you enter new data.

Part II

Using Functions in Your Formulas

Chapter 4

Introducing Worksheet Functions

IN THIS CHAPTER

◆ The advantages of using functions in your formulas

◆ The various types of arguments used by functions

◆ How to enter a function into a formula

◆ Excel's function categories

A thorough knowledge of Excel's worksheet functions is essential for anyone who wants to master the art of formulas. This chapter provides an overview of the functions available for use in formulas.

What Is a Function?

A *worksheet function* is a built-in tool that you use in a formula. A typical function (such as SUM) takes one or more arguments and then returns a result. The SUM function, for example, accepts a range argument and then returns the sum of the values in that range.

You'll find functions useful because they

- Simplify your formulas
- Permit formulas to perform otherwise impossible calculations

- Speed up some editing tasks

- Allow *conditional* execution of formulas — giving them rudimentary decision-making capability

The examples in the sections that follow demonstrate each of these points.

Simplify Formulas

Using a built-in function can simplify a formula significantly. For example, you might need to calculate the average of the values in 10 cells (A1:A10). Without the help of any functions, you would need to construct a formula like this:

```
=(A1+A2+A3+A4+A5+A6+A7+A8+A9+A10)/10
```

Not very pretty, is it? Even worse, you would need to edit this formula if you expanded the range to be summed. You can replace this formula with a much simpler one that uses one of Excel's built-in worksheet functions. For example, the following formula uses the AVERAGE function:

```
=AVERAGE(A1:A10)
```

Perform Otherwise Impossible Calculations

Functions permit formulas to perform impossible calculations. Perhaps you need to determine the largest value in a range. A formula can't tell you the answer without using a function. This simple formula uses the MAX function to return the largest value in the range A1:D100:

```
=MAX(A1:D100)
```

Speed Up Editing Tasks

Functions can sometimes eliminate manual editing. Assume that you have a worksheet that contains 1,000 names in cells A1:A1000 and that all the names appear in all-upper-case letters. Your boss sees the listing and informs you that you need to mail-merge the names with a form letter and that the use of all uppercase is not acceptable. For example, JOHN F. CRANE must appear as John F. Crane. You *could* spend the rest of the day reentering the list — or you could use a formula such as the following, which uses the PROPER function to convert the text in cell A1 to proper case:

```
=PROPER(A1)
```

1. Enter this formula in cell B1 and then copy it down to the next 999 rows.

2. Select B1:B1000 and use the Home⇨Clipboard⇨Copy command to copy the range to the Clipboard (or press Ctrl+C).

3. Activate cell A1 and use the Home⇨Clipboard⇨Paste⇨Paste Values command to convert the formulas to values.

4. Delete column B.

You're finished! With the help of a function, you just accomplished several hours of work in less than a minute.

Provide Decision-Making Capability

Functions can also give your formulas decision-making capability. Suppose you have a worksheet that calculates sales commissions. If a salesperson sells more than $100,000 of product, the commission rate reaches 7.5 percent; otherwise, the commission rate remains at 5.0 percent. Without using a function, you would need to create two different formulas and make sure that you use the correct formula for each sales amount. Note this formula that uses the IF function to check the value in cell A1 and make the appropriate commission calculation:

```
=IF(A1<100000,A1*5%,A1*7.5%)
```

This formula uses the IF function, which takes three arguments, each separated by a comma. These arguments provide input to the function. The formula is making a decision: If the value in cell A1 is less than 100,000, then return the value in cell A1 multiplied by 5 percent. Otherwise, return the value in cell A1 multiplied by 7.5 percent.

More about Functions

All told, Excel includes more than 300 functions. And if that's not enough, you can purchase additional specialized functions from third-party suppliers, and even create your own custom functions (using VBA).

 CROSS REF

If you're ready to create your own custom functions by using VBA, check out Part IV of this book.

The sheer number of available worksheet functions may overwhelm you, but you'll probably find that you use only a dozen or so of the functions on a regular basis. And as you'll see, the Excel Function Library Group on the Formula tab (described later in this chapter) makes it easy to locate and insert a function, even if you use it only rarely.

CROSS REF

Appendix A contains a complete listing of Excel's worksheet functions, with a brief description of each.

Function Argument Types

If you examine the preceding examples in this chapter, you'll notice that all the functions use a set of parentheses. The information within the parentheses is the function's *arguments*. Functions vary in how they use arguments. A function may use

- No arguments
- One argument
- A fixed number of arguments
- An indeterminate number of arguments
- Optional arguments

For example, the RAND function, which returns a random number between 0 and 1, doesn't use an argument. Even if a function doesn't require an argument, you must provide a set of empty parentheses, like this:

```
=RAND()
```

If a function uses more than one argument, a comma separates the arguments. For example, the LARGE function, which returns the *n*th largest value in a range, uses two arguments. The first argument represents the range; the second argument represents the value for *n*. The formula below returns the third-largest value in the range A1:A100:

```
=LARGE(A1:A100,3)
```

NOTE

The character used to separate function arguments can be something other than a comma—for example, a semicolon. This character is determined by the List Separator setting for your system, which is specified in the Regional Settings dialog box, accessible via the Control Panel.

The examples at the beginning of the chapter used cell or range references for arguments. Excel proves quite flexible when it comes to function arguments, however. The following sections demonstrate additional argument types for functions.

Accommodating Former Lotus 1-2-3 Users

If you've ever used any of the 1-2-3 spreadsheets (or any version of Corel's Quattro Pro), you might recall that these products require you to type an "at" sign (@) before a function name. Excel is smart enough to distinguish functions without you having to flag them with a symbol.

Because old habits die hard, however, Excel accepts @ symbols when you type functions in your formulas, but it removes them as soon as you enter the formula.

These competing products also use two dots (..) as a range reference operator—for example, A1..A10. Excel also enables you to use this notation when you type formulas, but Excel replaces the notation with its own range reference operator, a colon (:).

This accommodation goes only so far, however. Excel still insists that you use the standard Excel function names, and it doesn't recognize or translate the function names used in other spreadsheets. For example, if you enter the 1-2-3 @AVG function, Excel flags it as an error. (Excel's name for this function is AVERAGE.)

Names as Arguments

As you've seen, functions can use cell or range references for their arguments. When Excel calculates the formula, it simply uses the current contents of the cell or range to perform its calculations. The SUM function returns the sum of its argument(s). To calculate the sum of the values in A1:A20, you can use

```
=SUM(A1:A20)
```

And, not surprisingly, if you've defined a name for A1:A20 (such as *Sales*), you can use the name in place of the reference:

```
=SUM(Sales)
```

CROSS REF

For more information about defining and using names, refer to Chapter 3.

Full-Column or Full-Row as Arguments

In some cases, you may find it useful to use an entire column or row as an argument. For example, the following formula sums all values in column B:

```
=SUM(B:B)
```

Using full-column and full-row references is particularly useful if the range that you're summing changes — if you continually add new sales figures, for instance. If you do use an entire row or column, just make sure that the row or column doesn't contain extraneous information that you don't want included in the sum.

You might think that using such a large range (a column consists of 1,048,576 cells) might slow down calculation time. Not true. Excel keeps track of the last-used row and last-used column and will not use cells beyond them when computing a formula result that references an entire column or row.

Literal Values as Arguments

A *literal argument* refers to a value or text string that you enter directly. For example, the SQRT function, which calculates the square root of a number, takes one argument. In the following example, the formula uses a literal value for the function's argument:

```
=SQRT(225)
```

Using a literal argument with a simple function like this one usually defeats the purpose of using a formula. This formula always returns the same value, so you could just as easily replace it with the value 15. You may want to make an exception to this rule in the interest of clarity. For example, you might want to make it perfectly clear that you are computing the square root of 225.

Using literal arguments makes more sense with formulas that use more than one argument. For example, the LEFT function (which takes two arguments) returns characters from the beginning of its first argument; the second argument specifies the number of characters. If cell A1 contains the text Budget, the following formula returns the first letter, or B:

```
=LEFT(A1,1)
```

Expressions as Arguments

Excel also enables you to use expressions as arguments. Think of an *expression* as a formula within a formula. When Excel encounters an expression as a function's argument, it evaluates the expression and then uses the result as the argument's value. Here's an example:

```
=SQRT((A1^2)+(A2^2))
```

This formula uses the SQRT function, and its single argument appears as the following expression:

```
(A1^2)+(A2^2)
```

When Excel evaluates the formula, it first evaluates the expression in the argument and then computes the square root of the result.

Other Functions as Arguments

Because Excel can evaluate expressions as arguments, it shouldn't surprise you that these expressions can include other functions. Writing formulas that have functions within functions is sometimes known as *nesting* functions. Excel starts by evaluating the most deeply nested expression and works its way out. Note this example of a nested function:

```
=SIN(RADIANS(B9))
```

The RADIANS function converts degrees to *radians*, the unit used by all of the Excel trigonometric functions. If cell B9 contains an angle in degrees, the RADIANS function converts it to radians and then the SIN function computes the sine of the angle.

 NEW

A formula can contain up to 64 levels of nested functions, up from 7 in previous versions. If you exceed this level, Excel pops up an error message. In the vast majority of cases, this limit poses no problem. In the unlikely event that you need to exceed this limit, you may be able to use a lookup function instead. See Chapter 8 for more information about lookup functions.

Arrays as Arguments

A function can also use an array as an argument. An *array* is a series of values separated by a comma and enclosed in brackets. The formula below uses the OR function with an array as an argument. The formula returns TRUE if cell A1 contains 1, 3, or 5.

```
=OR(A1={1,3,5})
```

 CROSS REF

See Part IV of this book for more information about working with arrays.

Often, using arrays can help you simplify your formula. The formula below, for example, returns the same result but uses nested IF functions instead of an array:

```
=IF(A1=1,TRUE,IF(A1=3,TRUE,IF(A1=5,TRUE,FALSE)))
```

Ways to Enter a Function into a Formula

You can enter a function into a formula by typing it manually or by using the Insert Function dialog box.

Entering a Function Manually

If you're familiar with a particular function — you know its correct spelling and the types of arguments that it takes — you may choose simply to type the function and its arguments into your formula. Often, this method is the most efficient.

A new feature in Excel 2007 is Formula AutoComplete. When you type an equal sign and the first letter of a function in a cell, Excel displays a drop-down list box of all the functions that begin with that letter and a ScreenTip with a brief description for the function (see Figure 4-1). You can continue typing the function to limit the list or use the arrow keys to select the function from the list. After the desired function is selected, pressing Tab inserts the function and its opening parenthesis into the cell.

NOTE

In addition to displaying function names, the Formula AutoComplete feature also lists names and table references.

At this point, Excel displays another ScreenTip that shows the arguments for the function. The bold argument is the argument you are currently entering. Arguments shown in brackets are optional. Notice that the text in the ScreenTip is hyperlinked. The hyperlinks appear when you move the mouse pointer over the function name or the arguments. The function name is hyperlinked to the help file that explains that function. Each argument that is entered or is the current argument is also hyperlinked. Clicking an argument hyperlink selects that argument in the cell.

	A	B	C	D	E	F	G	H	I	J	K
1	Loan Amount:	24,500									
2	Interest Rate:	8.25%									
3	Laon Term:	48									
4	Monthly Payment:	=p									
5			*ƒ* PEARSON								
6			*ƒ* PERCENTILE								
7			*ƒ* PERCENTRANK								
8			*ƒ* PERMUT								
9			*ƒ* PI								
10			*ƒ* PMT	Calculates the payment for a loan based on constant payments and a constant interest rate							
11			*ƒ* POISSON								
12			*ƒ* POWER								
13			*ƒ* PPMT								
14			*ƒ* PRICE								
15			*ƒ* PRICEDISC								
16			*ƒ* PRICEMAT								

Figure 4-1: When you begin to enter a function, Excel lists available functions that begin with the typed letters.

If you omit the closing parenthesis for a function, Excel adds it for you automatically. For example, if you type =**SUM(A1:C12** and press Enter, Excel corrects the formula by adding the right parenthesis.

TIP

When you enter a function, Excel always converts the function's name to uppercase. Therefore, it's a good idea to use lowercase when you type functions. If Excel doesn't convert your text to uppercase when you press Enter, your entry isn't recognized as a function — which means that you spelled it incorrectly or the function isn't available. For example, it may be defined in an add-in not currently installed.

Using the Insert Function Dialog Box to Enter a Function

The Insert Function dialog box assists you by providing a way to enter a function and its arguments in a semi-automated manner. Using the Insert Function dialog ensures that you spell the function correctly and that it contains the proper number of arguments in the correct order.

To insert a function, select the function from the Insert Function dialog box, as shown in Figure 4-2. You access this dialog box by

- Choosing Formulas⇨Function Library⇨Insert Function
- Choosing Formulas⇨Function Library⇨AutoSum, and clicking More Functions in the drop-down list
- Clicking the *fx* icon to the left of the formula bar
- Pressing Shift+F3

When you select a category from the drop-down list, the list box displays the functions in the selected category. The Most Recently Used category lists the functions that you've used most recently. The All category lists all the functions available across all categories. Access this category if you know a function's name but not its category.

If you're not sure which function to use, you can search for a function. Use the field at the top of the Insert Function dialog box. Enter one or more keywords and click Go. Excel will display a list of functions that match your search criteria. For example, if you're looking for functions that are used for loan calculations, enter **loan** as the search term.

When you select a function in the Select a Function list box, notice that Excel displays the function (and its argument names) in the dialog box, along with a brief description of what the function does.

Part II

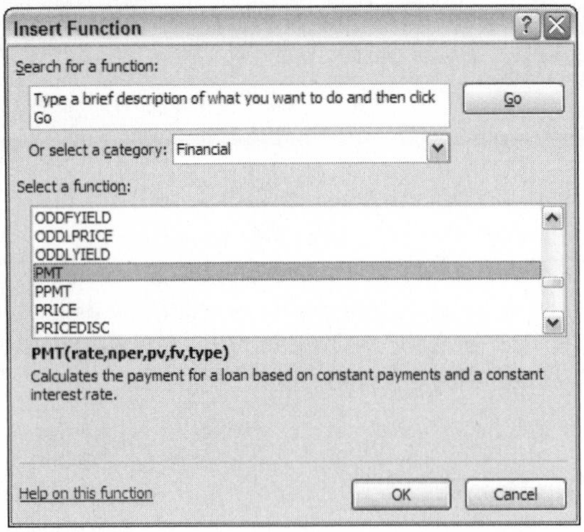

Figure 4-2: The Insert Function dialog box.

When you locate the function that you want to use, click OK. Excel's Function Arguments dialog box appears, as shown in Figure 4-3. Use the Function Arguments dialog box to specify the arguments for the function. You can easily specify a range argument by clicking the Collapse Dialog button (the icon at the right edge of each argument field). Excel temporarily collapses the Function Arguments dialog box to a thin box, so that you can select a range in the worksheet.

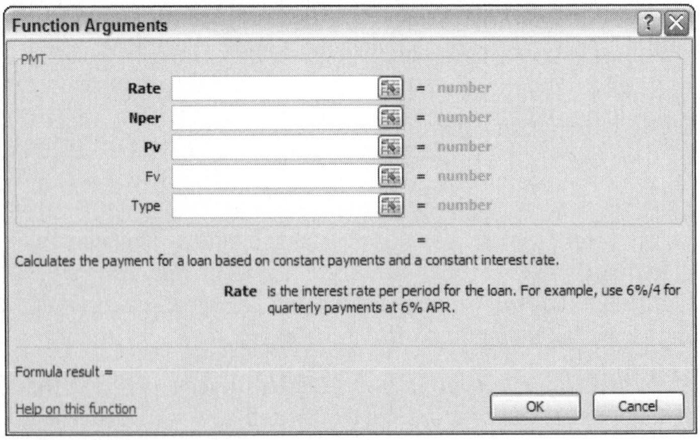

Figure 4-3: The Function Arguments dialog box.

The Function Library group on the Formulas tab contains several drop-downs for often-used function categories. If you select a function from one of these drop-downs, Excel skips the Insert Function dialog box and immediately displays the Function Arguments dialog box for the function selected.

Let Excel Insert Functions for You

Most of the time, you're on your own when it comes to inserting functions. However, at least three situations can arise in which Excel will enter functions for you automatically:

- When you choose Formulas⇨Function Library⇨AutoSum, Excel does a quick check of the surrounding cells. It then proposes a formula that uses the SUM function. If Excel guessed your intentions correctly, just press Enter to accept the proposed formula(s). If Excel guessed incorrectly, you can simply select the range with your mouse to override Excel's suggestion (or press Esc to cancel the AutoSum).

  You can preselect the cells to be included in an AutoSum rather than let Excel guess which cells you want. To insert a SUM function in cell A11 that sums A1:A10, select A1:A11 and click the AutoSum button.

  The AutoSum button displays an arrow that when clicked, displays additional functions. For example, you can use this button to insert a formula that uses the AVERAGE function.

- When you're working with a table (created by using Insert⇨Tables⇨Table), you can choose Table Tools⇨Design⇨Total Row, and Excel displays a new row at the bottom of the table that contains summary formulas for the columns. See Chapter 9 for more information about tables.

- When you choose the Data⇨Data Tools⇨Outline⇨Subtotal command, Excel displays a dialog box that enables you to specify some options. Then it proceeds to insert rows and enter some formulas automatically. These formulas use the SUBTOTAL function.

More Tips for Entering Functions

The following list contains some additional tips to keep in mind when you use the Insert Function dialog box to enter functions:

- Click the Help on This Function hyperlink at any time to get help about the function that you selected (see Figure 4-4).

- If the active cell already contains a formula that uses a function, clicking the Insert Function button displays the Function Arguments dialog box.

- You can use the Insert Function dialog box to insert a function into an existing formula. Just edit the formula and move the insertion point to the location where you want to insert the function. Then open the Insert Function dialog box and select the function.

- If you change your mind about entering a function, click Cancel.

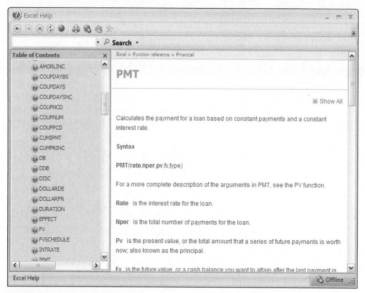

Figure 4-4: Don't forget about Excel's Help system. It's the most comprehensive function reference source available.

- The number of arguments used by the function that you selected determines the number of boxes you see in the Function Arguments dialog box. If a function uses no arguments, you won't see any boxes. If the function uses a variable number of arguments (as with the AVERAGE function), Excel adds a new box every time you enter an optional argument.

- On the right side of each box in the Function Arguments dialog box, you'll see the current value for each argument that's entered or the type of argument (such as text or number) for arguments yet to be entered.

- A few functions, such as INDEX, have more than one form. If you choose such a function, Excel displays the Select Arguments dialog box that enables you to choose which form you want to use.

- If you're entering a function manually and you need help remembering the function's arguments, type an equal sign and the function's name, and then press Ctrl+Shift+A. Excel inserts the function with descriptive placeholders for the arguments, as shown in Figure 4-5. You need to replace these placeholders with actual arguments.

- To locate a function quickly in the Function Name list that appears in the Insert Function dialog box, open the list box, type the first letter of the function name, and then scroll to the desired function. For example, if you select the All category and want to insert the SIN function, click anywhere on the Select a Function list box and press S. Excel selects the first function that begins with S. Keep pressing S until you reach the SIN function.

	A	B	C	D	E	F	G
1	Loan Amount:	24,500					
2	Interest Rate:	8.25%					
3	Laon Term:	48					
4	Monthly Payment:	=pmt(rate,nper,pv,fv,type)					
5		PMT(rate, nper, pv, [fv], [type])					
6							
7							
8							
9							
10							
11							

Figure 4-5: Press Ctrl+Shift+A to instruct Excel to display descriptive placeholders for a function.

- If the active cell contains a formula that uses one or more functions, the Function Arguments dialog box enables you to edit each function. In the formula bar, click the function that you want to edit and then click the Insert Function button.

Function Categories

I list and briefly describe Excel's function categories in the following sections.

CROSS REF

See subsequent chapters for specific examples of using the functions.

NEW

Excel 2007 incorporates all the functions that were formerly available in the Analysis Toolpak add-in.

Financial Functions

The financial functions enable you to perform common business calculations that deal with money. For example, you can use the PMT function to calculate the monthly payment for a car loan. (You need to provide the loan amount, interest rate, and loan term as arguments.)

Date & Time Functions

The functions in this category enable you to analyze and work with date and time values in formulas. For example, the TODAY function returns the current date (as stored in the system clock).

Math & Trig Functions

This category contains a wide variety of functions that perform mathematical and trigonometric calculations.

 NOTE

The trigonometric functions all assume radians for angles (not degrees). Use the RADIANS function to convert degrees to radians.

Statistical Functions

The functions in this category perform statistical analysis on ranges of data. For example, you can calculate statistics such as mean, mode, standard deviation, and variance.

Lookup and Reference Functions

Functions in this category are used to find (look up) values in lists or tables. A common example is a tax table. You can use the VLOOKUP function to determine a tax rate for a particular income level.

Database Functions

Functions in this category are useful when you need to summarize data in a list (also known as a worksheet database) that meets specific criteria. For example, assume you have a list that contains monthly sales information. You can use the DCOUNT function to count the number of records that describe sales in the Northern region with a value greater than 10,000.

Text Functions

The text functions enable you to manipulate text strings in formulas. For example, you can use the MID function to extract any number of characters beginning at any character position. Other functions enable you to change the case of text (convert to uppercase, for example).

Logical Functions

This category consists of only seven functions that enable you to test a condition (for logical TRUE or FALSE). You will find the IF function very useful because it gives your formulas simple decision-making capability.

Volatile Functions

Some Excel functions belong to a special class of functions called *volatile*. Excel recalculates a volatile function whenever it recalculates the workbook — even if the formula that contains the function is not involved in the recalculation.

The RAND function represents an example of a volatile function because it generates a new random number every time Excel calculates the worksheet. Other volatile functions include

AREAS	INDEX	OFFSET
CELL	INDIRECT	ROWS
COLUMNS	NOW	TODAY

As a side effect of using these volatile functions, Excel will always prompt you to save the workbook when you close it — even if you made no changes to it. For example, if you open a workbook that contains any of these volatile functions, scroll around a bit (but don't change anything), and then close the file, Excel will ask whether you want to save the workbook.

You can circumvent this behavior by using the Manual Recalculation mode, with the Recalculate Before Save option turned off. Change the recalculation mode in the Calculate section of the Formulas tab of the Excel Options dialog box (choose Office➪ Excel Options).

Information Functions

The functions in this category help you determine the type of data stored within a cell. For example, the ISTEXT function returns TRUE if a cell reference contains text. Or you can use the ISBLANK function to determine whether a cell is empty. The CELL function returns lots of potentially useful information about a particular cell.

User-Defined Functions

Functions that appear in this category are custom worksheet functions created using VBA. These functions can operate just like Excel's built-in functions. One difference, however, is that custom functions do not display a description of each argument in the Paste Function dialog box.

Engineering Functions

The functions in this category can prove useful for engineering applications. They enable you to work with complex numbers and to perform conversions between various numbering and measurement systems.

Cube Functions

The functions in this category allow you to manipulate data that is part of an OLAP data cube.

Other Function Categories

In addition to the function categories described previously, Excel includes four other categories that may not appear in the Paste Function dialog box: Commands, Customizing, Macro Control, and DDE/External. These categories appear to be holdovers from older versions of Excel. If you create a custom function, you can assign it to one of these categories. In addition, you may see other function categories created by macros.

 CROSS REF

See Chapter 23 for information about assigning your custom functions to a function category.

Chapter 5

Manipulating Text

IN THIS CHAPTER

◆ How Excel handles text entered into cells

◆ Excel's worksheet functions that handle text

◆ Examples of advanced text formulas

◆ Custom VBA text functions

Excel, of course, is best known for its ability to crunch numbers. However, it is also quite versatile when it comes to handling text. As you know, Excel enables you to enter text for things such as row and column headings, customer names and addresses, part numbers, and just about anything else. And, as you might expect, you can use formulas to manipulate the text contained in cells.

This chapter contains many examples of formulas that use functions to manipulate text. Some of these formulas perform feats you may not have thought possible.

A Few Words about Text

When you enter data into a cell, Excel immediately goes to work and determines whether you're entering a formula, a number (including a date or time), or anything else. Anything else is considered text.

> **NOTE**
>
> You may hear the term *string* used instead of *text*. You can use these terms interchange-ably. Sometimes, they even appear together, as in *text string*.

How Many Characters in a Cell?

A single cell can hold up to 32,000 characters. To put things into perspective, this chapter contains about 30,000 characters. I certainly don't recommend using a cell in lieu of a word processor, but you really don't have to lose much sleep worrying about filling up a cell with text.

Numbers as Text

As I mentioned, Excel distinguishes between numbers and text. If you want to "force" a number to be considered as text, you can do one of the following:

- Apply the Text number format to the cell. Select Text from the Number Format drop-down list, which can be found at Home➪Number. If you haven't applied other horizontal alignment formatting, the value will appear left-aligned in the cell (like normal text).

- Precede the number with an apostrophe. The apostrophe isn't displayed, but the cell entry will be treated as if it were text.

Even though a cell is formatted as Text (or uses an apostrophe), you can still perform some mathematical operations on the cell if the entry looks like a number. For example, assume cell A1 contains a value preceded by an apostrophe. The formula that follows will display the value in A1, incremented by 1:

```
=A1+1
```

The formula that follows, however, will treat the contents of cell A1 as 0:

```
=SUM(A1:A10)
```

When a Number Isn't Treated as a Number

If you import data into Excel, you may be aware of a common problem: Sometimes, the imported values are treated as text. Here's a quick way to convert these non-numbers to actual values. Activate any empty cell and choose Home➪Clipboard➪Copy. Then, select the range that contains the values you need to fix. Choose Home➪Clipboard➪Paste Special. In the Paste Special dialog box, select the Add option and click OK. By "adding zero" to the text, you force Excel to treat the non-numbers as actual values.

In some cases, treating text as a number can be useful. In other cases, it can cause problems. Bottom line? Just be aware of Excel's inconsistency in how it treats a number formatted as text.

NOTE

If background error checking is turned on, Excel flags numbers preceded by an apostrophe (and numbers formatted as Text) with a Smart Tag. You can use this Smart Tag to convert the "text" to an actual value. Just click the Smart Tag and choose Convert to Number. Background error checking is controlled in the Excel Options dialog box. Choose Office⇨Excel Options and navigate to the Error Checking section of the Formulas tab.

Text Functions

Excel has an excellent assortment of worksheet functions that can handle text. For your convenience, the Function Library group on the Formulas tab includes a Text drop-down that provides access to most of these functions. A few other functions that are relevant to text manipulation appear in other function categories. For example, the ISTEXT function is in the Information category (Formulas⇨Function Library⇨Other Functions⇨Information).

CROSS REF

Refer to Appendix A for a listing of the functions in the Text category.

Most of the text functions are not limited for use with text. In other words, these functions can also operate with cells that contain values. Excel is very accommodating when it comes to treating numbers as text and text as numbers.

The examples discussed in this section demonstrate some common (and useful) things you can do with text. You may need to adapt some of these examples for your own use.

Determining Whether a Cell Contains Text

In some situations, you may need a formula that determines the type of data contained in a particular cell. For example, you may use an IF function to return a result only if a cell contains text. The easiest way to make this determination is to use the ISTEXT function.

The ISTEXT function takes a single argument, returning TRUE if the argument contains text and FALSE if it doesn't contain text. The formula that follows returns TRUE if A1 contains a string:

```
=ISTEXT(A1)
```

The TYPE function takes a single argument and returns a value that indicates the type of data in a cell. If cell A1 contains a text string, the formula that follows returns 2 (the code number for text):

```
=TYPE(A1)
```

Working with Character Codes

Every character that you see on your screen has an associated code number. For Windows systems, Excel uses the standard ANSI (American National Standards Institute) character set. The ANSI character set consists of 255 characters, numbered from 1 to 255.

Figure 5-1 shows a portion of an Excel worksheet that displays all 255 characters. This example uses the Calibri font. (Other fonts may have different characters.)

Figure 5-1: The ANSI character set (for the Calibri font).

ON THE CD

The companion CD-ROM includes a copy of the workbook `character set.xlsm`. It has some simple macros that enable you to display the character set for any font installed on your system.

Two functions come into play when dealing with character codes: CODE and CHAR. These functions aren't very useful by themselves. However, they can prove quite useful in conjunction with other functions. I discuss these functions in the following sections.

NOTE

The CODE and CHAR functions work only with ANSI strings. These functions will not work with double-byte Unicode strings.

THE CODE FUNCTION

Excel's CODE function returns the character code for its argument. The formula that follows returns 65, the character code for uppercase A:

```
=CODE("A")
```

If the argument for CODE consists of more than one character, the function uses only the first character. Therefore, this formula also returns 65:

```
=CODE("Abbey Road")
```

THE CHAR FUNCTION

The CHAR function is essentially the opposite of the CODE function. Its argument should be a value between 1 and 255, and the function should return the corresponding character. The following formula, for example, returns the letter A:

```
=CHAR(65)
```

To demonstrate the opposing nature of the CODE and CHAR functions, try entering this formula:

```
=CHAR(CODE("A"))
```

This formula (illustrative rather than useful) returns the letter A. First, it converts the character to its code value (65) and then it converts this code back to the corresponding character.

Assume that cell A1 contains the letter A (uppercase). The following formula returns the letter *a* (lowercase):

```
=CHAR(CODE(A1)+32)
```

This formula takes advantage of the fact that the alphabetic characters all appear in alphabetical order within the character set, and the lowercase letters follow the uppercase letters (with a few other characters tossed in between). Each lowercase letter lies exactly 32 character positions higher than its corresponding uppercase letter.

Part II

How to Find Special Characters

Don't overlook the handy Symbol dialog box (which appears when you choose Insert➪Text➪Symbol). This dialog box makes it easy to insert special characters (including Unicode characters) into cells. For example, you might (for some strange reason) want to include a smiley face character in your spreadsheet. Access Excel's Symbol dialog box and select the Wingdings font (see the accompanying figure). Examine the characters, locate the smiley face, click Insert, and then click Cancel. You'll also find out that this character has a code of 74.

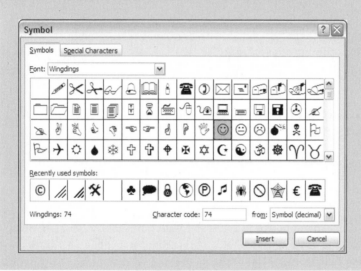

Determining Whether Two Strings Are Identical

You can set up a simple logical formula to determine whether two cells contain the same entry. For example, use this formula to determine whether cell A1 has the same contents as cell A2:

```
=A1=A2
```

Excel acts a bit lax in its comparisons when text is involved. Consider the case in which A1 contains the word *January* (initial capitalization), and A2 contains *JANUARY* (all uppercase). You'll find that the previous formula returns TRUE even though the contents of the two cells are not really the same. In other words, the comparison is not case sensitive.

In many cases, you don't need to worry about the case of the text. However, if you need to make an exact, case-sensitive comparison, you can use Excel's EXACT function. The formula that follows returns TRUE only if cells A1 and A2 contain exactly the same entry:

```
=EXACT(A1,A2)
```

The following formula returns FALSE because the first string contains a trailing space:

```
=EXACT("zero ","zero")
```

Joining Two or More Cells

Excel uses an ampersand as its concatenation operator. *Concatenation* is simply a fancy term that describes what happens when you join the contents of two or more cells. For example, if cell A1 contains the text *Tucson* and cell A2 contains the text *Arizona*, the following formula will return *TucsonArizona:*

```
=A1&A2
```

Notice that the two strings are joined together without an intervening space. To add a space between the two entries (to get *Tucson Arizona*), use a formula like this one:

```
=A1&" "&A2
```

Or, even better, use a comma and a space to produce *Tucson, Arizona:*

```
=A1&", "&A2
```

Another option is to eliminate the quote characters and use the CHAR function, with an appropriate argument. Note this example of using the CHAR function to represent a comma (44) and a space (32):

```
=A1&CHAR(44)&CHAR(32)&A2
```

If you'd like to force a line break between strings, concatenate the strings by using CHAR(10), which inserts a line break character. Also, make sure that you apply the wrap text format to the cell (choose Home⇨Alignment⇨Wrap Text). The following example joins the text in cell A1 and the text in cell B1, with a line break in between:

```
=A1&CHAR(10)&B1
```

Here's another example of the CHAR function. The following formula returns the string *Stop* by concatenating four characters returned by the CHAR function:

```
=CHAR(83)&CHAR(116)&CHAR(111)&CHAR(112)
```

Here's a final example of using the & operator. In this case, the formula combines text with the result of an expression that returns the maximum value in column C:

```
="The largest value in Column C is " &MAX(C:C)
```

Part II

NOTE
Excel also has a CONCATENATE function, which takes up to 255 arguments. This function simply combines the arguments into a single string. You can use this function if you like, but using the & operator is usually simpler.

Displaying Formatted Values as Text

The Excel TEXT function enables you to display a value in a specific number format. Although this function may appear to have dubious value, it does serve some useful purposes, as the examples in this section demonstrate. Figure 5-2 shows a simple worksheet. The formula in cell D1 is

```
="The net profit is " & B3
```

	A	B	C	D	E	F	G
1	Gross:	$155,609.84		The net profit is 104616.52			
2	Expenses:	$50,993.32					
3	Net:	$104,616.52					
4							
5							
6							

Sheet1

Figure 5-2: The formula in D1 doesn't display the formatted number.

This formula essentially combines a text string with the contents of cell B3 and displays the result. Note, however, that the contents of B3 are not formatted in any way. You might want to display B3's contents using a currency number format.

NOTE
Contrary to what you might expect, applying a number format to the cell that contains the formula has no effect. This is because the formula returns a string, not a value.

Note this revised formula that uses the TEXT function to apply formatting to the value in B3:

```
="The net profit is " & TEXT(B3,"$#,##0.00")
```

This formula displays the text along with a nicely formatted value: *The net profit is $104,616.52.*

The second argument for the TEXT function consists of a standard Excel number format string. You can enter any valid number format string for this argument.

The preceding example uses a simple cell reference (B3). You can, of course, use an expression instead. Here's an example that combines text with a number resulting from a computation:

```
="Average Expenditure: "& TEXT(AVERAGE(A:A),"$#,##0.00")
```

This formula might return a string such as *Average Expenditure: $7,794.57.*

Here's another example that uses the NOW function (which returns the current date and time). The TEXT function displays the date and time, nicely formatted.

```
="Report printed on "&TEXT(NOW(),"mmmm d, yyyy at h:mm AM/PM")
```

The formula might display the following: *Report printed on July 22, 2004 at 3:23 PM.*

 CROSS REF

Refer to Appendix B for details on Excel number formats.

Displaying Formatted Currency Values as Text

Excel's DOLLAR function converts a number to text using the currency format. It takes two arguments: the number to convert, and the number of decimal places to display. The DOLLAR function uses the regional currency symbol (for example, a $).

You can sometimes use the DOLLAR function in place of the TEXT function. The TEXT function, however, is much more flexible because it doesn't limit you to a specific number format.

The following formula returns *Total: $1,287.37.*

The second argument for the DOLLAR function specifies the number of decimal places.

```
="Total: " & DOLLAR(1287.367, 2)
```

Counting Characters in a String

The Excel LEN function takes one argument and returns the number of characters in the argument. For example, assume that cell A1 contains the string *September Sales.* The following formula returns 15:

```
=LEN(A1)
```

Notice that space characters are included in the character count. This can be useful for identifying strings with extraneous spaces. For instance, if A1 contains *Sales* and the preceding formula returns 6, there may be a leading or trailing space.

The following formula shortens text that is too long. If the text in A1 is more than ten characters in length, this formula returns the first nine characters plus an ellipsis (133 on the ANSI chart) as a continuation character. If it's ten or fewer, the whole string is returned:

```
=IF(LEN(A1)>10,LEFT(A1,9)&CHAR(133),A1)
```

CROSS REF

You will see example formulas that demonstrate how to count the number of specific characters within a string later in this chapter. Also, Chapter 7 contains additional counting techniques. Still more counting examples are provided in Chapter 15, which deals with array formulas.

Repeating a Character or String

The REPT function repeats a text string (first argument) any number of times you specify (second argument). For example, this formula returns *HoHoHo*:

```
=REPT("Ho",3)
```

You can also use this function to create crude vertical dividers between cells. This example displays a squiggly line, 20 characters in length:

```
=REPT("~",20)
```

Creating a Text Histogram

A clever use for the REPT function is to create a simple histogram (also known as a *frequency distribution*) directly in a worksheet (chart not required). Figure 5-3 shows an example of such a histogram. You'll find this type of graphical display especially useful when you need to visually summarize many values. In such a case, a standard chart may be unwieldy.

The formulas in columns E and G graphically depict monthly budget variances by displaying a series of characters in the Wingdings font. This example uses the character *n*, which displays as a small square in the Wingdings font. A formula using the REPT function determines the number of characters displayed. Key formulas include

```
E3: =IF(D3<0,REPT("n",-ROUND(D3*100,0)),"")
F3: =A3
G3: =IF(D3>0,REPT("n",ROUND(D3*100,0)),"")
```

	A	B	C	D	E	F	G	H
1								
2		Budget	Actual	Pct. Diff	Under Budget		Exceeded Budget	
3	Jan	300	311	3.7%		Jan	■■■■	
4	Feb	300	298	-0.7%	■	Feb		
5	Mar	300	305	1.7%		Mar	■■	
6	Apr	350	351	0.3%		Apr		
7	May	350	402	14.9%		May	■■■■■■■■■■■■■■	
8	Jun	350	409	16.9%		Jun	■■■■■■■■■■■■■■	
9	Jul	500	421	-15.8%	■■■■■■■■■■■■■■■■■	Jul		
10	Aug	500	454	-9.2%	■■■■■■■■■■	Aug		
11	Sep	500	474	-5.2%	■■■■■	Sep		
12	Oct	500	521	4.2%		Oct	■■■■	
13	Nov	500	476	-4.8%	■■■■■	Nov		
14	Dec	500	487	-2.6%	■■■	Dec		
15								

Sheet1 Sheet2

Figure 5-3: Using the REPT function to create a histogram in a worksheet range.

Assign the Wingdings font to cells E3 and G3, and then copy the formulas down the columns to accommodate all the data. Right-align the text in column E and adjust any other formatting. Depending on the numerical range of your data, you may need to change the scaling. Experiment by replacing the 100 value in the formulas. You can substitute any character you like for the *n* in the formulas to produce a different character in the chart.

NEW

The Data Bars conditional formatting option (new in Excel 2007) may be a better option for displaying a histogram in a range.

ON THE CD

The workbook shown in Figure 5-3, `text histogram.xlsx`, also appears on the companion CD-ROM.

Padding a Number

You're probably familiar with a common security measure (frequently used on printed checks) in which numbers are padded with asterisks on the right. The following formula displays the value in cell A1, along with enough asterisks to make 24 characters total:

```
=(A1 & REPT("*",24-LEN(A1)))
```

Or if you'd prefer to pad the number with asterisks on the left, use this formula:

```
=REPT("*",24-LEN(A1))&A1
```

The following formula displays asterisk padding on both sides of the number. It will return 24 characters when the number in cell A1 contains an even number of characters; otherwise, it returns 23 characters.

```
=REPT("*",12-LEN(A1)/2)&A1&REPT("*",12-LEN(A1)/2)
```

Part II

The preceding formulas are a bit deficient because they don't show any number formatting. Note this revised version that displays the value in A1 (formatted), along with the asterisk padding on the left:

```
=REPT("*",24-LEN(TEXT(A1,"$#,##0.00")))&TEXT(A1,"$#,##0.00")
```

Figure 5-4 shows this formula in action.

	A	B	C	D	E	F
1	143.55		****************$143.55			
2	9.8754		******************$9.88			
3	1933.43		**************$1,933.43			
4	-908.32		***************-$908.32			
5						
6						
7						

Sheet1 Sheet2

Figure 5-4: Using a formula to pad a number with asterisks.

You can also pad a number by using a custom number format. To repeat the next character in the format to fill the column width, include an asterisk (*) in the custom number format code. For example, use this number format to pad the number with dashes:

```
$#,##0.00*-
```

To pad the number with asterisks, use two asterisks, like this:

```
$#,##0.00**
```

CROSS REF

Refer to Appendix B for more information about custom number formats, including additional examples using the asterisk format code.

Removing Excess Spaces and Nonprinting Characters

Often, data imported into an Excel worksheet contains excess spaces or strange (often unprintable) characters. Excel provides you with two functions to help whip your data into shape: TRIM and CLEAN.

- **TRIM:** Removes all leading and trailing spaces, and replaces internal strings of multiple spaces by a single space.

- **CLEAN:** Removes all nonprinting characters from a string. These "garbage" characters often appear when you import certain types of data.

This example uses the TRIM function. The formula returns *Fourth Quarter Earnings* (with no excess spaces):

```
=TRIM("   Fourth    Quarter    Earnings    ")
```

Changing the Case of Text

Excel provides three handy functions to change the case of text:

- **UPPER:** Converts the text to ALL UPPERCASE.
- **LOWER:** Converts the text to all lowercase.
- **PROPER:** Converts the text to Proper Case. (The First Letter In Each Word Is Capitalized.)

These functions are quite straightforward. The formula that follows, for example, converts the text in cell A1 to proper case. If cell A1 contained the text *MR. JOHN Q. PUBLIC*, the formula would return *Mr. John Q. Public*.

```
=PROPER(A1)
```

These functions operate only on alphabetic characters; they simply ignore all other characters and return them unchanged.

Transforming Data with Formulas

Many of the examples in this chapter describe how to use functions to transform data in some way. For example, you can use the UPPER function to transform text into uppercase. Often, you'll want to replace the original data with the transformed data. To do so, Paste Values over the original text. Here's how:

1. Create your formulas to transform the original data.

2. Select the formula cells.

3. Choose Home⇨Clipboard⇨Copy (or press Ctrl+C).

4. Select the original data cells.

5. Choose Home⇨Clipboard⇨Paste⇨Paste Values

After performing these steps, you can delete the formulas.

CAUTION

The PROPER function will capitalize the first letter of every word, which isn't always desirable. Applying the PROPER function to *a tale of two cities* results in *A Tale Of Two Cities*. Normally, the preposition *of* wouldn't be capitalized. In addition, applying the PROPER function to a name such as *ED MCMAHON* results in *Ed Mcmahon* (not *Ed McMahon*).

Extracting Characters from a String

Excel users often need to extract characters from a string. For example, you may have a list of employee names (first and last names) and need to extract the last name from each cell. Excel provides several useful functions for extracting characters:

- **LEFT:** Returns a specified number of characters from the beginning of a string
- **RIGHT:** Returns a specified number of characters from the end of a string
- **MID:** Returns a specified number of characters beginning at any position within a string

The formula that follows returns the last ten characters from cell A1. If A1 contains fewer than ten characters, the formula returns all of the text in the cell.

```
=RIGHT(A1,10)
```

This next formula uses the MID function to return five characters from cell A1, beginning at character position 2. In other words, it returns characters 2–6.

```
=MID(A1,2,5)
```

The following example returns the text in cell A1, with only the first letter in uppercase (sometimes referred to as *sentence case*). It uses the LEFT function to extract the first character and convert it to uppercase. This then concatenates to another string that uses the RIGHT function to extract all but the first character (converted to lowercase).

```
=UPPER(LEFT(A1))&LOWER(RIGHT(A1,LEN(A1)-1))
```

If cell A1 contained the text *FIRST QUARTER*, the formula would return *First quarter.*

Replacing Text with Other Text

In some situations, you may need to replace a part of a text string with some other text. For example, you may import data that contains asterisks, and you need to convert the asterisks to some other character. You could use Excel's Find and Replace dialog box to make the replacement. If you prefer a formula-based solution, you can take advantage of either of two functions:

- **SUBSTITUTE:** Replaces specific text in a string. Use this function when you know the character(s) to be replaced, but not the position.

- **REPLACE:** Replaces text that occurs in a specific location within a string. Use this function when you know the position of the text to be replaced, but not the actual text.

The following formula uses the SUBSTITUTE function to replace *2006* with *2007* in the string *2006 Budget.* The formula returns *2007 Budget.*

```
=SUBSTITUTE("2006 Budget","2006","2007")
```

The following formula uses the SUBSTITUTE function to remove all spaces from a string. In other words, it replaces all space characters with an empty string. The formula returns the title of an excellent Liz Phair CD: *Whitechocolatespaceegg.*

```
=SUBSTITUTE("White chocolate space egg"," ","")
```

The following formula uses the REPLACE function to replace one character beginning at position 5 with nothing. In other words, it removes the fifth character (a hyphen) and returns *Part544.*

```
=REPLACE("Part-544",5,1,"")
```

You can, of course, nest these functions to perform multiple replacements in a single formula. The formula that follows demonstrates the power of nested SUBSTITUTE functions. The formula essentially strips out any of the following seven characters in cell A1: space, hyphen, colon, asterisk, underscore, left parenthesis, and right parenthesis.

```
=SUBSTITUTE(SUBSTITUTE(SUBSTITUTE(
SUBSTITUTE(SUBSTITUTE(SUBSTITUTE(SUBSTITUTE(
A1," ",""),"-",""),":",""),"*",""),"_",""),"(",""),")","")
```

Therefore, if cell A1 contains the string *Part-2A - Z(4M1)_A*,* the formula returns *Part2AZ4M1A.*

Finding and Searching within a String

The Excel FIND and SEARCH functions enable you to locate the starting position of a particular substring within a string:

- **FIND:** Finds a substring within another text string and returns the starting position of the substring. You can specify the character position at which to begin searching. Use this function for case-sensitive text comparisons. Wildcard comparisons are not supported.

- **SEARCH:** Finds a substring within another text string and returns the starting position of the substring. You can specify the character position at which to begin searching. Use this function for non–case-sensitive text or when you need to use wildcard characters.

The following formula uses the FIND function and returns 7, the position of the first *m* in the string. Notice that this formula is case sensitive.

```
=FIND("m","Big Mamma Thornton",1)
```

The formula that follows, which uses the SEARCH function, returns *5*, the position of the first m (either uppercase or lowercase):

```
=SEARCH("m","Big Mamma Thornton",1)
```

You can use the following wildcard characters within the first argument for the SEARCH function:

- **Question mark (?):** Matches any single character
- **Asterisk (*):** Matches any sequence of characters

TIP

If you want to find an actual question mark or asterisk character, type a tilde (~) before the question mark or asterisk.

The next formula examines the text in cell A1 and returns the position of the first three-character sequence that has a hyphen in the middle of it. In other words, it looks for any character followed by a hyphen and any other character. If cell A1 contains the text *Part-A90*, the formula returns 4.

```
=SEARCH("?-?",A1,1)
```

Searching and Replacing within a String

You can use the REPLACE function in conjunction with the SEARCH function to replace part of a text string with another string. In effect, you use the SEARCH function to find the starting location used by the REPLACE function.

For example, assume cell A1 contains the text *Annual Profit Figures*. The following formula searches for the word *Profit* and replaces those six characters it with the word *Loss:*

```
=REPLACE(A1,SEARCH("Profit",A1),6,"Loss")
```

This next formula uses the SUBSTITUTE function to accomplish the same effect in a more efficient manner:

```
=SUBSTITUTE(A1,"Profit","Loss")
```

Advanced Text Formulas

The examples in this section are more complex than the examples in the previous section. But, as you'll see, these formulas can perform some very useful text manipulations.

ON THE CD

You can access all the examples in this section on the companion CD-ROM in `text formula examples.xlsx` file.

Counting Specific Characters in a Cell

This formula counts the number of Bs (uppercase only) in the string in cell A1:

```
=LEN(A1)-LEN(SUBSTITUTE(A1,"B",""))
```

This formula uses the SUBSTITUTE function to create a new string (in memory) that has all the Bs removed. Then the length of this string is subtracted from the length of the original string. The result reveals the number of Bs in the original string.

The following formula is a bit more versatile. It counts the number of Bs (both upper- and lowercase) in the string in cell A1.

```
=LEN(A1)-LEN(SUBSTITUTE(SUBSTITUTE(A1,"B",""),"b",""))
```

Counting the Occurrences of a Substring in a Cell

The formulas in the preceding section count the number of occurrences of a particular character in a string. The following formula works with more than one character. It returns the number of occurrences of a particular substring (contained in cell B1) within a string (contained in cell A1). The substring can consist of any number of characters.

```
=(LEN(A1)-LEN(SUBSTITUTE(A1,B1,"")))/LEN(B1)
```

For example, if cell A1 contains the text *Blonde On Blonde* and B1 contains the text *Blonde*, the formula returns 2.

The comparison is case sensitive, so if B1 contains the text *blonde,* the formula returns 0. The following formula is a modified version that performs a case-insensitive comparison:

```
=(LEN(A1)-LEN(SUBSTITUTE(UPPER(A1),UPPER(B1),"")))/LEN(B1)
```

Expressing a Number as an Ordinal

You may need to express a value as an ordinal number. For example, *Today is the 21st day of the month.* In this case, the number 21 converts to an ordinal number by appending the characters *st* to the number.

The characters appended to a number depend on the number. There is no clear pattern, making the construction of a formula more difficult. Most numbers will use the *th* suffix. Exceptions occur for numbers that end with 1, 2, or 3 — except if the preceding number is a 1 (numbers that end with 11, 12, or 13). These may seem like fairly complex rules, but you can translate them into an Excel formula.

The formula that follows converts the number in cell A1 (assumed to be an integer) to an ordinal number:

```
=A1&IF(OR(VALUE(RIGHT(A1,2))={11,12,13}),"th",IF(OR(VALUE(RIGHT(A1))={1,2,3}),
CHOOSE(RIGHT(A1),"st","nd","rd"),"th"))
```

This is a rather complicated formula, so it may help to examine its components. Basically, the formula works as follows:

1. If the last two digits of the number are 11, 12, or 13, use *th*.

2. If Rule #1 does not apply, check the last digit. If the last digit is 1, use *st*. If the last digit is 2, use *nd*. If the last digit is 3, use *rd*.

3. If neither Rule #1 nor Rule #2 apply, use *th*.

 CROSS REF

The formula uses two arrays, specified by brackets. Refer to Chapter 14 for more information about using arrays in formulas.

Figure 5-5 shows the formula in use.

Determining a Column Letter for a Column Number

This next formula returns a worksheet column letter (ranging from A to XFD) for the value contained in cell A1. For example, if A1 contains *29,* the formula returns *AC.*

```
=LEFT(ADDRESS(1,A1,4),FIND(1,ADDRESS(1,A1,4))-1)
```

Note that the formula doesn't check for a valid column number. In other words, if A1 contains a value less than 1 or greater than 16,384, the formula will return an error. The following modification uses the new IFERROR function to display text *(Invalid Column)* instead of an error value.

```
=IFERROR(LEFT(ADDRESS(1,A1,4),FIND(1,ADDRESS(1,A1,4))-1),"Invalid Column")
```

	A	B	C	D
1	**Number**	**Ordinal**		
2	1	1st		
3	4	4th		
4	7	7th		
5	10	10th		
6	13	13th		
7	16	16th		
8	19	19th		
9	22	22nd		
10	25	25th		
11	28	28th		
12	31	31st		
13	34	34th		
14	37	37th		
15	40	40th		
16	43	43rd		
17	46	46th		
18	49	49th		
19	52	52nd		
20				

Ⅰ◀ ◀ ▶ ▶Ⅰ　Sheet1 ╱ Sheet2

Figure 5-5: Using a formula to express a number as an ordinal.

For compatibility with versions prior to Excel 2007, use this formula:

```
=IF(ISERR(LEFT(ADDRESS(1,A1,4),FIND(1,ADDRESS(1,A1,4))-1)),
"Invalid Column",LEFT(ADDRESS(1,A1,4),FIND(1,ADDRESS(1,A1,4))-1))
```

Extracting a Filename from a Path Specification

The following formula returns the filename `from` a full path specification. For example, if cell A1 contains *c:\windows\desktop\myfile.xlsx,* the formula returns *myfile.xlsx.*

```
=MID(A1,FIND("*",SUBSTITUTE(A1,"\","*",LEN(A1)-LEN(SUBSTITUTE(A1,"\",""))))+1,LEN(A1))
```

This formula assumes that the system path separator is a backslash (\). It essentially returns all the text following the last backslash character. If cell A1 doesn't contain a backslash character, the formula returns an error.

Extracting the First Word of a String

To extract the first word of a string, a formula must locate the position of the first space character, and then use this information as an argument for the LEFT function. The following formula does just that:

```
=LEFT(A1,FIND(" ",A1)-1)
```

This formula returns all of the text prior to the first space in cell A1. However, the formula has a slight problem: It returns an error if cell A1 consists of a single word. A simple modification solves the problem by using an IFERROR function to check for the error:

```
=IFERROR(LEFT(A1,FIND(" ",A1)-1),A1)
```

The IFERROR function is new to Excel 2007. For compatibility with previous versions, use this formula:

```
=IF(ISERR(FIND(" ",A1)),A1,LEFT(A1,FIND(" ",A1)-1))
```

Extracting the Last Word of a String

Extracting the last word of a string is more complicated because the FIND function only works from left to right. Therefore, the problem rests with locating the *last* space character. The formula that follows, however, solves this problem. It returns the last word of a string (all the text following the last space character):

```
=RIGHT(A1,LEN(A1)-FIND("*",SUBSTITUTE(A1," ","*",LEN(A1)-LEN(SUBSTITUTE(A1," ","")))))
```

This formula, however, has the same problem as the first formula in the preceding section: It fails if the string does not contain at least one space character. The following modified formula uses the IFERROR function to avoid the error value.

```
=IFERROR(RIGHT(A1,LEN(A1)-FIND("*",SUBSTITUTE(A1," ","*",LEN(A1)-
LEN(SUBSTITUTE(A1," ",""))))),A1)
```

For compatibility with previous Excel versions, use this formula:

```
=IF(ISERR(FIND(" ",A1)),A1,RIGHT(A1,LEN(A1)-FIND("*",SUBSTITUTE(A1,"
","*",LEN(A1)-LEN(SUBSTITUTE(A1," ",""))))))
```

Extracting All but the First Word of a String

The following formula returns the contents of cell A1, except for the first word:

```
=RIGHT(A1,LEN(A1)-FIND(" ",A1,1))
```

If cell A1 contains *2007 Operating Budget*, the formula returns *Operating Budget*.

This formula returns an error if the cell contains only one word. The formula below solves this problem and returns an empty string if the cell does not contain multiple words:

```
=IFERROR(RIGHT(A1,LEN(A1)-FIND(" ",A1,1)),"")
```

For compatibility with earlier versions of Excel, use this formula:

```
=IF(ISERR(FIND(" ",A1)),"",RIGHT(A1,LEN(A1)-FIND(" ",A1,1)))
```

Extracting First Names, Middle Names, and Last Names

Suppose you have a list consisting of people's names in a single column. You have to separate these names into three columns: one for the first name, one for the middle name or initial, and one for the last name. This task is more complicated than you may initially think because not every name in the column has a middle name or middle initial. However, you can still do it.

NOTE

The task becomes a *lot* more complicated if the list contains names with titles (such as Mrs. or Dr.) or names followed by additional details (such as Jr. or III). In fact, the following formulas will not handle these complex cases. However, they still give you a significant head start if you're willing to do a bit of manual editing to handle the special cases.

The formulas that follow all assume that the name appears in cell A1.

You can easily construct a formula to return the first name:

```
=IFERROR(LEFT(A1,FIND(" ",A1)-1),A1)
```

Returning the middle name or initial is much more complicated because not all names have a middle initial. This formula returns the middle name or initial (if it exists). Otherwise, it returns nothing.

```
=IF(LEN(A1)-LEN(SUBSTITUTE(A1," ",""))>1,MID(A1,FIND(" ",A1)+1,FIND("
",A1,FIND(" ",A1)+1)-(FIND(" ",A1)+1)),"")
```

Finally, this formula returns the last name:

```
=IFERROR(RIGHT(A1,LEN(A1)-FIND("*",SUBSTITUTE(A1," ","*",LEN(A1)-
LEN(SUBSTITUTE(A1," ",""))))),"")
```

The formula that follows is a much shorter way to extract the middle name. This formula is useful if you use the other formulas to extract the first name and the last name. It assumes that the first name is in B1 and the last name is in D1.

```
=IF(LEN(B1&D1)+2>=LEN(A1),"",MID(A1,LEN(B1)+2,LEN(A1)-LEN(B1&D1)-2))
```

Splitting Text Strings without Using Formulas

In many cases, you can eliminate the use of formulas and use Excel's Data⇨Data Tools⇨Convert Text to Table command to parse strings into their component parts. Selecting this command displays Excel's Convert Text to Columns Wizard (see the accompanying figure), which consists of a series of dialog boxes that walk you through the steps to convert a single column of data into multiple columns. Generally, you'll want to select the Delimited option (in Step 1) and use Space as the delimiter (in Step 2).

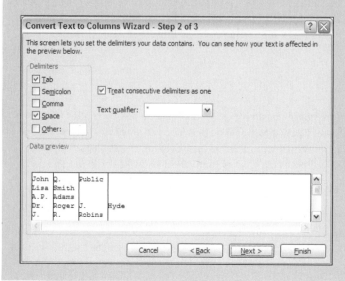

As you can see in Figure 5-6, the formulas work fairly well. There are a few problems, however — notably names that contain four "words." But, as I mentioned earlier, you can clean these cases up manually.

	A	B	C	D
1	**Full Name**	**First**	**Middle**	**Last**
2	John Q. Public	John	Q.	Public
3	Lisa Smith	Lisa		Smith
4	A.P. Adams	A.P.		Adams
5	Dr. Roger J. Hyde	Dr.	Roger	Hyde
6	J. R. Robins	J.	R.	Robins
7	Cher	Cher		
8	B.B. King	B.B.		King
9				
10				

Sheet1 / Sheet2 /

Figure 5-6: This worksheet uses formulas to extract the first name, middle name (or initial), and last name from a list of names in column A.

CROSS REF

If you want to know how I created these complex formulas, refer to Chapter 20 for a discussion of megaformulas.

Removing Titles from Names

You can use the formula that follows to remove four common titles (Mr., Dr., Ms., and Mrs.) from a name. For example, if cell A1 contains *Mr. Fred Munster,* the formula would return *Fred Munster.*

```
=IF(OR(LEFT(A1,2)={"Mr","Dr","Ms"}),RIGHT(A1,LEN(A1)-(FIND(".",A1)+1)),A1)
```

Counting the Number of Words in a Cell

The following formula returns the number of words in cell A1:

```
=LEN(TRIM(A1))-LEN(SUBSTITUTE((A1)," ",""))+1
```

The formula uses the TRIM function to remove excess spaces. It then uses the SUBSTITUTE function to create a new string (in memory) that has all the space characters removed. The length of this string is subtracted from the length of the original (trimmed) string to get the number of spaces. This value is then incremented by 1 to get the number of words.

Note that this formula will return 1 if the cell is empty. The following modification solves that problem:

```
=IF(LEN(A1)=0,0,LEN(TRIM(A1))-LEN(SUBSTITUTE(TRIM(A1)," ",""))+1)
```

Custom VBA Text Functions

Excel has many functions that work with text, but you're likely to run into a situation in which the appropriate function just doesn't exist. In such a case, you can often create your own worksheet function using VBA.

CROSS REF

Chapter 25 contains a number of custom text functions written in VBA.

Part II

Chapter 6

Working with Dates and Times

IN THIS CHAPTER

◆ An overview of using dates and times in Excel

◆ Excel's date-related functions

◆ Excel's time-related functions

Beginners often find that working with dates and times in Excel can be frustrating. To eliminate this frustration, you'll need a good understanding of how Excel handles time-based information. This chapter provides the information you need to create powerful formulas that manipulate dates and times.

NOTE

The dates in this chapter correspond to the U.S. English date format: month/day/year. For example, the date 3/1/1952 refers to March 1, 1952 — not January 3, 1952. I realize that this is very illogical, but that's how we Americans have been trained. I trust that the non-American readers of this book can make the adjustment.

How Excel Handles Dates and Times

This section presents a quick overview of how Excel deals with dates and times. It includes coverage of Excel's date and time serial number system and also offers tips for entering and formatting dates and times.

CROSS REF

Other chapters in this book contain additional date-related information. For example, refer to Chapter 7 for counting examples that use dates. Chapter 25 contains some VBA functions that work with dates.

Understanding Date Serial Numbers

To Excel, a date is simply a number. More precisely, a date is a serial number that represents the number of days since January 0, 1900. A serial number of 1 corresponds to January 1, 1900; a serial number of 2 corresponds to January 2, 1900, and so on. This system makes it possible to deal with dates in formulas. For example, you can create a formula to calculate the number of days between two dates.

Choose Your Date System: 1900 or 1904

Excel actually supports two date systems: the 1900 date system and the 1904 date system. Which system you use in a workbook determines what date serves as the basis for dates. The 1900 date system uses January 1, 1900 as the day assigned to date serial number 1. The 1904 date system uses January 1, 1904 as the base date. By default, Excel for Windows uses the 1900 date system, and Excel for Macintosh uses the 1904 date system. Excel for Windows supports the 1904 date system for compatibility with Macintosh files. You can choose to use the 1904 date system from the Excel Options dialog box. (Choose Office⇨Excel Options and navigate to the When Calculating This Workbook section of the Advanced tab.) You cannot change the date system if you use Excel for Macintosh.

Generally, you should use the default 1900 date system. And you should exercise caution if you use two different date systems in workbooks that are linked. For example, assume that Book1 uses the 1904 date system and contains the date 1/15/1999 in cell A1. Further assume that Book2 uses the 1900 date system and contains a link to cell A1 in Book1. Book2 will display the date as 1/14/1995. Both workbooks will use the same date serial number (34713), but they will be interpreted differently.

One advantage to using the 1904 date system is that it enables you to display negative time values. With the 1900 date system, a calculation that results in a negative time (for example, 4:00 PM–5:30 PM) cannot be displayed. When using the 1904 date system, the negative time displays as –1:30: that is, a difference of one hour and 30 minutes.

You may wonder about January 0, 1900. This non-date (which corresponds to date serial number 0) is actually used to represent times that are not associated with a particular day. This will become clear later in this chapter.

To view a date serial number as a date, you must format the cell as a date. Use the Format Cells dialog box (Number tab) to apply a date format.

NOTE

Excel 2000 and later versions support dates from January 1, 1900 through December 31, 9999 (serial number = 2,958,465). Versions prior to Excel 2000 support a much smaller range of dates: from January 1, 1900 through December 31, 2078 (serial number = 65,380).

Entering Dates

You can enter a date directly as a serial number (if you know it), but more often, you'll enter a date using any of several recognized date formats. Excel automatically converts your entry into the corresponding date serial number (which it uses for calculations) and also applies a date format to the cell so that it displays as an easily readable date rather than a cryptic serial number.

For example, if you need to enter June 18, 2007, you can simply enter the date by typing **June 18, 2007** (or use any of several different date formats). Excel interprets your entry and stores the value 39251, which is the date serial number for that date. It also applies one of several date formats depending on how the date is originally entered, so the cell contents may not appear exactly as you typed them.

NOTE

Depending on your regional settings, entering a date in a format such as **June 18, 2007** may be interpreted as a text string. In such a case, you would need to enter the date in a format that corresponds to your regional settings, such as **18 June, 2007**.

When you activate a cell that contains a date, the formula bar shows the cell contents formatted using the default date format — which corresponds to your system's short date style. The formula bar does not display the date's serial number. If you need to find out the serial number for a particular date, format the cell by using the General format.

TIP

To change the default date format, you need to change a system-wide setting. Access the Windows Control Panel and choose Regional and Language Options. Then click the Customize button to display the Customize Regional Options dialog box. Select the Date tab. The selected item for the Short date style format determines the default date format used by Excel.

Table 6-1 shows a sampling of the date formats that Excel recognizes (using the U.S. settings). Results will vary if you use a different regional setting.

TABLE 6-1   DATE ENTRY FORMATS RECOGNIZED BY EXCEL

Entry	Excel's Interpretation (U.S. Settings)	What Excel Displays
6-18-07	June 18, 2007	Windows short date
6-18-2007	June 18, 2007	Windows short date
6/18/07	June 18, 2007	Windows short date
6/18/2007	June 18, 2007	Windows short date
6-18/07	June 18, 2007	Windows short date
June 18, 2007	June 18, 2007	18-Jun-07
Jun 18	June 18 of the current year	18-Jun
June 18	June 18 of the current year	18-Jun
6/18	June 18 of the current year	18-Jun
6-18	June 18 of the current year	18-Jun
18-Jun-2007	June 18, 2007	18-Jun-07
2007/6/18	June 18, 2007	Windows short date

As you can see in Table 6-1, Excel is rather intelligent when it comes to recognizing dates entered into a cell. It's not perfect, however. For example, Excel does *not* recognize any of the following entries as dates:

- June 18 2007
- Jun-18 2007
- Jun-18/2007

Searching for Dates

If your worksheet uses many dates, you may need to search for a particular date by using Excel's Find dialog box (which you can access with the Home⇨Editing⇨Find & Select⇨ Find command, or Ctrl+F). You'll find that Excel is rather picky when it comes to finding dates. You must enter a full four-digit year into the Find What field in the Find dialog box. The format must correspond to how dates are displayed in the formula bar.

Rather, it interprets these entries as text. If you plan to use dates in formulas, make sure that Excel can recognize the date you enter as a date; otherwise, the formulas that refer to these dates will produce incorrect results.

If you attempt to enter a date that lies outside of the supported date range, Excel interprets it as text. If you attempt to format a serial number that lies outside of the supported range as a date, the value displays as a series of hash marks (#########).

Understanding Time Serial Numbers

When you need to work with time values, you simply extend Excel's date serial number system to include decimals. In other words, Excel works with times by using fractional days. For example, the date serial number for June 18, 2007, is 39234. Noon (halfway through the day) is represented internally as 39234.5.

The serial number equivalent of 1 minute is approximately 0.00069444. The formula that follows calculates this number by multiplying 24 hours by 60 minutes and then dividing the result into 1. The denominator consists of the number of minutes in a day (1,440).

```
=1/(24*60)
```

Similarly, the serial number equivalent of 1 second is approximately 0.00001157, obtained by the following formula (1 divided by 24 hours times 60 minutes times 60 seconds). In this case, the denominator represents the number of seconds in a day (86,400).

```
=1/(24*60*60)
```

In Excel, the smallest unit of time is one one-thousandth of a second. The time serial number shown here represents 23:59:59.999, or one one-thousandth of a second before midnight:

```
0.99999999
```

Table 6-2 shows various times of day, along with each associated time serial number.

TABLE 6-2   TIMES OF DAY AND THEIR CORRESPONDING SERIAL NUMBERS

Time of Day	Time Serial Number
12:00:00 AM (midnight)	0.0000
1:30:00 AM	0.0625
3:00:00 AM	0.1250
4:30:00 AM	0.1875

continued

TABLE 6-2   TIMES OF DAY AND THEIR CORRESPONDING SERIAL NUMBERS
(continued)

Time of Day	Time Serial Number
6:00:00 AM	0.2500
7:30:00 AM	0.3125
9:00:00 AM	0.3750
10:30:00 AM	0.4375
12:00:00 PM (noon)	0.5000
1:30:00 PM	0.5625
3:00:00 PM	0.6250
4:30:00 PM	0.6875
6:00:00 PM	0.7500
7:30:00 PM	0.8125
9:00:00 PM	0.8750
10:30:00 PM	0.9375

Entering Times

Like with entering dates, you normally don't have to worry about the actual time serial numbers. Just enter the time into a cell using a recognized format. Table 6-3 shows some examples of time formats that Excel recognizes.

TABLE 6-3   TIME ENTRY FORMATS RECOGNIZED BY EXCEL

Entry	Excel's Interpretation	What Excel Displays
11:30:00 am	11:30 AM	11:30:00 AM
11:30:00 AM	11:30 AM	11:30:00 AM
11:30 pm	11:30 PM	11:30 PM
11:30	11:30 AM	11:30
13:30	1:30 PM	13:30
11 AM	11:00 AM	11:00 AM

Because the preceding samples don't have a specific day associated with them, Excel (by default) uses a date serial number of 0, which corresponds to the non-day January 0, 1900.

NOTE

If you're using the 1904 date system, time values without an explicit date use January 1, 1904 as the date. The discussion that follows assumes that you are using the default 1900 date system.

Often, you'll want to combine a date and time. Do so by using a recognized date entry format, followed by a space, and then a recognized time-entry format. For example, if you enter the text that follows in a cell, Excel interprets it as 11:30 a.m. on June 18, 2007. Its date/time serial number is 39251.4791666667.

```
6/18/2007 11:30
```

When you enter a time that exceeds 24 hours, the associated date for the time increments accordingly. For example, if you enter the following time into a cell, it is interpreted as 1:00 AM on January 1, 1900. The day part of the entry increments because the time exceeds 24 hours. (Keep in mind that a time value entered without a date uses January 0, 1900 as the date.)

```
25:00:00
```

Similarly, if you enter a date *and* a time (and the time exceeds 24 hours), the date that you entered is adjusted. The following entry, for example, is interpreted as 9/2/2007 1:00:00 AM.

```
9/1/2007 25:00:00
```

If you enter a time only (without an associated date), you'll find that the maximum time that you can enter into a cell is 9999:59:59 (just under 10,000 hours). Excel adds the appropriate number of days. In this case, 9999:59:59 is interpreted as 3:59:59 PM on 02/19/1901. If you enter a time that exceeds 10,000 hours, the time appears as a text string.

Formatting Dates and Times

You have a great deal of flexibility in formatting cells that contain dates and times. For example, you can format the cell to display the date part only, the time part only, or both the date and time parts.

You format dates and times by selecting the cells and then using the Number Format control in the Home⇨Number group (see Figure 6-1). This control offers two date formats and one time format.

Part II

Figure 6-1: Use the Number Format drop-down list to change the appearance of dates and times.

TIP

When you create a formula that refers to a cell containing a date or a time, Excel automatically formats the formula cell as a date or a time. Sometimes, this is very helpful; other times, it's completely inappropriate and downright annoying. Unfortunately, you cannot turn off this automatic date formatting. You can, however, use a shortcut key combination to remove all number formatting from the cell and return to the default General format. Just select the cell and press Ctrl+Shift+~.

If none of the built-in formats meet your needs, you can create a custom number format. Select the More Number Formats option from the Number Format drop-down to display the Number tab of the Format Cells dialog box. The Date and Time categories provide many additional formatting choices. If none of these are satisfactory, select the Custom category and type the custom format codes into the Type box. (See Appendix B for information on creating custom number formats.)

TIP

A particularly useful custom number format for displaying times is

```
[h]:mm:ss
```

Using square brackets around the hour part of the format string causes Excel to display hours beyond 24 hours. You will find this useful when adding times that exceed 24 hours. For an example, see "Summing Times That Exceed 24 Hours," later in this chapter.

Problems with Dates

Excel has some problems when it comes to dates. Many of these problems stem from the fact that Excel was designed many years ago, before the acronym Y2K became a household term. And, as I describe, the Excel designers basically emulated the Lotus 1-2-3 limited date and time features, which contain a nasty bug duplicated intentionally in Excel. In addition, versions of Excel show inconsistency in how they interpret a cell entry that has a two-digit year. And finally, how Excel interprets a date entry depends on your regional date settings.

If Excel were being designed from scratch today, I'm sure it would be much more versatile in dealing with dates. Unfortunately, we're currently stuck with a product that leaves much to be desired in the area of dates.

THE EXCEL LEAP YEAR BUG

A *leap year,* which occurs every four years, contains an additional day (February 29). Although the year 1900 was not a leap year, Excel treats it as such. In other words, when you type the following into a cell, Excel does not complain. It interprets this as a valid date and assigns a serial number of 60:

2/29/1900

If you type the following invalid date, Excel correctly interprets it as a mistake and *doesn't* convert it to a date. Rather, it simply makes the cell entry a text string:

2/29/1901

How can a product used daily by millions of people contain such an obvious bug? The answer is historical. The original version of Lotus 1-2-3 contained a bug that caused it to consider 1900 as a leap year. When Excel was released some time later, the designers knew of this bug and chose to reproduce it in Excel to maintain compatibility with Lotus worksheet files.

Why does this bug still exist in later versions of Excel? Microsoft asserts that the disadvantages of correcting this bug outweigh the advantages. If the bug were eliminated, it would mess up hundreds of thousands of existing workbooks. In addition, correcting this problem would affect compatibility between Excel and other programs that use dates. As it stands, this bug really causes very few problems because most users do not use dates before March 1, 1900.

PRE-1900 DATES

The world, of course, didn't begin on January 1, 1900. People who work with historical information using Excel often need to work with dates before January 1, 1900. Unfortunately, the only way to work with pre-1900 dates is to enter the date into a cell as text. For example, you can enter the following into a cell, and Excel won't complain:

```
July 4, 1776
```

You can't, however, perform any manipulation on dates recognized as text. For example, you can't change its numeric formatting, you can't determine which day of the week this date occurred on, and you can't calculate the date that occurs seven days later.

 ## CROSS REF

In Chapter 25, I present some custom VBA functions that enable you to work with any date in the years 0100 through 9999.

INCONSISTENT DATE ENTRIES

You need to exercise caution when entering dates by using two digits for the year. When you do so, Excel has some rules that kick in to determine which century to use. And those rules vary, depending on the version of Excel that you use.

For Excel 97, two-digit years between 00 and 29 are interpreted as 21st century dates, and two-digit years between 30 and 99 are interpreted as 20th century dates. For example, if you enter 12/15/28, Excel interprets your entry as December 15, 2028. However, if you enter 12/15/30, Excel sees it as December 15, 1930. If you use Excel 2000 or later (running on Windows 98 or later), you can use the default boundary year of 2029. Or, change it via the Windows Control Panel; use the Date tab of the Customize Regional Options Properties dialog box.

For previous versions of Excel (Excel 3 through Excel 95), two-digit years between 00 and 19 are interpreted as 21st century dates, and two-digit years between 20 and 99 are interpreted as 20th century dates. For example, if you enter **12/5/19**, Excel interprets your entry as December 5, 2019. But if you enter **12/5/20**, Excel sees it as December 5, 1920.

If (for some unknown reason) you still use Excel 2, when you enter a two-digit date, it is *always* interpreted as a 20th century date. Table 6-4 summarizes these differences for various versions of Excel.

TABLE 6-4   HOW TWO-DIGIT YEARS ARE INTERPRETED IN VARIOUS EXCEL VERSIONS

Excel Version	20th Century Years	21st Century Years
2	00–99	N/A
3, 4, 5, 7 (95)	20–99	00–19
8 (97), 9 (2000), 10 (2002), 11 (2003), 12 (2007)	30–99	00–29

TIP

To avoid any surprises, you should simply enter *all* years using all four digits for the year.

Date-Related Functions

Excel has quite a few functions that work with dates. They are all listed under the Date & Time drop-down list in the Formulas⇨Function Library group.

Table 6-5 summarizes the date-related functions available in Excel.

TABLE 6-5   DATE-RELATED FUNCTIONS

Function	Description
DATE	Returns the serial number of a date given the year, month, and day
DATEDIF	Calculates the number of days, months, or years between two dates
DATEVALUE	Converts a date in the form of text to an actual date
DAY	Returns the day of the month for a given date
DAYS360	Calculates the number of days between two dates based on a 360-day year
EDATE	Returns the date that represents the indicated number of months before or after the start date

continued

Part II

TABLE 6-5   DATE-RELATED FUNCTIONS (continued)

Function	Description
EOMONTH	Returns the date of the last day of the month before or after a specified number of months
MONTH	Returns the month for a given date.
NETWORKDAYS*	Returns the number of whole workdays between two dates
NOW	Returns the current date and time
TODAY	Returns today's date
WEEKDAY	Returns the day of the week (expressed as a number) for a date
WEEKNUM*	Returns the week number of the year for a date
WORKDAY*	Returns the date before or after a specified number of workdays
YEAR	Returns the year for a given date
YEARFRAC*	Returns the year fraction representing the number of whole days between two dates

Prior to Excel 2007, this function required the Analysis ToolPak add-in installed.

Displaying the Current Date

The following function displays the current date in a cell:

```
=TODAY()
```

You can also display the date, combined with text. The formula that follows, for example, displays text such as *Today is Friday, September 14, 2007.*

```
="Today is "&TEXT(TODAY(),"dddd, mmmm d, yyyy")
```

It's important to understand that the TODAY function is updated whenever the worksheet is calculated. For example, if you enter either of the preceding formulas into a worksheet, the formulas will display the current date. When you open the workbook tomorrow, though, they will display the current date for that day (not the date when you entered the formula).

TIP

To enter a date stamp into a cell, press Ctrl+; (semicolon). This enters the date directly into the cell and does not use a formula. Therefore, the date will not change.

Displaying Any Date

As explained earlier in this chapter, you can easily enter a date into a cell by simply typing it, using any of the date formats that Excel recognizes. You can also create a date by using the DATE function, which takes three arguments: the year, the month, and the day. The following formula, for example, returns a date comprising the year in cell A1, the month in cell B1, and the day in cell C1:

```
=DATE(A1,B1,C1)
```

NOTE

The DATE function accepts invalid arguments and adjusts the result accordingly. For example, this next formula uses 13 as the month argument, and returns January 1, 2008. The month argument is automatically translated as month 1 of the following year.

```
=DATE(2007,13,1)
```

Often, you'll use the DATE function with other functions as arguments. For example, the formula that follows uses the YEAR and TODAY functions to return the date for Independence Day (July 4th) of the current year:

```
=DATE(YEAR(TODAY()),7,4)
```

The DATEVALUE function converts a text string that looks like a date into a date serial number. The following formula returns 39316, the date serial number for August 22, 2007:

```
=DATEVALUE("8/22/2007")
```

To view the result of this formula as a date, you need to apply a date number format to the cell.

CAUTION

Be careful when using the DATEVALUE function. A text string that looks like a date in your country may not look like a date in another country. The preceding example works fine if your system is set for U.S. date formats, but it returns an error for other regional date formats because Excel is looking for the eighth day of the 22nd month!

Generating a Series of Dates

Often, you'll want to insert a series of dates into a worksheet. For example, in tracking weekly sales, you may want to enter a series of dates, each separated by seven days. These dates will serve to identify the sales figures.

The most efficient way to enter a series of dates doesn't require any formulas — just use Excel's AutoFill feature to insert the dates. Enter the first date and then drag the cell's fill handle while pressing the right mouse button. (Right-drag the cell's fill handle.) Release the mouse button and select an option from the shortcut menu (see Figure 6-2).

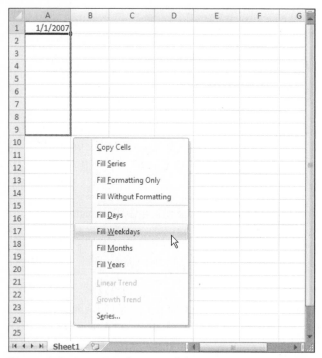

Figure 6-2: Using Excel's AutoFill feature to create a series of dates.

The advantage of using formulas (rather than the AutoFill feature) to create a series of dates is that you can change the first date, and the others will update automatically. You need to enter the starting date into a cell and then use formulas (copied down the column) to generate the additional dates.

The following examples assume that you entered the first date of the series into cell A1 and the formula into cell A2. You can then copy this formula down the column as many times as needed.

To generate a series of dates separated by seven days, use this formula:

```
=A1+7
```

To generate a series of dates separated by one month, use this formula:

```
=DATE(YEAR(A1),MONTH(A1)+1,DAY(A1))
```

To generate a series of dates separated by one year, use this formula:

```
=DATE(YEAR(A1)+1,MONTH(A1),DAY(A1))
```

To generate a series of weekdays only (no Saturdays or Sundays), use the formula that follows. This formula assumes that the date in cell A1 is not a weekend day:

```
=IF(WEEKDAY(A1)=6,A1+3,A1+1)
```

Converting a Non-Date String to a Date

You may import data that contains dates coded as text strings. For example, the following text represents August 21, 2007 (a four-digit year followed by a two-digit month, followed by a two-digit day):

```
20070821
```

To convert this string to an actual date, you can use a formula such as this one, which assumes the coded date is in cell A1:

```
=DATE(LEFT(A1,4),MID(A1,5,2),RIGHT(A1,2))
```

This formula uses text functions (LEFT, MID, and RIGHT) to extract the digits and then uses these extracted digits as arguments for the DATE function.

 CROSS REF

Refer to Chapter 5 for more information about using formulas to manipulate text.

Calculating the Number of Days between Two Dates

A common type of date calculation determines the number of days between two dates. For example, you may have a financial worksheet that calculates interest earned on a deposit account. The interest earned depends on how many days that the account is open. If your sheet contains the open date and the close date for the account, you can calculate the number of days the account was open.

Because dates store as consecutive serial numbers, you can use simple subtraction to calculate the number of days between two dates. For example, if cells A1 and B1 both contain a date, the following formula returns the number of days between these dates:

```
=A1-B1
```

Part II

Excel will automatically format this formula cell as a date rather than a numeric value. Therefore, you will need to change the number format so the result is displayed as a non-date. If cell B1 contains a more recent date than the date in cell A1, the result will be negative.

 NOTE

If this formula does not display the correct value, make sure that A1 and B1 both contain actual dates — not text that *looks* like dates.

Sometimes, calculating the difference between two days is more difficult. To demonstrate, consider the common "fence post" analogy. If somebody asks you how many units make up a fence, you can respond with either of two answers: the number of fence posts, or the number of gaps between the fence posts. The number of fence posts is always one more than the number of gaps between the posts.

To bring this analogy into the realm of dates, suppose you start a sales promotion on February 1 and end the promotion on February 9. How many days was the promotion in effect? Subtracting February 1 from February 9 produces an answer of eight days. However, the promotion actually lasted nine days. In this case, the correct answer involves counting the fence posts, as it were, and not the gaps. The formula to calculate the length of the promotion (assuming you have appropriately named cells) appears like this:

```
=EndDay-StartDay+1
```

Calculating the Number of Work Days between Two Dates

When calculating the difference between two dates, you may want to exclude weekends and holidays. For example, you may need to know how many business days fall in the month of November. This calculation should exclude Saturdays, Sundays, and holidays. Using the NETWORKDAYS function can help.

 NOTE

The NETWORKDAYS function has a very misleading name. This function has nothing to do with networks or networking. Rather, it calculates the net number of workdays between two dates.

The NETWORKDAYS function calculates the difference between two dates, excluding weekend days (Saturdays and Sundays). As an option, you can specify a range of cells that contain the dates of holidays, which are also excluded. Excel has absolutely no way of determining which days are holidays, so you must provide this information in a range.

Figure 6-3 shows a worksheet that calculates the workdays between two dates. The range A2:A11 contains a list of holiday dates. The formulas in column C calculate the workdays between the dates in column A and column B. For example, the formula in cell C15 is

```
=NETWORKDAYS(A15,B15,A2:A11)
```

	A	B	C	D
1	Date	Holiday		
2	1/1/2007	New Year's Day		
3	1/15/2007	Martin Luther King Jr. Day		
4	2/19/2007	Presidents' Day		
5	5/28/2007	Memorial Day		
6	7/4/2007	Independence Day		
7	9/3/2007	Labor Day		
8	10/8/2007	Columbus Day		
9	11/12/2007	Veterans Day		
10	11/22/2007	Thanksgiving Day		
11	12/25/2007	Christmas Day		
12				
13				
14	First Day	Last Day	Working Days	
15	Monday 1/1/2007	Sunday 1/7/2007	4	
16	Monday 1/1/2007	Monday 12/31/2007	251	
17				
18				

Sheet1

Figure 6-3: Using the NETWORKDAYS function to calculate the number of working days between two dates.

This formula returns 4, which means that the seven-day period beginning with January 1 contains four workdays. In other words, the calculation excludes one holiday, one Saturday, and one Sunday. The formula in cell C16 calculates the total number of workdays in the year.

 ON THE CD

This workbook, work days.xlsx, is available on the companion CD-ROM.

Offsetting a Date Using Only Work Days

The WORKDAY function is the opposite of the NETWORKDAYS function. For example, if you start a project on January 4 and the project requires ten working days to complete, the WORKDAY function can calculate the date you will finish the project.

The following formula uses the WORKDAY function to determine the date ten working days from January 8, 2007. A *working day* is a weekday (Monday through Friday).

```
=WORKDAY("1/8/2007",10)
```

The formula returns January 20, 2007; two weekend days fall between January 8 and January 20. Make sure that this formula cell is formatted to display a date format.

 CAUTION
The preceding formula may return a different result, depending on your regional date setting. (The hard-coded date may be interpreted as August 1, 2007.) A better formula is

```
=WORKDAY(DATE(2007,1,8),10)
```

The second argument for the WORKDAY function can be negative. And, as with the NETWORKDAYS function, the WORKDAY function accepts an optional third argument (a reference to a range that contains a list of holiday dates).

Calculating the Number of Years between Two Dates

The following formula calculates the number of years between two dates. This formula assumes that cells A1 and B1 both contain dates:

```
=YEAR(A1)-YEAR(B1)
```

This formula uses the YEAR function to extract the year from each date and then subtracts one year from the other. If cell B1 contains a more recent date than the date in cell A1, the result will be negative.

Note that this function doesn't calculate *full* years. For example, if cell A1 contains 12/31/2007 and cell B1 contains 01/01/2008, the formula returns a difference of one year, even though the dates differ by only one day.

You can also use the YEARFRAC function to calculate the number of years between two dates. This function returns the number of years, including partial years. For example

```
=YEARFRAC(A1,B1,1)
```

Because the YEARFRAC function is often used for financial applications, it uses an optional third argument that represents the "basis" for the year (for example, a 360-day year). A third argument of 1 indicates an actual year.

Calculating a Person's Age

A person's age indicates the number of full years that the person has been alive. The formula in the previous section (for calculating the number of years between two dates) won't calculate this value correctly. You can use two other formulas, however, to calculate a person's age.

Where's the DATEDIF Function?

In several places throughout this chapter, I refer to the DATEDIF function. You may notice that this function does not appear in the Insert Function dialog box, is not listed in the Date & Time drop-down, and does not appear in the Formula AutoComplete list. Therefore, to use this function, you must always enter it manually.

The DATEDIF function has its origins in Lotus 1-2-3, and apparently Excel provides it for compatibility purposes. For some reason, Microsoft wants to keep this function a secret. You won't even find the DATEDIF function in the Help files although it's available in all Excel versions. Strangely, DATEDIF made an appearance in the Excel 2000 Help files but hasn't been seen since.

DATEDIF is a handy function that calculates the number of days, months, or years between two dates. The function takes three arguments: start_date, end_date, and a code that represents the time unit of interest. The following table displays valid codes for the third argument. You must enclose the codes in quotation marks.

Unit Code	Returns
"y"	The number of complete years in the period.
"m"	The number of complete months in the period.
"d"	The number of days in the period.
"md"	The difference between the days in start_date and end_date. The months and years of the dates are ignored.
"ym"	The difference between the months in start_date and end_date. The days and years of the dates are ignored.
"yd"	The difference between the days of start_date and end_date. The years of the dates are ignored.

The start_date argument must be earlier than the end_date argument, or the function returns an error.

The following formula returns the age of the person whose date of birth you enter into cell A1. This formula uses the YEARFRAC function:

```
=INT(YEARFRAC(TODAY(),A1,1))
```

The following formula uses the DATEDIF function to calculate an age. (See the sidebar, "Where's the DATEDIF Function?".)

```
=DATEDIF(A1,TODAY(),"Y")
```

Determining the Day of the Year

January 1 is the first day of the year, and December 31 is the last day. But what about all of those days in between? The following formula returns the day of the year for a date stored in cell A1:

```
=A1-DATE(YEAR(A1),1,0)
```

The day argument supplied is zero, calling for the "0th" day of the first month. The DATE function interprets this as the day before the first day, or December 31 of the previous year in this example. Similarly, negative numbers can be supplied for the day argument.

The following formula returns the number of days remaining in the year from a particular date (assumed to be in cell A1):

```
=DATE(YEAR(A1),12,31)-A1
```

To convert a particular day of the year (for example, the 90th day of the year) to an actual date in a specified year, use the formula that follows. This formula assumes that the year is stored in cell A1 and that the day of the year is stored in cell B1.

```
=DATE(A1,1,B1)
```

Determining the Day of the Week

The WEEKDAY function accepts a date argument and returns an integer between 1 and 7 that corresponds to the day of the week. The following formula, for example, returns 2 because the first day of the year 2007 falls on a Monday:

```
=WEEKDAY(DATE(2007,1,1))
```

The WEEKDAY function uses an optional second argument that specifies the day numbering system for the result. If you specify 2 as the second argument, the function returns 1 for Monday, 2 for Tuesday, and so on. If you specify 3 as the second argument, the function returns 0 for Monday, 1 for Tuesday, and so on.

TIP

You can also determine the day of the week for a cell that contains a date by applying a custom number format. A cell that uses the following custom number format displays the day of the week, spelled out:

dddd

Determining the Date of the Most Recent Sunday

You can use the following formula to return the date for the previous Sunday. If the current day is a Sunday, the formula returns the current date. (You will need to format the cell to display as a date.)

```
=TODAY()-MOD(TODAY()-1,7)
```

To modify this formula to find the date of a day other than Sunday, change the 1 to a different number between 2 (for Monday) and 7 (for Saturday).

Determining the First Day of the Week after a Date

This next formula returns the specified day of the week that occurs after a particular date. For example, use this formula to determine the date of the first Monday after June 1, 2007. The formula assumes that cell A1 contains a date and that cell A2 contains a number between 1 and 7 (1 for Sunday, 2 for Monday, and so on).

```
=A1+A2-WEEKDAY(A1)+(A2<WEEKDAY(A1))*7
```

If cell A1 contains June 1, 2007 and cell A2 contains 2 (for Monday), the formula returns June 4, 2007. This is the first Monday after June 1, 2007 (which is a Friday).

Determining the *n*th Occurrence of a Day of the Week in a Month

You may need a formula to determine the date for a particular occurrence of a weekday. For example, suppose your company payday falls on the second Friday of each month, and you need to determine the paydays for each month of the year. The following formula will make this type of calculation:

```
=DATE(A1,A2,1)+A3-WEEKDAY(DATE(A1,A2,1))+
(A4-(A3>=WEEKDAY(DATE(A1,A2,1))))*7
```

The formula in this section assumes that

- Cell A1 contains a year.

- Cell A2 contains a month.

- Cell A3 contains a day number (1 for Sunday, 2 for Monday, and so on.).

- Cell A4 contains the occurrence number (for example, 2 to select the second occurrence of the weekday specified in cell A3).

If you use this formula to determine the date of the second Friday in June 2007, it returns June 8, 2007.

NOTE

If the value in cell A4 exceeds the number of the specified day in the month, the formula returns a date from a subsequent month. For example, if you attempt to determine the date of the sixth Friday in June 2007 (there is no such date), the formula returns the first Friday in July.

Counting the Occurrences of a Day of the Week

You can use the following formula to count the number of occurrences of a particular day of the week for a specified month. It assumes that cell A1 contains a date and that cell B1 contains a day number (1 for Sunday, 2 for Monday, and so on). The formula is an array formula, so you must enter it by using Ctrl+Shift+Enter.

```
{=SUM((WEEKDAY(DATE(YEAR(A1),MONTH(A1),ROW(INDIRECT("1:"&
DAY(DATE(YEAR(A1),MONTH(A1)+1,0))))))=B1)*1)}
```

If cell A1 contains the date January 8, 2007 and cell B1 contains the value 3 (for Tuesday), the formula returns 5, which reveals that January 2007 contains five Tuesdays.

The preceding array formula calculates the year and month by using the YEAR and MONTH functions. You can simplify the formula a bit if you store the year and month in separate cells. The following formula (also an array formula) assumes that the year appears in cell A1, the month in cell A2, and the day number in cell B1:

```
{=SUM((WEEKDAY(DATE(A1,A2,ROW(INDIRECT("1:"&
DAY(DATE(A1,A2+1,0))))))=B1)*1)}
```

CROSS REF

Refer to Chapters 14 and 15 for more information about array formulas.

Figure 6-4 shows this formula used in a worksheet. In this case, the formula uses mixed cell references so you can copy it. For example, the formula in cell C3 is

```
{=SUM((WEEKDAY(DATE($B$2,$A3,ROW(INDIRECT("1:"&
DAY(DATE($B$2,$A3+1,0))))))=C$1)*1)}
```

Additional formulas use the SUM function to calculate the number of days per month (column J) and the number of each weekday in the year (row 15).

		1	2	3	4	5	6	7	
YEAR ->	2007	Sun	Mon	Tue	Wed	Thu	Fri	Sat	Month
1	January	4	5	5	5	4	4	4	31
2	February	4	4	4	4	4	4	4	28
3	March	4	4	4	4	5	5	5	31
4	April	5	5	4	4	4	4	4	30
5	May	4	4	5	5	5	4	4	31
6	June	4	4	4	4	4	5	5	30
7	July	5	5	5	4	4	4	4	31
8	August	4	4	4	5	5	5	4	31
9	September	5	4	4	4	4	4	5	30
10	October	4	5	5	5	4	4	4	31
11	November	4	4	4	5	5	5	4	30
12	December	5	5	4	4	4	4	5	31
	Total Days:	52	53	52	52	52	52	52	365

Sheet1

Figure 6-4: Calculating the number of each weekday in each month of a year.

ON THE CD

The workbook shown in Figure 6-4, `day of the week count.xlsx`, is available on the companion CD-ROM.

Expressing a Date as an Ordinal Number

You may want to express the day portion of a date as an ordinal number. For example, you can display 4/16/2007 as *April 16th, 2007*. The following formula expresses the date in cell A1 as an ordinal date:

```
=TEXT(A1,"mmmm ")&DAY(A1)&IF(INT(MOD(DAY(A1),100)/10)=1,
"th",IF(MOD(DAY(A1),10)=1,"st",IF(MOD(DAY(A1),10)=2,"nd",IF(MOD(DAY(A1),10)=3,
"rd","th"))))&TEXT(A1,", yyyy")
```

CAUTION

The result of this formula is text, not an actual date.

The following formula shows a variation that expresses the date in cell A1 in day-month-year format. For example, 4/16/2007 would appear as *16th April, 2007*. Again, the result of this formula represents text, not an actual date.

```
=DAY(A1)&IF(INT(MOD(DAY(A1),100)/10)=1, "th",
IF(MOD(DAY(A1),10)=1, "st",IF(MOD(DAY(A1),10)=2,"nd",
IF(MOD(DAY(A1),10)=3, "rd","th"))))& " " &TEXT(A1,"mmmm, yyyy")
```

ON THE CD

The companion CD-ROM contains the workbook `ordinal dates.xlsx` that demonstrates the formulas for expressing dates as ordinal numbers.

Calculating Dates of Holidays

Determining the date for a particular holiday can be tricky. Some, such as New Year's Day and U.S. Independence Day, are no-brainers because they always occur on the same date. For these kinds of holidays, you can simply use the DATE function, which I covered earlier in this chapter. To enter New Year's Day (which always falls on January 1) for a specific year in cell A1, you can enter this function:

```
=DATE(A1,1,1)
```

Other holidays are defined in terms of a particular occurrence of a particular weekday in a particular month. For example, Labor Day in the United States falls on the first Monday in September.

Figure 6-5 shows a workbook with formulas to calculate the date for ten U.S. holidays. The formulas reference the year in cell A1. Notice that because New Year's Day, Independence Day, Veterans Day, and Christmas Day all fall on the same days of the year, their dates can be calculated by using the simple DATE function.

	A	B	C	D	E	F
1	2007	<-- Enter the year				
2						
3			**Holiday Calculations**			
4						
5		Holiday	Description	Date	Weekday	
6		New Year's Day	1st Day in January	January 1, 2007	Monday	
7		Martin Luther King Jr. Day	3rd Monday in January	January 15, 2007	Monday	
8		Presidents' Day	3rd Monday in February	February 19, 2007	Monday	
9		Memorial Day	Last Monday in May	May 28, 2007	Monday	
10		Independence Day	4th Day of July	July 4, 2007	Wednesday	
11		Labor Day	1st Monday in September	September 3, 2007	Monday	
12		Columbus Day	2nd Monday in October	October 8, 2007	Monday	
13		Veterans Day	11th Day of November	November 11, 2007	Sunday	
14		Thanksgiving Day	4thThursday in November	November 22, 2007	Thursday	
15		Christmas Day	25th Day of December	December 25, 2007	Tuesday	
16						

Figure 6-5: Using formulas to determine the date for various holidays.

ON THE CD

The workbook shown in Figure 6-5, `holidays.xlsx`, also appears on the companion CD-ROM.

NEW YEAR'S DAY

This holiday always falls on January 1:

```
=DATE(A1,1,1)
```

MARTIN LUTHER KING, JR. DAY

This holiday occurs on the third Monday in January. This formula calculates Martin Luther King, Jr. Day for the year in cell A1:

```
=DATE(A1,1,1)+IF(2<WEEKDAY(DATE(A1,1,1)),7-WEEKDAY
(DATE(A1,1,1))+2,2-WEEKDAY(DATE(A1,1,1)))+((3-1)*7)
```

PRESIDENTS' DAY

Presidents' Day occurs on the third Monday in February. This formula calculates Presidents' Day for the year in cell A1:

```
=DATE(A1,2,1)+IF(2<WEEKDAY(DATE(A1,2,1)),7-WEEKDAY
(DATE(A1,2,1))+2,2-WEEKDAY(DATE(A1,2,1)))+((3-1)*7)
```

MEMORIAL DAY

The last Monday in May is Memorial Day. This formula calculates Memorial Day for the year in cell A1:

```
=DATE(A1,6,1)+IF(2<WEEKDAY(DATE(A1,6,1)),7-WEEKDAY
(DATE(A1,6,1))+2,2-WEEKDAY(DATE(A1,6,1)))+((1-1)*7)-7
```

Notice that this formula actually calculates the first Monday in June and then subtracts 7 from the result to return the last Monday in May.

INDEPENDENCE DAY

This holiday always falls on July 4:

```
=DATE(A1,7,4)
```

LABOR DAY

Labor Day occurs on the first Monday in September. This formula calculates Labor Day for the year in cell A1:

```
=DATE(A1,9,1)+IF(2<WEEKDAY(DATE(A1,9,1)),7-WEEKDAY
(DATE(A1,9,1))+2,2-WEEKDAY(DATE(A1,9,1)))+((1-1)*7)
```

Part II

COLUMBUS DAY

This holiday occurs on the second Monday in October. This formula calculates Columbus Day for the year in cell A1:

```
=DATE(A1,10,1)+IF(2<WEEKDAY(DATE(A1,10,1)),7-WEEKDAY
(DATE(A1,10,1))+2,2-WEEKDAY(DATE(A1,10,1)))+((2-1)*7)
```

VETERANS DAY

This holiday always falls on November 11:

```
=DATE(A1,11,11)
```

THANKSGIVING DAY

Thanksgiving Day is celebrated on the fourth Thursday in November. This formula calculates Thanksgiving Day for the year in cell A1:

```
=DATE(A1,11,1)+IF(5<WEEKDAY(DATE(A1,11,1)),7-WEEKDAY
(DATE(A1,11,1))+5,5-WEEKDAY(DATE(A1,11,1)))+((4-1)*7)
```

CHRISTMAS DAY

This holiday always falls on December 25:

```
=DATE(A1,12,25)
```

Calculating Easter

You'll notice that I omitted Easter from the previous section. Easter is an unusual holiday because its date is determined based on the phase of the moon and not by the calendar. Because of this, determining when Easter occurs proves a bit of a challenge.

Hans Herber, an Excel master in Germany, once sponsored an Easter formula contest at his Web site. The goal was to create the shortest formula possible that correctly determined the date of Easter for the years 1900 through 2078.

Twenty formulas were submitted, ranging in length from 44 characters up to 154 characters. Some of these formulas, however, work only with European date settings. The following formula, submitted by Thomas Jansen, is the shortest formula that works with any date setting. This formula returns the date for Easter and assumes that the year is stored in cell A1:

```
=DOLLAR(("4/"&A1)/7+MOD(19*MOD(A1,19)-7,30)*14%,)*7-6
```

Please don't ask me to explain this formula. I haven't a clue!

Determining the Last Day of a Month

To determine the date that corresponds to the last day of a month, you can use the DATE function. However, you need to increment the month by 1, and use a day value of zero (0). In other words, the 0th day of the next month is the last day of the current month.

The following formula assumes that a date is stored in cell A1. The formula returns the date that corresponds to the last day of the month.

```
=DATE(YEAR(A1),MONTH(A1)+1,0)
```

You can use a variation of this formula to determine how many days make up a specified month. The formula that follows returns an integer that corresponds to the number of days in the month for the date in cell A1.

```
=DAY(DATE(YEAR(A1),MONTH(A1)+1,0))
```

Determining Whether a Year Is a Leap Year

To determine whether a particular year is a leap year, you can write a formula that determines whether the 29th day of February occurs in February or March. You can take advantage of the fact that Excel's DATE function adjusts the result when you supply an invalid argument — for example, a day of 29 when February contains only 28 days.

The following formula returns TRUE if the year of the date in cell A1 is a leap year. Otherwise, it returns FALSE.

```
=IF(MONTH(DATE(YEAR(A1),2,29))=2,TRUE,FALSE)
```

 CAUTION
This function returns the wrong result (TRUE) if the year is 1900. See "The Excel Leap Year Bug," earlier in this chapter.

Determining a Date's Quarter

For financial reports, you might find it useful to present information in terms of quarters. The following formula returns an integer between 1 and 4 that corresponds to the calendar quarter for the date in cell A1:

```
=ROUNDUP(MONTH(A1)/3,0)
```

This formula divides the month number by 3 and then rounds up the result.

Part II

Converting a Year to Roman Numerals

Fans of old movies will like this one. The following formula converts the year 1945 to Roman numerals: MCMXLV:

```
=ROMAN(1945)
```

This function returns a text string, so you can't perform any calculations using the result. Unfortunately, Excel doesn't provide a function to convert Roman numerals back to normal numbers.

Time-Related Functions

Excel, as you might expect, also includes a number of functions that enable you to work with time values in your formulas. This section contains examples that demonstrate the use of these functions.

Table 6-6 summarizes the time-related functions available in Excel. Like the date functions discussed earlier, time-related functions can be found under the Date & Time drop-down list via Formulas➪Function Library.

TABLE 6-6   TIME-RELATED FUNCTIONS

Function	Description
HOUR	Returns the hour of a time value
MINUTE	Returns the minute of a time value
NOW	Returns the current date and time
SECOND	Returns the second of a time
TIME	Returns a time for a specified hour, minute, and second
TIMEVALUE	Converts a time in the form of text to an actual time value

Displaying the Current Time

This formula displays the current time as a time serial number (or a serial number without an associated date):

```
=NOW()-TODAY()
```

You need to format the cell with a time format to view the result as a recognizable time. For example, you can apply the following number format:

```
hh:mm AM/PM
```

You can also display the time, combined with text. The formula that follows displays this text: *The current time is 6:28 PM.*

```
="The current time is "&TEXT(NOW(),"h:mm AM/PM")
```

NOTE

These formulas are updated only when the worksheet is calculated.

TIP

To enter a time stamp into a cell, press Ctrl+Shift+: (colon). Excel inserts the time as a *static value* (it does not change).

Displaying Any Time

Earlier in this chapter, I describe how to enter a time value into a cell: Just type it into a cell, making sure that you include at least one colon (:). You can also create a time by using the TIME function. For example, the following formula returns a time comprising the hour in cell A1, the minute in cell B1, and the second in cell C1:

```
=TIME(A1,B1,C1)
```

Like the DATE function, the TIME function accepts invalid arguments and adjusts the result accordingly. For example, the following formula uses 80 as the minute argument and returns 10:20:15 AM. The 80 minutes are simply added to the hour, with 20 minutes remaining.

```
=TIME(9,80,15)
```

CAUTION

If you enter a value greater than 24 as the first argument for the TIME function, the result may not be what you expect. Logically, a formula such as the one that follows should produce a date/time serial number of 1.041667 (that is, one day and one hour).

```
=TIME(25,0,0)
```

In fact, this formula is equivalent to the following:

```
=TIME(1,0,0)
```

You can also use the DATE function along with the TIME function in a single cell. The formula that follows generates 6:30 PM on December 4, 2007 (which is date/time serial number 39420.7708333333):

```
=DATE(2007,12,4)+TIME(18,30,0)
```

NOTE

When you enter the preceding formula, Excel formats the cell to display the date only. To see the time, you'll need to change the number format to one that displays a date and a time.

TIP

To enter the current date and time into a cell that doesn't change when the worksheet recalculates, press Ctrl+; (semicolon), space, Ctrl+Shift+: (colon), and then press Enter.

The TIMEVALUE function converts a text string that looks like a time into a time serial number. This formula returns 0.2395833333, which is the time serial number for 5:45 AM:

```
=TIMEVALUE("5:45 am")
```

To view the result of this formula as a time, you need to apply number formatting to the cell. The TIMEVALUE function doesn't recognize all common time formats. For example, the following formula returns an error because Excel doesn't like the periods in "a.m."

```
=TIMEVALUE("5:45 a.m.")
```

Summing Times That Exceed 24 Hours

Many people are surprised to discover that when you sum a series of times that exceed 24 hours, Excel doesn't display the correct total. Figure 6-6 shows an example. The range B2:B8 contains times that represent the hours and minutes worked each day. The formula in cell B9 is

```
=SUM(B2:B8)
```

As you can see, the formula returns a seemingly incorrect total (18 hours, 30 minutes). The total should read 42 hours, 30 minutes. The problem is that the formula is really displaying a date/time serial number of 1.770833, but the cell formatting is not displaying the "date" part of the date/time. In other words, cell B9 has an incorrect number format.

To view a time that exceeds 24 hours, you need to change the number format for the cell so square brackets surround the *hour* part of the format string. Applying the number format here to cell B9 displays the sum correctly:

```
[h]:mm
```

	A	B	C
1	**Day**	**Hours Worked**	
2	Sunday	0	
3	Monday	8:30	
4	Tuesday	8:00	
5	Wednesday	9:00	
6	Thursday	9:30	
7	Friday	4:30	
8	Saturday	3:00	
9	**Total for Week**	**18:30**	
10			
11			
12			

Sheet1

Figure 6-6: Incorrect cell formatting makes the total appear incorrectly.

Figure 6-7 shows another example of a worksheet that manipulates times. This worksheet keeps track of hours worked during a week (regular hours and overtime hours).

Employee Time Sheet

Employee Name: Gina Davison
Department: Tech Support
Start Day: 1/22/2007

Weekday	Date	Start Work	Time Out (Lunch)	Time In (Lunch)	End Work	Total Hours	Weekly Hours
Monday	1/22/2007	8:00 AM	12:00 PM	1:00 PM	6:00 PM	9:00	9:00
Tuesday	1/23/2007	10:00 AM	2:00 PM	2:30 PM	7:00 PM	8:30	17:30
Wednesday	1/24/2007	9:00 AM	12:00 PM	1:00 PM	6:30 PM	8:30	26:00
Thursday	1/25/2007	7:30 AM	11:30 AM	12:00 PM	6:30 PM	10:30	36:30
Friday	1/26/2007	9:30 AM	2:00 PM	3:30 PM	5:00 PM	6:00	42:30
Saturday	1/27/2007					0:00	42:30
Sunday	1/28/2007					0:00	42:30

WEEKLY TOTAL	
Total hours:	42:30
Regular hours:	40:00
Overtime hours:	2:30

Clear | Help

Overtime: 40:00

TimeSheet

Figure 6-7: An employee time sheet workbook.

The week's starting date appears in cell D5, and the formulas in column B fill in the dates for the days of the week. Times appear in the range D8:G14, and formulas in column H calculate the number of hours worked each day. For example, the formula in cell H8 is

```
=IF(E8<D8,E8+1-D8,E8-D8)+IF(G8<F8,G8+1-G8,G8-F8)
```

The first part of this formula subtracts the time in column D from the time in column E to get the total hours worked before lunch. The second part subtracts the time in column F from the time in column G to get the total hours worked after lunch. I use IF functions to accommodate graveyard shift cases that span midnight — for example, an employee may start work at 10:00 PM and begin lunch at 2:00 AM. Without the IF function, the formula returns a negative result.

The following formula in cell H17 calculates the weekly total by summing the daily totals in column H:

```
=SUM(H8:H14)
```

This worksheet assumes that hours that exceed 40 hours in a week are considered overtime hours. The worksheet contains a cell named *Overtime* (cell C23) that contains 40:00. If your standard workweek consists of something other than 40 hours, you can change the *Overtime* cell.

The following formula (in cell E18) calculates regular (non-overtime) hours. This formula returns the smaller of two values: the total hours, or the overtime hours.

```
=MIN(E17,Overtime)
```

The final formula, in cell E19, simply subtracts the regular hours from the total hours to yield the overtime hours:

```
=E17-E18
```

The times in H17:H19 may display time values that exceed 24 hours, so these cells use a custom number format:

```
[h]:mm
```

 ON THE CD

The workbook shown in Figure 6-7, `time sheet.xlsm`, also appears on the companion CD-ROM.

Calculating the Difference between Two Times

Because times are represented as serial numbers, you can subtract the earlier time from the later time to get the difference. For example, if cell A2 contains 5:30:00 and cell B2 contains 14:00:00, the following formula returns 08:30:00 (a difference of eight hours and 30 minutes):

```
=B2-A2
```

If the subtraction results in a negative value, however, it becomes an invalid time; Excel displays a series of hash marks (#######) because a time without a date has a date serial number of 0. A negative time results in a negative serial number, which is not permitted.

If the direction of the time difference doesn't matter, you can use the ABS function to return the absolute value of the difference:

```
=ABS(B2-A2)
```

This "negative time" problem often occurs when calculating an elapsed time — for example, calculating the number of hours worked given a start time and an end time. This presents no problem if the two times fall in the same day. If the work shift spans midnight, though, the result is an invalid negative time. For example, you may start work at 10:00 PM and end work at 6:00 AM the next day. Figure 6-8 shows a worksheet that calculates the hours worked. As you can see, the shift that spans midnight presents a problem.

	A	B	C	D
1	**Start Shift**	**End Shift**	**Hours Worked**	
2	8:00 AM	5:30 PM	9:30	
3	10:00 PM	6:00 AM	##################	
4				
5				
6				
7				

Sheet1 Sheet2

Figure 6-8: Calculating the number of hours worked returns an error if the shift spans midnight.

Using the ABS function (to calculate the absolute value) isn't an option in this case because it returns the wrong result (16 hours). The following formula, however, *does* work:

```
=IF(B2<A2,B2+1,B2)-A2
```

In fact, another formula (even simpler) can do the job:

```
=MOD(B2-A2,1)
```

TIP

Negative times are permitted if the workbook uses the 1904 date system. To switch to the 1904 date system, choose Office⇨Excel Options and then navigate to the When Calculating This Workbook section of the Advanced tab. Place a check mark next to the Use 1904 Date System option. But beware! When changing the workbook's date system, if the workbook uses dates, the dates will be off by four years.

Converting from Military Time

Military time is expressed as a four-digit number from 0000 to 2359. For example, 1:00 AM is expressed as 0100 hours, and 3:30 PM is expressed as 1530 hours. The following formula converts such a number (assumed to appear in cell A1) to a standard time:

```
=TIMEVALUE(LEFT(A1,2)&":"&RIGHT(A1,2))
```

The formula returns an incorrect result if the contents of cell A1 do not contain four digits. The following formula corrects the problem and returns a valid time for any military time value from 0 to 2359:

```
=TIMEVALUE(LEFT(TEXT(A1,"0000"),2)&":"&RIGHT(A1,2))
```

The following is a simpler formula that uses the TEXT function to return a formatted string and then uses the TIMEVALUE function to express the result in terms of a time.

```
=TIMEVALUE(TEXT(A1,"00\:00"))
```

Converting Decimal Hours, Minutes, or Seconds to a Time

To convert decimal hours to a time, divide the decimal hours by 24. For example, if cell A1 contains 9.25 (representing hours), this formula returns 09:15:00 (9 hours, 15 minutes):

```
=A1/24
```

To convert decimal minutes to a time, divide the decimal hours by 1,440 (the number of minutes in a day). For example, if cell A1 contains 500 (representing minutes), the following formula returns 08:20:00 (8 hours, 20 minutes):

```
=A1/1440
```

To convert decimal seconds to a time, divide the decimal hours by 86,400 (the number of seconds in a day). For example, if cell A1 contains 65,000 (representing seconds), the following formula returns 18:03:20 (18 hours, 3 minutes, and 20 seconds):

```
=A1/86400
```

Adding Hours, Minutes, or Seconds to a Time

You can use the TIME function to add any number of hours, minutes, or seconds to a time. For example, assume that cell A1 contains a time. The following formula adds two hours and 30 minutes to that time and displays the result:

```
=A1+TIME(2,30,0)
```

You can use the TIME function to fill a range of cells with incremental times. Figure 6-9 shows a worksheet with a series of times in ten-minute increments. Cell A1 contains a time that was entered directly. Cell A2 contains the following formula, which was copied down the column:

```
=A1+TIME(0,10,0)
```

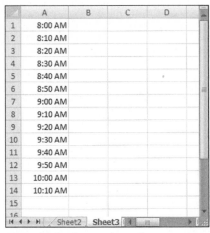

Figure 6-9: Using a formula to create a series of incremental times.

TIP

You can also use Excel AutoFill feature to fill a range with times. For example, to create a series of times with ten-minute increments, enter **8:00 AM** in cell A1 and **8:10 AM** in cell A2. Select both cells, and then drag the fill handle (in the lower-right corner of cell A2) down the column to create the series.

Converting between Time Zones

You may receive a worksheet that contains dates and times in Greenwich Mean Time (GMT), sometimes referred to as *Zulu time*), and you need to convert these values to local time. To convert dates and times into local times, you need to determine the difference in hours between the two time zones. For example, to convert GMT times to U.S. Central Standard Time (CST), the hour conversion factor is –6.

You can't use the TIME function with a negative argument, so you need to take a different approach. One hour equals $\frac{1}{24}$ of a day, so you can divide the time conversion factor by 24 and then add it to the time.

Figure 6-10 shows a worksheet set up to convert dates and times (expressed in GMT) to local times. Cell B1 contains the hour conversion factor (–5 hours for U.S. Eastern Standard Time; EST). The formula in B4, which copies down the column, is

```
=A4+($B$1/24)
```

ON THE CD

You can access the workbook shown in Figure 6-10, `gmt conversion.xlsx`, on the companion CD-ROM.

	A	B	C	D
1	**Conversion Factor:**	**-5 hours**		
2				
3	**GMT**	**Local Time**		
4	01/08/2007 01:00 AM	01/07/2007 08:00 PM		
5	01/08/2007 03:30 AM	01/07/2007 10:30 PM		
6	01/08/2007 06:00 AM	01/08/2007 01:00 AM		
7	01/08/2007 08:30 AM	01/08/2007 03:30 AM		
8	01/08/2007 11:00 AM	01/08/2007 06:00 AM		
9	01/08/2007 01:30 PM	01/08/2007 08:30 AM		
10	01/08/2007 04:00 PM	01/08/2007 11:00 AM		
11	01/08/2007 06:30 PM	01/08/2007 01:30 PM		
12	01/08/2007 09:00 PM	01/08/2007 04:00 PM		
13	01/08/2007 11:30 PM	01/08/2007 06:30 PM		
14	01/09/2007 02:00 AM	01/08/2007 09:00 PM		
15	01/09/2007 04:30 AM	01/08/2007 11:30 PM		
16	01/09/2007 07:00 AM	01/09/2007 02:00 AM		
17	01/09/2007 09:30 AM	01/09/2007 04:30 AM		
18	01/09/2007 12:00 PM	01/09/2007 07:00 AM		
19				
20				

Figure 6-10: This worksheet converts dates and times between time zones.

This formula effectively adds x hours to the date and time in column A. If cell B1 contains a negative hour value, the value subtracts from the date and time in column A. Note that, in some cases, this also affects the date.

Rounding Time Values

You may need to create a formula that rounds a time to a particular value. For example, you may need to enter your company's time records rounded to the nearest 15 minutes. This section presents examples of various ways to round a time value.

The following formula rounds the time in cell A1 to the nearest minute:

```
=ROUND(A1*1440,0)/1440
```

The formula works by multiplying the time by 1440 (to get total minutes). This value is passed to the ROUND function, and the result is divided by 1440. For example, if cell A1 contains 11:52:34, the formula returns 11:53:00.

The following formula resembles this example, except that it rounds the time in cell A1 to the nearest hour:

```
=ROUND(A1*24,0)/24
```

If cell A1 contains 5:21:31, the formula returns 5:00:00.

The following formula rounds the time in cell A1 to the nearest 15 minutes (quarter of an hour):

```
=ROUND(A1*24/0.25,0)*(0.25/24)
```

In this formula, 0.25 represents the fractional hour. To round a time to the nearest 30 minutes, change 0.25 to 0.5, as in the following formula:

```
=ROUND(A1*24/0.5,0)*(0.5/24)
```

Working with Non–Time-of-Day Values

Sometimes, you may want to work with time values that don't represent an actual time of day. For example, you might want to create a list of the finish times for a race, or record the time you spend jogging each day. Such times don't represent a time of day. Rather, a value represents the time for an event (in hours, minutes, and seconds). The time to complete a test, for instance, might be 35 minutes and 45 seconds. You can enter that value into a cell as

```
00:35:45
```

Excel interprets such an entry as 12:35:45 AM, which works fine (just make sure that you format the cell so it appears as you like). When you enter such times that do not have an hour component, you must include at least one zero for the hour. If you omit a leading zero for a missing hour, Excel interprets your entry as 35 hours and 45 minutes.

Figure 6-11 shows an example of a worksheet set up to keep track of someone's jogging activity. Column A contains simple dates. Column B contains the distance, in miles. Column C contains the time it took to run the distance. Column D contains formulas to calculate the speed, in miles per hour. For example, the formula in cell D2 is

```
=B2/(C2*24)
```

	A	B	C	D	E	F	G	H
1	Date	Distance	Time	Speed (mph)	Pace (min/mile)	YTD Distance	Cumulative Time	
2	1/1/2007	1.50	00:18:45	4.80	12.50	1.50	00:18:45	
3	1/2/2007	1.50	00:17:40	5.09	11.78	3.00	00:36:25	
4	1/3/2007	2.00	00:21:30	5.58	10.75	5.00	00:57:55	
5	1/4/2007	1.50	00:15:20	5.87	10.22	6.50	01:13:15	
6	1/5/2007	2.40	00:25:05	5.74	10.45	8.90	01:38:20	
7	1/6/2007	3.00	00:31:06	5.79	10.37	11.90	02:09:26	
8	1/7/2007	3.80	00:41:06	5.55	10.82	15.70	02:50:32	
9	1/8/2007	5.00	01:09:00	4.35	13.80	20.70	03:59:32	
10	1/9/2007	4.00	00:45:10	5.31	11.29	24.70	04:44:42	
11	1/10/2007	3.00	00:29:06	6.19	9.70	27.70	05:13:48	
12	1/11/2007	5.50	01:08:30	4.82	12.45	33.20	06:22:18	
13								
14								

Sheet1

Figure 6-11: This worksheet uses times not associated with a time of day.

Column E contains formulas to calculate the pace, in minutes per mile. For example, the formula in cell E2 is

```
=(C2*60*24)/B2
```

Columns F and G contain formulas that calculate the year-to-date distance (using column B) and the cumulative time (using column C). The cells in column G are formatted using the following number format (which permits time displays that exceed 24 hours):

```
[hh]:mm:ss
```

 ON THE CD

You can access the workbook shown in Figure 6-11, `jogging log.xlsx`, on the companion CD-ROM.

Chapter 7

Counting and Summing Techniques

IN THIS CHAPTER

- ◆ Information on counting and summing cells
- ◆ Information on counting and summing records in databases and pivot tables
- ◆ Basic counting formulas
- ◆ Advanced counting formulas
- ◆ Formulas for performing common summing tasks
- ◆ Conditional summing formulas using a single criterion
- ◆ Conditional summing formulas using multiple criteria
- ◆ The use of VBA to perform counting and summing tasks

Many of the most frequently asked spreadsheet questions involve counting and summing values and other worksheet elements. It seems that people are always looking for formulas to count or sum various items in a worksheet. If I've done my job, this chapter will answer the vast majority of such questions.

Counting and Summing Worksheet Cells

Generally, a *counting formula* returns the number of cells in a specified range that meet certain criteria. A *summing formula* returns the sum of the values of the cells in a range that meet certain criteria. The range you want counted or summed may or may not consist of a worksheet database or table.

Table 7-1 lists the worksheet functions that come into play when creating counting and summing formulas. If none of the functions in Table 7-1 can solve your problem, it's likely that an array formula can come to the rescue.

CROSS REF

See Part IV for detailed information and examples of array formulas used for counting and summing. In addition, refer to Chapter 9 for information about summing and counting data in a list.

TABLE 7-1   EXCEL'S COUNTING AND SUMMING FUNCTIONS

Function	Description
COUNT	Returns the number of cells in a range that contain a numeric value
COUNTA	Returns the number of nonblank cells in a range
COUNTBLANK	Returns the number of blank cells in a range
COUNTIF	Returns the number of cells in a range that meet a single specified criterion
COUNTIFS*	Returns the number of cells in a range that meet one or more specified criterion
DCOUNT	Counts the number of records in a worksheet database that meet specified criteria

Function	Description
DCOUNTA	Counts the number of nonblank records in a worksheet database that meet specified criteria
DEVSQ	Returns the sum of squares of deviations of data points from the sample mean; used primarily in statistical formulas
DSUM	Returns the sum of a column of values in a worksheet database that meet specified criteria
FREQUENCY	Calculates how often values occur within a range of values and returns a vertical array of numbers; used only in a multicell array formula
SUBTOTAL	When used with a first argument of 2 or 3, returns a count of cells that comprise a subtotal; when used with a first argument of 9, returns the sum of cells that comprise a subtotal
SUM	Returns the sum of its arguments
SUMIF	Returns the sum of cells in a range that meet a specified criterion
SUMIFS*	Returns the sum of the cells in a range that meet one or more specified criterion
SUMPRODUCT	Multiplies corresponding cells in two or more ranges and returns the sum of those products
SUMSQ	Returns the sum of the squares of its arguments; used primarily in statistical formulas
SUMX2PY2	Returns the sum of the sum of squares of corresponding values in two ranges; used primarily in statistical formulas
SUMXMY2	Returns the sum of squares of the differences of corresponding values in two ranges; used primarily in statistical formulas
SUMX2MY2	Returns the sum of the differences of squares of corresponding values in two ranges; used primarily in statistical formulas

*These are new functions, available only in Excel 2007.

Getting a Quick Count or Sum

In Excel 97, Microsoft introduced the AutoCalculate feature. This feature displays, in the status bar, information about the selected range. By default, Excel 2007 displays the average, count, and sum of the selected cells. You can, however, right-click the status bar to bring up the Status Bar Configuration menu with some other options.

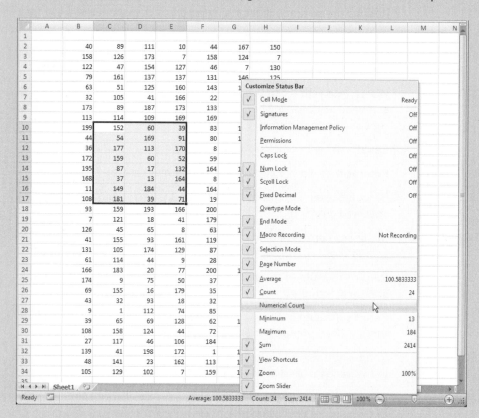

If you select Count, the status bar displays the number of nonempty cells in the selected range. If you select Numerical Count, the status bar displays the number of numeric cells in the selected range.

Counting or Summing Records in Databases and Pivot Tables

Special database functions and pivot tables provide additional ways to achieve counting and summing. Excel's DCOUNT and DSUM functions are database functions. They work in conjunction with a worksheet database and require a special criterion range that holds the counting or summing criteria.

CROSS REF

Chapter 9 covers the database functions and provides information about counting and summing using a worksheet database or table.

Creating a pivot table is a great way to get a count or sum of items without using formulas. Like the database function, using a pivot table is appropriate when your data is in the form of a worksheet database or table.

CROSS REF

Refer to Chapter 18 for information about pivot tables.

Part II

Basic Counting Formulas

The basic counting formulas presented here are all straightforward and relatively simple. They demonstrate how to count the number of cells in a range that meet specific criteria. Figure 7-1 shows a worksheet that uses formulas (in column E) to summarize the contents of range A1:B10 — a 20-cell range named *Data*.

	A	B	C	D	E	F
1	Jan	Feb		Total cells:	20	
2	525	718		Blank cells:	6	
3				Nonblank cells:	14	
4	3			Numeric values:	7	
5	552	911		Non-text cells:	17	
6	250	98		Text cells:	3	
7				Logical values:	2	
8	TRUE	FALSE		Error values:	2	
9		#DIV/0!		#N/A errors:	0	
10	Total	#NAME?		#NULL! errors:	0	
11				#DIV/0! errors:	1	
12				#VALUE! errors:	0	
13				#REF! errors:	0	
14				#NAME? errors:	1	
15				#NUM! errors:	0	
16						

Figure 7-1: Formulas provide various counts of the data in A1:B10.

ON THE CD

You can access the `basic counting.xlsx` workbook shown in Figure 7-1 on the companion CD-ROM.

About This Chapter's Examples

Some of the examples in this chapter use array formulas. An *array formula*, as explained in Chapter 14, is a special type of formula. You can spot an array formula because it is enclosed in brackets when it is displayed in the formula bar. For example

```
{=Data*2}
```

When you enter an array formula, press Ctrl+Shift+Enter (not just Enter). And don't type the brackets—Excel inserts the brackets for you. If you need to edit an array formula, don't forget to press Ctrl+Shift+Enter when you've finished editing. Otherwise, the array formula will revert to a normal formula, and it will return an incorrect result.

Counting the Total Number of Cells

To get a count of the total number of cells in a range, use the following formula. This formula returns the number of cells in a range named *Data*. It simply multiplies the number of rows (returned by the ROWS function) by the number of columns (returned by the COLUMNS function).

```
=ROWS(Data)*COLUMNS(Data)
```

Counting Blank Cells

The following formula returns the number of blank (empty) cells in a range named *Data:*

```
=COUNTBLANK(Data)
```

The COUNTBLANK function also counts cells containing a formula that returns an empty string. For example, the formula that follows returns an empty string if the value in cell A1 is greater than 5. If the cell meets this condition, the COUNTBLANK function counts that cell.

```
=IF(A1>5,"",A1)
```

NOTE

The COUNTBLANK function does not count cells that contain a zero value, even if you clear the Show a Zero in Cells That Have Zero Value option in the Excel Options dialog box. (Choose Office⇨ Excel Options and navigate to the Display Options for this Worksheet section of the Advanced tab.)

You can use the COUNTBLANK function with an argument that consists of entire rows or columns. For example, this next formula returns the number of blank cells in column A:

```
=COUNTBLANK(A:A)
```

The following formula returns the number of empty cells on the entire worksheet named Sheet1. You must enter this formula on a sheet other than Sheet1, or it will create a circular reference.

```
=COUNTBLANK(Sheet1!1:1048576)
```

Counting Nonblank Cells

The following formula uses the COUNTA function to return the number of nonblank cells in a range named *Data:*

```
=COUNTA(Data)
```

The COUNTA function counts cells that contain values, text, or logical values (TRUE or FALSE).

NOTE

If a cell contains a formula that returns an empty string, that cell is included in the count returned by COUNTA even though the cell appears to be blank.

Counting Numeric Cells

To count only the numeric cells in a range, use the following formula, which assumes that the range is named *Data:*

```
=COUNT(Data)
```

Cells that contain a date or a time are considered to be numeric cells. Cells that contain a logical value (TRUE or FALSE) are not considered to be numeric cells.

Counting Nontext Cells

The following array formula uses Excel's ISNONTEXT function, which returns TRUE if its argument refers to any nontext cell (including a blank cell). This formula returns the count of the number of cells not containing text (including blank cells):

```
{=SUM(IF(ISNONTEXT(Data),1))}
```

Counting Text Cells

To count the number of text cells in a range, you need to use an array formula. The array formula that follows returns the number of text cells in a range named *Data:*

```
{=SUM(IF(ISTEXT(Data),1))}
```

Counting Logical Values

The following array formula returns the number of logical values (TRUE or FALSE) in a range named *Data:*

```
{=SUM(IF(ISLOGICAL(Data),1))}
```

Counting Error Values in a Range

Excel has three functions that help you determine whether a cell contains an error value:

- **ISERROR:** Returns TRUE if the cell contains any error value (#N/A, #VALUE!, #REF!, #DIV/0!, #NUM!, #NAME?, or #NULL!)

- **ISERR:** Returns TRUE if the cell contains any error value except #N/A

- **ISNA:** Returns TRUE if the cell contains the #N/A error value

NOTE

Notice that the #N/A error value is treated separately. In most cases, #N/A is not a "real" error. #N/A is often used as a placeholder for missing data. You can enter the #N/A error value directly or use the NA function:

```
=NA()
```

You can use these functions in an array formula to count the number of error values in a range. The following array formula, for example, returns the total number of error values in a range named *Data:*

```
{=SUM(IF(ISERROR(Data),1))}
```

Depending on your needs, you can use the ISERR or ISNA function in place of ISERROR.

If you would like to count specific types of errors, you can use the COUNTIF function. The following formula, for example, returns the number of #DIV/0! error values in the range named *Data:*

```
=COUNTIF(Data,"#DIV/0!")
```

Advanced Counting Formulas

Most of the basic examples I presented previously use functions or formulas that perform conditional counting. The advanced counting formulas that I present here represent more complex examples for counting worksheet cells, based on various types of criteria.

Counting Cells by Using the COUNTIF Function

Excel's COUNTIF function is useful for single-criterion counting formulas. The COUNTIF function takes two arguments:

- **range:** The range that contains the values that determine whether to include a particular cell in the count

- **criteria:** The logical criteria that determine whether to include a particular cell in the count

Table 7-2 contains several examples of formulas that use the COUNTIF function. These formulas all work with a range named *Data*. As you can see, the *criteria* argument proves quite flexible. You can use constants, expressions, functions, cell references, and even wildcard characters (* and ?).

TABLE 7-2 EXAMPLES OF FORMULAS USING THE COUNTIF FUNCTION

=COUNTIF(Data,12)	Returns the number of cells containing the value 12
=COUNTIF(Data,"<0")	Returns the number of cells containing a negative value
=COUNTIF(Data,"<>0")	Returns the number of cells not equal to 0
=COUNTIF(Data,">5")	Returns the number of cells greater than 5
=COUNTIF(Data,A1)	Returns the number of cells equal to the contents of cell A1
=COUNTIF(Data,">"&A1)	Returns the number of cells greater than the value in cell A1
=COUNTIF(Data,"*")	Returns the number of cells containing text
=COUNTIF(Data,"???")	Returns the number of text cells containing exactly three characters
=COUNTIF(Data,"budget")	Returns the number of cells containing the single word *budget* and nothing else (not case sensitive)
=COUNTIF(Data,"*budget*")	Returns the number of cells containing the text *budget* anywhere within the text

continued

TABLE 7-2   EXAMPLES OF FORMULAS USING THE COUNTIF FUNCTION *(continued)*

=COUNTIF(Data,"A*")	Returns the number of cells containing text that begins with the letter A (not case sensitive)
=COUNTIF(Data,TODAY())	Returns the number of cells containing the current date
=COUNTIF(Data,">" &AVERAGE(Data))	Returns the number of cells with a value greater than the average
=COUNTIF(Data,">" &AVERAGE(Data)+ STDEV(Data)*3)	Returns the number of values exceeding three standard deviations above the mean
=COUNTIF(Data,3)+COUNTIF) (Data,-3	Returns the number of cells containing the value 3 or –3
=COUNTIF(Data,TRUE)	Returns the number of cells containing logical TRUE
=COUNTIF(Data,TRUE)+ COUNTIF(Data,FALSE)	Returns the number of cells containing a logical value (TRUE or FALSE)
=COUNTIF(Data,"#N/A")	Returns the number of cells containing the #N/A error value

Counting Cells That Meet Multiple Criteria

In many cases, your counting formula will need to count cells only if two or more criteria are met. These criteria can be based on the cells that are being counted or based on a range of corresponding cells.

Figure 7-2 shows a simple worksheet that I use for the examples in this section. This sheet shows sales data categorized by Month, SalesRep, and Type. The worksheet contains named ranges that correspond to the labels in Row 1.

ON THE CD

The workbook `multiple criteria counting.xlsx` is available on the companion CD-ROM.

NEW

Several of the examples in this section use the COUNTIFS function, which is new to Excel 2007. I also present alternative version of the formulas, which should be used if you plan to share your workbook with others who don't use Excel 2007.

Month	SalesRep	Type	Amount			
January	Albert	New	85		9	Amounts between 500 and 1000
January	Albert	New	675		9	Amounts between 500 and 1000 (array)
January	Brooks	New	130		2	Sales by Brooks in January greater than 1000 (COUNTIFS)
January	Cook	New	1350		2	Sales by Brooks in January greater than 1000 (array)
January	Cook	Existing	685		20	Sales by Brooks OR Cook
January	Brooks	New	1350		20	Sales by Brooks OR Cook (array)
January	Cook	New	475		16	Sales by Brooks OR in January OR greater than 1000
January	Brooks	New	1205		6	Brooks and Cooks January sales (COUNTIFS)
February	Brooks	Existing	450		6	Brooks and Cooks January sales (array)
February	Albert	New	495		900	Most frequent sales amount
February	Cook	New	210		3	Number of times most frequent sales amount appears
February	Cook	Existing	1050		10	Number of times most frequent sales rep appears
February	Albert	New	140	Brooks		Most frequent sales rep (first, if more than one)
February	Brooks	New	900			
February	Brooks	New	900			
February	Cook	New	95			
February	Cook	New	780			
March	Brooks	New	900			
March	Albert	Existing	875			
March	Brooks	New	50			
March	Brooks	New	875			
March	Cook	Existing	225			
March	Cook	New	175			
March	Brooks	Existing	400			
March	Albert	New	840			
March	Cook	New	132			

Figure 7-2: This worksheet demonstrates various counting techniques that use multiple criteria.

Using And Criteria

An And criterion counts cells if all specified conditions are met. A common example is a formula that counts the number of values that fall within a numerical range. For example, you may want to count cells that contain a value greater than 0 *and* less than or equal to 12. Any cell that has a positive value less than or equal to 12 will be included in the count. For this example, the COUNTIFS function will do the job:

```
=COUNTIFS(Amount,">0",Amount,"<=12")
```

NOTE

If the data is contained in a table, you can use the new Excel 2007 method of referencing data within a table. For example, if the table is named Table1, the preceding formula can be rewritten as

```
=COUNTIFS(Table1[Amount],">100",Table1[Amount],"<=200")
```

This method of writing formulas does not require named ranges.

The COUNTIFS function accepts any number of paired arguments. The first member of the pair is the range to be counted (in this case, the range named Amount); the second member of the pair is the criterion. The example above contains two sets of paired arguments and returns the number of cells in which Amount is greater than 100 and less than or equal to 200.

Part II

Prior to Excel 2007, you would need to use a formula like this:

```
=COUNTIF(Data,">0")-COUNTIF(Data,">12")
```

This formula counts the number of values that are greater than 0 and then subtracts the number of values that are greater than 12. The result is the number of cells that contain a value greater than 0 and less than or equal to 12.

Creating this type of formula can be confusing because the formula refers to a condition ">12" even though the goal is to count values that are less than or equal to 12. An alternate technique is to use an array formula, such as the one that follows. You may find creating this type of formula easier.

```
{=SUM((Data>0)*(Data<=12))}
```

 NOTE

When you enter an array formula, remember to use Ctrl+Shift+Enter — and don't type the brackets.

Sometimes, the counting criteria will be based on cells other than the cells being counted. You may, for example, want to count the number of sales that meet the following criteria:

- Month is January.

and

- SalesRep is Brooks.

and

- Amount is greater than 1,000.

The following formula (for Excel 2007 only) returns the number of items that meets all three criteria. Note that the COUNTIFS function uses three sets of pairs of arguments.

```
=COUNTIFS(Month,"January",SalesRep,"Brooks",Amount,">1000")
```

An alternative formula, which works with all version of Excel, uses the SUMPRODUCT function. The formula below returns the same result as the previous formula:

```
=SUMPRODUCT((Month="January")*(SalesRep="Brooks")*(Amount>1000))
```

Yet another way to perform this count is to use an array formula:

```
{=SUM((Month="January")*(SalesRep="Brooks")*(Amount>1000))}
```

Using Or Criteria

To count cells using an Or criterion, you can sometimes use multiple COUNTIF functions. The following formula, for example, counts the number of 1s, 3s, and 5s in the range named *Data:*

```
=COUNTIF(Data,1)+COUNTIF(Data,3)+COUNTIF(Data,5)
```

You can also use the COUNTIF function in an array formula. The following array formula, for example, returns the same result as the previous formula:

```
{=SUM(COUNTIF(Data,{1,3,5}))}
```

But if you base your Or criteria on cells other than the cells being counted, the COUNTIF function won't work. Refer to Figure 7-2. Suppose you want to count the number of sales that meet the following criteria:

- Month is January.

or

- SalesRep is Brooks.

or

- Amount is greater than 1,000.

The following array formula returns the correct count:

```
{=SUM(IF((Month="January")+(SalesRep="Brooks")+(Amount>1000),1))}
```

Combining And and Or Criteria

In some cases, you may need to combine And and Or criteria when counting. For example, perhaps you want to count sales that meet the following criteria:

- Month is January.

and

- SalesRep is Brooks.

or

- SalesRep is Cook.

You can add two COUNTIFS functions to get the desired result:

```
=COUNTIFS(Month,"January",SalesRep,"Brooks")+
COUNTIFS(Month,"January",SalesRep,"Cook")
```

Because you have to repeat the AND portion of the criteria in each function's arguments, using COUNTIFS can produce long formulas with more criteria. When you a lot of criteria, it makes sense to use an array formula, like this one that produces the same result:

```
{=SUM((Month="January")*((SalesRep="Brooks")+(SalesRep="Cook")))}
```

Counting the Most Frequently Occurring Entry

Excel's MODE function returns the most frequently occurring value in a range. Figure 7-3 shows a worksheet with values in range A1:A10 (named *Data*). The formula that follows returns 10 because that value appears most frequently in the *Data* range:

```
=MODE(Data)
```

The formula returns an #N/A error if the *Data* range contains no duplicated values.

	A	B	C	D
1	1		10	<-- Mode
2	4		3	<--Frequency of the Mode
3	7			
4	10			
5	10			
6	10			
7	12			
8	14			
9	16			
10	9			
11				
12				

Sheet1 Sheet2

Figure 7-3: The MODE function returns the most frequently occurring value in a range.

To count the number of times the most frequently occurring value appears in the range (in other words, the frequency of the mode), use the following formula:

```
=COUNTIF(Data,MODE(Data))
```

This formula returns 3 because the modal value (10) appears three times in the *Data* range.

The MODE function works only for numeric values. It simply ignores cells that contain text. To find the most frequently occurring text entry in a range, you need to use an array formula.

To count the number of times the most frequently occurring item (text or values) appears in a range named *Data*, use the following array formula:

```
{=MAX(COUNTIF(Data,Data))}
```

This next array formula operates like the MODE function except that it works with both text and values:

```
{=INDEX(Data,MATCH(MAX(COUNTIF(Data,Data)),COUNTIF(Data,Data),0))}
```

 CAUTION
If there is more than one most-frequent value, the preceding formula will return only the first in the list.

Counting the Occurrences of Specific Text

The examples in this section demonstrate various ways to count the occurrences of a character or text string in a range of cells. Figure 7-4 shows a worksheet used for these examples. Various text appears in the range A1:A10 (named *Data*); cell B1 is named *Text*.

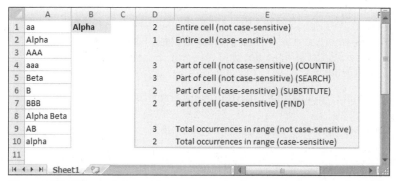

Figure 7-4: This worksheet demonstrates various ways to count characters in a range.

 ON THE CD
The companion CD-ROM contains a workbook named `counting text in a range.xlsx` that demonstrates the formulas in this section.

ENTIRE CELL CONTENTS

To count the number of cells containing the contents of the *Text* cell (and nothing else), you can use the COUNTIF function. The following formula demonstrates:

```
=COUNTIF(Data,Text)
```

For example, if the *Text* cell contains the string *Alpha*, the formula returns 2 because two cells in the Data range contain this text. This formula is not case sensitive, so it counts both *Alpha* (cell A2) and *alpha* (cell A10). Note, however, that it does not count the cell that contains *Alpha Beta* (cell A8).

The following array formula is similar to the preceding formula, but this one is case sensitive:

```
{=SUM(IF(EXACT(Data,Text),1))}
```

PARTIAL CELL CONTENTS

To count the number of cells that contain a string that includes the contents of the *Text* cell, use this formula:

```
=COUNTIF(Data,"*"&Text&"*")
```

For example, if the *Text* cell contains the text *Alpha*, the formula returns *3* because three cells in the *Data* range contain the text *alpha* (cells A2, A8, and A10). Note that the comparison is not case sensitive.

An alternative is a longer array formula that uses the SEARCH function:

```
{=SUM(IF(NOT(ISERROR(SEARCH(text,data))),1))}
```

The SEARCH function returns an error if *Text* is not found in *Data*. The preceding formula counts one for every cell where SEARCH does not find an error. Because SEARCH is not case sensitive, neither is this formula.

If you need a case-sensitive count, you can use the following array formula:

```
{=SUM(IF(LEN(Data)-LEN(SUBSTITUTE(Data,Text,""))>0,1))}
```

If the Text cells contain the text *Alpha*, the preceding formula returns *2* because the string appears in two cells (A2 and A8).

Like the SEARCH function, the FIND function will return an error if *Text* is not found in *Data*, as in this alternative array formula:

```
{=SUM(IF(NOT(ISERROR(FIND(text,data))),1))}
```

Unlike SEARCH, the FIND function is case sensitive.

TOTAL OCCURRENCES IN A RANGE

To count the total number of occurrences of a string within a range of cells, use the following array formula:

```
{=(SUM(LEN(Data))-SUM(LEN(SUBSTITUTE(Data,Text,""))))/
LEN(Text)}
```

If the *Text* cell contains the character *B*, the formula returns *7* because the range contains seven instances of the string. This formula is case sensitive.

The following array formula is a modified version that is not case sensitive:

```
{=(SUM(LEN(Data))-SUM(LEN(SUBSTITUTE(UPPER(Data),
UPPER(Text),"")))))/LEN(Text)}
```

Counting the Number of Unique Values

The following array formula returns the number of unique values in a range named *Data:*

```
{=SUM(1/COUNTIF(Data,Data))}
```

To understand how this formula works, you need a basic understanding of array formulas. (See Chapter 14 for an introduction to this topic.) In Figure 7-5, range A1:A12 is named *Data.* Range C1:C12 contains the following multicell array formula. A single formula was entered into all 12 cells in the range.

```
{=COUNTIF(Data,Data)}
```

	A	B	C	D	E	F	G	H
1	100		3	0.333333				
2	100		3	0.333333				
3	100		3	0.333333				
4	200		2	0.5				
5	200		2	0.5				
6	300		1	1				
7	400		2	0.5				
8	400		2	0.5				
9	500		4	0.25				
10	500		4	0.25				
11	500		4	0.25				
12	500		4	0.25				
13				5	<-- Unique items in Column A			
14								
15				5	<-- Single formula			
16				5	<-- Single formula, handles blank cells			
17								
18								

Figure 7-5: Using an array formula to count the number of unique values in a range.

ON THE CD

You can access the workbook `count unique.xlsx` shown in Figure 7-5 on the companion CD-ROM.

The array in range C1:C12 consists of the count of each value in *Data.* For example, the number 100 appears three times, so each array element that corresponds to a value of 100 in the *Data* range has a value of 3.

Range D1:D12 contains the following array formula:

```
{=1/C1:C12}
```

This array consists of each value in the array in range C1:C12, divided into 1. For example, each cell in the original *Data* range that contains a 200 has a value of 0.5 in the corresponding cell in D1:D12.

Summing the range D1:D12 gives the number of unique items in *Data.* The array formula presented at the beginning of this section essentially creates the array that occupies D1:D12 and sums the values.

This formula has a serious limitation: If the range contains any blank cells, it returns an error. The following array formula solves this problem:

```
{=SUM(IF(COUNTIF(Data,Data)=0,"",1/COUNTIF(Data,Data)))}
```

CROSS REF

To create an array formula that returns a list of unique items in a range, refer to Chapter 15.

Creating a Frequency Distribution

A *frequency distribution* basically comprises a summary table that shows the frequency of each value in a range. For example, an instructor may create a frequency distribution of test scores. The table would show the count of As, Bs, Cs, and so on. Excel provides a number of ways to create frequency distributions. You can

- Use the FREQUENCY function.
- Create your own formulas.
- Use the Analysis ToolPak add-in.

ON THE CD

The `frequency distribution.xlsx` workbook that demonstrates these three techniques appears on the companion CD-ROM.

CROSS REF

If your data is in the form of a worksheet database or table, you can also use a pivot table to create a frequency distribution. Refer to Chapter 18 for more information about pivot tables.

The **FREQUENCY** Function

Using Excel's FREQUENCY function presents the easiest way to create a frequency distribution. This function always returns an array, so you must use it in an array formula entered into a multicell range.

Figure 7-6 shows some data in range A1:E20 (named *Data*). These values range from 1 to 500. The range G2:G11 contains the bins used for the frequency distribution. Each cell in this bin range contains the upper limit for the bin. In this case, the bins consist of 1–50, 51–100, 101–150, and so on. See the sidebar, "Creating Bins for a Frequency Distribution" to discover an easy way to create a bin range.

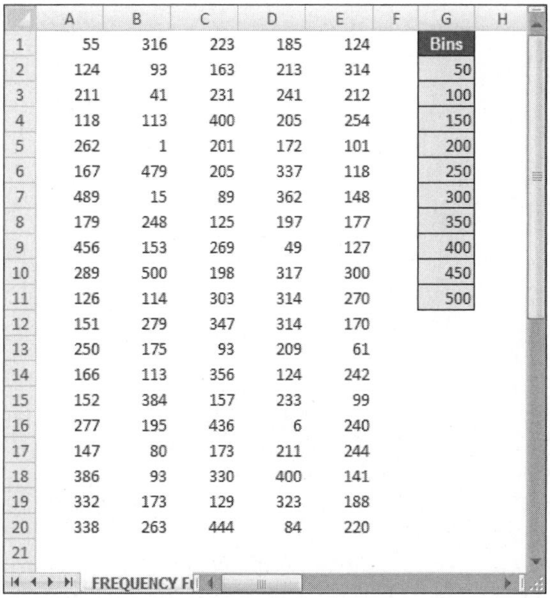

	A	B	C	D	E	F	G	H
1	55	316	223	185	124		Bins	
2	124	93	163	213	314		50	
3	211	41	231	241	212		100	
4	118	113	400	205	254		150	
5	262	1	201	172	101		200	
6	167	479	205	337	118		250	
7	489	15	89	362	148		300	
8	179	248	125	197	177		350	
9	456	153	269	49	127		400	
10	289	500	198	317	300		450	
11	126	114	303	314	270		500	
12	151	279	347	314	170			
13	250	175	93	209	61			
14	166	113	356	124	242			
15	152	384	157	233	99			
16	277	195	436	6	240			
17	147	80	173	211	244			
18	386	93	330	400	141			
19	332	173	129	323	188			
20	338	263	444	84	220			
21								

FREQUENCY F

Figure 7-6: Creating a frequency distribution for the data in A1:E20.

To create the frequency distribution, select a range of cells that correspond to the number of cells in the bin range. Then enter the following array formula:

```
{=FREQUENCY(Data,G2:G11)}
```

The array formula enters the count of values in the *Data* range that fall into each bin. To create a frequency distribution that consists of percentages, use the following array formula:

```
{=FREQUENCY(Data,G2:G11)/COUNT(Data)}
```

Figure 7-7 shows two frequency distributions — one in terms of counts, and one in terms of percentages. The figure also shows a chart (histogram) created from the frequency distribution.

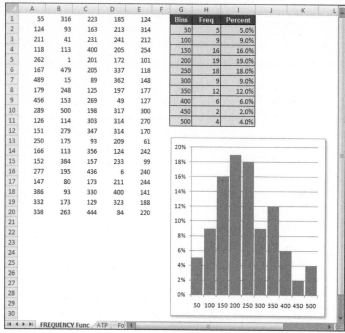

Figure 7-7: Frequency distributions created using the FREQUENCY function.

Creating Bins for a Frequency Distribution

When creating a frequency distribution, you must first enter the values into the bin range. The number of bins determines the number of categories in the distribution. Most of the time, each of these bins will represent an equal range of values.

To create ten evenly spaced bins for values in a range named *Data*, enter the following array formula into a range of ten cells in a column:

```
{=MIN(Data)+(ROW(INDIRECT("1:10"))*
(MAX(Data)-MIN(Data)+1)/10)-1}
```

This formula creates ten bins, based on the values in the *Data* range. The upper bin will always equal the maximum value in the range.

To create more or fewer bins, use a value other than 10 and enter the array formula into a range that contains the same number of cells. For example, to create five bins, enter the following array formula into a five-cell vertical range:

```
{=MIN(Data)+(ROW(INDIRECT("1:5"))*(MAX(Data)-MIN(Data)+1)/5)-1}
```

USING FORMULAS TO CREATE A FREQUENCY DISTRIBUTION

Figure 7-8 shows a worksheet that contains test scores for 50 students in column B. (The range is named *Grades*.) Formulas in columns G and H calculate a frequency distribution for letter grades. The minimum and maximum values for each letter grade appear in columns D and E. For example, a test score between 80 and 89 (inclusive) qualifies for a B.

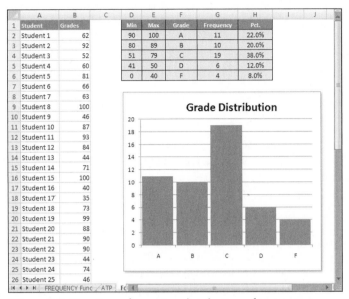

Figure 7-8: Creating a frequency distribution of test scores.

The formula in cell G2 that follows is an array formula that counts the number of scores that qualify for an A:

```
{=SUM((Grades>=D2)*(Grades<=E2))}
```

You may recognize this formula from a previous section in this chapter. (See "Counting Cells That Meet Multiple Criteria.") This formula was copied to the four cells below G2.

The formulas in column H calculate the percentage of scores for each letter grade. The formula in H2, which was copied to the four cells below H2, is

```
=G2/SUM($G$2:$G$6)
```

USING THE ANALYSIS TOOLPAK TO CREATE A FREQUENCY DISTRIBUTION

After you install the Analysis ToolPak add-in, you can use the Histogram option to create a frequency distribution. Start by entering your bin values in a range. Then choose Data⇨Analysis⇨Data Analysis to display the Data Analysis dialog box. Next, select Histogram and click OK. You should see the Histogram dialog box shown in Figure 7-9.

Part II

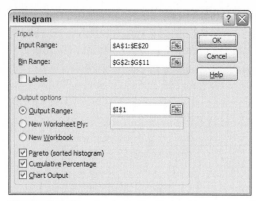

Figure 7-9: The Analysis ToolPak's Histogram dialog box.

Specify the ranges for your data *(Input Range)*, bins *(Bin Range)*, and results *(Output Range)*, and then select any options. Figure 7-10 shows a frequency distribution (and chart) created with the Histogram option.

CAUTION

Note that the frequency distribution consists of values, not formulas. Therefore, if you make any changes to your input data, you need to rerun the Histogram procedure to update the results.

Is the Analysis ToolPak Installed?

To make sure that the Analysis ToolPak add-in is installed, choose Add-Ins⇨Menu Commands. If Data Analysis appears in the group, you're all set. If not, you need to install it:

1. Choose Office⇨Excel Options to display the Excel Options dialog box.

2. Click the Add-ins tab on the left.

3. Select Excel Add-Ins from the Manage drop-down list.

4. Click Go to display the Add-Ins dialog box.

5. Place a check mark next to Analysis ToolPak.

6. Click OK.

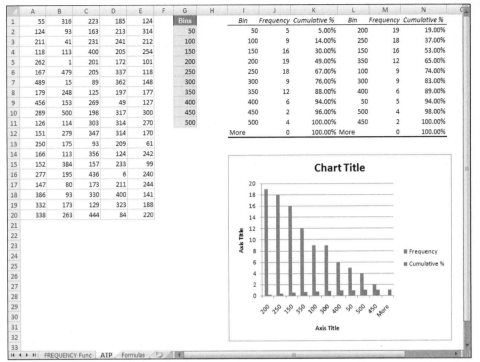

Figure 7-10: A frequency distribution and chart generated by the Analysis ToolPak's Histogram option.

USING ADJUSTABLE BINS TO CREATE A HISTOGRAM

Figure 7-11 shows a worksheet with student grades listed in column B (67 students total). Columns D and E contain formulas that calculate the upper and lower limits for bins, based on the entry in cell E1 (named *BinSize*). For example, if *BinSize* is 10 (as in the figure), then each bin contains ten scores (1–10, 11–20, and so on).

ON THE CD

The workbook adjustable bins.xlsx, shown in Figure 7-11, is available on the companion CD-ROM.

Part II

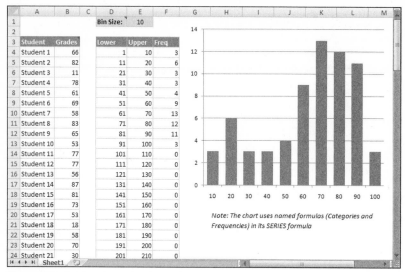

Figure 7-11: The chart displays a histogram; the contents of cell E1 determine the number of categories.

The chart uses two dynamic names in its SERIES formula. You can define the name *Categories* with the following formula:

```
=OFFSET(Sheet1!$E$4,0,0,ROUNDUP(100/BinSize,0))
```

You can define the name *Frequencies* with this formula:

```
=OFFSET(Sheet1!$F$4,0,0,ROUNDUP(100/BinSize,0))
```

The net effect is that the chart adjusts automatically when you change the *BinSize* cell.

CROSS REF

See Chapter 17 for more about creating a chart that uses dynamic names in its SERIES formula.

Summing Formulas

The examples in this section demonstrate how to perform common summing tasks by using formulas. The formulas range from very simple to relatively complex array formulas that compute sums of cells that match multiple criteria.

Summing All Cells in a Range

It doesn't get much simpler than this. The following formula returns the sum of all values in a range named *Data:*

```
=SUM(Data)
```

The SUM function can take up to 30 arguments. The following formula, for example, returns the sum of the values in five noncontiguous ranges:

```
=SUM(A1:A9,C1:C9,E1:E9,G1:G9,I1:I9)
```

You can use complete rows or columns as an argument for the SUM function. The formula that follows, for example, returns the sum of all values in column A. If this formula appears in a cell in column A, it generates a circular reference error.

```
=SUM(A:A)
```

The following formula returns the sum of all values on Sheet1. To avoid a circular reference error, this formula must appear on a sheet other than Sheet1.

```
=SUM(Sheet1!1:1048576)
```

The SUM function is very versatile. The arguments can be numerical values, cells, ranges, text representations of numbers (which are interpreted as values), logical values, array constants, and even embedded functions. For example, consider the following formula:

```
=SUM(B1,5,"6",,SQRT(4),{1,2,3},A1:A5,TRUE)
```

This formula, which is a perfectly valid formula, contains all the following types of arguments, listed here in the order of their presentation:

- A single cell reference
- A literal value
- A string that looks like a value

- A missing argument
- An expression that uses another function
- An array constant
- A range reference
- A logical TRUE value

CAUTION

The SUM function is versatile, but it's also inconsistent when you use logical values (TRUE or FALSE). Logical values stored in cells are always treated as 0. But logical TRUE, when used as an argument in the SUM function, is treated as 1.

Computing a Cumulative Sum

You may want to display a cumulative sum of values in a range — sometimes known as a *running total.* Figure 7-12 illustrates a cumulative sum. Column B shows the monthly amounts, and column C displays the cumulative (year-to-date) totals.

	A	B	C	D
1	Month	Amount	Year-to-Date	
2	January	850	850	
3	February	900	1,750	
4	March	750	2,500	
5	April	1,100	3,600	
6	May	600	4,200	
7	June	500	4,700	
8	July	1,200	5,900	
9	August		5,900	
10	September		5,900	
11	October		5,900	
12	November		5,900	
13	December		5,900	
14	TOTAL	5,900		
15				

Sheet1 / Sheet2

Figure 7-12: Simple formulas in column C display a cumulative sum of the values in column B.

The formula in cell C2 is

```
=SUM(B$2:B2)
```

Notice that this formula uses a *mixed reference.* The first cell in the range reference always refers to the same row (in this case, row 2). When this formula is copied down the column, the range argument adjusts such that the sum always starts with row 2 and ends with the current row. For example, after copying this formula down column C, the formula in cell C8 is

```
=SUM(B$2:B8)
```

You can use an IF function to hide the cumulative sums for rows in which data hasn't been entered. The following formula, entered in cell C2 and copied down the column, is

```
=IF(ISBLANK(B2),"",SUM(B$2:B2))
```

Figure 7-13 shows this formula at work.

	A	B	C	D
1	**Month**	**Amount**	**Year-to-Date**	
2	January	850	850	
3	February	900	1,750	
4	March	750	2,500	
5	April	1,100	3,600	
6	May	600	4,200	
7	June	500	4,700	
8	July	1,200	5,900	
9	August			
10	September			
11	October			
12	November			
13	December			
14	TOTAL	5,900		
15				

Sheet1 | Sheet2

Figure 7-13: Using an IF function to hide cumulative sums for missing data.

 ON THE CD

The workbook `cumulative sum.xlsx` is available on the companion CD-ROM.

Summing the "Top n" Values

In some situations, you may need to sum the *n* largest values in a range — for example, the top ten values. One approach is to sort the range in descending order and then use the SUM function with an argument consisting of the first *n* values in the sorted range. An array formula such as this one accomplishes the task without sorting:

```
{=SUM(LARGE(Data,{1,2,3,4,5,6,7,8,9,10}))}
```

This formula sums the ten largest values in a range named *Data*. To sum the ten smallest values, use the SMALL function instead of the LARGE function:

```
{=SUM(SMALL(Data,{1,2,3,4,5,6,7,8,9,10}))}
```

These formulas use an array constant comprising the arguments for the LARGE or SMALL function. If the value of *n* for your top-*n* calculation is large, you may prefer to use the following variation. This formula returns the sum of the top 30 values in the *Data* range. You can, of course, substitute a different value for 30.

```
{=SUM(LARGE(Data,ROW(INDIRECT("1:30"))))}
```

CROSS REF

See Chapter 14 for more information about array constants.

Conditional Sums Using a Single Criterion

Often, you need to calculate a conditional sum. With a *conditional sum,* values in a range that meet one or more conditions are included in the sum. This section presents examples of conditional summing using a single criterion.

The SUMIF function is very useful for single-criterion sum formulas. The SUMIF function takes three arguments:

- **range:** The range containing the values that determine whether to include a particular cell in the sum.

- **criteria:** An expression that determines whether to include a particular cell in the sum.

- **sum_range:** Optional. The range that contains the cells you want to sum. If you omit this argument, the function uses the range specified in the first argument.

The examples that follow demonstrate the use of the SUMIF function. These formulas are based on the worksheet shown in Figure 7-14, set up to track invoices. Column F contains a formula that subtracts the date in column E from the date in column D. A negative number in column F indicates a past-due payment. The worksheet uses named ranges that correspond to the labels in row 1. Various summing formulas begin in row 15.

ON THE CD

All the examples in this section also appear on the companion CD-ROM in the file named `conditional summing.xlsx`.

	A	B	C	D	E	F	G
1	**InvoiceNum**	**Office**	**Amount**	**DateDue**	**Today**	**Difference**	
2	AG-0145	Oregon	$5,000.00	4/1/2007	5/5/2007	-34	
3	AG-0189	California	$450.00	4/19/2007	5/5/2007	-16	
4	AG-0220	Washington	$3,211.56	4/28/2007	5/5/2007	-7	
5	AG-0310	Oregon	$250.00	4/30/2007	5/5/2007	-5	
6	AG-0355	Washington	$125.50	5/4/2007	5/5/2007	-1	
7	AG-0409	Washington	$3,000.00	5/10/2007	5/5/2007	5	
8	AG-0581	Oregon	$2,100.00	5/23/2007	5/5/2007	18	
9	AG-0600	Oregon	$335.39	5/23/2007	5/5/2007	18	
10	AG-0602	Washington	$65.00	5/28/2007	5/5/2007	23	
11	AG-0633	California	$250.00	5/30/2007	5/5/2007	25	
12	**TOTAL**		**$14,787.45**			26	
13							
14							
15		-63	Total past due days				
16		-63	Total past due days (array formula)				
17							
18		$9,037.06	Total amount past due				
19		$9,037.06	Total amount past due (array formula)				
20							
21		$7,685.39	Total for Oregon only				
22							
23		$7,102.06	Total for all except Oregon				
24							
25		$5,875.89	Total amount with due date beyond May 1				
26							
27		$5,250.00	Total past due amount for Oregon (Excel 2007 only)				
28		$5,250.00	Total past due amount for Oregon (array formula)				
29							
30		$5,000.00	Total past due amounts OR amounts for Oregon (array formula)				
31							
32		$5,700.00	Total past due amounts for Oregon and California (array formula)				
33							
34							

Figure 7-14: A negative value in column F indicates a past-due payment.

Summing Only Negative Values

The following formula returns the sum of the negative values in column F. In other words, it returns the total number of past-due days for all invoices. For this worksheet, the formula returns –58.

```
=SUMIF(Difference,"<0")
```

Because you omit the third argument, the second argument ("<0") applies to the values in the *Difference* range.

Let a Wizard Create Your Formula

Excel ships with the Conditional Sum Wizard add-in. After you install this add-in, you can invoke the wizard by choosing Formulas⇨Solutions⇨Conditional Sum.

You can specify various conditions for your summing, and the add-in creates the formula for you (always an array formula). The Conditional Sum Wizard add-in, although a handy tool, is not all that versatile. For example, you can combine multiple criteria by using an And condition but not an Or condition.

To install the Conditional Sum Wizard add-in

1. Choose File⇨Excel Options to display the Excel Options dialog box.

2. Click the Add-ins tab on the left.

3. Choose Excel Add-Ins from the Manage drop-down list.

4. Click Go to display the Add-Ins dialog box.

5. Place a check mark next to Conditional Sum Wizard.

6. Click OK.

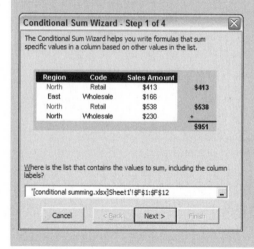

 NOTE

You can also use the following array formula to sum the negative values in the *Difference* range:

```
{=SUM(IF(Difference<0,Difference))}
```

You do not need to hard-code the arguments for the SUMIF function into your formula. For example, you can create a formula such as the following, which gets the criteria argument from the contents of cell G2:

```
=SUMIF(Difference,G2)
```

This formula returns a new result if you change the criteria in cell G2.

Summing Values Based on a Different Range

The following formula returns the sum of the past-due invoice amounts (in column C):

```
=SUMIF(Difference,"<0",Amount)
```

This formula uses the values in the *Difference* range to determine whether the corresponding values in the *Amount* range contribute to the sum.

 NOTE

You can also use the following array formula to return the sum of the values in the *Amount* range, where the corresponding value in the *Difference* range is negative:

```
{=SUM(IF(Difference<0,Amount))}
```

Summing Values Based on a Text Comparison

The following formula returns the total invoice amounts for the Oregon office:

```
=SUMIF(Office,"=Oregon",Amount)
```

Using the equal sign is optional. The following formula has the same result:

```
=SUMIF(Office,"Oregon",Amount)
```

To sum the invoice amounts for all offices *except* Oregon, use this formula:

```
=SUMIF(Office,"<>Oregon",Amount)
```

Summing Values Based on a Date Comparison

The following formula returns the total invoice amounts that have a due date after May 1, 2007:

```
=SUMIF(DateDue,">="&DATE(2007,5,1),Amount)
```

Notice that the second argument for the SUMIF function is an expression. The expression uses the DATE function, which returns a date. Also, the comparison operator, enclosed in quotation marks, is concatenated (using the & operator) with the result of the DATE function.

The formula that follows returns the total invoice amounts that have a future due date (including today):

```
=SUMIF(DateDue,">="&TODAY(),Amount)
```

Conditional Sums Using Multiple Criteria

The examples in the preceding section all use a single comparison criterion. The examples in this section involve summing cells based on multiple criteria. Because the SUMIF function does not work with multiple criteria, you need to use an array formula or the SUMIFS function (for Excel 2007 only). Figure 7-15 shows the sample worksheet again, for your reference.

	A	B	C	D	E	F
1	InvoiceNum	Office	Amount	DateDue	Today	Difference
2	AG-0145	Oregon	$5,000.00	4/1/2007	5/5/2007	-34
3	AG-0189	California	$450.00	4/19/2007	5/5/2007	-16
4	AG-0220	Washington	$3,211.56	4/28/2007	5/5/2007	-7
5	AG-0310	Oregon	$250.00	4/30/2007	5/5/2007	-5
6	AG-0355	Washington	$125.50	5/4/2007	5/5/2007	-1
7	AG-0409	Washington	$3,000.00	5/10/2007	5/5/2007	5
8	AG-0581	Oregon	$2,100.00	5/23/2007	5/5/2007	18
9	AG-0600	Oregon	$335.39	5/23/2007	5/5/2007	18
10	AG-0602	Washington	$65.00	5/28/2007	5/5/2007	23
11	AG-0633	California	$250.00	5/30/2007	5/5/2007	25
12	TOTAL		$14,787.45			26
13						

Sheet1

Figure 7-15: This worksheet demonstrates summing based on multiple criteria.

NEW

The SUMIFS function can be used to sum a range when multiple conditions are met. The first argument of SUMIFS is the range to be summed. The remaining arguments are 1 to 127 range/criterion pairs that determine which values in the sum range are included. In the following examples, alternatives to SUMIFS are presented for those workbooks that are required to work in versions prior to 2007.

Using And Criteria

Suppose you want to get a sum of both the invoice amounts that are past due as well as associated with the Oregon office. In other words, the value in the Amount range will be summed only if both of the following criteria are met:

- The corresponding value in the *Difference* range is negative.

- The corresponding text in the *Office* range is *Oregon*.

The SUMIFS function was designed for just this task:

```
=SUMIFS(Amount,Difference,"<0",Office,"Oregon")
```

In SUMIFS, the first argument is the range to be summed. The remaining arguments define the criteria and come in pairs. Each pair consists of the criteria range followed by the criteria.

For use with earlier versions of Excel, following array formula also does the job:

```
{=SUM((Difference<0)*(Office="Oregon")*Amount)}
```

This formula creates two new arrays (in memory):

- A Boolean array that consists of TRUE if the corresponding *Difference* value is less than zero; FALSE otherwise

- A Boolean array that consists of TRUE if the corresponding *Office* value equals *Oregon*; FALSE otherwise

Multiplying Boolean values results in the following:

```
TRUE * TRUE = 1
TRUE * FALSE = 0
FALSE * FALSE = 0
```

Therefore, the corresponding *Amount* value returns non-zero only if the corresponding values in the memory arrays are both TRUE. The result produces a sum of the *Amount* values that meet the specified criteria.

 NOTE

You may think that you can rewrite the previous array function as follows, using the SUMPRODUCT function to perform the multiplication and addition:

```
=SUMPRODUCT((Difference<0),(Office="Oregon"),Amount)
```

For some reason, the SUMPRODUCT function does not handle Boolean values properly, so the formula does not work. The following formula, which multiplies the Boolean values by 1, does work:

```
=SUMPRODUCT(1*(Difference<0),1*(Office="Oregon"),Amount)
```

Using Or Criteria

Suppose you want to get a sum of past-due invoice amounts, *or* ones associated with the Oregon office. In other words, the value in the *Amount* range will be summed if either of the following criteria is met:

- The corresponding value in the *Difference* range is negative.

- The corresponding text in the *Office* range is *Oregon.*

The following array formula does the job:

```
{=SUM(IF((Office="Oregon")+(Difference<0),1,0)*Amount)}
```

A plus sign (+) joins the conditions; you can include more than two conditions.

Using And and Or Criteria

As you might expect, things get a bit tricky when your criteria consists of both And and Or operations. For example, you may want to sum the values in the *Amount* range when both of the following conditions are met:

- The corresponding value in the *Difference* range is negative.

- The corresponding text in the *Office* range is *Oregon* or *California.*

Notice that the second condition actually consists of two conditions, joined with Or. Using multiple SUMIFS can accomplish this:

```
=SUMIFS(Amount,Difference,"<0",Office,"Oregon")
+SUMIFS(Amount,Difference,"<0",Office,"California")
```

The following array formula also does the trick:

```
{=SUM((Difference<0)*((Office="Oregon")+(Office="California"))*(Amount))}
```

Chapter 8

Using Lookup Functions

IN THIS CHAPTER

◆ An introduction to formulas that look up values in a table

◆ An overview of the worksheet functions used to perform lookups

◆ Basic lookup formulas

◆ More sophisticated lookup formulas

This chapter discusses various techniques that you can use to look up a value in a table. Excel has three functions (LOOKUP, VLOOKUP, and HLOOKUP) designed for this task, but you may find that these functions don't quite cut it. This chapter provides many lookup examples, including alternative techniques that go well beyond Excel's normal lookup capabilities.

What Is a Lookup Formula?

A *lookup formula* essentially returns a value from a table (in a range) by looking up another value. A common telephone directory provides a good analogy: If you want to find a person's telephone number, you first locate the name (look it up) and then retrieve the corresponding number.

Figure 8-1 shows a simple worksheet that uses several lookup formulas. This worksheet contains a table of employee data (named *EmpData*), beginning in row 7. When you enter a last name into cell B2, lookup formulas in C2:F2 retrieve the matching information from the table. The following lookup formulas use the VLOOKUP function.

Cell	Formula
C2	=VLOOKUP(B2,EmpData,2,FALSE)
D2	=VLOOKUP(B2,EmpData,3,FALSE)
E2	=VLOOKUP(B2,EmpData,4,FALSE)
F2	=VLOOKUP(B2,EmpData,5,FALSE)

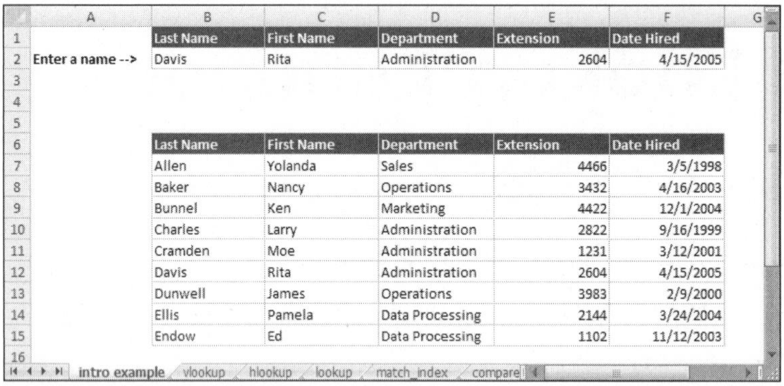

Figure 8-1: Lookup formulas in row 2 look up the information for the employee name in cell B2.

This particular example uses four formulas to return information from the *EmpData* range. In many cases, you'll only want a single value from the table, so use only one formula.

Functions Relevant to Lookups

Several Excel functions are useful when writing formulas to look up information in a table. Table 8-1 lists and describes these functions.

TABLE 8-1   FUNCTIONS USED IN LOOKUP FORMULAS

Function	Description
CHOOSE	Returns a specific value from a list of values (up to 29) supplied as arguments.
HLOOKUP	Horizontal lookup. Searches for a value in the top row of a table and returns a value in the same column from a row you specify in the table.

Function	Description
INDEX	Returns a value (or the reference to a value) from within a table or range.
LOOKUP	Returns a value either from a one-row or one-column range. Another form of the LOOKUP function works like VLOOKUP but is restricted to returning a value from the last column of a range.
MATCH	Returns the relative position of an item in a range that matches a specified value.
OFFSET	Returns a reference to a range that is a specified number of rows and columns from a cell or range of cells.
VLOOKUP	Vertical lookup. Searches for a value in the first column of a table and returns a value in the same row from a column you specify in the table.

The examples in this chapter use the functions listed in Table 8-1.

Basic Lookup Formulas

You can use Excel's basic lookup functions to search a column or row for a lookup value to return another value as a result. Excel provides three basic lookup functions: HLOOKUP, VLOOKUP, and LOOKUP. The MATCH and INDEX functions are often used together to return a cell or relative cell reference for a lookup value.

 ON THE CD

The examples in this section are available on the companion CD-ROM. The filename is
`basic lookup examples.xlsx`.

The VLOOKUP Function

The VLOOKUP function looks up the value in the first column of the lookup table and returns the corresponding value in a specified table column. The lookup table is arranged vertically. The syntax for the VLOOKUP function is

`VLOOKUP(lookup_value,table_array,col_index_num,range_lookup)`

The VLOOKUP function's arguments are as follows:

- **lookup_value:** The value to be looked up in the first column of the lookup table.

- **table_array:** The range that contains the lookup table.

- **col_index_num:** The column number within the table from which the matching value is returned.

- **range_lookup:** Optional. If TRUE or omitted, an approximate match is returned. (If an exact match is not found, the next largest value that is less than *lookup_value* is returned.) If FALSE, VLOOKUP will search for an exact match. If VLOOKUP cannot find an exact match, the function returns #N/A.

NOTE

If the *range_lookup* argument is TRUE or omitted, the first column of the lookup table must be in ascending order. If *lookup_value* is smaller than the smallest value in the first column of *table_array*, VLOOKUP returns #N/A. If the *range_lookup* argument is FALSE, the first column of the lookup table need not be in ascending order. If an exact match is not found, the function returns #N/A.

The classic example of a lookup formula involves an income tax rate schedule (see Figure 8-2). The tax rate schedule shows the income tax rates for various income levels. The following formula (in cell B3) returns the tax rate for the income in cell B2:

```
=VLOOKUP(B2,D2:F7,3)
```

	A	B	C	D	E	F
1				Income is Greater Than or Equal To...	But Less Than or Equal To...	Tax Rate
2	Enter Income:	$45,500		$0	$2,650	15.00%
3	The Tax Rate is:	31.00%		$2,651	$27,300	28.00%
4				$27,301	$58,500	31.00%
5				$58,501	$131,800	36.00%
6				$131,801	$284,700	39.60%
7				$284,701		45.25%
8						

intro example | **vlookup** | hlookup | lookup | match_in

Figure 8-2: Using VLOOKUP to look up a tax rate.

The lookup table resides in a range that consists of three columns (D2:F7). Because the third argument for the VLOOKUP function is 3, the formula returns the corresponding value in the third column of the lookup table.

Note that an exact match is not required. If an exact match is not found in the first column of the lookup table, the VLOOKUP function uses the next largest value that is less than the lookup value. In other words, the function uses the row in which the value you want to look up is greater than or equal to the row value, but less than the value in the next row. In the case of a tax table, this is exactly what you want to happen.

The HLOOKUP Function

The HLOOKUP function works just like the VLOOKUP function except that the lookup table is arranged horizontally instead of vertically. The HLOOKUP function looks up the value in the first row of the lookup table and returns the corresponding value in a specified table row.

The syntax for the HLOOKUP function is

```
HLOOKUP(lookup_value,table_array,row_index_num,range_lookup)
```

The HLOOKUP function's arguments are as follows:

- **lookup_value:** The value to be looked up in the first row of the lookup table.
- **table_array:** The range that contains the lookup table.
- **row_index_num:** The row number within the table from which the matching value is returned.
- **range_lookup:** Optional. If TRUE or omitted, an approximate match is returned. (If an exact match is not found, the next largest value less than *lookup_value* is returned.) If FALSE, VLOOKUP will search for an exact match. If VLOOKUP cannot find an exact match, the function returns #N/A.

TIP

If the *lookup_value* argument is text, it can include the wildcard characters * and ?. An asterisk matches any number of characters, and a question mark matches a single character.

Figure 8-3 shows the tax rate example with a horizontal lookup table (in the range E1:J3). The formula in cell B3 is

```
=HLOOKUP(B2,E1:J3,3)
```

Figure 8-3: Using HLOOKUP to look up a tax rate.

The LOOKUP Function

The LOOKUP function has the following syntax:

```
LOOKUP(lookup_value,lookup_vector,result_vector)
```

The function's arguments are as follows:

- **lookup_value:** The value to be looked up in the *lookup_vector*.
- **lookup_vector:** A single-column or single-row range that contains the values to be looked up. These values must be in ascending order.
- **result_vector:** The single-column or single-row range that contains the values to be returned. It must be the same size as the *lookup_vector*.

The LOOKUP function looks in a one-row or one-column range (*lookup_vector*) for a value (*lookup_value*) and returns a value from the same position in a second one-row or one-column range (*result_vector*).

CAUTION

Values in the *lookup_vector* must be in ascending order. If *lookup_value* is smaller than the smallest value in *lookup_vector*, LOOKUP returns #N/A.

NOTE

The Help system also lists an "array" syntax for the LOOKUP function. This alternative syntax is included for compatibility with other spreadsheet products. In general, you can use the VLOOKUP or HLOOKUP functions rather than the array syntax.

Figure 8-4 shows the tax table again. This time, the formula in cell B3 uses the LOOKUP function to return the corresponding tax rate. The formula in B3 is

```
=LOOKUP(B2,D2:D7,G4:G9)
```

	A	B	C	D	E	F	G	H
1				Income is Greater Than or Equal To...	But Less Than...			
2	Enter Income:	$123,409		$0	$2,650			
3	The Tax Rate is:	36.00%		$2,651	$27,300		Tax Rate	
4				$27,301	$58,500		15.00%	
5				$58,501	$131,800		28.00%	
6				$131,801	$284,700		31.00%	
7				$284,701			36.00%	
8							39.60%	
9							45.25%	
10								
11								

intro example / vlookup / hlookup / **lookup** / match_index

Figure 8-4: Using LOOKUP to look up a tax rate.

CAUTION
If the values in the first column are not arranged in ascending order, the LOOKUP function may return an incorrect value.

Note that LOOKUP (as opposed to VLOOKUP) can return a value that's on a different row than the matched value. If your *lookup_vector* and your *result_vector* are not part of the same table, LOOKUP can be a useful function. If, however, they are part of the same table, VLOOKUP is usually a better choice if for no other reason than that LOOKUP will not work on unsorted data.

Combining the MATCH and INDEX Functions

The MATCH and INDEX functions are often used together to perform lookups. The MATCH function returns the relative position of a cell in a range that matches a specified value. The syntax for MATCH is

```
MATCH(lookup_value,lookup_array,match_type)
```

The MATCH function's arguments are as follows:

- **lookup_value:** The value you want to match in *lookup_array*. If *match_type* is 0 and the *lookup_value* is text, this argument can include the wildcard characters * and ?.

- **lookup_array:** The range being searched.

- **match_type:** An integer (–1, 0, or 1) that specifies how the match is determined.

 NOTE
If match_type is 1, MATCH finds the largest value less than or equal to *lookup_value*. (*lookup_array* must be in ascending order.) If *match_type* is 0, MATCH finds the first value exactly equal to *lookup_value*. If *match_type* is –1, MATCH finds the smallest value greater than or equal to *lookup_value* (*lookup_array* must be in descending order). If you omit the *match_type* argument, this argument is assumed to be 1.

The INDEX function returns a cell from a range. The syntax for the INDEX function is

```
INDEX(array,row_num,column_num)
```

The INDEX function's arguments are as follows:

- **array:** A range
- **row_num:** A row number within the array argument
- **column_num:** A column number within the array argument

Part II

NOTE

If array contains only one row or column, the corresponding *row_num* or *column_num* argument is optional.

Figure 8-5 shows a worksheet with dates, day names, and amounts in columns D, E, and F. When you enter a date in cell B1, the following formula (in cell B2) searches the dates in column D and returns the corresponding amount from column F. The formula in B2 is

```
=INDEX(F2:F21,MATCH(B1,D2:D21,0))
```

	A	B	C	D	E	F	G
1	Date:	1/12/2007		Date	Weekday	Amount	
2	Amount:	189		1/1/2007	Monday	23	
3				1/2/2007	Tuesday	179	
4				1/3/2007	Wednesday	149	
5				1/4/2007	Thursday	196	
6				1/5/2007	Friday	131	
7				1/6/2007	Saturday	179	
8				1/7/2007	Sunday	134	
9				1/8/2007	Monday	179	
10				1/9/2007	Tuesday	193	
11				1/10/2007	Wednesday	191	
12				1/11/2007	Thursday	176	
13				1/12/2007	Friday	189	
14				1/13/2007	Saturday	163	
15				1/14/2007	Sunday	121	
16				1/15/2007	Monday	100	
17				1/16/2007	Tuesday	109	
18				1/17/2007	Wednesday	151	
19				1/18/2007	Thursday	138	
20				1/19/2007	Friday	114	
21				1/20/2007	Saturday	156	
22							

Figure 8-5: Using the INDEX and MATCH functions to perform a lookup.

To understand how this works, start with the MATCH function. This function searches the range D2:D21 for the date in cell B1. It returns the relative row number where the date is found. This value is then used as the second argument for the INDEX function. The result is the corresponding value in F2:F21.

Specialized Lookup Formulas

You can use some additional types of lookup formulas to perform more specialized lookups. For instance, you can look up an exact value, search in another column besides the first in a lookup table, perform a case-sensitive lookup, return a value from among multiple lookup tables, and perform other specialized and complex lookups.

When a Blank Is Not a Zero

Excel's lookup functions treat empty cells in the result range as zeros. The worksheet in the accompanying figure contains a two-column lookup table, and this formula looks up the name in cell B1 and returns the corresponding amount:

```
=VLOOKUP(B1,D2:E8,2)
```

Note that the Amount cell for Charlie is blank, but the formula returns a 0.

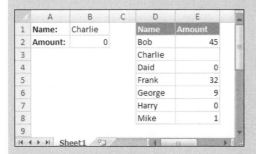

If you need to distinguish zeros from blank cells, you must modify the lookup formula by adding an IF function to check whether the length of the returned value is 0. When the looked up value is blank, the length of the return value is 0. In all other cases, the length of the returned value is non-zero. The following formula displays an empty string (a blank) whenever the length of the looked-up value is zero, and the actual value whenever the length is anything but zero:

```
=IF(LEN(VLOOKUP(B1,D2:E8,2))=0,"",(VLOOKUP(B1,D2:E8,2)))
```

Alternatively, you can specifically check for a blank cell, as in the following formula:

```
=IF(ISBLANK(VLOOKUP(B1,D2:E8,2)),"",(VLOOKUP(B1,D2:E8,2)))
```

ON THE CD

The examples in this section are available on the companion CD-ROM. The filename is `specialized lookup examples.xlsx`.

Looking Up an Exact Value

As demonstrated in the previous examples, VLOOKUP and HLOOKUP don't necessarily require an exact match between the value to be looked up and the values in the lookup table. An example of an approximate match is looking up a tax rate in a tax table. In some cases, you may require a perfect match. For example, when looking up an employee number, you would probably require a perfect match for the number.

To look up an exact value only, use the VLOOKUP (or HLOOKUP) function with the optional fourth argument set to FALSE.

Figure 8-6 shows a worksheet with a lookup table that contains employee numbers (column C) and employee names (column D). The lookup table is named *EmpList.* The formula in cell B2, which follows, looks up the employee number entered in cell B1 and returns the corresponding employee name:

```
=VLOOKUP(B1,EmpList,2,FALSE)
```

	A	B	C	D
1	**Employee No.:**	1101	**Employee Number**	**Employee Name**
2	**Employee Name:**	Melinda Hindquest	873	Charles K. Barkley
3			1109	Francis Jenikins
4			1549	James Brackman
5			1334	Linda Harper
6			1643	Louise Victor
7			1101	Melinda Hindquest
8			1873	Michael Orenthal
9			983	Peter Yates
10			972	Sally Rice
11			1398	Walter Franklin
12				

exact value / lookup to left / case sensitive / multiple tables / grade lookup 1 / grade (

Figure 8-6: This lookup table requires an exact match.

Because the last argument for the VLOOKUP function is FALSE, the function returns an employee name only if an exact match is found. If the employee number is not found, the formula returns #N/A. This, of course, is exactly what you want to happen because returning an approximate match for an employee number makes no sense. Also, notice that the employee numbers in column C are not in ascending order. If the last argument for VLOOKUP is FALSE, the values need not be in ascending order.

NEW

If you prefer to see something other than #N/A when the employee number is not found, you can use the new IFERROR function to test for #NA. The syntax for IFERROR is

```
IFERROR(value, value_if_error)
```

- **value:** Any expression, usually a formula that can result in an error
- **value_if_error:** Any expression including numbers, text, cell references or formulas

IFERROR returns *value* if it's not an error and value_if_error if it is. The following formula displays the text Not Found rather than #N/A:

```
=IFERROR(VLOOKUP(B1,EmpList,2,FALSE) "Not Found")
```

Looking Up a Value to the Left

The VLOOKUP function always looks up a value in the first column of the lookup range. But what if you want to look up a value in a column other than the first column? It would be helpful if you could supply a negative value for the third argument for VLOOKUP — but you can't.

Figure 8-7 illustrates the problem. Suppose you want to look up the batting average (column B, in a range named *Averages*) of a player in column C (in a range named *Players*). The player you want data for appears in a cell named *LookupValue.* The VLOOKUP function won't work because the data is not arranged correctly. One option is to rearrange your data, but sometimes that's not possible.

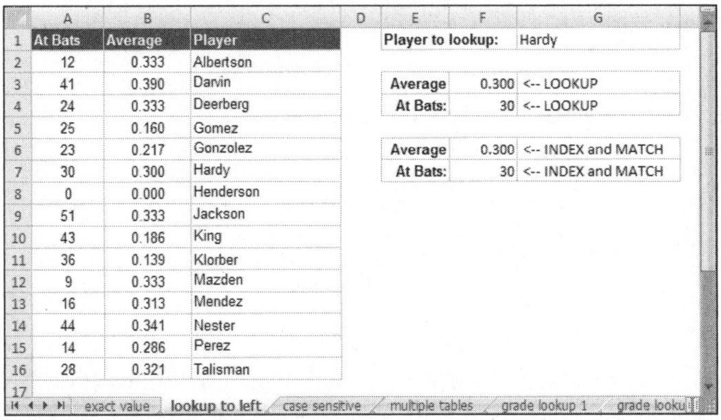

	A	B	C	D	E	F	G
1	At Bats	Average	Player		Player to lookup:	Hardy	
2	12	0.333	Albertson				
3	41	0.390	Darvin		Average	0.300	<-- LOOKUP
4	24	0.333	Deerberg		At Bats:	30	<-- LOOKUP
5	25	0.160	Gomez				
6	23	0.217	Gonzolez		Average	0.300	<-- INDEX and MATCH
7	30	0.300	Hardy		At Bats:	30	<-- INDEX and MATCH
8	0	0.000	Henderson				
9	51	0.333	Jackson				
10	43	0.186	King				
11	36	0.139	Klorber				
12	9	0.333	Mazden				
13	16	0.313	Mendez				
14	44	0.341	Nester				
15	14	0.286	Perez				
16	28	0.321	Talisman				

Figure 8-7: The VLOOKUP function can't look up a value in column B, based on a value in column C.

Another solution is to use the LOOKUP function, which requires two range arguments. The following formula (in cell F3) returns the batting average from column B of the player name contained in the cell named *LookupValue:*

```
=LOOKUP(LookupValue,Players,Averages)
```

Using the LOOKUP function requires that the lookup range (in this case, the *Players* range) is in ascending order. In addition to this limitation, the formula suffers from a slight problem: If you enter a nonexistent player (in other words, the *LookupValue* cell contains a value not found in the *Players* range), the formula returns an erroneous result.

A better solution uses the INDEX and MATCH functions. The formula that follows works just like the previous one except that it returns #N/A if the player is not found. Another advantage to using this formula is that the player names need not be sorted.

```
=INDEX(Averages,MATCH(LookupValue,Players,0))
```

Performing a Case-Sensitive Lookup

Excel's lookup functions (LOOKUP, VLOOKUP, and HLOOKUP) are not case sensitive. For example, if you write a lookup formula to look up the text *budget,* the formula considers any of the following a match: *BUDGET, Budget,* or *BuDgEt.*

Figure 8-8 shows a simple example. Range D2:D7 is named *Range1*, and range E2:E7 is named *Range2*. The word to be looked up appears in cell B1 (named *Value*).

	A	B	C	D	E
1	Word	DOG		Range1	Range2
2	Result:	300		APPLE	100
3				apple	200
4				DOG	300
5				dog	400
6				CANDY	500
7				candy	600
8					

exact value　lookup to left　**case sensitive**

Figure 8-8: Using an array formula to perform a case-sensitive lookup.

The array formula that follows is in cell B2. This formula does a case-sensitive lookup in *Range1* and returns the corresponding value in *Range2*.

```
{=INDEX(Range2,MATCH(TRUE,EXACT(Value,Range1),0))}
```

The formula looks up the word *DOG* (uppercase) and returns 300. The following standard LOOKUP formula (which is not case sensitive) returns 400:

```
=LOOKUP(Value,Range1,Range2)
```

NOTE

When entering an array formula, remember to use Ctrl+Shift+Enter.

Choosing among Multiple Lookup Tables

You can, of course, have any number of lookup tables in a worksheet. In some cases, your formula may need to decide which lookup table to use. Figure 8-9 shows an example.

	A	B	C	D	E	F	G	H	I	J	K
1	Sales Rep	Years	Sales	Comm. Rate	Commission		<3 Years Tenure			3+ Years Tenure	
2	Benson	2	120,000	7.00%	8,400		Amt Sold	Rate		Amt Sold	Rate
3	Davidson	1	210,921	7.00%	14,764		0	1.50%		0	2.00%
4	Ellison	1	100,000	7.00%	7,000		5,000	3.25%		50,000	6.25%
5	Gomez	2	87,401	6.00%	5,244		10,000	3.50%		100,000	7.25%
6	Hernandez	6	310,983	9.25%	28,766		20,000	5.00%		200,000	8.25%
7	Kelly	3	43,902	2.00%	878		50,000	6.00%		300,000	9.25%
8	Martin	2	121,021	7.00%	8,471		100,000	7.00%		500,000	10.00%
9	Oswald	3	908	2.00%	18		250,000	8.00%			
10	Reginald	1	0	1.50%	0						
11	Veras	4	359,832	9.25%	33,284						
12	Wilmington	4	502,983	10.00%	50,298						
13											

exact value　lookup to left　case sensitive　**multiple tables**　grade lookup 1　grade lookup 2　GPA 1

Figure 8-9: This worksheet demonstrates the use of multiple lookup tables.

This workbook calculates sales commission and contains two lookup tables: G3:H9 (named *Table1*) and J3:K8 (named *Table2*). The commission rate for a particular sales representative depends on two factors: the sales rep's years of service (column B) and the amount sold (column C). Column D contains formulas that look up the commission rate from the appropriate table. For example, the formula in cell D2 is

```
=VLOOKUP(C2,IF(B2<3,Table1,Table2),2)
```

The second argument for the VLOOKUP function consists of an IF formula that uses the value in column B to determine which lookup table to use.

The formula in column E simply multiplies the sales amount in column C by the commission rate in column D. The formula in cell E2, for example, is

```
=C2*D2
```

Determining Letter Grades for Test Scores

A common use of a lookup table is to assign letter grades for test scores. Figure 8-10 shows a worksheet with student test scores. The range E2:F6 (named *GradeList*) displays a lookup table used to assign a letter grade to a test score.

	A	B	C	D	E	F
1	Student	Score	Grade		Score	Grade
2	Adams	36	F		0	F
3	Baker	68	D		40	D
4	Camden	50	D		70	C
5	Dailey	77	C		80	B
6	Gomez	92	A		90	A
7	Hernandez	100	A			
8	Jackson	74	C			
9	Maplethorpe	45	D			
10	Paulson	60	D			
11	Ramirez	89	B			
12	Sosa	99	A			
13	Thompson	91	A			
14	Wilson	59	D			
15						

grade lookup / GPA 1 / GPA 2 / 2-way lookup / 2-col

Figure 8-10: Looking up letter grades for test scores.

Column C contains formulas that use the VLOOKUP function and the lookup table to assign a grade based on the score in column B. The formula in C2, for example, is

```
=VLOOKUP(B2,GradeList,2)
```

When the lookup table is small (as in the example shown in Figure 8-10), you can use a literal array in place of the lookup table. The formula that follows, for example, returns a letter grade without using a lookup table. Rather, the information in the lookup table is hard-coded into an array constant. See Chapter 14 for more information about array constants.

```
=VLOOKUP(B2,{0,"F";40,"D";70,"C";80,"B";90,"A"},2)
```

Another approach, which uses a more legible formula, is to use the LOOKUP function with two array arguments:

```
=LOOKUP(B2,{0,40,70,80,90},{"F","D","C","B","A"})
```

Finally, whenever you can easily convert your input, the number grade in this case, into the integers 1 to 29, the CHOOSE function becomes an option. The number grades are divided by 10, the decimal is stripped off, and 1 is added to it to produce the numbers 1 to 11. The remaining arguments define the return values for those 11 options.

```
=CHOOSE(TRUNC(B2/10)+1,"F","F","F","F","D","D","D","C","B","A","A")
```

Calculating a Grade Point Average

A student's *grade point average* (GPA) is a numerical measure of the average grade received for classes taken. This discussion assumes a letter grade system, in which each letter grade is assigned a numeric value (A=4, B=3, C=2, D=1, and F=0). The GPA comprises an average of the numeric grade values, weighted by the credit hours of the course. A one-hour course, for example, receives less weight than a three-hour course. The GPA ranges from 0 (all Fs) to 4.00 (all As).

Figure 8-11 shows a worksheet with information for a student. This student took five courses, for a total of 13 credit hours. Range B2:B6 is named *CreditHours*. The grades for each course appear in column C (Range C2:C6 is named *Grades*). Column D uses a lookup formula to calculate the grade value for each course. The lookup formula in cell D2, for example, follows. This formula uses the lookup table in G2:H6 (named *GradeTable*).

```
=VLOOKUP(C2,GradeTable,2,FALSE)
```

	A	B	C	D	E	F	G	H
1	Course	Credit Hrs	Grade	Grade Val	Weighted Val		GradeTable	
2	Psych 101	3	A	4	12		A	4
3	PhysEd	2	C	2	4		B	3
4	PoliSci 101	4	B	3	12		C	2
5	IndepStudy	1	A	4	4		D	1
6	IntroMath	3	A	4	12		F	0
7								
8	GPA:	3.38		<-- Requires multiple formulas and lookup table				
9								
10		3.38		<--Array formula				

grade lookup | GPA | 2-way lookup | 2-column lookup | cell address | closest m

Figure 8-11: Using multiple formulas to calculate a GPA.

Formulas in column E calculate the weighted values. The formula in E2 is

```
=D2*B2
```

Cell B8 computes the GPA by using the following formula:

```
=SUM(E2:E6)/SUM(B2:B6)
```

The preceding formulas work fine, but you can streamline the GPA calculation quite a bit. In fact, you can use a single array formula to make this calculation and avoid using the lookup table and the formulas in columns D and E. This array formula does the job:

```
{=SUM((MATCH(Grades,{"F","D","C","B","A"},0)-1)*CreditHours)
/SUM(CreditHours)}
```

Performing a Two-Way Lookup

Figure 8-12 shows a worksheet with a table that displays product sales by month. To retrieve sales for a particular month and product, the user enters a month in cell B1 and a product name in cell B2.

	A	B	C	D	E	F	G	H	I
					Widgets	**Sprockets**	**Snapholytes**	**Combined**	
1	Month:	July		January	2,892	1,771	4,718	9,381	
2	Product:	Sprockets		February	3,380	4,711	2,615	10,706	
3				March	3,744	3,223	5,312	12,279	
4	Month Offset:	8		April	3,221	2,438	1,108	6,767	
5	Product Offset:	3		May	4,839	1,999	1,994	8,832	
6	Sales:	3,337		June	3,767	5,140	3,830	12,737	
7				July	5,467	3,337	3,232	12,036	
8				August	3,154	4,895	1,607	9,656	
9	Single-formula -->	3,337		September	1,718	2,040	1,563	5,321	
10				October	1,548	1,061	2,590	5,199	
11				November	5,083	3,558	3,960	12,601	
12				December	5,753	2,839	3,013	11,605	
13				Total	44,566	37,012	35,542	117,120	
14									
15									

grade lookup / GPA / 2-way lookup / 2-column lookup / cell address / closest match

Figure 8-12: This table demonstrates a two-way lookup.

To simplify things, the worksheet uses the following named ranges:

Name	Refers To
Month	B1
Product	B2
Table	D1:H14
MonthList	D1:D14
ProductList	D1:H1

The following formula (in cell B4) uses the MATCH function to return the position of the Month within the *MonthList* range. For example, if the month is January, the formula returns 2 because January is the second item in the *MonthList* range. (The first item is a blank cell, D1.)

```
=MATCH(Month,MonthList,0)
```

The formula in cell B5 works similarly but uses the *ProductList* range:

```
=MATCH(Product,ProductList,0)
```

The final formula, in cell B6, returns the corresponding sales amount. It uses the INDEX function with the results from cells B4 and B5.

```
=INDEX(Table,B4,B5)
```

You can, of course, combine these formulas into a single formula, as shown here:

```
=INDEX(Table,MATCH(Month,MonthList,0),MATCH(Product,ProductList,0))
```

TIP

You can use the Lookup Wizard add-in to create this type of formula (see Figure 8-13). The Lookup Wizard add-in is distributed with Excel. After installing the add-in, access the Lookup Wizard by choosing Formulas⇨Solutions⇨Lookup.

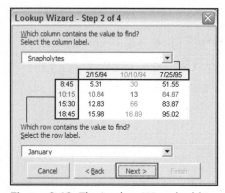

Figure 8-13: The Lookup Wizard add-in can create a formula that performs a two-way lookup.

TIP

Another way to accomplish a two-way lookup is to provide a name for each row and column of the table. A quick way to do this is to select the table and use Formulas⇨

Defined Names➪Create from Selection. After creating the names, you can use a simple formula to perform the two-way lookup, such as

```
=Sprockets July
```

This formula, which uses the range intersection operator (a space), returns July sales for Sprockets. To refer to the cells where the month and product are entered, use

```
=INDIRECT(Month) INDIRECT(Product)
```

This formula converts the values in the cells Month and Product into range references and finds the intersection. See Chapter 3 for details about the range intersection operator.

Performing a Two-Column Lookup

Some situations may require a lookup based on the values in two columns. Figure 8-14 shows an example.

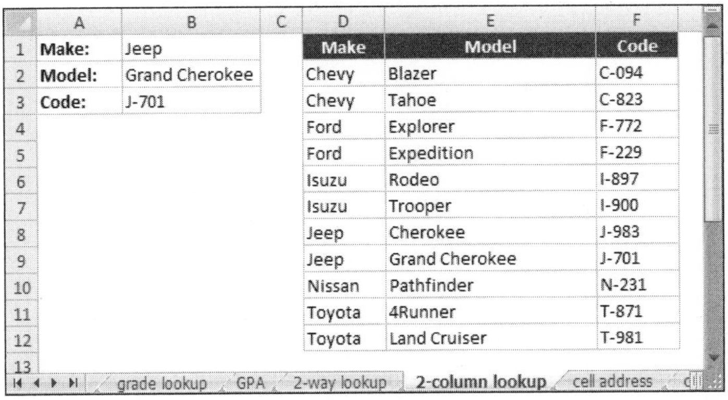

	A	B	C	D	E	F
1	Make:	Jeep		Make	Model	Code
2	Model:	Grand Cherokee		Chevy	Blazer	C-094
3	Code:	J-701		Chevy	Tahoe	C-823
4				Ford	Explorer	F-772
5				Ford	Expedition	F-229
6				Isuzu	Rodeo	I-897
7				Isuzu	Trooper	I-900
8				Jeep	Cherokee	J-983
9				Jeep	Grand Cherokee	J-701
10				Nissan	Pathfinder	N-231
11				Toyota	4Runner	T-871
12				Toyota	Land Cruiser	T-981
13						

Figure 8-14: This workbook performs a lookup by using information in two columns (D and E).

The lookup table contains automobile makes and models, and a corresponding code for each. The worksheet uses named ranges, as shown here:

F2:F12	*Code*
B1	*Make*
B2	*Model*
D2:D12	*Range1*
E2:E12	*Range2*

The following array formula displays the corresponding code for an automobile make and model:

```
{=INDEX(Code,MATCH(Make&Model,Range1&Range2,0))}
```

This formula works by concatenating the contents of *Make* and *Model,* and then searching for this text in an array consisting of the concatenated corresponding text in *Range1* and *Range2.*

Determining the Address of a Value within a Range

Most of the time, you want your lookup formula to return a value. You may, however, need to determine the cell address of a particular value within a range. For example, Figure 8-15 shows a worksheet with a range of numbers that occupy a single column (named *Data*). Cell B1, which contains the value to look up, is named *Target.*

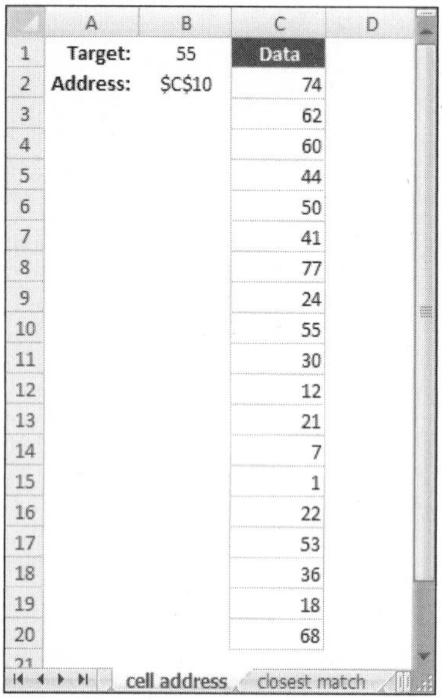

Figure 8-15: The formula in cell B2 returns the address in the *Data* range for the value in cell B1.

The formula in cell B2, which follows, returns the address of the cell in the *Data* range that contains the *Target* value:

```
=ADDRESS(ROW(Data)+MATCH(Target,Data,0)-1,COLUMN(Data))
```

If the *Data* range occupies a single row, use this formula to return the address of the *Target* value:

```
=ADDRESS(ROW(Data),COLUMN(Data)+MATCH(Target,Data,0)-1)
```

If the *Data* range contains more than one instance of the *Target* value, the address of the first occurrence is returned. If the *Target* value is not found in the *Data* range, the formula returns #N/A.

Looking Up a Value by Using the Closest Match

The VLOOKUP and HLOOKUP functions are useful in the following situations:

- You need to identify an exact match for a target value. Use FALSE as the function's fourth argument.

- You need to locate an approximate match. If the function's fourth argument is TRUE or omitted and an exact match is not found, the next largest value that is less than the lookup value is returned.

But what if you need to look up a value based on the *closest* match? Neither VLOOKUP nor HLOOKUP can do the job.

Figure 8-16 shows a worksheet with student names in column A and values in column B. Range B2:B20 is named *Data*. Cell E2, named *Target,* contains a value to search for in the *Data* range. Cell E3, named *ColOffset,* contains a value that represents the column offset from the *Data* range.

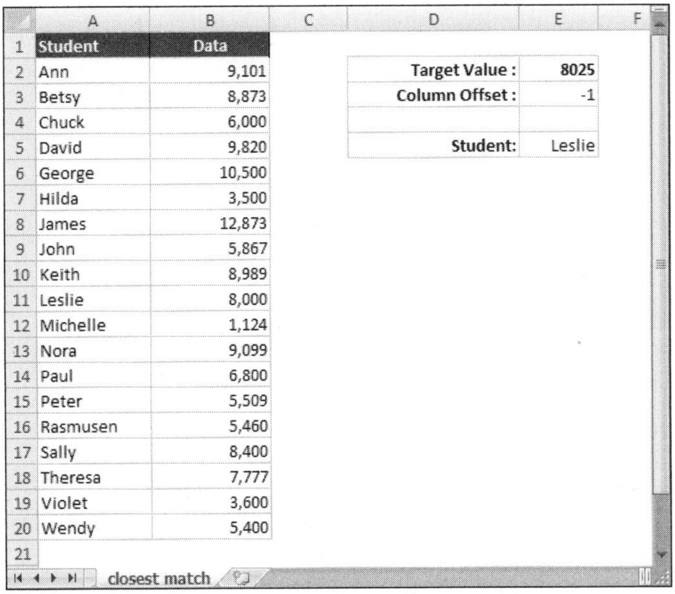

	A	B	C	D	E	F
1	Student	Data				
2	Ann	9,101		Target Value :	8025	
3	Betsy	8,873		Column Offset :	-1	
4	Chuck	6,000				
5	David	9,820		Student:	Leslie	
6	George	10,500				
7	Hilda	3,500				
8	James	12,873				
9	John	5,867				
10	Keith	8,989				
11	Leslie	8,000				
12	Michelle	1,124				
13	Nora	9,099				
14	Paul	6,800				
15	Peter	5,509				
16	Rasmusen	5,460				
17	Sally	8,400				
18	Theresa	7,777				
19	Violet	3,600				
20	Wendy	5,400				
21						

closest match

Figure 8-16: This workbook demonstrates how to perform a lookup by using the closest match.

The array formula that follows identifies the closest match to the *Target* value in the *Data* range and returns the names of the corresponding student in column A (that is, the column with an offset of –1). The formula returns *Leslie* (with a matching value of 8,000, which is the one closest to the *Target* value of 8,025).

```
{=INDIRECT(ADDRESS(ROW(Data)+MATCH(MIN(ABS(Target-Data)),
ABS(Target-Data),0)-1,COLUMN(Data)+ColOffset))}
```

If two values in the *Data* range are equidistant from the *Target* value, the formula uses the first one in the list.

The value in *ColOffset* can be negative (for a column to the left of *Data*), positive (for a column to the right of *Data*), or 0 (for the actual closest match value in the *Data* range).

To understand how this formula works, you need to understand the INDIRECT function. This function's first argument is a text string in the form of a cell reference (or a reference to a cell that contains a text string). In this example, the text string is created by the ADDRESS function, which accepts a row and column reference and returns a cell address.

Looking Up a Value Using Linear Interpolation

Interpolation refers to the process of estimating a missing value by using existing values. For an illustration of this concept, see Figure 8-17. Column D contains a list of values (named *x*) and column E contains corresponding values (named *y*).

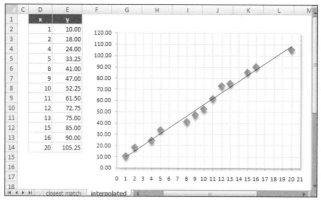

Figure 8-17: This workbook demonstrates a table lookup using linear interpolation.

The worksheet also contains a chart that depicts the relationship between the *x* range and the *y* range graphically. As you can see, there is an approximate linear relationship between the corresponding values in the *x* and *y* ranges: As *x* increases, so does *y*. Notice that the values in the *x* range are not strictly consecutive. For example, the *x* range doesn't contain the following values: 3, 6, 7, 14, 17, 18, and 19.

You can create a lookup formula that looks up a value in the *x* range and returns the corresponding value from the *y* range. But what if you want to estimate the *y* value for a missing *x* value? A normal lookup formula does not return a very good result because it simply returns an existing *y* value (not an estimated *y* value). For example, the following formula looks up the value 3 and returns 18.00 (the value that corresponds to 2 in the *x* range):

```
=LOOKUP(3,x,y)
```

In such a case, you probably want to interpolate. In other words, because the lookup value (3) is halfway between existing *x* values (2 and 4), you want the formula to return a *y* value of 21.00 — a value halfway between the corresponding *y* values 18.00 and 24.00.

FORMULAS TO PERFORM A LINEAR INTERPOLATION

Figure 8-18 shows a worksheet with formulas in column B. The value to be looked up is entered into cell B1. The final formula, in cell B16, returns the result. If the value in B3 is found in the *x* range, the corresponding *y* value is returned. If the value in B3 is not found, the formula in B16 returns an estimated *y* value, obtained using linear interpolation.

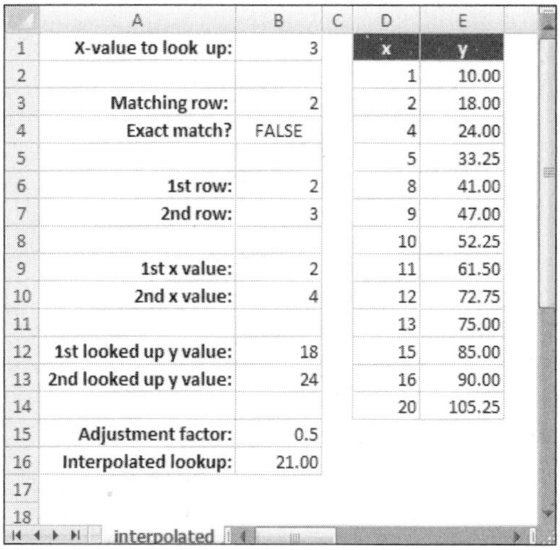

	A	B	C	D	E
1	X-value to look up:	3		**x**	**y**
2				1	10.00
3	Matching row:	2		2	18.00
4	Exact match?	FALSE		4	24.00
5				5	33.25
6	1st row:	2		8	41.00
7	2nd row:	3		9	47.00
8				10	52.25
9	1st x value:	2		11	61.50
10	2nd x value:	4		12	72.75
11				13	75.00
12	1st looked up y value:	18		15	85.00
13	2nd looked up y value:	24		16	90.00
14				20	105.25
15	Adjustment factor:	0.5			
16	Interpolated lookup:	21.00			
17					
18					

interpolated

Figure 8-18: Column B contains formulas that perform a lookup using linear interpolation.

It's critical that the values in the *x* range appear in ascending order. If B1 contains a value less than the lowest value in *x* or greater than the largest value in *x*, the formula returns an error value. Table 8-2 lists and describes these formulas.

TABLE 8-2   FORMULAS FOR A LOOKUP USING LINEAR INTERPOLATION

Cell	Formula	Description
B3	=LOOKUP(B1,x,x)	Performs a standard lookup on the *x* range and returns the looked-up value.
B4	=B1=B3	Returns TRUE if the looked-up value equals the value to be looked up.
B6	=MATCH(B3,x,0)	Returns the row number of the *x* range that contains the matching value.
B7	=IF(B4,B6,B6+1)	Returns the same row as the formula in B6 if an exact match is found. Otherwise, it adds 1 to the result in B6.
B9	=INDEX(x,B6)	Returns the *x* value that corresponds to the row in B6.
B10	=INDEX(x,B7)	Returns the *x* value that corresponds to the row in B7.

continued

Part II

TABLE 8-2   FORMULAS FOR A LOOKUP USING LINEAR INTERPOLATION
(continued)

Cell	Formula	Description
B12	=LOOKUP(B9,x,y)	Returns the *y* value that corresponds to the *x* value in B9.
B13	=LOOKUP(B10,x,y)	Returns the *y* value that corresponds to the *x* value in B10.
B15	=IF(B4,0,(B1-B3)/(B10-B9))	Calculates an adjustment factor based on the difference between the *x* values.
B16	=B12+((B13-B12)*B15)	Calculates the estimated *y* value using the adjustment factor in B15.

COMBINING THE LOOKUP AND TREND FUNCTIONS

Another slightly different approach, which you may find preferable to performing lookup using linear interpolation, uses the LOOKUP and TREND functions. One advantage is that it requires only one formula (see Figure 8-19).

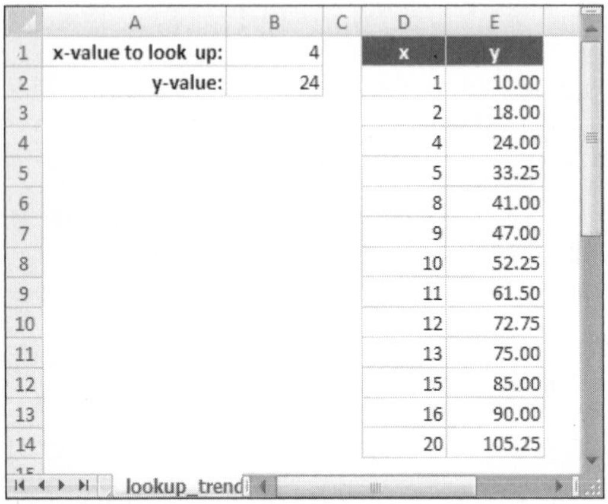

Figure 8-19: This worksheet uses a formula that uses the LOOKUP function and the TREND function.

The formula in cell B3 follows. This formula uses an IF function to make a decision. If an exact match is found in the *x* range, the formula returns the corresponding *y* value (using the LOOKUP function). If an exact match is not found, the formula uses the TREND function to return the calculated "best-fit" *y* value. (It does not perform a linear interpolation.)

```
=IF(B1=LOOKUP(B1,x,x),LOOKUP(INDEX(x,MATCH
(LOOKUP(B1,x,x),x,0)),x,y),TREND(y,x,B1))
```

Chapter 9

Tables and Worksheet Databases

IN THIS CHAPTER

◆ Using the new Excel 2007 table feature

◆ Basic information about using tables and worksheet databases

◆ Filtering data using simple criteria

◆ Using advanced filtering to filter data by specifying more complex criteria

◆ Understanding how to create a criteria range for use with advanced filtering or database functions

◆ Using the SUBTOTAL function to summarize data in a table

One of the most significant new features in Excel 2007 is tables. A *table* is a rectangular range of data that usually has a row of text headings to describe the contents of each column. Excel, of course, has always supported tables, but the new implementation lets you designate a range as an "official" table, which makes common tasks much easier. More importantly, the new table features may help eliminate some common errors.

This chapter discusses the new Excel 2007 table features and also covers what I refer to as *worksheet databases,* which are essentially tables of data that have not been converted to an official table.

Tables and Terminology

It seems that Microsoft can't quite make up its mind when it comes to naming some of Excel's features. Excel 2003 introduced a feature called *lists*, which is a way of working with what is often called a *worksheet database*. In Excel 2007, the list features evolved into a much more useful feature called *tables*. To confuse the issue even more, Excel also has a feature called *data tables*, which has nothing at all to do with the table feature. In this section, I define the terms that I use throughout this chapter.

- **Worksheet database:** An organized collection of information contained in a rectangular range of cells. More specifically, a worksheet database consists of a row of headers (descriptive text), followed by additional rows of data comprising values or text. I use the term *database* loosely. An Excel worksheet database is more like a single table in a standard database. Unlike a conventional database, Excel does not allow you to set up relationships between tables.

- **Table:** A worksheet database that has been converted to a special range by using the Insert➪Tables➪Table command. Converting a worksheet database into an official table offers several advantages (and a few disadvantages), as I explain in this chapter.

A Worksheet Database Example

Figure 9-1 shows a small worksheet database that contains employee information. It consists of 1 header row, 6 columns, and 20 rows of data. Notice that the data consists of several different types: text, numerical values, dates, and logical values. Column C contains a formula that calculates the monthly salary from the value in column B.

In database terminology, the columns in a worksheet database are *fields,* and the rows are *records.* Using this terminology, the range shown in the figure has 6 fields (Name, Annual Salary, Monthly Salary, Location, Date Hired, and Exempt) and 20 records.

The size of a database that you develop in Excel is limited by the size of a single worksheet. In theory, a worksheet database can have more than 16,000 fields and can consist of more than one million records. In practice, you cannot create a database of this size because it requires an enormous amount of memory, and the weight will cause even a state-of-the-art computer to slow to a crawl.

A Table Example

Figure 9-2 shows the employee worksheet database after I converted it to a table, using Insert➪Tables➪Table.

	Name	Annual Salary	Monthly Salary	Location	Date Hired	Exempt
2	Joe Morrison	$140,000	$11,667	Seattle	1/29/2000	TRUE
3	Douglas Williams	$89,900	$7,492	Portland	10/10/2006	TRUE
4	Clark Bickerson	$82,900	$6,908	Los Angeles	7/31/2003	TRUE
5	James millen	$79,700	$6,642	Los Angeles	4/21/2000	FALSE
6	Chris Poundsworth	$79,200	$6,600	Seattle	5/24/2000	TRUE
7	Phillip A. Todd	$78,200	$6,517	Portland	6/18/2007	FALSE
8	Richard E. Card	$75,700	$6,308	Seattle	3/6/2005	FALSE
9	Steven H. Katz	$75,200	$6,267	Los Angeles	11/13/1999	TRUE
10	Stephen C. Carter	$72,400	$6,033	Los Angeles	11/14/2003	TRUE
12	Charles S. Billings	$62,200	$5,183	Los Angeles	6/20/2001	FALSE
13	Michael Hayden	$53,400	$4,450	Seattle	4/9/2006	FALSE
14	Ivan Silberstein	$50,900	$4,242	Los Angeles	12/9/2006	FALSE
15	Tom Brown	$49,700	$4,142	Seattle	3/17/2006	FALSE
16	Robert H. Miller	$40,000	$3,333	Portland	1/10/1999	FALSE
17	Kurt Kamichoff	$35,600	$2,967	Los Angeles	2/27/2002	FALSE
18	John T. Foster	$35,000	$2,917	Seattle	10/6/2002	FALSE
19	Thomas E. Abbott	$32,300	$2,692	Los Angeles	5/21/2002	FALSE
20	Rick Fogerty	$28,100	$2,342	Portland	5/21/2004	FALSE
21	Jeffrey P. Jones	$27,800	$2,317	Seattle	8/30/2003	FALSE

Figure 9-1: A typical worksheet database.

	Name	Annual Salary	Monthly Salary	Location	Date Hired	Exempt
2	Joe Morrison	$140,000	$11,667	Seattle	1/29/2000	TRUE
3	Douglas Williams	$89,900	$7,492	Portland	10/10/2006	TRUE
4	Clark Bickerson	$82,900	$6,908	Los Angeles	7/31/2003	TRUE
5	James millen	$79,700	$6,642	Los Angeles	4/21/2000	FALSE
6	Chris Poundsworth	$79,200	$6,600	Seattle	5/24/2000	TRUE
7	Phillip A. Todd	$78,200	$6,517	Portland	6/18/2007	FALSE
8	Richard E. Card	$75,700	$6,308	Seattle	3/6/2005	FALSE
9	Steven H. Katz	$75,200	$6,267	Los Angeles	11/13/1999	TRUE
10	Stephen C. Carter	$72,400	$6,033	Los Angeles	11/14/2003	TRUE
12	Charles S. Billings	$62,200	$5,183	Los Angeles	6/20/2001	FALSE
13	Michael Hayden	$53,400	$4,450	Seattle	4/9/2006	FALSE
14	Ivan Silberstein	$50,900	$4,242	Los Angeles	12/9/2006	FALSE
15	Tom Brown	$49,700	$4,142	Seattle	3/17/2006	FALSE
16	Robert H. Miller	$40,000	$3,333	Portland	1/10/1999	FALSE
17	Kurt Kamichoff	$35,600	$2,967	Los Angeles	2/27/2002	FALSE
18	John T. Foster	$35,000	$2,917	Seattle	10/6/2002	FALSE
19	Thomas E. Abbott	$32,300	$2,692	Los Angeles	5/21/2002	FALSE
20	Rick Fogerty	$28,100	$2,342	Portland	5/21/2004	FALSE
21	Jeffrey P. Jones	$27,800	$2,317	Seattle	8/30/2003	FALSE

Figure 9-2: A worksheet database, converted to a table.

Part II

What's the difference between a worksheet database and a table?

- Activating any cell in the table gives you access to a new Table Tools context tab on the Ribbon.

- The cells contain background color and text color formatting, applied automatically by Excel. This formatting is optional.

- Each column header contains a button that, when clicked, displays a drop-down with sorting and filtering options.

- If you scroll the worksheet down so that the header row disappears, the table headers replace the column letters in the worksheet header.

- Tables support calculated columns. A single formula entered in a column is propagated automatically to all cells in the column.

- Tables support structured references. Rather than using cell references, formulas can use table names and column headers.

- The lower-right corner of the lower-right cell contains a small control that you can click and drag to extend the table's size, either horizontally (add more columns) or vertically (add more rows).

- Excel is able to remove duplicate rows automatically.

- Selecting rows and columns within the table is simplified.

Uses For Worksheet Databases and Tables

People use worksheet databases (or tables) for a wide variety of purposes. For some users, a worksheet database simply keeps track of information (for example, customer information); others use a database to store data that ultimately appears in a summary report. Common database operations include

- Entering data into the database

- Filtering the database to display only the rows that meet certain criteria

- Sorting the database

- Inserting formulas to calculate subtotals

- Creating formulas to calculate results on the data, filtered by certain criteria

- Creating a summary table of the data in the table (often done by using a pivot table)

When creating a worksheet database or table, it helps to plan the organization of your information. See the sidebar, "Designing a Worksheet Database or Table," for guidelines to help you create tables.

Designing a Worksheet Database or Table

Although Excel is quite accommodating with regard to the information that is stored in a worksheet database, planning the organization of your information is important and makes the data easier to work with. Remember the following guidelines when you create a worksheet database or table:

- **Insert descriptive labels (one for each column) in the first row (the *header row*).** If you use lengthy labels, consider using the Wrap Text format so that you don't have to widen the columns.

- **Make sure that each column contains only one type of information.** For example, don't mix dates and text in a single column.

- **Consider using formulas that perform calculations on other fields in the same record.** If you use formulas that refer to cells outside the database, make these absolute references; otherwise, you get unexpected results when you sort the table.

- **Don't leave any empty rows within the worksheet database.** For normal worksheet database operations, Excel determines the database boundaries automatically, and an empty row signals the end of the data. If you're working with a table, empty rows are allowed because Excel keeps track of the table dimensions.

- **Freeze the first row.** Select the cell in the first column and first row of your table and then choose View⇨Freeze Panes⇨Freeze Top Row to make sure that you can see the headings when you scroll the table. This action is not necessary with a table because table headers replace the column letters when you scroll down.

Don't worry if you later discover that your worksheet database or table needs one or more additional columns. Excel is very flexible, and adding new columns is easy.

Working with Tables

It may take you a while to get use to working with tables, but you'll soon discover that a table offers many advantages over a standard worksheet database.

A major advantage of using a table is the ease with which you can format the table as well as change the formatting. See "Changing the Look of a Table," later in this chapter.

If you normally use a lot of named ranges in your formulas, you may find the table syntax to be a welcome alternative to creating names for each column and the table as a whole — not to mention the advantage having named ranges that adjust automatically as the table changes.

A similar advantage is apparent when working with charts. If you create a chart from data in a table, the chart series expands automatically when you add new data. If the chart data isn't in a table, you need to edit the chart series definitions manually (or resort to a few tricks) when new data is added.

If your company happens to use Microsoft's SharePoint service, you'll see yet another advantage. You can easily publish a table to your SharePoint server. To do so, choose Table Tools Design⇨External Table Data⇨Export⇨Export Table to SharePoint List. This command displays a dialog box in which you enter the address of your server and provide additional information necessary to publish your designated table.

Tables, however, do have a few limitations compared to worksheet database. (See the sidebar, "Table Limitations.")

The sections that follow cover common operations that you perform with a table in Excel 2007.

Creating a Table

Although Excel allows you to create a table from an empty range, most of the time, you'll create a table from an existing range of data (a worksheet database). The following instructions assume that you already have a range of data that's suitable for a table.

Table Limitations

An Excel 2007 table offers several advantages over a normal worksheet database. For some reason, the Excel designers imposed some restrictions and limitations on tables. Among them are that

- If a worksheet contains a table, you cannot create or use custom views (View⇨Workbook Views⇨Custom Views).

- A table cannot contain multicell array formulas.

- You cannot insert automatic subtotals (Data⇨Outline⇨Subtotal).

- You cannot share a workbook that contains a table (Review⇨Changes⇨Protect and Share Workbook).

- You cannot track changes in a workbook that contains a table (Review⇨Changes⇨Track Changes).

- You cannot use the Home⇨Alignment⇨Merge & Center command cells in a table (which makes sense because doing so would break up the rows or columns).

If you encounter any of these limitations, just convert the table back to a worksheet database by using Table Tools⇨Design⇨Convert To Range.

1. Make sure that the range doesn't contain any completely blank rows or columns.

2. Activate any cell within the range.

3. Choose Insert⇨Tables⇨Table (or press Ctrl+T). Excel responds with its Create Table dialog box. Excel tries to guess the range and also whether the table has a header row. Most of the time, it guesses correctly. If not, make your corrections before you click OK.

After you click OK, the table is automatically formatted, and Filter mode for the table is enabled. In addition, Excel displays its Table Tools⇨contextual tab (as shown in Figure 9-3). The controls on this tab are relevant to working with a table.

Figure 9-3: When you select a cell in a table, you can use the commands on the Table Tools contextual menu.

TIP

Another method for converting a range into a table is Home⇨Styles⇨Format as Table. By selecting a format, you force Excel to first designate the range as a table.

In the Create Table dialog box, Excel may guess the table's dimensions incorrectly if the table isn't separated from other information by at least one empty row or column. If Excel guesses incorrectly, just specify the exact range for the table in the dialog box. Or, click Cancel and rearrange your worksheet such that the table is separated from your other data by at least one blank row or column.

Changing the Look of a Table

When you create a table, Excel applies the default table style. The actual appearance depends on which document theme is used in the workbook. If you prefer a different look, you can easily change the entire look of the table.

Select any cell in the table and choose Table Tools⇨Design⇨Table Styles. The Ribbon shows one row of styles, but if you click the bottom of the vertical scrollbar, the table styles group expands, as shown in Figure 9-4. The styles are grouped into three categories: Light, Medium, and Dark. Notice that you get a live preview as you move your mouse among the styles. When you see one you like, just click to make it permanent.

For a different set of color choices, use Page Layout⇨Themes⇨Themes to select a different document theme.

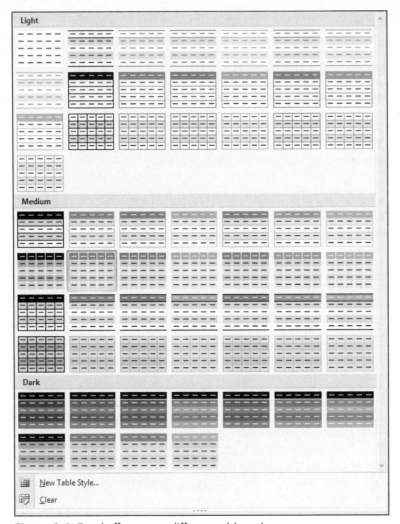

Figure 9-4: Excel offers many different table styles.

TIP

If applying table styles isn't working, the range was probably already formatted before you converted it to a table. (Table formatting doesn't override normal formatting.) To clear the existing background fill colors, select the entire table and choose Home⇨ Font⇨Fill Color⇨No Fill. To clear the existing font colors, choose Home⇨Font⇨Font Color⇨Automatic. After you issue these commands, the table styles should work as expected.

Navigating and Selecting in a Table

Moving among cells in a table works just like moving among cells in a normal range. One difference is when you use the Tab key. Pressing Tab moves to the cell to the right; when you reach the last column, pressing Tab again moves to the first cell in the next row.

When you move your mouse around in a table, you may notice that the pointer changes shapes. These shapes help you select various parts of the table.

- **To select an entire column:** Move the mouse to the top of a cell in the header row, and the mouse pointer changes to a down-pointing arrow. Click to select the data in the column. Click a second time to select the entire table column (including the header). You can also press Ctrl+spacebar (once or twice) to select a column.

- **To select an entire row:** Move the mouse to the left of a cell in the first column, and the mouse pointer changes to a right-pointing arrow. Click to select the entire table row. You can also press Shift+spacebar to select a table row.

- **To select the entire table:** Move the mouse to the upper-left part of the upper-left cell. When the mouse pointer turns into a diagonal arrow, click to select the data area of the table. Click a second time to select the entire table (including the Header Row and the Totals Row). You can also press Ctrl+A (once or twice) to select the entire table.

TIP

Right-clicking a cell in a table displays several selection options in the shortcut menu.

Adding New Rows or Columns

To add a new column to the end of a table, just active a cell in the column to the right of the table and start entering the data. Excel automatically extends the table horizontally.

Similarly, if you enter data in the row below a table, Excel extends the table vertically to include the new row. An exception to automatically extending tables is when the table is displaying a Total Row. If you enter data below the Total Row, the table will not be extended.

To add rows or columns within the table, right-click and choose Insert from the shortcut menu. The Insert shortcut menu command displays additional menu items that describe where to add the rows or columns.

TIP

When the cell pointer is in the bottom-right cell of a table, pressing Tab inserts a new row at the bottom.

When you move your mouse to the resize handle at bottom-right cell of a table, the mouse pointer turns into a diagonal line with two arrow heads. Click and drag down to add more rows to the table. Click and drag to the right to add more columns.

When you insert a new column, the Header Row displays a generic description, such as Column 1, Column 2, and so on. Normally, you'll want to change these names to more descriptive labels.

Deleting Rows or Columns

To delete a row (or column) in a table, select any cell in the row (or column) to be deleted. If you want to delete multiple rows or columns, select them all. Then right-click and choose Delete⇨Table Rows (or Delete⇨Table Columns).

Moving a Table

To move a table to a new location in the same worksheet, move the mouse pointer to any of its borders. When the mouse pointer turns into a cross with four arrows, click and drag the table to its new location.

To move a table to a different worksheet (in the same workbook, or in a different workbook), do the following:

1. Press Alt+A *twice* to select the entire table.

2. Press Ctrl+X to cut the selected cells.

3. Activate the new worksheet and select the upper-left cell for the table.

4. Press Ctrl+V to paste the table.

Excel Remembers

When you do something with a complete column in a table, Excel remembers that and extends that "something" to all new entries added to that column. For example, if you apply currency formatting to a column and then add a new row, Excel applies currency formatting to the new value in that column.

The same thing applies to other operations, such as conditional formatting, cell protection, data validation, and so on. And if you create a chart using the data in a table, the chart will be extended automatically if you add new data to the table. Those who have used a previous version of Excel will appreciate this feature the most.

Using a Data Form

Excel can display a dialog box to help you work with a worksheet database or table. This dialog box enables you to enter new data, delete rows, and search for rows that match certain criteria. This data form works with either a database or with a range that has been designated as a table (choosing the Insert⇨Tables⇨Table command).

Unfortunately, the command to access the data form is not in the Ribbon. To use the data form, you must add it to your Quick Access toolbar (QAT):

1. Right-click the QAT and choose Customize Quick Access Toolbar. Excel displays the Customization Customize panel of the Excel Options dialog box appears.

2. From the Choose Commands From drop-down list, choose Commands Not in the Ribbon.

3. In the list box on the left, select Form.

4. Click the Add button to add the selected command to your QAT.

5. Click OK to close the Excel Options dialog box.

After performing these steps, a new icon will appears on your QAT.

Excel's Data Form is handy but is by no means ideal. If you like the idea of using a dialog box to work with data in a table, check out my Enhanced Data Form add-in. It offers many advantages over Excel's Data Form. Download a free copy from my Web site: www.j-walk.com/ss.

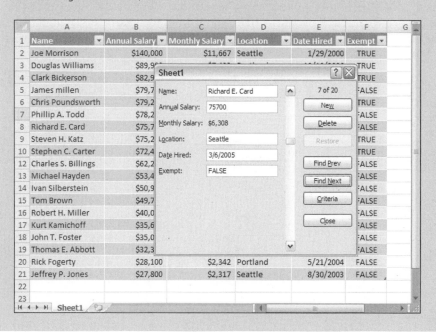

Setting Table Options

The Table Tools⇨Design⇨Table Style Options group contains several check boxes that determine whether various elements of the table are displayed and also whether some formatting options are in effect:

- **Header Row:** Toggles the display of the Header Row
- **Totals Row:** Toggles the display of the Totals Row
- **First Column:** Toggles special formatting for the first column
- **Last Column:** Toggles special formatting for the last column
- **Banded Rows:** Toggles the display of *banded* (alternating color) rows
- **Banded Columns:** Toggles the display of banded (alternating color) columns

Removing Duplicate Rows from a Table

If you have a table that contains duplicate items, you may want to eliminate the duplicates. In the past, removing duplicate data was essentially a manual task, but Excel 2007 makes it very easy.

Start by selecting any cell in your table. Then choose Table Tools⇨Design⇨Remove Duplicates. Excel responds with the dialog box shown in Figure 9-5. The dialog box lists all the columns in your table. Place a check mark next to the columns that you want to be included in the duplicate search. Most of the time, you'll want to select all the columns, which is the default. Click OK, and Excel weeds out the duplicate rows and displays a message that tells you how many duplicates it removed.

Unfortunately, Excel does not provide a way for you to review the duplicate records before deleting them. You can, however, use Undo (or press Ctrl+Z) if the result isn't what you expected.

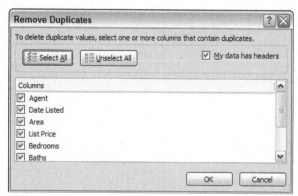

Figure 9-5: Removing duplicate rows from a table is easy.

TIP

If you want to remove duplicates from worksheet database that's not a table, choose Data⇨Data Tools⇨Remove Duplicates.

CAUTION

Duplicate values are determined by the value *displayed* in the cell — not necessarily the value *stored* in the cell. For example, assume that two cells contain the same date. One of the dates is formatted to display as 5/15/2007, and the other is formatted to display as May 15, 2007. When removing duplicates, Excel considers these dates to be different.

Sorting and Filtering a Table

The Header Row of a table contains a drop-down arrow that when clicked, displays sorting and filtering options (see Figure 9-6).

	A	B	C	D	E	F	G	H	I
1	Agent	Date Listed	Area	List Price	Bedrooms	Baths	SqFt	Type	Pool	Sc
2	Adams	10/9/2007				2.5	1,510	Condo	FALSE	F
3	Adams	8/19/2007		Sort Smallest to Largest		2.5	1,862	Single Family	TRUE	F
4	Adams	4/28/2007		Sort Largest to Smallest		3	1,905	Single Family	FALSE	F
5	Adams	7/19/2007				2.5	1,911	Single Family	FALSE	F
6	Adams	2/6/2007		Sort by Color ▶		2	1,552	Single Family	TRUE	T
7	Adams	8/1/2007		Clear Filter From "Bedrooms"		3	2,800	Single Family	TRUE	F
8	Adams	1/15/2007				2.5	1,752	Single Family	FALSE	T
9	Jenkins	1/29/2007		Filter by Color ▶		5	4,696	Single Family	TRUE	F
10	Romero	4/4/2007		Number Filters ▶		5	4,800	Single Family	FALSE	F
11	Hamilton	2/24/2007				3	2,414	Single Family	TRUE	F
12	Randolph	4/24/2007		☑ (Select All)		3	2,444	Single Family	TRUE	T
13	Adams	4/21/2007		☑ 1		3	2,207	Single Family	TRUE	T
14	Shasta	3/24/2007		☑ 2		2.5	2,620	Single Family	FALSE	F
15	Kelly	6/9/2007		☑ 3		2	1,971	Single Family	FALSE	F
16	Shasta	8/17/2007		☑ 4		3	3,109	Single Family	FALSE	F
17	Adams	6/6/2007		☑ 5		2.5	2,468	Condo	FALSE	F
18	Adams	2/8/2007		☑ 6		3	2,354	Condo	FALSE	T
19	Robinson	3/30/2007				3	3,000	Single Family	FALSE	F
20	Barnes	6/26/2007				2	1,800	Single Family	FALSE	F
21	Bennet	5/12/2007				3	2,041	Single Family	FALSE	T
22	Bennet	5/9/2007				3	1,940	Single Family	TRUE	F
23	Shasta	7/15/2007				3	3,927	Single Family	FALSE	F
24	Lang	5/3/2007				2.5	2,030	Condo	TRUE	F
25	Romero	1/28/2007				3	1,988	Condo	FALSE	T
26	Bennet	6/26/2007		OK Cancel		2.5	1,580	Single Family	TRUE	F
27	Chung	7/8/2007	Central	$236,900	3	2	1,700	Single Family	FALSE	F
28	Chung	8/27/2007	Central	$339,900	4	2	2,238	Single Family	FALSE	F
29	Chung	4/21/2007	Central	$375,000	4	3	2,467	Single Family	TRUE	F
30	Chung	3/22/2007	S. County	$205,000	3	2.5	2,001	Single Family	TRUE	F
31	Chung	8/3/2007	S. County	$229,500	4	2.5	2,284	Condo	FALSE	F

Sheet1

Figure 9-6: Each column in a table contains sorting and filtering options.

Part II

TIP

If you're working with a worksheet database (rather than a table), use Data⇨Sort & Filter⇨Filter to add the drop-down arrows to the top row of your database. This command is a toggle, so you can hide the drop-down arrows by selecting that command again. You can also use Data⇨Sort & Filter⇨Filter to hide the drop-down arrows in a table.

SORTING A TABLE

Sorting a table rearranges the rows based on the contents of a particular column. You may want to sort a table to put names in alphabetical order. Or, maybe you want to sort your sales staff by the totals sales made.

To sort a table by a particular column, click the drop-down in the column header and choose one of the sort commands. The exact command varies, depending on the type of data in the column. Sort A to Z and Sort Z to A are the captions that show when the columns contain text. The captions for columns that contain numeric data or True/False are Sort Smallest to Largest and Sort Largest to Smallest. Columns that contain dates change the captions into Sort Oldest to Newest and Sort Newest to Oldest.

You can also select Sort By Color to sort the rows based on the background or text color of the data. This option is relevant only if you've overridden the table style colors with custom colors, or if you've used conditional formatting to apply colors based on the cell contents.

TIP

When a column is sorted, the drop-down in the header row displays a different graphic to remind you that the table is sorted by that column.

You can sort on any number of columns. The trick is to sort the least significant column first and then proceed until the most significant column is sorted lasted.

For example, in the real estate listing table, you may want the list to be sorted by agent. And within each agent's group, the rows should be sorted by area. And within each area, the rows should be sorted by list price. For this type of sort, first sort by the List Price column, then sort by the Area column, and then sort by the Agent column. Figure 9-7 shows the table sorted in this manner.

ON THE CD

This workbook, named `real estate table.xlsx`, is available on the companion CD-ROM.

Another way of performing a multiple-column sort is to use the Sort dialog box. To display this dialog box, choose Home⇨Editing⇨Sort & Filter⇨Custom Sort. Or, right-click any cell in the table and choose Sort⇨Custom Sort from the shortcut menu.

	Agent	Date Listed	Area	List Price	Bedrooms	Baths	SqFt	Type	Pool	Sold
2	Adams	10/9/2007	Central	$199,000	3	2.5	1,510	Condo	FALSE	FALSE
3	Adams	8/19/2007	Central	$214,500	4	2.5	1,862	Single Family	TRUE	FALSE
4	Adams	4/28/2007	Central	$265,000	4	3	1,905	Single Family	FALSE	FALSE
5	Adams	7/19/2007	Central	$268,500	4	2.5	1,911	Single Family	FALSE	FALSE
6	Adams	2/6/2007	Central	$273,500	2	2	1,552	Single Family	TRUE	TRUE
7	Adams	8/1/2007	Central	$309,950	4	3	2,800	Single Family	TRUE	FALSE
8	Adams	1/15/2007	Central	$325,000	3	2.5	1,752	Single Family	FALSE	TRUE
9	Adams	4/15/2007	N. County	$339,900	3	2	1,828	Single Family	TRUE	TRUE
10	Adams	5/24/2007	N. County	$349,000	4	2.5	2,730	Condo	TRUE	TRUE
11	Adams	2/8/2007	N. County	$379,000	3	3	2,354	Condo	FALSE	TRUE
12	Adams	6/6/2007	N. County	$379,900	3	2.5	2,468	Condo	FALSE	FALSE
13	Adams	4/21/2007	S. County	$208,750	4	3	2,207	Single Family	TRUE	TRUE
14	Barnes	9/27/2007	N. County	$239,900	4	3	2,041	Condo	FALSE	FALSE
15	Barnes	3/14/2007	N. County	$264,900	3	3	2,495	Condo	FALSE	FALSE
16	Barnes	3/7/2007	N. County	$299,000	3	2	2,050	Condo	FALSE	FALSE
17	Barnes	8/10/2007	N. County	$345,000	4	3	2,388	Condo	TRUE	TRUE
18	Barnes	3/22/2007	N. County	$350,000	3	2.5	1,991	Condo	FALSE	TRUE
19	Barnes	6/26/2007	N. County	$355,000	4	2.5	2,647	Condo	TRUE	FALSE
20	Barnes	6/26/2007	S. County	$208,750	4	2	1,800	Single Family	FALSE	FALSE
21	Bennet	5/12/2007	Central	$229,500	4	3	2,041	Single Family	FALSE	TRUE
22	Bennet	5/9/2007	Central	$549,000	4	3	1,940	Single Family	TRUE	FALSE
23	Bennet	7/1/2007	N. County	$229,500	6	3	2,700	Single Family	TRUE	FALSE
24	Bennet	4/21/2007	N. County	$229,900	3	3	2,266	Condo	FALSE	FALSE
25	Bennet	5/27/2007	N. County	$229,900	4	3	2,041	Condo	FALSE	FALSE
26	Bennet	6/26/2007	S. County	$229,900	3	2.5	1,580	Single Family	TRUE	FALSE
27	Chung	7/8/2007	Central	$236,900	3	2	1,700	Single Family	FALSE	FALSE
28	Chung	8/27/2007	Central	$339,900	4	2	2,238	Single Family	FALSE	FALSE

Sheet1

Figure 9-7: A table, after performing a three-column sort.

In the Sort dialog box, use the drop-down lists to specify the first search specifications. Note that the searching is opposite of what I described in the previous paragraph. In this example, you start with Agent. Then, click the Add Level button to insert another set of search controls. In this new set of controls, specify the sort specifications for the Area column. Then, add another level and enter the specifications for the List Price column. Figure 9-8 shows the dialog box after entering the specifications for the three-column sort. This technique produces exactly the same sort as described in the previous paragraph.

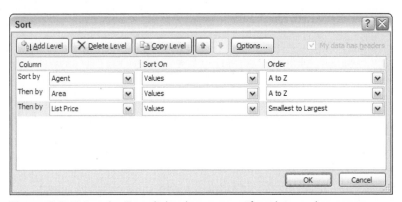

Figure 9-8: Using the Sort dialog box to specify a three-column sort.

FILTERING A TABLE

Filtering a table refers to displaying only the rows that meet certain conditions. (The other rows are hidden.)

 NOTE

Excel provides two ways to filter a table. This section discusses standard filtering (formerly known as AutoFiltering), which is adequate for most filtering requirements. For more complex filter criteria, you may need to use advanced filtering (discussed later in this chapter).

Using the real estate table, assume that you're only interested in the data for the N. County area. Click the drop-down in the Area Row header and remove the check mark from Select All, which unselects everything. Then, place a check mark next to N. County and click OK. The table, shown in Figure 9-9, is now filtered to display only the listings in the N. County area. Notice that some row numbers are missing; these rows contain the filtered (hidden) data.

Also notice that the drop-down arrow in the Area column now shows a different graphic — an icon that indicates the column is filtered.

	Agent	Date Listed	Area	List Price	Bedrooms	Baths	SqFt	Type	Pool	Sold
9	Adams	4/15/2007	N. County	$339,900	3	2	1,828	Single Family	TRUE	TRUE
10	Adams	5/24/2007	N. County	$349,000	4	2.5	2,730	Condo	TRUE	TRUE
11	Adams	2/8/2007	N. County	$379,000	3	3	2,354	Condo	FALSE	TRUE
12	Adams	6/6/2007	N. County	$379,900	3	2.5	2,468	Condo	FALSE	FALSE
14	Barnes	9/27/2007	N. County	$239,900	4	3	2,041	Condo	FALSE	FALSE
15	Barnes	3/14/2007	N. County	$264,900	3	3	2,495	Condo	FALSE	FALSE
16	Barnes	3/7/2007	N. County	$299,000	3	2	2,050	Condo	FALSE	FALSE
17	Barnes	8/10/2007	N. County	$345,000	4	3	2,388	Condo	TRUE	TRUE
18	Barnes	3/22/2007	N. County	$350,000	3	2.5	1,991	Condo	FALSE	TRUE
19	Barnes	6/26/2007	N. County	$355,000	4	2.5	2,647	Condo	TRUE	FALSE
23	Bennet	7/1/2007	N. County	$229,500	6	3	2,700	Single Family	TRUE	FALSE
24	Bennet	4/21/2007	N. County	$229,900	3	3	2,266	Condo	FALSE	FALSE
25	Bennet	5/27/2007	N. County	$229,900	4	3	2,041	Condo	FALSE	FALSE
44	Hamilton	2/24/2007	N. County	$425,900	5	3	2,414	Single Family	TRUE	FALSE
47	Jenkins	4/22/2007	N. County	$238,000	4	2.5	1,590	Condo	FALSE	TRUE
48	Jenkins	4/9/2007	N. County	$248,500	4	2.5	2,101	Single Family	TRUE	TRUE
49	Jenkins	5/1/2007	N. County	$349,900	4	3	2,290	Single Family	TRUE	TRUE
50	Jenkins	1/29/2007	N. County	$1,200,500	5	5	4,696	Single Family	TRUE	FALSE
56	Kelly	6/9/2007	N. County	$389,500	4	2	1,971	Single Family	FALSE	FALSE
62	Lang	8/23/2007	N. County	$264,900	3	2.5	2,062	Condo	FALSE	FALSE
63	Lang	7/22/2007	N. County	$349,000	4	3	3,930	Single Family	TRUE	FALSE
64	Lang	6/23/2007	N. County	$359,000	3	2.5	2,210	Single Family	FALSE	FALSE
65	Lang	5/3/2007	N. County	$369,900	3	2.5	2,030	Condo	TRUE	FALSE
74	Peterson	6/18/2007	N. County	$235,990	4	2	1,656	Condo	TRUE	FALSE

Figure 9-9: This table is filtered to show only the information for N. County.

You can filter by multiple values — for example, filter the table to show only N. Country and Central.

You can filter a table using any number of columns. For example, you may want to see only the N. County listings in which the Type is Single Family. Just repeat the operation using the Type column. All tables then display only the rows in which the Area is N. County and the Type is Single Family.

For additional filtering options, select Text Filters (or Number Filters, if the column contains values). The options are fairly self explanatory, and you have a great deal of flexibility in displaying only the rows that you're interested in.

In addition, you can right-click a cell and use the Filter command on the shortcut menu. This menu item leads to several additional filtering options.

NOTE

As you may expect, the Total row is updated to show the total for the visible rows only.

Some of the standard spreadsheet operations work differently with a filtered table. For example, you might use the Home⇨Cells⇨Format⇨Hide & Unhide⇨Hide Rows command to hide rows. If you then copy a range that includes those hidden rows, all the data gets copied (even the hidden rows). When you copy data in a filtered table, though, only the visible rows are copied. This filtering makes it very easy to copy a subset of a larger table and paste it to another area of your worksheet. Keep in mind that the pasted data is not a table — it's just a normal range.

Similarly, you can select and delete the visible rows in the table, and the rows hidden by filtering will not be affected.

To remove filtering for a column, click the drop-down in the Row Header and choose Clear Filter. If you've filtered using multiple columns, it may be faster to remove all filters by choosing Home⇨Editing⇨Sort & Filter⇨Clear.

Working with the Total Row

The Total Row is an optional table element that contains formulas that summarize the information in the columns. Normally, the Total Row isn't displayed. To display the Total Row, choose Table Tools⇨Design⇨Table Style Options⇨ Total Row. This command is a toggle that turns the Total Row on and off.

By default, the Total Row displays the sum of the values in a column of numbers. In many cases, you'll want a different type of summary formula. When you select a cell in the Total Row, a drop-down arrow appears, and you can select from a number of other summary formulas (see Figure 9-10):

- **None:** No formula.

- **Average:** Displays the average of the numbers in the column.

- **Count:** Displays the number of entries in the column. (Blank cells are not counted.)

- **Count Numbers:** Displays the number of numeric values in the column. (Blank cells, text cells, and error cells are not counted.)

- **Max:** Displays the maximum value in the column.

- **Min:** Displays the minimum value in the column.

- **Sum:** Displays the sum of the values in the column.

- **StdDev:** Displays the standard deviation of the values in the column. *Standard deviation* is a statistical measure of how "spread out" the values are.

- **Var:** Displays the variance of the values in the column. Variance is another statistical measure of how "spread out" the values are.

- **More Functions:** Displays the Insert Function dialog box so that you can select a function that isn't in the list.

	Date Listed	Area	List Price	Bedrooms	Baths	SqFt	Type	Pool	Sold
119	8/17/2007	N. County	$389,000	4	3	3,109	Single Family	FALSE	FALSE
120	3/24/2007	N. County	$398,000	4	2.5	2,620	Single Family	FALSE	FALSE
121	9/16/2007	S. County	$205,500	4	2.5	2,036	Condo	FALSE	TRUE
122	4/25/2007	S. County	$236,900	1	2	1,483	Condo	FALSE	FALSE
123	7/22/2007	S. County	$238,000	3	2.5	2,300	Single Family	TRUE	FALSE
124	9/28/2007	S. County	$249,000	4	2.5	1,902	Single Family	FALSE	FALSE
125	8/8/2007	S. County	$249,900	3	2	2,050	Single Family	FALSE	TRUE
126	6/4/2007	S. County	$574,900	5	4	4,700	Single Family	FALSE	FALSE
127			$308,037	3.648 ▾	2.634				
128				None					
129				Average					
130				Count					
131				Count Numbers					
132				Max					
133				Min					
134				Sum					
135				StdDev					
136				Var					
				More Functions…					

H ◀ ▶ H   Sheet1

Figure 9-10: Several types of summary functions are available for the Totals Row.

The drop-down choices insert the SUBTOTAL function and refer to the table's column using a special structured syntax (described later). The first argument of the SUBTOTAL function determines the type of summary displayed. For example, if the first argument is 109, the function displays the sum. You can override the formula inserted by Excel and enter any formula you like in the Total row cell. For more information, see the sidebar, "About the SUBTOTAL Function."

 CAUTION

The SUBTOTAL function is the only function that ignores data hidden by filtering. If you have other formulas that refer to data in a filtered table, these formulas don't adjust to use only the visible cells. For example, if you use the SUM function to add the values in column C and some rows are hidden because of filtering, the formula continues to show the sum for all the values in column C—not just those in the visible rows.

About the SUBTOTAL Function

The SUBTOTAL function is very versatile, but it's also one of the most confusing functions in Excel's arsenal. First of all, it has a misleading name because it does a lot more than addition. The first argument for this function requires an arbitrary (and impossible to remember) number that determines the type of result that's returned. Fortunately, the Excel 2007 formula AutoComplete feature helps you insert these numbers.

In addition, the SUBTOTAL function was enhanced in Excel 2003 with an increase in the number of choices for its first argument, which opens the door to compatibility problems if you share your workbook with someone who uses an earlier version of Excel.

The first argument for the SUBTOTAL function determines the actual function used. For example, when the first argument is 1, the SUBTOTAL function works like the AVERAGE function. The following table shows the possible values for the first argument for the SUBTOTAL function:

Value	Function
1	AVERAGE
2	COUNT
3	COUNTA
4	MAX
5	MIN
6	PRODUCT
7	STDEV
8	STDEVP
9	SUM
10	VAR
11	VARP
101*	AVERAGE
102*	COUNT
103*	COUNTA
104*	MAX

continued

Part II

continued

Value	Function
105*	MIN
106*	PRODUCT
107*	STDEV
108*	STDEVP
109*	SUM
110*	VAR
111*	VARP

*Excel 2003 and Excel 2007 only

When the first argument is greater than 100, the SUBTOTAL function behaves a bit differently. Specifically, it does not include data in rows that were hidden manually. When the first argument is less than 100, the SUBTOTAL function includes data in rows that were hidden manually but excludes data in rows that were hidden as a result of filtering or using an outline.

To add to the confusion, a manually hidden row is not always treated the same. If a row is manually hidden in a range that already contains rows hidden via a filter, Excel treats the manually hidden rows as filtered rows. After a filter is applied, Excel can't seem to tell the difference between filtered rows and manually hidden rows. The SUBTOTAL function with a first argument over 100 behaves the same as those with a first argument under 100, and removing the filter shows all rows—even the manually hidden ones.

The ability to use a first argument that's greater than 100 was new to Excel 2003. You can use this updated version of the SUBTOTAL function anywhere in your workbook; that is, it's not limited to tables. Be aware, however, that this function is not backward compatible. If you share your workbook with someone who is using a version prior to Excel 2003, the SUBTOTAL function will display an error if you use a first argument greater than 100.

Another interesting characteristic of the SUBTOTAL function is its ability to produce an accurate grand total. It does this by ignoring any cells that already contain a formula with SUBTOTAL in it. For a demonstration of this ability, see "Inserting Subtotals" later in this chapter.

CAUTION

If you have a formula that refers to a value in the Total Row of a table, the formula returns an error if you hide the Total Row. However, if you make the Total Row visible again, the formula works as it should.

Using Formulas within a Table

Adding a Total Row to a table is an easy way to summarize the values in a table column. In many cases, you'll want to use formulas *within* a table. For example, in the table shown in Figure 9-11, you might want to add a column that shows the difference between the Actual and Projected amounts. As you'll see, Excel 2007 makes this very easy.

ON THE CD

This workbook, named `table formulas.xlsx`, is available on the companion CD-ROM.

	A	B	C	D	E	F
1						
2		Month	Projected	Actual		
3		Jan	4,000	3,255		
4		Feb	4,000	4,102		
5		Mar	4,000	3,982		
6		Apr	5,000	4,598		
7		May	5,000	5,873		
8		Jun	5,000	4,783		
9		Jul	5,000	5,109		
10		Aug	6,000	5,982		
11		Sep	6,000	6,201		
12		Oct	7,000	6,833		
13		Nov	8,000	7,983		
14		Dec	9,000	9,821		
15		Total	68,000	68,522		
16						

Sheet1 / Sheet2

Figure 9-11: Adding a calculated column to this table is easy.

1. Activate cell E2 and type **Difference** for the column header. Excel automatically expands the table to include a new column.

2. Move to cell E3 and type an equal sign to signify the beginning of a formula.

3. Press the left-arrow key, and Excel displays `=[Actual]`, which is the column heading, in the formula bar.

4. Type a minus sign and then press left arrow twice. Excel displays `=[[Actual]-Projected]` in your formula.

5. Press Enter to end the formula.

Excel copies the formula to all rows in the table.

Figure 9-12 shows the table with the new column.

	A	B	C	D	E	F
1						
2		Month	Projected	Actual	Difference	
3		Jan	4,000	3,255	-745	
4		Feb	4,000	4,102	102	
5		Mar	4,000	3,982	-18	
6		Apr	5,000	4,598	-402	
7		May	5,000	5,873	873	
8		Jun	5,000	4,783	-217	
9		Jul	5,000	5,109	109	
10		Aug	6,000	5,982	-18	
11		Sep	6,000	6,201	201	
12		Oct	7,000	6,833	-167	
13		Nov	8,000	7,983	-17	
14		Dec	9,000	9,821	821	
15		Total	68,000	68,522		
16						

Sheet1 / Sheet2

Figure 9-12: The Difference column contains a formula.

If you examine the table, you'll find this formula for all cells in the Difference column:

```
=[Actual]-[Projected]
```

Keep in mind that I didn't define any names in this worksheet. The formula uses table references that are based on the column names. If you change the text in a column header, any formulas that refer to that data will update automatically.

Although I entered the formula into the first data row of the table, that's not necessary. Any time a formula is entered into any cell in an empty table column, it will automatically fill all the cells in that column. And if you need to edit the formula, edit the copy in any row, and Excel will automatically copy the edited formula to the other cells in the column.

The preceding steps used the pointing technique to create the formula. Alternatively, you could have entered the formula manually using standard cell references. For example, you could enter the following formula in cell E3:

```
=D3-C3
```

If you type the formulas using cell references, Excel still copies the formula to the other cells automatically: It just doesn't use the column headings.

TIP

When Excel inserts a calculated column formula, it also displays a Smart Tag, with some options, one of which is Stop Automatically Creating Calculated Columns. Select this option if you prefer to do your own copying within a column.

Referencing Data in a Table

The preceding section described how to create a column of formulas within a table. What about formulas outside of a table that refer to data inside of a table? You can take advantage of the new structured table referencing that uses the table name, column headers, and other table elements. You no longer need to create names for these items.

The table itself has a name (for example, Table1), and you can refer to data within the table by using column headers.

You can, of course, use standard cell references to refer to data in a table, but the new method has a distinct advantage: The names adjust automatically if the table size changes by adding or deleting rows.

Refer to Figure 9-13, which shows a simple table that contains regional sales information. Excel named this table Table2 when it was created; it was the second table in the workbook. To calculate the sum of all the values in the table, use this formula:

```
=SUM(Table2)
```

	A	B	C	D	E	F
1						
2		Month	Region	Sales		
3		Jan	Region 1	789,345		
4		Jan	Region 2	431,263		
5		Feb	Region 1	812,302		
6		Feb	Region 2	509,239		
7		Mar	Region 1	871,902		
8		Mar	Region 2	411,287		
9				3,825,338		
10						
11						

Sheet1 Sheet2

Figure 9-13: This table shows sales by month and by region.

This formula will always return the sum of all the data, even if rows or columns are added or deleted. And if you change the name of the table, Excel adjusts all formulas that refer to that table automatically. For example, if you renamed Table1 to be Q1Data, the preceding formula would be changed to

```
=SUM(Q1Data)
```

TIP

To change the name of a table, select any cell in the table, use the Table Name box in the Table Tools⇨Design⇨Properties group. Or, you can use the Name Manger to change the name of a table (Formulas⇨Defined Names⇨Name Manger).

Most of the time, your formulas will refer to a specific column in the table, rather than the entire table. The following formula returns the sum of the data in the Sales column:

```
=SUM(Table2[Sales])
```

Notice that the column name is enclosed in square brackets. Again, the formula adjusts automatically if you change the text in the column heading.

CAUTION

Keep in mind that the preceding formula does not adjust if table rows are hidden as a result of filtering. SUBTOTAL is the only function that changes its result to ignore hidden rows. Use the following formula instead:

```
=SUBTOTAL(109,Table2[Sales])
```

Even better, Excel provides some helpful assistance when you create a formula that refers to data within a table. Figure 9-14 shows the formula AutoComplete feature helping create a formula by showing a list of the elements in the table.

Figure 9-14: The formula AutoComplete feature is useful when creating a formula that refers to data in a table.

Here's another example that returns the sum of the January sales:

```
=SUMIF(Table2[Month],"Jan",Table2[Sales])
```

 ## CROSS REF

For an explanation of the SUMIF worksheet function, refer to Chapter 7.

Using this structured table syntax is optional — you can use actual range references if you like. For example, the following formula returns the same result as the preceding one:

```
=SUMIF(B3:B8,"Jan",D3:D8)
```

To refer to a cell in the Total row of a table, use a formula like this:

```
=Table2[[#Totals],[Sales]]
```

If the Total row in Table2 is not displayed, the preceding formula returns a #REF error.

This formula returns the value in the Total row of the Sales column in Table2.

To count the total number of rows in Table2, use the following formula:

```
=ROWS(Table2[#All])
```

The preceding formula counts all rows, including the Header row and Total row. To count only the data rows, use a formula like this:

```
=ROWS(Table2[#Data])
```

A formula that's in the same row as a table can use a #This Row reference to refer to table data that's in the same row. For example, assume the following formula is in row 3, in a column outside Table2. The formula counts the number of entries in the row 3 of Table2:

```
=COUNTA(Table2[#This Row])
```

You can also combine row and column references by nesting brackets and including multiple references separated by commas. The following example returns Sales from the current row divided by the total sales:

```
=Table2[[#This Row],[Sales]]/Table2[[#Totals],[Sales]]
```

A formula like the preceding one is much easier to create if you use the pointing method.

Table 9-1 summarizes the row identifiers for table references and also describes which ranges they represent.

Part II

TABLE 9-1 TABLE ROW REFERENCES

Row Identifier	Description
#All	Returns the range that includes the header row, all data rows, and the total row.
#Data	Returns the range that includes the data rows but not the header or total rows.
#Headers	Returns the range that includes the header row only. Returns the #REF! error if there is no header row.
#Totals	Returns the range that includes the total row only. Returns the #REF! error if there is no total row.
#This Row	Returns the range that is the intersection of the active row and the table's data rows. If the active row does not intersect with the table or it's the same row as the header or total row, the #VALUE! error is returned.

Filling in the Gaps

When you import data, you can end up with a worksheet that looks something like the one in the accompanying figure. In this example, an entry in column A applies to several rows of data. If you sort such a range, you can end up with a mess, and you won't be able to tell who sold what.

Monthly Sales Report

Sales Rep	Month	Units Sold	Amount	New Clients
Bob	Jan	324	$22,356	5
	Feb	331	$22,839	6
	Mar	290	$20,010	3
Karen	Jan	189	$13,041	12
	Feb	234	$16,146	11
	Mar	398	$27,462	6
Elizabeth	Jan	541	$37,329	16
	Feb	212	$14,628	21
	Mar	681	$46,989	7
Stan	Jan	771	$53,199	14
	Feb	322	$22,218	3
	Mar	821	$56,649	11

Sheet1

When you have a small range, you can enter the missing cell values manually. If your worksheet database has hundreds of rows, though, you need a better way of filling in those cell values. Here's how:

1. Select the range (A3:A14 in this example).

2. Choose Home⇨Editing⇨Find & Select⇨Go To Special to display the Go To Special dialog box.

3. In the Go To Special dialog box, select the Blanks option.

4. Click OK to close the Go To Special dialog box.

5. In the Formula bar, type =, followed by the address of the first cell with an entry in the column (=**A3** in this example), and then press Ctrl+Enter to copy that formula to all selected cells

6. Press Escape to cancel the selection.

7. Reselect the range and then choose Home⇨Clipboard⇨Paste Values.

Each blank cell in the column is filled with data from above.

TIP

You can use the SUBTOTAL function to generate consecutive numbers for nonhidden rows in a filtered table. The numbering will adjust as you apply filtering to hide or display rows. If your table has the field names in row 1, enter this formula in cell A2 and then copy it down for each row in your table:

```
=SUBTOTAL(3,B$2:B2)
```

Converting a Table to a Worksheet Database

If you need to convert a table back to a normal worksheet database, just select a cell in the table and choose Table Tools⇨Design⇨Tools⇨Convert To Range. The table style formatting remains intact, but the range no longer functions as a table.

Formulas inside and outside the table that use structured table references are converted, so they use range addresses rather than table items.

Using Advanced Filtering

In many cases, standard filtering does the job just fine. If you run up against its limitations, you need to use advanced filtering. Advanced filtering is much more flexible than standard filtering, but it takes a bit of up-front work to use it. Advanced filtering provides you with the following capabilities.

- You can specify more complex filtering criteria.

- You can specify computed filtering criteria.

- You can extract a copy of the rows that meet the criteria and place them in another location.

You can use advanced filtering with a worksheet database or with a table.

The examples in this section use a real estate listing worksheet database (shown in Figure 9-15), which has 125 records and 10 fields. This database contains a good assortment of data types: values, text strings, logicals, and dates. The database occupies the range A8:H133. (Rows above the table are used for the criteria range.)

	A	B	C	D	E	F	G	H	I	J
6										
7										
8	Agent	Date Listed	Area	List Price	Bedrooms	Baths	SqFt	Type	Pool	Sold
9	Shasta	10/2/2007	N. County	$349,000	3	2.5	1,727	Condo	TRUE	TRUE
10	Peterson	4/25/2007	S. County	$240,000	3	2.5	1,595	Condo	FALSE	TRUE
11	Jenkins	3/3/2007	S. County	$338,876	4	2.5	2,612	Single Family	FALSE	FALSE
12	Peterson	4/15/2007	N. County	$259,900	4	3	1,734	Condo	FALSE	TRUE
13	Daily	10/3/2007	Central	$340,000	4	2.5	2,517	Condo	FALSE	FALSE
14	Bennet	7/1/2007	N. County	$229,500	6	3	2,700	Single Family	TRUE	FALSE
15	Lang	4/19/2007	S. County	$325,000	4	3	2,800	Condo	TRUE	TRUE
16	Shasta	8/17/2007	N. County	$389,000	4	3	3,109	Single Family	FALSE	FALSE
17	Adams	2/8/2007	N. County	$379,000	3	3	2,354	Condo	FALSE	TRUE
18	Adams	8/19/2007	Central	$214,500	4	2.5	1,862	Single Family	TRUE	FALSE
19	Bennet	5/12/2007	Central	$229,500	4	3	2,041	Single Family	FALSE	TRUE
20	Chung	9/2/2007	S. County	$245,000	4	3	2,084	Single Family	FALSE	FALSE
21	Peterson	10/9/2007	Central	$227,500	4	3	1,990	Single Family	TRUE	FALSE
22	Romero	7/29/2007	N. County	$215,000	4	2.5	1,640	Condo	TRUE	FALSE
23	Lang	7/22/2007	N. County	$349,000	4	3	3,930	Single Family	TRUE	FALSE
24	Peterson	3/14/2007	Central	$364,900	4	2.5	2,507	Single Family	FALSE	FALSE
25	Peterson	6/26/2007	S. County	$225,000	4	3	2,013	Single Family	TRUE	FALSE
26	Jenkins	5/26/2007	S. County	$249,000	3	2.5	1,730	Condo	FALSE	TRUE
27	Lang	5/3/2007	S. County	$225,911	4	2.5	1,908	Single Family	TRUE	FALSE

Figure 9-15: This real estate listing database is used to demonstrate advanced filtering.

ON THE CD

This workbook, named `real estate database.xlsx`, is available on the companion CD-ROM.

Setting Up a Criteria Range

Before you can use the advanced filtering feature, you must set up a *criteria range*, which is a range on a worksheet that conforms to certain requirements. The criteria range holds the information that Excel uses to filter the table. The criteria range must conform to the following specifications:

- It must consist of at least two rows, and the first row must contain some or all field names from the table. An exception to this is when you use computed criteria. Computed criteria can use an empty header row. (See "Specifying Computed Criteria," later in this chapter.)

- The other rows of the criteria range must consist of your filtering criteria.

You can put the criteria range anywhere in the worksheet or even in a different worksheet. However, you should avoid putting the criteria range in rows that are occupied by the worksheet database or table. Because Excel may hide some of these rows when filtering, you may find that your criteria range is no longer visible after filtering. Therefore, you should generally place the criteria range above or below the table.

Figure 9-16 shows a criteria range in A1:B2, above the worksheet database that it uses. Notice that the criteria range does not include all the field names from the table. You can include only the field names for fields that you use in the selection criteria.

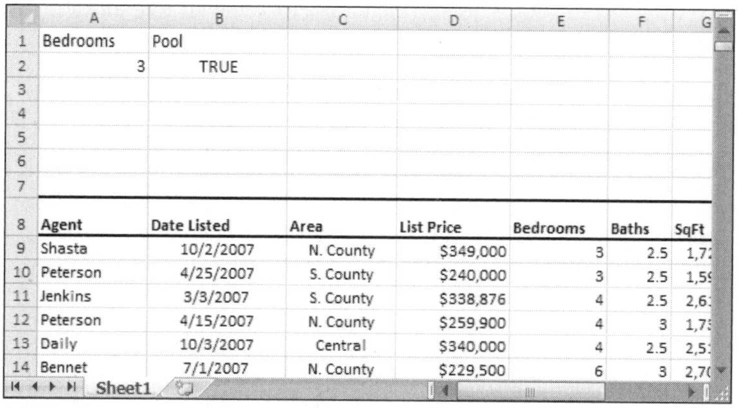

Part II

Figure 9-16: A criteria range for advanced filtering.

In this example, the criteria range has only one row of criteria. The fields in each row of the criteria range (except for the header row) are joined with an AND operator. Therefore, after applying the advanced filter, the worksheet database shows only the rows in which the Bedrooms field is 3 and the Pool field is TRUE. In other words, it shows only the listings for three-bedroom homes with a pool.

You may find specifying criteria in the criteria range a bit tricky. I discuss this topic in detail later in this chapter, in the section, "Specifying Advanced Filter Criteria."

Applying an Advanced Filter

To perform the advanced filtering:

1. Ensure that you've set up a criteria range.

2. Choose Data⇨Sort & Filter⇨Advanced. Excel displays the Advanced Filter dialog box, as shown in Figure 9-17.

Figure 9-17: The Advanced Filter dialog box.

3. Excel guesses your database range if the active cell is within or adjacent to a block of data, but you can change it if necessary.

4. Specify the criteria range. If you happen to have a named range with the name Criteria, Excel will insert that range in the Criteria range box — you can also change this range if you like.

5. To filter the database in place (that is, to hide rows that don't qualify), select the option labeled Filter the List, In-Place. If you select the Copy to Another Location option, you need to specify a range in the Copy To box.

6. Click OK, and Excel filters the table by the criteria that you specify.

Figure 9-18 shows the worksheet database after applying the advanced filter that displays three-bedroom homes with a pool.

TIP

When you select the Copy to Another Location option, you can specify which columns to include in the copy. Before displaying the Advanced Filter dialog box, copy the desired field labels to the first row of the area where you plan to paste the filtered rows. In the Advanced Filter dialog box, specify a reference to the copied column labels in the Copy To box. The copied rows then include only the columns for which you copied the labels.

Clearing an Advanced Filter

When you apply an advanced filter, Excel hides all row that don't meet the criteria you specified. To clear the advanced filter and display all rows, choose Data⇨Sort & Filter⇨ Clear.

	A	B	C	D	E	F	G	H	I	J
1	Bedrooms	Pool								
2	3	TRUE								
3										
4										
5										
6										
7										
8	Agent	Date Listed	Area	List Price	Bedrooms	Baths	SqFt	Type	Pool	Sold
9	Shasta	10/2/2007	N. County	$349,000	3	2.5	1,727	Condo	TRUE	TRUE
31	Romero	8/3/2007	N. County	$359,900	3	2	2,198	Condo	TRUE	FALSE
35	Bennet	6/26/2007	S. County	$229,900	3	2.5	580	Single Family	TRUE	FALSE
38	Lang	5/3/2007	N. County	$369,900	3	2.5	2,030	Condo	TRUE	FALSE
39	Shasta	2/10/2007	Central	$350,000	3	2	2,275	Single Family	TRUE	FALSE
45	Shasta	5/19/2007	Central	$335,000	3	2.5	2,000	Single Family	TRUE	TRUE
61	Shasta	3/24/2007	Central	$215,000	3	1.75	2,157	Single Family	TRUE	TRUE
101	Shasta	9/13/2007	N. County	$349,000	3	2	1,810	Condo	TRUE	TRUE
111	Shasta	7/22/2007	S. County	$238,000	3	2.5	2,300	Single Family	TRUE	FALSE
120	Shasta	8/5/2007	N. County	$349,000	3	2.5	2,000	Single Family	TRUE	FALSE
132	Chung	3/22/2007	S. County	$205,000	3	2.5	2,001	Single Family	TRUE	FALSE
133	Adams	4/15/2007	N. County	$339,900	3	2	1,828	Single Family	TRUE	TRUE
134										
135										

Sheet1

Figure 9-18: The result of applying an advanced filter.

Specifying Advanced Filter Criteria

The key to using advanced filtering is knowing how to set up the criteria range — which is the focus of the sections that follow. As you see, you have a great deal of flexibility, but you also see that some of the options are not exactly intuitive. Here you'll find plenty of examples to help you understand how to create a criteria range that extracts the information you need.

NOTE

The use of a separate criteria range for advanced filtering originated with the original version of Lotus 1-2-3, more than 20 years ago. Excel adapted this method, and it has never been changed, despite the fact that specifying advanced filtering criteria remains one of the most confusing aspects of Excel. Fortunately, however, Excel's standard filtering is sufficient for most needs.

Specifying a Single Criterion

The examples in this section use a single-selection criterion. In other words, the contents of a single field determine the record selection.

NOTE

You also can use standard filtering to perform this type of filtering.

To select only the records that contain a specific value in a specific field, enter the field name in the first row of the criteria range and the value to match in the second row. Figure 9-19, for example, shows the criteria range (A1:A2) that selects records containing the value 4 in the Bedrooms field.

	A	B	C	D	E	F	G
1	Bedrooms						
2	4						
3							
4							
5							
6							
7							
8	**Agent**	**Date Listed**	**Area**	**List Price**	**Bedrooms**	**Baths**	**SqFt**	**Type**
9	Shasta	10/2/2007	N. County	$349,000	3	2.5	1,727	Condo
31	Romero	8/3/2007	N. County	$359,900	3	2	2,198	Condo
35	Bennet	6/26/2007	S. County	$229,900	3	2.5	1,580	Single
38	Lang	5/3/2007	N. County	$369,900	3	2.5	2,030	Condo
39	Shasta	2/10/2007	Central	$350,000	3	2	2,275	Single
45	Shasta	5/19/2007	Central	$335,000	3	2.5	2,000	Single
61	Shasta	3/24/2007	Central	$215,000	3	1.75	2,157	Single

Sheet1

Figure 9-19: The criteria range (A1:A2) selects records that describe homes with four bedrooms.

Note that the criteria range does not need to include all the fields from the database. If you work with different sets of criteria, you may find it more convenient to list all the field names in the first row of your criteria range.

USING COMPARISON OPERATORS

You can use comparison operators to refine your record selection. For example, you can select records based on any of the following:

- Homes that have at least four bedrooms
- Homes with a square footage less than 2,000
- Homes with a table price of no more than $200,000

To select the records that describe homes that have at least four bedrooms, enter **Bedrooms** in cell A1 and then enter **>=4** in cell A2 of the criterion range.

Table 9-2 lists the comparison operators that you can use with text or value criteria. If you don't use a comparison operator, Excel assumes the equal sign operator (=).

TABLE 9-2   COMPARISON OPERATORS

Operator	Comparison Type
=	Equal to
>	Greater than
>=	Greater than or equal to
<	Less than
<=	Less than or equal to
< >	Not equal to

USING WILDCARD CHARACTERS

Criteria that use text also can make use of two wildcard characters: An asterisk (*) matches any number of characters; a question mark (?) matches any single character.

Table 9-3 shows examples of criteria that use text. Some of these are a bit counter-intuitive. For example, to select records that match a single character, you must enter the criterion as a formula (refer to the last entry in the table).

TABLE 9-3   EXAMPLES OF TEXT CRITERIA

Criteria	Selects
="=January"	Records that contain the text *January* (and nothing else). You enter this exactly as shown: as a formula, with an initial equal sign. Alternatively, you can use a leading apostrophe and omit the quotes: '=January
January	Records that begin with the text *January.*
C	Records that contain text that begins with the letter C.
<>C*	Records that contain any text, except text that begins with the letter C.
>=L	Records that contain text that begins with the letters L through Z.
County	Records that contain text that includes the word *county.*
Sm*	Records that contain text that begins with the letters SM.

continued

TABLE 9-3 EXAMPLES OF TEXT CRITERIA *(continued)*

Criteria	Selects
s*s	Records that contain text that begins with S and have a subsequent occurrence of the letter S.
s?s	Records that contain text that begins with S and has another S as its third character. Note that this does *not* select only three-character words.
="=s*s"	Records that contain text that begins and ends with S. You enter this exactly as shown: as a formula, with an initial equal sign. Alternatively, you can use a leading apostrophe and omit the quotes: '=s*s
<>*c	Records that contain text that does not end with the letter C.
=????	Records that contain exactly four letters.
<>?????	All records that don't contain exactly five letters.
<>*c*	Records that do not contain the letter C.
~?	Records that contain a single question mark character. (The tilde character overrides the wildcard question mark character.)
=	Records that contain a blank.
<>	Records that contain any nonblank entry.
="=c"	Records that contain the single character C. You enter this exactly as shown: as a formula, with an initial equal sign. Alternatively, you can use a leading apostrophe and omit the quotes: '=c

NOTE

The text comparisons are not case sensitive. For example, se* matches *Seligman, seller*, and SEC.

Specifying Multiple Criteria

Often, you may want to select records based on criteria that use more than one field or multiple values within a single field. These selection criteria involve logical OR or AND comparisons. Following are a few examples of the types of multiple criteria that you can apply to the real estate database:

- A list price less than $250,000, and square footage of at least 2,000

- A single-family home with a pool

- At least four bedrooms, at least three bathrooms, and square footage less than 3,000

- A home that has been listed for no more than two months, with a list price greater than $300,000

- A condominium with square footage between 1,000 and 1,500

- A single-family home listed in the month of March

To join criteria with an AND operator, use multiple columns in the criteria range. Figure 9-20 shows a criteria range that selects records with a list price of less than $250,000 and square footage of at least 2,000.

	A	B	C	D	E	F	G	H
1	List Price	SqFt						
2	<250000	>=2000						
3								
4								
5								
6								
7								
8	Agent	Date Listed	Area	List Price	Bedrooms	Baths	SqFt	Type
9	Shasta	10/2/2007	N. County	$349,000	3	2.5	1,727	Condo
31	Romero	8/3/2007	N. County	$359,900	3	2	2,198	Condo
35	Bennet	6/26/2007	S. County	$229,900	3	2.5	1,580	Single Fa
38	Lang	5/3/2007	N. County	$369,900	3	2.5	2,030	Condo
39	Shasta	2/10/2007	Central	$350,000	3	2	2,275	Single Fa
45	Shasta	5/19/2007	Central	$335,000	3	2.5	2,000	Single Fa
61	Shasta	3/24/2007	Central	$215,000	3	1.75	2,157	Single Fa

Sheet1

Figure 9-20: This criteria range uses multiple columns that select records using a logical AND operation.

Figure 9-21 shows another example. This criteria range displays listing that were listed in the month of March. Notice that the field name (Date Listed) appears twice in the criteria range. The criteria selects the records in which the Date Listed date is greater than or equal to March 1, and the Date Listed date is less than or equal to March 31.

CAUTION

The date selection criteria may not work properly for systems that don't use the U.S. date formats. To ensure compatibility with different date systems, use the DATE function to define such criteria, as in the following formulas:

```
=">="&DATE(2007,3,1)
="<="&DATE(2007,3,31)
```

	A	B	C	D	E	F	G
1	Date Listed	Date Listed					
2	>=3/1/2007	<=3/31/2007					
3							
4							
5							
6							
7							
8	Agent	Date Listed	Area	List Price	Bedrooms	Baths	SqFt
9	Shasta	10/2/2007	N. County	$349,000	3	2.5	1,727
31	Romero	8/3/2007	N. County	$359,900	3	2	2,198
35	Bennet	6/26/2007	S. County	$229,900	3	2.5	1,580
38	Lang	5/3/2007	N. County	$369,900	3	2.5	2,030
39	Shasta	2/10/2007	Central	$350,000	3	2	2,275

Sheet1

Figure 9-21: This criteria range selects records that describe properties that were listed in the month of March.

To join criteria with a logical OR operator, use more than one row in the criteria range. A criteria range can have any number of rows, each of which joins with the others via an OR operator. Figure 9-22 shows a criteria range (A1:C3) with two rows of criteria.

	A	B	C	D	E	F	G	H
1	Type	SqFt	List Price					
2	Condo	>=1800						
3	Single Family		<210000					
4								
5								
6								
7								
8	Agent	Date Listed	Area	List Price	Bedrooms	Baths	SqFt	Type
11	Jenkins	3/3/2007	S. County	$338,876	4	2.5	2,612	Single Family
24	Peterson	3/14/2007	Central	$364,900	4	2.5	2,507	Single Family
29	Lang	3/8/2007	Central	$229,900	4	3	2,006	Single Family
36	Jenkins	3/26/2007	S. County	$247,500	4	3	2,000	Single Family
44	Barnes	3/14/2007	N. County	$264,900	3	3	2,495	Condo
59	Shasta	3/24/2007	N. County	$398,000	4	2.5	2,620	Single Family
61	Shasta	3/24/2007	Central	$215,000	3	1.75	2,157	Single Family
66	Robinson	3/30/2007	N. County	$379,000	4	3	3,000	Single Family
76	Lang	3/23/2007	S. County	$325,000	4	3	2,770	Single Family
82	Romero	3/16/2007	Central	$235,910	4	3	2,285	Single Family
92	Barnes	3/23/2007	N. County	$350,000	3	2.5	1,991	Condo

Sheet1

Figure 9-22: This criteria range has two sets of criteria, each of which is in a separate row.

In this example, the filtered table shows the rows that meet either of the following conditions:

- A condo with a square footage of at least 1,800

    or

- A single-family home with a table price less than $210,000

NOTE

This is an example of the type of filtering that you cannot perform by using standard (non-advanced) filtering.

You can repeat a value on multiple rows to include the same criteria in two or more AND criteria. Suppose you want a condo in the Central area, but you would be willing to consider a condo in another area as long as it has a pool and at least three bedrooms. Figure 9-23 shows how you use the OR operator between the Area and the Pool and Bedrooms criteria but still limit your search to only one Type.

	A	B	C	D	E	F	G	
1	Type	Area	Pool	Bedrooms				
2	Condo	Central						
3	Condo		TRUE	>=3				
4								
5								
6								
7								
8	**Agent**	**Date Listed**	**Area**	**List Price**	**Bedrooms**	**Baths**	**SqFt**	**Ty**
9	Shasta	10/2/2007	N. County	$349,000	3	2.5	1,727	Co
10	Peterson	4/25/2007	S. County	$240,000	3	2.5	1,595	Co
11	Jenkins	3/3/2007	S. County	$338,876	4	2.5	2,612	Si
12	Peterson	4/15/2007	N. County	$259,900	4	3	1,734	Co
13	Daily	10/3/2007	Central	$340,000	4	2.5	2,517	Co
14	Bennet	7/1/2007	N. County	$229,500	6	3	2,700	Si
15	Lang	4/19/2007	S. County	$325,000	4	3	2,800	Co

◄ ► ► ► Sheet1

Figure 9-23: Repeating values in the criteria range applies the OR operator to only those criteria that aren't repeated.

Specifying Computed Criteria

Using computed criteria can make filtering even more powerful. Computed criteria filter the table based on one or more calculations. For example, you can specify computed criteria that displays only the rows in which the List Price (column D) is greater than average.

```
=D9>AVERAGE(D:D)
```

Notice that this formula uses a reference to the first data cell in the List Price column. Also, when you use computed criteria, the cell above it must *not* contain a field name. You can leave the top row blank or provide a descriptive label, such as Above Average.

By the way, you can also use a standard filter to display data that's above (or below) average.

The next computed criteria example displays the rows in which the price per square foot is less that $100. Cell D9 is the first data cell in the List Price column, and cell G9 is the first data cell in the SqFt column. The computed criteria formula is

```
=(D9/G9)<100
```

Part II

Figure 9-24 shows the real estate database after filtering to show only those listings that have a price per square foot less then $100. I added some formulas in column L to verify that the filtering is accurate.

	A	B	C	D	E	F	G	H	I	J	K	L
1	Under $100/SqFt											
2	FALSE											
3												
4												
5												
6												
7												
8	Agent	Date Listed	Area	List Price	Bedrooms	Baths	SqFt	Type	Pool	Sold		Per Sq Ft
16	Adams	4/21/2007	S. County	$208,750	4	3	2,207	Single Family	TRUE	TRUE		$94.59
20	Shasta	3/24/2007	Central	$215,000	3	1.75	2,157	Single Family	TRUE	TRUE		$99.68
25	Hamilton	8/29/2007	Central	$225,911	4	3	2,285	Single Family	TRUE	FALSE		$98.87
28	Bennet	7/1/2007	N. County	$229,500	6	3	2,700	Single Family	TRUE	FALSE		$85.00
38	Chung	9/30/2007	S. County	$235,990	5	3	2,723	Condo	FALSE	FALSE		$86.67
96	Lang	7/22/2007	N. County	$349,000	4	3	3,930	Single Family	TRUE	FALSE		$88.80
113	Peterson	9/1/2007	S. County	$365,000	5	3	3,938	Single Family	FALSE	FALSE		$92.69
117	Shasta	7/15/2007	N. County	$374,900	4	3	3,927	Single Family	FALSE	FALSE		$95.47
134												

Figure 9-24: Using computed criteria with advanced filtering.

Following is another example of a computed criteria formula. This formula displays the records listed within the past 60 days:

```
=B9>TODAY()-60
```

Keep these following points in mind when using computed criteria:

- Computed criteria formulas are always logical formulas: They must return either TRUE or FALSE.

- When referring to columns, use a reference to the cell in the first data row in the field of interest (not a reference to the cell that contains the field name).

- When you use computed criteria, do not use an existing field label in your criteria range. A computed criterion essentially computes a new field for the table. Therefore, you must supply a new field name in the first row of the criteria range. Or, if you prefer, you can simply leave the field name cell blank.

- You can use any number of computed criteria and mix and match them with noncomputed criteria.

- If your computed formula refers to a value outside the table, use an absolute reference rather than a relative reference. For example, use $C$1 rather than C1.

- In many cases, you may find it easier to add a new calculated column to your worksheet database or table and avoid using computed criteria.

Using Database Functions

To create formulas that return results based on a criteria range, use Excel's database worksheet functions. These functions all begin with the letter D, and they are listed in the Database category of the Insert Function dialog box.

Table 9-4 lists Excel's database functions. Each of these functions operates on a single field in the database.

TABLE 9-4   EXCEL'S DATABASE WORKSHEET FUNCTIONS

Function	Description
DAVERAGE	Returns the average of database entries that match the criteria
DCOUNT	Counts the cells containing numbers from the specified database and criteria
DCOUNTA	Counts nonblank cells from the specified database and criteria
DGET	Extracts from a database a single field from a single record that matches the specified criteria
DMAX	Returns the maximum value from selected database entries
DMIN	Returns the minimum value from selected database entries
DPRODUCT	Multiplies the values in a particular field of records that match the criteria in a database
DSTDEV	Estimates the standard deviation of the selected database entries (assumes that the data is a sample from a population) of selected database entries
DSTDEVP	Calculates the standard deviation of the selected database entries, based on the entire population of selected database entries
DSUM	Adds the numbers in the field column of records in the database that match the criteria
DVAR	Estimates the variance from selected database entries (assumes that the data is a sample from a population)
DVARP	Calculates the variance, based on the entire population of selected database entries

The database functions all require a separate criteria range, which is specified as the last argument for the function. The database functions use exactly the same type of criteria range as discussed earlier in "Specifying Advanced Filter Criteria."

Part II

See Figure 9-25. The formula in cell B24, which follows, uses the DSUM function to calculate the sum of values in a table that meet certain criteria. Specifically, the formula returns the sum of the Sales column for records in which the Month is Feb and the Region is North.

```
=DSUM(B6:G21,F6,Criteria)
```

	A	B	C	D	E	F	G	
1		Month	Region					
2		Feb	North					
3								
4								
5								
6		Month ▾	Sales Rep ▾	Region ▾	Contacts ▾	Sales ▾	Annualized ▾	
7		Jan	Bob	North	58	283,800	3,405,600	
8		Jan	Frank	North	35	507,200	6,086,400	
9		Jan	Paul	South	25	107,600	1,291,200	
11		Jan	Mary	South	39	226,700	2,720,400	
12		Feb	Bob	North	44	558,400	6,700,800	
13		Feb	Jill	North	46	350,400	4,204,800	
14		Feb	Frank	North	74	411,800	4,941,600	
15		Feb	Paul	South	29	154,200	1,850,400	
16		Feb	Randy	South	45	258,000	3,096,000	
17		Feb	Mary	South	52	233,800	2,805,600	
18		Mar	Bob	North	30	353,100	4,237,200	
19		Mar	Jill	North	44	532,100	6,385,200	
20		Mar	Frank	North	57	258,400	3,100,800	
21		Mar	Mary	South	36	134,300	1,611,600	
22								
23								
24		1,320,600	DSUM					
25								

Figure 9-25: Using the DSUM function to sum a table using a criteria range.

In this case, B6:G21 is the entire table, F6 is the column heading for Sales, and Criteria is the name for B1:C2 (the criteria range).

Following is an alternative version of this formula that uses structured table references:

```
=DSUM(Table1[#All],Table1[[#Headers],[Sales]],Criteria)
```

 ON THE CD

This workbook is available on the companion CD-ROM. The filename is `database formulas.xlsx`.

NOTE

You may find it cumbersome to set up a criteria range every time you need to use a database function. Fortunately, Excel provides some alternative ways to perform conditional sums and counts. Refer to Chapter 7 for examples that use SUMIF, COUNTIF, and various other techniques.

If you're an array formula aficionado, you might be tempted to use a literal array in place of the criteria range. In theory, the following array formula *should* work (and would eliminate the need for a separate criteria range). Unfortunately, the database functions do not support arrays, and this formula simply returns a #VALUE! error.

```
=DSUM(B6:G21,F6, {"Month","Region";"Feb","North"})
```

Inserting Subtotals

Excel's Data⇨Outline⇨Subtotal command is a handy tool that inserts formulas into a worksheet database automatically. These formulas use the SUBTOTAL function. To use this feature, your database must be sorted because the formulas are inserted whenever the value in a specified field changes. For more information about the SUBTOTAL function, refer to the sidebar, "About the SUBTOTAL Function," earlier in this chapter.

NOTE

When a table is selected, the Data⇨Outline⇨Subtotal command is not available. Therefore, this section applies only to worksheet databases. If your data is in a table and you need to insert subtotals automatically, convert the table to a range by using Table Tools⇨Design⇨Tools⇨Convert To Range. After you insert the subtotals, you can convert the range back to a table by using Insert⇨Tables⇨Table.

Figure 9-26 shows an example of a range that is appropriate for subtotals. This database is sorted by the Month field, and the Region field is sorted within months.

ON THE CD

This workbook, named `nested subtotals.xlsx`, is available on the companion CD-ROM.

To insert subtotal formulas into a worksheet database automatically, move the cell pointer anywhere in the database and choose Data⇨Outline⇨Subtotal. You will see the Subtotal dialog box, as shown in Figure 9-27.

	A	B	C	D	E	F
1	Month	State	Region	Contacts	Sales	
2	Jan	California	West	58	283,800	
3	Jan	Washington	West	35	507,200	
4	Jan	Oregon	West	39	226,700	
5	Jan	New York	East	25	107,600	
6	Jan	New Jersey	East	47	391,600	
7	Feb	California	West	44	558,400	
8	Feb	Washington	West	74	411,800	
9	Feb	Oregon	West	46	350,400	
10	Feb	New York	East	52	233,800	
11	Feb	New Jersey	East	29	154,200	
12	Mar	California	West	30	353,100	
13	Mar	Washington	West	57	258,400	
14	Mar	Oregon	West	44	532,100	
15	Mar	New York	East	36	134,300	
16	Mar	New Jersey	East	14	162,200	
17						
18						

Sheet1

Figure 9-26: This database is a good candidate for subtotals, which are inserted at each change of the month and at each change of the region.

Figure 9-27: The Subtotal dialog box automatically inserts subtotal formulas into a sorted table.

The Subtotal dialog box offers the following choices:

- **At Each Change In:** This drop-down table displays all fields in your table. You must have sorted the table by the field that you choose.

- **Use Function:** Choose from 11 functions. (Sum is the default.)

- **Add Subtotal To:** This list box shows all the fields in your table. Place a check mark next to the field or fields that you want to subtotal.

- **Replace Current Subtotals:** If checked, Excel removes any existing subtotal formulas and replaces them with the new subtotals.

- **Page Break between Groups:** If checked, Excel inserts a manual page break after each subtotal.

- **Summary below Data:** If checked, Excel places the subtotals below the data (the default). Otherwise, the subtotal formulas appear above the data.

- **Remove All:** This button removes all subtotal formulas in the table.

When you click OK, Excel analyzes the database and inserts formulas as specified — and even creates an outline for you. Figure 9-28 shows a worksheet after adding two sets of subtotals: one that summarizes by month, and another that summarizes by region. You can, of course, use the SUBTOTAL function in formulas that you create manually. Using the Data⇨Outline⇨Subtotals command is usually easier.

	Month	State	Region	Contacts	Sales
1	**Month**	**State**	**Region**	**Contacts**	**Sales**
2	Jan	California	West	58	283,800
3	Jan	Washington	West	35	507,200
4	Jan	Oregon	West	39	226,700
5			**West Total**	132	1,017,700
6	Jan	New York	East	25	107,600
7	Jan	New Jersey	East	47	391,600
8			**East Total**	72	499,200
9	**Jan Total**			204	1,516,900
10	Feb	California	West	44	558,400
11	Feb	Washington	West	74	411,800
12	Feb	Oregon	West	46	350,400
13			**West Total**	164	1,320,600
14	Feb	New York	East	52	233,800
15	Feb	New Jersey	East	29	154,200
16			**East Total**	81	388,000
17	**Feb Total**			245	1,708,600
18	Mar	California	West	30	353,100
19	Mar	Washington	West	57	258,400
20	Mar	Oregon	West	44	532,100
21			**West Total**	131	1,143,600
22	Mar	New York	East	36	134,300
23	Mar	New Jersey	East	14	162,200
24			**East Total**	50	296,500
25	**Mar Total**			181	1,440,100
26	**Grand Total**			630	4,665,600
27					

Figure 9-28: Excel adds the subtotal formulas automatically and creates an outline.

Part II

CAUTION

If you add subtotals to a filtered database, the subtotals may no longer be accurate when you remove the filter.

TIP

When you apply the second subtotal, remember to clear the Replace Current Subtotals check box on the Subtotal dialog box.

The formulas all use the SUBTOTAL worksheet function. For example, the formula in cell E9 (total sales for January) is as follows:

```
=SUBTOTAL(9,E2:E7)
```

Although this formula refers to two other cells that contain a SUBTOTAL formula (E5 and E8), those cells are not included in the sum to avoid double-counting.

You can use the outline controls to adjust the level of detail shown. Figure 9-29, for example, shows only the summary rows from the subtotaled table. These rows contain the SUBTOTAL formulas. I did column B because it shows only empty cells.

		A	C	D	E	F
	1	Month	Region	Contacts	Sales	
+	5		West Total	132	1,017,700	
+	8		East Total	72	499,200	
−	9	Jan Total		204	1,516,900	
+	13		West Total	164	1,320,600	
+	16		East Total	81	388,000	
−	17	Feb Total		245	1,708,600	
+	21		West Total	131	1,143,600	
+	24		East Total	50	296,500	
−	25	Mar Total		181	1,440,100	
−	26	Grand Total		630	4,665,600	
	27					
	28					

Figure 9-29: Use the outline controls to hide the detail and display only the summary rows.

Chapter 10

Miscellaneous Calculations

IN THIS CHAPTER

- ◆ Converting between measurement units
- ◆ Formulas for calculating the various parts of a right triangle
- ◆ Calculations for area, surface, circumference, and volume
- ◆ Matrix functions to solve simultaneous equations
- ◆ Formulas that demonstrate various ways to round numbers

This chapter contains reference information that may be useful to you at some point. Consider it a cheat sheet to help you remember the stuff you may have learned but have long since forgotten.

Unit Conversions

You know the distance from New York to London in miles, but your European office needs the numbers in kilometers. What's the conversion factor?

Excel's CONVERT function can convert between a variety of measurements in the following categories:

- • Weight and mass
- • Distance

- Time

- Pressure

- Force

- Energy

- Power

- Magnetism

- Temperature

- Liquid measures

 NEW

In previous versions of Excel, the CONVERT function required the Analysis TookPak add-in. In Excel 2007, this useful function is built in.

The CONVERT function requires three arguments: the value to be converted, the from-unit, and the to-unit. For example, if cell A1 contains a distance expressed in miles, use this formula to convert miles to kilometers:

```
=CONVERT(A1,"mi","km")
```

The second and third arguments are unit abbreviations, which are listed in the Help system. Some of the abbreviations are commonly used, but others aren't. And, of course, you must use the *exact* abbreviation. Furthermore, the unit abbreviations are case sensitive, so the following formula returns an error:

```
=CONVERT(A1,"Mi","km")
```

The CONVERT function is even more versatile than it seems. When using metric units, you can apply a multiplier. In fact, the first example I presented uses a multiplier. The actual unit abbreviation for the third argument is m for meters. I added the kilo-multipler — k — to express the result in kilometers.

In some situations, the CONVERT function requires some creativity. For example, what if you need to convert ten square yards to square feet? Neither of these units are available, but the following formula will do the job:

```
=CONVERT(CONVERT(10,"yd","ft"),"yd","ft")
```

The nested instance of CONVERT converts ten yards into feet, and this result (30) is used as the first argument of the outer instance of the function. Similarly, to convert ten cubic yards into unit cubic feet, use this formula:

```
=CONVERT(CONVERT(CONVERT(10,"yd","ft"),"yd","ft"),"yd","ft")
```

Need to Convert Other Units?

The CONVERT function, of course, doesn't handle every possible unit conversion. To calculate other unit conversions, you need to find the appropriate conversion factor. The Internet is a good source for such information. Use any Web search engine and enter search terms that correspond to the units you use. Likely, you'll find the information you need.

Also, you can download a copy of Josh Madison's popular (and free) Convert software. This excellent program can handle just about any conceivable unit conversion you throw at it. The URL is as follows:

```
www.joshmadison.com/software
```

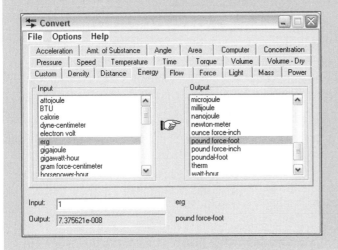

ON THE CD

The companion CD-ROM includes a workbook named `unit conversion tables.xlsx` that contains conversion factors for a number of units. This workbook uses hard-coded conversion factors and does not use the CONVERT function.

Solving Right Triangles

A *right triangle* has six components: three sides and three angles. Figure 10-1 shows a right triangle with its various parts labeled. Angles are labeled A, B, and C; sides are labeled Hypotenuse, Base, and Height. Angle C is always 90 degrees (or PI/2 radians). If you know any two of these components (excluding Angle C, which is always known), you can use formulas to solve for the others.

The Pythagorean theorem states that

```
Height^2 + Base^2 = Hypotenuse^2
```

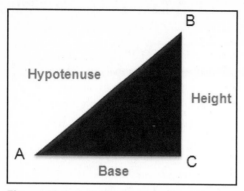

Figure 10-1: A right triangle's components.

Therefore, if you know two sides of a right triangle, you can calculate the remaining side. The formula to calculate a right triangle's height (given the length of the hypotenuse and base) is as follows:

```
=SQRT((hypotenuse^2)-(base^2))
```

The formula to calculate a right triangle's base (given the length of the hypotenuse and height) is as follows:

```
=SQRT((hypotenuse^2)-(height^2))
```

The formula to calculate a right triangle's hypotenuse (given the length of the base and height) is as follows:

```
=SQRT((height^2)+(base^2))
```

Other useful trigonometric identities are

```
SIN(A) = Height/Hypotenuse
SIN(B) = Base/Hypotenuse
COS(A) = Base/Hypotenuse
COS(B) = Height/Hypotenuse
TAN(A) = Height/Base
SIN(A) = Base/Height
```

 NOTE

Excel's trigonometric functions all assume that the angle arguments are in radians. To convert degrees to radians, use the RADIANS function. To convert radians to degrees, use the DEGREES function.

If you know the height and base, you can use the following formula to calculate the angle formed by the hypotenuse and base (angle A).

```
=ATAN(height/base)
```

The preceding formula returns radians. To convert to degrees, use this formula:

```
=DEGREES(ATAN(height/base))
```

If you know the height and base, you can use the following formula to calculate the angle formed by the hypotenuse and height (angle B):

```
=PI()/2-ATAN(height/base)
```

The preceding formula returns radians. To convert to degrees, use this formula:

```
=90-DEGREES(ATAN(height/base))
```

ON THE CD

The companion CD-ROM contains a workbook, `solve right triangle.xlsm`, with formulas that calculate various parts of a right triangle, given two known parts. These formulas give you some insight on working with right triangles. The workbook uses a simple VBA macro to enable you to specify the known parts of the triangle.

Figure 10-2 shows a workbook containing formulas to calculate the various parts of a right triangle.

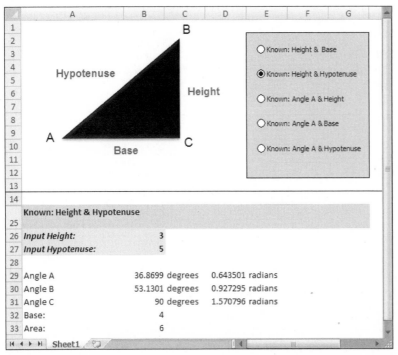

Figure 10-2: This workbook is useful for working with right triangles.

Part II

Area, Surface, Circumference, and Volume Calculations

This section contains formulas for calculating the area, surface, circumference, and volume for common two- and three-dimensional shapes.

Calculating the Area and Perimeter of a Square

To calculate the area of a square, square the length of one side. The following formula calculates the area of a square for a cell named *side:*

```
=side^2
```

To calculate the perimeter of a square, multiply one side by 4. The following formula uses a cell named *side* to calculate the perimeter of a square:

```
=side*4
```

Calculating the Area and Perimeter of a Rectangle

To calculate the area of a rectangle, multiply its height by its base. The following formula returns the area of a rectangle, using cells named *height* and *base:*

```
=height*base
```

To calculate the perimeter of a rectangle, multiply the height by 2 and then add it to the width multiplied by 2. The following formula returns the perimeter of a rectangle, using cells named *height* and *width:*

```
=(height*2)+(width*2)
```

Calculating the Area and Perimeter of a Circle

To calculate the area of a circle, multiply the square of the radius by Π. The following formula returns the area of a circle. It assumes that a cell named *radius* contains the circle's radius:

```
=PI()*(radius^2)
```

The radius of a circle is equal to one-half of the diameter.

To calculate the circumference of a circle, multiply the diameter of the circle by Π. The following formula calculates the circumference of a circle using a cell named *diameter:*

```
=diameter*PI()
```

The diameter of a circle is the radius times 2.

Calculating the Area of a Trapezoid

To calculate the area of a trapezoid, add the two parallel sides, multiply by the height, and then divide by 2. The following formula calculates the area of a trapezoid, using cells named *parallel side 1, parallel side 2,* and *height:*

```
=((parallel side 1+parallel side 2)*height)/2
```

Calculating the Area of a Triangle

To calculate the area of a triangle, multiply the base by the height and then divide by 2. The following formula calculates the area of a triangle, using cells named *base* and *height:*

```
=(base*height)/2
```

Calculating the Surface and Volume of a Sphere

To calculate the surface of a sphere, multiply the square of the radius by Π and then multiply by 4. The following formula returns the surface of a sphere, the radius of which is in a cell named *radius:*

```
=PI()*(radius^2)*4
```

To calculate the volume of a sphere, multiply the cube of the radius by 4 times Π and then divide by 3. The following formula calculates the volume of a sphere. The cell named *radius* contains the sphere's radius.

```
=((radius^3)*(4*PI()))/3
```

Calculating the Surface and Volume of a Cube

To calculate the surface area of a cube, square one side and multiply by 6. The following formula calculates the surface of a cube using a cell named *side,* which contains the length of a side of the cube:

```
=(side^2)*6
```

To calculate the volume of a cube, raise the length of one side to the third power. The following formula returns the volume of a cube, using a cell named *side:*

```
=side^3
```

Calculating the Surface and Volume of a Cone

The following formula calculates the surface of a cone (including the surface of the base). This formula uses cells named *radius* and *height:*

```
=PI()*radius*(SQRT(height^2+radius^2)+radius))
```

To calculate the volume of a cone, multiply the square of the radius of the base by Π, multiply by the height, and then divide by 3. The following formula returns the volume of a cone, using cells named *radius* and *height:*

```
=(PI()*(radius^2)*height)/3
```

Calculating the Volume of a Cylinder

To calculate the volume of a cylinder, multiply the square of the radius of the base by Π and then multiply by the height. The following formula calculates the volume of a cylinder, using cells named *radius* and *height:*

```
=(PI()*(radius^2)*height)
```

Calculating the Volume of a Pyramid

Calculate the area of the base, multiply by the height, and then divide by 3. This next formula calculates the volume of a pyramid. It assumes cells named *width* (the width of the base), *length* (the length of the base), and *height* (the height of the pyramid).

```
=(width*length*height)/3
```

Solving Simultaneous Equations

This section describes how to use formulas to solve simultaneous linear equations. The following is an example of a set of simultaneous linear equations:

```
3x + 4y = 8
4x + 8y = 1
```

Solving a set of simultaneous equations involves finding the values for x and y that satisfy both equations. For this set of equations, the solution is as follows:

```
x = 7.5
y = -3.625
```

The number of variables in the set of equations must be equal to the number of equations. The preceding example uses two equations with two variables. Three equations are required to solve for three variables (x, y, and z).

The general steps for solving a set of simultaneous equations follow. See Figure 10-3, which uses the equations presented at the beginning of this section.

1. Express the equations in standard form. If necessary, use simple algebra to rewrite the equations such that the variables all appear on the left side of the equal sign. The two equations that follow are identical, but the second one is in standard form:

```
3x -8 = -4y
3x + 4y = 8
```

2. Place the coefficients in an *n* x *n* range of cells, where *n* represents the number of equations. In Figure 10-3, the coefficients are in the range I2:J3.

3. Place the constants (the numbers on the right side of the equal sign) in a vertical range of cells. In Figure 10-3, the constants are in the range L2:L3.

4. Use an array formula to calculate the inverse of the coefficient matrix. In Figure 10-3, the following array formula is entered into the range I6:J7. (Remember to use Ctrl+Shift+Enter to enter an array formula.)

```
{=MINVERSE(I2:J3)}
```

5. Use an array formula to multiply the inverse of the coefficient matrix by the constant matrix. In Figure 10-3, the following array formula is entered into the range J10:J11. This range holds the solution.

```
{=MMULT(I6:J7,L2:L3)}
```

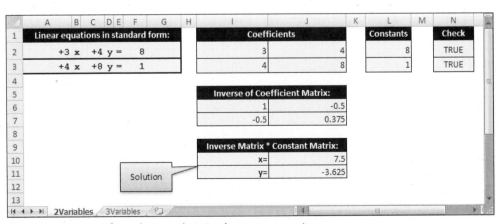

Figure 10-3: Using formulas to solve simultaneous equations.

Part II

CROSS REF

Refer to Chapter 14 for more information on array formulas. Chapter 16 demonstrates how to use iteration to solve some simultaneous equations.

ON THE CD

You can access the workbook, `simultaneous equations.xlsx`, shown in Figure 10-3, on the companion CD-ROM. This workbook solves simultaneous equations with two or three variables.

Rounding Numbers

Excel provides quite a few functions that round values in various ways. Table 10-1 summarizes these functions.

CAUTION

It's important to understand the difference between rounding a value and formatting a value. When you format a number to display a specific number of decimal places, formulas that refer to that number use the actual value, which may differ from the displayed value. When you round a number, formulas that refer to that value use the rounded number.

TABLE 10-1   EXCEL ROUNDING FUNCTIONS

Function	Description
CEILING	Rounds a number up (away from zero) to the nearest specified multiple
DOLLARDE	Converts a dollar price expressed as a fraction into a decimal number
DOLLARFR	Converts a dollar price expressed as a decimal into a fractional number
EVEN	Rounds a number up (away from zero) to the nearest even integer
FLOOR	Rounds a number down (toward zero) to the nearest specified multiple
INT	Rounds a number down to make it an integer
MROUND	Rounds a number to a specified multiple
ODD	Rounds a number up (away from zero) to the nearest odd integer

Function	Description
ROUND	Rounds a number to a specified number of digits
ROUNDDOWN	Rounds a number down (toward zero) to a specified number of digits
ROUNDUP	Rounds a number up (away from zero) to a specified number of digits
TRUNC	Truncates a number to a specified number of significant digits

CROSS REF

Chapter 6 contains examples of rounding time values.

The following sections provide examples of formulas that use various types of rounding.

Basic Rounding Formulas

The ROUND function is useful for basic rounding to a specified number of digits. You specify the number of digits in the second argument for the ROUND function. For example, the formula that follows returns 123.40 (the value is rounded to one decimal place):

```
=ROUND(123.37,1)
```

If the second argument for the ROUND function is zero, the value is rounded to the nearest integer. The formula that follows, for example, returns 123.00:

```
=ROUND(123.37,0)
```

The second argument for the ROUND function can also be negative. In such a case, the number is rounded to the left of the decimal point. The following formula, for example, returns 120.00:

```
=ROUND(123.37,-1)
```

The ROUND function rounds either up or down. But how does it handle a number such as 12.5, rounded to no decimal places? You'll find that the ROUND function rounds such numbers away from zero. The formula that follows, for instance, returns 13.0:

```
=ROUND(12.5,0)
```

The next formula returns −13.00 (the rounding occurs away from zero):

```
=ROUND(-12.5,0)
```

Part II

To force rounding to occur in a particular direction, use the ROUNDUP or ROUNDDOWN functions. The following formula, for example, returns 12.0. The value rounds down.

```
=ROUNDDOWN(12.5,0)
```

The formula that follows returns 13.0. The value rounds up to the nearest whole value.

```
=ROUNDUP(12.43,0)
```

Rounding to the Nearest Multiple

The MROUND function is useful for rounding values to the nearest multiple. For example, you can use this function to round a number to the nearest 5. The following formula returns 135:

```
=MROUND(133,5)
```

Rounding Currency Values

Often, you need to round currency values. For example, you may need to round a dollar amount to the nearest penny. A calculated price may be something like $45.78923. In such a case, you'll want to round the calculated price to the nearest penny. This may sound simple, but there are actually three ways to round such a value:

- Round it up to the nearest penny.
- Round it down to the nearest penny.
- Round it to the nearest penny (the rounding may be up or down).

The following formula assumes a dollar and cents value is in cell A1. The formula rounds the value to the nearest penny. For example, if cell A1 contains $12.421, the formula returns $12.42.

```
=ROUND(A1,2)
```

If you need to round the value up to the nearest penny, use the CEILING function. The following formula rounds the value in cell A1 up to the nearest penny. For example, if cell A1 contains $12.421, the formula returns $12.43.

```
=CEILING(A1,0.01)
```

To round a dollar value down, use the FLOOR function. The following formula, for example, rounds the dollar value in cell A1 down to the nearest penny. If cell A1 contains $12.421, the formula returns $12.42.

```
=FLOOR(A1,0.01)
```

To round a dollar value up to the nearest nickel, use this formula:

```
=CEILING(A1,0.05)
```

You've probably noticed that many retail prices end in $0.99. If you have an even dollar price and you want it to end in $0.99, just subtract .01 from the price. Some higher-ticket items are always priced to end with $9.99. To round a price to the nearest $9.99, first round it to the nearest $10.00 and then subtract a penny. If cell A1 contains a price, use a formula like this to convert it to a price that ends in $9.99:

```
=ROUND(A1/10,0)*10-0.01
```

For example, if cell A1 contains $345.78, the formula returns $349.99.

A simpler approach uses the MROUND function:

```
=MROUND(A1,10)-0.01
```

Working with Fractional Dollars

The DOLLARFR and DOLLARDE functions are useful when working with fractional dollar value, as in stock market quotes.

Consider the value $9.25. You can express the decimal part as a fractional value ($9 1/4, $9 2/8, $9 4/16, and so on). The DOLLARFR function takes two arguments: the dollar amount and the denominator for the fractional part. The following formula, for example, returns 9.1 (the .1 decimal represents 1/4):

```
=DOLLARFR(9.25,4)
```

 CAUTION

In most situations, you won't use the value returned by the DOLLARFR function in other calculations. In the preceding example, the result of the function will be interpreted as 9.1, not 9.25. To perform calculations on such a value, you need to convert it back to a decimal value by using the DOLLARDE function.

The DOLLARDE function converts a dollar value expressed as a fraction to a decimal amount. It also uses a second argument to specify the denominator of the fractional part. The following formula, for example, returns 9.25:

```
=DOLLARDE(9.1,4)
```

TIP
The DOLLARDE and DOLLARFR functions aren't limited to dollar values. For example, you can use these functions to work with feet and inches. You might have a value that represents 8.5 feet. Use the following formula to express this value in terms of feet and inches. The formula returns 8.06 (which represents 8 feet, 6 inches).

```
=DOLLARFR(8.5,12)
```

Another example is baseball statistics. A pitcher may work 6⅔ innings, and this is usually represented as 6.2. The following formula displays 6.2:

```
=DOLLARFR(6+2/3,3)
```

Using the INT and TRUNC Functions

On the surface, the INT and TRUNC functions seem similar. Both convert a value to an integer. The TRUNC function simply removes the fractional part of a number. The INT function rounds a number down to the nearest integer, based on the value of the fractional part of the number.

In practice, INT and TRUNC return different results only when using negative numbers. For example, the following formula returns –14.0:

```
=TRUNC(-14.2)
```

The next formula returns –15.0 because –14.3 is rounded down to the next lower integer:

```
=INT(-14.2)
```

The TRUNC function takes an additional (optional) argument that's useful for truncating decimal values. For example, the formula that follows returns 54.33 (the value truncated to two decimal places):

```
=TRUNC(54.3333333,2)
```

Rounding to an Even or Odd Integer

The ODD and EVEN functions are provided for situations in which you need to round a number up to the nearest odd or even integer. These functions take a single argument and return an integer value. The EVEN function rounds its argument up to the nearest even integer. The ODD function rounds its argument up to the nearest odd integer. Table 10-2 shows some examples of these functions.

TABLE 10-2 RESULTS USING THE EVEN AND ODD FUNCTIONS

Number	EVEN Function	ODD Function
–3.6	–4	–5
–3.0	–4	–3
–2.4	–4	–3
–1.8	–2	–3
–1.2	–2	–3
–0.6	–2	–1
0.0	0	1
0.6	2	1
1.2	2	3
1.8	2	3
2.4	4	3
3.0	4	3
3.6	4	5

Rounding to *n* Significant Digits

In some cases, you may need to round a value to a particular number of significant digits. For example, you might want to express the value 1,432,187 in terms of two significant digits (that is, as 1,400,000). The value 9,187,877 expressed in terms of three significant digits is 9,180,000.

If the value is a positive number with no decimal places, the following formula does the job. This formula rounds the number in cell A1 to two significant digits. To round to a different number of significant digits, replace the 2 in this formula with a different number.

```
=ROUNDDOWN(A1,2-LEN(A1))
```

For non-integers and negative numbers, the solution gets a bit trickier. The formula that follows provides a more general solution that rounds the value in cell A1 to the number of significant digits specified in cell A2. This formula works for positive and negative integers and non-integers.

```
=ROUND(A1,A2-1-INT(LOG10(ABS(A1))))
```

For example, if cell A1 contains 1.27845 and cell A2 contains 3, the formula returns 1.28000 (the value, rounded to three significant digits).

Part III

Financial Formulas

Chapter 11

Borrowing and Investing Formulas

IN THIS CHAPTER

- ◆ Introducing the fundamental concept of time value of money
- ◆ Explaining financial terms
- ◆ Using the basic financial functions
- ◆ Calculating the interest and principal components of payments
- ◆ Converting between different types of interest rates
- ◆ Understanding the limitations of the Excel financial functions
- ◆ Calculating price and yield of bonds

It's a safe bet that the most common use of Excel is to perform calculations involving money. Every day, people make hundreds of thousands of financial decisions based on the numbers that are calculated in a spreadsheet. These decisions range from simple (*Can I afford to buy a new car?*) to complex (*Will purchasing XYZ Corporation result in a positive cash flow in the next 18 months?*). This is the first of three chapters that discuss financial calculations that you can perform with the assistance of Excel.

Financial Concepts

Before you start using Excel's financial functions, you must be familiar with some basic concepts. These concepts are not specific to Excel, but they are necessary when constructing financial formulas. If you're already well versed in finance and financial terminology, a quick skim of this section is all that is needed. If you're new to creating financial formulas, make sure you have a solid understanding of the following concepts.

Time Value of Money

The concept of Time Value of Money, or TVM, simply means that money has a different value depending on what time it is. That is, not the time of day, but the time relative to right now (or some other defined time). If I give you $1,000 today, it's worth precisely $1,000. However, if I give you $1,000 in a year, that money will be worth $1,000 when I give to you, but it's worth something different today.

If you had the $1,000 today, you could put it in a savings account, invest it in stocks and bonds, or go on a wild shopping spree. You would have control over the money, and you could put it to work for you. Because you're not going to get the money for a year, it's worth less to you now. In fact, you may be willing to take a lesser amount if you got paid today.

These are all practical implementation of the concept of TVM:

- Banks charge and pay interest.
- Lotteries pay out less when you take the lump sum option.
- Vendors give a discount when you pay earlier than the normal terms.

Cash In and Cash Out

All financial formulas are based on cash flows: that is, cash that is flowing out *(payments)* and cash that is flowing in *(receipts)*. Even those financial transactions that don't seem to be dealing with cash flows, really are. If you buy a car on credit, you get a car, and the bank gets a promise. No cash, right? From a financial perspective, the bank is giving you cash to buy a car (positive cash flow to you); and, in the future, you will pay back that money (negative cash flow to you). The fact that the money was used to buy a car doesn't change the underlying financial transaction. Always think in terms of cash in or out.

The first decision you make when constructing a financial formula is who is asking the question. Because you must designate the cash flows as either positive or negative, you need to determine from whose pocket the cash will be flowing:

- If you buy a house and calculate your mortgage payments, the cash flows are from your perspective:

- When you borrow the money for the house, it's a positive cash flow.

- When you make mortgage payments, it's a negative cash flow.

- The cash flows are the opposite if the bank is doing the calculation.

In Excel's financial functions, positive cash flows are shown as positive values, and negative cash flows are shows as negative values.

TIP

When a formula returns a result that you know is wrong, the first place to look is at the signs in front of the cash flow numbers.

Matching Time Periods

A common problem that you may encounter when working with Excel's financial functions is the matching of time periods. It's a simple concept, but it is often overlooked. Simply put, the time period that your payment covers must match the time period of your interest rate. If you put a monthly payment into a financial function, along with an annual interest rate, the result will be wrong. In this case, you need to convert the interest rate to a monthly rate so it matches the payment frequency.

The examples in this chapter deal with the issue of matching time periods explicitly. When you see an interest rate divided by 12, it probably means that an annual interest rate is being converted into a monthly interest rate.

Timing of the First Payment

The final concept to keep in mind when constructing financial formulas is the timing of the first payment. Sometimes the first payment is made right away. Usually, the first payment is made after the first month (or whatever period payments are normally made). For example, if you get a car loan on May 15, you probably don't have to make the first payment until June 15.

In Excel formulas, first payment timing is handled in the Type argument of various functions:

- If the first payment is made *in arrears* (after the first period), you use a Type of 0 (zero), which is generally the default.

- If the first payment is made in advance, use a Type of 1.

NOTE

Down payments are not considered regular payments, so they don't affect which Type argument you specify. Many of the examples in this chapter use down payments, and their handling is discussed then.

The Basic Excel Financial Functions

Excel has five basic financial functions: PV, FV, PMT, RATE, and NPER. I discuss each of these functions in this section, and also provide examples.

 NOTE
All these functions are related in that they are all looking at different sides of the same situation. Many of the arguments are the same from function to function.

Calculating Present Value

The PV function returns the present value of future cash flows. We know that money in the future has a different value than money today. This function tells us how much that future money is worth right now. Its syntax, with required arguments in bold, is

PV(**rate, nper, pmt**, fv, type)

The example in this section computes the present value of a series of future receipts, sometimes called an *annuity*. You get one payment of $1,200 each year for ten years. The value of those payments right now is $6,780.27.

```
=PV(.12,10,1200,0,0)
```

In other words, if the payer offered you more than $6,800 right now (so he wouldn't have to make the payments to you in the future), you would take it. If he offered you less, you would pass and wait for the regular payments.

 ON THE CD
The file `basic financial formulas.xlsx` on the companion CD-ROM contains all the examples in this section.

You may have noticed that in the preceding formula, the interest rate (12%) appeared out of thin air. The PV function is usually used to determine how much a specific future amount is worth today. A specific interest rate is not available in those situations.

 NOTE
There are a lot of opinions on what discount rate you should use, and which one you choose depends a lot on your personality. Some say that you should use the interest rate you would get from a bank if you borrowed the money with no collateral. Others say you should use the interest rate you would receive if you made a risk-free investment, like in a U.S. Treasury bill. In this example, I use the rate of return you would make if you invested the money in the stock market—because I know you're a shrewd investor.

Financial Function Arguments

The five basic Excel financial functions have many common arguments. The arguments and their meanings are listed here:

- **Rate:** The interest rate, expressed as a percentage, that is paid on a loan or used to discount future cash flows.

  The period that the interest rate covers must be the same period used for Nper and Pmt.

- **Nper:** The number of periods. This could be the number of payments on a loan or the number of years that money is kept in a savings account.

  The number of periods must be expressed in the same terms as Rate and Pmt. A 30-year mortgage with monthly payments, for instance, would have an Nper of 360. Three-hundred-sixty months is the number of periods, not 30 years.

- **Pmt:** The amount of each payment. For these financial functions, the payments must be the same amount and made at regular intervals.

  The payment amount is normally made up of both principal and interest.

- **Fv:** The future value. This is the last cash flow that settles the transaction. In many cases, the payments settle the transaction (for example, pay off the loan), so there is no future value.

- **Pv:** The present value. This is the first cash flow that starts the transaction, such as borrowing money on a loan or putting money into a savings account.

  If the transaction is made up of just payments, there may not be a present value.

- **Type:** Whether the payments are made in arrears (0 or default) or in advance (1).

  See the preceding section, "Financial Concepts," for more detailed information on Type.

- **Guess:** An approximation of the result. When computing an interest rate, Excel must perform many iterations to get the answer.

  You can help Excel by specifying a Guess argument that's close to the expected result.

By choosing 12% in this example, I'm saying that you can take the $6,800, invest it so that you make a 12% return, and you'll be in the same financial position as if you had just waited for the $1,200 payments. If the payer offers you $7,000, you can invest that and be in a better position.

Now let's turn the tables and say that you have an obligation to pay someone $1,200 per year for ten years. That formula looks like this:

```
=PV(.12,10,-1200,0,0)
```

Instead of a positive cash flow, this formula shows a negative cash flow. The result, $6,780.27, is also oppositely signed from the previous result. In both examples, the sum total of the payments constitutes the entire transaction, so there is no future value. Also, the default value of zero for the Type argument is included. Both the Fv argument and the Type argument are optional, but they are included here for clarity. Figure 11-1 shows these examples in a workbook.

NOTE

For simplicity, the formulas presented in this chapter use literal values for function arguments. In most cases, you'll use cell references for the arguments.

	A	B	C	D
1		**PV, Annuity**		**PV, Annuity**
2	Rate:	12.0%		12.0%
3	Period:	10		10
4	Payment:	$1,200.00		($1,200.00)
5	Future Value:	$0.00		$0.00
6	Type:	0		0
7				
8	Present Value:	($6,780.27)		$6,780.27
9				
10				
11				
12				
13				
14				
15				

Present Value / Future Value

Figure 11-1: Some present value calculations.

CAUTION

When entering numeric data as function arguments, make sure that you don't insert thousands separators. For example, type **1000**, not **1,000**. Depending on your regional settings, the thousands separator may be the same character as the argument separator.

PRESENT VALUE OF A LUMP SUM

The previous examples dealt with a series of future cash flows, but sometimes there's just one big future cash flow.

For the next example, assume a wealthy relative wants to give you $100,000, but that you can't collect it until your fortieth birthday. If you are 25 years old now, the value of that future gift would be $31,524.17 and is computed as follows:

```
=PV(.08,15,0,100000)
```

The payment is an inflow (a positive $100,000) that will occur 15 years from now. If you had some money now, you think you could make 8% investing it. Because there are no payments, the Type argument is irrelevant.

The result of this formula means that if you did have $31,500 now and you invested it at 8%, it would be worth $100,000 in 15 years. See Figure 11-2.

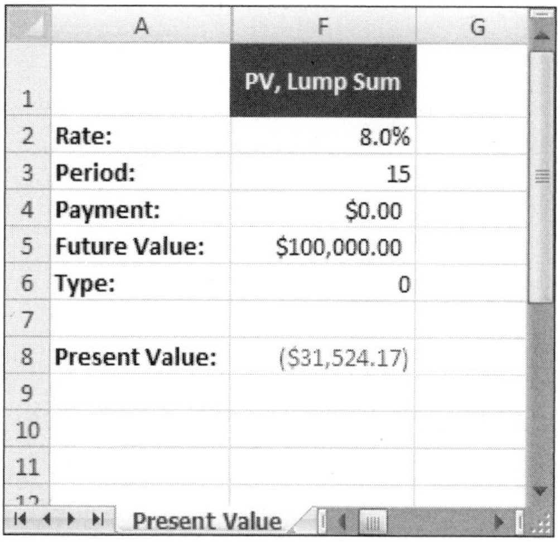

	A	F	G
1		**PV, Lump Sum**	
2	Rate:	8.0%	
3	Period:	15	
4	Payment:	$0.00	
5	Future Value:	$100,000.00	
6	Type:	0	
7			
8	Present Value:	($31,524.17)	
9			
10			
11			

Present Value

Figure 11-2: Calculating the present value of a lump sum.

PRESENT VALUE OF AN ANNUITY WITH A LUMP SUM

In some cases, future cash flows are followed by a single big future cash flow.

Assume that your brother-in-law wants you to invest in his carpet cleaning business. If you'll invest $50,000 now, he will pay you $200 per month for five years and then also pay you $60,000 at the end of the five years. To determine whether this is a good deal, find the present value of all your future cash inflows:

```
=PV(.1/12,60,200,60000,1)
```

Let's look at each of these arguments (see Figure 11-3):

- You determined that you could make 10% on your money elsewhere, so 10% is the discount rate.

- All the arguments must cover the same time period. Because the $200 payment is made monthly, all the arguments must be converted to months:

  - The **Rate argument** is divided by 12 (for 12 months).

  - The **Nper argument** is expressed as 60 (for 60 months; not 5 for 5 years).

- The payment amount and the lump sum amount were laid out in the deal.

- The Type argument is 1 because I assume he'll want the first payment now (in advance).

	A	H	I	J
1		PV, Annuity, Lump Sum		
2	Rate:	0.8%		
3	Period:	60		
4	Payment:	$200.00		
5	Future Value:	$60,000.00		
6	Type:	1		
7				
8	Present Value:	($45,958.83)		
9				
10				

Figure 11-3: Calculating a present value of an annuity with a lump sum.

The formula tells us that the value of all those future cash flows is $45,958.83. According to the terms of this deal and your assumptions, you could make more money investing your $50,000 elsewhere.

TIP

You can plug in different values for the arguments until you find a solution that is favorable — and then make a counter proposal to your brother-in-law. You can even use Excel's goal seek feature (Data⇨Data Tools⇨What-If Analysis⇨Goal Seek) to find the value of an argument that results in your desired present value.

Calculating Future Value

The future value is the other side of time value of money coin. It calculates how much a known quantity of money (or a known series of payments) will be worth at some point in the future. The syntax for the FV function follows. Arguments in bold are required arguments.

```
FV(rate, nper, pmt, pv, type)
```

FUTURE VALUE OF PAYMENTS

For this example, assume you start a savings account for your new baby's college education. Starting next month, you'll put $50 per month in the account, and you'll earn 3% interest. The formula that follows shows that, in 18 years, the account will have $14,297.02 (see Figure 11-4).

```
=FV(.03/12,18*12,-50,0,0)
```

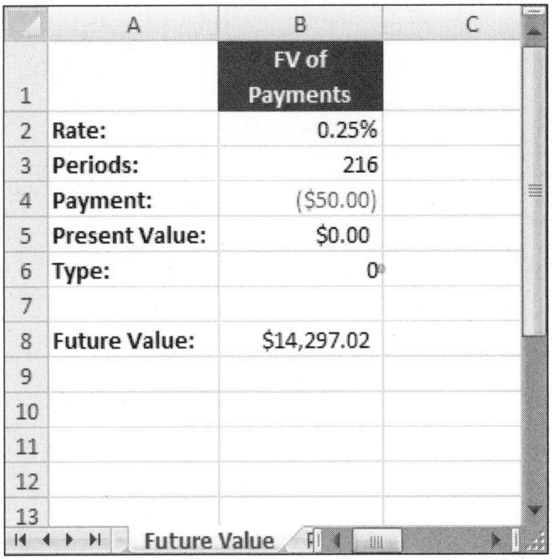

	A	B	C
1		**FV of Payments**	
2	Rate:	0.25%	
3	Periods:	216	
4	Payment:	($50.00)	
5	Present Value:	$0.00	
6	Type:	0	
7			
8	Future Value:	$14,297.02	
9			
10			
11			
12			
13			

Figure 11-4: Calculating the future value of payments.

The 3% annual percentage rate is converted into a monthly rate, and the 18 years is converted into months. There is no present value because you just opened the account, and the Type is 0 (zero) because you're starting next month (in arrears).

FUTURE VALUE OF A LUMP SUM

The next example computes the future value of a sum of money to which you don't intend to add any money or take any money out.

Assume you roll your 401(k) account into an IRA, but you don't plan to make any more contributions. This formula computes how much your $20,000 will be worth in 15 years when you plan to retire (see Figure 11-5):

```
=FV(.08,15,0,-20000,0)
```

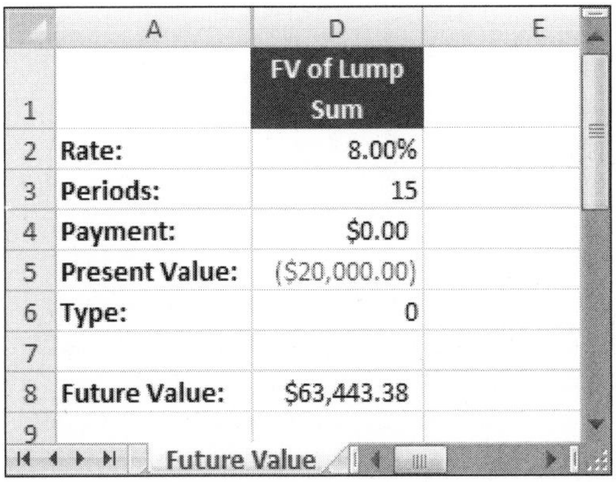

	A	D	E
1		**FV of Lump Sum**	
2	Rate:	8.00%	
3	Periods:	15	
4	Payment:	$0.00	
5	Present Value:	($20,000.00)	
6	Type:	0	
7			
8	Future Value:	$63,443.38	
9			

Figure 11-5: Calculating the future value a lump sum.

Rounding of Financial Formulas

When you're working with financial formulas, the issue of rounding is almost certain to arise. Excel offers several relevant functions, including ROUND, ROUNDUP, and ROUNDDOWN.

To help prevent cumulative errors, round only the final calculated value. In other words, avoid rounding any intermediate, non-reported calculations.

In general, financial calculations rarely display more than two decimal places, and they often display only full dollar values. For intermediate calculations, this means that you format to the nearest cent (or dollar) and thus retain the fully accurate figure for subsequent calculations.

In some cases, calculations will be based on approximated data or from data based upon subjective opinions or adjusted data (such as rental values), A common professional practice is to report rounded figures to avoid misleading readers. For example, you may have a rental value of $43.55 per square foot, based on an average of recent transactions. If this rate is applied to an area of 1,537 square feet, the calculated rental value is $66,936.35. However, the rental rate is actually an approximation (it may actually be between $42 and $45). To avoid giving an impression of extreme accuracy, you may want to round the calculated rental value to the nearest $100 or even nearest $1,000.

One problem of the accuracy allowed by modern technology is a danger of being seduced by the precision of point estimates.

This example assumes you will average an 8% annual return on your IRA. The –$20,000 represents $20,000 that's flowing away from you and into the IRA. The result, $63,443,38, represents money that's flowing to you from the IRA.

FUTURE VALUE OF PAYMENTS AND A LUMP SUM

It's also possible to compute the future value when there's an existing amount and you plan to add to or subtract from that amount.

In this example, you are going to make monthly payments of $900 against your $150,000 mortgage. If your mortgage interest rate is 5.75%, this formula will compute how much you will still owe on your house in 5 years (see Figure 11-6):

```
=FV(.0575/12,5*12,-900,150000,0)
```

The payments are monthly, so the other arguments are converted to months – the annual interest rate is divided by 12, and the Nper expressed in years is multiplied by 12. The current balance of the mortgage is shown as a cash inflow in this example even though no cash is actually flowing in. There was a cash inflow when you originally bought the house.

That is, someone paid you a large sum of money in exchange for a promise to pay it back, and you turned around and bought a house with the money. Because the scope of your problem is from now until five years from now, it doesn't contemplate the time when the funds actually flowed in.

	A	F	G
1		**FV Payments & Lump Sum**	
2	Rate:	0.479%	
3	Periods:	60	
4	Payment:	($900.00)	
5	Present Value:	$150,000.00	
6	Type:	0	
7			
8	Future Value:	($137,435.10)	
9			
10			
11			

Future Value / P

Figure 11-6: Calculating the future value of payments and a lump sum.

TIP

One way to think of it is that someone loaned you $150,000 right now to pay off your mortgage, even though that didn't really happen. The –$137,435.10 is the computed outflow to pay that money back at the end of the five years.

Calculating Payments

The PMT function computes payments required to get a certain balance (pv) down to zero, or some other number (fv). Its syntax is

```
PMT(rate, nper, pv, fv, type)
```

COMPUTING LOAN PAYMENTS

When borrowing money, the key question is the periodic payment amount.

In this example, you want to buy a $32,000 car, and you need to compute how much your monthly payments will be. You will make a down payment of $4,000, and the car dealership is offering 2.1% financing for a four-year loan (see Figure 11-7).

```
=PMT(.021/12,4*12,28000,0,0)
```

Part III

	A	B	C
1		**Loan Payments**	
2	Rate:	0.175%	
3	Periods:	48	
4	Present Value:	$28,000	
5	Future Value:	$0	
6	Type:	0	
7			
8	Payment:	($608.69)	
9			
10			

Figure 11-7: Calculating a loan payment.

The formula returns $608.69. So, if you can handle such a monthly outflow, you can get the $28,000 that you borrowed down to zero in 48 payments.

CAUTION

If you get a #NUM! error or a result that is obviously incorrect on any of these basic financial functions, the first place to look is the direction of the cash flows. Pay close attention to the signs on the amounts in this section's examples to get a better understanding of how to sign the arguments.

COMPUTING RETIREMENT PAYMENTS

For some payment calculations, you may have to include a future value amount.

For this example, assume you have $700,000 in a retirement account. If you need to draw out payments to live on for the next 20 years — and still want $100,000 left to leave to heirs — this formula computes how much you can take out every month (see Figure 11-8):

```
=PMT(.06/12,20*12,-700000,100000,0)
```

If your estimated 6% annual return on your money is accurate, you can withdraw $4,798.59 per month, and still have $100,000 in the account 20 years from now.

Calculating Rates

The RATE function computes the interest or discount rate on future cash flows. For transactions where the interest rate is not specifically stated, the RATE function can be used to compute the implicit interest rate (the rate that occurred whether stated or not). Its syntax is

```
RATE(nper, pmt, pv, fv, type, guess)
```

	A	D	E
1		**Retirement Payments**	
2	Rate:	0.500%	
3	Periods:	240	
4	Present Value:	($700,000)	
5	Future Value:	$100,000	
6	Type:	0	
7			
8	Payment:	$4,798.59	
9			

Payment / Rat

Figure 11-8: Calculating retirement payments.

PAYDAY LOAN RATES

Payday loans are extremely short-term loans. Generally they are paid back in 14 days (the next paycheck date), and lenders typically charge $15 for every $100 borrowed.

If you borrow $200 and agree to pay $230 in 14 days, the interest rate is calculated with the following formula (see Figure 11-9):

```
=RATE(1,0,200,-230,0,.01)*365/14
```

The period is set to one because the loan has only one payment. The period of one actually represents a 14-day period, so the rate is converted to an annual percentage rate by dividing by 14 days and multiplying by 365 days. The result, 391%, is so large because the term is so short.

	A	B	C
1		**Payday Loan**	
2	Period:	1	
3	Payment:	$0	
4	Present Value:	$200	
5	Future Value:	($230)	
6	Type:	0	
7	Guess:	1.00%	
8			
9	Rate:	391.07%	
10			
11			

Rate / Period

Figure 11-9: Calculating the interest rate on a short-term loan.

Part III

NOTE

Interest rates are often stated as annual percentage rates (APRs), even if the term of the loan is more or less than a year. Converting rates to APR, regardless of term, allows you to compare different loans. If you try to compare a monthly interest rate to an annual interest rate, the monthly interest rate will look much smaller but may not actually be.

GROWTH RATES

A common use of the RATE function is to calculate the growth rate on a retirement account.

Assume for this example that you have a $40,000 balance in your 401(k) at the beginning of the year and $62,000 at the end of the year. You put $200 per paycheck into the account all year (26 payments). This formula shows how your investments performed (see Figure 11-10):

```
=RATE(26,-200,-40000,62000,0,.01)*26
```

The RATE function returns the growth rate over each of the 26 periods, so you must multiply it by 26 to get the annual growth rate of 33.62%.

	A	D	E
1		**Growth Rate**	
2	Period:	26	
3	Payment:	($200)	
4	Present Value:	($40,000)	
5	Future Value:	$62,000	
6	Type:	0	
7	Guess:	1.00%	
8			
9	Rate:	33.62%	
10			
11			

Rate / Period

Figure 11-10: Calculating a growth rate.

NOTE

The Guess argument is used by several financial functions. You can omit this argument and let Excel use the default value, or you can explicitly provide a value. If the result is not close to what it should be, you can try using a different value for the guess argument.

INTEREST-FREE LOANS

Interest-free loans are rarely free because the interest the merchant would receive for lending you the money is built into the price.

Assume that you want to purchase a $3,000 leather couch, and you can pay for it in 12 monthly payments with no interest. A little comparison shopping reveals that you can get the same couch for $2,500 if you pay cash. So, in essence, you're paying $500 in interest on a $2,500 loan, or 35.07%.

```
=RATE(12,-3000/12,2500,0,0,.01)*12
```

You can check the results of the rate function by creating an amortization schedule (see Figure 11-11). If the balance goes to zero, the rate is correct.

	A	D	E	F	G	H	I	J
1		Interest Free Loan			Amortization Schedule			
2	Period:	12		Interest Rate:	35.07%			
3	Payment:	($250)						
4	Present Value:	$2,500		Payment No.	Payment Amount	Interest Portion	Principal Portion	Balance
5	Future Value:	$0						2,500.00
6	Type:	0		1	250.00	73.07	176.93	2,323.07
7	Guess:	1.00%		2	250.00	67.90	182.10	2,140.97
8				3	250.00	62.58	187.42	1,953.55
9	Rate:	35.07%		4	250.00	57.10	192.90	1,760.65
10				5	250.00	51.46	198.54	1,562.11
11				6	250.00	45.66	204.34	1,357.77
12				7	250.00	39.69	210.31	1,147.45
13				8	250.00	33.54	216.46	930.99
14				9	250.00	27.21	222.79	708.20
15				10	250.00	20.70	229.30	478.90
16				11	250.00	14.00	236.00	242.90
17				12	250.00	7.10	242.90	(0.00)
18								

Rate / Period

Figure 11-11: An amortization schedule to verify the results of the RATE function.

Calculating Periods

The NPER function is used to determine how many payments are necessary to pay off a loan, or to fund an account to a certain amount. Its syntax is

```
NPER(rate, pmt, pv, fv, type)
```

YEARS UNTIL RETIREMENT

If you know how much money you need to retire and you're making regular payments to a retirement account, you can use the NPER function to determine the age at which you can retire.

Part III

Assume you'll need $500,000 to retire, and you're putting away $100 per month. Further assume that your retirement account has a balance of $350,000. This formula will return the number of years until you can retire:

```
=NPER(.1/12,-100,-350000,500000,0)
```

Assuming you can earn 10% on your investments, NPER returns 41.8 months (or 3.5 years). You can combine NPER and PV if you know how much you need to live on each week, as in this formula:

```
=NPER(.1/12,-100,-350000,PV(.1/52,20*52,-1000,0,0),0)
```

The PV function used in the Fv arguments assumes that you'll make 10% (converted to weeks), that you'll need to withdraw money for 20 years (converted to weeks), that you'll need $1,000 per week, and that there will be nothing left. If you can live on $1,000 per week, you can retire in 2.4 years.

The two formulas in this section are shown in Figure 11-12.

	A	B	C	D	E
1		**Years Until Retirement**		**$1,000 Per Week**	
2	Rate:	0.833%		0.833%	
3	Payment:	($100)		($100)	
4	Present Value:	($350,000)		($350,000)	
5	Future Value:	$500,000		$449,490	
6	Type:	0		0	
7					
8	Period (months):	41.8		29.3	
9	Period (years):	3.5		2.4	
10					
11					

Figure 11-12: Using the NPER function for retirement calculations.

EARLY LOAN PAYOFF

In recent years, many people have refinanced their home mortgages to take advantage of falling interest rates. You can use NPER to calculate how many fewer payments you would have to make due to refinancing.

This example assumes a $200,000 mortgage at 7.5%, with monthly payments of $1,611.19 for the next 20 years. If you refinance to 5.75% but keep making the same payment, this formula computes how many years you can shave off of the loan (see Figure 11-13):

```
=(20*12)-NPER(.0575/12,PMT(0.075/12,20*12,200000,0),200000,0,0)
```

The pmt argument is a PMT function that computes the $1,611.19 that you're paying based on the terms of your existing mortgage. Subtracting the result from 240 (20 years of 12 months) shows that you can reduce your mortgage term by 51 months by refinancing under these terms.

	A	F	G	H
1		**Early Loan Payoff**		
2	Rate:	0.479%		
3	Payment:	($1,611)		
4	Present Value:	$200,000		
5	Future Value:	$0		
6	Type:	0		
7				
8	Period (months):	51.0		
9	Period (years):	4.3		
10				
11				

| ◄ ◄ ► ►| / Rate / Period / |

Figure 11-13: Calculating the effect of an early loan payoff.

NOTE

Although NPER can produce fraction results (for example, 4.26 months), you probably would not make a payment 26% of the way through a month. Instead, you would make a payment on the fifth month for an amount that's less than the payments you made previously.

Calculating the Interest and Principal Components

This section discusses four Excel functions that enable you to

- Calculate the interest or principal components of a particular payment.
- Calculate cumulative interest or principal components between any two time periods.

ON THE CD

The examples in this section are available on the companion CD-ROM in a file named `payment components.xlsx`.

Using the IPMT and PPMT Functions

You may need to know (or simply be curious about) how much of a particular payment constitutes interest, and how much of the payment goes toward paying off the debt (the principal). The portion of the payment that pays down the debt is smaller in the beginning of the loan because the interest portion is higher (because of the higher balance).

> **NOTE**
>
> If you've created an amortization schedule, these functions are not particularly useful because you can simply refer to the schedule. The IPMT (interest payment) and PPMT (principal payment) functions are most useful when you need to determine the interest/principal breakdown of a particular payment.

The syntax for these two functions is as follows (bold arguments are required):

IPMT(**rate**,**per**,**nper**,**pv**,fv,type)
PPMT(**rate**,**per**,**nper**,**pv**,fv,type)

As with all amortization functions, the Rate, Per, and Nper arguments must match in terms of the time period. If the loan term is measured in months, the Rate argument must be the effective rate per month, and the Per argument (that is, the period of interest) must be a particular month.

The example in Figure 11-14 shows calculations for three payments toward a 30-year mortgage: the first payment, a payment at month 180, and the last payment (month 360). The formulas for computing the amounts for payment number 1 are

=IPMT(.055/12,1,30*12,350000)
=PPMT(.055/12,1,30*12,350000)

	A	B	C	D	E
1	Loan Amt:	$350,000.00			
2	Interest:	5.50%			
3	Years:	30			
4					
5			**Payment Number**		
6		**1**	**180**	**360**	
7	IPMT:	($1,604.17)	($1,118.71)	($9.07)	
8	PPMT:	($383.09)	($868.55)	($1,978.19)	
9	SUM:	($1,987.26)	($1,987.26)	($1,987.26)	
10					
11	PMT:	($1,987.26)	($1,987.26)	($1,987.26)	
12					

Sheet1 / Sheet2

Figure 11-14: Calculating the principal and interest component of selected payments.

The formulas for the other payments are the same except that the Per argument reflects the payment being computed. Summing the IMPT and the PPMT amounts returns the same result as using the PMT function.

NOTE

It's interesting (and a little disheartening) to see how little of that first payment goes toward paying off the debt.

Using the CUMIPMT and CUMPRINC Functions

The IPMT and PPMT functions show the interest and principal components for a single payment. The CUMIPMT and CUMPRINC functions show the same components but for a specified series of payments.

The syntax for these functions is shown here (all arguments are required):

```
CUMIPMT(rate, nper, pv, start_period, end_period, type)
CUMPRINC(rate, nper, pv, start_period, end_period, type)
```

The following example computes the amount of interest paid on a home mortgage in 2006. It assumes a $220,000 mortgage that originated in October of 2004 and carries an interest rate of 6%.

```
=CUMIPMT(.06/12,30*12,220000,16,27,0)
```

January, 2006 represents the 16th payment and December, 2006 is the 27th payment. The interest paid between those two payments, inclusive, comes to $12,916.64.

The following formula calculates how much the principal has decreased over that same time period ($2,911.50):

```
=CUMPRINC(.06/12,30*12,220000,16,27,0)
```

Figure 11-15 shows a workbook that's set up to calculate the cumulative interest and principal for any series of payment periods. Enter the starting payment in cell B4 and the ending payment in cell B5. Cell E4 uses the CUMIPMT function to calculate the cumulate interest, and cell D5 uses the CUMPRINC to calculate the cumulative principal.

TIP

The worksheet has an amortization schedule so you can verify the calculations.

Part III

	A	B	C	D	E	F
1	Principal:	$220,000				
2	Interest:	6.00%				
3	Term:	30				
4	Starting Payment:	16		Interest:	($12,916.64)	
5	Ending Payment:	27		Principal:	($2,911.50)	
6						
7						
8						
9						
10	Pmt No.	Date	Payment	Interest	Principal	Balance
11						220,000.00
12	1	10/1/2004	1,319.01	1,100.00	219.01	219,780.99
13	2	11/1/2004	1,319.01	1,098.90	220.11	219,560.88
14	3	12/1/2004	1,319.01	1,097.80	221.21	219,339.68
15	4	1/1/2005	1,319.01	1,096.70	222.31	219,117.36
16	5	2/1/2005	1,319.01	1,095.59	223.42	218,893.94
17	6	3/1/2005	1,319.01	1,094.47	224.54	218,669.40
18	7	4/1/2005	1,319.01	1,093.35	225.66	218,443.73
19	8	5/1/2005	1,319.01	1,092.22	226.79	218,216.94
20	9	6/1/2005	1,319.01	1,091.08	227.93	217,989.01
21	10	7/1/2005	1,319.01	1,089.95	229.07	217,759.95
22	11	8/1/2005	1,319.01	1,088.80	230.21	217,529.74

Sheet1 Sheet2

Figure 11-15: Using the CUMIPMT and CUMPRINC functions.

Converting Interest Rates

The previous examples in this chapter used a simplified method of converting interest rates. They either used a nominal rate that matched the payment terms nicely, or the rates were estimated. The nominal rates were assumed to compound with the same frequency as the payment — say monthly. No conversion was necessary in that case.

In the discounting examples where discount rates where estimated (such as assuming an 8% return on your IRA), it makes no sense to convert those rates. Converting an estimated interest rate in those examples makes it appear that there is some level of accuracy in the rate – and there isn't. In some situations, however, you may need to convert a rate. This section describes different types of rates and how to convert them.

Methods of Quoting Interest Rates

The three commonly used methods of quoting interest rates are

- **Nominal rate:** This is the quoted rate. It is quoted on an annual basis, along with a compounding frequency per year — for example, 6% APR compounded monthly.

- **Annual effective rate:** This is the actual rate paid or earned annualized. For example, a nominal rate of 6% APR compounded monthly results in $61.68 of interest on a $1,000 loan. That's an effective rate of 6.168%.

- **Periodic effective rate:** This rate is applied to the principal over the compounding period, usually less than a year. For example, 6% APR compounded monthly implies a periodic rate of .5% per month.

Conversion Formulas

An interest rate quoted using any of these three methods can be converted to any of the other three methods. Excel provides two functions, EFFECT and NOMINAL, to aid in conversion. The periodic rate is simply the nominal rate divided by the stated compounding period, so no special function is provided for it. The syntax for NOMINAL and EFFECT is

```
EFFECT(nominal_rate,npery)
NOMINAL(effect_rate,npery)
```

NOTE

Most banks and financial institutions quote interest on a nominal basis compounded monthly. However, when reporting returns from investments or when comparing interest rates, it's common to quote annual effective returns, which makes it easier to compare rates. For example, you know that 12% per year compounded monthly is more than 12% per year compounded quarterly—but you don't know (without an intermediate conversion calculation) how *much* more it is.

A nominal rate of 12% compounded monthly is converted to a periodic rate as follows:

```
=.12/12
```

That results in .01, meaning 1% per month. To convert it to an effective rate, use this formula:

```
=EFFECT(.12,12)
```

ON THE CD

A file named `rate conversion.xlsx` contains the examples in this chapter and can be found on the companion CD-ROM.

The result of 12.6825% represents the actual interest that's paid or earned in a year. You can also use the FV function to determine the effective rate using a present value of –1, such as

```
=FV(0.12/12,12,0,-1)-1
```

If you know you paid $56.41 in interest last year on a $1,000 loan, you can compute the nominal interest with the following formula:

```
=NOMINAL(56.41/1000,12)
```

This calculation results in a 5.5% APR compounded monthly.

Limitations of Excel's Financial Functions

Excel's primary financial functions (PV, FV, PMT, RATE, NPER, CUMIPMT, and CUMPRINC) are very useful, but they have two common limitations:

- They can handle only one level of interest rate.
- They can handle only one level of payment.

For example, the NPER function cannot handle the variations in payments that arise with credit card calculations. In such calculations, the monthly payment is based upon a reducing outstanding balance and may also be subject to a minimum amount rule.

The common solution to the problem of varying payments is to create a cash flow schedule and use other financial functions that can handle multiple payments and rates. Examples of the process appear in the next two chapters. Briefly, the functions involved are

- FVSCHEDULE, which calculates a future value when the interest rate is variable
- IRR, which calculates a rate of return from a varying level of cash flow received at regular intervals
- NPV, which calculates the sum of the present values of a varying level of cash flow received at regular intervals
- MIRR, which is a modified IRR that considers cash flows that are reinvested
- XIRR, which calculates a single rate from irregular cash flows
- XNPV, which calculates the net present value of irregular cash flows

In a situation that involves only slight variations, you can combine and nest Excel's financial functions.

 ON THE CD

The examples in this section can be found in the file named `extending basic functions.xlsx` on the companion CD-ROM.

Deferred Start to a Series of Regular Payments

In some cases, a series of cash flows may have a deferred start. You can calculate the PV of a regular series of cash flows with a deferred start by nesting PV functions.

In this example, you get a loan to start a business. You can afford to pay $7,000 per month, and you negotiate a deal with the bank to defer the first payment for 12 months. If the bank quotes an 8% rate on a ten-year loan, this formula will tell you how much you can borrow (see Figure 11-16):

```
=PV(0.08/12,12,0,-PV(0.08/12,10*12,-7000))
```

	A	B	C	D	E
1	Step 1: Compute the PV of the payments				
2	Rate	8%			
3	Period	10			
4	Payment	($7,000)			
5	Present Value	$576,950.37	.	=PV(B2/12,B3*12,B4)	
6					
7					
8	Step 2: The above PV becomes the FV of the next calculation. Find				
9	the PV of the above over the deferral period				
10	Deferral Period	1			
11	Payment	$0			
12	Present Value	$532,733.73		=PV(B2/12,B10*12,B11,-B5)	
13					
14					

Deferred Start / Variable Pmts

Figure 11-16: Calculating the present value of regular payments with a deferred start is a two-step process.

First, calculate the present value, which is $576,950. This value is used as the future value argument of the outer function. The outer function further discounts this amount over the year deferral period, and results in $532,733. In other words, if you borrow $532,733 now, the amount will increase to $576,950 in one year with no payments, and it will reduce to zero in ten years with a $7,000 monthly payment.

Valuing a Series of Variable Payments

This example calculates the present value when the payments change over time. Assume that you want to buy your way out of a property lease, and you need to know how much it's worth. There's nine years left on the lease, and the payment schedule is

- Years 1–3: $5,000/month
- Years 4– 6: $6,500/month
- Years 7– 9: $8,500/month

Part III

The following formula will calculate the value of the lease assuming a 10% discount rate:

```
=PV(.1/12,36,-5000)+
PV(.1/12,3*12,0,-PV(.1/12,36,-6500))+
PV(.1/12,6*12,0,-PV(.1/12,36,-8500))
```

The result of $449,305 is calculated in three steps:

1. Compute the present value of three years of rent payments.

2. The second three years is the same as the preceding deferred start example. The present value of its payments are computed, and that becomes the future value argument to a different PV function. That future value is discounted over a three year deferred period (while the $5,000 rent payments are being made).

3. The last three years of payments are similarly discounted but this time over a six-year deferral period.

Bond Calculations

Excel provides worksheet functions that are used to calculate various aspects of bonds. A *bond* is a financial instrument in which the buyer loans money to the bond issuer – usually a corporation or a government. Many of the functions that deal with securities (such as bonds) are beyond the scope of this book. However, examples of some of the more common functions are provided in this section.

 ON THE CD

The examples in this section can be found on the companion CD-ROM in the file named `bond calculations.xlsx`.

Bonds have certain properties that are worth reviewing, mostly because those properties are also arguments in many of the bond related functions:

- **Settlement:** The date the security is transferred to the buyer.
- **Maturity:** The date the loan (represented by the bond) is repaid to the buyer.
- **Rate:** Also known as the *coupon:* the interest rate the issuer is paying on the bond.
- **Yield:** The rate of return the buyer receives, including the interest payments and the discount.
- **Redemption:** The amount the buyer receives at maturity, per $100 of face value. In typical cases, the buyer gets the face value, so this argument is 100.
- **Frequency:** The number of times per year that interest is paid.

Pricing Bonds

Bond issuers set the properties of the bond before it is issued based on current market conditions. As market conditions change, the value of the bonds change as well.

For example, Company X issues bonds with a $100 face value, 10-year maturity date, and a 6% interest rate paid twice per year:

- **If interest rates rise**: Earning 6% isn't so attractive anymore, and buyers will not be willing to pay $100. They will, however, be willing to *pay* something less.

- **If interest rates fall:** The 6% coupon looks like a great deal, and the bonds will be in demand. In that case, buyers will pay more than the face value.

The PRICE function calculates the price an investor should pay for a bond to achieve a specified return on his money. The syntax for PRICE, with required arguments in bold, is

```
PRICE(settlement,maturity,rate,yld,redemption,frequency,basis)
```

Given the preceding facts, an investor who requires a 7.5% return on his money would use the following formula to determine what price to pay for a bond that matures in eight years:

```
=PRICE(TODAY(),TODAY()+DATE(8,1,0),.06,.075,100,2)
```

The result of $91.10 is what the investor should pay so that his yield is 7.5%. He will get $6.00 in interest per year (6% × $100), plus he will earn an addition $8.90 when the bond matures and he is paid the $100 face value. These two components — the interest and the discount — make up *yield*.

The actual dates used for settlement and maturity are irrelevant as long as the time between the dates is correct. In this example, Company X issued the bonds two years earlier, but the investor didn't buy them until today. Because they were issued as ten-year bonds, they would mature in eight years from the day the investor bought them.

If instead, interest rates had fallen since the bonds were issued, and the investor required only a 5.2% return on his money, the formula would change slightly:

```
=PRICE(TODAY(),TODAY()+DATE(8,1,0),.06,.052,100,2)
```

Under these circumstances, the investor will be willing to pay $105.18 per $100 face value bond.

Figure 11-17 shows these calculations in a worksheet.

Part III

	A	B	C	D	E
1		Example 1		Example 2	
2	Date Purchased:	10/7/2006		10/7/2006	
3	Maturity:	10/7/2014		10/7/2014	
4	Coupon:	6%		6%	
5	Desired Return:	7.50%		5.20%	
6	Face Value:	$100		$100	
7	Frequency:	2		2	
8					
9	Price:	$91.10		$105.18	
10					
11					

Pricing Bonds / Yield

Figure 11-17: Using the PRICE function.

Calculating Yield

In the previous section, an investor knew what yield he wanted and calculated the price to pay to get it. If instead, he knows what price he is willing to pay, the YIELD function will tell him what his rate of return on his investment will be. The syntax for YIELD is

```
YIELD(settlement,maturity,rate,pr,redemption,frequency,basis)
```

The investor is still interested in buying the ten-year bond with a 6% coupon paid twice per year, but this time, he wishes to only pay $93.95 for each $100 face value bond. The following formula will calculate his rate of return over the eight years remaining until the bond matures:

```
=YIELD(TODAY(),TODAY()+DATE(8,1,0),.06,93.95,100,2)
```

The investor will make 7% on his investment if he pays $93.95 for these bonds. Had he been willing to pay more than the $100 face value, the resulting yield would be lower than the 6% coupon rate, as shown in Figure 11-18.

	A	B	C	D	E
1		Example 1		Example 2	
2	Date Purchased:	10/7/2006		10/7/2006	
3	Maturity:	10/7/2014		10/7/2014	
4	Coupon:	6%		6%	
5	Price:	$93.95		$104.58	
6	Face Value:	$100.00		$100.00	
7	Frequency:	2		2	
8					
9	Yield:	7.00%		5.29%	
10					
11					

Pricing Bonds / Yield

Figure 11-18: When the price is higher than face value, the yield is lower than the coupon.

Chapter 12

Discounting and Depreciation Formulas

IN THIS CHAPTER

◆ Calculating the net present value of future cash flows

◆ Understanding the various approaches for cash flows

◆ Using cross-checking to verify results

◆ Calculating the internal rate of return

◆ Dealing with multiple internal rates of return

◆ Calculating the net present value of irregular cash flows

◆ Finding the internal rate of return on irregular cash flows

◆ Using the NPV function to calculate accumulated values

◆ Using the depreciation functions

The NPV (Net Present Value) and IRR (Internal Rate of Return) functions are perhaps the most commonly used financial analysis functions. This chapter provides many examples that use these functions for various types of financial analysis.

Using the NPV Function

The NPV function returns the sum of a series of cash flows, discounted to the present day using a single discount rate. The cash flows don't have to be the same amount, but they do have to be at regular intervals (for example, monthly). The syntax for Excel's NPV function is shown here; arguments in bold are required:

```
NPV(rate,value1,value2, ...)
```

Cash inflows are represented as positive values, and cash outflows are negative values. The NPV function is subject to the same restrictions that apply to financial functions, such as PV, PMT, FV, NPER, and RATE.

If the discounted negative flows exceed the discounted positive flows, the function will return a negative amount. Alternatively, if the discounted positive flows exceed the discounted negative flows, the NPV function will return a positive amount.

The *rate* argument is the discount rate — the rate at which future cash flows are discounted. It represents the rate of return the investor requires. If NPV returns zero, this indicates that the future cash flows will provide a rate of return exactly equal to the specified discount rate.

If the NPV is positive, this indicates that the future cash flows provide a better rate of return than the specified discount rate. The positive amount returned by NPV is the amount that the investor could add to the initial cash flow (called *Point 0*) to get the exact rate of return specified.

As you may have guessed, a negative NPV indicates that the investor does not get the required discount rate, often called a *hurdle rate.* To achieve the desired rate, the investor would have to reduce the initial cash outflow (or increase the initial cash inflow) by the amount returned by the negative NPV.

NOTE

The discount rate used must be a single effective rate for the period used for the cash flows. Therefore, if flows are set out monthly, you must use the monthly effective rate.

Definition of NPV

Excel's NPV function assumes that the first cash flow is received at the *end* of the first period.

CAUTION

This assumption differs from the definition used by most financial calculators, and it is also at odds with the definition used by institutions such as the Appraisal Institute of America (AIA). For example, the AIA defines NPV as the difference between the present value of positive cash flows and the present value of negative cash flows. If you use Excel's NPV function without making an adjustment, the result will not adhere to this definition.

The point of a NPV calculation is to determine whether an investment will provide an appropriate return. The typical sequence of cash flows is an initial cash outflow followed by a series of cash inflows. For example, you buy a hot dog cart and some hot dogs (initial outflow) and spend the summer months selling them on a street corner (series of inflows). If you include the initial cash flow as an argument, NPV will assume the initial investment isn't made right now but instead at the end of the first month (or some other time period).

Figure 12-1 shows three calculations using the same cash flows: a $20,000 initial outflow, a series of monthly inflows, and an 8% discount rate.

	A	B	C	D	E
1		Cash Flow Calculations			
2					
3	Month	Cash Flows	Cash Flows	Cash Flows	
4	Initial Investment	(20,000.00)	(20,000.00)	(20,000.00)	
5	June	4,000.00	4,000.00	4,000.00	
6	July	5,000.00	5,000.00	5,000.00	
7	August	10,000.00	10,000.00	10,000.00	
8	September	2,000.00	2,000.00	2,000.00	
9		($2,408.54)	($2,601.22)	($2,601.22)	
10		-- Caution --			
11					
12					

End_of_Period Initial_Investment

Figure 12-1: Three methods of computing net present value.

The formulas in row 9 are as follows:

```
B9:   =NPV(0.08,B4:B8)
C9:   =NPV(0.08,C5:C8)+C4
D9:   =NPV(0.08,D4:D8)*(1+0.08)
```

The formula in B9 produces a result that's different than the other two. It assumes the $20,000 investment is made one month from now. There are applications where this is useful, but they rarely if ever involve an initial investment. The other two formulas answer the question of whether a $20,000 investment right now will earn 8%, assuming the future cash flows. The formulas in C9 and D9 produce the same result and can be used interchangeably.

NPV Function Examples

This section contains a number of examples that demonstrate the NPV function.

ON THE CD

All the examples in this section are available in the workbook `net present value .xlsx` on the companion CD-ROM.

INITIAL INVESTMENT

Many NPV calculation start with an initial cash outlay followed by a series of inflows. In this example, the Time 0 cash flow is the purchase of a snow plow. Over the next ten years, the plow will be used to plow driveways and earn revenue. Experience shows that such a snow plow lasts ten years. After that time, it will be broken-down and worthless. Figure 12-2 shows a worksheet set up to calculate the net present value of the future cash flows associated with buying the plow.

	A	B	C
1	NPV Example		
2			
3	Discount Rate:	10%	
4			
5	Time	Cash Flow	
6	0	($200,000.00)	
7	1	20,000.00	
8	2	22,500.00	
9	3	25,000.00	
10	4	27,500.00	
11	5	30,000.00	
12	6	32,500.00	
13	7	35,000.00	
14	8	37,500.00	
15	9	40,000.00	
16	10	42,500.00	
17			
18	NPV =	($19,880.30)	
19			
20			

Initial_Investment

Figure 12-2: An initial investment returns positive future cash flows.

The NPV calculation in cell B18 uses the following formula, which returns –$19,880.30:

```
=NPV($B$3,B7:B16)+B6
```

The NPV is negative, so this analysis indicates that buying the snow plow is not a good investment. Several factors that influence the result:

- First, I defined a "good investment" as one that returns 10% when I set the discount rate. If you settle for a lesser return, the result might be satisfactory.

- The future cash flows are generally, but not always, estimates. In this case, the potential plow owner assumes increasing revenue over the ten-year period. Unless he has a ten-year contract to plow snow that sets forth the exact amounts to be received, the future cash flows are educated guesses at how much money can be made.

- Finally, if you can get the snow plow dealer to lower his price, the ten-year investment may prove worthwhile.

NO INITIAL INVESTMENT

You can look at the snow plow example in another way. In the previous example, you knew the cost of the snow plow and included that as the initial investment. That example tells you whether the initial investment would produce a 10% return. You can also use NPV to tell what initial investment is required to produce the required return. That is, how much should you pay for the snow plow. Figure 12-3 shows the calculation of the net present value of a series of cash flow with no initial investment.

	A	B	C	D
1	Calculating a Required Initial Investment			
2				
3	Discount Rate:	10%		
4				
5				
6	Time	Cash Flow		
7	0	$0.00		
8	1	20,000.00		
9	2	22,500.00		
10	3	25,000.00		
11	4	27,500.00		
12	5	30,000.00		
13	6	32,500.00		
14	7	35,000.00		
15	8	37,500.00		
16	9	40,000.00		
17	10	42,500.00		
18				
19				
20	NPV=	$180,119.70		
21				

No_Initial_Investment

Figure 12-3: The NPV function can be used to determine the initial investment required.

The NPV calculation in cell B20 uses the following formula:

```
=NPV($B$3,B8:B17)+B7
```

Part III

If the future snow plow owner can buy the snow plow for $180,119.70, it will result in a 10% rate of return (assuming the cash flow projections are accurate, of course). The formula adds the value in B7 to the end to be consistent with the formula from the previous example. Obviously, because the initial cash flow is zero, adding B7 is superfluous.

INITIAL CASH INFLOW

Figure 12-4 shows an example in which the initial cash flow (the Time 0 cash flow) is an inflow. Like the previous example, this calculation returns the amount of an initial investment that will be necessary to achieve the desired rate of return. In this example, however, the initial investment entitles you to receive the first inflow immediately.

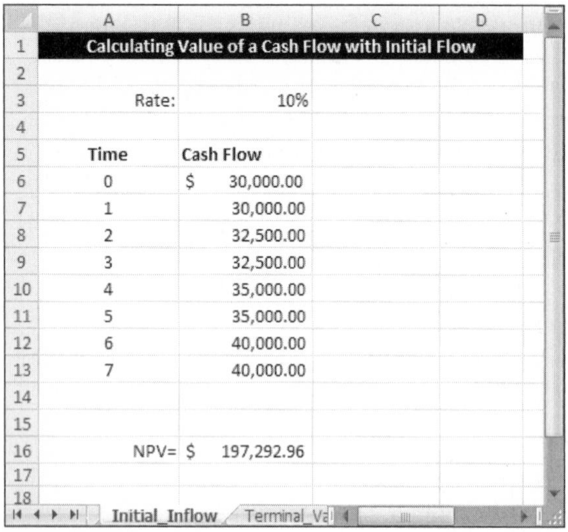

	A	B	C	D
1	Calculating Value of a Cash Flow with Initial Flow			
2				
3	Rate:	10%		
4				
5	Time	Cash Flow		
6	0	$ 30,000.00		
7	1	30,000.00		
8	2	32,500.00		
9	3	32,500.00		
10	4	35,000.00		
11	5	35,000.00		
12	6	40,000.00		
13	7	40,000.00		
14				
15				
16	NPV= $	197,292.96		
17				
18				

Initial_Inflow   Terminal_Va

Figure 12-4: Some NPV calculations include an initial cash inflow.

The net present value calculation is in cell B16, which contains the following formula:

```
=NPV(B3,B7:B13)+B6
```

This example might seem unusual, but it is common in real estate situations in which rent is paid in advance. This calculation indicates that you can pay $197,292.96 for a rental property that pays back the future cash flows in rent. The first year's rent, however, is due immediately. Therefore, the first year's rent is shown at Time 0.

TERMINAL VALUES

The previous example is missing one key element: namely, the disposition of the property after seven years. You could keep renting it forever, in which case you need to increase the number of cash flows in the calculation. Or you could sell it, as shown in Figure 12-5.

	A	B	C	D	E
1		Cash Flows with Terminal Values			
2					
3	Rate:	10%			
4					
5	Time	Income Flow	Capital Flow	Cash Flow	
6	0	$ 30,000.00		$ 30,000.00	
7	1	30,000.00		30,000.00	
8	2	32,500.00		32,500.00	
9	3	32,500.00		32,500.00	
10	4	35,000.00		35,000.00	
11	5	35,000.00		35,000.00	
12	6	40,000.00		40,000.00	
13	7	40,000.00	450,000.00	490,000.00	
14					
15			NPV=	$ 428,214.11	
16					

Terminal_Value / Inital and Termin

Figure 12-5: The initial investment may still have value at the end of the cash flows.

The NPV calculation in cell D15 is

```
=NPV(B3,D7:D13)+D6
```

In this example, the investor can pay $428,214.11 for the rental property, collect rent for seven years, sell the property for $450,000, and make 10% on his investment.

Initial and Terminal Values

This example uses the same cash flows as the previous example except that you know how much the owner of the investment property wants. It represents a typical investment example in which the aim is to determine if, and by how much, an asking price exceeds a desired rate of return, as you can see in Figure 12-6.

	A	B	C	D	E
1		Cash Flows with a Terminal Value			
2					
3	Rate:	10%			
4					
5	Time	Income Flow	Capital Flow	Cash Flow	
6	0	$ 30,000.00	($360,000.00)	$ (330,000.00)	
7	1	30,000.00		30,000.00	
8	2	32,500.00		32,500.00	
9	3	32,500.00		32,500.00	
10	4	35,000.00		35,000.00	
11	5	35,000.00		35,000.00	
12	6	40,000.00		40,000.00	
13	7	40,000.00	450,000.00	490,000.00	
14					
15			NPV=	$ 68,214.11	
16					

Inital and Terminal / Multiple_Ou

Figure 12-6: The NPV function can include an initial value and a terminal value.

The following formula indicates that at a $360,000 asking price, the discounted positive cash at the desired rate of return is $68,214.11:

```
=NPV(B3,D9:D15)+D8
```

The resulting positive net present value means that the investor can pay the asking price and make more than his desired rate of return. In fact, he could pay $68,214.11 more than the asking price and still meet his objective.

FUTURE OUTFLOWS

Although the typical investment decision may consist of an initial cash outflow resulting in periodic inflows, that's certainly not always the case. The flexibility of NPV is that you can have varying amounts, both positive and negative, at all the points in the cash flow schedule.

In this example, a company wants to roll out a new product. It needs to purchase equipment for $475,000 and will need to spend another $225,000 to overhaul the equipment after five years. Also, the new product won't be profitable at first but will be eventually.

Figure 12-7 shows a worksheet set up to account for all of these varying cash flows.

	A	B	C	D	E
1			Multiple Outflows		
2					
3	Rate:	10%			
4					
5	Time	Capital Flow	Gross Margin	Fixed Expenses	Cash Flow
6	0	$ (475,000.00)	$ -	$ (25,000.00)	$ (500,000.00)
7	1	-	-	(25,000.00)	(25,000.00)
8	2	-	20,000.00	(25,000.00)	(5,000.00)
9	3	-	40,000.00	(25,000.00)	15,000.00
10	4	-	100,000.00	(25,000.00)	75,000.00
11	5	(225,000.00)	175,000.00	(25,000.00)	(75,000.00)
12	6	-	200,000.00	(25,000.00)	175,000.00
13	7	-	250,000.00	(25,000.00)	225,000.00
14	8	-	275,000.00	(25,000.00)	250,000.00
15	9	-	275,000.00	(25,000.00)	250,000.00
16	10	-	275,000.00	(25,000.00)	250,000.00
17					
18					
19			NPV=		$ 22,347.71
20					

Multiple_Outflows / Convert_Interest

Figure 12-7: The NPV function can accept multiple positive and negative cash flows.

The positive net present value indicates that the company should invest in the equipment and start producing the new product. If it does, and the estimates of gross margin and expenses are accurate, the company will earn better than 10% on its investment.

MISMATCHED INTEREST RATE PERIODS

In the previous examples, the discount rate conveniently matched the time periods used in the cash flow. Often, you'll be faced with a mismatch of rate and time periods. The most common situation occurs when the desired rate of return is an annual effective rate and cash flows are monthly or quarterly. In this case, you need to convert the discount rate to the appropriate period.

CROSS REF

See Chapter 11 for a discussion on interest rate conversion.

Figure 12-8 shows a rental of $12,000 paid quarterly in advance. It also shows an initial price of $700,000 and a sale (after three years) for $900,000. Note that because rent is paid in advance, the purchaser gets a cash adjustment to the price. However, at the end of three years (12 quarters), the same rule applies, and the rent payable for the next quarter is received by the new owner. If you discount at 7% per annum effective, this shows an NPV of $166,099.72.

Part III

	A	B	C	D	E
1			**Non-Annual Cash Flows**		
2					
3	Effective Annual Interest Rate		7%		
4	Cash Flow Frequency		4		
5	Interest Rate Per Period		1.70585% Quarterly		
6					
7	Period	Revenue Flow	Capital Flow	Cash Flow	
8	0	$ 12,000.00	$ (700,000.00)	$ (688,000.00)	
9	1	12,000.00		12,000.00	
10	2	12,000.00		12,000.00	
11	3	12,000.00		12,000.00	
12	4	12,000.00		12,000.00	
13	5	12,000.00		12,000.00	
14	6	12,000.00		12,000.00	
15	7	12,000.00		12,000.00	
16	8	12,000.00		12,000.00	
17	9	12,000.00		12,000.00	
18	10	12,000.00		12,000.00	
19	11	12,000.00		12,000.00	
20	12		900,000.00	900,000.00	
21					
22			NPV: $	166,099.72	

Convert_Interest / Future_Value

Figure 12-8: Calculating the NPV using quarterly cash flows.

In some situations, determining the frequency of cash flows is simple. With rent, for instance, the lease agreement spells out how often rent is paid. When the future cash flow is revenue from the sale of a product, the figures are usually estimates. In those cases, determining whether to state the cash flows monthly, quarterly, or annually is not so clear. Generally, you should use a frequency that matches the accuracy of your data. That is, if you estimate sales on an annual basis, don't divide that number by 12 to arrive at a monthly estimate.

For an illustration of the difference that can result from different frequencies, see Figure 12-9. It shows the same data, but this time, the calculations are based on the assumption that the rent of $48,000 per annum is paid annually in arrears. Still discounting at 7% per annum effective, you get an NPV of $160,635.26.

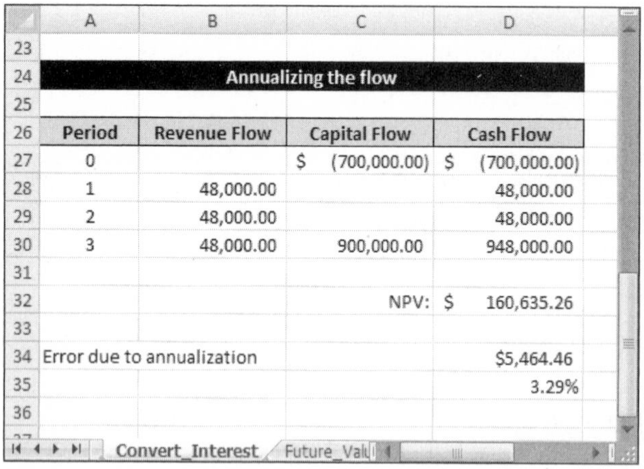

	A	B	C	D
23				
24		Annualizing the flow		
25				
26	Period	Revenue Flow	Capital Flow	Cash Flow
27	0		$ (700,000.00)	$ (700,000.00)
28	1	48,000.00		48,000.00
29	2	48,000.00		48,000.00
30	3	48,000.00	900,000.00	948,000.00
31				
32			NPV: $	160,635.26
33				
34	Error due to annualization			$5,464.46
35				3.29%
36				

Figure 12-9: Calculating the NPV by annualizing quarterly cash flows.

Using the NPV Function to Calculate Accumulated Amounts

This section presents two examples that use the NPV function to calculate future values or accumulations. These examples take advantage of the fact that

```
FV = PV * (1 + Rate)
```

CALCULATING FUTURE VALUE

The data for this example is shown in Figure 12-10. The net present value calculation is performed by the formula in cell B15:

```
=NPV(B3,B7:B13)+B6
```

	A	B	C	D	E
1		Calculating FV using NPV Function			
2					
3	Rate:	10%			
4					
5	Time	Cash Flow	Interest	Cumulative Balance	
6	0	$ 100,000.00		$ 100,000.00	
7	1	40,000.00	10,000.00	150,000.00	
8	2	30,000.00	15,000.00	195,000.00	
9	3	20,000.00	19,500.00	234,500.00	
10	4	50,000.00	23,450.00	307,950.00	
11	5	20,000.00	30,795.00	358,745.00	
12	6	50,000.00	35,874.50	444,619.50	
13	7	30,000.00	44,461.95	519,081.45	
14					
15	NPV= $	266,370.86			
16					
17	Future Value $	519,081.45	*(Checks with final balance)*		
18					

Future_Value / Payments

Figure 12-10: Calculating FV using the NPV function.

The future value is calculated using the following formula (in cell B17):

```
=(NPV(B3,B7:B13)+B6)*(1+B3)^7
```

The result is also computed in column D, in which formulas calculate a running balance of the interest. Interest is calculated using the interest rate multiplied by the previous month's balance. The running balance is the sum of the previous balance, interest, and the current month's cash flow.

It is important to properly sign the cash flows. Then, if the running balance for the previous month is negative, the interest will be negative. Signing the flows properly and using addition is preferable to using the signs in the formulas for interest and balance.

SMOOTHING PAYMENTS

Chapter 11 covers the use of the PMT function to calculate payments equivalent to a given present value. Similarly, you can use the NPV function, nested in a PMT function, to calculate an equivalent single-level payment to a series of changing payments.

This is a typical problem where you require a time-weighted average single payment to replace a series of varying payments. An example is an agreement in which a schedule of rising rental payments is replaced by a single payment amount. In the example shown in Figure 12-11, the following formula (in cell C25) returns $10,923.24, which is the payment amount that would substitute for the varying payment amounts in column B:

```
=PMT(C5,C4,-B23,0,C6)
```

Part III

	A	B	C	D	E
1	Calculating Equivalent Payments with NPV				
2					
3	Interest Rate:		7%		
4	Cash Flow Frequency:		12		
5	Interest Rate Per Period:		0.56541%	Monthly	
6	Payment Type:		1		
7					
8	Time	Cash Flow			
9	0	$10,000.00			
10	1	$10,000.00			
11	2	$10,000.00			
12	3	$10,500.00			
13	4	$10,500.00			
14	5	$10,500.00			
15	6	$11,250.00			
16	7	$11,250.00			
17	8	$11,250.00			
18	9	$12,000.00			
19	10	$12,000.00			
20	11	$12,000.00			
21	12				
22					
23	NPV=	$127,100.53			
24					
25	Equivalent Single Payment:		$10,923.24		
26					
27	Check using PV:		$127,100.53		
28					

Future_Value | **Payments**

Figure 12-11: Calculating equivalent payments with NPV.

Using the IRR Function

Excel's IRR function returns the discount rate that makes the net present value of an investment zero. In other words, the IRR function is a special-case NPV.

The syntax of the IRR function is

IRR(**range**,guess)

CAUTION

The range argument must contain values. Empty cells are not treated as zero. If the range contains empty cells or text, the IRR function does not return an error. Rather, it will return an incorrect result.

In most cases, the IRR can only be calculated by iteration. The guess argument, if supplied, acts as a "seed" for the iteration process. It has been found that a guess of –0.9 will almost always produce an answer. Other guesses, such as 0, usually (but not always) produce an answer.

An essential requirement of the IRR function is that there must be both negative and positive income flows: To get a return, there must be an outlay, and there must be a payback. There is no essential requirement for the outlay to come first. For a loan analysis using IRR, the loan amount will be positive (and come first), and the repayments that follow will be negative.

The IRR is a very powerful tool, and its uses extend beyond simply calculating the return from an investment. This function can be used in any situation in which you need to calculate a time- and data-weighted average return.

ON THE CD

The examples in this section are in a workbook named `internal rate of return.xlsx`, which is available on the companion CD-ROM.

Rate of Return

This example sets up a basic IRR calculation (see Figure 12-12). An important consideration when calculating IRR is the payment frequency. If the cash flows are monthly, the IRR will be monthly. In general, you'll want to convert the IRR to an annual rate. The example uses data validation in cell C3 to allow the user to select the type of flow (annual, monthly, daily, and so on), which displays in cell D3. That choice determines the appropriate interest conversion calculation; it also affects the labels in row 5, which contain formulas that reference the text in cell D3.

Cell D20 contains this formula:

```
=IRR(D6:D18,-0.9)
```

Cell D21 contains this formula:

```
=FV(D20,C3,0,-1)-1
```

The following formula, in cell D23, is a validity check:

```
=NPV(D20,D7:D18)+D6
```

The IRR is the rate at which the discounting of the cash flow produces an NPV of zero. The formula in cell D23 uses the IRR in an NPV function applied to the same cash flow. The NPV discounting at the IRR (per quarter) is $0.00 — so the calculation checks.

Part III

	A	B	C	D	E	F
1			Calculation of IRR			
2						
3		Cash Flow Frequency:		12 Monthly		
4						
5	Monthly Number	Monthly Income Flow	Capital Flow	Net Monthly Flow		
6	0	$0.00	($2,000,000.00)	($2,000,000.00)		
7	1	$50,000.00		$50,000.00		
8	2	$50,000.00		$50,000.00		
9	3	$50,000.00		$50,000.00		
10	4	$50,000.00		$50,000.00		
11	5	$50,000.00		$50,000.00		
12	6	$50,000.00		$50,000.00		
13	7	$50,000.00		$50,000.00		
14	8	$50,000.00		$50,000.00		
15	9	$50,000.00		$50,000.00		
16	10	$50,000.00		$50,000.00		
17	11	$50,000.00		$50,000.00		
18	12	$50,000.00	$2,500,000.00	$2,550,000.00		
19						
20		IRR of Net Quarterly Flow:		4.14958%	Monthly	
21		IRR p.a.		62.88844%	per annum	
22						
23		Check NPV:		($0.00)		
24						

|◀ ◀ ▶ ▶| Rate of Return / Geometric / Check Re ◀

Figure 12-12: The IRR returns the rate based on the cash flow frequency and should be converted into an annual rate.

Geometric Growth Rates

You may have a need to calculate an average growth rate, or average rate of return. Because of compounding, a simple arithmetic average does not yield the correct answer. Even worse, if the flows are different, an arithmetic average will not take these variations into account.

A solution uses the IRR function to calculate a *geometric* average rate of return. This is simply a calculation that determines the single percentage rate per period that exactly replaces the varying ones.

This example (see Figure 12-13) shows the IRR function being used to calculate a geometric average return based upon index data (in column B). The calculations of the growth rate for each year are in column C. For example, the formula in cell C5 is

```
=(B5/B4)-1
```

The remaining columns show the geometric average growth rate between different periods. The formulas in Row 10 use the IRR function to calculate the internal rate of return. For example, the formula in cell F10, which returns 5.241%, is

```
=IRR(F4:F8,-0.9)
```

In other words, the growth rates of 5.21%, 4.86%, and 5.66% are equivalent to a geometric average growth rate of 5.241%.

The IRR calculation takes into account the direction of flow and places a greater value on the larger flows.

	A	B	C	D	E	F	G	H
1	IRR to Calculate Geometric Average Growth							
2								
3	Year	Index	Growth P.A.	2003-2004	2004-2005	2005-2006	2006-2007	
4	2003	100.00		-100.00	-100.00	-100.00	-100.00	
5	2004	105.21	5.21%	105.21	0	0	0	
6	2005	110.32	4.86%		110.32	0	0	
7	2006	116.56	5.66%			116.56	0	
8	2007	119.94	2.90%				119.94	
9								
10	Average Growth Since 2003:			5.210%	5.033%	5.241%	4.650%	
11								
12								

Rate of Return | Geometric | Check Results

Figure 12-13: Using the IRR function to calculate geometric average growth.

Part III

Checking Results

Figure 12-14 shows a worksheet that demonstrates the relationship between IRR, NPV, and PV by verifying the results of some calculations. This verification is based on the definition of IRR: The rate at which the sum of positive and negative discounted flows is 0.

	A	B	C	D	E
1	Checking IRR & NPV Using Sum of PV Approach				
2					
3	Discount Rate for NPV:			10%	
4					
5	Period	Flow	PV IRR Check	PV NPV Check	
6	0	$(100,000.00)	$ (100,000.00)	$ (100,000.00)	
7	1	14,000.00	13,570.24	12,727.27	
8	2	14,000.00	13,153.68	11,570.25	
9	3	14,000.00	12,749.90	10,518.41	
10	4	14,000.00	12,358.52	9,562.19	
11	5	14,000.00	11,979.15	8,692.90	
12	6	15,000.00	12,440.82	8,467.11	
13	7	15,000.00	12,058.92	7,697.37	
14	8	15,000.00	11,688.75	6,997.61	
15					
16	NPV	$ (23,766.89)	$ -	$ (23,766.89)	
17	IRR	3.167%			
18					
19					

Geometric | Check Results

Figure 12-14: Checking IRR and NPV using sum of PV approach.

The net present value is calculated in cell B16:

```
=NPV(D3,B7:B14)+B6
```

The internal rate of return is calculated in cell B17:

```
=IRR(B6:B14,-0.9)
```

In column C, formulas calculate the present value. They use the IRR (calculated in cell B17) as the discount rate, and use the period number (in column A) for the *nper*. For example, the formula in cell C6 is

```
=PV($B$17,A6,0,-B6)
```

The sum of the values in column C is 0, which verifies that the IRR calculation is accurate.

The formulas in column D use the discount rate (in cell D3) to calculate the present values. For example, the formula in cell D6 is

```
=PV($D$3,A6,0,-B6)
```

The sum of the values in column D is equal to the net present value.

For serious applications of NPV and IRR functions, it is an excellent idea to use this type of cross-checking.

Multiple Rates of IRR and the MIRR Function

In standard cash flows, there is only one sign change: from negative to positive, or from positive to negative. However, there are cash flows in which the sign can change more than once. In those cases, it is possible that more than one IRR can exist.

Multiple IRRs

Figure 12-15 shows an example that has two IRR calculations, each of which uses a different "seed" value for the guess argument. As you can see, the formula produces different results.

 ON THE CD

You can find the workbook with all of the examples in this section, `multiple irr.xlsx`, on the companion CD-ROM.

	A	B	C	D	E	F	G	H
1				Multiple Internal Rate of Returns				
2								
3	Seed 1:	11.00%						
4	Seed 2:	-90.00%						
5								
6	Period	Flow		Interest @ 13.88%	Balance		Interest @ 7.04%	Balance
7	0	$ (14,375.00)	$	-	$ (14,375.00)	$	-	$ (14,375.00)
8	1	6,250.00		(1,995.53)	(10,120.53)		(1,012.58)	(9,137.58)
9	2	6,250.00		(1,404.93)	(5,275.46)		(643.65)	(3,531.23)
10	3	6,250.00		(732.34)	242.20		(248.74)	2,470.03
11	4	6,250.00		33.62	6,525.82		173.99	8,894.02
12	5	-		905.91	7,431.73		626.50	9,520.52
13	6	-		1,031.67	8,463.40		670.63	10,191.14
14	7	-		1,174.89	9,638.29		717.87	10,909.01
15	8	-		1,337.98	10,976.28		768.43	11,677.44
16	9	(12,500.00)		1,523.72	(0.00)		822.56	(0.00)
17								
18		Total:	$	1,875.00	Total:	$	1,875.00	
19								
20				NPV @ IRR				
21	IRR 1:	13.882%		($0.00)				
22	IRR 2:	7.044%		($0.00)				
23								

H ◀ ▶ H   **Multiple IRRs**   Seperating Flows   Balances   ▷⏐

Figure 12-15: The same cash flows can have multiple IRRs.

The IRR formula in cell B21 (which returns a result of 13.88%) is

```
=IRR(B7:B16,B3)
```

The IRR formula in cell B22 (which returns a result of 7.04%) is

```
=IRR(B7:B16,B4)
```

So which rate is correct? Unfortunately, *both* are correct. Figure 12-15 shows the interest and running balance calculations for both of these IRR calculations. Both show that the investor can pay and receive either rate of interest, and can secure a (definitional) final balance of $0. Interestingly, the total interest received ($1,875) is also the same.

But there's a flaw. This example illustrates a worst-case scenario of the practical fallacy of many IRR calculations. NPV and IRR analyses make two assumptions:

- You can actually get the assumed (for NPV) or calculated (for IRR) interest on the out-standing balance.

- Interest does not vary according to whether the running balance is positive or negative.

Part III

The first assumption may or may not be correct. It's possible that balances could be reinvested. However, in forward-projections in times of changing interest rates, this might not be the case. The real problem is with the second assumption. Banks simply do not charge the same rate for borrowing that they pay for deposits.

Separating Flows

The MIRR function attempts to resolve this multiple rate of return problem. The example in this section demonstrates the use of the MIRR function.

Figure 12-16 shows a worksheet that uses the same data as in the previous example. Rates are provided for borrowing (cell B3) and for deposits (cell B4). These are used as arguments for the MIRR function (cell B19), and the result is 6.1279%:

```
=MIRR(B7:B16,B3,B4)
```

	A	B	C	D	E	F
1	Multiple Internal Rate of Returns					
2						
3	Finance Rate:	9%				
4	Deposit Rate:	5%				
5			5%	9%		
6	Period		Positive Flow	Negative Flow	Revised Flow	
7	0	($14,375.00)	$0.00	($14,375.00)	($20,130.35)	
8	1	$6,250.00	$6,250.00	$0.00	$0.00	
9	2	$6,250.00	$6,250.00	$0.00	$0.00	
10	3	$6,250.00	$6,250.00	$0.00	$0.00	
11	4	$6,250.00	$6,250.00	$0.00	$0.00	
12	5	$0.00	$0.00	$0.00	$0.00	
13	6	$0.00	$0.00	$0.00	$0.00	
14	7	$0.00	$0.00	$0.00	$0.00	
15	8	$0.00	$0.00	$0.00	$0.00	
16	9	($12,500.00)	$0.00	($12,500.00)	$34,380.83	
17		NPVs	$22,162.19	($20,130.35)		
18						
19	MIRR:	6.1279%		IRR (Revised Flow):	6.1279%	
20						

Multiple IRRs | **Seperating Flows** | Balances

Figure 12-16: Multiple internal rate of return.

The MIRR function works by separating negative and positive flows, and discounting them at the appropriate rate — the finance rate for negative flows and the deposit rate for positive flows.

You can replicate the MIRR algorithm by setting up a revised flow, which compares the two NPVs (refer to Figure 12-16, columns C:E). The negative flow NPV is placed at Period 0, and the positive flow is expressed as its equivalent future value (by accumulating it at the deposit rate) at the end of the investment term. The IRR of the revised flow is the same as the MIRR of the original (source) flow.

This example reveals that the methodology is suspect. In separating negative and positive flows, the MIRR implies that interest is charged on flows. Banks, of course, charge interest on balances. An attempt at resolving the problem is shown in the next example.

Using Balances Instead of Flows

The MIRR function uses two rates: one for negative flows, and one for positive flows. In reality, interest rates are charged on *balances* and not on flows. The example in this section applies different rates on negative and positive balances. The interest calculation uses an IF function to determine which rate to use.

When analyzing a project in which interest is paid and received, the end balance must be 0 (as shown in Figure 12-17). If it is greater than 0, you have actually received more than the stated deposit rate. If it is less than 0, you still owe money, and the finance rate has been underestimated. This example assumes a fixed finance rate and calculates the deposit rate needed to secure a 0 final balance.

In the Risk Rate Equivalent IRR method, the finance rate is fixed (at 9% in this example). The interest received on positive balances is found by using the Data⇨Data Tools⇨ What-If Analysis⇨Goal Seek command. In this example, cell D21 was set to zero by changing cell C6.

	A	B	C	D	E	F
1			**Multiple Internal Rate of Returns**			
2						
3	**Accumulating Balance Approach**					
4						
5	Finance Rate:		9%			
6	Risk Rate Equivalent IRR:		8.579%	(found by Goal Seek)		
7						
8	Risk Free Rate:	5.000%				
9	Risk Premium:	3.579%				
10						
11	Period		Interest	Balance	Flow	
12	0	($14,375.00)	$0.00	($14,375.00)	($14,375.00)	
13	1	$6,250.00	($1,293.75)	($9,418.75)	$4,956.25	
14	2	$6,250.00	($847.69)	($4,016.44)	$5,402.31	
15	3	$6,250.00	($361.48)	$1,872.08	$5,888.52	
16	4	$6,250.00	$160.61	$8,282.70	$6,410.61	
17	5	$0.00	$710.61	$8,993.31	$710.61	
18	6	$0.00	$771.58	$9,764.88	$771.58	
19	7	$0.00	$837.77	$10,602.66	$837.77	
20	8	$0.00	$909.65	$11,512.31	$909.65	
21	9	($12,500.00)	$987.69	$0.00	($11,512.31)	
22						
23				IRR:	0.0000%	
24						
25						

Seperating Flows | **Balances**

Figure 12-17: Accumulating balance approach for multiple IRRs.

The series of flows then becomes the change in the balances, rather than the original given cash flows. The internal rate of return on these balanced-derived flows is zero, or very close to zero. I've already taken into account all the financing and reinvesting necessary for the project, and the resulting interest and return is shown in the flows. The Risk Rate Equivalent IRR may be compared with a different rate such as the Risk Free Rate of Return (traditionally 90-day Treasury bills) to determine the relative risk of the project.

But what does this all mean? If you pay 9% on negative balances, this project returns an 8.579% rate to you on positive balances. The name "Risk Rate Equivalent IRR" refers to the fact that it determines how the project compares with the return on money invested in a bank or 90-day Treasury bills.

There is no requirement that the finance rate be fixed. A bank may do calculations in the same way but fix the deposit rate and allow the Goal Seek feature to calculate the equivalent lending rate.

Irregular Cash Flows

All the functions discussed so far — NPV, IRR, and MIRR — deal with cash flows that are *regular*. That is, they occur monthly, quarterly, yearly, or at some other periodic interval. Excel provides two functions for dealing with cash flows that don't occur regularly: XNPV and XIRR.

Net Present Value

The syntax for XNPV is

```
XNPV(rate,values,dates)
```

The difference between XNPV and NPV is that XNPV requires a series of *dates* to which the *values* relate. In the example shown in Figure 12-18, the net present value of a series of irregular cash flows is found using XNPV.

 ON THE CD

The companion CD-ROM contains the workbook `irregular cash flows.xlsx`, which contains all the examples in this section.

The formula in cell B17 is

```
=NPV(B3,B6:B15,A6:A15)
```

Similar to NPV, the result of XNPV can be checked by duplicating the cash flows and netting the result with the first cash flow. The XNPV of the revised cash flows will be zero.

	A	B	C	D
1		The XNPV Function		
2				
3	Interest Rate:	8.00%		
4				
5	Date	Flow	Revised Flow	
6	Oct-09-2006	$ 250.00	$ (3,026.49)	
7	Oct-29-2006	250.00	250.00	
8	Nov-28-2006	250.00	250.00	
9	Jan-07-2007	500.00	500.00	
10	Jan-17-2007	500.00	500.00	
11	Feb-16-2007	600.00	600.00	
12	Mar-08-2007	400.00	400.00	
13	Mar-13-2007	200.00	200.00	
14	Apr-02-2007	200.00	200.00	
15	Apr-12-2007	200.00	200.00	
16				
17	XNPV:	$ 3,276.49	$ 0.00	
18				

◄ ◄ ► ►◄ **XNPV** / XIRR

Figure 12-18: The XNPV function works with irregular cash flows.

NOTE

Unlike the NPV function, XNPV assumes the cash flows are at the beginning of each period instead of the end. With NPV, I had to exclude the initial cash flow from the arguments and add it to the end of the formula. With XNPV, there is no need to do that.

Internal Rate of Return

The syntax for the XIRR function is

XIRR(**value,dates,**guess)

Just like XNPV, XIRR differs from its regular cousin by requiring dates. Figure 12-19 shows an example of computing the internal rate of return on a series of irregular cash flows.

The formula in B15 is

=XIRR(B4:B13,A4:A13)

CAUTION

The XIRR function has the same problem with multiple rates of return as IRR. It expects that the cash flow changes signs only once: that is, goes from negative to positive or from positive to negative. If the sign changes more than once, it is essential that you plug the XIRR result back into an XNPV function to verify that it returns zero. Figure 12-19 shows such a verification although the sign only changes once in that example.

Part III

	A	B	C
1	The XIRR Function		
2			
3	Date	Flow	
4	Oct-09-2006	($3,000.00)	
5	Oct-29-2006	$250.00	
6	Nov-28-2006	$250.00	
7	Jan-07-2007	$500.00	
8	Jan-17-2007	$500.00	
9	Feb-16-2007	$600.00	
10	Mar-08-2007	$400.00	
11	Mar-13-2007	$200.00	
12	Apr-02-2007	$200.00	
13	Apr-12-2007	$200.00	
14			
15	XIRR:	11.0966%	
16	Check XNPV:	($0.00)	
17			

Figure 12-19: The XIRR function works with irregular cash flows.

Using the FVSCHEDULE Function

The FVSCHEDULE function calculates the future value of an initial amount, after applying a series of varying rates over time. Its syntax is

```
FVSCHEDULE(principal,schedule)
```

Calculating an Annual Return

The FVSCHEDULE function can be used to convert a series of monthly returns into an annual return. Figure 12-20 shows the monthly returns for a mutual fund.

ON THE CD

The example in this section can be found on the companion CD-ROM in a workbook named FVSCHEDULE.xlsx.

For the year, this fund returned 37.83%. The formula to calculate the annual return is

```
=FVSCHEDULE(1,B5:B16)-1
```

	A	B	C
1		Annual Return	
2			
3			
4	**Month**	**Return**	
5	Jan	5.50%	
6	Feb	7.50%	
7	Mar	-1.75%	
8	Apr	9.40%	
9	May	0.63%	
10	Jun	-4.70%	
11	Jul	6.00%	
12	Aug	1.35%	
13	Sep	1.43%	
14	Oct	1.35%	
15	Nov	3.30%	
16	Dec	3.35%	
17			
18	Annual:	37.83%	
19			
20			

Sheet1

Figure 12-20: Monthly returns for a mutual fund.

A principal of 1 is used because I'm interested only in the rate of the return, not the actual balance of the mutual fund. The principal is subtracted from the end, so the result is the increase for only the year.

CAUTION

Note that the FVSCHEDULE function does not follow the sign convention. It returns a future value with the same sign as the present value.

Depreciation Calculations

Depreciation is an accounting concept whereby the value of an asset is expensed over time. Some expenditures affect only the current period and are expensed fully in that period. Other expenditures, however, affect multiple periods. These expenditures are *capitalized* (made into an asset) and *depreciated* (written off a little each period). A forklift, for example, may be useful for five years. Expensing the full cost of the forklift in the year it was purchased would not put the correct cost into the correct years. Instead, the forklift is capitalized and one-fifth of its cost is expensed in each year of its useful life.

Table 12-1 summarizes Excel's depreciation functions and the arguments used by each. For complete details, consult Excel's Help system.

TABLE 12-1   EXCEL DEPRECIATION FUNCTIONS

Function	Depreciation Method	Arguments*
SLN	Straight-line. The asset depreciates by the same amount each year of its life.	Cost, Salvage, Life
DB	Declining balance. Computes depreciation at a fixed rate.	Cost, Salvage, Life, Period, [Month]
DDB	Double-declining balance. Computes depreciation at an accelerated rate. Depreciation is highest in the first period and decreases in successive periods.	Cost, Salvage, Life, Period, Month, [Factor]
SYD	Sum of the year's digits. Allocates a larger depreciation in the earlier years of an asset's life.	Cost, Salvage, Life, Period
VDB	Variable-declining balance. Computes the depreciation of an asset for any period (including partial periods) using the double-declining balance method or some other method you specify.	Cost, Salvage, Life, Start Period, End Period, [Factor], [No Switch]

Arguments in brackets are optional.

The arguments for the depreciation functions are described as follows:

- **Cost:** Original cost of the asset.
- **Salvage:** Salvage cost of the asset after it has fully depreciated.
- **Life:** Number of periods over which the asset will depreciate.
- **Period:** Period in the Life for which the calculation is being made.
- **Month:** Number of months in the first year; if omitted, Excel uses 12.
- **Factor:** Rate at which the balance declines; if omitted, it is assumed to be 2 (that is, double-declining).
- **Rate:** Interest rate per period. If you make payments monthly, for example, you must divide the annual interest rate by 12.
- **No Switch:** True or False. Specifies whether to switch to straight-line depreciation when depreciation is greater than the declining balance calculation.

Figure 12-21 shows depreciation calculations using the SLN, DB, DDB, and SYD functions. The asset's original cost, $10,000, is assumed to have a useful life of ten years, with a salvage value of $1,000. The range labeled Depreciation Amount shows the annual depreciation of the asset. The range labeled Value of Asset shows the asset's depreciated value over its life.

	A	B	C	D	E
1	Asset:	Office Furniture			
2	Original Cost:	$10,000			
3	Life (years):	10			
4	Salvage Value:	$1,000			
5					
6	**Depreciation Amount**				
7	Year	SLN	DB	DDB	SYD
8	1	$900.00	$2,060.00	$2,000.00	$1,636.36
9	2	$900.00	$1,635.64	$1,600.00	$1,472.73
10	3	$900.00	$1,298.70	$1,280.00	$1,309.09
11	4	$900.00	$1,031.17	$1,024.00	$1,145.45
12	5	$900.00	$818.75	$819.20	$981.82
13	6	$900.00	$650.08	$655.36	$818.18
14	7	$900.00	$516.17	$524.29	$654.55
15	8	$900.00	$409.84	$419.43	$490.91
16	9	$900.00	$325.41	$335.54	$327.27
17	10	$900.00	$258.38	$268.44	$163.64
18					
19					
20	**Value of Asset**				
21	Year	SLN	DB	DDB	SYD
22	0	$10,000.00	$10,000.00	$10,000.00	$10,000.00
23	1	$9,100.00	$7,940.00	$8,000.00	$8,363.64
24	2	$8,200.00	$6,304.36	$6,400.00	$6,890.91
25	3	$7,300.00	$5,005.66	$5,120.00	$5,581.82
26	4	$6,400.00	$3,974.50	$4,096.00	$4,436.36
27	5	$5,500.00	$3,155.75	$3,276.80	$3,454.55
28	6	$4,600.00	$2,505.67	$2,621.44	$2,636.36
29	7	$3,700.00	$1,989.50	$2,097.15	$1,981.82
30	8	$2,800.00	$1,579.66	$1,677.72	$1,490.91
31	9	$1,900.00	$1,254.25	$1,342.18	$1,163.64
32	10	$1,000.00	$995.88	$1,073.74	$1,000.00
33					

Depreciation / VDB

Figure 12-21: A comparison of four depreciation functions.

ON THE CD

The companion CD-ROM contains `depreciation.xlsx`, the workbook shown in Figure 12-21.

Figure 12-22 shows a chart that graphs the asset's value. As you can see, the SLN function produces a straight line; the other functions produce curved lines because the depreciation is greater in the earlier years of the asset's life.

The VDB (variable declining balance) function is useful if you need to calculate depreciation for multiple periods, such as when you need to figure accumulated depreciation on an asset that has been sold. Figure 12-23 shows a worksheet set up to calculate the gain or loss on the sale of some office furniture. The formula in cell B12 is

```
=VDB(B2,B4,B3,0,DATEDIF(B5,B6,"y"),B7,B8)
```

Depreciation Functions

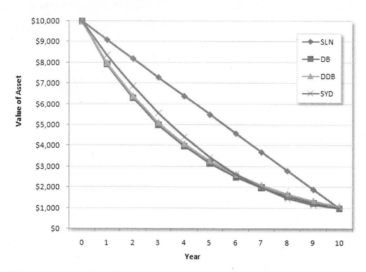

Figure 12-22: This chart shows an asset's value over time, using four depreciation functions.

	A	B	C	D
1	Asset:	Office Furniture		
2	Original Cost:	$ 10,000.00		
3	Life (years):	10		
4	Salvage Value:	$ 1,000.00		
5	Purchase Date:	3/15/2006		
6	Disposal Date:	3/15/2009		
7	Factor:	2		
8	No-Switch:	TRUE		
9				
10	Proceeds:		$5,875.00	
11	Cost:	10,000.00		
12	Accumulated Depreciation:	4,880.00		
13	Net Asset Value:		5,120.00	
14	Gain on sale of asset:		$755.00	
15				
16				

| ◄ ◄ ► ►| | Depreciation | VDB |

Figure 12-23: Using the VDB function to calculate accumulated depreciation.

The formula computes the depreciation taken on the asset from the date it was purchased until the date it was sold. The DATEDIF function is used to determine how many years the asset has been in service.

Chapter 13

Financial Schedules

IN THIS CHAPTER

◆ Setting up a basic amortization schedule

◆ Setting up a dynamic amortization schedule

◆ Evaluating loan options with a data table

◆ Creating two-way data tables

◆ Creating financial statements

◆ Understanding credit card repayment calculations

◆ Calculating and evaluating financial ratios

◆ Creating indices

This chapter, which makes use of much of the information contained in the two previous chapters, contains useful examples of a wide variety of financial calculations.

Creating Financial Schedules

Financial schedules present financial information in many different forms. Some present a summary of information, such as a Profit & Loss Statement, which presents the results of operations of a company. Others present a detail list, such as an amortization schedule, which schedules the payments of a loan.

Financial schedules can be static or dynamic. Static schedules generally use a few Excel functions but mainly exist in Excel to take advantage of its grid system, which lends itself well for formatting schedules. Dynamic schedules, on the other hand, usually contain an area for user input. A user can change certain input parameters and affect the results.

The sections that follow demonstrate summary and detail schedules as well as static and dynamic schedules.

Creating Amortization Schedules

In its simplest form, an *amortization schedule* tracks the payments (including interest and principal components) and the loan balance for a particular loan. This section presents several examples of amortization schedules.

A Simple Amortization Schedule

This example uses a simple loan to demonstrate the basic concepts involved in creating a dynamic schedule. Refer to the worksheet in Figure 13-1. Notice that rows 19 through 369 are hidden, so only the first five payments and last five payments are visible.

	A	B	C	D	E
1	**Amortization Schedule**				
2	**Input Area**				
3	Purchase Price	$225,000.00			
4	Down Payment	45,000.00			
5	Amount Financed	180,000.00			
6					
7	Annual Interest Rate	5.90%			
8	Term (years)	30			
9	Monthly Payment	$1,067.65			
10	Loan Date	3/15/2007			
11					
12	**Date**	**Payment**	**Interest**	**Principal**	**Balance**
13	Totals	$384,354.00	$204,349.93	$180,004.07	
14	3/15/2007				$180,000.00
15	4/15/2007	1,067.65	885.00	182.65	179,817.35
16	5/15/2007	1,067.65	884.10	183.55	179,633.80
17	6/15/2007	1,067.65	883.20	184.45	179,449.35
18	7/15/2007	1,067.65	882.29	185.36	179,263.99
370	11/15/2036	1,067.65	25.84	1,041.81	4,214.64
371	12/15/2036	1,067.65	20.72	1,046.93	3,167.71
372	1/15/2037	1,067.65	15.57	1,052.08	2,115.63
373	2/15/2037	1,067.65	10.40	1,057.25	1,058.38
374	3/15/2037	1,067.65	5.20	1,062.45	(4.07)
375					

H ◀ ▶ H   Simple / Flexible / Tables / Credit Card

Figure 13-1: A simple amortization schedule.

ON THE CD

All the examples in this section are available on the companion CD-ROM in the workbook `amortization.xlsx`.

USER INPUT SECTION

The area above the schedule contains cells for user input and for intermediate calculations. The user input cells are shaded, so it's easy to determine what can be changed and what has a formula.

The user can enter the purchase price and the down payment. The amount financed is calculated for use in the amortization calculation. The formula in cell B5 is

```
=Purchase_Price-Down_Payment
```

 TIP

Descriptively named ranges are used to make the formulas more readable.

The other calculation necessary to complete the schedule is the monthly payment. The formula in B9 is

```
=-ROUND(PMT(Rate/12,Term*12,Amount_Financed),2)
```

 CROSS REF

More information on named cells and ranges is in Chapter 3.

The PMT function is used to determine the monthly payment amount. The rate (B7) is divided by 12, and the term (B8) is multiplied by 12, so that the arguments are on a monthly basis. This ensures that the result of PMT is also on a monthly basis.

The ROUND function rounds the result of PMT to two decimal places. t is an attractive proposition not to round this number so that the result is accurate to the penny. However, because you will not be paying the bank fractions of pennies, you shouldn't have them in your schedule.

SUMMARY INFORMATION

The first line of the schedule, after the header information, contains summary formulas. In this example, only the totals are shown. However, you could include totals by year, quarter, or any other interval you like. The formula in B13, and copied across, is

```
=SUM(B14:B381)
```

TIP

Placing the summary information above the schedule itself eliminates the need to scroll to the end of the worksheet.

THE SCHEDULE

The schedule starts in row 14 with the amount financed as the beginning balance. The first payment is deemed to be made exactly one month after the loan is initiated. The first payment row (row 15) and all subsequent rows contain the same formulas, which are described below. The formula in E14 is

```
=Amount_Financed
```

To increment the date for the payment rows, the DATE function is used. The formula in A15 is

```
=DATE(YEAR(A14),MONTH(A14)+1,DAY(A14))
```

The DATE function constructs a date from the year, month, and day arguments. The arguments are derived from the cell above, and the month is increment by one.

The payment column simply references the PMT function from the user input section. Because that formula was rounded, no further rounding is necessary.

The interest column computes a monthly interest based on the previous balance. The formula in C15 is

```
=ROUND(E14*Rate/12,2)
```

The previous balance, in cell E14, is multiplied by the annual interest rate which is divided by 12. The annual interest rate is in cell B7, named Rate. Each month's balance must be rounded to the penny, so every interest calculation is rounded as you go.

Whatever portion of the payment doesn't go toward interest goes toward reducing the principal balance. The formula in D15 is

```
=B15-C15
```

Finally, the balance is updated to reflect the principal portion of the payment. The formula in E15 is

```
=E14-D15
```

Loan amortization schedules are self-checking. If everything is set up correctly, the final balance at the end of the term is 0 (or very close to 0, given rounding errors).

TIP

Another check is to add the Principal components. The sum of these values should equal the original loan amount.

LIMITATIONS

This type of schedule is excellent for loans that will likely never change. It can be set up one time and referred to throughout the life of the loan. Further, it can be copied to create new loan with just a few adjustments. However, it leaves a little to be desired.

You may have noticed that the balance at the end of the loan, as well as the total principal paid in the summary section, is off by $4.07. This is because of the rounding of each month's payment and interest calculation. Although rounding those results is necessary, a more flexible schedule would allow you to adjust the final payment so the balance is zero when the final payment is made.

This schedule lacks flexibility in other ways as well:

- The payment is computed and applied every month but cannot account for over- or under-payments.

- Many loans have variable interest rates, and this schedule provides no way to adjust the interest rate per period.

- Although the user is allowed to specify a term, the rows in the schedule are fixed. Specifying a shorter or longer term would require that formulas be deleted or added to compensate.

In the next section, I address some of the flexibility issues and create a more dynamic amortization schedule.

A Dynamic Amortization Schedule

The example in this section builds on the previous example. Figure 13-2 shows a loan amortization schedule that allows the user to define input parameters beyond the amount, rate, and term. Notice that rows 22 through 124 are hidden.

The first difference you'll notice is that this schedule has more shaded cells, meaning there are more cells that the user can change. Also, a column has been added for the annual percentage rate, which now can be different for every period.

USER INPUT SECTION

Not much has changed in this section. The interest rate is labeled *Starting Rate,* and the payment is labeled *Computed Payment,* indicating that they are subject to change.

Part III

	A	B	C	D	E	F	G
1	**Amortization Schedule**						
2		**Input Area**					
3	Purchase Price	$225,000.00					
4	Down Payment	45,000.00					
5	Amount Financed	180,000.00					
6							
7	Starting Rate	5.90%					
8	Term (years)	10					
9	Computed Payment	$1,989.34					
10	Loan Date	3/15/2007					
11							
12	**Date**	**APR**	**Payment**	**Addt'l Pymt**	**Interest**	**Principal**	**Balance**
13	Totals		$224,247.84	$500.00	$44,747.84	$180,000.00	
14	3/15/2007						$180,000.00
15	4/15/2007	5.90%	1,989.34		901.97	1,087.37	178,912.63
16	5/15/2007	5.90%	1,989.34		867.60	1,121.74	177,790.89
17	6/25/2007	5.90%	1,989.34		1,178.29	811.05	176,979.84
18	7/15/2007	5.90%	1,989.34		572.15	1,417.19	175,562.65
19	8/15/2007	4.80%	1,989.34		715.72	1,273.62	174,289.03
20	9/15/2007	4.80%	1,989.34	500.00	710.53	1,778.81	172,510.22
21	10/15/2007	4.80%	1,989.34		680.59	1,308.75	171,201.47
125	6/15/2016	4.80%	1,989.34		21.93	1,967.41	3,411.79
126	7/15/2016	4.80%	1,989.34		13.46	1,975.88	1,435.91
127	8/15/2016	4.80%	1,441.76		5.85	1,435.91	-
128							

I◄ ◄ ► ►I   Simple   **Flexible**   Tables   Credit Card

Figure 13-2: A dynamic amortization schedule.

SUMMARY INFORMATION

The user can now change the term; the interest rates; and the payments, which can and usually will change the maturity date. For the summary information, you want to sum only the relevant rows. The formula in C13 is

```
=SUMIF($F15:$F374,">=0",C15:C374)
```

After the *Balance* in column F is zero, the amortization is complete. This SUMIF function sums only those payments up until that point. This formula is copied across to the interest and principal columns, and the absolute column reference ensures the new formulas still point to column F.

THE SCHEDULE

With so many user changeable fields in the schedule, many of the formulas had to change to account for different conditions. An amortization schedule has two kinds of user input data:

- Data that changes for one payment only
- Data that changes for all subsequent payments

When the interest rate changes for one payment, it changes for all subsequent payment — at least, until it changes again. It doesn't go back to the old rate. For that reason, the APR column relies on the data directly above it. The formula in B15 pulls the starting interest rate from the user input section. This formula, in B16 and copied down, simply repeats the previous month's rate:

```
=B15
```

This allows the user to enter a new rate when it changes and have that rate continue down until it's manually changed again. In this example, the bank informed you that the rate was reduced to 4.8% for the fifth payment (row 19). That rate was entered in B19, and all rates after that reflect the change.

The payment date is an example of data that changes for one payment. If a payment is made late, it doesn't mean that all subsequent payments will be late. In this example, the third payment (row 17) was made ten days late. This had no effect on the next month's payment, which was made on time. For this type of data, the increments need to be made against a base that doesn't change. The formula in A15 is

```
=DATE(YEAR(Loan_Date),MONTH(Loan_Date)+ROW()-14,DAY(Loan_Date))
```

This formula is copied down to all the rows. Unlike the previous example, it doesn't rely on the date above it. Rather, it uses the *Loan_Date* range as its base. Because the payments start in row 15, the current row less 14 is used to increment the month.

The point of these formulas is to allow the user to overwrite the formula with a literal date value and not affect the rest of the dates. In Cell A17, the user replaced the formula by entering a new date, which changed the calculation for that payment but did not affect future payments.

Because you provide a separate column for an additional payment, the payment should never change — except that it needs to account for any previous rounding errors in the last payment. The formula in C15 is

```
=IF(G127+E128-Monthly_Payment-D128<5,G127+E128-D128,Monthly_Payment)
```

Normally, if the remaining balance is less than the normal payment, just the balance (plus interest) is paid. However, in this example, I don't want a last payment of less than $5. If a normal payment would leave such a balance, it is just added to the last payment. There's nothing wrong with a really small final payments. If you don't mind them, you can simplify the formula to

```
=IF(G127+E128<Monthly_Payment+D128,G127+E128-D128,Monthly_Payment)
```

The interest calculation now has to account for the fact that the user may make a payment early or late. Instead of dividing the rate by 12, as in the last example, the rate is multiplied by a ratio of the number of days outstanding to 365. The formula in E15 is

```
=ROUND(G14*B15*(A15-A14)/365,2)
```

The principal column calculation is similar to the previous example except that any additional payment must be added in. The formula in F15 is

```
=C15+D15-E15
```

The balance is computed by subtracting the principal portion of the current payment from the previous balance, exactly as it was in the previous example.

FINISHING TOUCHES

As you can see in Figure 13-2 (which hides rows in the middle so you can see the last payment), the final payment is represented in row 127, and there are no calculations below that. I didn't just guess right, however. All the cells in the schedule, starting in row 15, have conditional formatting applied to them. If column G of the row above is zero or less, both the background color and the font color are white, rendering them invisible.

To apply conditional formatting, select the range A15:G374 and choose the Home⇨Styles⇨Conditional Formatting command. Add a formula rule with this formula:

```
=$G14<=0
```

The absolute column means that every column in the selection will refer to column G; the relative row means the row applies to the row above, regardless of which row you're in.

CROSS REF

For more information on conditional formatting, refer to Chapter 19.

The formulas are present in row beyond row 127 (they exist for up to 360 months) but are hidden using conditional formatting to make the table size dynamic as well.

Using Payment and Interest Tables

The preceding example allows the user to input data directly in the calculation and reporting section of the schedule. This affords maximum flexibility and adds a level of intuitiveness to customizing the schedule. Depending on the intended user, however, it could be dangerous and lead to errors. In particular, overwriting formulas, like changing the interest rate in the last example, does not lend itself to undoing or correcting errors. Unless the user is intimately familiar with the workings of the spreadsheet, those hard-coded values can stick around when the user thinks they're formulas.

Another method — and some would argue a better method — is to keep the user input section separate from the calculation and report section. If all user inputs are relegated to one area, it's easier to determine what has been inputted and whether any inputs are missing.

This example uses the same basic data as the previous two examples. It adds an additional payment table, an interest rate table, and a late payment table in the user input\section, and the formulas are adjusted. Figure 13-3 shows the user input section of this flexible schedule.

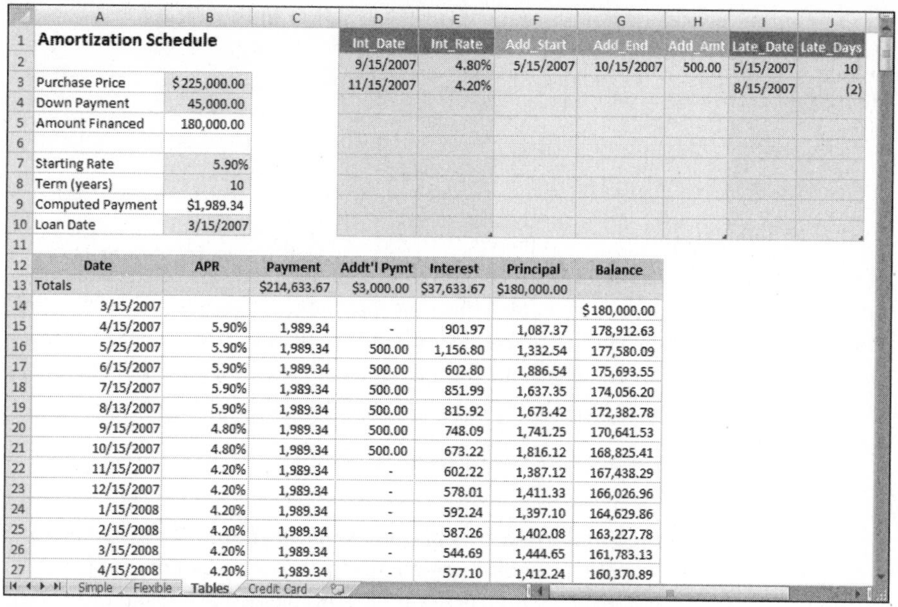

	A	B	C	D	E	F	G	H	I	J
1	**Amortization Schedule**			Int_Date	Int_Rate	Add_Start	Add_End	Add_Amt	Late_Date	Late_Days
2				9/15/2007	4.80%	5/15/2007	10/15/2007	500.00	5/15/2007	10
3	Purchase Price	$225,000.00		11/15/2007	4.20%				8/15/2007	(2)
4	Down Payment	45,000.00								
5	Amount Financed	180,000.00								
6										
7	Starting Rate	5.90%								
8	Term (years)	10								
9	Computed Payment	$1,989.34								
10	Loan Date	3/15/2007								
11										
12	Date	APR	Payment	Addt'l Pymt	Interest	Principal	Balance			
13	Totals		$214,633.67	$3,000.00	$37,633.67	$180,000.00				
14	3/15/2007						$180,000.00			
15	4/15/2007	5.90%	1,989.34	-	901.97	1,087.37	178,912.63			
16	5/25/2007	5.90%	1,989.34	500.00	1,156.80	1,332.54	177,580.09			
17	6/15/2007	5.90%	1,989.34	500.00	602.80	1,886.54	175,693.55			
18	7/15/2007	5.90%	1,989.34	500.00	851.99	1,637.35	174,056.20			
19	8/13/2007	5.90%	1,989.34	500.00	815.92	1,673.42	172,382.78			
20	9/15/2007	4.80%	1,989.34	500.00	748.09	1,741.25	170,641.53			
21	10/15/2007	4.80%	1,989.34	500.00	673.22	1,816.12	168,825.41			
22	11/15/2007	4.20%	1,989.34	-	602.22	1,387.12	167,438.29			
23	12/15/2007	4.20%	1,989.34	-	578.01	1,411.33	166,026.96			
24	1/15/2008	4.20%	1,989.34	-	592.24	1,397.10	164,629.86			
25	2/15/2008	4.20%	1,989.34	-	587.26	1,402.08	163,227.78			
26	3/15/2008	4.20%	1,989.34	-	544.69	1,444.65	161,783.13			
27	4/15/2008	4.20%	1,989.34	-	577.10	1,412.24	160,370.89			

Simple / Flexible / **Tables** / Credit Card

Figure 13-3: Keeping the user input isolated in its own area.

Nothing in the schedule can be updated by the user. Changes to the amortization table must be made in the inputs in column B or in one of the three tables to the right of that. The new formulas in the schedule are discussed in the following sections. Formulas not listed have not changed from the previous example.

DATE

```
=DATE(YEAR(Loan_Date),MONTH(Loan_Date)+ROW()-14,
DAY(Loan_Date))+IFERROR(VLOOKUP(DATE(YEAR(Loan_Date),
MONTH(Loan_Date)+ROW()-14,DAY(Loan_Date)),tblLate,2,FALSE),0)
```

This formula looks a little daunting, but it's not too bad. It starts with the same DATE function used in the preceding example and adds the number of late days from tblLate. The VLOOKUP function looks for an exact match in the first column of tblDate; the number in the second column, either plus or minus, is added to the originally computed date. The IFERROR function is used to return a zero if no match is found, meaning the originally computed date is used.

APR

```
=IFERROR(VLOOKUP(A15,tblRate,2),Rate)
```

The table tblRate contains a list of interest rate changes. The VLOOKUP function is used with an omitted fourth argument so that the rate change persists until it is changed again. This means that the dates in tblRate must be sorted.

The IFERROR statement returns the starting rate if no value is found in tblRate.

ADDITIONAL PAYMENT

```
=SUMIFS(tblAdd[Add_Amt],tblAdd[Add_Start],
"<="&A15,tblAdd[Add_End],">="&A15)
```

The table tblAdd is a listing of additional payments, the date they become effective, and the date they expire. To add a one-time additional payment, the user can make the start and end dates the same. To schedule a series of additional payments, however, this method allows the user to add them quickly. The SUMIFS formula adds the additional amount for every row in the table where the current payment date is in between the start and end dates. That means that more than one additional payment can be made for one date.

 CROSS REF

You can find more information on referring to tables in formulas in Chapter 9. Summing and counting functions, like SUMIFS, are discussed in Chapter 7. And examples of lookup functions, such as VLOOKUP, as well as the IFERROR function are given in Chapter 8.

Credit Card Calculations

The final type of loan amortization schedule is for credit card loans. Credit cards are different beasts because the minimum payment varies, based on the outstanding balance. You could use the preceding Payment Table method, but it offers only nine rows of varying payments – probably not enough for most applications. You could also use the method where the payments are entered directly in the schedule. When the payments are different every time, however, the schedule loses its value as a predictor or planner. You need a schedule that can predict the future payments of a credit card loan.

Credit card calculations represent several nonstandard problems. Excel's financial functions (PV, FV, RATE, and NPER) require that the regular payments are at a single level. In addition, the PMT function returns a single level of payments. With IRR and NPV analysis, the user inserts the varying payments into a cash flow.

Credit card companies calculate payments based on the following relatively standard set of criteria:

- **A minimum payment is required.** For example, a credit card account might require a minimum payment of $25.

- **The payment must be at least equal to a base percentage of the outstanding debt.** Usually, the payment is a percentage of the outstanding balance but not less than a specified amount.

- **The payment is rounded,** usually to the nearest $0.05.

- **Interest is invariably quoted at a given rate per month.**

Figure 13-4 shows a worksheet set up to calculate credit card payments.

	A	B	C	D	E	F
1	**Credit Card Amortization**					
2		Input Area				
3	Starting Balance			$ 3,200.00		
4	Starting Date			2/3/2007		
5	Monthly Interest Rate			1.500%		
6	Minimum Payment Percent			3.000%		
7	Minimum Payment Dollars			$ 25.00		
8	Payment Rounding			$ 0.05		
9						
10	Date	Minimum Payment	Additional Payment	Interest	Principal	Balance
11	Totals	$5,896.92	$0.00	$2,696.92	$3,200.00	
12	2/3/2007					$ 3,200.00
13	3/3/2007	96.00		48.00	48.00	3,152.00
14	4/3/2007	94.55		47.28	47.27	3,104.73
15	5/3/2007	93.15		46.57	46.58	3,058.15
16	6/3/2007	91.75		45.87	45.88	3,012.27
17	7/3/2007	90.35		45.18	45.17	2,967.10
18	8/3/2007	89.00		44.51	44.49	2,922.61
19	9/3/2007	87.70		43.84	43.86	2,878.75
20	10/3/2007	86.35		43.18	43.17	2,835.58
21	11/3/2007	85.05		42.53	42.52	2,793.06
22	12/3/2007	83.80		41.90	41.90	2,751.16
23	1/3/2008	82.55		41.27	41.28	2,709.88
24	2/3/2008	81.30		40.65	40.65	2,669.23
25	3/3/2008	80.10		40.04	40.06	2,629.17
26	4/3/2008	78.90		39.44	39.46	2,589.71
27	5/3/2008	77.70		38.85	38.85	2,550.86
28	6/3/2008	76.55		38.26	38.29	2,512.57

Simple / Flexible / Tables / Credit Card

Figure 13-4: Calculating a credit card payment schedule.

The formula for the minimum payment is rather complicated — just like the terms of a credit card. This example uses a minimum payment amount of $25 or 3% of the balance, which results in a very long payback. If this borrower ever hopes to get rid of that balance in a reasonable amount of time, he'll need to use that additional payment column.

The minimum payment formula, such as the one in B13, is

```
=MIN(F12+D13,MROUND(MAX(MinDol,ROUND(MinPct*F12,2)),PayRnd))
```

From the inside out: The larger of the minimum dollar amount and the minimum percent is calculated. The result of that is rounded to the nearest five cents. This rounded amount is then compared with the outstanding balance, and the lesser of the two is used.

Of course, things get much more complicated when additional charges are made. In such a case, the formulas would need to account for "grace periods" for purchases (but not cash withdrawals). A further complication is that interest is calculated on the daily outstanding balance at the daily effective equivalent of the quoted rate.

Part III

Summarizing Loan Options Using a Data Table

If you're faced with making a decision about borrowing money, you have to choose between many variables, not the least of which is the interest rate. Fortunately, Excel's Data Table command (Data⇨Data Tools⇨What-If Analysis⇨Data Table) can help by summarizing the results of calculations using different inputs.

ON THE CD

The workbook `loan data tables.xlsx` contains the examples in this section and can be found on the companion CD-ROM.

The data table feature is one of Excel's most under-utilized tools. A data table is a dynamic range that summarizes formula cells for varying input cells. You can create a data table fairly easily, but data tables have some limitations. In particular, a data table can deal with only one or two input cells at a time. This limitation becomes clear as you view the examples.

Creating a One-Way Data Table

A *one-way data table* shows the results of any number of calculations for different values of a single input cell. Figure 13-5 shows the general layout for a one-way data table.

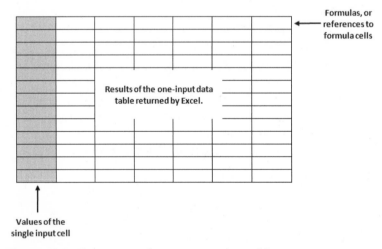

Results of the one-input data table returned by Excel.

Formulas, or references to formula cells

Values of the single input cell

Figure 13-5: The structure for a one-way data table.

Figure 13-6 shows a one-way data table (in D2:G9) that displays three calculations (payment amount, total payments, and total interest) for a loan, using eight interest rates ranging from 6.75% to 8.50%. In this example, the input cell is cell B2. Note that the range E1:G1 is not part of the data table. These cells contain descriptive labels.

	A	B	C	D	E	F	G
1	Loan Amount:	$10,000.00			Payment Amt	Total Payments	Total Interest
2	Annual Interest Rate:	6.75%		6.75%	$307.63	$11,074.65	$1,074.65
3	Pmt. Period (mos):	1		7.00%	$308.77	$11,115.75	$1,115.75
4	No. of Periods:	36		7.25%	$309.92	$11,156.95	$1,156.95
5				7.50%	$311.06	$11,198.24	$1,198.24
6	Payment Amount:	$307.63		7.75%	$312.21	$11,239.62	$1,239.62
7	Total Payments:	$11,074.65		8.00%	$313.36	$11,281.09	$1,281.09
8	Total Interest:	$1,074.65		8.25%	$314.52	$11,322.66	$1,322.66
9				8.50%	$315.68	$11,364.31	$1,364.31
10							
11							

1-way / 2-way

Figure 13-6: Using a one-way data table to display three loan calculations for various interest rates.

To create this one-way data table, follow these steps:

1. **In the first row of the data table, enter the formulas that are used to return the results.**

   The interest rate will vary in the data table, but it doesn't matter which interest rate you use for the calculations, as long as the calculations are correct. In this example, the formulas in E2:G2 contain references to other formulas in column B

   ```
   E2:  =B6
   F2:  =B7
   G2:  =B8
   ```

2. **In the first column of the data table, enter various values for a single input cell.**

   In this example, the input value is interest rate, and the values for various interest rates appear in D2:D9. Note that the first row of the data table (row 2) displays the results for the first input value (in cell D2).

3. **Select the range that contains the entries from the previous steps.**

   In this example, select D2:G9.

4. **Choose the Data⇨Data Tools ⇨What-If Analysis⇨Data Table.**

   Excel displays the Data Table dialog box, as shown in Figure 13-7.

Figure 13-7: The Excel Data Table dialog box.

5. For the Row Input Cell field, specify the formula cell that corresponds to the input variable.

   In this example, the Column Input Cell is B2.

6. Leave the Row Input Cell field empty, and click OK.

   Excel inserts an array formula that uses the TABLE function with a single argument.

TIP

If you like, you can format the data table. For example, you might want to apply shading to the row and column headers.

Note that the array formula is not entered into the entire range that you selected in Step 4. The first column and first row of your selection are not changed.

Creating a Two-Way Data Table

A *two-way data table* shows the results of a single calculation for different values of two input cells. Figure 13-8 shows the general layout of a two-way data table.

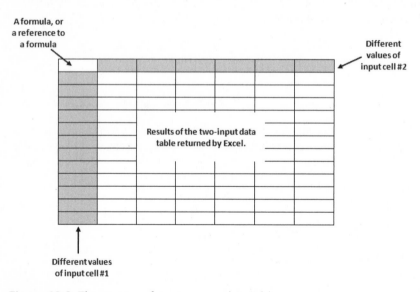

Figure 13-8: The structure for a two-way data table.

Figure 13-9 shows a two-way data table (in B7:J16) that displays a calculation (payment amount) for a loan, using eight interest rates and nine loan amounts.

	A	B	C	D	E	F	G	H	I
1	Loan Amount:	$10,000.00							
2	Annual Interest Rate:	7.25%							
3	Pmt. Period (mos):	1							
4	No. of Periods:	36							
5									
6						*Interest Rate*			
7		$309.92	7.00%	7.25%	7.50%	7.75%	8.00%	8.25%	8.50%
8		$9,000.00	$277.89	$278.92	$279.96	$280.99	$282.03	$283.07	$284.11
9		$9,500.00	$293.33	$294.42	$295.51	$296.60	$297.70	$298.79	$299.89
10		$10,000.00	$308.77	$309.92	$311.06	$312.21	$313.36	$314.52	$315.68
11		$10,500.00	$324.21	$325.41	$326.62	$327.82	$329.03	$330.24	$331.46
12		$11,000.00	$339.65	$340.91	$342.17	$343.43	$344.70	$345.97	$347.24
13		$11,500.00	$355.09	$356.40	$357.72	$359.04	$360.37	$361.70	$363.03
14									

H ◄ ► H   1-way   2-way

Figure 13-9: Using a two-way data table to display payment amounts for various loan amounts and interest rates.

To create this two-way data table, follow these steps:

1. Enter a formula that returns the results that will be used in the data table.

   In this example, the formula is in cell B7 is a reference to cell B5, which contains the payment calculation: *B7: =B5*

2. Enter various values for the first input in successive columns of the first row of the data table.

   In this example, the first input value is interest rate, and the values for various interest rates appear in C7:J7.

3. Enter various values for the second input cell in successive rows of the first column of the data table.

   In this example, the second input value is the loan amount, and the values for various loan amounts are in B8:B16.

4. Select the range that contains the entries from the preceding steps.

   In this example, select B7:J16.

5. Choose the Data⇨Data Tools ⇨What-If Analysis⇨Data Table.

   Excel displays the Data Table dialog box.

6. For the Row Input Cell field, specify the cell reference that corresponds to the first input cell.

   In this example, the Row Input Cell is B2.

7. For the Column Input Cell field, specify the cell reference that corresponds to the second input cell.

   In this example, the Row Input Cell is B1.

8. Click OK.

Excel inserts an array formula that uses the TABLE function with two arguments.

After you create the two-way data table, you can change the formula in the upper-left cell of the data table. In this example, you can change the formula in cell B7 to

```
=PMT(B2*(B3/12),B4,-B1)*B4-B1
```

This causes the TABLE function to displays total interest rather than payment amounts.

TIP

If you find that using data tables slows down the calculation of your workbook, choose Formulas⇨Calculation⇨Calculation Options⇨Automatic Except for Data Tables.

Financial Statements and Ratios

Many companies use Excel to evaluate their financial health and report financial results. Financial statements and financial ratios are two types of analyses a company can use to accomplish those goals. Excel is well suited for financial statements because its grid interface allows for easy adjustment of columns. Ratios are simply financial calculations — something Excel was designed for.

Basic Financial Statements

Financial statements summarize the financial transactions of a business. The two primary financial statements are the balance sheet and the income statement:

- The *balance sheet* reports the state of a company at a particular moment in time. It shows

  - *Assets:* What the company owns

  - *Liabilities:* What the company owes

  - *Equity:* What the company is worth

- The *income statement* summarizes the transactions of a company over a certain period of time, such as a month, quarter, or year

  A typical income statement reports the sales, costs, and net income (or loss) of the company.

CONVERTING TRIAL BALANCES

Most accounting software will produce financial statements for you. However, many of those applications do not give you the flexibility and formatting options that you have in Excel. One way to produce your own financial statements is to export the trial balance from your accounting software package and use Excel to summarize the transactions for you. Figure 13-10 shows part of a trial balance, which lists all the accounts and their balances.

Figure 13-11 shows a balance sheet that summarizes the balance sheet accounts from the trial balance.

Account Name	Account No.	Balance	Class
Cash-Petty Cash	1010	449.87	Cash
Checking Account	1110	2412.23	Cash
Investment Account	1115	327283.53	Marketable Securities
Accounts Receivable	1210	16586.25	Accounts Receivable
Prepaid Expenses	1420	2587.5	Prepaid and Other
Prepaid Insurance	1425	1000	Prepaid and Other
Inventory Asset	1310	46005.75	Inventory
Property and Equipment	1510	65000	Property and Equipment
Accum. Depr.Property and Equipment	1511	-6750	Accumulated Depreciation
Office/Store Furniture and Fixtures	1520	12000	Property and Equipment
Accum. Depr. Furniture and Fixtures	1521	-9525	Accumulated Depreciation
Accounts Payable	2010	-15502.62	Accounts Payable
Pending Item Receipts	2015	-846.59	Accrued Expenses
Sales Tax Payable	2110	-11426.42	Accrued Expenses
Federal Tax Liability	2210	-1517.3	Accrued Expenses
Federal Tax Liability (FUTA)	2215	-145	Accrued Expenses
State Tax Liability	2220	-740	Accrued Expenses
401 (k) Liability	2230	-2000	Accrued Expenses
Union Dues Liability	2240	-85	Accrued Expenses
Medical/Dental Liability	2250	-990	Accrued Expenses
Other Payables	2310	-500	Accrued Expenses
Interest Payable	2315	-2000	Accrued Expenses
Visa Credit Card	2610	-300	Accrued Expenses
Note Payable to Bank	2710	-20000	Long Term Debt
Common Stock	3015	-1000	Common Stock
APIC	3016	-36000	Additional Paid in Capital
Owners' Withdrawals	3020	12000	Dividends
Retained Earnings	3025	-76484.48	Beginning Retained Earnings

Trial Balance / Balance Sheet / Income Statement / CS B

Figure 13-10: A trial balance lists all accounts and balances.

The *class* column of the trial balance is used to classify that account on the balance sheet or income statement. The formula in cell B4 on the balance sheet is

```
=SUMIF(Class,A4,Balance)
```

ON THE CD

The file `financial statements.xlsx` contains all the examples in this chapter and can be found on the companion CD-ROM.

	A	B	C	D
1	Balance Sheet			
2				
3	Assets			
4	Cash	$ 2,862.10	0.63%	
5	Marketable Securities	327,283.53	71.61%	
6	Accounts Receivable	16,586.25	3.63%	
7	Inventory	46,005.75	10.07%	
8	Prepaid and Other	3,587.50	0.78%	
9	Total Current Assets	$ 396,325.13	86.71%	
10				
11	Property and Equipment	$ 77,000.00	16.85%	
12	Accumulated Depreciation	16,275.00	3.56%	
13	Net PP&E	$ 60,725.00	13.29%	
14				
15	Total Assets	$ 457,050.13	100.00%	
16				
17	Liabilities			
18	Accounts Payable	$ 15,502.62	3.39%	
19	Accrued Expenses	20,550.31	4.50%	
20	Total Current Liabilities	$ 36,052.93	7.89%	
21				
22	Long Term Debt	$ 20,000.00	4.38%	
23				
24	Equity			
25	Common Stock	$ 1,000.00	0.22%	
26	Additional Paid in Capital	36,000.00	7.88%	
27	Retained Earnings	363,997.20	79.64%	
28				
29	Total Liabilities and Equity	$ 457,050.13	100.00%	
30				
31	Balanced			
32				

Income Statement   CS Balance Sheet

Figure 13-11: A balance sheet summarizes certain accounts.

For all the accounts on the trial balance whose class equals Cash, their total is summed here. The formula is repeated for every financial statement classification on both the balance sheet and income statement. For classifications that typically have a credit balance — such as liabilities, equity, and revenue — the formula starts with a negative sign. The formula for Accounts Payable, cell B18, is

```
=-SUMIF(Class,A18,Balance)
```

The account that ties the balance sheet and income statement together is Retained Earnings. Figure 13-12 shows an income statement that includes a statement of retained earning at the bottom.

	A	B	C
1	**Income Statement**		
2	**with Statement of Retained Earnings**		
3			
4	Revenue	$ 1,195,450.25	
5	Cost of Goods Sold	870,175.83	
6	Gross Margin	$ 325,274.42	
7			
8	Overhead	29,879.65	
9	Net Ordinary Income (Loss)	$ 295,394.77	
10			
11	Interest Expense	1,269.08	
12	Interest Income	5,387.03	
13	Net Income (Loss)	$ 299,512.72	
14			
15	Beginning Retained Earnings	$ 76,484.48	
16	Net Income (Loss)	299,512.72	
17	Dividends	(12,000.00)	
18	Ending Retained Earnings	$ 363,997.20	
19			
20			

Income Statement / CS Balance S

Figure 13-12: The income statement can include a statement of retained earnings.

The Retained Earning classification on the balance sheet refers to the Ending Retained Earnings classification on the income statement. Ending Retained Earnings is computed by taking Beginning Retained Earnings, adding net income (or subtracting net loss), and subtracting dividends.

Finally, the balance sheet must be in balance: hence, the name. Total assets must equal total liabilities and equity. This error-checking formula is used in cell B31 on the balance sheet:

```
=IF(ABS(B29-B15)>0.01,"Out of Balance","Balanced")
```

If the difference between assets and liabilities and equity is more than a penny, an error message is displayed below the schedule. The ABS function is used to check for assets being more or less than liabilities and equity. Because the balance sheet is in balance, the formula returns an empty string.

COMMON SIZE FINANCIAL STATEMENTS

Comparing financial statements from different companies can be difficult. One such difficulty is comparing companies of different sizes. A small retailer might show $1 million is revenue, but a multinational retailer might show $1 billion. The sheer scale of the numbers makes it difficult to compare the health and results of operations of these very different companies.

Common-size financial statements summarize accounts relative to a single number. For balance sheets, all entries are shown relative to total assets. For the income statement, all entries are shown relative to total sales. Figure 13-13 shows a common-size income statement.

Part III

	A	B	C	D	E
1		Income Statement			
3					
4	Revenue	$1,195,450.25	100.00%		
5	Cost of Goods Sold	870,175.83	72.79%		
6	Gross Margin	$ 325,274.42	27.21%		
7					
8	Overhead	29,879.65	2.50%		
9	Net Ordinary Income (Loss)	$ 295,394.77	24.71%		
10					
11	Interest Expense	1,269.08	0.11%		
12	Interest Income	5,387.03	0.45%		
13	Net Income (Loss)	$ 299,512.72	25.05%		
14					
19					

CS Balance Sheet   CS Inc Statement

Figure 13-13: Entries on a common size income statement are shown relative to revenue.

The formula in cell C4 is

```
=B4/$B$4
```

The denominator is absolute with respect to both rows and columns so that when this formula is copied to other areas of the income statement, it shows the percentage of revenue. To display only the percentage figures, you can hide column B.

Ratio Analysis

Financial ratios are calculations that are derived from the financial statements and other financial data to measure various aspects of a company. They can be compared with other companies or to industry standards. This section demonstrates how to calculate several financial ratios. See Figure 13-14.

LIQUIDITY RATIOS

Liquidity ratios measure a company's ability to pay its bills in the short term.

CAUTION
Poor liquidity ratios may indicate that the company has a high cost of financing or is on the verge of bankruptcy.

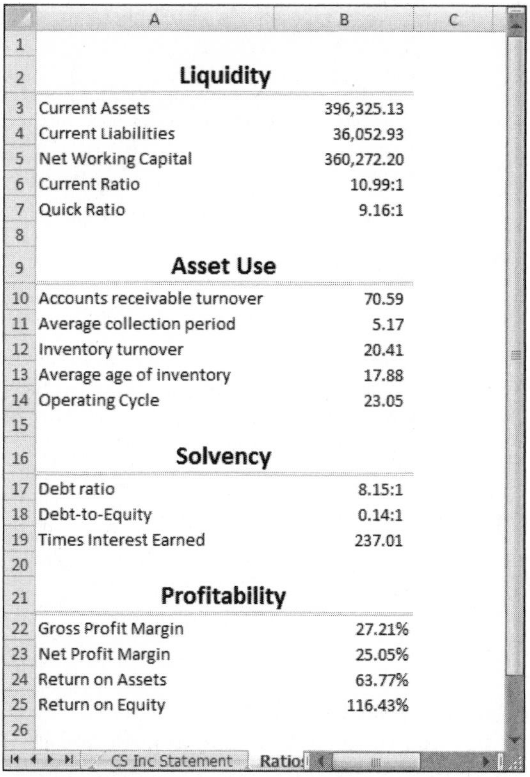

	A	B	C
1			
2	**Liquidity**		
3	Current Assets	396,325.13	
4	Current Liabilities	36,052.93	
5	Net Working Capital	360,272.20	
6	Current Ratio	10.99:1	
7	Quick Ratio	9.16:1	
8			
9	**Asset Use**		
10	Accounts receivable turnover	70.59	
11	Average collection period	5.17	
12	Inventory turnover	20.41	
13	Average age of inventory	17.88	
14	Operating Cycle	23.05	
15			
16	**Solvency**		
17	Debt ratio	8.15:1	
18	Debt-to-Equity	0.14:1	
19	Times Interest Earned	237.01	
20			
21	**Profitability**		
22	Gross Profit Margin	27.21%	
23	Net Profit Margin	25.05%	
24	Return on Assets	63.77%	
25	Return on Equity	116.43%	
26			

CS Inc Statement　Ratio

Figure 13-14: Various financial ratio calculations.

Net Working Capital is computed by subtracting current liabilities from current assets:

```
=Total_Current_Assets-Total_Current_Liabilities
```

Current assets are turned into cash within one accounting period (usually one year). *Current liabilities* are debts that will be paid within one period. A positive number here indicates that the company has enough assets to pay for its short-term liabilities.

The Current Ratio is a similar measure that divides current assets by current liabilities:

```
=Total_Current_Assets/Total_Current_Liabilities
```

When this ratio is greater than 1:1, it's the same as when Net Working Capital is positive.

The final liquidity ratio is the Quick Ratio. Although the Current Ratio includes assets, such as inventory and accounts receivable that will be converted into cash in a short time, the Quick Ratio includes only cash and assets that can be converted into cash immediately.

```
=(Cash+Marketable_Securities)/Total_Current_Liabilities
```

Part III

A Quick Ratio greater than 1:1 indicates that the company can pay all its short-term liabilities right now.

TIP

The custom number format

```
0.00":1"_)
```

can be used to format the result of the Current Ratio and Quick Ratio.

ASSET USE RATIOS

Asset use ratios measure how efficiently a company is using its assets: that is, how quickly the company is turning its assets back into cash. The accounts Receivable Turnover ratio divides sales by average accounts receivable:

```
=Revenue/((Account_Receivable+LastYear_Accounts_Receivable)/2)
```

Accounts Receivable Turnover is then used to compute the Average Collection Period:

```
=365/Accounts_receivable_turnover
```

The Average Collection Period is generally compared against the company's credit terms. If the company allows 30 days for its customers to pay and the Average Collection Period is greater than 30 days, it can indicate a problem with the company's credit policies or collection efforts.

The efficiency with which the company uses its inventory can be similarly computed. Inventory Turnover divides cost of sales by average inventory:

```
=Cost_of_Goods_Sold/((Inventory+LastYear_Inventory)/2)
```

The Average Age of Inventory tells how many days inventory is in stock before it is sold:

```
=365/Inventory_turnover
```

By adding the Average Collection Period to the Average Age of Inventory, the total days to convert inventory into cash can be computed. This is the Operating Cycle and is computed as follows:

```
=Average_collection_period+Average_age_of_inventory
```

SOLVENCY RATIOS

Whereas *liquidity ratios* compute a company's ability to pay short-term debt, *solvency ratios* compute its ability to pay long-term debt. The Debt Ratio compares total assets with total liabilities:

```
=Total_Assets/(Total_Current_Liabilities+Long_Term_Debt)
```

The Debt-to-Equity Ratio divides total liabilities by total equity. It's used to determine whether a company is primarily equity financed or debt financed:

```
=(Total_Current_Liabilities+Long_Term_Debt)/
(Common_Stock+Additional_Paid_in_Capital+Retained_Earnings)
```

The Times Interest Earned Ratio computes how many times a company's profit would cover its interest expense:

```
=(Net_Income__Loss+Interest_Expense)/Interest_Expense
```

PROFITABILITY RATIOS

As you might guess, *profitability ratios* measure how much profit a company makes. Gross Profit Margin and Net Profit Margin can be seen on the earlier common size financial statements because they are both ratios computed relative to sales. The formulas for Gross Profit Margin and Net Profit Margin are

```
=Gross_Margin/Revenue
=Net_Income__Loss/Revenue
```

The Return on Assets computes how well a company uses its assets to produce profits:

```
=Net_Income__Loss/((Total_Assets+LastYear_Total_Assets)/2)
```

The Return on Equity computes how well the owners' investments are performing:

```
=Net_Income__Loss/((Total_Equity+LastYear_Total_Equity)/2)
```

Creating Indices

The final topic in this chapter demonstrates how to create an index from schedules of changing values. An index is commonly used to compare how data changes over time. An index allows easy cross-comparison between different periods and between different data sets.

For example, consumer price changes are recorded in an index in which the initial "shopping basket" is set to an index of 100. All subsequent changes are made relative to that base. Therefore, any two points in time show the cumulative effect of increases.

TIP

Using indices makes it easier to compare data that use vastly different scales — such as comparing a consumer price index with a wage index.

Perhaps the best approach is to use a two-step illustration:

1. Convert the second and subsequent data in the series to percentage increases from the previous item.

2. Set up a column where the first entry is 100 and successive entries increase by the percentage increases previously determined.

Although a two-step approach is not required, a major advantage is that the calculation of the percentage changes is often very useful data in its own right.

The example, shown in Figure 13-15, involves rentals per square foot of different types of space between 2000 and 2006. The raw data is contained in the first table. This data is converted to percentage changes in the second table, and this information is used to create the indices in the third table.

ON THE CD

This example is available on the companion CD-ROM in the workbook `indices.xlsx`.

Creating an Index from Growth Data

Rentals Per Square Foot

	2000	2001	2002	2003	2004	2005	2006
Retail	89	88	97	148	159	187	201
Office	60	58	60	84	84	92	101
Industrial	12	11	12	18	18	19	20
Other	33	32	35	52	53	66	75
All Property	38	38	40	58	60	69	74

Growth Data

	2000	2001	2002	2003	2004	2005	2006	Average
Retail		-0.92%	8.83%	34.52%	6.73%	15.13%	7.14%	11.39%
Office		-2.97%	3.10%	28.68%	-0.55%	8.98%	9.01%	7.24%
Industrial		-5.14%	9.41%	31.15%	-0.20%	7.78%	4.58%	7.36%
Other		-2.79%	8.79%	31.76%	2.14%	20.72%	11.63%	11.47%
All Property		-2.43%	6.29%	31.43%	2.91%	12.34%	7.68%	9.21%

Index Data

	2000	2001	2002	2003	2004	2005	2006	Average
Retail	100	99.08	107.83	145.05	154.81	178.24	190.97	11.39%
Office	100	97.03	100.04	128.74	128.03	139.52	152.09	7.24%
Industrial	100	94.86	103.79	136.12	135.84	146.41	153.11	7.36%
Other	100	97.21	105.76	139.35	142.33	171.83	191.80	11.47%
All Property	100	97.57	103.71	136.30	140.27	157.59	169.68	9.21%

Figure 13-15: Creating an index from growth data.

The formulas for calculating the growth rates (in the second table) are simple. For example, the formula in cell C14 is as follows:

```
=(C5-B5)/B5
```

This formula returns –0.92%, which represents the change in retail space (from $89 to $88). This formula is copied to the other cells in the table (range C14:H18). This information is useful, but it is difficult to track overall performance between periods of more than a year. That's why indices are required.

Calculating the indices in the third table is also straightforward. The 2000 index is set at 100 (column B) and is the base for the indices. The formula in cell C23 is

```
=B23*(1+C14)
```

This formula is copied to the other cells in the table (range C23:H27).

These indices make it possible to compare performance of, say, offices between any two years, and to track the relative performance over any two years of any two types of property. So it is clear, for example, that retail property rental grew faster than office rentals between 2000 and 2006.

The average figures (column I) are calculated by using the RATE function. This results in an annual growth rate over the entire period.

The formula in I23 that calculates the average growth rate over the term is

```
=RATE(6,0,B23,-H23,0)
```

The *nper* argument is 6 in the formula because that is the number of years since the base date.

Part IV

Array Formulas

Chapter 14

Introducing Arrays

IN THIS CHAPTER

◆ The definition of an array and an array formula

◆ One-dimensional versus two-dimensional arrays

◆ How to work with array constants

◆ Techniques for working with array formulas

◆ Examples of multicell array formulas

◆ Examples of array formulas that occupy a single cell

One of Excel's most interesting (and most powerful) features is its ability to work with arrays in a formula. When you understand this concept, you'll be able to create elegant formulas that appear to perform magic. This chapter introduces the concept of arrays and is required reading for anyone who wants to become a master of Excel formulas. Chapter 15 continues with lots of useful examples.

Introducing Array Formulas

If you do any computer programming, you've probably been exposed to the concept of an array. An *array* is simply a collection of items operated on collectively or individually. In Excel, an array can be one-dimensional or two-dimensional. These dimensions correspond to rows and columns. For example, a *one-dimensional array* can be stored in a range that consists of one row (a horizontal array) or one column (a vertical array). A *two-dimensional array* can be stored in a rectangular range of cells. Excel doesn't support three-dimensional arrays (although its VBA programming language does).

As you'll see, though, arrays need not be stored in cells. You can also work with arrays that exist only in Excel's memory. You can then use an *array formula* to manipulate this information and return a result. An array formula can occupy multiple cells or reside in a single cell.

This section presents two array formula examples: an array formula that occupies multiple cells, and another array formula that occupies only one cell.

A Multicell Array Formula

Figure 14-1 shows a simple worksheet set up to calculate product sales. Normally, you would calculate the value in column D (total sales per product) with a formula such as the one that follows, and then copy this formula down the column.

```
=B2*C2
```

After copying the formula, the worksheet contains six formulas in column D.

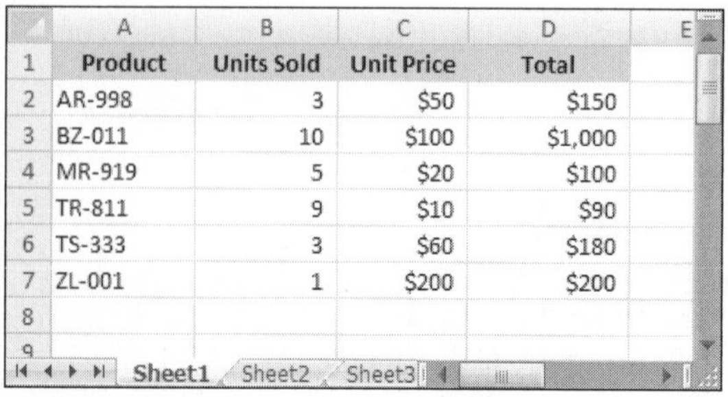

	A	B	C	D	E
1	Product	Units Sold	Unit Price	Total	
2	AR-998	3	$50	$150	
3	BZ-011	10	$100	$1,000	
4	MR-919	5	$20	$100	
5	TR-811	9	$10	$90	
6	TS-333	3	$60	$180	
7	ZL-001	1	$200	$200	
8					
9					

Sheet1 / Sheet2 / Sheet3

Figure 14-1: Column D contains formulas to calculate the total for each product.

Another alternative uses a *single* formula (an array formula) to calculate all six values in D2:D7. This single formula occupies six cells and returns an array of six values.

To create a single array formula to perform the calculations, follow these steps:

1. Select a range to hold the results. In this example, the range is D2:D7.

2. Enter the following formula:

   ```
   =B2:B7*C2:C7
   ```

3. Normally, you press Enter to enter a formula. Because this is an array formula, however, you press Ctrl+Shift+Enter.

The formula is entered into all six selected cells. If you examine the formula bar, you'll see the following:

```
{=B2:B7*C2:C7}
```

Excel places curly brackets around the formula to indicate that it's an array formula.

This formula performs its calculations and returns a six-item array. The array formula actually works with two other arrays, both of which happen to be stored in ranges. The values for the first array are stored in B2:B7, and the values for the second array are stored in C2:C7.

Because displaying more than one value in a single cell is not possible, six cells are required to display the resulting array. That explains why you selected six cells before you entered the array formula.

This array formula, of course, returns exactly the same values as these six normal formulas entered into individual cells in D2:D7:

```
=B2*C2
=B3*C3
=B4*C4
=B5*C5
=B6*C6
=B7*C7
```

Using a single array formula rather than individual formulas does offer a few advantages:

- It's a good way of ensuring that all formulas in a range are identical.
- Using a multicell array formula makes it less likely you will overwrite a formula accidentally. You cannot change one cell in a multicell array formula.
- Using a multicell array formula will almost certainly prevent novices from tampering with your formulas.

A Single-Cell Array Formula

Now it's time to take a look at a single-cell array formula. Refer again to Figure 14-1. The following array formula occupies a single cell:

```
{=SUM(B2:B7*C2:C7)}
```

You can enter this formula into any cell. Remember: When you enter this formula, make sure you press Ctrl+Shift+Enter (and don't type the curly brackets).

Part IV

This array formula returns the sum of the total product sales. It's important to understand that this formula does not rely on the information in column D. In fact, you can delete column D, and the formula will still work.

This formula works with two arrays, both of which are stored in cells. The first array is stored in B2:B7, and the second array is stored in C2:C7. The formula multiplies the corresponding values in these two arrays and creates a new array (which exists only in memory). The SUM function then operates on this new array and returns the sum of its values.

NOTE

In this case, you can use Excel's SUMPRODUCT function to obtain the same result without using an array formula:

```
=SUMPRODUCT(B2:B7,C2:C7)
```

As you'll see, however, array formulas allow many other types of calculations that are otherwise not possible.

Creating an Array Constant

The examples in the previous section used arrays stored in worksheet ranges. The examples in this section demonstrate an important concept: An array does not have to be stored in a range of cells. This type of array, which is stored in memory, is referred to as an *array constant*.

You create an array constant by listing its items and surrounding them with curly brackets. Here's an example of a five-item vertical array constant:

```
{1,0,1,0,1}
```

The following formula uses the SUM function, with the preceding array constant as its argument. The formula returns the sum of the values in the array (which is 3). Notice that this formula uses an array, but it is not an array formula. Therefore, you do not use Ctrl+Shift+Enter to enter the formula.

```
=SUM({1,0,1,0,1})
```

NOTE

When you specify an array directly (as shown previously), you must provide the curly brackets around the array elements. When you enter an array formula, on the other hand, you do not supply the curly brackets.

At this point, you probably don't see any advantage to using an array constant. The formula that follows, for example, returns the same result as the previous formula:

```
=SUM(1,0,1,0,1)
```

Keep reading, and the advantages will become apparent.

Following is a formula that uses two array constants:

```
=SUM({1,2,3,4}*{5,6,7,8})
```

This formula creates a new array (in memory) that consists of the product of the corresponding elements in the two arrays. The new array is as follows:

```
{5,12,21,32}
```

This new array is then used as an argument for the SUM function, which returns the result (70). The formula is equivalent to the following formula, which doesn't use arrays:

```
=SUM(1*5,2*6,3*7,4*8)
```

A formula can work with both an array constant and an array stored in a range. The following formula, for example, returns the sum of the values in A1:D1, each multiplied by the corresponding element in the array constant:

```
=SUM((A1:D1*{1,2,3,4}))
```

This formula is equivalent to

```
=SUM(A1*1,B1*2,C1*3,D1*4)
```

Part IV

Array Constant Elements

An array constant can contain numbers, text, logical values (TRUE or FALSE), and even error values such as #N/A. Numbers can be in integer, decimal, or scientific format. You must enclose text in double quotation marks (for example, "Tuesday"). You can use different types of values in the same array constant, as in this example:

```
{1,2,3,TRUE,FALSE,TRUE,"Moe","Larry","Curly"}
```

An array constant cannot contain formulas, functions, or other arrays. Numeric values cannot contain dollar signs, commas, parentheses, or percent signs. For example, the following is an invalid array constant:

```
{SQRT(32),$56.32,12.5%}
```

Understanding the Dimensions of an Array

As stated previously, an array can be either one-dimensional or two-dimensional. A one-dimensional array's orientation can be either vertical or horizontal.

One-Dimensional Horizontal Arrays

The elements in a one-dimensional horizontal array are separated by commas. The following example is a one-dimensional horizontal array constant:

```
{1,2,3,4,5}
```

To display this array in a range requires five consecutive cells in a single row. To enter this array into a range, select a range of cells that consists of one row and five columns. Then enter ={**1,2,3,4,5**} and press Ctrl+Shift+Enter.

If you enter this array into a horizontal range that consists of more than five cells, the extra cells will contain #N/A (which denotes unavailable values). If you enter this array into a *vertical* range of cells, only the first item (1) will appear in each cell.

The following example is another horizontal array; it has seven elements and is made up of text strings:

```
{"Sun","Mon","Tue","Wed","Thu","Fri","Sat"}
```

To enter this array, select seven cells in one row and then type the following (followed by pressing Ctrl+Shift+Enter):

```
={"Sun","Mon","Tue","Wed","Thu","Fri","Sat"}
```

One-Dimensional Vertical Arrays

The elements in a one-dimensional vertical array are separated by semicolons. The following is a six-element vertical array constant:

```
{10;20;30;40;50;60}
```

Displaying this array in a range requires six cells in a single column. To enter this array into a range, select a range of cells that consists of six rows and one column. Then enter the following formula, followed by pressing Ctrl+Shift+Enter:

```
={10;20;30;40;50;60}
```

The following is another example of a vertical array; this one has four elements:

```
{"Widgets";"Sprockets";"Do-Dads";"Thing-A-Majigs"}
```

To enter this array into a range, select four cells in a column, enter the following formula and then press Ctrl+Shift+Enter:

```
={"Widgets";"Sprockets";"Do-Dads";"Thing-A-Majigs"}
```

Two-Dimensional Arrays

A *two-dimensional array* uses commas to separate its horizontal elements, and semicolons to separate its vertical elements. The following example shows a 3 x 4 array constant:

```
{1,2,3,4;5,6,7,8;9,10,11,12}
```

To display this array in a range requires 12 cells. To enter this array into a range, select a range of cells that consists of three rows and four columns. Then type the following formula, followed by pressing Ctrl+Shift+Enter:

```
={1,2,3,4;5,6,7,8;9,10,11,12}
```

Figure 14-2 shows how this array appears when entered into a range (in this case, B3:E5).

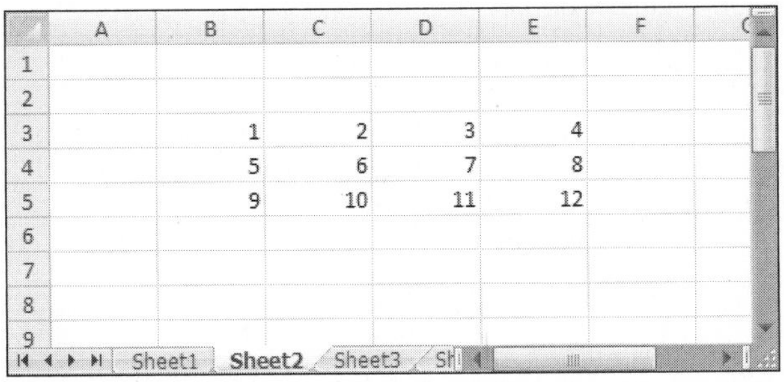

Figure 14-2: A 3 x 4 array, entered into a range of cells.

If you enter an array into a range that has more cells than array elements, Excel displays #N/A in the extra cells. Figure 14-3 shows a 3 x 4 array entered into a 10 x 5 cell range.

Each row of a two-dimensional array must contain the same number of items. The array that follows, for example, is not valid because the third row contains only three items:

```
{1,2,3,4;5,6,7,8;9,10,11}
```

Excel will not allow you to enter a formula that contains an invalid array.

	A	B	C	D	E	F	G
1							
2							
3		1	2	3	4	#N/A	
4		5	6	7	8	#N/A	
5		9	10	11	12	#N/A	
6		#N/A	#N/A	#N/A	#N/A	#N/A	
7		#N/A	#N/A	#N/A	#N/A	#N/A	
8		#N/A	#N/A	#N/A	#N/A	#N/A	
9		#N/A	#N/A	#N/A	#N/A	#N/A	
10		#N/A	#N/A	#N/A	#N/A	#N/A	
11		#N/A	#N/A	#N/A	#N/A	#N/A	
12		#N/A	#N/A	#N/A	#N/A	#N/A	
13							

Sheet1 / Sheet2 / **Sheet3** / Shee

Figure 14-3: A 3 x 4 array, entered into a 10 x 5 cell range.

Naming Array Constants

You can create an array constant, give it a name, and then use this named array in a formula. Technically, a named array is a named formula.

CROSS REF

Chapter 3 covers names and named formulas in detail.

Figure 14-4 shows a named array being created by using the New Name dialog box, which is displayed when you choose Formulas⇨Defined Names⇨Define Name. The name of the array is *DayNames*, and it refers to the following array constant:

```
{"Sun","Mon","Tue","Wed","Thu","Fri","Sat"}
```

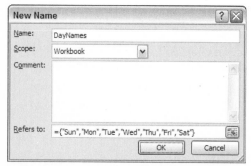

Figure 14-4: Creating a named array constant.

Notice that in the New Name dialog box, the array is defined by using a leading equal sign (=). Without this equal sign, the array is interpreted as a text string rather than an array. Also, you must type the curly brackets when defining a named array constant; Excel does not enter them for you.

After creating this named array, you can use it in a formula. Figure 14-5 shows a worksheet that contains a single array formula entered into the range A1:G1. The formula is

```
{=DayNames}
```

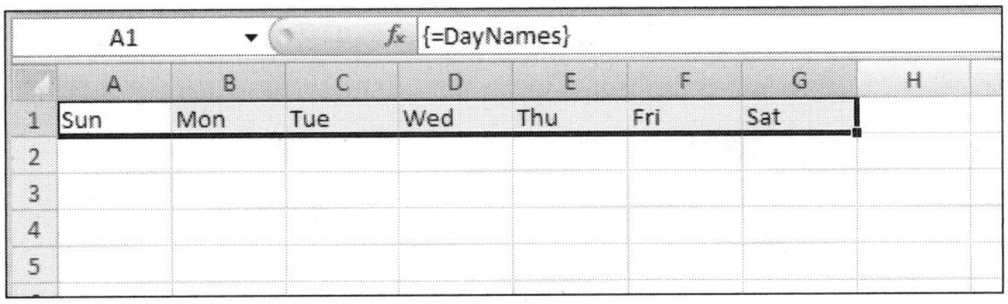

Figure 14-5: Using a named array in an array formula.

Because commas separate the array elements, the array has a horizontal orientation. Use semicolons to create a vertical array. Or, you can use Excel's TRANSPOSE function to insert a horizontal array into a vertical range of cells. (See "Transposing an Array," later in this chapter.) The following array formula, which is entered into a seven-cell vertical range, uses the TRANSPOSE function:

```
{=TRANSPOSE(DayNames)}
```

You also can access individual elements from the array by using Excel's INDEX function. The following formula, for example, returns *Wed*, the fourth item in the *DayNames* array:

```
=INDEX(DayNames,4)
```

Working with Array Formulas

This section deals with the mechanics of selecting cells that contain arrays as well as entering and editing array formulas. These procedures differ a bit from working with ordinary ranges and formulas.

Entering an Array Formula

When you enter an array formula into a cell or range, you must follow a special procedure so Excel knows that you want an array formula rather than a normal formula. You enter a normal formula into a cell by pressing Enter. You enter an array formula into one or more cells by pressing Ctrl+Shift+Enter.

You can easily identify an array formula because the formula is enclosed in curly brackets in the formula bar. The following formula, for example, is an array formula:

```
{=SUM(LEN(A1:A5))}
```

Don't enter the curly brackets when you create an array formula; Excel inserts them for you after you press Ctrl+Shift+Enter. If the result of an array formula consists of more than one value, you must select all of the cells in the results range *before* you enter the formula. If you fail to do this, only the first element of the result is returned.

Selecting an Array Formula Range

You can select the cells that contain a multicell array formula manually by using the normal cell selection procedures. Alternatively, you can use either of the following methods:

- Activate any cell in the array formula range. Choose Home⇨Editing⇨Find & Select⇨ Go To Special, and then choose the Current Array option. When you click OK to close the dialog box, Excel selects the array.

- Activate any cell in the array formula range and press Ctrl+/ to select the entire array.

Editing an Array Formula

If an array formula occupies multiple cells, you must edit the entire range as though it were a single cell. The key point to remember is that you can't change just one element of an array formula. If you attempt to do so, Excel displays the message shown in Figure 14-6. Press Esc to exit Edit mode; then select the entire range and try again.

Figure 14-6: Excel's warning message reminds you that you can't edit just one cell of a multicell array formula.

The following rules apply to multicell array formulas. If you try to do any of these things, Excel lets you know about it:

- You can't change the contents of any individual cell that make up an array formula.

- You can't move cells that make up part of an array formula (although you can move an entire array formula).

- You can't delete cells that form part of an array formula (although you can delete an entire array).

- You can't insert new cells into an array range. This rule includes inserting rows or columns that would add new cells to an array range.

To edit an array formula, select all the cells in the array range and activate the formula bar as usual (click it or press F2). Excel removes the brackets from the formula while you edit it. Edit the formula and then press Ctrl+Shift+Enter to enter the changes. Excel adds the curly brackets, and all the cells in the array now reflect your editing changes.

 CAUTION

If you accidentally press Ctrl+Enter (instead of Ctrl+Shift+Enter) after editing an array formula, the formula will be entered into each selected cell, but it will no longer be an array formula.

Array Formulas: The Downside

If you've read straight through to this point in the chapter, you probably understand some of the advantages of using array formulas. The main advantage, of course, is that an array formula enables you to perform otherwise impossible calculations. As you gain more experience with arrays, you undoubtedly will discover some disadvantages.

Array formulas are one of the least understood features of Excel. Consequently, if you plan to share a workbook with someone who may need to make modifications, you should probably avoid using array formulas. Encountering an array formula when you don't know what it is can be very confusing.

You might also discover that you can easily forget to enter an array formula by pressing Ctrl+Shift+Enter. If you edit an existing array, you still must use these keys to complete the edits. Except for logical errors, this is probably the most common problem that users have with array formulas. If you press Enter by mistake after editing an array formula, just press F2 to get back into Edit mode and then press Ctrl+Shift+Enter.

Another potential problem with array formulas is that they can slow your worksheet's recalculations, especially if you use very large arrays. On a faster system, this may not be a problem. But, conversely, using an array formula is almost always faster than using a custom VBA function. (Part VI of this book covers custom VBA functions.)

Part IV

Although you can't change any individual cell that makes up a multicell array formula, you can apply formatting to the entire array or to only parts of it.

Expanding or Contracting a Multicell Array Formula

Often, you may need to expand a multicell array formula (to include more cells) or contract it (to include fewer cells). Doing so requires a few steps:

1. Select the entire range that contains the array formula. You can use Ctrl+/ to automatically select the cells in an array that includes the active cell.

2. Press F2 to enter Edit mode.

3. Press Ctrl+Enter. This step enters an identical (non-array) formula into each selected cell.

4. Change your range selection to include additional or fewer cells.

5. Press F2 to reenter Edit mode.

6. Press Ctrl+Shift+Enter.

Using Multicell Array Formulas

This section contains examples that demonstrate additional features of multicell array formulas (array formulas that are entered into a range of cells). These features include creating arrays from values, performing operations, using functions, transposing arrays, and generating consecutive integers.

Creating an Array from Values in a Range

The following array formula creates an array from a range of cells. Figure 14-7 shows a workbook with some data entered into A1:C4. The range D8:F11 contains a single array formula:

```
{=A1:C4}
```

The array in D8:F11 is linked to the range A1:C4. Change any value in A1:C4, and the corresponding cell in D8:F11 reflects that change.

Creating an Array Constant from Values in a Range

In the previous example, the array formula in D8:F11 essentially created a link to the cells in A1:C4. It's possible to sever this link and create an array constant made up of the values in A1:C4.

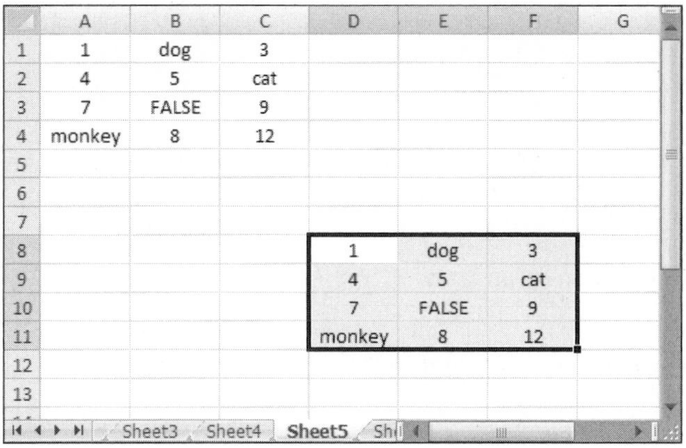

	A	B	C	D	E	F	G
1	1	dog	3				
2	4	5	cat				
3	7	FALSE	9				
4	monkey	8	12				
5							
6							
7							
8				1	dog	3	
9				4	5	cat	
10				7	FALSE	9	
11				monkey	8	12	
12							
13							

Figure 14-7: Creating an array from a range.

To do so, select the cells that contain the array formula (the range D8:F11, in this example). Then press F2 to edit the array formula. Press F9 to convert the cell references to values. Press Ctrl+Shift+Enter to reenter the array formula (which now uses an array constant). The array constant is as follows:

```
{1,"dog",3;4,5,"cat";7,8,9;"monkey",11,12}
```

Figure 14-8 shows how this looks in the formula bar.

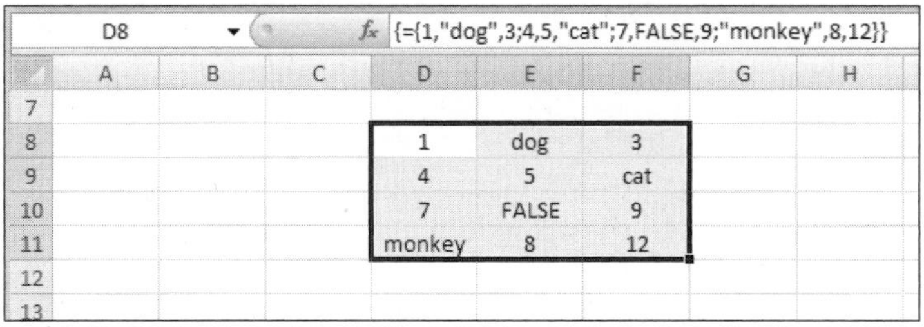

	A	B	C	D	E	F	G	H
7								
8				1	dog	3		
9				4	5	cat		
10				7	FALSE	9		
11				monkey	8	12		
12								
13								

Figure 14-8: After you press F9, the formula bar displays the array constant.

Performing Operations on an Array

So far, most of the examples in this chapter simply entered arrays into ranges. The following array formula creates a rectangular array and multiplies each array element by 2:

```
{={1,2,3,4;5,6,7,8;9,10,11,12}*2}
```

Figure 14-9 shows the result when you enter this formula into a range.

	A	B	C	D	E	F
1						
2						
3		2	4	6	8	
4		10	12	14	16	
5		18	20	22	24	
6						
7						

Sheet5 | Sheet6 | Sheet7

Figure 14-9: Performing a mathematical operation on an array.

The following array formula multiplies each array element by itself. Figure 14-10 shows the result when you enter this formula into a range:

`{={1,2,3,4;5,6,7,8;9,10,11,12}*{1,2,3,4;5,6,7,8;9,10,11,12}}`

	A	B	C	D	E	F
7						
8		1	4	9	16	
9		25	36	49	64	
10		81	100	121	144	
11						
12						
13						

Sheet5 | Sheet6 | Sheet7

Figure 14-10: Multiplying each array element by itself.

The following array formula is a simpler way of obtaining the same result:

`{={1,2,3,4;5,6,7,8;9,10,11,12}^2}`

If the array is stored in a range (such as A1:C4), the array formula returns the square of each value in the range, as follows:

`{=A1:C4^2}`

TIP

In some of these examples are brackets that you must enter to define an array constant as well as brackets that Excel enters when you define an array by pressing Control+Shift+Enter. An easy way to tell whether you must enter the brackets is to note the position of the opening curly bracket. If it's before the equal sign, Excel enters the bracket. If it's after the equal sign, you enter them.

Using Functions with an Array

As you might expect, you also can use functions with an array. The following array formula, which you can enter into a ten-cell vertical range, calculates the square root of each array element in the array constant:

```
{=SQRT({1;2;3;4;5;6;7;8;9;10})}
```

If the array is stored in a range, an array formula such as the one that follows returns the square root of each value in the range:

```
{=SQRT(A1:A10)}
```

Transposing an Array

When you transpose an array, you essentially convert rows to columns and columns to rows. In other words, you can convert a horizontal array to a vertical array and vice versa. Use Excel's TRANSPOSE function to transpose an array.

Consider the following one-dimensional horizontal array constant:

```
{1,2,3,4,5}
```

You can enter this array into a vertical range of cells by using the TRANSPOSE function. To do so, select a range of five cells that occupy five rows and one column. Then enter the following formula and press Ctrl+Shift+Enter:

```
=TRANSPOSE({1,2,3,4,5})
```

The horizontal array is transposed, and the array elements appear in the vertical range.

Transposing a two-dimensional array works in a similar manner. Figure 14-11 shows a two-dimensional array entered into a range normally and entered into a range using the TRANSPOSE function. The formula in A1:D3 is

```
{={1,2,3,4;5,6,7,8;9,10,11,12}}
```

The formula in A6:C9 is

```
{=TRANSPOSE({1,2,3,4;5,6,7,8;9,10,11,12})}
```

You can, of course, use the TRANSPOSE function to transpose an array stored in a range. The following formula, for example, uses an array stored in A1:C4 (four rows, three columns). You can enter this array formula into a range that consists of three rows and four columns:

```
{=TRANSPOSE(A1:C4)}
```

Part IV

Worksheet Functions That Return an Array

Several of Excel's worksheet functions use arrays; you must enter a formula that uses one of these functions into multiple cells as an array formula. These functions are as follows: FORECAST, FREQUENCY, GROWTH, LINEST, LOGEST, MINVERSE, MMULT, and TREND. Consult the online help for more information.

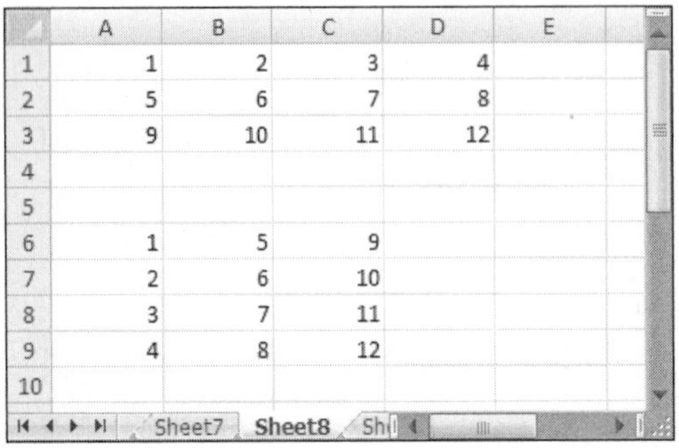

Figure 14-11: Using the TRANSPOSE function to transpose a rectangular array.

Generating an Array of Consecutive Integers

As you will see in Chapter 15, it's often useful to generate an array of consecutive integers for use in an array formula. Excel's ROW function, which returns a row number, is ideal for this. Consider the array formula shown here, entered into a vertical range of 12 cells:

```
{=ROW(1:12)}
```

This formula generates a 12-element array that contains integers from 1 to 12. To demonstrate, select a range that consists of 12 rows and 1 column, and then enter the array formula into the range. You'll find that the range is filled with 12 consecutive integers (see Figure 14-12).

If you want to generate an array of consecutive integers, a formula like the one shown previously is good — but not perfect. To see the problem, insert a new row above the range that contains the array formula. You'll find that Excel adjusts the row references so the array formula now reads:

```
{=ROW(2:13)}
```

The formula that originally generated integers from 1 to 12 now generates integers from 2 to 13.

	A	B	C	D	E
1					
2		1			
3		2			
4		3			
5		4			
6		5			
7		6			
8		7.			
9		8			
10		9			
11		10			
12		11			
13		12			
14					

Sheet8   Sheet9

Figure 14-12: Using an array formula to generate consecutive integers.

For a better solution, use this formula:

```
{=ROW(INDIRECT("1:12"))}
```

This formula uses the INDIRECT function, which takes a text string as its argument. Excel does not adjust the references contained in the argument for the INDIRECT function. Therefore, this array formula *always* returns integers from 1 to 12.

CROSS REF

Chapter 15 contains several examples that use the technique for generating consecutive integers.

Using Single-Cell Array Formulas

The examples in the previous section all used a multicell array formula — a single array formula entered into a range of cells. The real power of using arrays becomes apparent when you use single-cell array formulas. This section contains examples of array formulas that occupy a single cell.

Counting Characters in a Range

Suppose you have a range of cells that contains text entries (see Figure 14-13). If you need to get a count of the total number of characters in that range, the "traditional" method involves creating a formula like the one that follows and copying it down the column:

```
=LEN(A1)
```

Part IV

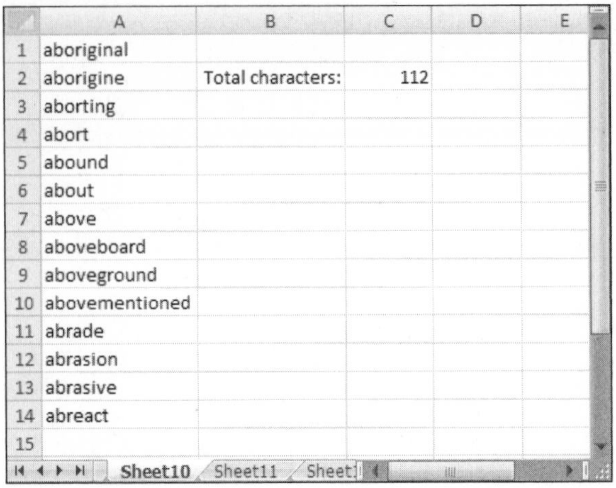

	A	B	C	D	E
1	aboriginal				
2	aborigine	Total characters:	112		
3	aborting				
4	abort				
5	abound				
6	about				
7	above				
8	aboveboard				
9	aboveground				
10	abovementioned				
11	abrade				
12	abrasion				
13	abrasive				
14	abreact				
15					

Sheet10 / Sheet11 / Sheet1

Figure 14-13: The goal is to count the number of characters in a range of text.

Then, you use a SUM formula to calculate the sum of the values returned by the intermediate formulas.

The following array formula does the job without using any intermediate formulas:

```
{=SUM(LEN(A1:A14))}
```

The array formula uses the LEN function to create a new array (in memory) that consists of the number of characters in each cell of the range. In this case, the new array is

```
{10,9,8,5,6,5,5,10,11,14,6,8,8,7}
```

The array formula is then reduced to the following:

```
=SUM({10,9,8,5,6,5,5,10,11,14,6,8,8,7})
```

Summing the Three Smallest Values in a Range

The following formula returns the sum of the three smallest values in a range named *Data*:

```
{=SUM(SMALL(Data,{1,2,3}))}
```

The function uses an array constant as the second argument for the SMALL function. This generates a new array, which consists of the three smallest values in the range. This array is then passed to the SUM function, which returns the sum of the values in the new array.

Figure 14-14 shows an example in which the range A1:A10 is named *Data*. The SMALL function is evaluated three times, each time with a different second argument. The first time, the SMALL function has a second argument of 1, and it returns –5. The second time, the second argument for the SMALL function is 2, and it returns 0 (the second-smallest value in the range). The third time, the SMALL function has a second argument of 3, and returns the third-smallest value of 2.

	A	B	C	D	E	F
1	12					
2	-5		Sum of three smallest:	-3		
3	3					
4	2					
5	0					
6	6					
7	13					
8	7					
9	4					
10	8					
11						
12						
13						

Sheet10   **Sheet11**   Sheet12

Figure 14-14: An array formula returns the sum of the three smallest values in A1:A10.

Therefore, the array that's passed to the SUM function is

```
{-5,0,2}
```

The formula returns the sum of the array (–3).

Counting Text Cells in a Range

The following array formula uses the IF function to examine each cell in a range. It then creates a new array (of the same size and dimensions as the original range) that consists of 1s and 0s, depending on whether the cell contains text. This new array is then passed to the SUM function, which returns the sum of the items in the array. The result is a count of the number of text cells in the range.

```
{=SUM(IF(ISTEXT(A1:D5),1,0))}
```

CROSS REF

This general array formula type (that is, an IF function nested in a SUM function) is very useful for counting. Refer to Chapter 7 for additional examples.

Figure 14-15 shows an example of the preceding formula in cell C8. The array created by the IF function is as follows:

```
{0,1,1,1;1,0,0,0;1,0,0,0;1,0,0,0;1,0,0,0}
```

TRUE and FALSE in Array Formulas

When your arrays return Boolean values (True or False), you must coerce these Boolean values into numbers. Excel's SUM function ignores Booleans, but you can still perform mathematical operation on them. In Excel, True is equivalent to a value of 1 and False to a value of 0. Converting True and False to these values ensures the SUM function treats them appropriately.

You can use three mathematical operations to convert True and False to numbers without changing their values, called *identity operations*.

- Multiply by 1: (x * 1 = x)

- Add zero: (x + 0 = x)

- Double negative: (-- x = x)

Applying any of these operations to a Boolean value will cause Excel to convert it to a number. The following formulas all return the same answer:

```
{=SUM(ISTEXT(A1:D5)*1)}
{=SUM(ISTEXT(A1:D5)+0)}
{=SUM(--ISTEXT(A1:D5))}
```

There is no "best" way to convert Boolean values to numbers. Pick a method that you like and use that. However, be aware of all three methods so that you can identify them in other people's spreadsheets.

	A	B	C	D	E
1		Jan	Feb	Mar	
2	Region 1	7	4	9	
3	Region 2	8	2	8	
4	Region 3	12	1	9	
5	Region 4	14	6	10	
6					
7	No. of text cells:		7		

Figure 14-15: An array formula returns the number of text cells in the range.

Notice that this array contains four rows of three elements (the same dimensions as the range).

A variation on this formula follows:

```
{=SUM(ISTEXT(A1:D5)*1)}
```

This formula eliminates the need for the IF function and takes advantage of the fact that

```
TRUE * 1 = 1
```

and

```
FALSE * 1 = 0
```

Eliminating Intermediate Formulas

One of the main benefits of using an array formula is that you can eliminate intermediate formulas in your worksheet. This makes your worksheet more compact and eliminates the need to display irrelevant calculations. Figure 14-16 shows a worksheet that contains pre-test and post-test scores for students. Column D contains formulas that calculate the changes between the pre-test and the post-test scores. Cell D17 contains the following formula, which calculates the average of the values in column D:

```
=AVERAGE(D2:D15)
```

	A	B	C	D	E
1	Student	Pre-Test	Post-Test	Change	
2	Andy	56	67	11	
3	Beth	59	74	15	
4	Cindy	98	92	(6)	
5	Duane	78	79	1	
6	Eddy	81	100	19	
7	Francis	92	94	2	
8	Georgia	100	100	-	
9	Hilda	92	99	7	
10	Isabel	54	69	15	
11	Jack	91	92	1	
12	Kent	80	88	8	
13	Linda	45	68	23	
14	Michelle	71	92	21	
15	Nancy	94	83	(11)	
16					
17		Average Change:		7.57	
18					

Sheet13 / Sheet14

Figure 14-16: Without an array formula, calculating the average change requires intermediate formulas in column D.

With an array formula, you can eliminate column D. The following array formula calculates the average of the changes but does not require the formulas in column D:

```
{=AVERAGE(C2:C15-B2:B15)}
```

How does it work? The formula uses two arrays, the values of which are stored in two ranges (B2:B15 and C2:C15). The formula creates a *new* array that consists of the differences between each corresponding element in the other arrays. This new array is stored in Excel's memory, not in a range. The AVERAGE function then uses this new array as its argument and returns the result.

The new array consists of the following elements:

```
{11,15,-6,1,19,2,0,7,15,1,8,23,21,-11}
```

The formula, therefore, is reduced to the following:

```
=AVERAGE({11,15,-6,1,19,2,0,7,15,1,8,23,21,-11})
```

You can use additional array formulas to calculate other measures for the data in this example. For instance, the following array formula returns the largest change (that is, the greatest improvement). This formula returns 23, which represents Linda's test scores:

```
{=MAX(C2:C15-B2:B15)}
```

The following array formula returns the smallest change (that is, the least improvement). This formula returns –11, which represents Nancy's test scores.

```
{=MIN(C2:C15-B2:B15)}
```

Using an Array in Lieu of a Range Reference

If your formula uses a function that requires a range reference, you may be able to replace that range reference with an array constant. This is useful in situations in which the values in the referenced range do not change.

 NOTE

A notable exception to using an array constant in place of a range reference in a function is with the database functions that use a reference to a criteria range (for example, DSUM). Unfortunately, using an array constant instead of a reference to a criteria range does not work.

Figure 14-17 shows a worksheet that uses a lookup table to display a word that corresponds to an integer. For example, looking up a value of 9 returns *Nine* from the lookup table in D1:E10. The formula in cell C1 is

```
=VLOOKUP(B1,D1:E10,2,FALSE)
```

You can use a two-dimensional array in place of the lookup range. The following formula returns the same result as the previous formula, but it does not require the lookup range in D1:E1:

```
=VLOOKUP(B1,{1,"One";2,"Two";3,"Three";4,"Four";5,"Five";
6,"Six";7,"Seven";8,"Eight";9,"Nine";10,"Ten"},2,FALSE)
```

	A	B	C	D	E	F	G
1	Number ->	9	Nine	1	One		
2				2	Two		
3				3	Three		
4				4	Four		
5				5	Five		
6				6	Six		
7				7	Seven		
8				8	Eight		
9				9	Nine		
10				10	Ten		
11							
12							

Sheet13 Sheet14

Figure 14-17: You can replace the lookup table in D1:E10 with an array constant.

Chapter 15

Performing Magic with Array Formulas

IN THIS CHAPTER

◆ More examples of single-cell array formulas

◆ More examples of multicell array formulas

The previous chapter provided an introduction to arrays and array formulas, and also presented some basic examples to whet your appetite. This chapter continues the saga and provides many useful examples that further demonstrate the power of this feature.

I selected the examples in this chapter to provide a good assortment of the various uses for array formulas. Most can be used as-is. You will, of course, need to adjust the range names or references used. Also, you can modify many of the examples easily to work in a slightly different manner.

 ON THE CD
The examples in this section are demonstrated in workbook named `single-cell array formulas.xlsx`, which is available on the companion CD-ROM.

Working with Single-Cell Array Formulas

As I describe in the previous chapter, you enter single-cell array formulas into a single cell (not into a range of cells). These array formulas work with arrays contained in a range or that exist in memory. This section provides some additional examples of such array formulas.

Summing a Range That Contains Errors

You've probably discovered that Excel's SUM function doesn't work if you attempt to sum a range that contains one or more error values (such as #DIV/0! or #N/A). Figure 15-1 shows an example. The SUM formula in cell C11 returns an error value because the range that it sums (C4:C10, named Data) contains errors.

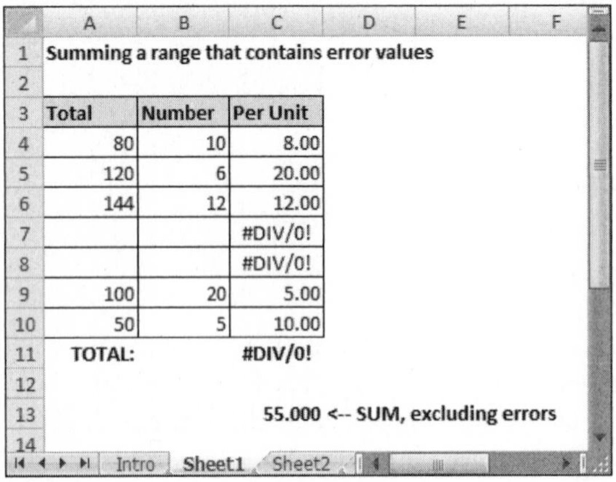

	A	B	C	D	E	F
1	Summing a range that contains error values					
2						
3	Total	Number	Per Unit			
4	80	10	8.00			
5	120	6	20.00			
6	144	12	12.00			
7			#DIV/0!			
8			#DIV/0!			
9	100	20	5.00			
10	50	5	10.00			
11	TOTAL:		#DIV/0!			
12						
13			55.000 <-- SUM, excluding errors			
14						

Figure 15-1: An array formula can sum a range of values, even if the range contains errors.

The following array formula returns a sum of the values in a range named *Data*, even if the range contains error values:

```
=SUM(IFERROR(Data,""))
```

About the Examples in This Chapter

This chapter contains many examples of array formulas. Keep in mind that you press Ctrl+Shift+Enter to enter an array formula. Excel places curly brackets around the formula to remind you that it's an array formula. The array formula examples shown here are surrounded by curly brackets, but you should not enter the brackets because Excel will do that for you when the formula is entered.

The preceding function uses the IFERROR function, which is introduced in Excel 2007. Following is a formula that's compatible with earlier versions:

```
{=SUM(IF(ISERROR(Data),"",Data))}
```

This formula works by creating a new array (in memory, not in a range). This array contains the original values but without the errors. The IFERROR function effectively filters out error values by replacing them with an empty string. The SUM function treats strings as zeros, effectively ignoring those entries in the array. This technique also works with other functions, such as MIN and MAX.

In this example, the SUM function operates on this array:

```
{8, 20, 12, "", "", 5, 10}
```

 NOTE

You may want to use a function other than ISERROR. The ISERROR function returns TRUE for any error value: #N/A, #VALUE!, #REF!, #DIV/0!, #NUM!, #NAME?, or #NULL!. The ISERR function returns TRUE for any error except #N/A. The ISNA function returns TRUE only if the cell contains #N/A.

Counting the Number of Error Values in a Range

The following array formula is similar to the previous example, but it returns a count of the number of error values in a range named *Data*:

```
{=SUM(IF(ISERROR(Data),1,0))}
```

This formula creates an array that consists of 1s (if the corresponding cell contains an error) and 0s (if the corresponding cell does not contain an error value).

You can simplify the formula a bit by removing the third argument for the IF function. If this argument is not specified, the IF function returns FALSE if the condition is not satisfied (that is, the cell does not contain an error value). In this context, Excel treats FALSE as a 0 value. The array formula shown here performs exactly like the previous formula, but it doesn't use the third argument for the IF function:

```
{=SUM(IF(ISERROR(Data),1))}
```

Actually, you can simplify the formula even more:

```
{=SUM(ISERROR(Data)*1)}
```

This version of the formula relies on the fact that

```
TRUE * 1 = 1
```

and

```
FALSE * 1 = 0
```

Summing Based on a Condition

Often, you need to sum values based on one or more conditions. The array formula that follows, for example, returns the sum of the positive values (it excludes negative values) in a range named *Data:*

```
{=SUM(IF(Data>0,Data))}
```

The IF function creates a new array that consists only of positive values and False values. This array is passed to the SUM function, which ignores the False values and returns the sum of the positive values. The *Data* range can consist of any number of rows and columns.

You can also use Excel's SUMIF function for this example. The following formula, which is not an array formula, returns the same result as the previous array formula:

```
=SUMIF(Data,">0")
```

For multiple conditions, the non-array solution uses the new SUMIFS function. For example, if you want to sum only values that are greater than 0 and less than or equal to 5, you can use this non-array formula:

```
=SUMIFS(Data,Data,"<=5",Data,">0")
```

Following is an array formula that performs the same calculation and is compatible with earlier versions of Excel:

```
{=SUM((Data>0)*(Data<=5)*Data)}
```

This formula calculates three arrays:

- (Data>0)
- (Data<=5)
- Data

The formula then multiplies the three arrays together and calculates the sum of the products. The first two arrays consist of TRUE (1) or FALSE (0) values.

This formula also has a limitation: It will return an error if the *Data* range contains one or more non-numeric cells.

CAUTION

Contrary to what you might expect, you cannot use the AND function in an array formula. The following array formula, while quite logical, doesn't return the correct result:

```
{=SUM(IF(AND(Data>0,Data<=5),Data))}
```

You can also write an array formula that combines criteria using an OR condition. For example, to sum the values that are less than 0 or greater than 5, use the following array formula:

```
{=SUM(IF((Data<0)+(Data>5),Data))}
```

To understand how this formula works, keep in mind that the argument for the IF function returns TRUE if either *Data*<0 or *Data*>5. Otherwise, the argument returns FALSE. If it's FALSE, the item of the *Data* range is not included in the sum.

CAUTION

As with the AND function, you cannot use the OR function in an array formula. The following formula, for example, does not return the correct result:

```
{=SUM(IF(OR(Data<0,Data>5),Data))}
```

For an explanation of the workarounds required for using logical functions in an array formula, see the sidebar, "Illogical Behavior from Logical Functions."

Part IV

Illogical Behavior from Logical Functions

Excel's AND and OR functions are logical functions that return TRUE or FALSE. Unfortunately, these functions do not perform as expected when used in an array formula.

As shown here, columns A and B contain logical values. The AND function returns TRUE if all its arguments are TRUE. Column C contains non-array formulas that work as expected. For example, cell C3 contains the following function:

```
=AND(A3,B3)
```

continued

continued

	A	B	C	D	E
1			Non-Array	Array with AND	Array formula:
2	Condition 1	Condition 2	Formulas	{=AND(A3:A6,B3:B6)}	{=A3:A6*B3:B6}
3	TRUE	TRUE	TRUE	FALSE	1
4	TRUE	FALSE	FALSE	FALSE	0
5	FALSE	TRUE	FALSE	FALSE	0
6	FALSE	FALSE	FALSE	FALSE	0
7					

Sheet1

ON THE CD

This workbook, named `logical functions.xlsx`, is available on the companion CD-ROM.

The range D3:D6 contains this array formula:

```
{=AND(A3:A6,B3:B6)}
```

You might expect this array formula to return the following array:

```
{TRUE,FALSE,FALSE,FALSE}
```

Rather, it returns only a single item: FALSE. In fact, both the AND function and the OR function always return a single result (never an array). Even when using array constants, the AND function still returns only a single value. For example, this array formula does not return an array:

```
{=AND({TRUE,TRUE,FALSE,FALSE},{TRUE,FALSE,TRUE,FALSE})}
```

I don't know whether this is by design or whether it's a bug. In any case, it certainly is inconsistent with how the other functions operate.

Column E contains another array formula, which follows, that returns an array of 0s and 1s. These 0s and 1s correspond to FALSE and TRUE, respectively.

```
{=A3:A6*B3:B6}
```

In array formulas, you must use this syntax in place of the AND function.

The following array formula, which uses the OR function, does not return an array (as you might expect):

```
=OR(A3:A6,B3:B6)
```

Rather, you can use a formula such as the following, which *does* return an array comprising logical OR, using the corresponding elements in the ranges:

```
{=A3:A6+B3:B6}
```

Summing the *n* Largest Values in a Range

The following array formula returns the sum of the ten largest values in a range named *Data*:

```
{=SUM(LARGE(Data,ROW(INDIRECT("1:10"))))}
```

The LARGE function is evaluated ten times, each time with a different second argument (1, 2, 3, and so on up to 10). The results of these calculations are stored in a new array, and that array is used as the argument for the SUM function.

To sum a different number of values, replace the 10 in the argument for the INDIRECT function with another value. To sum the *n smallest* values in a range, use the SMALL function instead of the LARGE function.

> **⚠ CAUTION**
> Both LARGE and SMALL return a #NUM! error if you supply a second argument that's greater than the number of cells in the first argument.

Computing an Average That Excludes Zeros

Figure 15-2 shows a simple worksheet that calculates average sales. Range B5:B12 is named *Data*. The formula in cell B14 is as follows:

```
=AVERAGE(Data)
```

	A	B	C	D	E	F
1	Exclude zero from average					
2						
3						
4	Sales Person	Sales				
5	Abner	23,991				
6	Baker	15,092				
7	Charleston	0				
8	Davis	11,893				
9	Ellerman	32,116				
10	Flugelhart	29,089				
11	Gallaway	0				
12	Harrison	33,211				
13						
14		18,174 <-- Average with zeros				
15		24,232 <-- Average without zeros (array formula)				

Sheet3 / Sheet4 / **Sheet5** / Shee

Figure 15-2: Calculating an average excluding cells that contain a 0.

Part IV

This formula, of course, calculates the average of the values in the range named *Data*. Two of the sales staff had the week off, however, so this average doesn't accurately describe the average sales per representative.

NOTE

The AVERAGE function ignores blank cells but does not ignore cells that contain 0.

The following array formula returns the average of the range but excludes the cells containing 0:

```
{=AVERAGE(IF(Data<>0,Data))}
```

This formula creates a new array that consists of the nonzero values in the range and the value FALSE for any cells that do contain zero. The AVERAGE function then uses this new array, properly ignoring the FALSE values, as its argument. You can get the same result with a regular (non-array) formula:

```
=SUM(Data)/COUNTIF(Data,"<>0")
```

This formula uses the COUNTIF function to count the number of nonzero values in the range. This value is divided into the sum of the values.

Determining Whether a Particular Value Appears in a Range

To determine whether a particular value appears in a range of cells, you can choose the Home⇨Editing⇨Find & Select⇨Find command and do a search of the worksheet. You also can make this determination by using an array formula.

Figure 15-3 shows a worksheet with a list of names in A5:E24 (named *NameList*). An array formula in cell D3 checks the name entered into cell C3 (named *TheName*). If the name exists in the list of names, the formula displays the text *Found*. Otherwise, it displays *Not Found*.

The array formula in cell D3 is

```
{=IF(OR(TheName=NameList),"Found","Not Found")}
```

This formula compares *TheName* to each cell in the *NameList* range. It builds a new array that consists of logical TRUE or FALSE values. The OR function returns TRUE if any one of the values in the new array is TRUE. The IF function uses this result to determine which message to display.

A simpler form of this formula follows. This formula displays TRUE if the name is found and returns FALSE otherwise:

```
{=OR(TheName=NameList)}
```

Figure 15-3: Using an array formula to determine whether a range contains a particular value.

Another approach uses the COUNTIF function in a non-array formula:

```
=IF(COUNTIF(NameList,TheName)>0,"Found","Not Found")
```

Counting the Number of Differences in Two Ranges

The following array formula compares the corresponding values in two ranges (named *MyData* and *YourData*) and returns the number of differences in the two ranges. If the contents of the two ranges are identical, the formula returns 0 (no differences):

```
{=SUM(IF(MyData=YourData,0,1))}
```

The two ranges must be the same size and of the same dimensions.

This formula works by creating a new array of the same size as the ranges being compared. The IF function fills this new array with 0s and 1s (1 if a difference is found; 0 if the corresponding cells are the same). The SUM function then returns the sum of the values in the array.

The following formula, which is simpler, is another way of calculating the same result:

```
{=SUM(1*(MyData<>YourData))}
```

This version of the formula relies on the fact that

```
TRUE * 1 = 1
```

and

```
FALSE * 1 = 0
```

Returning the Location of the Maximum Value in a Range

The following array formula returns the row number of the maximum value in a single-column range named *Data:*

```
{=MIN(IF(Data=MAX(Data),ROW(Data), ""))}
```

The IF function creates a new array that corresponds to the *Data* range. If the corresponding cell contains the maximum value in *Data,* the array contains the row number; otherwise, it contains an empty string. The MIN function uses this new array as its second argument and returns the smallest value, which corresponds to the row number of the maximum value in *Data.*

If the *Data* range contains more than one cell that has the maximum value, the row of the first maximum cell is returned.

The following array formula is similar to the previous one, but it returns the actual cell address of the maximum value in the *Data* range. It uses the ADDRESS function, which takes two arguments: a row number and a column number.

```
{=ADDRESS(MIN(IF(Data=MAX(Data),ROW(Data), "")),COLUMN(Data))}
```

If *Data* spans more than one column, the following array formula will return the correct address.

```
{=ADDRESS(MIN(IF(Data=MAX(Data),ROW(Data),"")),
MIN(IF(Data=MAX(Data),COLUMN(Data),"")))}
```

Finding the Row of a Value's *n*th Occurrence in a Range

The following array formula returns the row number within a single-column range named *Data* that contains the *n*th occurrence of the value in a cell named *Value:*

```
{=SMALL(IF(Data=Value,ROW(Data), ""),n)}
```

The IF function creates a new array that consists of the row number of values from the *Data* range that are equal to *Value*. Values from the Data range that are not equal to *Value* are replaced with an empty string. The SMALL function works on this new array and returns the *n*th smallest row number.

The formula returns #NUM! if the *Value* is not found or if *n* exceeds the number of the values in the range.

Returning the Longest Text in a Range

The following array formula displays the text string in a range (named *Data*) that has the most characters. If multiple cells contain the longest text string, the first cell is returned.

```
{=INDEX(Data,MATCH(MAX(LEN(Data)),LEN(Data),FALSE),1)}
```

This formula works with two arrays, both of which contain the length of each item in the *Data* range. The MAX function determines the largest value, which corresponds to the longest text item. The MATCH function calculates the offset of the cell that contains the maximum length. The INDEX function returns the contents of the cell containing the most characters. This function works only if the *Data* range consists of a single column.

Determining Whether a Range Contains Valid Values

You might have a list of items that you need to check against another list. For example, you might import a list of part numbers into a range named *MyList,* and you want to ensure that all the part numbers are valid. You can do this by comparing the items in the imported list with the items in a master list of part numbers (named *Master*).

The following array formula returns TRUE if every item in the range named *MyList* is found in the range named *Master.* Both of these ranges must consist of a single column, but they don't need to contain the same number of rows.

```
{=ISNA(MATCH(TRUE,ISNA(MATCH(MyList,Master,0)),0))}
```

The inside MATCH function compares each element of *MyList* against *Master,* returning an array of numbers and #NA! errors for those that don't match. That array is fed into ISNA, which converts it into an array of True and False values. The outer MATCH function attempts to find a True value in the array. If it finds a True, a number is returned, and the outer ISNA returns False. If no True values are found, ISNA returns True.

The array formula that follows returns the number of invalid items. In other words, it returns the number of items in *MyList* that do not appear in *Master.*

```
{=SUM(1*ISNA(MATCH(MyList,Master,0)))}
```

To return the first invalid item in *MyList,* use the following array formula:

```
{=INDEX(MyList,MATCH(TRUE,ISNA(MATCH(MyList,Master,0)),0))}
```

Part IV

Summing the Digits of an Integer

I can't think of any practical application for the example in this section, but it's a good demonstration of the power of an array formula. The following array formula calculates the sum of the digits in a positive integer, which is stored in cell A1. For example, if cell A1 contains the value 409, the formula returns 13 (the sum of 4, 0, and 9).

```
{=SUM(MID(A1,ROW(INDIRECT("1:"&LEN(A1))),1)*1)}
```

To understand how this formula works, start with the ROW function, shown here:

```
{=ROW(INDIRECT("1:"&LEN(A1)))}
```

This function returns an array of consecutive integers beginning with 1 and ending with the number of digits in the value in cell A1. For example, if cell A1 contains the value 409, the LEN function returns 3, and the array generated by the ROW functions is

```
{1,2,3}
```

CROSS REF

For more information about using the INDIRECT function to return this array, see Chapter 14.

This array is then used as the second argument for the MID function. The MID part of the formula, simplified a bit and expressed as values, is the following:

```
{=MID(409,{1,2,3},1)*1}
```

This function generates an array with three elements:

```
{4,0,9}
```

By simplifying again and adding the SUM function, the formula looks like this:

```
{=SUM({4,0,9})}
```

This produces the result of 13.

NOTE

The values in the array created by the MID function are multiplied by 1 because the MID function returns a string. Multiplying by 1 forces a numeric value result. Alternatively, you can use the VALUE function to force a numeric string to become a numeric value.

Notice that the formula does not work with a negative value because the negative sign is not a numeric value. The following formula solves this problem by using the ABS function to return the absolute value of the number. Figure 15-4 shows a worksheet that uses this formula in cell B4.

```
{=SUM(VALUE(MID(ABS(A4),ROW(INDIRECT("1:"&LEN(ABS(A4)))),1)))}
```

The formula was copied down to calculate the sum of the digits for other values in column A.

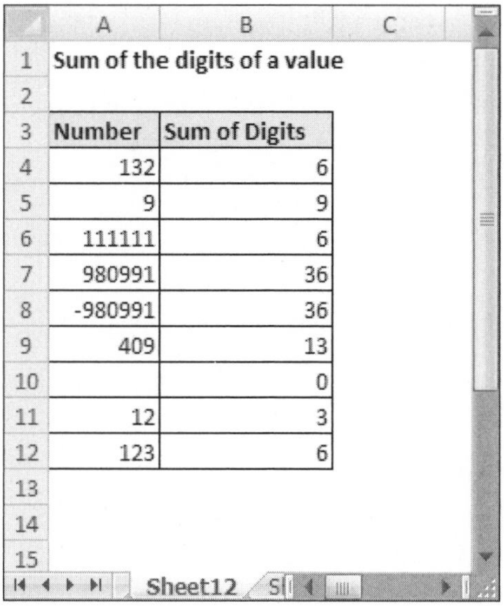

	A	B	C
1	Sum of the digits of a value		
2			
3	Number	Sum of Digits	
4	132	6	
5	9	9	
6	111111	6	
7	980991	36	
8	-980991	36	
9	409	13	
10		0	
11	12	3	
12	123	6	
13			
14			
15			

Figure 15-4: An array formula calculates the sum of the digits in an integer.

Part IV

Summing Rounded Values

Figure 15-5 shows a simple worksheet that demonstrates a common spreadsheet problem: rounding errors. As you can see, the grand total in cell E7 appears to display an incorrect amount; that is, it's off by a penny. The values in column E use a number format that displays two decimal places. The actual values, however, consist of additional decimal places that do not display because of rounding (as a result of the number format). The net effect of these rounding errors is a seemingly incorrect total. The total, which is actually $168.320997, displays as $168.32.

The following array formula creates a new array that consists of values in column E, rounded to two decimal places:

```
=SUM(ROUND(E4:E6,2))
```

This formula returns $168.31.

	A	B	C	D	E
1	Summing rounded values				
2					
3	Description	Quantity	Unit Price	Discount	Total
4	Widgets	6	$11.69	5.23%	$66.47
5	Sprockets	8	$9.74	5.23%	$73.84
6	Snapholytes	3	$9.85	5.23%	$28.00
7	GRAND TOTAL				$168.32
8					
9				Sum of rounded values:	$168.31
10					

Sheet12 / Sheet13 / Sheet14

Figure 15-5: Using an array formula to correct rounding errors.

You also can eliminate these types of rounding errors by using the ROUND function in the formula that calculates each row total in column E. This technique does not require an array formula.

 CROSS REF

Refer to Chapter 10 for more information about Excel's functions that are relevant to rounding.

Summing Every nth Value in a Range

Suppose you have a range of values and you want to compute the sum of every third value in the list — the first, the fourth, the seventh, and so on. One solution is to hard-code the cell addresses in a formula. A better solution, though, is to use an array formula.

Refer to the data in Figure 15-6. The values are stored in a range named *Data,* and the value of n is in cell D2 (named n).

The following array formula returns the sum of every nth value in the range:

```
{SUM(IF(MOD(ROW(INDIRECT("1:"&COUNT(Data)))-1,n)=0,Data,""))}
```

This formula generates an array of consecutive integers, and the MOD function uses this array as its first argument. The second argument for the MOD function is the value of n. The MOD function creates another array that consists of the remainders when each row number is divided by n. When the array item is 0 (that is, the row is evenly divisible by n), the corresponding item in the *Data* range will be included in the sum.

You'll find that this formula fails when n is 0 (that is, sums no items). The modified array formula that follows uses an IF function to handle this case:

```
{=IF(n=0,0,SUM(IF(MOD(ROW(INDIRECT("1:"&COUNT(data)))-1,n)=0,data,"")))}
```

This formula works only when the *Data* range consists of a single column of values. It does not work for a multicolumn range nor for a single row of values.

	A	B	C	D	E	F	G
1	Summing every nth value						
2							
3		Data					
4		1		5	=nth		
5		2		34	= Result		
6		3					
7		4		30	Alternate method		
8		5					
9		6					
10		7					
11		8					
12		9					
13		10					
14		11					
15		12					
16		13					
17		14					
18		15					
19		16					
20		17					
21		18					
22		19					
23							

Figure 15-6: An array formula returns the sum of every *n*th value in the range.

The preceding formula always includes the first item in the count. For example, when *n* is 5, the elements summed are 1, 6, 11, and 16. Following is a slightly modified version that begins summing with the *n*th element. When n is 5, the formula sums the following elements: 5, 10, and 15.

```
{=IF(n=0,0,SUM(IF(MOD(ROW(INDIRECT("1:"&COUNT(Data)))-n,n)=0,Data,"")))}
```

To make the formula work with a horizontal range, you need to transpose the array of integers generated by the ROW function. Excel's TRANSPOSE function is just the ticket. The modified array formula that follows works only with a horizontal *Data* range:

```
{=IF(n=0,0,SUM(IF(MOD(TRANSPOSE(ROW(INDIRECT
("1:"&COUNT(Data))))-1,n)=0,Data,"")))}
```

Removing Non-Numeric Characters from a String

The following array formula extracts a number from a string that contains text. For example, consider the string *ABC145Z*. The formula returns the numeric part — 145.

```
{=MID(A1,MATCH(0,(ISERROR(MID(A1,ROW(INDIRECT("1:"&LEN(A1))),1)
*1)*1),0),LEN(A1)-SUM((ISERROR(MID(A1,ROW
(INDIRECT("1:"&LEN(A1))),1)*1)*1)))}
```

Part IV

Using Excel's Formula Evaluator

If you would like to better understand how some of these complex array formulas work, consider using a handy tool: the Formula Evaluator. Select the cell that contains the formula and then choose Formulas⇨Formula Auditing⇨Evaluate Formula. You'll see the Evaluate Formula dialog box shown in the accompanying figure. Click the Evaluate button repeatedly to see the intermediate results as the formula is being calculated. It's like watching a formula calculate in slow motion.

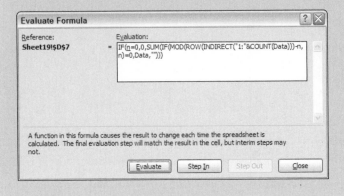

This formula works only with a single embedded number. For example, it fails with a string such as *X45Z99* (returning *45Z9*).

Determining the Closest Value in a Range

The array formula that follows returns the value in a range named *Data* that is closest to another value (named *Target*):

```
{=INDEX(Data,MATCH(SMALL(ABS(Target-Data),1),ABS(Target-Data),0))}
```

If two values in the *Data* range are equidistant from the *Target* value, the formula returns the first one in the list. Figure 15-7 shows an example of this formula. In this case, the *Target* value is 45. The array formula in cell D5 returns 48 — the value closest to 45.

Returning the Last Value in a Column

Suppose you have a worksheet that you update frequently by adding new data to columns. You might need a way to reference the last value in column A (the value most recently entered). If column A contains no empty cells, the solution is relatively simple and doesn't require an array formula:

```
=OFFSET(A1,COUNTA(A:A)-1,0)
```

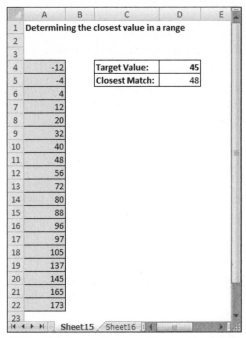

Figure 15-7: An array formula returns the closest match.

This formula uses the COUNTA function to count the number of nonempty cells in column A. This value (minus 1) is used as the second argument for the OFFSET function. For example, if the last value is in row 100, COUNTA returns 100. The OFFSET function returns the value in the cell 99 rows down from cell A1, in the same column.

If column A has one or more empty cells interspersed, which is frequently the case, the preceding formula won't work because the COUNTA function doesn't count the empty cells.

The following array formula returns the contents of the last nonempty cell in the first 500 rows of column A:

```
{=INDEX(A1:A500,MAX(ROW(A1:A500)*(A1:A500<>"")))}
```

You can, of course, modify the formula to work with a column other than column A. To use a different column, change the four column references from A to whatever column you need. If the last nonempty cell occurs in a row beyond row 500, you need to change the two instances of 500 to a larger number. The fewer rows referenced in the formula, the faster the calculation speed.

CAUTION
You cannot use this formula, as written, in the same column with which it's working. Attempting to do so generates a circular reference. You can, however, modify it. For example, to use the function in cell A1, change the references so they begin with row 2.

Part IV

NEW

In versions prior to Excel 2007, you could not use whole column or row references in an array formula, such as A:A or 3:3. In Excel 2007, you are allowed to use such references. The previous formula can be written as

```
=INDEX(A:A,MAX(ROW(A:A)*(A:A<>"")))
```

However, with the increase in the number of cells in a worksheet, using whole column or row references can significantly increase calculation time.

Returning the Last Value in a Row

The following array formula is similar to the previous formula, but it returns the last non-empty cell in the first 200 columns of a row (in this case, row 1):

```
{=INDEX(A1:GR1,MAX(COLUMN(A1:GR1)*(A1:GR1<>"")))}
```

Column GR is column 200. To use this formula for a different row, change the A1:GR1 reference to correspond to the range to check. A simpler (but slower) version of this formula that checks all 16,384 columns is

```
{=INDEX(1:1,MAX(COLUMN(1:1)*(1:1<>"")))}
```

Ranking Data with an Array Formula

Often, computing the rank orders for the values in a range of data is helpful. If you have a worksheet containing the annual sales figures for 20 salespeople, for example, you may want to know how each person ranks, from highest to lowest.

If you've used Excel's RANK function, you may have noticed that the ranks produced by this function don't handle ties the way that you may like. For example, if two values are tied for third place, the RANK function gives both of them a rank of 3. You may prefer a commonly used approach that assigns each an average (or midpoint) of the ranks — in other words, a rank of 3.5 for both values tied for third place.

Figure 15-8 shows a worksheet that uses two methods to rank a column of values (named *Sales*). The first method (column C) uses Excel's RANK function. Column D uses array formulas to compute the ranks.

The following is the array formula in cell D5:

```
=SUM(1*(B5<=Sales))-(SUM(1*(B5=Sales))-1)/2
```

This formula is copied to the cells below it.

	Salesperson	Sales	Excel's Rank Function	Ranks With Array Formula	
	Ranking data with an array formula				
5	Adams	123,000	6	6	
6	Bigelow	98,000	9	10	
7	Fredericks	98,000	9	10	Assigned middle rank
8	Georgio	98,000	9	10	
9	Jensen	25,000	12	12	
10	Juarez	101,000	8	8	
11	Klein	305,000	1	1	
12	Lynch	145,000	3	3.5	
13	Mayne	145,000	3	3.5	Assigned average rank
14	Roberton	121,000	7	7	
15	Slokum	124,000	5	5	
16	Wu	150,000	2	2	

Sheet15 Sheet16 **Sheet17** Sheet

Figure 15-8: Ranking data with Excel's RANK function and with array formulas.

NOTE

Each ranking is computed with a separate array formula, not with an array formula entered into multiple cells.

Each array function works by computing the number of higher values and subtracting one half of the number of equal values minus 1.

Creating a Dynamic Crosstab Table

A crosstab table tabulates or summarizes data across two dimensions. Take a look at the data in Figure 15-9. This worksheet shows a simple expense account listing. Each item consists of the date, the expense category, and the amount spent. Each column of data is a named range, indicated in the first row.

Array formulas summarize this information into a handy table that shows the total expenses — by category — for each day. Cell F6 contains the following array formula, which is copied to the remaining 14 cells in the table:

```
=SUM(($E6=Date)*(F$5=Category)*Amount)
```

These array formulas display the totals for each day, by category.

The formula sums the values in the *Amount* range, but does so only if the row and column names in the summary table match the corresponding entries in the *Date* and *Category* ranges. It does so by multiplying two Boolean values by the *Amount*. If both Boolean values are True, the result is the Amount. If one or both of the Boolean values is False, the result is 0.

Part IV

	A	B	C	D	E	F	G	H
1	Dynamic crosstabulation							
2								
3								
4	Date	Category	Amount			Transp	Food	Lodging
5	1/4/2007	Food	23.50		4-Jan	160.50	49.57	65.95
6	1/4/2007	Transp	15.00		5-Jan	20.00	27.80	89.00
7	1/4/2007	Food	9.12		6-Jan	0.00	101.96	75.30
8	1/4/2007	Food	16.95		7-Jan	11.50	25.00	112.00
9	1/4/2007	Transp	145.50					
10	1/4/2007	Lodging	65.95					
11	1/5/2007	Transp	20.00					
12	1/5/2007	Food	7.80					
13	1/5/2007	Food	20.00					
14	1/5/2007	Lodging	89.00					
15	1/6/2007	Food	9.00					
16	1/6/2007	Food	3.50					
17	1/6/2007	Food	11.02					
18	1/6/2007	Food	78.44					
19	1/6/2007	Lodging	75.30					
20	1/7/2007	Transp	11.50					
21	1/7/2007	Food	15.50					
22	1/7/2007	Food	9.50					
23	1/7/2007	Lodging	112.00					
24								

Sheet13 / Sheet14 / Sheet15 / Sheet

Figure 15-9: You can use array formulas to summarize data such as this in a dynamic crosstab table.

You can customize this technique to hold any number of different categories and any number of dates. You can eliminate the dates, in fact, and substitute people's names, departments, regions, and so on.

NOTE

You also can use Excel's pivot table feature to summarize data in this way. However, pivot tables do not update automatically when the data changes, so the array formula method described here has at least one advantage. See Chapter 18 for more information about pivot tables.

Working with Multicell Array Formulas

The previous chapter introduced array formulas entered into multicell ranges. In this section, I present a few more array multicell formulas. Most of these formulas return some of or all the values in a range, but rearranged in some way.

ON THE CD

Each of the examples in this section is demonstrated in `multi-cell array formulas .xlsx`, a file on the companion CD-ROM.

Returning Only Positive Values from a Range

The following array formula works with a single-column vertical range (named *Data*). The array formula is entered into a range that's the same size as *Data,* and it returns only the positive values in the *Data* range (0s and negative numbers are ignored).

```
{=INDEX(Data,SMALL(IF(Data>0,ROW(INDIRECT("1:"&ROWS(Data)))),
ROW(INDIRECT("1:"&ROWS(Data)))))}
```

As you can see in column C in Figure 15-10, this formula works albeit not perfectly. The *Data* range is A5:A24, and the array formula is entered into C5:C24. However, the array formula displays #NUM! error values for cells that don't contain a value.

	A	B	C	D	E	F
1	Return only positive values from a range					
2						
3						
4	Data		Positive Vals		Positive Vals	
5	33		33		33	
6	-33		44		44	
7	44		4		4	
8	4		43		43	
9	-5		99		99	
10	0		5		5	
11	43		6		6	
12	-1		7		7	
13	-2		8		8	
14	-3		9		9	
15	-33		10		10	
16	99		11		11	
17	5		12		12	
18	6		#NUM!			
19	7		#NUM!			
20	8		#NUM!			
21	9		#NUM!			
22	10		#NUM!			
23	11		#NUM!			
24	12		#NUM!			
25						

Intro Sheet1 Sheet2

Figure 15-10: Using an array formula to return only the positive values in a range.

Part IV

This modified array formula, entered into range E5:E24, uses the IFERROR function to avoid the error value display:

```
{=IFERROR(INDEX(Data,SMALL(IF(Data>0,ROW(INDIRECT
("1:"&ROWS(Data)))),ROW(INDIRECT("1:"&ROWS(Data))))),"")}
```

The IFERROR function is new to Excel 2007. For compatibility with older versions, use this formula:

```
{=IF(ISERR(SMALL(IF(Data>0,ROW(INDIRECT("1:"&ROWS(Data)))),
ROW(INDIRECT("1:"&ROWS(Data))))),"",INDEX(Data,SMALL(IF
(Data>0,ROW(INDIRECT("1:"&ROWS(Data)))),ROW(INDIRECT
("1:"&ROWS(Data))))))}
```

Returning Nonblank Cells from a Range

The following formula is a variation on the formula in the previous section. This array formula works with a single-column vertical range named *Data*. The array formula is entered into a range of the same size as *Data*, and it returns only the nonblank cell in the *Data* range.

```
{=IFERROR(INDEX(Data,SMALL(IF(Data<>"",ROW(INDIRECT
("1:"&ROWS(Data)))),ROW(INDIRECT("1:"&ROWS(Data))))),"")}
```

For compatibility with versions prior to Excel 2007, use this formula:

```
{=IF(ISERR(SMALL(IF(Data<>"",ROW(INDIRECT("1:"&ROWS(Data)))),
ROW(INDIRECT("1:"&ROWS(Data))))),"",INDEX(Data,SMALL(IF(Data
<>"",ROW(INDIRECT("1:"&ROWS(Data)))),ROW(INDIRECT("1:"&ROWS
(Data))))))}
```

Reversing the Order of the Cells in a Range

The following array formula works with a single-column vertical range (named *Data*). The array formula, which is entered into a range of the same size as *Data*, returns the values in *Data*, but in reverse order.

```
{=IF(INDEX(Data,ROWS(data)-ROW(INDIRECT("1:"&ROWS(Data)))+1)
="","",INDEX(Data,ROWS(Data)-ROW(INDIRECT("1:"&ROWS(Data)))
+1))}
```

Figure 15-11 shows this formula in action. The range A5:A14 is named *Data*, and the array formula is entered into the range C5:C14.

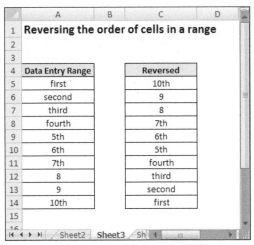

Figure 15-11: A multicell array formula reverses the order of the values in the range.

Sorting a Range of Values Dynamically

Suppose your worksheet contains a single-column vertical range named *Data*. The following array formula, entered into a range with the same number of rows as *Data*, returns the values in *Data*, sorted from highest to lowest. This formula works only with numeric values, not with text.

```
{=LARGE(Data,ROW(INDIRECT("1:"&ROWS(Data))))}
```

Figure 15-12 shows an example. The input range is in column A; the multicell array formula is in column C.

This formula can be useful if you need to have your data entry sorted immediately. Start by defining the range name *Data* as your data entry range. Then enter the array formula into another range with the same number of rows as *Data*.

The array formula returns #NUM! for cells that don't have a value. The modified version, which follows, uses Excel 2007's IFERROR function to eliminate the error display. This formula is used in column E in Figure 15-12:

```
{=IFERROR(LARGE(Data,ROW(INDIRECT("1:"&ROWS(Data)))),"")}
```

For compatibility with earlier versions, use this more complex formula:

```
{=IF(ISERR(LARGE(Data,ROW(INDIRECT("1:"&ROWS(Data))))),"",
LARGE(Data,ROW(INDIRECT("1:"&ROWS(Data)))))}
```

To sort the values in *Data* from lowest to highest, use the SMALL function in place of the LARGE function.

Part IV

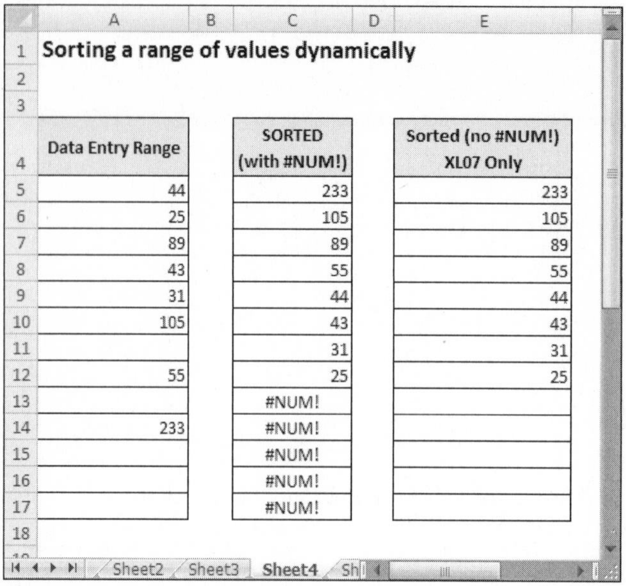

	Data Entry Range	SORTED (with #NUM!)	Sorted (no #NUM!) XL07 Only
1	Sorting a range of values dynamically		
2			
3			
5	44	233	233
6	25	105	105
7	89	89	89
8	43	55	55
9	31	44	44
10	105	43	43
11		31	31
12	55	25	25
13		#NUM!	
14	233	#NUM!	
15		#NUM!	
16		#NUM!	
17		#NUM!	
18			

Figure 15-12: A multicell array formula in column C sorts the values entered into column A.

Returning a List of Unique Items in a Range

If you have a single-column range named *Data*, the following array formula returns a list of the unique (non-duplicated) items in the range:

```
{=INDEX(Data,SMALL(IF(MATCH(Data,Data,0)=ROW(INDIRECT("1:"&ROWS(Data))),
MATCH(Data,Data,0),""),ROW(INDIRECT("1:"&ROWS(Data))))))}
```

This formula does not work if the *Data* range contains any blank cells. Figure 15-13 shows an example. Range A5:A23 is named *Data*, and the array formula is entered into range C5:C23. Note that the unfilled cells of the array formula display #NUM!.

The modified version, which follows, eliminates the #NUM! display by using the Excel 2007 IFERROR function:

```
{=IFERROR(INDEX(Data,SMALL(IF(MATCH(Data,Data,0)=ROW(INDIRECT
("1:"&ROWS(data))),MATCH(Data,Data,0),""),ROW(INDIRECT
("1:"&ROWS(Data))))),"")}
```

For compatibility with earlier versions, use this formula:

```
=INDEX(Data,SMALL(IF(MATCH(Data,Data,0)=ROW(INDIRECT
("1:"&ROWS(Data))),MATCH(Data,Data,0),""),ROW(INDIRECT
("1:"&ROWS(Data)))))
```

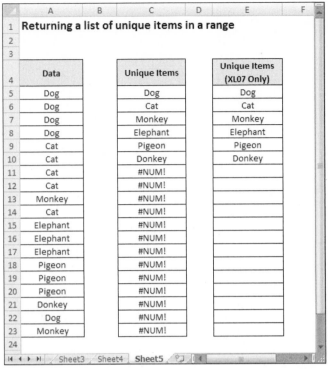

Figure 15-13: Using an array formula to return unique items from a list.

Displaying a Calendar in a Range

Figure 15-14 shows the results of one of my favorite multicell array formulas, a "live" calendar displayed in a range of cells. If you change the date at the top, the calendar recalculates to display the dates for the month and year.

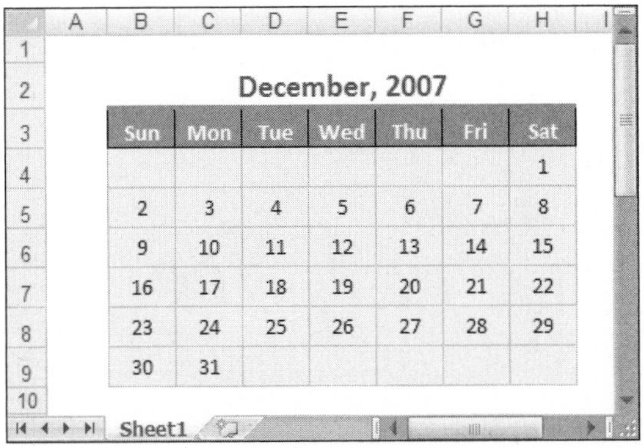

Figure 15-14: Displaying a calendar using a single array formula.

ON THE CD

This workbook is available on the companion CD-ROM. The file is named `array formula calendar.xlsx`.

To create this calendar in the range B2:H9, follow these steps:

1. Select B2:H2 and merge the cells by choosing Home⇨Alignment⇨Merge & Center.

2. Enter a date into the merged range. The day of the month isn't important.

3. Enter the abbreviated day names in the range B3:H3.

4. Select B4:H9 and enter this array formula. Remember, to enter an array formula, use Ctrl+Shift+Enter (not just Enter).

   ```
   {=IF(MONTH(DATE(YEAR(B2),MONTH(B2),1))<>MONTH(DATE(YEAR(B2),
   MONTH(B2),1)-(WEEKDAY(DATE(YEAR(B2),MONTH(B2),1))-1)+
   {0;1;2;3;4;5}*7+{1,2,3,4,5,6,7}-1),"",
   DATE(YEAR(B2),MONTH(B2),1)-(WEEKDAY(DATE(YEAR(B2),MONTH(B2),1))-1)+
   {0;1;2;3;4;5}*7+{1,2,3,4,5,6,7}-1)}
   ```

5. Format the range B4:H9 to use this custom number format: d. This step formats the dates to show only the day. Use the Custom category in the Number tab of the Format Cells dialog box to specify this custom number format.

6. Adjust the column widths and format the cells as you like.

Change the month and year in cell B2, and the calendar will update automatically. After creating this calendar, you can copy the range to any other worksheet or workbook.

The array formula actually returns date values, but the cells are formatted to display only the day portion of the date. Also, notice that the array formula uses array constants.

Following is another version of the formula. The IF function in the original formula checks each date to make sure it's in the current month. If not, the IF function returns an empty string.

You can simplify the array formula quite a bit by removing the IF function.

```
=DATE(YEAR(B2),MONTH(B2),1)-(WEEKDAY(DATE(YEAR(B2),MONTH(B2),
1))-1)+{0;7;14;21;28;35}+{0,1,2,3,4,5,6}
```

CROSS REF

See Chapter 14 for more information about array constants.

This version of the formula displays the days from the preceding month and the next month, as shown in Figure 15-15.

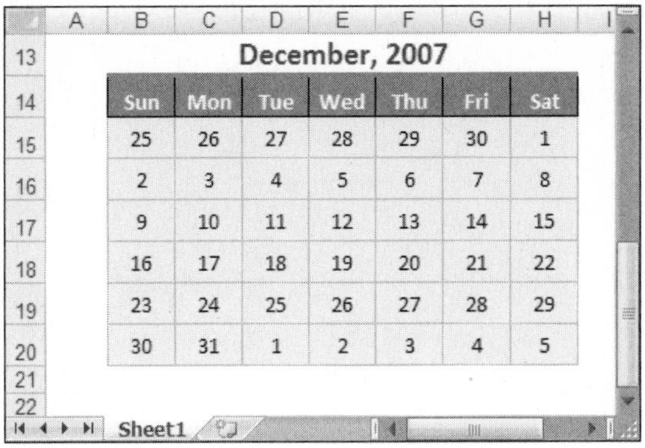

Figure 15-15: A simpler version of the formula also displays dates from the preceding and subsequent month.

Part

Miscellaneous Formula Techniques

Chapter 16

Intentional Circular References

IN THIS CHAPTER

◆ General information regarding how Excel handles circular references

◆ Why you might want to use an intentional circular reference

◆ How Excel determines calculation and iteration settings

◆ Examples of formulas that use intentional circular references

◆ Potential problems when using intentional circular references

When most spreadsheet users hear the term *circular reference,* they immediately think of an error condition. In the vast majority of situations, a circular reference represents an accident — something that you need to correct. Sometimes, however, a circular reference can be a good thing. This chapter presents some examples that demonstrate intentional circular references.

What Are Circular References?

When entering formulas in a worksheet, you occasionally may see a message from Excel, such as the one shown in Figure 16-1. This message is Excel's way of telling you that the formula you just entered will result in a *circular reference.* A circular reference occurs when a formula refers to its own cell, either directly or indirectly. For example, you create a circular reference if you enter the following formula into cell A10 because the formula refers to the cell that contains the formula:

```
=SUM(A1:A10)
```

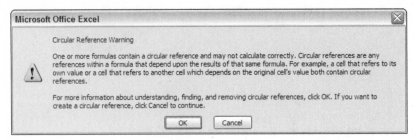

Figure 16-1: Excel's way of telling you that your formula contains a circular reference.

Every time the formula in A10 is calculated, it must be recalculated because A10 has changed. In theory, the calculation could continue forever while the value in cell A10 tried to reach infinity.

Correcting an Accidental Circular Reference

When you see the circular reference message after entering a formula, Excel gives you two options:

- Click OK to attempt to locate the circular reference. This also has the annoying side effect of displaying a help screen whether you need it or not.

- Click Cancel to enter the formula as is.

Most circular reference errors are caused by simple typographical errors or incorrect range specifications. For example, when creating a SUM formula in cell B10, you might accidentally specify an argument of B1:B10 instead of B1:B9.

If you know the source of the problem, click Cancel. Excel displays a message in the status bar to remind you that a circular reference exists. In this case, the message reads `Circular References: B10`. If you activate a different workbook or worksheet, the message simply displays `Circular References` (without the cell reference). At this point, you can then edit the formula and fix the problem.

If you get the circular message error but you don't know what formula caused the problem, you can click OK in response to the dialog box alert. When you do so, Excel shows the Help topic on circular references and also draws errors on the worksheet, which may help you identify the problem. For more help, choose Formulas⇨Formula Auditing⇨Error Checking⇨ Circular References to see a list of cells involved in the circular reference (see Figure 16-2). Click the first cell in the list to move to that cell, and examine its formula. If you cannot determine whether that cell caused the circular reference, move to the next cell by selecting it from the list. Continue to review the formulas until the status bar no longer displays Circular References.

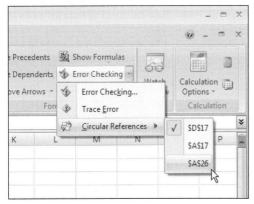

Figure 16-2: The Circular Reference command displays a list of cells involved in a circular reference.

NOTE

The Circular References command on the Ribbon will not be available if you have the Enable Iterative Calculation setting turned on. You can check this setting in the Excel Options dialog box (in the Formulas section). I discuss more about this setting later in this chapter.

Understanding Indirect Circular References

Often, finding the source of a circular reference is easy to identify and correct. Sometimes, however, circular references are indirect. In other words, one formula may refer to another formula that refers to a formula that refers back to the original formula. In some cases, you need to conduct a bit of detective work to figure out the problem.

CROSS REF

For more information about tracking down a circular reference, see Chapter 21.

About Circular References

For a practical, real-life demonstration of a circular reference, see the sidebar "More about Circular References," later in this chapter.

Intentional Circular References

As mentioned previously, you can use a circular reference to your advantage in some situations. A circular reference, if set up properly, can serve as the functional equivalent of a Do-Loop construct used in a programming language, such as VBA. An intentional circular reference introduces recursion or iteration into a problem. Each intermediate "answer" from a circular reference calculation functions in the subsequent calculation. Eventually, the solution converges to the final value.

By default, Excel does not permit iterative calculations. You must explicitly tell Excel that you want it to perform iterative calculations in your workbook. You do this by checking Enable Iterative Calculation in the Formulas section of the Excel Options dialog box (see Figure 16-3).

Figure 16-4 shows a simple example of a worksheet that uses an intentional circular reference. A company has a policy of contributing five percent of its net profit to charity. The contribution itself, however, is considered an expense and is therefore subtracted from the net profit figure — producing a circular reference.

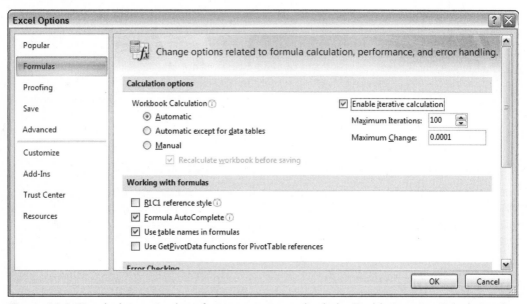

Figure 16-3: To calculate a circular reference, you must check the Enable Iterative Calculation check box.

	A	B	C	D	E	F
1	Gross Income	1,040,034				
2	Expenses	475,489				
3	Contributions	40,476	5% of Net Profit			
4	Net Profit	809,524	Gross Income - Expenses - Contributions			
5						
6						
7						

Sheet1

Figure 16-4: The company also deducts the 5 percent contribution of net profits as an expense (shown in cell B3), creating an intentional circular reference.

NOTE

You cannot resolve the circular reference unless you turn on the Enable Iterative Calculation setting.

The text in column A corresponds to the named cells in column B, and cell C3 is named *Pct.* The *Contributions* cell (B3) contains the following formula:

```
=Pct*Net_Profit
```

The *Net_Profit* cell (B4) contains the following formula:

```
=Gross_Income-Expenses-Contributions
```

These formulas produce a resolvable circular reference. When you change either the Gross_Income or the Expenses cell, Excel keeps calculating until the formula results converge on a solution.

NOTE

A reader of the first edition of this book pointed out another way to approach this problem without using a circular reference. Use the following formula to calculate the *Net_Profit* cell:

```
=(Gross_Income-Expenses)/(1+Pct)
```

Then calculate the Contributions cell using this formula:

```
=Pct*Net_Profit
```

ON THE CD

You can access the workbook, net profit (circular).xlsm, shown in Figure 16-4, on the companion CD-ROM. For your convenience, the worksheet includes a button that when clicked, executes a macro that displays a dialog box that lets you toggle the

Part V

iteration setting. This makes it easy to experiment with various iteration settings. Depending on your security settings, you may see a Security Warning when you open this workbook. In addition, the CD-ROM contains a file that demonstrates how to perform this calculation without using a circular reference, named `net profit (not circular).xlsm`.

The Formula tab of the Excel Options dialog box includes three controls relevant to circular references:

- **Enable Iterative Calculation check box:** If unchecked, Excel does not perform iterative calculations, and Excel displays a warning dialog box if you create a formula that has a circular reference. By default, this box is unchecked. When creating an intentional circular reference, you must check this check box.

- **Maximum iterations:** Determines the maximum number of iterations that Excel will perform. This value cannot exceed 32,767 and cannot be less than 1.

- **Maximum change:** Determines when iteration stops. For example, if this setting is .01, iterations stops when a calculation produces a result that differs by less than 1 percent of the previous value.

NOTE

Calculation continues until Excel reaches the number of iterations specified in the Maximum iterations box, or until a recalculation changes all cells by less than the amount you set in the Maximum change box (whichever is reached first). Depending on your application, you may need to adjust the settings in the Maximum iterations field or the Maximum change field. For a more accurate solution, make the Maximum change field smaller. If the result doesn't converge after 100 iterations, you can increase the Maximum iterations field.

To get a feel for how this works, open the example workbook presented in the previous section (refer to Figure 16-4). Then perform the following steps:

1. Ensure the Enable Iterative Calculation check box is checked as described above.

2. Set the Maximum iterations setting to 1.

3. Set the Maximum change setting to .001.

4. Enter a different value into the *Gross_Income* cell (cell B1).

5. Press F9 to calculate the sheet.

Because the Maximum iteration setting is 1, pressing F9 performs just one iteration. You'll find that the *Contributions* cell has not converged. Press F9 a few more times, and you'll see the result converge on the solution. When the solution is found, pressing F9 has no noticeable effect. If the Maximum iterations setting reflects a large value, the solution appears almost immediately (unless it involves some slow calculations).

How Excel Determines Calculation and Iteration Settings

You should understand that all open workbooks use the same calculation and iteration settings. For example, if you have two workbooks open, you cannot have one of them set to automatic calculation and the other set to manual calculation. Although you can save a workbook with particular settings (for example, manual calculation with no iterations), those settings can change if you open another workbook.

Excel follows these general rules to determine which calculation and iteration settings to use:

- The first workbook opened uses the calculation mode saved with that workbook. If you open other workbooks, they use the same calculation mode.

  For example, suppose you have two workbooks: Book1 and Book2. Book1 has its Iteration setting turned off (the default setting), and Book2 (which uses intentional circular references) has its Iteration setting turned on. If you open Book1 and then Book2, both workbooks will have the iteration setting turned off. If you open Book2 and then Book1, both workbooks will have their iteration setting turned on.

- Changing the calculation mode for one workbook changes the mode for all workbooks.

  If you have both Book1 and Book2 open, changing the calculation mode or Iteration setting of either workbook affects both workbooks.

- All worksheets in a workbook use the same mode of calculation.

- If you have all workbooks closed and you create a new workbook, the new workbook uses the same calculation mode as the last closed workbook. The exception is if you create the workbook from a template, the workbook uses the calculation mode specified in the template.

- If the mode of calculation in a workbook changes and you save the file, the current mode of calculation saves with the workbook.

Bottom line? When you open a workbook that uses iteration, there is no guarantee that the setting saved with your workbook will be the setting that is in effect when you open the workbook.

CAUTION

When the Enable Iterative Calculation setting is in effect, Excel will never display the Circular References warning dialog box and will not display the Circular References message in the status bar. Therefore, you may create an unintentional circular reference and not even know about it.

Part V

Circular Reference Examples

Following are a few more examples of using intentional circular references. They demonstrate creating circular references for entering unique random numbers, solving a recursive equation, solving simultaneous equations, and animating a chart.

NOTE

For these examples to work properly, the Enable Iterative Calculation setting must be in effect. Choose Excel Options, navigate to the Formulas section, and mark the Enable Iterative Calculation check box.

Generating Unique Random Integers

This example demonstrates how to take advantage of a circular reference to generate unique (nonduplicated) random integers in a range. The worksheet in Figure 16-5 generates 15 random integers between the values specified in the Lowest (E1) and Highest (E2) cells. A.

	A	B	C	D	E	F
1	74	1		Lowest:	1	
2	19	1		Highest:	100	
3	38	1				
4	40	1				
5	89	1				
6	49	1				
7	1	1				
8	61	1				
9	95	1				
10	52	1				
11	88	1				
12	80	1				
13	36	1				
14	72	1				
15	39	1				
16						
17	Dupes:	0		SOLUTION FOUND		
18						
19						

Figure 16-5: Using circular reference formulas to generate unique random integers in column A.

Column B contains formulas that count the number of times a particular number appears in the range A1:A15 (named *RandomNumbers*). For example, the formula in cell B1 follows. This formula displays the number of times the value in cell A1 appears in the *RandomNumbers* range:

```
=COUNTIF(RandomNumbers,A1)
```

Cell B17, named *Dupes,* displays the number of duplicated values using this formula:

```
=SUM(B1:B15)-COUNTA(B1:B15)
```

Each formula in column A contains a circular reference. The formula in cell A1, which was copied down the column, is

```
=IF(OR(Dupes<>0,(AND(A1>=Lowest,A1<=Highest))),
RANDBETWEEN(Lowest,Highest),A1)
```

The formula examines the value of the *Dupes* cell; if this value does not equal 0 — or, if the value in the cell is not between Lowest and Highest — a new random integer generates. When *Dupes* equals zero, all cells in the *RandomNumbers* range are different, and they are all within the specified value range.

Cell D17, which follows, contains a formula that displays the status. If the *Dupes* cell is not 0, the formula displays the text CALC AGAIN (press F9 to perform more iterations). When the *Dupes* cell is zero, the formula displays SOLUTION FOUND.

```
=IF(Dupes<>0,"CALC AGAIN","SOLUTION FOUND")
```

To generate a new set of random integers, press F9. The number of calculations required depends on

- The Maximum Iterations setting in the Formulas section of the Excel Options dialog box. If you specify a higher number of iterations, you have a better chance of finding unique values.

- The number of possible values (specified in the *Lowest* and *Highest* cells). Fewer calculations are required if, for example, you request the 15 unique values from a pool of 100.

Solving a Recursive Equation

A *recursive equation* is an equation in which a variable appears on both sides of the equal sign. The following equations are examples of recursive equations:

```
x = 1/(x+1)
x = COS(x)
x = SQRT(X+5)
x = 2^(1/x)
x = 5 + (1/x)
```

You can solve a recursive equation by using a circular reference. First, make sure that you turn on the Enable Iterative Calculation setting. Then convert the equation into a self-referencing formula. To solve the first equation, enter the following formula into cell A1:

```
=1/(A1+1)
```

The formula converges at 0.618033989, which is the value of x that satisfies the equation.

Sometimes, this technique doesn't work. For example, the formula allows the possibility of a division by zero error. The solution is to check for an error. If the formula displays an error, modify the iterated value slightly. For example, the preceding formula can be rewritten using Excel 2007's new IFERROR function:

```
=IFERROR(1/(A1+1),A1+0.01)
```

Following is a version of the formula that's compatible with previous versions of Excel:

```
=IF(ISERR(1/(A1+1)),A1+0.01,1/(A1+1))
```

Figure 16-6 shows a worksheet that calculates several recursive equations in column B. The formulas in column D provide a check of the results. For example, the formula in column D2 is

```
=1/(B2+1)
```

Formulas in column E display the difference between the values in column B and column D. If the solution is correct, column E displays a zero (or a value very close to zero).

	A	B	C	D	E	F
1	Equation	Circular Ref Formula		Check	Difference	
2	x = 1/(x+1)	0.618033989		0.6180340	0.000000000	
3	x = COS(x)	0.739085133		0.7390851	0.000000000	
4	x = SQRT(X+5)	2.791287847		2.7912878	0.000000000	
5	x = 2^(1/x)	1.559610455		1.5596105	-0.000000021	
6	x = 5 + (1/x)	5.192582403		5.1925824	-0.000000001	
7						

Figure 16-6: This workbook uses circular references to calculate several recursive equations.

 ON THE CD

You can access `recursive equations.xlsx`, the workbook shown in Figure 16-6, on the companion CD-ROM.

Solving Simultaneous Equations Using a Circular Reference

In some cases, you can use circular references to solve simultaneous equations. Consider the two simultaneous equations listed here:

```
3x + 4y = 8
3x + 8y = 20
```

You need to find the value of x and the value of y that satisfies both equations. First, rewrite the equations to express them in terms of x and y. The following represents the first equation, expressed in terms of x:

```
x = (8 - 4y)/3
```

The following equation represents the second equation, expressed in terms of y:

```
y = (20 - 3x)/8
```

As shown in Figure 16-7, cell B5 is named *X,* and cell B6 is named *Y.* The formulas in these cells mirror the previous equations. The formula in B5 (X) is

```
=(8-(4*Y))/3
```

The formula is cell B6 (Y) is

```
=(20-(3*X))/8
```

The figure also shows a chart that plots the two equations. The intersection of the two lines represents the values of X and Y that solve the equations.

Note the circular reference. The X cell refers to the Y cell, and the Y cell refers to the X cell. These cells converge to display the solution:

```
X = -1.333
Y = 3.000
```

Using intentional circular references to solve simultaneous equations is more of an interesting demonstration than a practical approach. You'll find that some iterative calculations never converge. In other words, successive recalculations will never hone in on a solution. For example, consider the simultaneous equations that follow. A solution does indeed exist, but you cannot use circular references to find it.

```
x = 4 - y/2
y = 3 + 2x
```

Part V

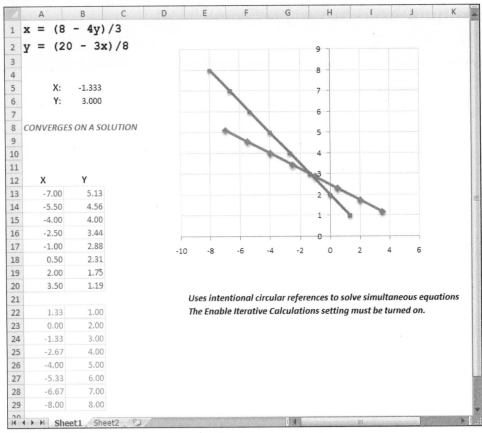

Figure 16-7: This worksheet solves two simultaneous equations.

CROSS REF

Using matrices is a better approach for solving simultaneous equations with Excel. See Chapter 10 for examples.

ON THE CD

The companion CD-ROM contains the workbook `simultaneous equations.xlsx` with two sets of simultaneous equations. You can solve one set by using intentional circular references; you cannot solve the other set using this technique.

More about Circular References

For a practical, real-life demonstration of a circular reference, refer to the sidebar, "About Circular References," earlier in this chapter.

Animating a Chart Using Iteration

The final intentional circular reference example involves a chart (see Figure 16-8). It's certainly not a practical example, but it may help you understand how circular references work.

The line series on the chart displays the COS function for values ranging from 0 to approximately 12.6, using the data in A6:B24.

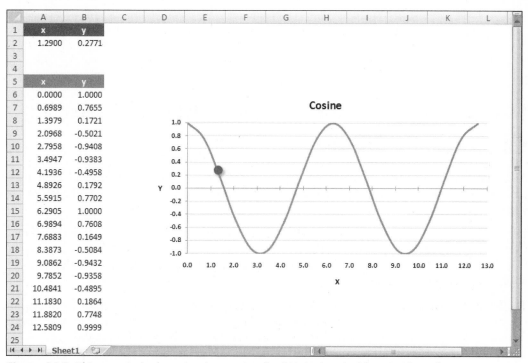

Figure 16-8: This uses a single-point data series that's calculated with a circular reference formulas.

The chart has an additional data series, consisting of a single point, in range A2:B2. This data series displays as a single large round marker on the chart. The circular reference formula in cell A2 is

```
=IF(A2>12.6,0,A2+0.005)
```

The formula in cell B2 is

```
=COS(A2)
```

When you press F9 to calculate the worksheet, the value in A2 increments, thereby changing the position of the round marker on the chart. Press F9 repeatedly and watch the marker move along the line. The amount of marker movement depends on two factors:

Part V

- The increment value in the formula (set at .005)
- The Maximum Iterations setting, in the Formula tab of the Excel Options dialog box

When Maximum Iterations is 100 and the increment is .005, each calculation increases the value in cell A2 by 0.5. The IF function in the formula resets the value to 0 when it exceeds 12.6. Therefore, the marker returns to the left side of the chart and starts over.

ON THE CD

This example, named `iterative chart animation.xlsx`, is available on the companion CD-ROM.

Potential Problems with Intentional Circular References

Although intentional circular references can be useful, using this feature has some potential problems. Perhaps the best advice is to use this feature with caution, and make sure you understand how it works.

To take advantage of an intentional circular reference, you must have the Enable Iterative Calculation setting in effect. When that setting is in effect, Excel does not warn you of circular references. Therefore, you run the risk of creating an accidental circular reference without even knowing about it.

The number of iterations specified in the Maximum iteration field applies to all formulas in the workbook, not just those that use circular references. If your workbook contains many complex formulas, these additional iterations can slow things down considerably. Therefore, when you use intentional circular references, keep your worksheets very simple and close all workbooks that you aren't using.

You may need to distribute a workbook that uses intentional circular references to other users. If Excel's Iteration setting is not active when you open the workbook, Excel displays the circular reference error message, which probably confuses all but the most sophisticated users.

Chapter 17

Charting Techniques

IN THIS CHAPTER

◆ Creating charts from any number of worksheets or different workbooks

◆ Plotting functions with one and two variables

◆ Creating awesome designs with formulas

◆ Working with linear and nonlinear trendlines

◆ Useful charting tricks for working with charts

When most people think of Excel, they think of analyzing rows and columns of numbers. As you probably know already, though, Excel is no slouch when it comes to presenting data visually in the form of a chart. In fact, it's a safe bet that Excel is the most commonly used software for creating charts.

After you've created a chart, you have almost complete control over nearly every aspect of each chart. This chapter, which assumes that you're familiar with Excel's charting feature, demonstrates some useful charting techniques — most of which involve formulas.

Understanding the SERIES Formula

You create charts from numbers that appear in a worksheet. You can enter these numbers directly, or you can derive them as the result of formulas.

Normally, the data used by a chart resides in a single worksheet, within one file, but that's not a strict requirement. A single chart can use data from any number of worksheets, or even from different workbooks.

A *chart* consists of one or more data series, and each data series appears as a line, column, bar, and so on. Each series in a chart has a SERIES formula. When you select a data series in a chart, Excel highlights the data with an outline, and its SERIES formula appears in the formula bar (see Figure 17-1).

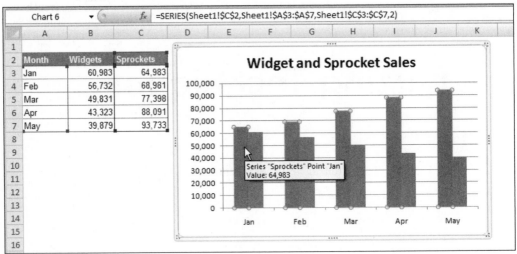

Figure 17-1: The formula bar displays the SERIES formula for the selected data series in a chart.

 NOTE

A SERIES formula is not a "real" formula. In other words, you can't use it in a cell, and you can't use worksheet functions within the SERIES formula. You can, however, edit the arguments in the SERIES formula to change the data that's used by the chart. You can also drag the outlines in the worksheet to change the chart's data.

A SERIES formula has the following syntax:

```
=SERIES(series_name, category_labels, values, order, sizes)
```

The arguments you can use in the SERIES formula include

- **series_name:** (Optional) A reference to the cell that contains the series name used in the legend. If the chart has only one series, the series_name argument is used as the title. The series_name argument can also consist of text, in quotation marks. If omitted, Excel creates a default series name (for example, Series 1).

- **category_labels:** (Optional) A reference to the range that contains the labels for the category axis. If omitted, Excel uses consecutive integers beginning with 1. For XY charts, this argument specifies the *x* values. A noncontiguous range reference is also valid. (The range's addresses are separated by a comma and enclosed in parentheses.) The argument may also consist of an array of comma-separated values (or text in quotation marks) enclosed in curly brackets.

- **values:** (Required) A reference to the range that contains the values for the series. For XY charts, this argument specifies the *y* values. A non-contiguous range reference is also valid. (The range's addresses are separated by a comma and enclosed in parentheses.) The argument may also consist of an array of comma-separated values enclosed in curly brackets.

- **order:** (Required) An integer that specifies the plotting order of the series. This argument is relevant only if the chart has more than one series. Using a reference to a cell is not allowed.

- **sizes:** (Only for bubble charts) A reference to the range that contains the values for the size of the bubbles in a bubble chart. A noncontiguous range reference is also valid. (The range's addresses are separated by a comma and enclosed in parentheses.) The argument may also consist of an array of values enclosed in curly brackets.

Range references in a SERIES formula are always absolute, and they always include the sheet name. For example

```
=SERIES(Sheet1!$B$1,,Sheet1!$B$2:$B$7,1)
```

A range reference can consist of a noncontiguous range. If so, each range is separated by a comma, and the argument is enclosed in parentheses. In the following SERIES formula, the values range consists of B2:B3 and B5:B7:

```
=SERIES(,,(Sheet1!$B$2:$B$3,Sheet1!$B$5:$B$7),1)
```

Although a SERIES formula can refer to data in other worksheets, all the data for a series must reside on a single sheet. The following SERIES formula, for example, is not valid because the data series references two different worksheets:

```
=SERIES(,,(Sheet1!$B$2,Sheet2!$B$2),1)
```

Using Names in a SERIES Formula

You can substitute range names for the range references in a SERIES formula. When you do so, Excel changes the reference in the SERIES formula to include the workbook name. For example, the SERIES formula shown here uses a range named *MyData* (located in a workbook named `budget.xlsx`). Excel added the workbook name and exclamation point.

```
=SERIES(Sheet1!$B$1,,budget.xlsx!MyData,1)
```

Part V

Chart-Making Tips

Here I present a number of chart-making tips that you might find helpful:

- Right-click any chart element and choose Format *xxxx*, where *xxxx* represents the element's name (or press Ctrl+1). Excel displays its Format dialog box, which remains open until you close it. The formatting controls in the Format dialog box enable you to perform actions that aren't available in the Ribbon.

- To create a chart with a single keystroke, select the data you want to chart and press Alt+F1. The result is an embedded chart of the default chart type. To create the chart on a chart sheet, press Alt+F11 instead of Alt+F1.

- If you have many charts of the same type to create, create and format the first chart and make a template from that chart by choosing Chart Tools⇨Design⇨ Type⇨Save as Template. When you create your additional charts, use Insert⇨ Charts⇨Other Charts⇨All Chart Types, and then choose your template from the list.

- To print an embedded chart on a separate sheet of paper, select the chart and choose Office⇨Print. Excel prints the chart on a page by itself and does *not* print the worksheet.

- If you don't want a particular embedded chart to appear on your printout, select the chart and click the dialog box launcher in the Chart Tools⇨Format⇨Size group to display the Size And Properties dialog box. Click the Properties tab and remove the check mark from the Print Object check box.

- Sometimes, using a mouse to select a particular chart element is tricky. You may find it easier to use the keyboard to select a chart element. When a chart is activated, press the up arrow or down arrow to cycle through all parts in the chart. When a data series is selected, press the right arrow or left arrow to select individual points in the series. Or, select the chart element by using the Chart Tools⇨ Format⇨Chart Elements drop-down control. This control is useful for selecting chart elements, and it also displays the name of the selected element. Better yet, put this control in your Quick Access toolbar so it's always visible.

- You can delete all data series from a chart. If you do so, the chart appears empty. It retains its settings, however. Therefore, you can add a data series to an empty chart, and it again looks like a chart.

- For more control over positioning your chart, press Ctrl while you click the chart. Then use the arrow keys to move the chart 1 pixel at a time.

Using names in a series formula provides a significant advantage: If you change the range reference for the name, the chart automatically displays the new data. In the preceding SERIES formula, for example, assume the range named *MyData* refers to A1:A20. The chart displays the 20 values in that range. You can then use the Name Manger to redefine

MyData as a different range — say, A1:A30. The chart then displays the 30 data points defined by *MyData*. (No chart editing is necessary.)

As I noted previously, a SERIES formula cannot use worksheet functions. You *can*, however, create named formulas (which use functions) and use these named formulas in your SERIES formula. As you see later in this chapter, this technique enables you to perform some useful charting tricks.

Unlinking a Chart Series from Its Data Range

Normally, an Excel chart uses data stored in a range. If you change the data in the range, the chart updates automatically. In some cases, you may want to "unlink" the chart from its data ranges and produce a *static chart* — a chart that never changes. For example, if you plot data generated by various what-if scenarios, you may want to save a chart that represents some baseline so you can compare it with other scenarios. There are two ways to create such a chart:

- **Paste it as a picture.** Activate the chart and then choose Home⇨Clipboard⇨Paste⇨As Picture⇨CopyAs Picture. (Accept the default settings in the Copy Picture dialog box.) Then, activate any cell and choose Home⇨Clipboard⇨Paste⇨As Pictur⇨Paste As Picture (or press Ctrl+V). The result is a picture of the copied chart. You can then delete the original chart if you like.

- **Convert the range references to arrays.** Click a chart series and then click the formula bar to activate the SERIES formula. Press F9 to convert the ranges to arrays (see Figure 17-2). Repeat this for each series in the chart. This technique (as opposed to creating a picture) enables you to continue to edit and format the chart. This technique will not work for large amounts of data because Excel imposes a limit on the length of a SERIES formula (about 1,024 characters).

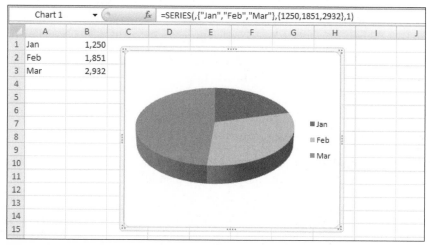

Figure 17-2: A SERIES formula that uses arrays rather than ranges.

Part V

Creating Links to Cells

You can add cell links to various elements of a chart. Adding cell links can make your charts more dynamic. You can set dynamic links for chart titles, data labels, and axis labels. In addition, you can insert a text box that links to a cell.

Adding a Chart Title Link

The chart title is normally not linked to a cell. In other words, it contain static text that changes only when you edit the title manually. You can, however, create a link so a title refers to a worksheet cell.

To create a linked title, first make sure the chart contains the chart element title that you want. (Use the controls in the Chart Tools⇨Layout⇨Labels group.) Next, select the title, type an equal sign, click the cell that contains the title text, and press Enter. The result is a formula that contains the sheet reference and the cell reference as an absolute reference (for example, =Sheet1!$A$1). Figure 17-3 shows a chart in which the chart title is linked to cell A1.

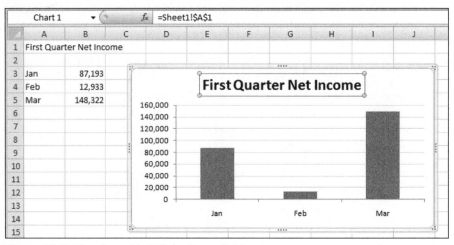

Figure 17-3: The chart title is linked to cell A1.

Adding Axis Title Links

The axis titles are optional and are used to describe the data for an axis. The process for adding a link to an axis title is identical to that described in the previous section for a chart title.

Adding Links to Data Labels

You probably know that Excel enables you to label each data point in a chart. You do this by using Chart Tools⇨Labels⇨Data Labels. Unfortunately, this feature isn't very flexible. For example, you can't specify a range that contains the labels.

You can, however, edit individual data labels. To do so, click any data label to select them all, and then click a second time to select the single data label. When a single data label is selected, you can add any text you like. Or, you can specify a link to a cell by typing an equal sign and clicking a cell to create a reference formula (such as =Sheet1!$A$1).

NEW

Excel 2007 no longer supports linked text boxes in charts.

Adding Text Links

You can also add a linked text box to a chart. The process is a bit tricky, however. Follow these steps exactly:

1. Select the chart and then choose Insert⇨Text⇨Text Box.
2. Drag the mouse inside the chart to create the text box.
3. Press Esc to exit text entry mode and select the text box object.
4. Click in the formula bar and then type an equal sign (=).
5. Use your mouse and click the cell that will be linked.
6. Press Enter.

You can apply any type of formatting you like.

TIP

After you add a text box to a chart, you can change it to any other shape that supports text. Select the text box and choose Drawing Tools⇨Format⇨Insert Shapes⇨Edit Shape⇨Change Shape. Then choose a new shape from the gallery.

Chart Examples

This section contains a variety of chart examples that you may find useful or informative.

Charting Progress toward a Goal

You're probably familiar with a thermometer-type display that shows the percentage of a task that's completed. Creating such a display in Excel is very easy. The trick involves creating a chart that uses a single cell (which holds a percentage value) as a data series.

Figure 17-4 shows a worksheet set up to track daily progress toward a goal: 1,000 new customers in a 15-day period. Cell B18 contains the goal value, and cell B19 sums the values in column B. Cell B21 contains a simple formula that calculates the percent of goal:

```
=B19/B18
```

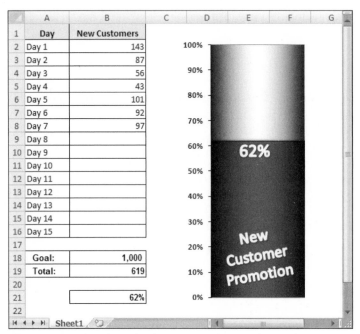

Figure 17-4: This chart displays progress toward a goal.

As you enter new data in column B, the formulas display the current results.

To make the thermometer chart, select cell B21 and create a column chart from that single cell. Notice the blank cell above cell B21. Without this blank cell, Excel uses the entire data block for the chart, not just the single cell. Because B21 is isolated from the other data, the data series consists of a single cell.

Other changes required are

- Select the horizontal category axis and press Delete to remove the category axis from the chart.

- Add a chart title. (I formatted it to display at an angle and then moved it to the bottom of the chart.)

- Remove the legend.

- Add data labels to the chart to display the percent accomplished.

- In the Format Data Series dialog box (Series Options tab), set the Gap width to 0, which makes the column occupy the entire width of the plot area.

- Select the Value Axis and display the Format Value Axis dialog box. In the Axis Options tab, set the Minimum to 0 and the Maximum to 1.

You can make other cosmetic changes as you like. For example, you may want to change the chart's width to make it look more like a thermometer, as well as adjust fonts, colors, and so on.

ON THE CD

This example, named `thermometer chart.xlsx`, is available on the companion CD-ROM.

Creating a Gauge Chart

Figure 17-5 shows another chart based on a single cell. It's a pie chart set up to resemble a gauge. Although this chart displays only one value (entered in cell B1), it actually uses three data points (in A4:A6).

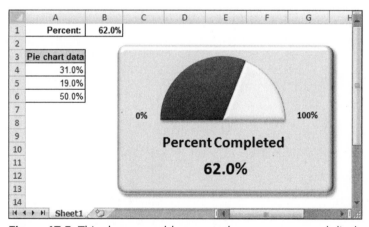

Figure 17-5: This chart resembles a speedometer gauge and displays a value between 0 and 100 percent.

ON THE CD

A workbook with this example is available on the companion CD-ROM. The filename is `gauge chart.xlsx`.

One slice of the pie — the slice at the bottom — always consists of 50 percent, and that slice is hidden (by using the No Fill and No Outline settings). The other two slices are apportioned based on the value in cell B1. The formula in cell 44 is

```
=MIN(B1,100%)/2
```

This formula uses the MIN function to display the smaller of two values: either the value in cell B1 or 100 percent. It then divides this value by 2 because only the top half of the pie is relevant. Using the MIN function prevents the chart from displaying more than 100 percent.

The formula in cell A5 simply calculates the remaining part of the pie — the part to the right of the gauge's needle:

```
=50%-A4
```

The chart's title was moved below the half-pie. The chart also includes data labels. I deleted two of the data labels and added a link to the remaining one so that it displays the percent completed value in cell B1.

Displaying Conditional Colors in a Column Chart

The Fill tab of the Format Data Series dialog box has an option labeled Vary Colors by Point. This option simply uses more colors for the data series. Unfortunately, the colors aren't related to the values of the data series.

This section describes how to create a column chart in which the color of each column depends on the value that it's displaying. Figure 17-6 shows such a chart. (It's more impressive when you see it in color.) The data used to create the chart is in range A1:F14.

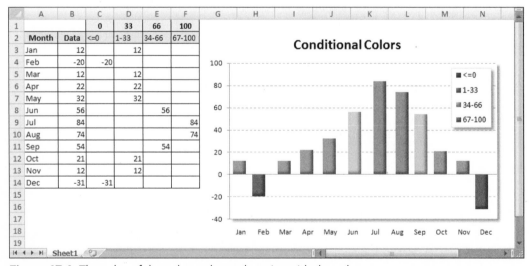

Figure 17-6: The color of the column depends varies with the value.

ON THE CD

A workbook with this example is available on the companion CD-ROM. The filename is `conditional colors.xlsx`.

This chart displays four data series, but some data is missing for each series. The data for the chart is entered in column B. Formulas in columns C:F determine which series the number belongs to by referencing the bins in Row 1. For example, the formula in cell C3 is

```
=IF(B3<=$C$1,B3,"")
```

If the value in column B is less than the value in cell C1, the value goes in this column. The formulas are set up such that a value in column B goes into only one column in the row.

The formula in cell D3 is a bit more complex because it must determine whether cell C3 is greater than the value in cell C1 and less than or equal to the value in cell D1:

```
=IF(AND($B3>C$1,$B3<=D$1),$B3,"")
```

The four data series are overlaid on top of each other in the chart. The trick involves setting the Series Overlap value to a large number. This setting determines the spacing between the series. Use the Series Options tab of the Format Data Series dialog box to adjust this setting

NOTE

Series Overlap is a single setting for the chart. If you change the setting for one series, the other series change to the same value.

Creating a Comparative Histogram

With a bit of creativity, you can create charts that you may have considered impossible. For example, Figure 17-7 shows a chart sometimes referred to as a *comparative histogram chart*. Such charts often display population data.

ON THE CD

A workbook with this example is available on the companion CD-ROM. The filename is `comparative histogram.xlsx`.

Here's how to create the chart:

1. Enter the data in A1:C8, as shown in Figure 17-7. Notice that the values for females are entered as negative values, which is very important.

2. Select A1:C8 and create a bar chart. Use the subtype labeled Clustered Bar.

3. Select the horizontal axis and display the Format Axis dialog box.

Part V

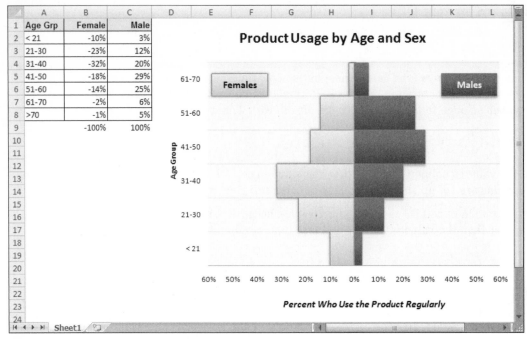

Figure 17-7: A comparative histogram.

4. Click the Number tab and specify the following custom number format:

0%;0%;0%

This custom format eliminates the negative signs in the percentages.

5. Select the vertical axis and display the Format Axis dialog box.

6. In the Axis Options tab, set all tick marks to None and set the Axis Labels option to Low. This setting keeps the vertical axis in the center of the chart but displays the axis labels at the left side.

7. Select either of the data series and display the Format Data Series dialog box.

8. In the Series Options tab, set the Series Overlap to 100% and the Gap Width to 0%.

9. Delete the legend and add two text boxes to the chart (Females and Males) to substitute for the legend.

10. Apply other formatting and labels as desired.

Creating a Gantt Chart

A *Gantt chart* is a horizontal bar chart often used in project management applications. Although Excel doesn't support Gantt charts per se, creating a simple Gantt chart is fairly easy. The key is getting your data set up properly.

Handling Missing Data

Sometimes, data that you're charting may be missing one or more data points. As shown in the accompanying figure, Excel offers three ways to handle the missing data:

- **Gaps:** Missing data is simply ignored, and the data series will have a gap.

  This is the default.

- **Zero:** Missing data is treated as zero.

- **Connect with Line:** Missing data is interpolated—calculated by using data on either side of the missing point(s).

  This option is available only for line charts, area charts, and XY charts.

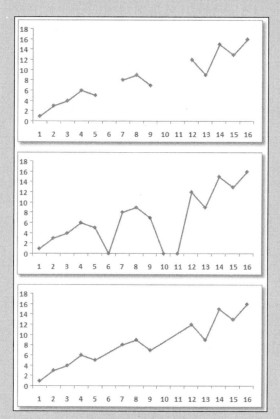

continued

continued

To specify how to deal with missing data for a chart, choose Chart Tools⇨Design⇨
Data⇨Select Data. In the Select Data Source, click the Hidden and Empty Cells button.
Excel displays its Hidden and Empty Cell Settings dialog box. Make your choice in the
dialog box. The option that you choose applies to the entire chart, and you can't set a
different option for different series in the same chart.

Normally, a chart doesn't display data that's in a hidden row or columns. You can use
the Hidden and Empty Cell Settings dialog box to force a chart to use hidden data.

Figure 17-8 shows a Gantt chart that depicts the schedule for a project, which is in the
range A2:C13. The horizontal axis represents the total time span of the project, and each
bar represents a project task. The viewer can quickly see the duration for each task and
identify overlapping tasks.

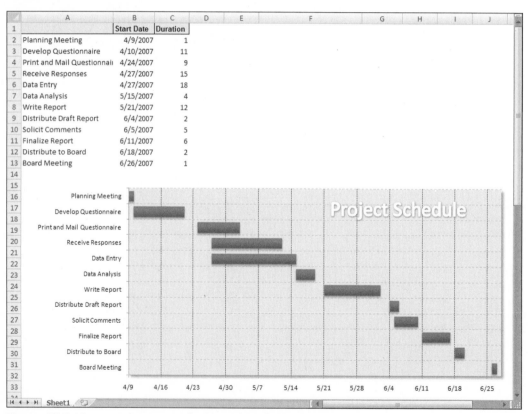

Figure 17-8: You can create a simple Gantt chart from a bar chart.

ON THE CD

A workbook with this example is available on the companion CD-ROM. The filename is `gantt chart.xlsx`.

Column A contains the task name, column B contains the corresponding start date, and column C contains the duration of the task, in days.

Follow these steps to create this chart:

1. Select the range A2:C13, and create a Stacked Bar Chart.

2. Delete the legend.

3. Select the category (vertical) axis, and display the Format Axis dialog box.

4. In the Format Axis dialog box, specify Categories in Reverse Order to display the tasks in order, starting at the top. Choose Horizontal Axis Crosses at Maximum Category to display the dates at the bottom.

5. Select the Start Date data series, and display the Format Data Series dialog box.

6. In the Format Data Series dialog box, click the Series Options tab and set the Series Overlap to 100%. Click the Fill tab, and specify No Fill. Click the Border Color tab and specify No Line. These steps effectively hide the data series.

7. Select the value (horizontal) axis and display the Format Axis dialog box.

8. In the Format Axis dialog box, adjust the Minimum and Maximum settings to accommodate the dates that you want to display on the axis.

   Unfortunately, you must enter these values as date serial numbers, not actual dates. In this example, the Minimum is 39181 (April 9, 2007) and the Maximum is 39261 (June 28, 2007). Specify 7 for the Major Unit, to display one week intervals. Use the number tab to specify a date format for the axis labels.

9. Apply other formatting as desired.

Creating a Box Plot

A *box plot* (sometimes known as a *quartile plot*) is often used to summarize data. Figure 17-9 shows a box plot created for four groups of data. The raw data appears in columns A through D. The range G2:J7, used in the chart, contains formulas that summarize the data. Table 17-1 shows the formulas in column G (which were copied to the three columns to the right).

ON THE CD

A workbook with this example is available on the companion CD-ROM. The filename is `box plot.xlsx`.

Part V

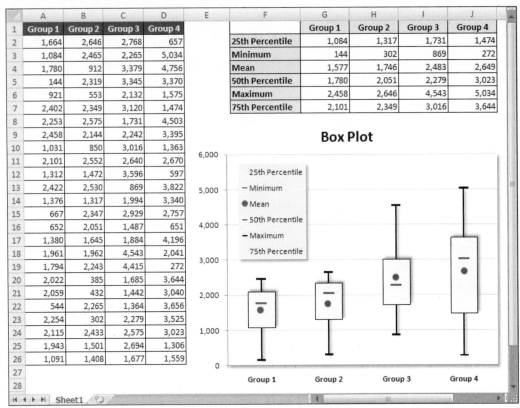

Figure 17-9: This box plot summarizes the data in columns A through D.

TABLE 17-1   FORMULAS USED TO CREATE A BOX PLOT

Cell	Calculation	Formula
G2	25th Percentile	=QUARTILE(A2:A26,1)
G3	Minimum	=MIN(A2:A26)
G4	Mean	=AVERAGE(A2:A26)
G5	50th Percentile	=QUARTILE(A2:A26,2)
G6	Maximum	=MAX(A2:A26)
G7	75th Percentile	=QUARTILE(A2:A26,3)

Follow these steps to create the box plot:

1. Select the range F1:J7.

2. Choose Insert⇨Charts⇨Line, and select the fourth subtype, Line with Markers.

3. Choose Chart Tools⇨Design⇨Data⇨Switch Row/Column to change the orientation of the chart.

4. Choose Chart Tools⇨Layout⇨Analysis⇨Up/Down Bars⇨Up/Down Bars to add up/down bars that connect the first data series (25th Percentile) with the last data series (75th Percentile).

5. Remove the markers from the 25th Percentile series and the 75th percentile series.

6. Choose Chart Tools⇨Layout⇨Analysis⇨Lines⇨Hi-Lo Lines to add a vertical line between the each point to connect the Minimum and Maximum data series.

7. Remove the lines from each of the six data series.

8. Change the series marker to a horizontal line for the following series: Minimum, Maximum, and 50th Percentile.

9. Make other formatting changes as required.

TIP

After performing all these steps, you may want to create a template to simplify the creation of additional box plots. Activate the chart, and choose Chart Tools⇨Design⇨ Type⇨Save As Template.

The legend for this chart displays the series in the order in which they are plotted — which is not the optimal order and may be confusing. Unfortunately, you can't change the plot order because the order is important. (The up/down bars use the first and last series.) If you find that the legend is confusing, you may want to delete all the legend entries except for Mean and 50th Percentile.

Plotting Every *n*th Data Point

Normally, Excel doesn't plot data that resides in a hidden row or column. You can sometimes use this to your advantage because it's an easy way to control what data appears in the chart.

Suppose you have a lot of data in a column, and you want to plot only every tenth data point. One way to accomplish this is to use filtering in conjunction with a formula. Figure 17-10 shows a two-column table with filtering in effect. The chart plots only the data in the visible (filtered) rows and ignores the values in the hidden rows.

ON THE CD

The example in this section, named `plot every nth data point.xlsx`, is available on the companion CD-ROM.

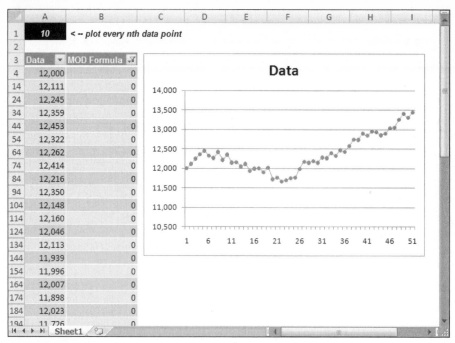

Figure 17-10: This chart plots every *n*th data point (specified in A1) by ignoring data in the rows hidden by filtering.

Cell A1 contains the value 10. The value in this cell determines which rows to hide. Column B contains identical formulas that use the value in cell A1. For example, the formula in cell B4 is as follows:

```
=MOD(ROW()-ROW($A$4),$A$1)
```

This formula subtracts the current row number from the first data row number in the table, and uses the MOD function to calculate the remainder when that value is divided by the value in A1. As a result, every *n*th cell (beginning with row 4) contains 0. Use the filter drop-down in cell B3 specify a filter that shows only the rows that contain a 0 in column B.

 NOTE

If you change the value in cell A1, you need to respecify the filter criteria for column B. (The rows will not hide automatically.)

Although this example uses a table (created using Insert⇨Tables⇨Table), the technique also works with a normal range of data as long as it has column headers. Choose Data⇨ Sort & Filter⇨Filter to enable filtering.

Plotting the Last *n* Data Points

You can use a technique that makes your chart show only the most recent data points in a column. For example, you can create a chart that always displays the most recent six months of data (see Figure 17-11).

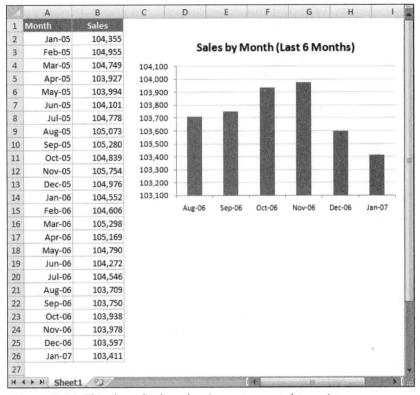

	A	B
1	**Month**	**Sales**
2	Jan-05	104,355
3	Feb-05	104,955
4	Mar-05	104,749
5	Apr-05	103,927
6	May-05	103,994
7	Jun-05	104,101
8	Jul-05	104,778
9	Aug-05	105,073
10	Sep-05	105,280
11	Oct-05	104,839
12	Nov-05	105,754
13	Dec-05	104,976
14	Jan-06	104,552
15	Feb-06	104,606
16	Mar-06	105,298
17	Apr-06	105,169
18	May-06	104,790
19	Jun-06	104,272
20	Jul-06	104,546
21	Aug-06	103,709
22	Sep-06	103,750
23	Oct-06	103,938
24	Nov-06	103,978
25	Dec-06	103,597
26	Jan-07	103,411
27		

Figure 17-11: This chart displays the six most recent data points.

The instructions that follow describe how to create the chart in this figure:

1. Create a worksheet like the one shown in Figure 17-11, and create a chart that uses the data in A1: B26.

2. Choose Formulas⇨Defined Names⇨Name Manager to bring up the Name Manager dialog box.

3. Click New to display the New Name dialog box.

4. In the Name field, enter **Dates**. In the Refers To field, enter this formula:

   ```
   =OFFSET(Sheet1!$A$1,COUNTA(Sheet1!$A:$A)-6,0,6,0)
   ```

   Notice that the OFFSET function refers to cell A1 (not the cell with the first month).

5. Click OK to close the New Name dialog box.

Part V

6. Click New to define the second name.

7. In the New Name dialog box, type **Sales** in the Names in Workbook field. Enter this formula in the Refers To field:

```
=OFFSET(Sheet1!$B$1,COUNTA(Sheet1!$B:$B)-6,0,6,1)
```

8. Click OK, and then click Close to close the dialog box Name Manager dialog box.

9. Activate the chart and select the data series.

10. In the SERIES formula, replace the range references with the names that you defined in Steps 4 and 7. The formula should read:

```
=SERIES(,Sheet1!Dates,Sheet1!Sales,1)
```

 NOTE

To plot a different number of data points, adjust the formulas entered in Steps 4 and 7. Replace all occurrences of 6 with your new value.

 ON THE CD

The example in this section, named `plot last n data points.xlsx`, is available on the companion CD-ROM.

Selecting a Series from a Combo Box

Figure 17-12 shows a chart that displays data as specified by a drop-down control (known as a *combo box*). The chart uses the data in A1:D2, but the month selected in the combo box determines the contents of these cells. Range A6:D17 contains the monthly data, and formulas in A2:D2 display the data using the value in cell F1 (which is linked to the combo box). For example, when cell F1 contains the value 4, the chart displays data for April (the fourth month).

The formula in cell A2 is

```
=INDEX(A6:A17,$F$1)
```

This formula was copied to B2:D2.

The key here is to get the combo box to display the month names and place the selected month index into cell F1. To create the combo box, follow these steps:

1. Make sure that Excel's Developer tab is displayed. If you don't see this tab, choose Office Button⇨Excel Options. Click the Popular tab and place a check mark next to Show Developer Tab in the Ribbon.

2. Choose Developer⇨Controls⇨Insert, and click the Combo Box icon in the Form Controls section.

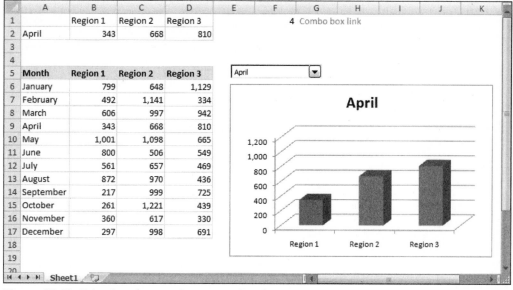

Figure 17-12: Selecting data to plot using a Combo Box.

3. Drag in the worksheet to create the control.

4. Right-click the combo box and choose Format Control to display the Format Control dialog box.

5. In the Format Control dialog box, click the Control tab.

6. Specify A6:A17 as the Input Range, and F1 as the Cell link.

After you perform these steps, the combo box displays the month names and places the index number of the selected month into cell F1. The formulas in row 2 display the appropriate data, which displays in the chart.

ON THE CD

This example is available on the companion CD-ROM. The filename is `chart from combo box.xlsx`.

Plotting Mathematical Functions

The examples in this section demonstrate how to plot mathematical functions that use one variable (a 2-D line chart) and two variables (a 3-D surface chart). The examples make use of Excel's Data Table feature, which enables you to evaluate a formula with varying input values.

NOTE

A Data Table is not the same as a table, created using Insert➪Tables➪Table.

PLOTTING FUNCTIONS WITH ONE VARIABLE

An XY chart is useful for plotting various mathematical and trigonometric functions. For example, Figure 17-13 shows a plot of the SIN function. The chart plots y for values of x (expressed in radians) from –5 to +5 in increments of 0.5. Each pair of x and y values appears as a data point in the chart, and the points connect with a line.

TIP

Excel's trigonometric functions use angles expressed in radians. To convert degrees to radians, use the RADIANS function.

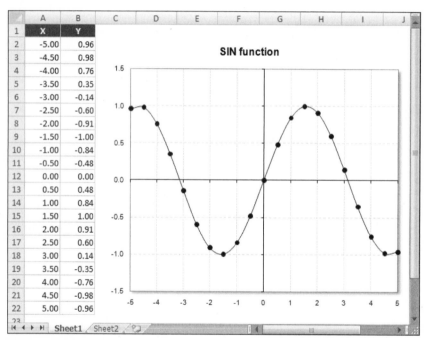

Figure 17-13: This chart plots the SIN(x).

The function is expressed as

```
y = SIN(x)
```

The corresponding formula in cell B2 (which is copied to the cells below) is

```
=SIN(A2)
```

Figure 17-14 shows a general-purpose, single-variable plotting application. The data for the chart is calculated by a Data Table in columns I:J. Follow these steps to use this application:

1. Enter a formula in cell B7. The formula should contain at least one x variable. In the figure, the formula in cell B3 is

   ```
   =SIN(PI() *x) * (PI() *x)
   ```

2. Enter the minimum value for x in cell B8.

3. Enter the maximum value for x cell B9.

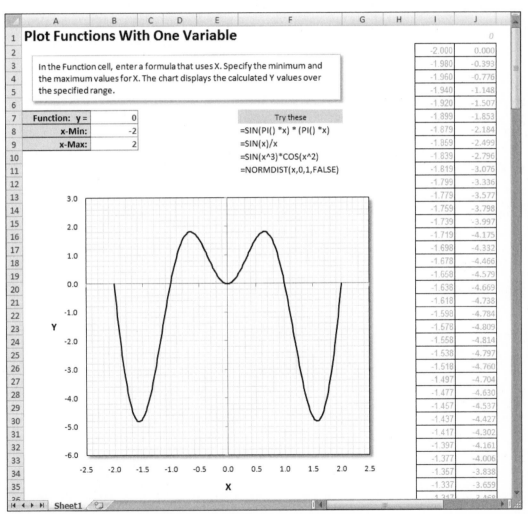

Figure 17-14: A general-purpose, single-variable plotting workbook.

The formula in cell B3 displays the value of y for the minimum value of x. The Data Table, however, evaluates the formula for 200 equally spaced values of x, and these values appear in the chart.

ON THE CD

This workbook, named `function plot 2D.xlsx`, is available on the companion CD-ROM.

PLOTTING FUNCTIONS WITH TWO VARIABLES

The preceding section describes how to plot functions that use a single variable (x). You also can plot functions that use two variables. For example, the following function calculates a value of z for various values of two variables $(x$ and $y)$:

```
z = SIN(x)*COS(y)
```

Figure 17-15 shows a surface chart that plots the value of z for 21 x values ranging from 2 to 5 (in 0.15 increments) and for 21 y values ranging from −3 to 0 (also in 0.15 increments).

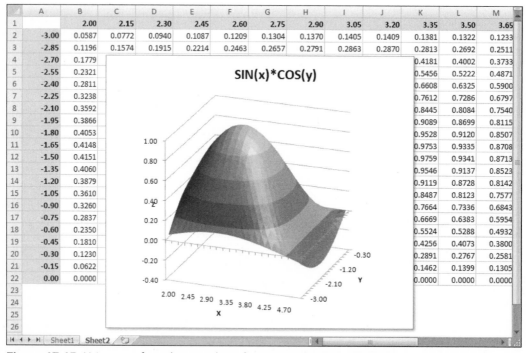

Figure 17-15: Using a surface chart to plot a function with two variables.

Figure 17-16 shows a general-purpose, two-variable plotting application, similar to the single-variable workbook described in the previous section. The data for the chart is a 25 x 25 data table in range M7:AL32 (not shown in the figure). To use this application

1. Enter a formula in cell B3. The formula should contain at least one x variable and at least one y variable. In the figure, the formula in cell B3 is

   =COS(y*x)

2. Enter the minimum x value in cell B4 and the maximum x value in cell B5.

3. Enter the minimum y value in cell B6 and the maximum y value in cell B7.

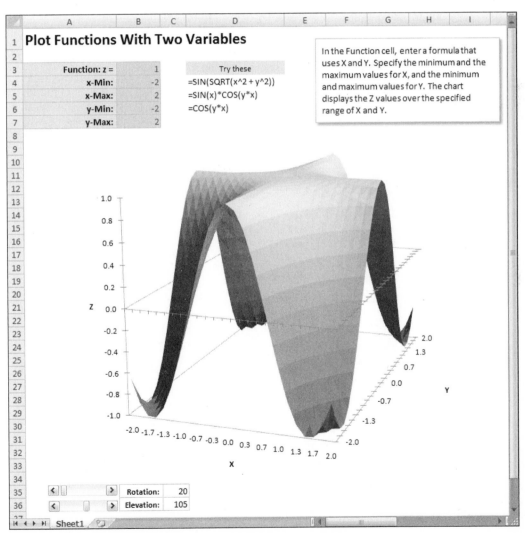

Figure 17-16: A general-purpose, two-variable plotting workbook.

Part V

The formula in cell B3 displays the value of z for the minimum values of x and y. The data table evaluates the formula for 25 equally spaced values of x and 25 equally spaced values of y. These values are plotted in the surface chart.

ON THE CD

This workbook, which is available on the companion CD-ROM, contains simple macros that enable you to easily change the rotation and elevation of the chart by using scroll-bars. The file is named `function plot 3D.xlsm`.

Plotting a Circle

You can create an XY chart that draws a perfect circle. To do so, you need two ranges: one for the x values and another for the y values. The number of data points in the series determines the smoothness of the circle. Or you can simply select the Smoothed Line option in the Format Data Series dialog box (Line Style tab) for the data series.

Figure 17-17 shows a chart that uses 13 points to create a circle. If you work in degrees, generate a series of values such as the ones shown in column A. The series starts with 0 and increases in 30-degree increments. If you work in radians (column B), the first series starts with 0 and increments by $\Pi/6$.

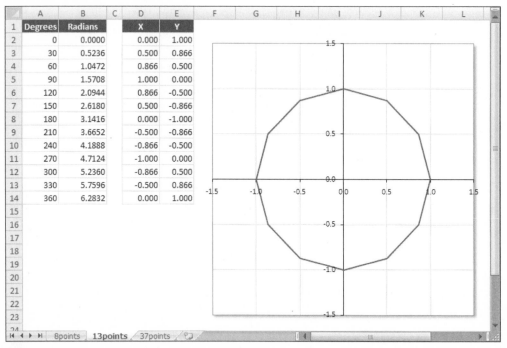

Figure 17-17: Creating a circle using an XY chart.

The ranges used in the chart appear in columns D and E. If you work in degrees, the formula in cell D2 is

```
=SIN(RADIANS(A2))
```

The formula in cell E2 is

```
=COS(RADIANS(A2))
```

If you work in radians, use this formula in cell D2:

```
=SIN(A2)
```

And use this formula in cell E2:

```
=COS(A2)
```

The formulas in cells D2 and E2 are copied down to subsequent rows.

To plot a circle with more data points, you need to adjust the increment value and the number of data points in column A (or column B if working in radians). The final value should be the same as those shown in row 14. In degrees, the increment is 360 divided by the number of data points minus 1. In radians, the increment is Π divided by the number of data points minus 1, divided by 2.

Figure 17-18 shows a general circle plotting application that uses 37 data points. In range H27:H29, you can specify the *x* origin, the *y* origin, and the radius for the circle (these are named cells). In the figure, the circle's origin is at 1,3 and it has a radius of 7.25.

The formula in cell D2 is:

```
=(SIN(RADIANS(A2))*radius)+x_origin
```

The formula in cell E2 is:

```
=(COS(RADIANS(A2))*radius)+y_origin
```

ON THE CD

This example, named `plot circles.xlsx`, is available on the companion CD-ROM.

Creating a Clock Chart

Figure 17-19 shows an XY chart formatted to look like a clock. It not only looks like a clock, but it also functions like a clock. There is really no reason why anyone would need to display a clock such as this on a worksheet, but creating the workbook was challenging, and you may find it instructive.

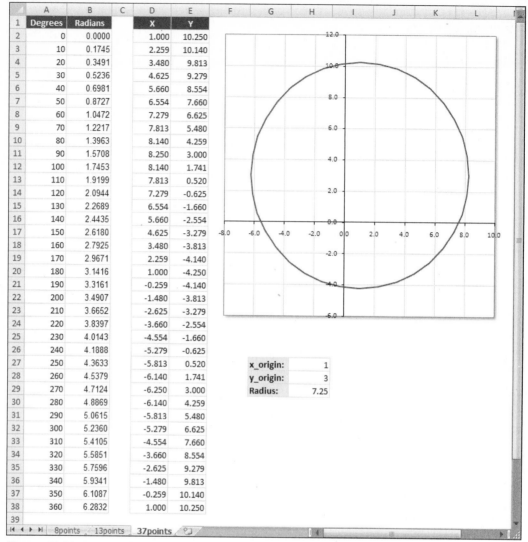

Figure 17-18: A general circle plotting application.

The chart uses four data series: one for the hour hand, one for the minute hand, one for the second hand, and one for the numbers. The last data series draws a circle with 12 points (but no line). The numbers consist of manually entered data labels. In addition, I added an oval shape on top of the chart.

The formulas listed in Table 17-2 use basic trigonometry to calculate the data series for the clock hands. (The range G4:L4 contains zero values, not formulas.)

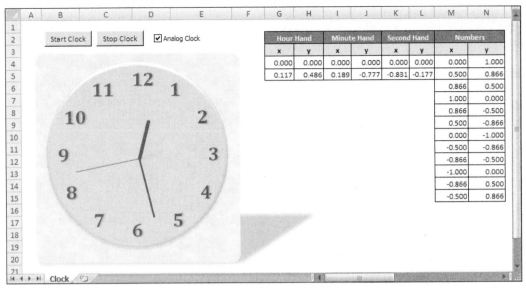

Figure 17-19: This fully functional clock is actually an XY chart in disguise.

TABLE 17-2 FORMULAS USED TO GENERATE A CLOCK CHART

Cell	Description	Formula
G5	Origin of hour hand	`=0.5*SIN((HOUR(NOW())+(MINUTE(NOW())/60))*(2*PI()/12))`
H5	End of hour hand	`=0.5*COS((HOUR(NOW())+(MINUTE(NOW())/60))*(2*PI()/12))`
I5	Origin of minute hand	`=0.8*SIN((MINUTE(NOW())+(SECOND(NOW())/60))*(2*PI()/60))`
J5	End of minute hand	`=0.8*COS((MINUTE(NOW())+(SECOND(NOW())/60))*(2*PI()/60))`
K5	Origin of second hand	`=0.85*SIN(SECOND(NOW())*(2*PI()/60))`
L5	End of second hand	`=0.85*COS(SECOND(NOW())*(2*PI()/60))`

This workbook uses a simple VBA procedure that schedules an event every second, which causes the clock to run.

Part V

In addition to the clock chart, the workbook contains a text box that displays the time using the NOW() function, as shown in Figure 17-20. Normally hidden behind the analog clock, you can display this text box by deselecting the Analog Clock check box. A simple VBA procedure attached to the check box hides and unhides the chart, depending on the status of the check box.

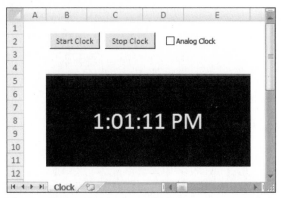

Figure 17-20: Displaying a digital clock in a worksheet is much easier but not as fun to create.

 ## ON THE CD

The workbook with the animated clock example appears on the companion CD-ROM. The filename is `clock chart.xlsx`.

When you examine the workbook, keep the following points in mind:

- The ChartObject, named *ClockChart,* covers up a range named *DigitalClock,* which is used to display the time digitally.

- The two buttons on the worksheet are from the Forms group (Developer⇨Controls⇨ Insert), and each has a VBA procedure assigned to it (`StartClock` and `StopClock`).

- Clicking the check box control executes a procedure named `cbClockType_Click`, which simply toggles the `Visible` property of the chart. When the chart is hidden, the digital clock is revealed.

- The `UpdateClock` procedure uses the `OnTime` method of the `Application` object. This method enables you to execute a procedure at a specific time. Before the `UpdateClock` procedure ends, it sets up a new `OnTime` event that occurs in one second. In other words, the `UpdateClock` procedure is called every second.

- The `UpdateClock` procedure inserts the following formula into the cell named *DigitalClock:*

  ```
  =NOW()
  ```

Inserting this formula causes the workbook to calculate, updating the clock.

Creating Awesome Designs

Figure 17-21 shows an example of an XY chart that displays hypocycloid curves using random values. This type of curve is the same as that generated by Hasbro's popular Spirograph toy, which you may remember from childhood.

	A	B	C	D	E	F	G	H	I	J	K
1		*Press F9 for*		a_inc:	8.80						
2		*a new chart*		b_inc:	5.50						
3				t_inc:	-2.10						
4											
5	**a**	**b**	**t**	**x**	**y**						
6	1.0	1.0	0.0	1.0	0.0						
7	9.8	6.5	-2.1	1.5	2.8						
8	18.6	12.0	-4.2	-11.3	14.6						
9	27.4	17.5	-6.3	-6.1	-7.3						
10	36.2	23.0	-8.4	-4.4	-34.1						
11	45.0	28.5	-10.5	20.1	8.7						
12	53.8	34.0	-12.6	36.6	28.9						
13	62.6	39.5	-14.7	-39.0	9.6						
14	71.4	45.0	-16.8	-53.0	4.6						
15	80.2	50.5	-18.9	35.7	-51.6						
16	89.0	56.0	-21.0	36.9	-38.3						
17	97.8	61.5	-23.1	13.4	86.4						
18	106.6	67.0	-25.2	-6.5	46.0						
19	115.4	72.5	-27.3	-89.5	-66.8						
20	124.2	78.0	-29.4	-9.4	-35.6						
21	133.0	83.5	-31.5	131.5	-18.8						
22	141.8	89.0	-33.6	11.3	35.5						

Sheet1

Figure 17-21: A hypocycloid curve.

ON THE CD

The companion CD-ROM contains two hypocycloid workbooks: the simple example shown in Figure 17-18 (named `hypocycloid chart.xlsx`), and a much more complex example (named `hypocycloid animated.xlsm`) that adds animation and a few other accoutrements. The animated version uses VBA macros.

The chart uses data in columns D and E (the *x* and *y* ranges). These columns contain formulas that rely on data in columns A through C. The formulas in columns A through C rely on the values stored in E1:E3. The data column for the *x* values (column D) consists of the following formula:

```
=(A6-B6)*COS(C6)+B6*COS((A6/B6-1)*C6)
```

The formula in the *y* values (column E) is as follows:

```
=(A6-B6)*SIN(C6)-B6*SIN((A6/B6-1)*C6)
```

Pressing F9 recalculates the worksheet, which generates new random increment values for E1:E3, and creates a new display in the chart. The variety (and beauty) of charts generated using these formulas may amaze you.

Part V

Working with Trendlines

With some charts, you may want to plot a trendline that describes the data. A *trendline* points out general trends in your data. In some cases, you can forecast future data with trendlines. A single series can have more than one trendline.

To add a trendline, select the chart series and then choose Chart Tools⇨Layout⇨ Analysis⇨Trendline. This drop-down control displays options for four types of trendlines. For additional options (and more control over the trendline) choose More Trendline Options, which displays the Trendline Options tab of the Format Trendline dialog box (see Figure 17-22).

Figure 17-22: The Format Trendline dialog box offers several types of automatic trendlines.

The type of trendline that you choose depends on your data. Linear trends are the most common type, but you can describe some data more effectively with another type.

The Trendline Options tab enables you to specify a name to appear in the legend and the number of periods that you want to forecast (if any). Additional options enable you to set the intercept value, specify that the equation used for the trendline should appear on the chart, and choose whether the R-squared value appears on the chart.

When Excel inserts a trendline, it may look like a new data series, but it's not. It's a new chart element with a name, such as Series 1 Trendline 1. And, of course, a trendline does not have a corresponding SERIES formula.

Linear Trendlines

Figure 17-23 shows two charts. The chart on the left depicts a data series without a trendline. As you can see, the data seems to be "linear" over time. The chart on the right is the same chart but with a linear trendline that shows the trend in the data.

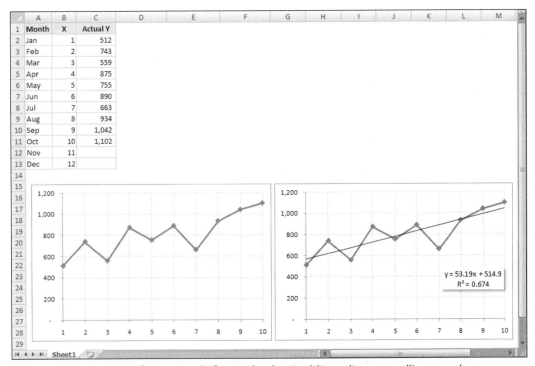

Figure 17-23: Before (left chart) and after (right chart) adding a linear trendline to a chart.

ON THE CD

The workbook used in this example is available on the companion CD-ROM. The file is named `linear trendline.xlsx`.

The second chart also uses the options to display the equation and the R-squared value. In this example, the equation is as follows:

```
y = 53.19x + 514.9
```

The R-squared value is 0.674

What do these numbers mean? You can describe a straight line with an equation of the form:

```
y = mx +b
```

For each value of x (the horizontal axis), you can calculate the predicted value of y (the value on the trendline) by using this equation. The variable m represents the slope of the line and b represents the y-intercept. For example, when x is 3 (for March) the predicted value of y is 674.47, calculated with this formula:

```
=(53.19*3)+514.9
```

The R-squared value, sometimes referred to as the *coefficient of determination,* ranges in value from 0 to 1. This value indicates how closely the estimated values for the trendline correspond to the actual data. A trendline is most reliable when its R-squared value is at or near 1.

CALCULATING THE SLOPE AND Y-INTERCEPT

As you know, Excel can display the equation for the trendline in a chart. This equation shows the slope *(m)* and y-intercept *(b)* of the best-fit trendline. You can calculate the value of the slope and y-intercept yourself, using the LINEST function in a formula.

Figure 17-24 shows 10 data points (x values in column B, y values in column C).

	A	B	C	D	E	F	G	H
1	Month	X	Actual Y				m	b
2	Jan	1	512				53.19394	514.9333
3	Feb	2	743					
4	Mar	3	559					
5	Apr	4	875					
6	May	5	755					
7	Jun	6	890					
8	Jul	7	663					
9	Aug	8	934					
10	Sep	9	1,042					
11	Oct	10	1,102					
12	Nov	11						
13	Dec	12						
14								

Figure 17-24: Using the LINEST function to calculate slope and y-intercept.

The formula that follows is a multicell array formula that displays its result (the slope and y-intercept) in two cells:

```
{=LINEST(C2:C11,B2:B11)}
```

To enter this formula, start by selecting two cells (in this example, G2:H2). Then type the formula (without the curly brackets), and press Ctrl+Shift+Enter. Cell G2 displays the slope; cell H2 displays the y-intercept.

CALCULATING PREDICTED VALUES

After you know the values for the slope and y-intercept, you can calculate the predicted y value for each x. Figure 17-25 shows the result. Cell E2 contains the following formula, which is copied down the column:

```
=(B2*$G$2)+$H$2
```

	A	B	C	D	E	F	G	H
1	Month	X	Actual Y		Predicted Y		m	b
2	Jan	1	512		568.13		53.19394	514.9333
3	Feb	2	743		621.32			
4	Mar	3	559		674.52			
5	Apr	4	875		727.71			
6	May	5	755		780.90			
7	Jun	6	890		834.10			
8	Jul	7	663		887.29			
9	Aug	8	934		940.48			
10	Sep	9	1,042		993.68			
11	Oct	10	1,102		1,046.87			
12	Nov	11			1,100.07			
13	Dec	12			1,153.26			
14								

Sheet1

Figure 17-25: Column E contains formulas that calculate the predicted values for y.

The calculated values in column E represent the values used to plot the linear trendline.

You can also calculate predicted values of y without first computing the slope and y-intercept. You do so with an array formula that uses the TREND function. Select D2:D11, type the following formula (without the curly brackets), and press Ctrl+Shift+Enter:

```
{=TREND(C2:C11,B2:B11)}
```

LINEAR FORECASTING

When your chart contains a trendline, you can instruct Excel to forecast and plot additional values. You do this on the Trendline Options tab in the Format Trendline dialog box. Just specify the number of periods to forecast. Figure 17-26 shows a chart that forecasts results for two subsequent periods.

If you know the values of the slope and y-intercept (see "Calculating the Slope and y-Intercept," earlier in the chapter), you can calculate forecasts for other values of x. For example, to calculate the value of y when $x = 11$ (November), use the following formula:

```
=(53.194*11)+514.93
```

Part V

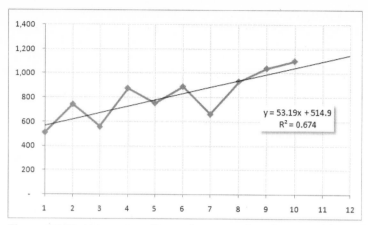

Figure 17-26: Using a trendline to forecast values for two additional periods of time.

You can also forecast values by using the FORECAST function. The following formula, for example, forecasts the value for November (that is, $x = 11$) using known x and known y values:

```
=FORECAST(11,C2:C11,B2:B11)
```

CALCULATING R-SQUARED

The accuracy of forecasted values depends on how well the linear trendline fits your actual data. The value of R-squared represents the degree of fit. R-squared values closer to 1 indicate a better fit — and more accurate predictions. In other words, you can interpret R-squared as the proportion of the variance in y attributable to the variance in x.

As described previously, you can instruct Excel to display the R-squared value in the chart. Or you can calculate it directly in your worksheet using the RSQ function. The following formula calculates R-squared for x values in B2:B11 and y values for C2:C11.

```
=RSQ(B2:B11,C2:C11)
```

 CAUTION

The value of R-squared calculated by the RSQ function is valid only for a linear trendline.

Working with Nonlinear Trendlines

Besides linear trendlines, an Excel chart can display trendlines of the following types:

- **Logarithmic:** Used when the rate of change in the data increases or decreases quickly, and then flattens out.

- **Power:** Used when the data consists of measurements that increase at a specific rate. The data cannot contain zero or negative values.

- **Exponential:** Used when data values rise or fall at increasingly higher rates. The data cannot contain zero or negative values.

- **Polynomial:** Used when data fluctuates. You can specify the order of the polynomial (from 2 to 6) depending on the number of fluctuations in the data.

NOTE

The Trendline Options tab in the Format Trendline dialog box offers the option of Moving Average, which really isn't a trendline. This option, however, can be useful for smoothing out "noisy" data. The Moving Average option enables you to specify the number of data points to include in each average. For example, if you select 5, Excel averages every group of five data points, and displays the points on a trendline.

Earlier in this chapter, I describe how to calculate the slope and y-intercept for the linear equation that describes a linear trendline. Nonlinear trendlines also have equations, as described in the sections that follow.

ON THE CD

The companion CD-ROM contains a workbook with the nonlinear trendline examples described in this section. The file is named `nonlinear trendlines.xlsx`.

LOGARITHMIC TRENDLINE

The equation for a logarithmic trendline is as follows:

```
y = (c * LN(x)) - b
```

Figure 17-27 shows a chart with a logarithmic trendline added. A single array formula in E2:F2 calculates the values for c and b. The formula is

```
{=LINEST(C2:C11,LN(B2:B11))}
```

Column C shows the predicted y values for each value of x, using the calculated values for b and c. For example, the formula in cell C2 is

```
=($E$2*LN(A2))+$F$2
```

As you can see, a logarithmic trendline does not provide a good fit for this data. The R-square value is low, and the trendline does not match the data.

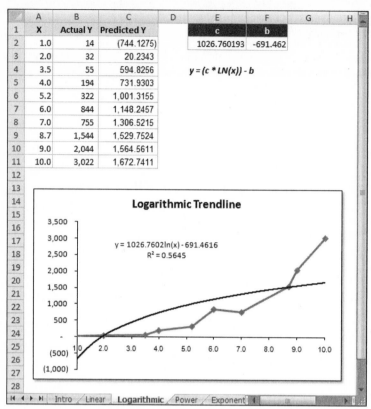

Figure 17-27: A chart displaying a logarithmic trendline.

POWER TRENDLINE

The equation for a power trendline looks like this:

```
y = c * x^b
```

Figure 17-28 shows a chart with a power trendline added. The first element in a two-cell array formula in E2:F2 calculates the values for b. The formula is

```
=LINEST(LN(B2:B11),LN(A2:A11),,TRUE)
```

The following formula, in cell F3, calculates the value for c:

```
=EXP(F2)
```

Column C shows the predicted y values for each value of x, using the calculated values for b and c. For example, the formula in cell C2 is as follows:

```
=$F$3*(A2^$E$2)
```

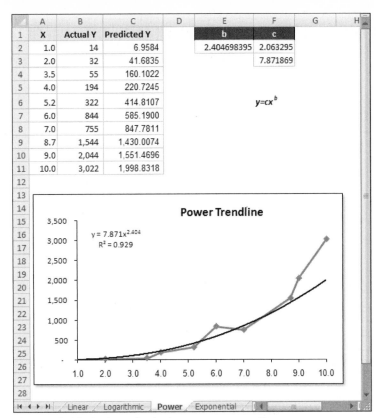

Figure 17-28: A chart displaying a power trendline.

EXPONENTIAL TRENDLINE

The equation for an exponential trendline looks like this:

```
y = c * EXP(b * x)
```

Figure 17-29 shows a chart with an exponential trendline added. The first element in a two-cell array formula in F2:G2 calculates the values for *b*. The formula is

```
{=LINEST(LN(B2:B11),A2:A11)}
```

The following formula, in cell G3, calculates the value for *c*:

```
=EXP(G2)
```

Column C shows the predicted *y* values for each value of *x*, using the calculated values for *b* and *c*. For example, the formula in cell C2 is as follows:

```
=$G$3*EXP($F$2*A2)
```

Part V

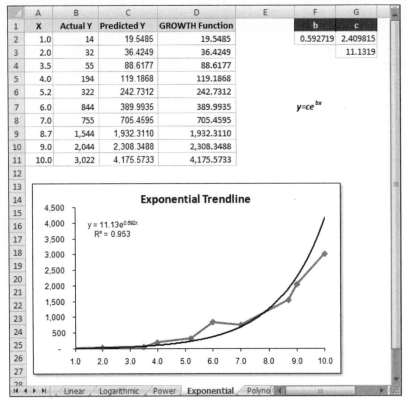

Figure 17-29: A chart displaying an exponential trendline.

Column D uses the GROWTH function in an array formula to generate predicted y values. The array formula, entered in D2:D10, appears like this:

```
{=GROWTH(B2:B11,A2:A11)}
```

POLYNOMIAL TRENDLINE

When you request a polynomial trendline, you also need to specify the order of the polynomial (ranging from 2 through 6). The equation for a polynomial trendline depends on the order. The following equation, for example, is for a third-order polynomial trendline:

```
y = (c3 * x^3) + (c2 * x^2) + (c1 * x^1) + b
```

Notice that there are three c coefficients (one for each order).

Figure 17-30 shows a chart with a third-order polynomial trendline added. A four-element array formula entered in F2:I2 calculates the values for each of three c coefficients and the b coefficient. The formula is

```
{=LINEST(B2:B11,A2:A11^{1,2,3})}
```

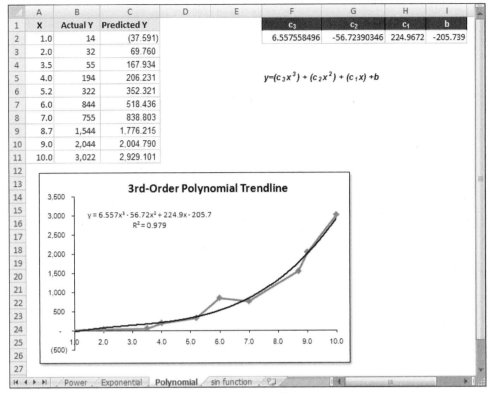

	A	B	C	D	E	F	G	H	I
1	**X**	**Actual Y**	**Predicted Y**			c_3	c_2	c_1	b
2	1.0	14	(37.591)			6.557558496	-56.72390346	224.9672	-205.739
3	2.0	32	69.760						
4	3.5	55	167.934						
5	4.0	194	206.231			$y=(c_3x^3)+(c_2x^2)+(c_1x)+b$			
6	5.2	322	352.321						
7	6.0	844	518.436						
8	7.0	755	838.803						
9	8.7	1,544	1,776.215						
10	9.0	2,044	2,004.790						
11	10.0	3,022	2,929.101						

3rd-Order Polynomial Trendline

$y = 6.557x^3 - 56.72x^2 + 224.9x - 205.7$
$R^2 = 0.979$

Power Exponential **Polynomial** sin function

Figure 17-30: A chart displaying a polynomial trendline.

Column C shows the predicted y values for each value of x, using the calculated values for b and the three c coefficients. For example, the formula in cell C2 is

```
=($F$2*A2^3)+($G$2*A2^2)+($H$2*A2)+$I$2
```

Chapter 18

Pivot Tables

IN THIS CHAPTER

◆ An introduction to pivot tables

◆ How to create a pivot table from a worksheet database or table

◆ How to group items in a pivot table

◆ How to create a calculated field or a calculated item in a pivot table

Excel's pivot table feature is perhaps the most technologically sophisticated component in Excel. This chapter may seem a bit out of place in a book devoted to formulas. After all, a pivot table does its job *without* using formulas. That's exactly the point. If you haven't yet discovered the power of pivot tables, this chapter will demonstrate how using a pivot table can serve as an excellent alternative to creating many complex formulas.

About Pivot Tables

A *pivot table* is essentially a dynamic summary report generated from a database. The database can reside in a worksheet or in an external file. A pivot table can help transform endless rows and columns of numbers into a meaningful presentation of the data.

For example, a pivot table can create frequency distributions and cross-tabulations of several different data dimensions. In addition, you can display subtotals and any level of detail that you want. Perhaps the most innovative aspect of a pivot table lies in its interactivity. After you create a pivot table, you can rearrange the information in almost any way imaginable and also insert special formulas that perform new calculations. You even can create post hoc groupings of summary items: for example, combine Northern Region totals with Western Region totals. And the icing on the cake is that with but a few mouse clicks, you can apply formatting to a pivot table to convert it to boardroom-quality-attractive.

Pivot tables have been around since Excel 97. Unfortunately, many users ignore this feature because they that think creating a pivot table is too complicated. The pivot table feature in Excel 2007 is vastly improved, and creating and working with pivot tables is easier than ever. One minor drawback to using a pivot table is that unlike a formula-based summary report, a pivot table does not update automatically when you change the source data. This does not pose a serious problem, however, because a single click of the Refresh button forces a pivot table to use the latest data.

A Pivot Table Example

The best way to understand the concept of a pivot table is to see one. Start with Figure 18-1, which shows a portion of the data used in creating the pivot table in this chapter.

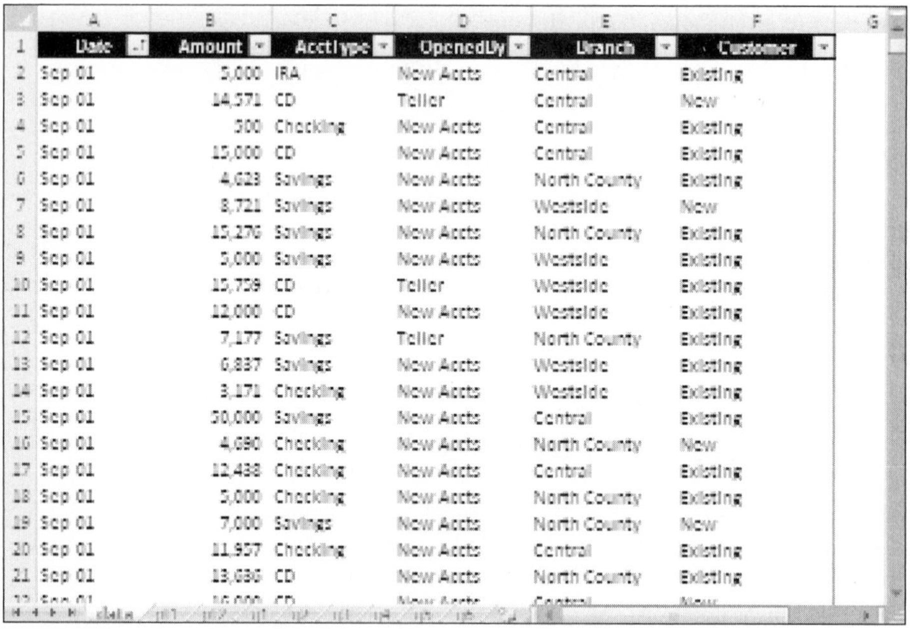

	A	B	C	D	E	F
1	Date	Amount	AcctType	OpenedBy	Branch	Customer
2	Sep 01	5,000	IRA	New Accts	Central	Existing
3	Sep 01	14,571	CD	Teller	Central	New
4	Sep 01	500	Checking	New Accts	Central	Existing
5	Sep 01	15,000	CD	New Accts	Central	Existing
6	Sep 01	4,623	Savings	New Accts	North County	Existing
7	Sep 01	8,721	Savings	New Accts	Westside	New
8	Sep 01	15,276	Savings	New Accts	North County	Existing
9	Sep 01	5,000	Savings	New Accts	Westside	Existing
10	Sep 01	15,759	CD	Teller	Westside	Existing
11	Sep 01	12,000	CD	New Accts	Westside	Existing
12	Sep 01	7,177	Savings	Teller	North County	Existing
13	Sep 01	6,837	Savings	New Accts	Westside	Existing
14	Sep 01	3,171	Checking	New Accts	Westside	Existing
15	Sep 01	50,000	Savings	New Accts	Central	Existing
16	Sep 01	4,690	Checking	New Accts	North County	New
17	Sep 01	12,438	Checking	New Accts	Central	Existing
18	Sep 01	5,000	Checking	New Accts	North County	Existing
19	Sep 01	7,000	Savings	New Accts	North County	New
20	Sep 01	11,957	Checking	New Accts	Central	Existing
21	Sep 01	13,686	CD	New Accts	North County	Existing

Figure 18-1: This table is used to create a pivot table.

This table comprises a month's worth of new account information for a three-branch bank. The table contains 712 rows, and each row represents a new account. The table has the following columns:

- The date when the account was opened

- The opening amount

- The account type: CD, checking, savings, or IRA (Individual Retirement Account)

- Who opened the account: a teller or a new-account representative

- The branch at which it was opened: Central, Westside, or North County

- The type of customer: An existing customer or a new customer

 ON THE CD

This workbook, named `bank accounts.xlsx`, is available on the companion CD-ROM.

The bank accounts database contains quite a bit of information, but in its current form, the data doesn't reveal much. To make the data more useful, you need to summarize it. Summarizing a database is essentially the process of answering questions about the data. Following are a few questions that may be of interest to the bank's management:

- What is the daily total new deposit amount for each branch?

- How many accounts were opened at each branch, broken down by account type?

- What's the dollar distribution of the different account types?

- What types of accounts do tellers open most often?

- How does the Central branch compare to the other two branches?

- In which branch do tellers open the most checking accounts for new customers?

You can, of course, spend time sorting the data and creating formulas to answer these questions. Often, however, a pivot table is a much better choice. Creating a pivot table takes only a few seconds, doesn't require a single formula, and produces a nice-looking report. In addition, pivot tables are much less prone to error than creating formulas.

By the way, I provide answers to these questions later in the chapter by presenting several additional pivot tables created from the data.

Figure 18-2 shows a pivot table created from the bank data. This pivot table shows the amount of new deposits, broken down by branch and account type. This particular summary represents one of dozens of summaries that you can produce from this data.

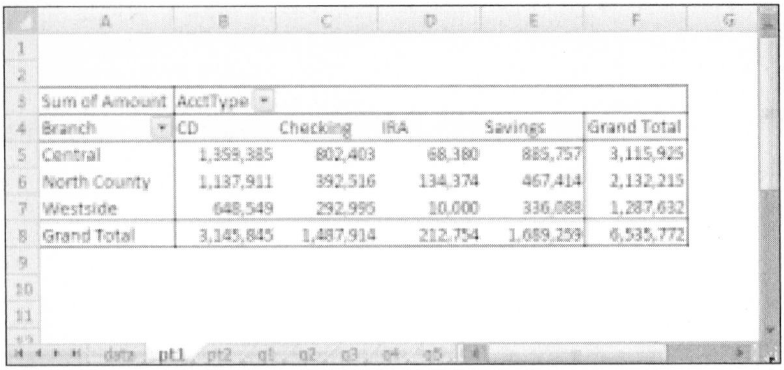

Sum of Amount	AcctType				
Branch	CD	Checking	IRA	Savings	Grand Total
Central	1,359,385	802,403	68,380	885,757	3,115,925
North County	1,137,911	392,516	134,374	467,414	2,132,215
Westside	648,549	292,995	10,000	336,088	1,287,632
Grand Total	3,145,845	1,487,914	212,754	1,689,259	6,535,772

Figure 18-2: A simple pivot table.

Figure 18-3 shows another pivot table generated from the bank data. This pivot table uses a drop-down Report Filter for the Customer item (in row 1). In the figure, the pivot table displays the data only for Existing customers. (The user can also select New or All from the drop-down control.) Notice the change in the orientation of the table. For this pivot table, branches appear as column labels, and account types appear as row labels. This change, which took about five seconds to make, is another example of the flexibility of a pivot table.

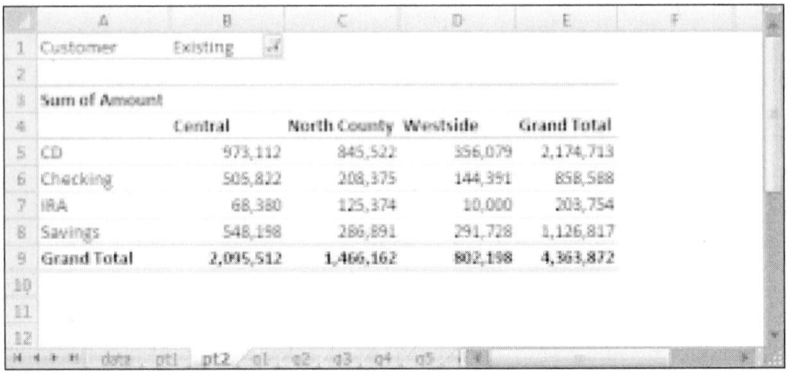

Customer	Existing			
Sum of Amount				
	Central	North County	Westside	Grand Total
CD	973,112	845,522	356,079	2,174,713
Checking	505,822	208,375	144,391	858,588
IRA	68,380	125,374	10,000	203,754
Savings	548,198	286,891	291,728	1,126,817
Grand Total	2,095,512	1,466,162	802,198	4,363,872

Figure 18-3: A pivot table that uses a report filter.

Data Appropriate for a Pivot Table

A pivot table requires that your data be in the form of a rectangular database. You can store the database in either a worksheet range (which can be a normal range, or a table created by using Insert⇨Tables⇨Table) or an external database file. Although Excel can generate a pivot table from any database, not all databases benefit.

Pivot Table Terminology

Understanding the terminology associated with pivot tables is the first step in mastering this feature. Refer to the accompanying figure to get your bearings.

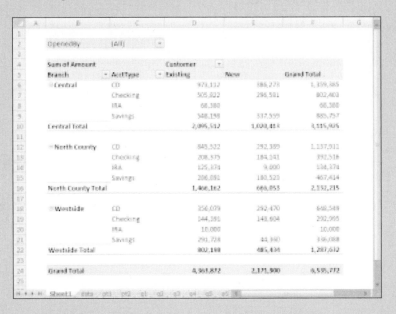

- **Column labels:** A field that has a column orientation in the pivot table. Each item in the field occupies a column. In the figure, Customer represents a column field that contains two items (Existing and New). You can have nested column fields.

- **Grand totals:** A row or column that displays totals for all cells in a row or column in a pivot table. You can specify that grand totals be calculated for rows, columns, or both (or neither). The pivot table in the figure shows grand totals for both rows and columns.

- **Group:** A collection of items treated as a single item. You can group items manually or automatically (group dates into months, for example). The pivot table in the figure does not have any defined groups.

- **Item:** An element in a field that appears as a row or column header in a pivot table. In the figure, Existing and New are items for the Customer field. The Branch field has three items: Central, North County, and Westside. AcctType has four items: CD, Checking, IRA, and Savings.

- **Refresh:** Recalculates the pivot table after making changes to the source data.

continued

continued

- **Row labels:** A field that has a row orientation in the pivot table. Each item in the field occupies a row. You can have nested row fields. In the figure, Branch and AcctType both represent row fields.

- **Source data:** The data used to create a pivot table. It can reside in a worksheet or an external database.

- **Subtotals:** A row or column that displays subtotals for detail cells in a row or column in a pivot table. The pivot table in the figure displays subtotals for each branch.

- **Table Filter:** A field that has a page orientation in the pivot table — similar to a slice of a three-dimensional cube. You can any number of items (or all items) in a page field at one time. In the figure, OpenedBy represents a page field that displays the New Accts item. In previous version of Excel, a table filter was known as a Page field.

- **Values area:** The cells in a pivot table that contain the summary data. Excel offers several ways to summarize the data (sum, average, count, and so on).

Generally speaking, fields in the database table consist of two types:

- **Data:** Contains a value or data to be summarized. For the bank account example, the Amount field is a data field.

- **Category:** Describes the data. For the bank account data, the Date, AcctType, OpenedBy, Branch, and Customer fields are category fields because they describe the data in the Amount field.

A single database table can have any number of data fields and category fields. When you create a pivot table, you usually want to summarize one or more of the data fields. Conversely, the values in the category fields appear in the pivot table as rows, columns, or filters.

Exceptions exist, however, and you may find Excel's pivot table feature useful even for a database that doesn't contain numerical data fields. In such a case, the pivot table provides counts rather than sums.

Figure 18-4 shows an example of an Excel range that is *not* appropriate for a pivot table. This range contains descriptive information about each value, but it's not set up as a table. In fact, this range resembles a pivot table summary.

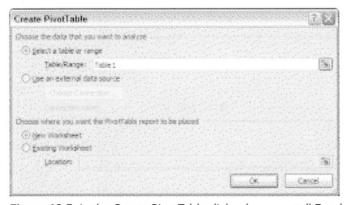

	A	B	C	D	E	F	G	H
1								
2			North	South	East	West		
3		Jan	132	233	314	441		
4		Feb	143	251	314	447		
5		Mar	172	252	345	450		
6		Apr	184	290	365	452		
7		May	212	299	401	453		
8		Jun	239	317	413	457		
9		Jul	249	350	427	460		
10		Aug	263	354	448	468		
11		Sep	291	373	367	472		
12		Oct	294	401	392	479		
13		Nov	302	437	495	484		
14		Dec	305	466	504	490		
15								

Figure 18-4: This range is not appropriate for a pivot table.

Creating a Pivot Table

In this section, I describe the basic steps required to create a pivot table, using the bank account data. Creating a pivot table is an interactive process. It's not at all uncommon to experiment with various layouts until you find one that you're satisfied with.

Specifying the Data

If your data is in a worksheet range or table, select any cell in that range and then choose Insert⇨Tables⇨PivotTable, which displays the dialog box shown in Figure 18-5.

Figure 18-5: In the Create PivotTable dialog box, you tell Excel where the data is and then specify a location for the pivot table.

Excel attempts to guess the range, based on the location of the active cell. If you're creating a pivot table from an external data source, you need to select that option and then click Choose Connection to specify the data source.

 TIP

If you're creating a pivot table from data in a worksheet, it's a good idea to first create a table for the range (by choosing Insert⇨Tables⇨Table). Then, if you expand the table by adding new rows of data, Excel will refresh the pivot table without the need to manually indicate the new data range.

Specifying the Location for the Pivot Table

Use the bottom section of the Create PivotTable dialog box to indicate the location for your pivot table. The default location is on a new worksheet, but you can specify any range on any worksheet, including the worksheet that contains the data.

Click OK, and Excel creates an empty pivot table and displays its PivotTable Field List, as shown in Figure 18-6.

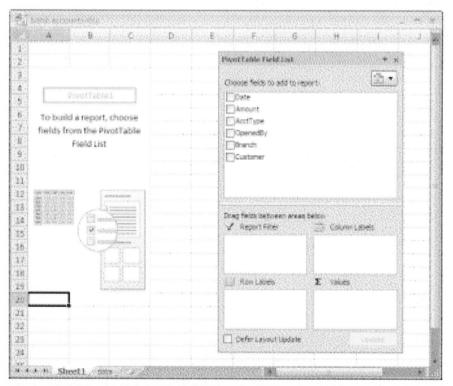

Figure 18-6: Use the PivotTable Field List to build the pivot table.

TIP

The PivotTable Field List is normally docked on the right side of Excel's window. By dragging its title bar, you can move it anywhere you like. Also, if you click a cell outside the pivot table, the PivotTable Field List is hidden.

Laying Out the Pivot Table

Next, set up the actual layout of the pivot table. You can do so by using either of these techniques:

- Drag the field names to one of the four boxes in the PivotTable Field List.
- Right-click a field name and choose its location from the shortcut menu.

NOTE

In previous versions of Excel, you could drag items from the field list directly into the appropriate area of the pivot table. This feature is still available, but it's turned off by default. To enable this feature, choose PivotTable Tools⇨Options⇨PivotTable Options⇨ Options to display the PivotTable Options dialog box. Click the Display tab and add a check mark next to Classic PivotTable Layout.

The following steps create the pivot table presented earlier in this chapter (see "A Pivot Table Example"). For this example, I drag the items from the top of the PivotTable Field List to the areas in the bottom of the PivotTable Field List.

1. Drag the Amount field into the Values area. At this point, the pivot table displays the total of all the values in the Amount column.

2. Drag the AcctType field into the Row Labels area. Now the pivot table shows the total amount for each of the account types.

3. Drag the Branch field into the Column Labels area. The pivot table shows the amount for each account type, crosstabulated by branch (see Figure 18-7).

Formatting the Pivot Table

Notice that the pivot table uses General number formatting. To change the number format used, select any value and choose PivotTable Tools⇨Options⇨Active Field⇨Field Settings to display the Data Field Settings dialog box. Click the Number Format button and change the number format.

You can apply any of several built-in styles to a pivot table. Select any cell in the pivot table and choose PivotTable Tools⇨Design⇨PivotTable Styles to select a style.

Part V

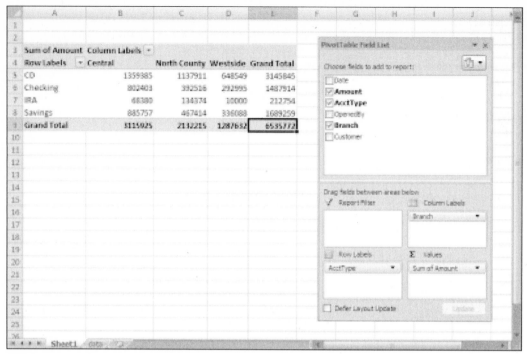

Figure 18-7: After a few simple steps, the pivot table shows a summary of the data.

Pivot Table Calculations

Pivot table data is most frequently summarized by using a sum. However, you can display your data using a number of different summary techniques. Select any cell in the Values area of your pivot table and then choose PivotTable Tools➪Options➪Active Field➪Field Settings to display the Data Field Settings dialog box. This dialog box has two tabs: Summarize By and Show Values As.

Use the Summarize By tab to select a different summary function. Your choices are Sum, Count, Average, Max, Min, Product, Count Numbers, StdDev, StdDevp, Var, and Varp.

To display your values in a different form, use the drop-down control in the Show Values As tab. Your choices are described in the following table.

Function	Result
Difference From	Displays data as the difference from the value of the Base item in the Base field
% Of	Displays data as a percentage of the value of the Base item in the Base field
% Difference From	Displays data as the percentage difference from the value of the Base item in the Base field
Running Total in	Displays the data for successive items in the Base field as a running total
% Of Row	Displays the data in each row or category as a percentage of the total for the row or category
% Of Column	Displays all the data in each column or series as a percentage of the total for the column or series
% Of Total	Displays data as a percentage of the grand total of all the data or data points in the report
Index	Calculates data as follows: ((value in cell) x (Grand Total of Grand Totals)) / ((Grand Row Total) x (Grand Column Total))

You also can use the controls in the PivotTable⇨Design⇨Layout group to control various elements in the pivot table. For example, you can choose to hide the grand totals if you prefer.

The PivotTable Tools⇨Options Show/Hide group contains additional options that affect the appearance of your pivot table. For example, you use the Show Field Headers button to toggle the display of the field headings.

Still more pivot table options are available in the PivotTable Options dialog box, shown in Figure 18-8. To display this dialog box, choose PivotTable Tools⇨Options⇨PivotTable Options⇨Options. Or, right-click any cell in the pivot table and choose Table Options from the shortcut menu.

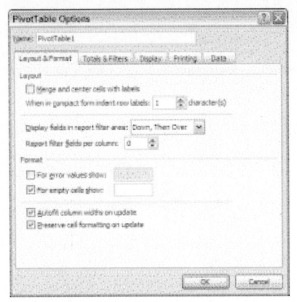

Figure 18-8: The PivotTable Options dialog box.

Modifying the Pivot Table

After you create a pivot table, changing it is easy. For example, you can add further summary information by using the PivotTable Field List. Figure 18-9 shows the pivot table after I dragged a second field (OpenedBy) to the Row Labels section in the PivotTable Field List.

Following are some tips on other pivot table modifications you can make:

- To remove a field from the pivot, select it in the bottom part of the PivotTable Field List and drag it away.

- If an area has more than one field, you can change the order in which the fields are listed by dragging the field names. Doing so affects the appearance of the pivot table.

- To temporarily remove a field from the pivot table, remove the check mark from the field name in the top part of the PivotTable Field List. The pivot table is redisplayed without that field. Place the check mark back on the field name, and it appears in its previous section.

- If you add a field to the Report Filter section, the field items appear in a drop-down list, which allows you to filter the displayed data by one or more items. Figure 18-10 shows an example. I dragged the Date field to the Report Filter area. The report is now showing the data only for a single day (which I selected from the drop-down list).

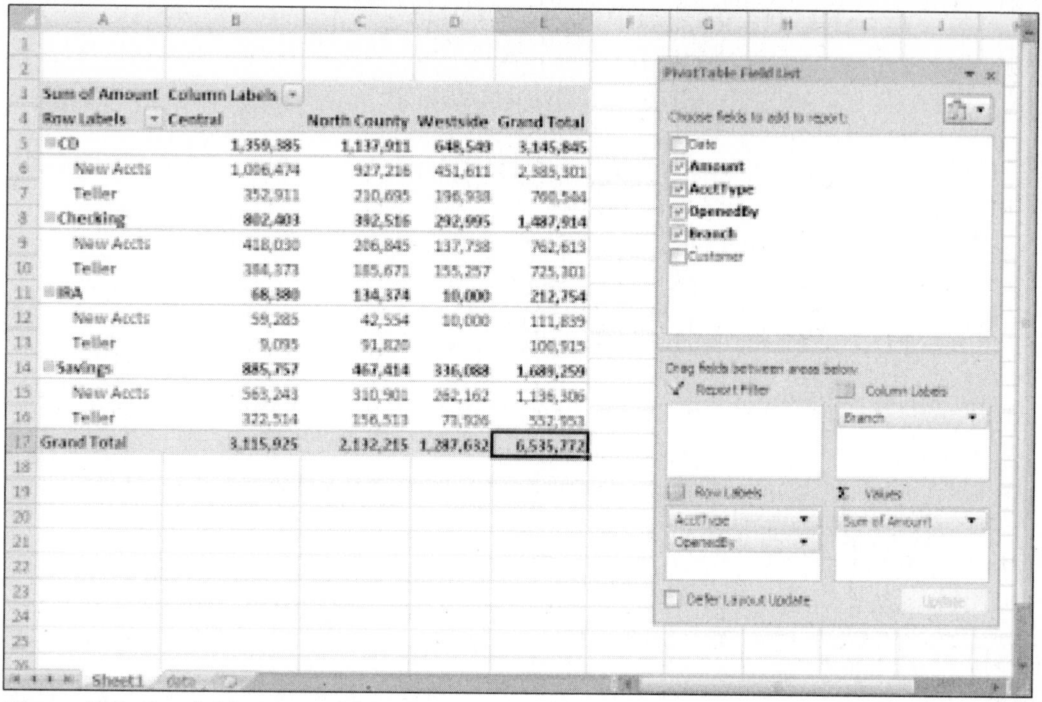

Figure 18-9: Two fields are used for row labels.

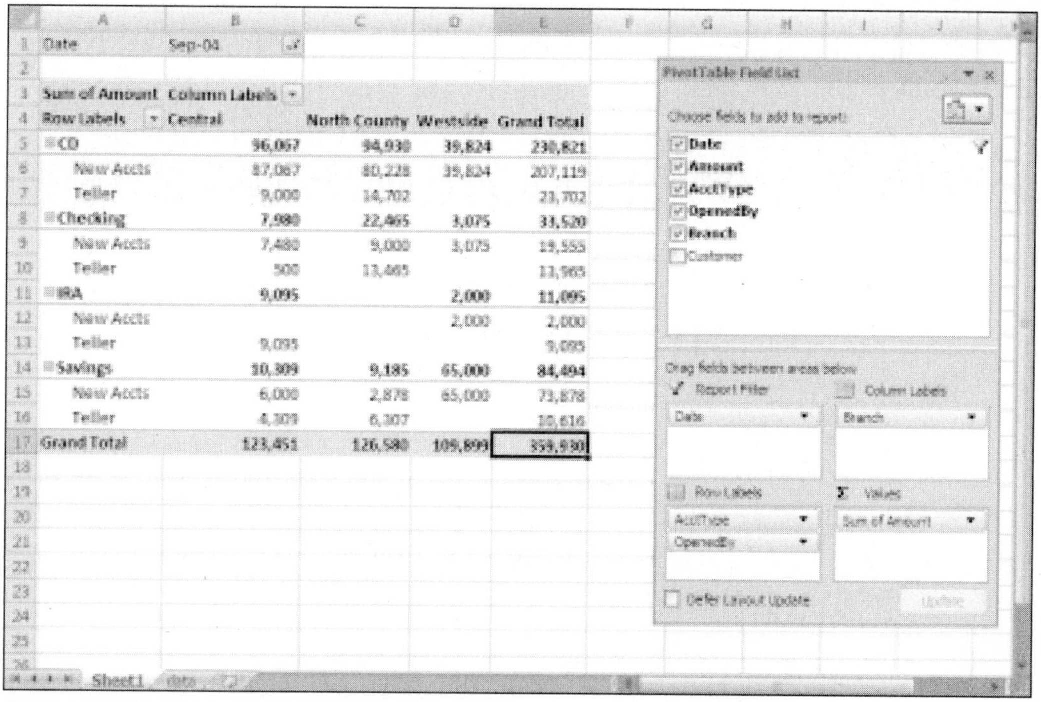

Figure 18-10: The pivot table is filtered by date.

Copying a Pivot Table

A pivot table is very flexible, but it does have some limitations. For example, you can't insert new rows or column, change any of the calculated values, or enter formulas within the pivot table. If you want to manipulate a pivot table in ways not normally permitted, make a copy of it.

To copy a pivot table, select the entire table and choose Home⇨Clipboard⇨Copy (or press Ctrl+C). Then select a new worksheet and choose Home⇨Clipboard⇨ Paste⇨Paste Values. The contents of the pivot table are copied to the new location so that you can do whatever you like to them. You also may want to copy the formats from the pivot table. Select the entire pivot table and then choose Home⇨ Clipboard⇨Format Painter. Then click the upper-left corner of the copied range.

Note that the copied information is not a pivot table, and it is no longer linked to the source data. If the source data changes, your copied pivot table does not reflect these changes.

More Pivot Table Examples

To demonstrate the flexibility of pivot tables, I've created some additional pivot tables. The examples use the bank account data and answer the questions posed earlier in this chapter (see "A Pivot Table Example").

Question 1

What is the daily total new deposit amount for each branch?

Figure 18-11 shows the pivot table that answers this question.

- The Branch field is in the Column Labels section.
- The Date field is in the Row Labels section.
- The Amount field is in the Value section and is summarized by Sum.

Note that the pivot table can also be sorted by any column. For example, you can sort the Grand Total column in descending order to find out which day of the month had the large amount of new funds. To sort, just right-click any cell in the column to sort and choose Sort from the shortcut menu.

Sum of Amount	Branch			
Date	Central	North County	Westside	Grand Total
Sep-01	135,345	57,402	51,488	244,235
Sep-02	79,642	81,794		161,436
Sep-03	59,119	65,530	20,117	144,766
Sep-04	123,451	126,580	109,899	359,930
Sep-05	101,480	50,294	97,415	249,189
Sep-06	188,018	91,724	52,738	332,480
Sep-07	271,227	196,188	53,525	520,940
Sep-08	67,999	24,123	47,329	139,451
Sep-09	14,475	41,248	36,172	91,895
Sep-10	91,367	24,238	8,512	124,117
Sep-11	104,166	32,018	89,258	225,442
Sep-12	70,300	43,621	39,797	153,718
Sep-13	143,921	176,698	29,075	349,694
Sep-14	117,800	114,418	36,064	268,282
Sep-15	88,566	41,635	78,481	208,682
Sep-16	79,579	21,152	6,534	107,265
Sep-17	56,187	29,380	7,037	92,604
Sep-18	46,673	42,882	41,300	130,855
Sep-19	208,916	213,728	53,721	476,365
Sep-20	125,276	140,739	56,444	322,459
Sep-21	79,355	35,753	3,419	118,527
Sep-22	132,403	149,447	97,210	379,060
Sep-23	56,106	15,823		71,929
Sep-24	75,606	23,285	28,457	127,348
Sep-25	143,283	111,740	57,371	314,194
Sep-26	150,139	29,040	94,310	271,489
Sep-27	56,379	72,948	43,472	172,799
Sep-28	62,192	43,217	12,128	117,537
Sep-29	186,955	33,570	36,359	256,884
Grand Total	3,115,925	2,132,215	1,287,632	6,535,772

Figure 18-11: This pivot table shows daily totals for each branch.

Question 2

How many accounts were opened at each branch, broken down by account type?

Figure 18-12 shows a pivot table that answers this question.

- The AcctType field is in the Column Labels section.
- The Branch field is in the Row Labels section.
- The Amount field is in the Value section and is summarized by Count.

	A	B	C	D	E	F
2						
3	Count of Amount	AcctType				
4	Branch		CD	Checking	IRA	Savings	Grand Total
5	Central		97	158	8	99	362
6	North County		60	61	15	61	197
7	Westside		54	59	5	35	153
8	Grand Total		211	278	28	195	712
9						
10						

Figure 18-12: This pivot table uses the Count function to summarize the data.

The most common summary function used in pivot tables is Sum. In this case, I changed the summary function to Count. To change the summary function to Count, right-click any cell in the Value area and choose Summarize Data By⇨Count from the shortcut menu.

Question 3

What's the dollar distribution of the different account types?

Figure 18-13 shows a pivot table that answers this question. For example, 253 of the new accounts were for an amount of $5,000 or less.

	A	B	C	D
2				
3		Data		
4	Amount	No. Accounts	Pct.	
5	1-5000	253	35.53%	
6	5001-10000	193	27.11%	
7	10001-15000	222	31.18%	
8	15001-20000	19	2.67%	
9	20001-25000	3	0.42%	
10	25001-30000	1	0.14%	
11	30001-35000	3	0.42%	
12	40001-45000	3	0.42%	
13	45001-50000	5	0.70%	
14	60001-65000	2	0.28%	
15	70001-75000	5	0.70%	
16	85001-90000	3	0.42%	
17	Grand Total	712	100.00%	
18				

Figure 18-13: This pivot table counts the number of accounts that fall into each value range.

This pivot table is unusual because it uses only one field: Amount.

- The Amount field is in the Row Labels section (grouped).

- The Amount field is also in the Values section and is summarized by Count.

- A third instance of the Amount field is the Values section, summarized by Percent of Total.

When I initially added the Amount field to the Row Labels section, the pivot table showed a row for each unique dollar amount. I right-clicked one of the Row Labels and chose Group. Then I used Excel's Grouping dialog box to set up bins of $5,000 increments.

The second instance of the Amount field (in the Values section) is summarized by Count. I right-clicked a value and chose Summarize Data By⇨Count.

I added another instance of Amount to the Values section, and I set it up to display the percentage. I used the Show Values As tab of the Data Field Settings dialog box and specified % of Total. To display the Data Field Settings dialog box, right-click any cell and choose Summarize Data As⇨More Options.

Question 4

What types of accounts do tellers open most often?

Figure 18-14 shows that the most common account opened by tellers is a Checking account.

- The AcctType field is in the Row Labels section.

- The OpenedBy field is in the Report Filters section.

- The Amount field is in the Values section (summarized by Count).

- A second instance of the Amount field is in the Values section (summarized by Percent of Total).

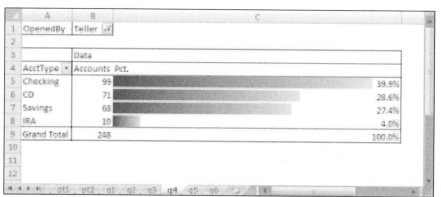

Figure 18-14: This pivot table uses a Report Filter to show only the Teller data.

This pivot table uses the OpenedBy field as a Report Filter and is showing the data only for Tellers. I sorted the data so that the largest value is at the top, and I also used conditional formatting to display data bars for the percentages.

 CROSS REF

Refer to Chapter 21 for more information about conditional formatting.

Question 5

How does the Central branch compare to the other two branches?

Figure 18-15 shows a pivot table that sheds some light on this rather vague question. It simply shows how the Central branch compares with the other two branches combined.

- The AcctType field is in the Row Labels section.

- The Branch field is in the Column Labels section.

- The Amount field is in the Values section.

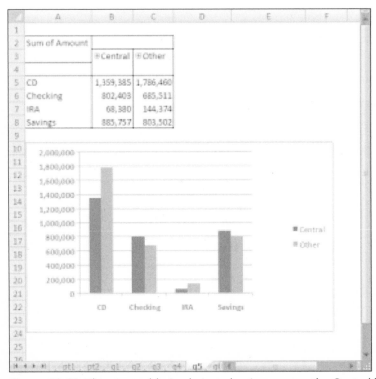

Figure 18-15: This pivot table (and pivot chart) compares the Central branch with the other two branches combined.

I grouped the North County and Westside branches together and named the group Other. The pivot table shows the amount, by account type. I also created a pivot chart for good measure.

Question 6

In which branch do tellers open the most checking accounts for new customers?

Figure 18-16 shows a pivot table that answers this question. At the Central branch, tellers opened 23 checking accounts for new customers.

- The Customer field is in the Report Filters section.
- The OpenedBy field is in the Report Filters section.
- The AcctType field is in the Report Filters section.
- The Branch field is in the Row Labels section.
- The Amount field is in the Values section, summarized by Count.

	A	B	C
1	Customer	New	
2	OpenedBy	Teller	
3	AcctType	Checking	
4			
5	Count of Amount		
6	Branch	Total	
7	Central	23	
8	North County	10	
9	Westside	10	
10	Grand Total	43	
11			
12			

Figure 18-16: This pivot table uses three report filters.

This pivot table uses three report filters. The Customer field is filtered to show only New, the OpenedBy field is filtered to show only Teller, and the AcctType field is filtered to show only Checking.

Part V

Grouping Pivot Table Items

One of the more useful features of a pivot table is the ability to combine items into groups. You can group items that appear as Row Labels or Column Labels. Excel offers two ways to group items:

- **Manually:** After creating the pivot table, select the items to be grouped and then choose PivotTable Tools⇨Options⇨Group⇨Group Selection. Or, you can right-click and choose Group from the shortcut menu.

- **Automatically:** If the items are numeric (or dates), use the Grouping dialog box to specify how you would like to group the items. Select any item in the Row Labels or Column Labels and then choose PivotTable Tools⇨Options⇨Group⇨Group Selection. Or, you can right-click and choose Group from the shortcut menu. In either case, Excel displays its Grouping dialog box.

A Manual Grouping Example

Figure 18-17 shows a pivot table created from an employee list in columns A:C, which has the following fields: Employee, Location, and Sex. The pivot table, in columns E:H shows the number of employees in each of six states, cross-tabulated by sex.

	A	B	C	D	E	F	G	H
1	Employee	Location	Sex		Count			
2	Al Grubbs	California	Male			Female	Male	Grand Total
3	Sarah Parks	New York	Female		Arizona	5	15	20
4	Cheryl Cory	California	Female		California	44	64	108
5	Gregory Steiger	California	Male		Massachusetts	43	47	90
6	Sheila Wigfall	California	Female		New York	51	40	91
7	Pedro H. Nicholson	Arizona	Male		Pennsylvania	17	29	46
8	Howard Keach	California	Male		Washington	16	29	45
9	Heather Lichtenstein	Washington	Female		Grand Total	176	224	400
10	Janet Woodson	Arizona	Female					
11	Hosea Pierson	New York	Male					
12	Nadine Blankenship	New York	Female					
13	Roy Greene	New York	Male					
14	William N. Campbell	New York	Male					
15	Stephen Foster	New York	Male					
16	Charles S. Billings	Pennsylvania	Male					

Figure 18-17: A pivot table before creating groups of states.

The goal is to create two groups of states: Western Region (Arizona, California, and Washington), and Eastern Region (Massachusetts, New York, and Pennsylvania). To create the first group, I held the Ctrl key while I selected Arizona, California, and Washington.

Then I right-clicked and chose Group from the shortcut menu. I repeated the operation to create the second group. Then I replaced the default group names (Group 1 and Group 2) with more meaningful names (Eastern Region and Western Region). Figure 18-18 shows the result of the grouping.

Count		Female	Male	Grand Total	
⊟ Western Region					
	Arizona	5	15	20	
	California	44	64	108	
	Washington	16	29	45	
⊟ Eastern Region					
	Massachusetts	43	47	90	
	New York	51	40	91	
	Pennsylvania	17	29	46	
Grand Total		176	224	400	

Figure 18-18: A pivot table with two groups and subtotals for the groups.

You can create any number of groups and even create groups of groups.

ON THE CD

The workbook used in this example is available on the companion CD-ROM. The file is named `employee list.xlsx`.

Viewing Grouped Data

Excel provides a number of options for displaying a pivot table, and you may want to experiment with these options when you use groups. These commands are in the PivotTable Tools⇨Design tab of the Ribbon. There are no rules for these options. The key is to try a few and see which makes your pivot table look the best. In addition, try various PivotTable Styles, with options for banded rows or banded columns. Often, the style that you choose can greatly enhance readability.

Figure 18-19 shows pivot tables using various options for displaying subtotals, grand totals, and styles.

Automatic Grouping Examples

When a field contains numbers, dates, or times, Excel can create groups automatically. The two examples in this section demonstrate automatic grouping.

Part V

	A	B	C	D	E	F	G	H	I
1						Count			
2	Count						Female	Male	Grand Total
3		Female	Male			Western Region	65	108	173
4	Western Region					Arizona	5	15	20
5	Arizona	5	15			California	44	64	108
6	California	44	64			Washington	16	29	45
7	Washington	16	29						
8	Eastern Region					Eastern Region	111	116	227
9	Massachusetts	43	47			Massachusetts	43	47	90
10	New York	51	40			New York	51	40	91
11	Pennsylvania	17	29			Pennsylvania	17	29	46
12									
13						Grand Total	176	224	400
14									
15									
16									
17	Count					Count			
18		Female	Male	Grand Total			Female	Male	Grand Total
19	Western Region					Western Region			
20	Arizona	5	15	20		Arizona	5	15	20
21	California	44	64	108		California	44	64	108
22	Washington	16	29	45		Washington	16	29	45
23	Western Region Total	65	108	173		Western Region Total	65	108	173
24									
25	Eastern Region					Eastern Region			
26	Massachusetts	43	47	90		Massachusetts	43	47	90
27	New York	51	40	91		New York	51	40	91
28	Pennsylvania	17	29	46		Pennsylvania	17	29	46
29	Eastern Region Total	111	116	227		Eastern Region Total	111	116	227
30									

Sheet2 / Sheet3

Figure 18-19: Pivot tables with options for subtotals and grand totals.

GROUPING BY DATE

Figure 18-20 shows a portion of a simple table with two fields: Date and Sales. This table has 730 rows and covers the dates between January 1, 2005, and December 31, 2006. The goal is to summarize the sales information by month.

 ON THE CD

A workbook demonstrating how to group pivot table items by date is available on the companion CD-ROM. The file is named `sales by date.xlsx`.

Figure 18-21 shows part of a pivot table created from the data. The Date field is in the Row Labels section, and the Sales field is in the Values section. Not surprisingly, the pivot table looks exactly like the input data because the dates have not been grouped.

	A	B	C
1	Date	Sales	
2	1/1/2005	1,277	
3	1/2/2005	1,255	
4	1/3/2005	1,454	
5	1/4/2005	1,223	
6	1/5/2005	1,314	
7	1/6/2005	1,496	
8	1/7/2005	1,472	
9	1/8/2005	1,124	
10	1/9/2005	1,210	
11	1/10/2005	1,516	
12	1/11/2005	1,831	
13	1/12/2005	1,902	
14	1/13/2005	2,193	
15	1/14/2005	2,111	
16	1/15/2005	2,034	
17	1/16/2005	1,763	
18	1/17/2005	1,783	
19	1/18/2005	1,938	
20	1/19/2005	2,167	
21	1/20/2005	2,171	
22	1/21/2005	1,990	

Figure 18-20: You can use a pivot table to summarize the sales data by month.

	A	B	C
1			
2	Date	Sum of Sales	
3	1/1/2005	1,277	
4	1/2/2005	1,255	
5	1/3/2005	1,454	
6	1/4/2005	1,223	
7	1/5/2005	1,314	
8	1/6/2005	1,496	
9	1/7/2005	1,472	
10	1/8/2005	1,124	
11	1/9/2005	1,210	
12	1/10/2005	1,516	
13	1/11/2005	1,831	
14	1/12/2005	1,902	
15	1/13/2005	2,193	
16	1/14/2005	2,111	

Figure 18-21: The pivot table, before grouping by month.

Part V

To group the items by month, select any date and choose PivotTable Tools⇨Options⇨ Group⇨Group Field (or, right-click and choose Group from the shortcut menu). You see the Grouping dialog box, shown in Figure 18-22.

Figure 18-22: Use the Grouping dialog box to group pivot table items by dates.

In the By list box, select Months and Years and verify that the starting and ending dates are correct. Click OK. The Date items in the pivot table are grouped by years and by months, as shown in Figure 18-23.

 NOTE

If you select only Months in the Grouping list box, months in different years combine together. For example, the January item would display sales for both 2005 and 2006.

Figure 18-24 shows another view of the data, grouped by quarter and by year.

GROUPING BY TIME

Figure 18-25 shows a set of data in columns A:B. Each row is a reading from an instrument, taken at one-minute intervals throughout an entire day. The table has 1,440 rows, each representing one minute. The pivot table summarizes the data by hour.

 ON THE CD

This workbook, named `hourly readings.xlsx`, is available on the companion CD-ROM.

Years	Date	Sum of Sales
2005	Jan	55,876
	Feb	45,943
	Mar	71,634
	Apr	33,626
	May	52,670
	Jun	39,218
	Jul	98,417
	Aug	172,990
	Sep	204,226
	Oct	233,286
	Nov	287,696
	Dec	323,482
2006	Jan	324,877
	Feb	323,233
	Mar	360,533
	Apr	327,771
	May	348,109
	Jun	310,027
	Jul	320,520
	Aug	312,812
	Sep	325,169
	Oct	316,041
	Nov	316,832
	Dec	302,131
Grand Total		5,507,118

Figure 18-23: The pivot table, after grouping by month and year.

Years	Date	Sum of Sales
2005	Qtr1	173,453
	Qtr2	125,513
	Qtr3	475,633
	Qtr4	844,464
2006	Qtr1	1,008,643
	Qtr2	985,906
	Qtr3	958,501
	Qtr4	935,005
Grand Total		5,507,118

Figure 18-24: This pivot table shows sales by quarter and by year.

Part V

	A	B	C	D	E	F	G
1	Time	Reading			Avg of Reading	Min of Reading	Max of Reading
2	6/15/2006 0:00	105.32		12 AM	110.50	104.37	116.21
3	6/15/2006 0:01	105.35		1 AM	118.57	112.72	127.14
4	6/15/2006 0:02	104.37		2 AM	124.39	115.75	130.36
5	6/15/2006 0:03	106.40		3 AM	122.74	112.85	132.90
6	6/15/2006 0:04	106.42		4 AM	129.29	123.99	133.52
7	6/15/2006 0:05	105.43		5 AM	132.91	125.88	141.04
8	6/15/2006 0:06	107.46		6 AM	139.67	132.69	146.06
9	6/15/2006 0:07	109.49		7 AM	128.18	117.53	139.65
10	6/15/2006 0:08	110.54		8 AM	119.24	112.10	129.38
11	6/15/2006 0:09	110.54		9 AM	134.36	129.11	142.79
12	6/15/2006 0:10	110.55		10 AM	136.16	130.91	142.89
13	6/15/2006 0:11	109.56		11 AM	122.79	108.63	138.10
14	6/15/2006 0:12	107.60		12 PM	111.76	106.43	116.71
15	6/15/2006 0:13	107.68		1 PM	104.91	98.48	111.86
16	6/15/2006 0:14	109.69		2 PM	119.71	110.37	130.55
17	6/15/2006 0:15	107.76		3 PM	131.83	121.92	139.65
18	6/15/2006 0:16	107.81		4 PM	131.05	123.36	137.94
19	6/15/2006 0:17	108.83		5 PM	138.90	133.05	145.06
20	6/15/2006 0:18	109.85		6 PM	134.71	129.29	139.89
21	6/15/2006 0:19	111.94		7 PM	123.09	113.97	135.21
22	6/15/2006 0:20	114.04		8 PM	118.13	112.64	125.65
23	6/15/2006 0:21	112.12		9 PM	112.64	108.09	117.72
24	6/15/2006 0:22	112.21		10 PM	101.19	98.13	110.49
25	6/15/2006 0:23	112.25		11 PM	106.01	100.03	111.76
26	6/15/2006 0:24	113.34		Grand Total	121.11	98.13	146.06
27	6/15/2006 0:25	112.41					

Sheet1

Figure 18-25: This pivot table is grouped by Hours.

Following are the settings I used for this pivot table:

- The values area has three instances of the Reading field. I used the Data Field Setting dialog box (Summarize By tab) to summarize the first instance by Average, the second instance by Min, and the third instance by Max.

- The Time field is in the Row Labels section, and I used the Grouping dialog box to group by Hours.

Creating a Frequency Distribution

Excel provides a number of ways to create a frequency distribution, but none of those methods is easier than using a pivot table. Figure 18-26 shows part of a table of 221 students and the test score for each. The goal is to determine how many students are in each ten-point range (1–10, 11–20, and so on).

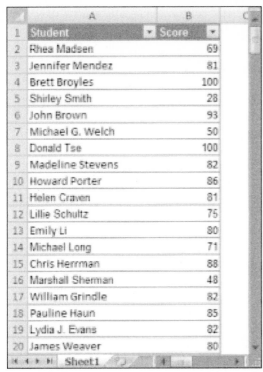

	A	B	C
1	Student	Score	
2	Rhea Madsen	69	
3	Jennifer Mendez	81	
4	Brett Broyles	100	
5	Shirley Smith	28	
6	John Brown	93	
7	Michael G. Welch	50	
8	Donald Tse	100	
9	Madeline Stevens	82	
10	Howard Porter	86	
11	Helen Craven	81	
12	Lillie Schultz	75	
13	Emily Li	80	
14	Michael Long	71	
15	Chris Herrman	88	
16	Marshall Sherman	48	
17	William Grindle	82	
18	Pauline Haun	85	
19	Lydia J. Evans	82	
20	James Weaver	80	

Figure 18-26: Creating a frequency distribution for these test scores is simple.

ON THE CD

This workbook, named `test scores.xlsx`, is available on the companion CD-ROM.

The pivot table is simple:

- The Score field is in the Row Labels section (grouped).
- Another instance of the Score field is in the Values section (summarized by Count).

The Grouping dialog box that generated the bins specified that the groups start at 1, end at 100, and are incremented by 10.

NOTE

By default, Excel does not display items with a zero value. In this example, no test scores are below 21, so the 1–10 and 11–20 items are hidden. To override this setting, access the PivotTable Options dialog box, click the Display tab, and put a check mark next to Display Item Labels When No Fields Are in the Values Area.

Part V

Figure 18-27 show the frequency distribution of the test scores, along with a pivot chart, created by choosing PivotTable Tools⇨Options⇨Tools⇨PivotChart.

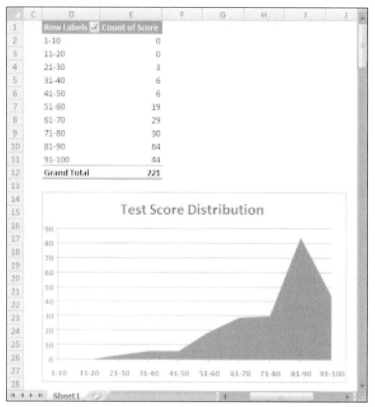

Figure 18-27: The pivot table and pivot chart shows the frequency distribution for the test scores.

NOTE

This example used Excel's Grouping dialog box to create the groups automatically. If you don't want to group in equal-sized bins, you can create your own groups. For example, you may want to assign letter grades based on the test score. Select the rows for the first group and then choose Group from the shortcut menu. Repeat these steps for each additional group. Then replace the default group names with more meaningful names.

Creating a Calculated Field or Calculated Item

Perhaps the most confusing aspect of pivot tables is calculated fields versus calculated items. Many pivot table users simply avoid dealing with calculated fields and items. However, these features can be useful, and they really aren't that complicated after you understand how they work.

First, some basic definitions:

- **A calculated field:** A new field created from other fields in the pivot table. If your pivot table source is a worksheet table, an alternative to using a calculated field is to add a new column to the table and then create a formula to perform the desired calculation. A calculated field must reside in the Values area of the pivot table. You can't use a calculated field in Column Labels, Row Labels, or a Report Filter.

- **A calculated item:** A calculated item uses the contents of other items within a field of the pivot table. If your pivot table source is a worksheet table, an alternative to using a calculate item is to insert one or more rows and write formulas that use values in other rows. A calculated item must reside in the Column Labels, Row Labels, or Report Filter area of a pivot table. You can't use a calculated item in the Values area.

The formulas used to create calculated fields and calculated items aren't standard Excel formulas. In other words, you don't enter the formulas into cells. Rather, you enter these formulas in a dialog box, and they're stored along with the pivot table data.

The examples in this section use the worksheet table shown in Figure 18-28. The table consists of five fields and 48 rows. Each row describes monthly sales information for a particular sales representative. For example, Amy is a sales rep for the North region, and she sold 239 units in January for total sales of $23,040.

ON THE CD

A workbook that demonstrates calculated fields and items is available on the companion CD-ROM. The file is named `calculated fields and items.xlsx`.

Figure 18-29 shows a pivot table created from the data. This pivot table shows Sales (Values area), cross-tabulated by Month (Row Labels) and by SalesRep (Column Labels).

The examples that follow create

- A calculated field, to compute average sales per unit
- Four calculated items, to compute the quarterly sales commission

SalesRep	Region	Month	Sales	Units Sold
Amy	North	Jan	$23,040	239
Amy	North	Feb	$24,131	79
Amy	North	Mar	$24,646	71
Amy	North	Apr	$22,047	71
Amy	North	May	$24,971	157
Amy	North	Jun	$24,218	92
Amy	North	Jul	$25,735	175
Amy	North	Aug	$23,638	87
Amy	North	Sep	$25,749	557
Amy	North	Oct	$24,437	95
Amy	North	Nov	$25,355	706
Amy	North	Dec	$25,899	180
Bob	North	Jan	$20,024	103
Bob	North	Feb	$23,822	267
Bob	North	Mar	$24,854	96
Bob	North	Apr	$22,838	74
Bob	North	May	$25,320	231
Bob	North	Jun	$24,733	164
Bob	North	Jul	$21,184	68

Figure 18-28: This data demonstrates calculated fields and calculated items.

Tot Sales				
	Amy	Bob	Chuck	Doug
Jan	23,040	20,024	19,886	26,264
Feb	24,131	23,822	23,494	29,953
Mar	24,646	24,854	21,824	25,041
Apr	22,047	22,838	22,058	29,338
May	24,971	25,320	20,280	25,150
Jun	24,218	24,733	23,965	27,371
Jul	25,735	21,184	23,032	25,044
Aug	23,638	21,174	21,273	29,506
Sep	25,749	25,999	21,584	29,061
Oct	24,437	22,639	19,625	27,113
Nov	25,355	23,949	19,832	25,953
Dec	25,899	23,179	20,583	28,670
Grand Total	**293,866**	**281,715**	**257,436**	**328,464**

Figure 18-29: This pivot table was created from the sales data.

Creating a Calculated Field

Because a pivot table is a special type of range, you can't insert new rows or columns within the pivot table, which means that you can't insert formulas to perform calculations with the data in a pivot table. However, you can create calculated fields for a pivot table. A *calculated field* consists of a calculation that can involve other fields.

A calculated field is basically a way to display new information in a pivot table. It essentially presents an alternative to creating a new column field in your source data. In many cases, you may find it easier to insert a new column in the source range with a formula that performs the desired calculation. A calculated field is most useful when the data comes from a source that you can't easily manipulate — such as an external database.

In the sales example, for example, suppose that you want to calculate the average sales amount per unit. You can compute this value by dividing the Sales field by the Units Sold field. The result shows a new field (a calculated field) for the pivot table.

Use the following procedure to create a calculated field that consists of the Sales field divided by the Units Sold field:

1. Select any cell within the pivot table.

2. Choose PivotTable Tools⇨Options ⇨Tools⇨Formulas⇨Calculated Field. Excel displays the Insert Calculated Field dialog box.

3. Enter a descriptive name in the Name box and specify the formula in the Formula box (see Figure 18-30). The formula can use worksheet functions and other fields from the data source. For this example, the calculated field name is Avg Unit Price, and the formula is

```
=Sales/'Units Sold'
```

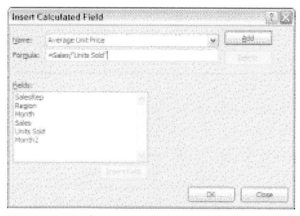

Figure 18-30: The Insert Calculated Field dialog box.

4. Click Add to add this new field.

5. Click OK to close the Insert Calculated Field dialog box.

NOTE

You can create the formula manually by typing it or by double-clicking items in the Fields list box. Double-clicking an item transfers it to the Formula field. Because the Units Sold field contains a space, Excel adds single quotes around the field name.

After you create the calculated field, Excel adds it to the Values area of the pivot table (and it also appears in the PivotTable Field List). You can treat it just like any other field, with one exception: You can't move it to the Row Labels, Column Labels, or Report Filter areas. It must remain in the Values area.

Figure 18-31 shows the pivot table after adding the calculated field. The new field displayed Sum of Avg Unit Price, but I changed this label to Avg Price. I also changed the style to display banded columns.

	A	B	C	D	E	F	G	H	I
1									
2									
3									
4		Amy		Bob		Chuck		Doug	
5		Tot Sales	Avg Price	Tot Sales	Avg Price	Tot Sales	Avg Price	Tot Sales	Avg Price
6	Jan	23,040	96	20,024	194	19,886	209	26,264	285
7	Feb	24,131	305	23,822	89	23,494	159	29,953	35
8	Mar	24,646	347	24,854	259	21,824	263	25,041	291
9	Apr	22,047	311	22,838	309	22,058	230	29,338	132
10	May	24,971	159	25,320	110	20,280	45	25,150	104
11	Jun	24,218	263	24,733	151	23,965	32	27,371	288
12	Jul	25,735	147	21,184	312	23,032	149	25,044	305
13	Aug	23,638	272	23,174	203	21,273	28	29,506	286
14	Sep	25,749	46	25,999	310	21,584	189	29,061	199
15	Oct	24,437	257	22,639	87	19,625	236	27,113	226
16	Nov	25,355	36	23,949	220	19,832	283	25,953	320
17	Dec	25,899	144	23,179	50	20,583	116	28,670	145
18	Grand Total	293,866	117	281,715	138	257,436	86	328,464	142
19									
20									

Sheet1 / Data

Figure 18-31: This pivot table uses a calculated field.

TIP

The formulas that you develop can also use worksheet functions, but the functions can't refer to cells or named ranges.

Inserting a Calculated Item

The preceding section describes how to create a calculated field. Excel also enables you to create a *calculated item* for a pivot table field. Keep in mind that a calculated field can be an alternative to adding a new field to your data source. A calculated item, on the other hand, is an alternative to adding new rows to the data source — rows that contains formulas that refer to other rows.

In this example, you create four calculated items. Each item represents the commission earned on the quarter's sales, according to the following schedule:

- **Quarter 1:** 10% of January, February, and March sales
- **Quarter 2:** 11% of April, May, and June sales
- **Quarter 3:** 12% of July, August, and September sales
- **Quarter 4:** 12.5% of October, November, and December sales

NOTE
Modifying the source data to obtain this information would require inserting 16 new rows, each with formulas. So, for this example, creating four calculated items may be an easier task.

To create a calculated item to compute the commission for January, February, and March, follow these steps:

1. Move the cell pointer to the Row Labels or Column Labels area of the pivot table and choose PivotTable Tools⇨Options⇨Tools⇨Formulas⇨Calculated Item. Excel displays the Insert Calculated Item dialog box.

2. Enter a name for the new item in the Name box and specify the formula in the Formula box (see Figure 18-32). The formula can use items in other fields, but it can't use worksheet functions. For this example, the new item is named Qtr1 Commission, and the formula appears as follows:

```
=10%*(Jan+Feb+Mar)
```

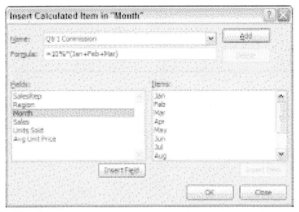

Figure 18-32: The Insert Calculated Item dialog box.

3. Click Add.

4. Repeat Steps 2 and 3 to create three additional calculated items:

- Qtr2 Commission: =11%*(Apr+May+Jun)

- Qtr3 Commission: =12%*(Jul+Aug+Sep)

- Qtr4 Commission: =12.5%*(Oct+Nov+Dec)

5. Click OK to close the dialog box.

NOTE

A calculated item, unlike a calculated field, does not appear in the PivotTable Field List. Only fields appear in the field list.

CAUTION

If you use a calculated item in your pivot table, you may need to turn off the Grand Total display for columns to avoid double counting. In this example, the Grand Total includes the calculated item, so the commission amounts are included with the sales amounts. To turn off Grand Totals, choose PivotTable Tools⇨Design⇨Layout⇨Grand Totals.

After you create the calculated items, they appear in the pivot table. Figure 18-33 shows the pivot table after adding the four calculated items. Notice that the calculated items are added to the end of the Month items. You can rearrange the items by selecting the cell and dragging its border. Another option is to create two groups: One for the sales numbers and one for the commission calculations. Figure 18-34 shows the pivot table after creating the two groups and adding subtotals.

	A	B	C	D	E	F	G
2							
3	Sum of Sales						
4		Amy	Bob	Chuck	Doug	Grand Total	
5	Jan	23,040	20,024	19,886	26,264	89,214	
6	Feb	24,131	23,822	23,494	29,953	101,400	
7	Mar	24,646	24,854	21,824	25,041	96,365	
8	Apr	22,047	22,338	22,058	29,338	96,281	
9	May	24,971	25,320	20,280	25,150	95,721	
10	Jun	24,218	24,733	23,965	27,371	100,287	
11	Jul	25,735	21,184	23,032	25,044	94,995	
12	Aug	23,638	23,174	21,273	29,506	97,591	
13	Sep	25,749	25,999	21,584	29,061	102,393	
14	Oct	24,437	22,639	19,625	27,113	93,814	
15	Nov	25,355	23,949	19,832	25,953	95,089	
16	Dec	25,899	23,179	20,583	28,670	98,331	
17	Qtr1 Commission	7,182	6,870	6,520	8,126	28,698	
18	Qtr2 Commission	7,836	8,018	7,293	9,004	32,152	
19	Qtr3 Commission	9,015	8,441	7,907	10,011	35,397	
20	Qtr4 Commission	9,461	8,721	7,505	10,217	35,904	
21							
22							

Sheet1 / Data

Figure 18-33: This pivot table uses calculated items for quarterly totals.

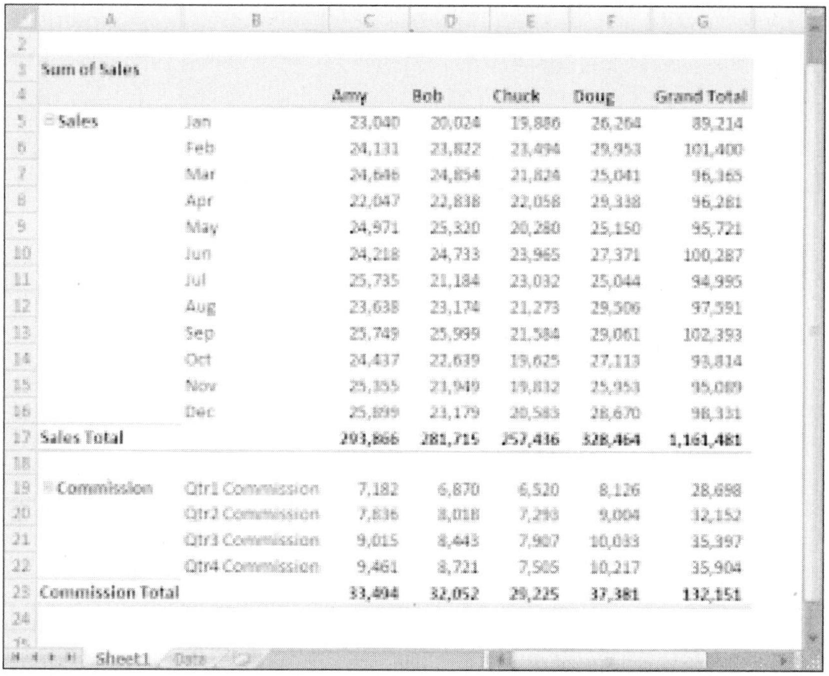

Figure 18-34: The pivot table, after creating two groups and adding subtotals.

Referencing Cells within a Pivot Table

In some cases, you may want to create a formula that references one or more cells within a pivot table. Figure 18-35 shows a simple pivot table that displays income and expense information for three years. In this pivot table, the Month field is hidden, so the pivot table shows the year totals.

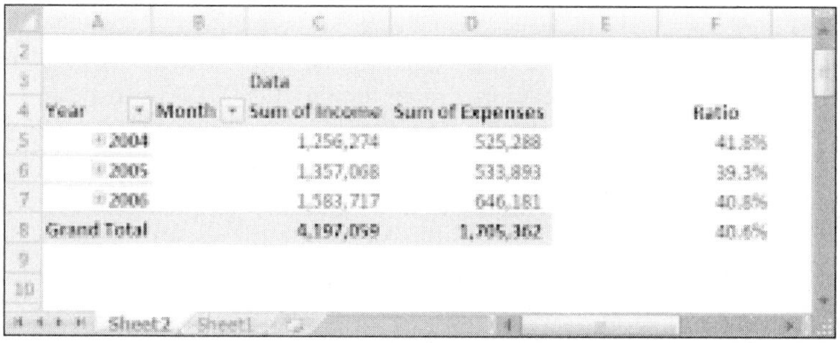

Figure 18-35: The formulas in column F reference cells in the pivot table.

ON THE CD

This workbook, named `income and expenses.xlsx`, is available on the companion CD-ROM.

Column F contains formulas and this column is not part of the pivot table. These formulas calculate the expense-to-income ratio for each year. I created these formulas by pointing to the cells. You may expect to see this formula in cell F5:

```
=D5/C5
```

In fact, the formula in cell F5 is

```
=GETPIVOTDATA("Sum of Expenses",$A$3,"Year",2004)/
GETPIVOTDATA("Sum of Income",$A$3,"Year",2004)
```

When you use the pointing technique to create a formula that references a cell in a pivot table, Excel replaces those simple cell references with a much more complicated GETPIVOTDATA function. If you type the cell references manually (rather than pointing to them), Excel does not use the GETPIVOTDATA function.

The reason? Using the GETPIVOTDATA function helps ensure that the formula will continue to reference the intended cells if the pivot table layout is changed. Figure 18-36 shows the pivot table after expanding the years to show the month detail. As you can see, the formulas in column F still show the correct result even though the references cells are in a different location. Had I used simple cell references, the formula would return incorrect results after expanding the years.

CAUTION

Using the GETPIVOTDATA function has one caveat: The data that it retrieves must be visible in the pivot table. If you modify the pivot table so that the value returned by GETPIVOTDATA is no longer visible, the formula returns an error.

TIP

If (for some reason) you want to prevent Excel from using the GETPIVOTDATA function when you point to pivot table cells when creating a formula, access the Excel Options dialog box, select the Formulas tab, and remove the check mark from Use GetPivotData Function For PivotTable References.

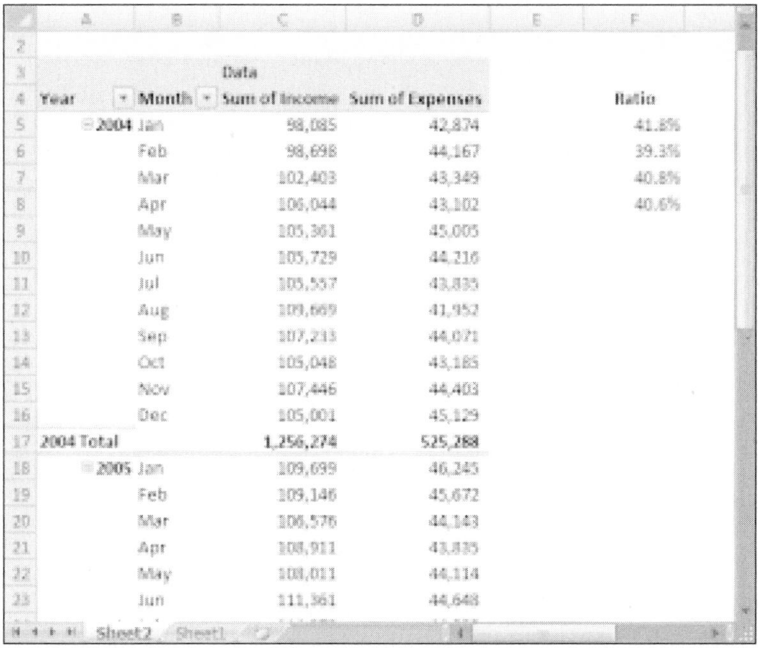

Year	Month	Sum of Income	Sum of Expenses		Ratio
		Data			
2004	Jan	98,085	42,874		41.8%
	Feb	98,698	44,167		39.3%
	Mar	102,403	43,349		40.8%
	Apr	106,044	43,102		40.6%
	May	105,361	45,005		
	Jun	105,729	44,216		
	Jul	105,557	43,835		
	Aug	109,669	41,952		
	Sep	107,213	44,071		
	Oct	105,048	43,185		
	Nov	107,446	44,403		
	Dec	105,001	45,129		
2004 Total		1,256,274	525,288		
2005	Jan	109,699	46,245		
	Feb	109,146	45,672		
	Mar	106,576	44,143		
	Apr	108,911	43,835		
	May	108,011	44,114		
	Jun	111,361	44,648		

Figure 18-36: After expanding the pivot table, formulas that use the GETPIVOTDATA function continue to display the correct result.

Another Pivot Table Example

The pivot table example in this section demonstrates some useful ways to work with pivot tables. Figure 18-37 shows a table with 3,144 data rows, one for each county in the United States. The fields are

- **County:** The name of the county
- **State Name:** The state of the county
- **Region:** The region (Roman number ranging from I–XII)
- **Census 2000:** The population of the county, according to the 2000 Census
- **Census 1990:** The population of the county, according to the 1990 Census
- **Land Area:** The area, in square miles (excluding water-covered area)
- **Water Area:** The area, in square miles, covered by water

	A	B	C	D	E	F	G
1	County	State Name	Region	Census 2000	Census 1990	Land Area	WaterArea
2	Los Angeles	California	Region IX	9,519,338	8,863,164	4,060.87	691.45
3	Cook	Illinois	Region V	5,376,741	5,105,067	945.68	689.36
4	Harris	Texas	Region VII	3,400,578	2,818,199	1,728.83	48.87
5	San Diego	California	Region IX	2,813,833	2,498,016	4,199.89	325.62
6	Orange	California	Region IX	2,846,289	2,410,556	788.40	158.57
7	Kings	New York	Region II	2,465,326	2,300,664	70.61	26.29
8	Maricopa	Arizona	Region IX	3,072,149	2,122,101	9,203.14	21.11
9	Wayne	Michigan	Region V	2,061,162	2,111,687	614.15	58.05
10	Queens	New York	Region II	2,229,379	1,951,598	109.24	69.04
11	Dade	Florida	Region IV	2,253,362	1,937,094	1,946.21	77.85
12	Dallas	Texas	Region VI	2,218,899	1,852,810	879.60	28.96
13	Philadelphia	Pennsylvania	Region III	1,517,550	1,585,577	135.09	7.55
14	King	Washington	Region X	1,737,034	1,507,319	2,126.04	180.48
15	Santa Clara	California	Region IX	1,682,585	1,497,577	1,290.69	11.12
16	New York	New York	Region II	1,537,195	1,487,536	22.96	10.81
17	San Bernardino	California	Region IX	1,709,434	1,418,380	20,052.50	52.82
18	Cuyahoga	Ohio	Region V	1,393,978	1,412,140	458.49	787.07
19	Middlesex	Massachusetts	Region I	1,465,396	1,398,468	823.46	24.08
20	Allegheny	Pennsylvania	Region III	1,281,666	1,336,449	730.17	14.54
21	Suffolk	New York	Region II	1,419,369	1,321,864	912.20	1,460.87
22	Nassau	New York	Region II	1,334,544	1,287,348	286.69	166.39
23	Alameda	California	Region IX	1,443,741	1,279,182	717.57	83.57
24	Broward	Florida	Region IV	1,623,018	1,255,488	1,205.40	114.24

Figure 18-37: This table contains data for each county in the United States.

ON THE CD

This workbook, named `county data.xlsx`, is available on the companion CD-ROM.

Figure 18-38 shows a pivot table created from the county data. The pivot table uses the Region and State Name fields for the Row Labels and uses Census 2000 and Census 1990 as the Column Labels.

I created three calculated fields to display additional information:

- **Change** (displayed as Pop Change): The difference between Census 2000 and Census 1990

- **Pct Change** (displayed as Pct Pop Change): The population change expressed as a percentage of the 1990 population

- **Density** (displayed as Pop/Sq Mile): The population per square mile of land.

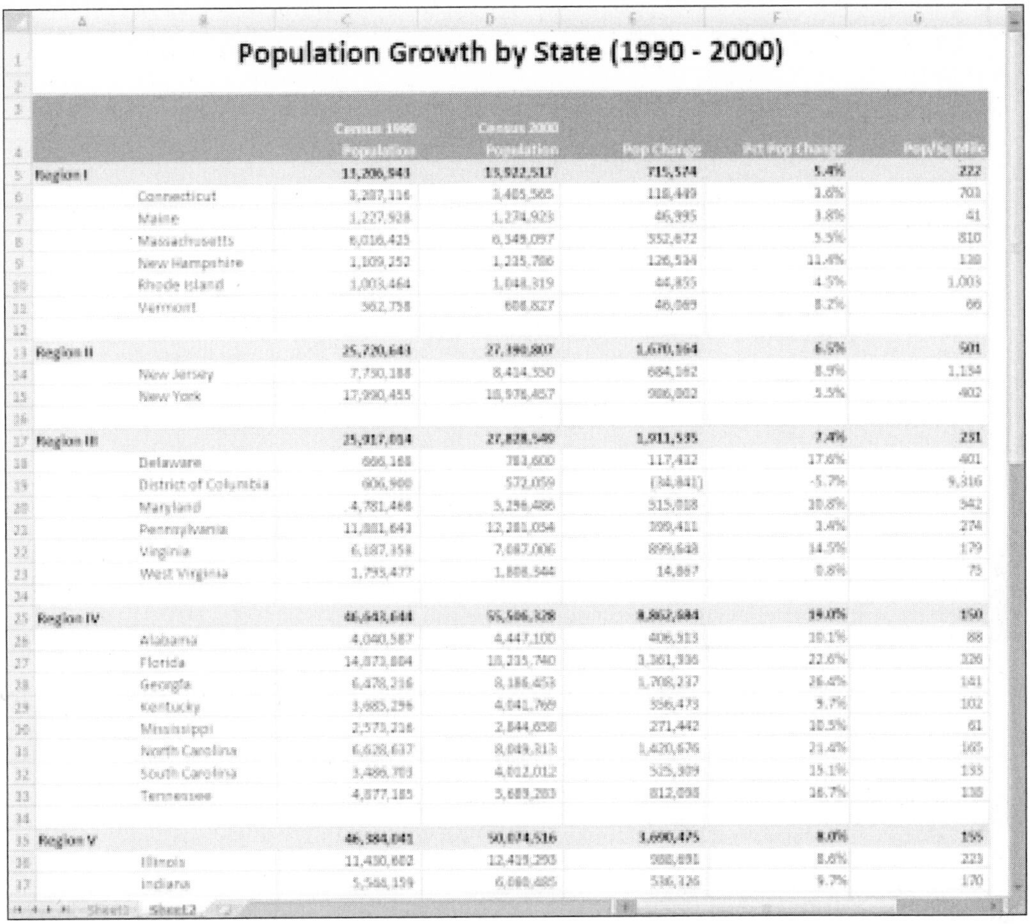

Population Growth by State (1990 - 2000)

		Census 1990 Population	Census 2000 Population	Pop Change	Pct Pop Change	Pop/Sq Mile
Region I		**13,206,943**	**13,922,517**	**715,574**	**5.4%**	**222**
	Connecticut	3,287,116	3,405,565	118,449	3.6%	703
	Maine	1,227,928	1,274,923	46,995	3.8%	41
	Massachusetts	6,016,425	6,349,097	332,672	5.5%	810
	New Hampshire	1,109,252	1,235,786	126,534	11.4%	138
	Rhode Island	1,003,464	1,048,319	44,855	4.5%	1,003
	Vermont	562,758	608,827	46,069	8.2%	66
Region II		**25,720,643**	**27,390,807**	**1,670,164**	**6.5%**	**501**
	New Jersey	7,730,188	8,414,350	684,162	8.9%	1,134
	New York	17,990,455	18,976,457	986,002	5.5%	402
Region III		**25,917,014**	**27,828,549**	**1,911,535**	**7.4%**	**251**
	Delaware	666,168	783,600	117,432	17.6%	401
	District of Columbia	606,900	572,059	(34,841)	-5.7%	9,316
	Maryland	4,781,468	5,296,486	515,018	10.8%	542
	Pennsylvania	11,881,643	12,281,054	399,411	3.4%	274
	Virginia	6,187,358	7,087,006	899,648	14.5%	179
	West Virginia	1,793,477	1,808,344	14,867	0.8%	75
Region IV		**46,643,644**	**55,506,328**	**8,862,684**	**19.0%**	**150**
	Alabama	4,040,587	4,447,100	406,513	10.1%	88
	Florida	14,873,804	18,235,740	3,361,936	22.6%	326
	Georgia	6,478,216	8,186,453	1,708,237	26.4%	141
	Kentucky	3,685,296	4,041,769	356,473	9.7%	102
	Mississippi	2,573,216	2,844,658	271,442	10.5%	61
	North Carolina	6,628,637	8,049,313	1,420,676	21.4%	165
	South Carolina	3,486,703	4,012,012	525,309	15.1%	133
	Tennessee	4,877,185	5,689,283	812,098	16.7%	138
Region V		**46,384,041**	**50,074,516**	**3,690,475**	**8.0%**	**155**
	Illinois	11,430,602	12,419,293	988,691	8.6%	223
	Indiana	5,544,159	6,080,485	536,326	9.7%	170

Figure 18-38: This pivot table was created from the county data.

A new feature in Excel 2007 lets you document your calculated fields and calculated items. Choose PivotTable Tools⇨Options⇨Tools⇨Formulas⇨List Formulas, and Excel inserts a new worksheet with information about your calculated fields and items. Figure 18-39 shows an example.

This pivot table is sorted on two columns. The main sort is by Region, and states within each region are sorted alphabetically. To sort, just select a cell that contains a data point to be included in the sort. Right-click and choose from the shortcut menu.

Sorting by Region required some additional effort because Roman numerals are not in alphabetical order. Therefore, I had to create a custom list. To create a custom sort list, access the Excel Options dialog box, click the Personalize tab, and click Edit Custom Lists. Click New List, type your list entries, and click Add. Figure 18-40 shows the custom list I created for the region names.

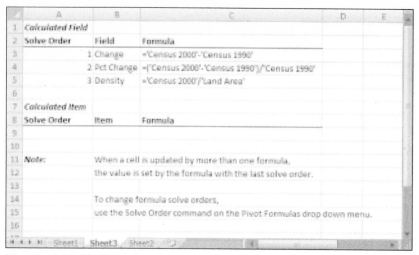

Figure 18-39: This worksheet lists calculated fields and items for the pivot table.

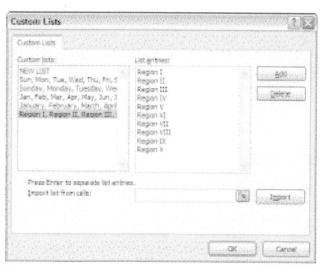

Figure 18-40: This custom list ensures that the Region names are sorted correctly.

Producing a Report with a Pivot Table

By using a pivot table, you can convert a huge table of data into an attractive printed report. Figure 18-41 shows a small portion of a pivot table that I created from a table that has 25,664 rows of data. This data happens to be my digital music collection, and each row contains information about a single music file: the genre, artist, album, filename, file size, and duration.

			D	E	F
133					
134	**Tony Rice**		12	59 Mb	0:37:18
135		California Autumn	12	59 Mb	0:37:18
136					
137	**Various - Bluegrass**		135	688 Mb	7:40:48
138		Adventures In Music #15 Bluegrass	18	58 Mb	0:59:51
139		Dawg Tales_ Acoustic Tribute to David Grisman	12	79 Mb	0:50:44
140		Hand-Picked (CD 1) 25 Years of Bluegrass on Rounder Records	26	115 Mb	1:13:45
141		Hand-Picked (CD 2) 25 Years of Bluegrass on Rounder Records	23	120 Mb	1:16:23
142		Heartland An Appalachian Anthology	16	105 Mb	1:06:07
143		O Brother, Where Art Thou	19	95 Mb	1:00:27
144		The Great Dobro Sessions	21	117 Mb	1:13:31
145					
146	**Wayne Henderson**		27	130 Mb	1:21:24
147		Les Pick	13	71 Mb	0:44:36
148		Rugby Guitar	14	60 Mb	0:36:48
149					
150	**Blues Acoustic**		219	1,099 Mb	12:22:04
151	**Alberta Hunter**		10	61 Mb	0:39:26
152		Amtrak Blues	10	61 Mb	0:39:26
153					
154	**Beth Scalet**		1	4 Mb	0:03:48
155		Blues In Paradise	1	4 Mb	0:03:48
156					
157	**Big Joe Duskin**		7	29 Mb	0:18:15
158		Big Joe Jumps Again!	7	29 Mb	0:18:15
159					
160	**Black Ace**		23	84 Mb	1:09:41
161		I'm The Boss Card In Your Hand	23	84 Mb	1:09:41
162					
163	**Bluff City Backsliders**		12	71 Mb	0:45:47
164		Bluff City Backsliders	12	71 Mb	0:45:47
165					

H ◄ ► H Sheet1 SongData

Figure 18-41: A 119-page pivot table report.

The pivot table report created from this data is 119 pages long, and it took about five minutes to set up (and a little longer to fine-tune it).

ON THE CD

This workbook, named `music list .xlsx`, is available on the companion CD-ROM.

Here's a quick summary of how I created this report:

1. I selected a cell in the table and chose Insert⇨Tables⇨PivotTable.

2. In the Create PivotTable dialog box, I clicked OK to accept the default settings.

3. In the new worksheet, I used the PivotTable Field List and dragged the following fields to the Row Labels area: Genre, Artist, and Album.

4. I dragged these fields to the Values area: Song, Size, and Duration.

5. I used the Data Field Settings dialog box to summarize Song as Count, Size as Sum, and Duration as Sum.

6. I wanted the information in the Size column to display in megabytes, so I formatted the column using this custom number format:

   `###,###, "Mb";;`

7. I wanted the information in the Duration column to display as hours, minutes, and seconds, so I formatted the column using this custom number format:

   `[h]:mm:ss;;`

8. I edited the column headings. For example, I replaced Count of Song with No. Songs.

9. I changed the layout to outline format by choosing PivotTable Tools⇨Design⇨Layout⇨ Report Layout.

10. I turned off the field headers by choosing PivotTable Tools⇨Options⇨Show/Hide⇨ Show Field Headers.

11. I turned off the buttons by choosing PivotTable Tools⇨Options⇨Show/Hide⇨ +/- Buttons.

12. I displayed a blank row after each artist by choosing PivotTable Tools⇨Design⇨ Layout⇨Blank Rows.

13. I applied a built-in style by choosing PivotTable Tools⇨Design⇨PivotTable Styles.

14. I increased the font size for the Genre.

15. I went into Page Layout View, and I adjusted the column widths so that the report would fit horizontally on the page.

 NOTE

Step 14 was actually kind of tricky. I wanted to increase the size of the genre names but leave the subtotals in the same font size. Therefore, I couldn't modify the style for the PivotTable Style I chose. I selected the entire column A and pressed Ctrl+G to bring up the Go To dialog box. I clicked Special to display the Go To Special dialog box. Then I selected the Constants option and clicked OK, which selected only the nonempty cells in column A. I then adjusted the font size for the selected cells.

Chapter 19

Conditional Formatting and Data Validation

This chapter explores two very useful Excel features: conditional formatting and data validation. You may not think these features have much to do with formulas. As you'll see, though, when you toss formulas into the mix, conditional formatting and data validation can perform some amazing feats.

Conditional Formatting

Conditional formatting enables you to apply cell formatting selectively and automatically, based on the contents of the cells. For example, you can set things up such that all negative values in a range have a light yellow background color. When you enter or change a value in the range, Excel examines the value and evaluates the conditional formatting rules for the cell. If the value is negative, the background is shaded. If not, no formatting is applied.

NEW

Conditional formatting has improved significantly in Excel 2007 and is now even more useful for visualizing numeric data. In some cases, you may be able to use conditional formatting in lieu of using a chart.

Conditional formatting is a useful way to quickly identifying erroneous cell entries or cells of a particular type. You can use a format (such as bright red cell shading) to make particular cells easy to identify.

Figure 19-1 shows a worksheet with nine ranges, each with a different type of conditional formatting rule applied. Here's a brief explanation of each:

- **Greater than 10:** Values greater than 10 are highlighted with a different background color. This rule is just one of many numeric value related rules that you can apply.

- **Above average:** Values that are higher than the average value are highlighted.

- **Duplicate values:** Values that appear more than one time are highlighted.

- **Words that contain X:** If the cell contains the letter X (upper- or lowercase), the cell is highlighted.

- **Data bars:** Each cell displays a horizontal bar, proportional to its value.

- **Color Scale:** The background color varies, depending on the value of the cells. You can choose from several different color scales or create your own.

- **Icon Set:** This is one of many icon sets, which display a small graphic in the cell. The graphic varies, depending on the cell value.

- **Icon Set:** This is another icon set.

- **Custom Rule:** The rule for this checkerboard pattern is based on a formula:

  ```
  =MOD(ROW(),2)=MOD(COLUMN(),2)
  ```

Specifying Conditional Formatting

To apply a conditional formatting rule to a cell or range, select the cells and then use one of the commands on the Home⇨Styles⇨Conditional Formatting drop-down to specify a rule. The choices are

- **Highlight Cell Rules:** Examples rules include highlighting cells that are greater than a particular value, are between two values, contain specific text string, or are duplicated.

- **Top Bottom Rules:** Examples include highlighting the top ten items, the items in the bottom 20 percent, or items that are above average.

- **Data Bars:** This applies graphic bars directly in the cells, proportional to the cell's value.

Greater than 10 / Above average / Duplicate values

A	B	C		E	F	G		I	J	K
5	9	2		80	9	77		45	62	48
8	10	10		52	22	71		94	57	74
12	9	10		62	69	74		84	74	61
3	10	8		62	59	73		68	85	89
12	12	2		5	68	16		15	12	47
9	12	5		60	9	72		11	36	99
5	12	11		76	95	97		46	14	81
2	1	9		8	29	24		18	28	57
9	5	8		60	42	96		94	40	46
4	12	3		24	75	53		5	60	87

Words that contain X / Data Bars / Color Scale

A	B	C		E	F	G		I	J	K
apple	kite	urn		3	3	9		1	11	21
baby	light	violin		7	6	1		2	12	22
cry	max	wax		9	7	2		3	13	23
dog	night	X-ray		5	8	7		4	14	24
elf	oxen	young		5	3	4		5	15	25
fox	purple	zebra		3	9	9		6	16	26
garage	quaint	angle		3	3	3		7	17	27
hex	right	boy		3	2	10		8	18	28
icon	sled	chump		9	7	8		9	19	29
jewel	turtle	dusty		3	7	3		10	20	30

Icon Set / Icon Set / Custom Rule

A	B	C	D		E	F	G
99	50	12			1	3	2
97	59	40			1	1	1
97	15	38			1	3	1
58	4	24			2	2	3
17	96	19			3	3	2
67	72	35			1	2	3
51	97	13			1	2	2
43	19	98			3	2	2
19	95	69			1	3	1
3	59	70			2	2	3
69	79	67			2	2	2

Sheet1

Figure 19-1: This worksheet demonstrates a few conditional formatting rules.

- **Color Scales:** This applies background color, proportional to the cell's value.
- **Icon Sets:** This displays icons directly in the cells. The icons depend on the cell's value.
- **New Rule:** This enables you to specify other conditional formatting rules, including rules based on a logical formula.
- **Clear Rules:** This deletes all the conditional formatting rules from the selected cells.
- **Manage Rules:** This displays the Conditional Formatting Rules Manager dialog box, in which you create new conditional formatting rules, edit rules, or delete rules.

Part V

Excel 2007 Improvements

If you've used conditional formatting in a previous version of Excel, you'll find lots of improvements in Excel 2007, and the feature is now much easier to use. Many conditional formatting rules that previously required a formula are now built in. Improvements include the following:

- In the past, it was far too easy to accidentally wipe out conditional formatting by copying and pasting a range of cells to cells that contain conditional formatting. This problem has been corrected in Excel 2007.

- Excel 2007 includes conditional formatting visualizations based on a range of data. These visualizations include data bars, color scales, and icon sets.

- You're no longer limited to three conditional formatting rules per cell. In fact, you can specify any number of rules.

- In the past, if more than one conditional formatting rule evaluated to true, only the first conditional format was applied. In Excel 2007, all the format rules are applied. For example, assume that you have a cell with two rules: One rule makes the cell's contents italic, and another rules makes the background color green. If both conditions are true, both formats are applied. When conflicts arise, (for example, red background versus green background), the first rule is used.

- Excel 2007 allows number formatting to result from conditional formatting.

- In previous versions, a conditional formatting formula could not reference cells in a different worksheet. Excel 2007 removes that restriction.

FORMATTING TYPES YOU CAN APPLY

When you select a conditional formatting rule, Excel displays a dialog box that's specific to that rule. These dialog boxes have one thing in a common: a drop-down list with common formatting suggestions. Figure 19-2 shows the dialog box that appears when you choose Home⇨Styles⇨Conditional Formatting⇨Highlight Cells Rules⇨Between. This particular rule applies the formatting if the value in the cell falls between two specified values. In this case, you enter the two values (or enter cell references) and then use the drop-down control to choose the type of formatting to display if the condition is met.

Figure 19-2: One of several different conditional formatting dialog boxes.

The formatting suggestions in the drop-down control are just a few of thousands of different formatting combinations. In most cases, none of Excel's suggestions are what you want, so you choose the Custom Format option to display the Format Cells dialog box. You can specify the format in any or all of the four tabs: Number, Font, Border, and Fill.

NOTE

The Format Cells dialog box used for conditional formatting is a modified version of the standard Format Cells dialog box. It doesn't have the Number, Alignment, and Protection tabs; and, some of the Font formatting options are disabled. The dialog box also includes a Clear button that clears any formatting already selected.

MAKING YOUR OWN RULES

For do-it-yourself types, Excel provides the New Formatting Rule dialog box, shown in Figure 19-3. Access this dialog box by choosing Home⇨Styles⇨Conditional Formatting⇨New Rules.

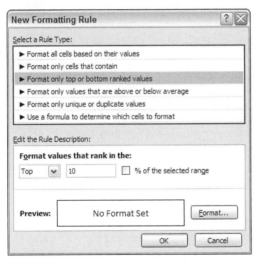

Figure 19-3: Use the New Formatting Rule dialog box to create your own conditional formatting rules.

The New Formatting Rule dialog box lets you re-create all the conditional format rules available via the Ribbon as well as create new rules.

First, select a general rule type from the list at the top of the dialog box. The bottom part of the dialog box varies, depending on your selection at the top. After you specify the rule, click the Format button to specify the type of formatting to apply if the condition is met. An exception is the first rule type, which doesn't have a Format button. (It uses graphics rather than cell formatting.)

Following is a summary of the rule types:

- **Format All Cells Based on Their Values:** Use this rule type to create rules that display data bars, color scales, or icon sets.

- **Format Only Cells That Contain:** Use this rule type to create rules that format cells based on mathematical comparisons (greater than, less than, greater than or equal to, less than or equal to, equal to, not equal to, between, or not between). You can also create rules based on text, dates, blanks, nonblanks, and errors. This rule type is very similar to how conditional formatting was set up in previous versions of Excel.

- **Format Only Top or Bottom Ranked Values:** Use this rule type to create rules that involve identifying cells in the top *n*, top *n* percent, bottom *n*, and bottom *n* percent.

- **Format Only Values That Are Above or Below Average:** Use this rule type to create rules that identify cells that are above average, below average, or within a specified standard deviation from the average.

- **Format Only Unique or Duplicate Values:** Use this rule type to create rules that format unique or duplicate values in a range.

- **Use a Formula to Determine Which Cells to Format:** Use this rule type to create rules based on a logical formula. See "Creating Formula-Based Rules," later in this chapter.

Conditional Formats That Use Graphics

This section describes the three conditional formatting options that are new to Excel 2007: data bars, color scales, and icon sets. These types of conditional formatting can be useful for visualizing the values in a range.

USING DATA BARS

The *data bars conditional format* displays horizontal bars directly in the cell. Length of the bar is based on the value of the cell, relative to the other values in the range.

Figure 19-4 shows a simple example of data bars. It's a list of customers and sales amounts. I applied data bar conditional formatting to the values in column B. You can tell at a glance where the higher values are.

 ON THE CD

The examples in the section are available on the companion CD-ROM. The workbook is named data bars examples.xlsx.

	A	B
1	**Customer**	**Sale Amount**
2	Albert N. Crumrine	59.95
3	Aliza Petrosky	25.00
4	Ana Howe	59.95
5	Andrew Faught	59.95
6	Angel T. Austin	0.00
7	Annette Davis	20.00
8	Bernice Williams	39.95
9	Betty Beard	64.95
10	Betty Shelton	39.95
11	Carl H. Sargent	47.90
12	Carmelita Nickel	39.95
13	Carol Valdez	39.95
14	Charles Guyer	5.00
15	Christian Dove	20.00
16	Christopher Cotton	39.95
17	Cynthia Baker	5.00
18	Danny F. Rutherford	26.00
19	David A. Ramos	5.00
20	David Burns	39.95
21	Debbie R. Krach	39.95
22	Debra L. Eldridge	26.00

‖◄ ◄ ► ►‖ **Sheet1** ╱ Sheet2 ╱ ╲

Figure 19-4: The length of the data bars is proportional to the value in the cell.

TIP

The differences between the bar lengths become more prominent when you increase the column width.

Excel provides quick access to six data bar colors via the Home⇨Styles⇨Conditional Formatting⇨Data Bars command. For additional choices, click the More Rules option, which displays the New Formatting Rule dialog box. Use this dialog box to

- Show the bar only (hide the numbers).
- Adjust how the bars relate to the values (use the Type and Value controls).
- Change the color of the bars.

NOTE

Data bars are always displayed as a color gradient (from dark to light), and you can't change the display style. Also, the colors used are not theme colors. If you apply a new document theme, the data bar colors do not change.

If you make adjustments in this dialog box, you can use the Preview button to see the formats before you commit to them by clicking OK.

 NOTE

You may notice something odd about the data bars in Figure 19-4. Contrary to what you may expect, a cell with a zero value displays a data bar. Data bar conditional formatting always displays a bar for every cell, even for zero values. The smallest value in the range always has a bar length equal to ten percent of the cell's width. Unfortunately, Excel provides no direct way to modify the minimum percent setting. However, if you're familiar with VBA, you can use a statement like the following to set the minimum display width for a range that uses conditional formatting data bars:

```
Range("B2:B123").FormatConditions(1).PercentMin = 1
```

After executing this statement, the minimum value in the range will display a bar length equal to one percent of the cell's width—and zero value cells will not display a data bar.

USING DATA BARS IN LIEU OF A CHART

Using the data bars conditional formatting can sometimes serve as a quick alternative to creating a chart. Figure 19-5 shows a three-column table of data, with data bars applied in the third column. The third column of the table contains references to the values in the second column. The conditional formatting in the third column uses the Show Bars Only option.

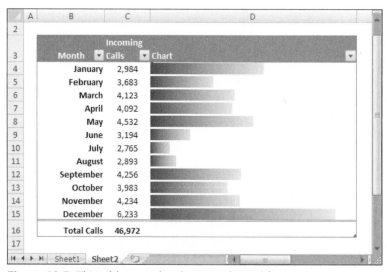

Figure 19-5: This table uses data bars conditional formatting.

Figure 19-6 shows an actual bar chart created from the same data. The bar chart takes about the same amount of time to create and is a lot more flexible. But for a quick-and-dirty chart, data bars are a good option — especially when you need to create several such charts.

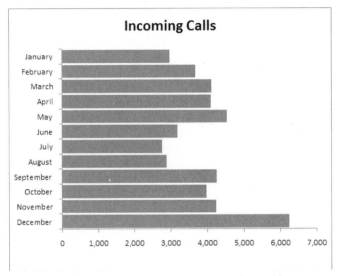

Figure 19-6: A real Excel bar chart (not conditional formatting data bars).

USING COLOR SCALES

The *color scale conditional formatting option* varies the background color of a cell based on the cell's value, relative to other cells in the range.

Figure 19-7 shows a range of cells that use color scale conditional formatting. It depicts the number of employees on each day of the year. This is a three-color scale that uses red for the lowest value, yellow for the midpoint, and green for the highest value. Values in between are displayed using a color within the gradient.

ON THE CD

This workbook, named `daily staffing level.xlsx`, is available on the companion CD-ROM.

Excel provides four two-color scale presets and four three-color scales presets, which you can apply to the selected range by choosing Home⇨Styles⇨Conditional Formatting⇨Color Scales.

To customize the colors and other options, choose Home⇨Styles⇨Conditional Formatting⇨Color Scales⇨More Rules. This command displays the New Formatting Rule dialog box, shown in Figure 19-8.

Part V

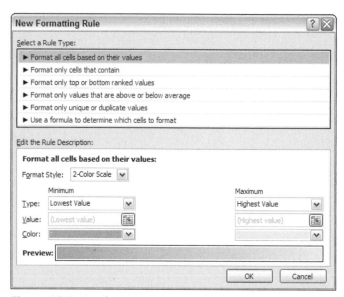

	A	1	2	3	4	5	6	7	8	9	10	11	12	13	14	15	16	17	18	19	20	21	22	23	24	25	26	27	28	29	30	31
1	Daily Staffing Level																															
2																																
3		1	2	3	4	5	6	7	8	9	10	11	12	13	14	15	16	17	18	19	20	21	22	23	24	25	26	27	28	29	30	31
4	January	80	80	80	80	80	80	80	79	79	79	79	79	79	80	82	82	82	82	82	82	82	82	82	82	84	84	84	84	84	84	84
5	February	84	84	84	84	84	84	84	84	83	83	83	82	82	82	82	82	82	82	82	82	82	82	82	82	85	85	85				
6	March	85	85	85	85	85	85	85	85	85	85	85	85	86	86	86	86	86	86	86	86	86	86	86	86	86	86	86	86	86	86	86
7	April	88	88	88	88	88	88	88	88	88	88	88	88	88	88	89	89	89	89	89	88	88	88	88	88	88	88	88	88	88	88	
8	May	88	88	88	88	88	88	88	88	88	88	89	89	89	89	89	89	89	89	89	89	89	89	89	89	89	92	92	92	92	92	92
9	June	92	92	92	92	92	92	92	92	92	92	92	92	91	91	91	91	91	91	91	91	91	91	92	92	92	92	92	92	92	92	
10	July	92	92	92	92	92	92	92	92	92	92	92	93	95	95	95	95	96	98	98	98	96	94	94	94	94	94	92	92	92	92	92
11	August	92	92	92	92	91	90	90	90	90	91	92	92	92	92	92	92	92	92	92	92	92	92	92	92	92	92	92	92	92	92	92
12	September	92	93	93	93	93	93	93	93	93	93	93	93	93	93	93	93	94	94	94	94	94	94	94	94	94	94	95	95	95		
13	October	95	95	95	95	95	95	94	94	94	94	94	95	95	95	95	95	96	96	96	96	96	96	96	96	96	96	97	97	97	97	
14	November	97	97	97	97	97	97	97	96	96	96	96	97	97	97	99	99	99	99	99	99	99	99	99	99	99	99	99	99	99	99	
15	December	101	101	101	101	101	101	101	101	102	102	102	102	102	102	102	102	102	102	101	101	101	101	101	101	101	101	101	101	101	101	101
16																																

Figure 19-7: A range that uses color scale conditional formatting.

Figure 19-8: Use the New Formatting Rule dialog box to customize a color scale.

It's important to understand that color scale conditional formatting uses a gradient. For example, if you format a range with a two-color scale, you will get a lot more than two colors because you'll get colors with the gradient between the two specified colors.

Figure 19-9 shows an extreme example that uses color scale conditional formatting on a range of 10,000 cells (100 rows x 100 columns). The worksheet is zoomed down to 20% to display a very smooth three-color gradient. The range contains formulas like this one, in cell C5:

```
=SIN($A2)+COS(B$1)Values
```

in column A and row 1 range from 0 to 4.0, in increments of 0.04.

Figure 19-9: This worksheet, which uses color scale conditional formatting, is zoomed to 20%.

The result, when viewed on your, screen is stunning. (It loses a lot when converted to grayscale.)

 ## ON THE CD

This workbook, named `extreme color scale.xlsx`, is available on the companion CD-ROM.

 ## NOTE

You can't hide the cell contents when using a color scale rule, so I formatted the cells using this custom number format:

```
;;;
```

USING ICON SETS

Yet another conditional formatting option is to display an icon in the cell. The icon displayed depends on the value of the cells.

To assign an icon set to a range, select the cells and choose Home⇨Styles⇨Conditional Formatting⇨Icon Sets. Excel provides 17 icon sets to choose from. *Note:* You can't create your set of icons. The number of icons in the sets ranges from 3–5.

Figure 19-10 shows a simple example that uses the icon set named Three Symbols (Uncircled). The symbols graphically depict the status of each project, based on the value in column C.

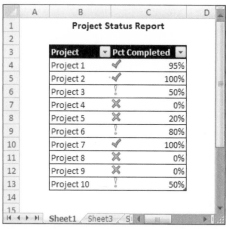

Figure 19-10: Using an icon set to indicate the status of projects.

 ON THE CD

All the icon set examples in this section are available on the companion CD-ROM. The workbook is named icon set examples.xlsx.

By default, the symbols are assigned using percentiles. For a three-symbol set, the items are grouped into three percentiles. For a four-symbol set, they're grouped into four percentiles. And for a five-symbol set, the items are grouped into five percentiles.

If you would like more control over how the icons are assigned, choose Home⇨Styles⇨ Conditional Formatting⇨Icon Sets⇨More Rules to display the New Formatting Rule dialog box. Figure 19-11 shows how to modify the icon set rules such that only projects that are 100% completed get check mark icons. Projects that are 0% completed get an X icon. All other projects get an exclamation point icon.

Figure 19-12 shows the task list after making this change.

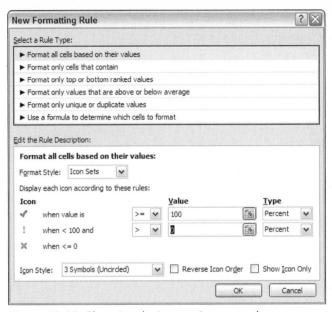

Figure 19-11: Changing the icon assignment rule.

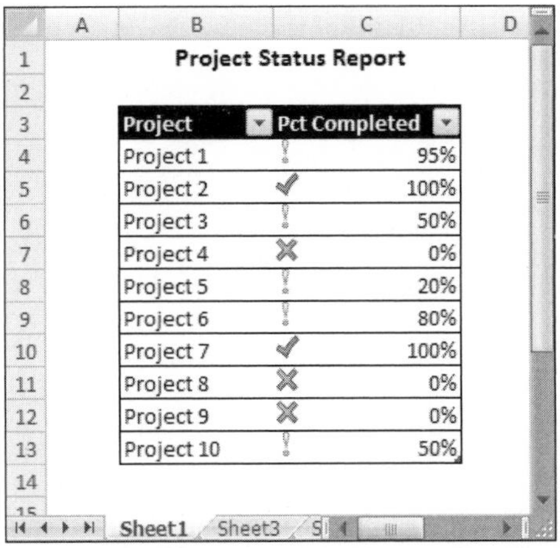

Figure 19-12: Using a customized icon set to indicate the status of projects.

Figure 19-13 shows a table that contains two test scores for each student. The Change column contains a formula that calculates the difference between the two tests. The Trend column uses an icon set to display the trend graphically.

	A	B	C	D	E	F
1						
2	Student ▼	Test 1 ▼	Test 2 ▼	Change ▼	Trend ▼	
3	Amy	59	65	6	⬆	
4	Bob	82	78	-4	⇨	
5	Calvind	98	92	-6	⬇	
6	Doug	56	69	13	⬆	
7	Ephraim	98	89	-9	⬇	
8	Frank	67	75	8	⬆	
9	Gretta	78	87	9	⬆	
10	Harold	87	95	8	⬆	
11	Inez	56	85	29	⬆	
12	June	87	72	-15	⬇	
13	Kenny	87	88	1	⇨	
14	Lance	92	92	0	⇨	
15	Marvin	82	73	-9	⬇	
16	Noel	98	100	2	⇨	
17	Opie	84	73	-11	⬇	
18	Paul	94	93	-1	⇨	
19	Quinton	68	92	24	⬆	
20	Rasmus	91	90	-1	⇨	
21	Sam	85	86	1	⇨	
22	Ted	72	92	20	⬆	
23	Ursie	80	71	-9	⬇	
24	Valerie	77	65	-12	⬇	
25	Wally	64	45	-19	⬇	
26	Xerxes	59	63	4	⇨	
27	Yolanda	89	99	10	⬆	
28	Zippy	85	82	-3	⇨	
29						

⊮ ◀ ▶ ▶⊯ Sheet1 **Sheet3** Sheet2 Sh ◀

Figure 19-13: The arrows depict the trend from Test 1 to Test 2.

This example uses the icon set named 3 Arrows, and I customized the rule:

- **Up Arrow:** When value is >=5
- **Level Arrow:** When value <5 and >= -5
- **Down Arrow:** When value is >=5

In other words, difference of five points or less in either direction is considered an even trend. An improvement of more than five points is considered a positive trend, and a decline of more than five points is considered a negative trend.

NOTE

The Trend column contains a formula that references the Change column. I used the Show Icon Only option in the Trend column, which also centers the icon in the column.

In some cases, you may want to display only one icon from an icon set. Excel doesn't provide this option directly, but displaying a single icon is possible if you use two rules. Figure 19-14 shows a range of values. Only the values greater than or equal to 80 display an icon.

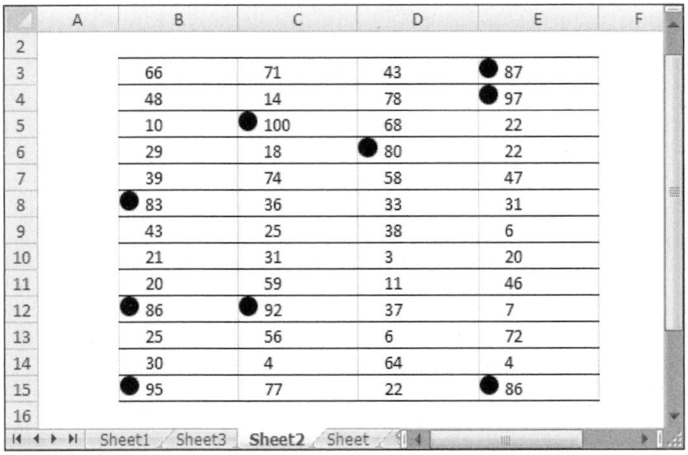

	A	B	C	D	E	F
2						
3		66	71	43	87	
4		48	14	78	97	
5		10	100	68	22	
6		29	18	80	22	
7		39	74	58	47	
8		83	36	33	31	
9		43	25	38	6	
10		21	31	3	20	
11		20	59	11	46	
12		86	92	37	7	
13		25	56	6	72	
14		30	4	64	4	
15		95	77	22	86	
16						

Figure 19-14: Displaying only one icon from an icon set.

Here's how to set up an icon set such that only values greater than or equal to 80 display an icon:

1. Select the cells, choose Home➪Styles➪Conditional Formatting➪Icon Sets, and select any icon set. Keep in mind that only the last icon of the set will be used.
2. With the range selected, choose Home➪Styles➪Conditional Formatting➪Manage Rules. Excel displays its Conditional Formatting Rules Manager dialog box.
3. Click Edit Rule to display the Edit Formatting Rule dialog box.
4. Change the first icon setting to When Value Is >= 80 and specify Number as the Type. Leave the other icon settings as they are, and then click OK to return to the Conditional Formatting Rules Manager.
5. Click New Rule and then choose this rule type: Format Only Cells That Contain.
6. In the bottom section of the dialog box, specify Cell Value Less Than 80 and then click OK to return to the Conditional Formatting Rules Manager. The range now has two rules.
7. Place a check mark next to Stop If True for the first rule. Figure 19-15 shows the completed dialog box.
8. Click OK.

Figure 19-15: The Conditional Formatting Rules Manager dialog box.

The first rule checks whether the value is less than 80. If so, rule checking stops, and no conditional formatting is applied. If the value is greater than or equal to 80, the second rule kicks in. This rule indicates that values greater than or equal to 80 are displayed with an icon.

Working with Conditional Formats

This section describes some additional information about conditional formatting that you may find useful.

MANAGING RULES

The Conditional Formatting Rules Manager dialog box is useful for checking, editing, deleting, and adding conditional formats. Access this dialog box by choosing Home⇨Styles⇨Conditional Formatting⇨Manage Rules.

You can specify as many rules as you like by clicking the New Rule button. As you can see in Figure 19-16, cells can even use data bars, color scales, and icon sets all at the same time — although I can't think of a good reason to do so.

COPYING CELLS THAT CONTAIN CONDITIONAL FORMATTING

Conditional formatting information is stored with a cell much like how standard formatting information is stored with a cell. As a result, when you copy a cell that contains conditional formatting, you also copy the conditional formatting.

TIP

To copy only the formatting (including conditional formatting), use the Paste Special dialog box and select the Formats option.

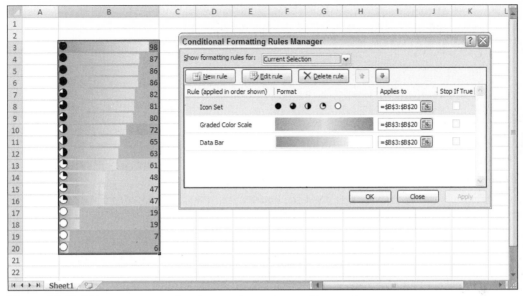

Figure 19-16: This ranges uses data bars, color scales, and icon sets.

Inserting rows or columns within a range that contains conditional formatting causes the new cells to have the same conditional formatting.

DELETING CONDITIONAL FORMATTING

When you press Delete to delete the contents of a cell, you do not delete the conditional formatting for the cell (if any). To remove all conditional formats (as well as all other cell formatting), select the cells and choose Home⇨Editing⇨Clear⇨Clear Formats. Or, choose Home⇨Editing⇨Clear⇨Clear All to delete the cell contents and the conditional formatting.

To remove only conditional formatting (and leave the other formatting intact), use Home⇨ Styles⇨Conditional Formatting⇨Clear Rules.

FIND AND REPLACE LIMITATIONS

Excel's Find And Replace dialog box includes a feature that allows you to search your worksheet to locate cells that contain specific formatting. This feature does *not* locate cells that contain formatting resulting from conditional formatting.

LOCATING CELLS THAT CONTAIN CONDITIONAL FORMATTING

Just by looking at a cell, you can't tell whether it contains conditional formatting. You can, however, use Excel's Go To dialog box to select such cells.

1. Choose Home⇨Editing⇨Find & Select⇨Go To Special.

2. In the Go To Special dialog box, select the Conditional Formats option.

Part V

3. To select all cells on the worksheet containing conditional formatting, select the All option. To select only the cells that contain the same conditional formatting as the active cell, select the Same option.

4. Click OK. Excel selects the cells for you.

Creating Formula-Based Rules

Excel's conditional formatting feature is versatile, but sometimes it's just not quite versatile enough. Fortunately, you can extend its versatility by writing conditional formatting formulas.

The examples later in this section describe how to create conditional formatting formulas for the following:

- To identify text entries
- To identify dates that fall on a weekend
- To format cells that are in odd-numbered rows or columns (for dynamic alternate row or columns shading)
- To format groups of rows (for example, shading every group of two rows)
- To display a sum only when all precedent cells contain values
- To identify text cells that begin with the same first letter as a letter in a cell
- To identify cells that contain a value that meets a criterion entered in a cell

Some of these formulas may be useful to you. If not, they may inspire you to create other conditional formatting formulas.

To specify conditional formatting based on a formula, select the cells and then choose Home⇨Styles⇨Conditional Formatting⇨New Rule. This command displays the New Formatting Rule dialog box. Click the rule type labeled Use A Formula To Determine Which Cells To Format, and you'll be able to specify the formula.

You can type the formula directly into the box, or you can enter a reference to an existing formula. As with normal Excel formulas, the formula you enter here must begin with an equal sign (=).

 NOTE

The formula must be a logical formula that returns either TRUE or FALSE. If the formula evaluates to TRUE, the condition is satisfied, and the conditional formatting is applied. If the formula evaluates to FALSE, the conditional formatting is not applied.

UNDERSTANDING RELATIVE AND ABSOLUTE REFERENCES

If the formula that you enter into the Conditional Formatting dialog box contains a cell reference, that reference is considered a *relative reference*, based on the upper-left cell in the selected range.

For example, suppose that you want to set up a conditional formatting condition that applies shading to cells in range A1:B10 only if the cell contains text. None of Excel's conditional formatting options can do this task, so you need to create a formula that will return TRUE if the cell contains text and FALSE otherwise. Follow these steps:

1. Select the range A1:B10 and ensure that cell A1 is the active cell.

2. Choose Home⇨Styles⇨Conditional Formatting⇨New Rule to display the New Formatting Rule dialog box.

3. Click the rule type labeled Use a Formula to Determine Which Cells to Format.

4. Enter the following formula in the Formula box:

   ```
   =ISTEXT(A1)
   ```

5. Click the Format button to display the Format Cells dialog box.

6. In the Format Cells dialog box, click the Fill tab and specify the cell shading that will be applied if the formula returns TRUE.

7. Click OK to return to the New Formatting Rule dialog box (see Figure 19-17).

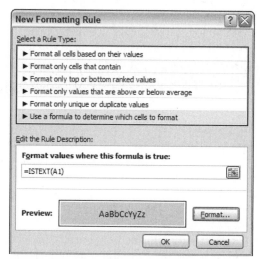

Figure 19-17: Creating a conditional formatting rule based on a formula.

8. In the New Formatting Rule dialog box, click the Preview button to make sure that the formula is working correctly and to see a preview of your selected formatting.

9. If the preview looks correct, click OK to close the New Formatting Rule dialog box.

Part V

Notice that the formula entered in Step 4 contains a relative reference to the upper-left cell in the selected range.

Generally, when entering a conditional formatting formula for a range of cells, you'll use a reference to the active cell, which is normally the upper-left cell in the selected range. One exception is when you need to refer to a specific cell. For example, suppose that you select range A1:B10, and you want to apply formatting to all cells in the range that exceed the value in cell C1. Enter this conditional formatting formula:

```
=A1>$C$1
```

In this case, the reference to cell C1 is an *absolute reference:* It will not be adjusted for the cells in the selected range. In other words, the conditional formatting formula for cell A2 looks like this:

```
=A2>$C$1
```

The relative cell reference is adjusted, but the absolute cell reference is not.

USING REFERENCES TO OTHER SHEETS

If you enter a conditional formatting formula that uses one or more references to other sheets, Excel responds with an error message. If you need to refer to a cell on a different sheet, you must create a reference to that cell on the sheet that contains the conditional formatting. For example, if your conditional formatting formula needs to refer to cell A1 on Sheet3, you can insert the following formula into a cell on the active sheet:

```
=Sheet3!A1
```

Then use a reference to that cell in your conditional formatting formula.

TIP

Another option is to create a name for the cell (by using Formulas⇨Defined Names⇨ Define Name). After defining the name, you can use the name in place of the cell reference in your conditional formatting formula. If you use this technique, the named cell can be in any worksheet in the workbook.

CONDITIONAL FORMATTING FORMULA EXAMPLES

Each of these examples uses a formula entered directly into the New Formatting Rule dialog box, after selecting the rule type labeled Use a Formula to Determine Which Cells to Format. You decide the type of formatting that you apply conditionally.

ON THE CD

The companion CD-ROM contains all the examples in this section. The file is named `conditional formatting formulas.xlsx`.

Identifying Weekend Days

Excel provides a number of conditional formatting rules that deal with dates, but it doesn't let you identify dates that fall on a weekend. Use this formula to identify weekend dates:

```
=OR(WEEKDAY(A1)=7,WEEKDAY(A1)=1)
```

This formula assumes that a range is selected and also that cell A1 is the active cell.

Identifying Cells Containing More Than One Word

You also can use conditional formatting with text. For example, you can use the following conditional formatting formula to apply formatting to cells that contain more than one word:

```
=LEN(TRIM(A1))-LEN(SUBSTITUTE(A1," ",""))>0
```

This formula assumes that the selected range begins in cell A1. The formula works by counting the space characters in the cell (using the TRIM function to strip out multiple spaces). If the count is greater than 0, the formula returns TRUE, and the conditional formatting is applied.

Displaying Alternate-Row Shading

The conditional formatting formula that follows was applied to the range A1:D18, as shown in Figure 19-18, to apply shading to alternate rows:

```
=MOD(ROW(),2)=0
```

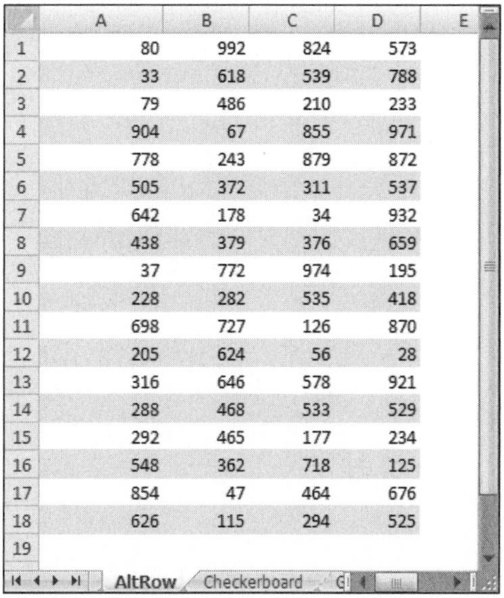

	A	B	C	D	E
1	80	992	824	573	
2	33	618	539	788	
3	79	486	210	233	
4	904	67	855	971	
5	778	243	879	872	
6	505	372	311	537	
7	642	178	34	932	
8	438	379	376	659	
9	37	772	974	195	
10	228	282	535	418	
11	698	727	126	870	
12	205	624	56	28	
13	316	646	578	921	
14	288	468	533	529	
15	292	465	177	234	
16	548	362	718	125	
17	854	47	464	676	
18	626	115	294	525	
19					

AltRow / Checkerboard

Figure 19-18: Using conditional formatting to apply formatting to alternate rows.

Part V

Alternate row shading can make your spreadsheets easier to read. If you add or delete rows within the conditional formatting area, the shading is updated automatically.

This formula uses the ROW function (which returns the row number) and the MOD function (which returns the remainder of its first argument divided by its second argument). For cells in even-numbered rows, the MOD function returns 0, and cells in that row are formatted.

For alternate shading of columns, use the COLUMN function instead of the ROW function.

Creating Checkerboard Shading

The following formula is a variation on the example in the preceding section. It applies formatting to alternate rows and columns, creating a checkerboard effect.

```
=MOD(ROW(),2)=MOD(COLUMN(),2)
```

Shading Groups of Rows

Here's another rows shading variation. The following formula shades alternate groups of rows. It produces four rows of shaded rows, followed by four rows of unshaded rows, followed by four more shaded rows, and so on.

```
=MOD(INT((ROW()-1)/4)+1,2)
```

Figure 19-19 shows an example.

	A	B	C	D
1	385	235	181	311
2	104	326	610	981
3	858	480	898	210
4	195	797	145	548
5	469	963	347	992
6	769	890	919	412
7	188	913	432	816
8	881	396	639	699
9	621	187	555	803
10	696	346	906	605
11	561	627	462	771
12	364	154	402	953
13	179	216	883	677
14	108	60	983	321
15	73	848	8	210
16	614	297	195	456
17	806	670	265	589
18	103	196	343	699
19	611	910	22	379
20	520	96	440	440
21	856	129	643	567
22	545	71	204	930
23				

Groups4 / AllData

Figure 19-19: Conditional formatting produces these groups of alternate shaded rows.

For different sized groups, change the 4 to some other value. For example, use this formula to shade alternate groups of two rows:

```
=MOD(INT((ROW()-1)/2)+1,2)
```

Displaying a Total Only When All Values Are Entered

Figure 19-20 shows a range with a formula that uses the SUM function in cell C6. Conditional formatting is used to hide the sum if any of the four cells above is blank. The conditional formatting formula for cell C6 (and cell C5, which contains a label) is

```
=COUNT($C$2:$C$5)=4
```

This formula returns TRUE only if C2:C5 contains no empty cells.

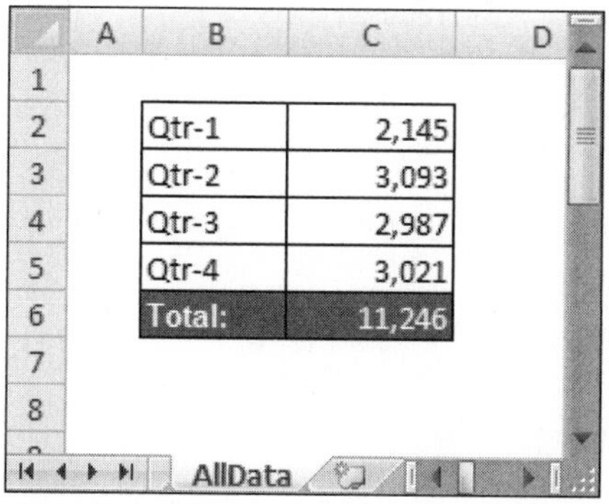

Figure 19-20: The sum is displayed only when all four values have been entered.

Figure 19-21 shows the worksheet when one of the values is missing.

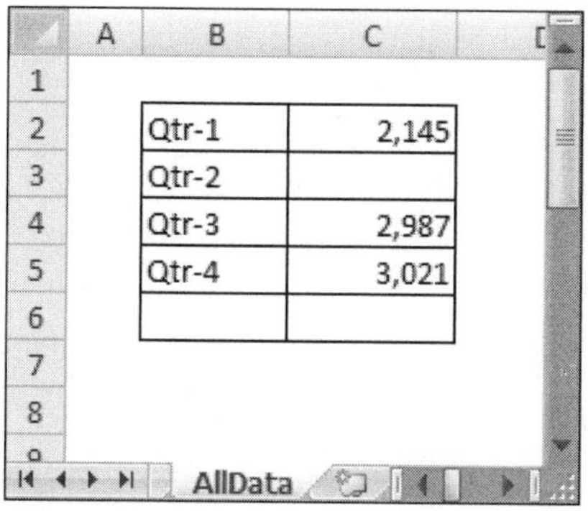

Figure 19-21: A missing value causes the sum to be hidden.

Part V

Identifing Text Cells That Begin with a Certain Letter

The worksheet shown in Figure 19-22 contains a list of names in the range A5:G32. Cell A1 contains a letter of the alphabet. A conditional formatting formula highlights the names that begin with the letter in cell A1.

The conditional formatting formula for the range A5:G32 is

```
=LEFT(A5)=LEFT($A$1)
```

	A	B	C	D	E	F
1	W	<--- Enter a letter				
2						
3						
4						
5	Alan Gillingham	Tammy Philpot	Wendy Lauver	Diane Willis	David Martin	Frank Mcmu
6	Mary Repass	Claudette Juarez	Laticia Rosenberger	Joseph Parks	James Gentry	Willie U. Po
7	Ethel Spencer	Caroline Mcguire	Scott P. Flynn	David J. Bowley	Mary England	Charles B. G
8	Deanna I. Davis	Rachel Shaffer	Richard E. Fredericks	David Flowers	Marvin H. Mcquillen	Isidro E. Jen
9	Jeanne Cosme	Maureen S. Hudson	Amy Brown	Francisco Elder	Violet Lee	Christopher
10	Mary Dailey	Elizabeth Brown	Taylor Rice	Thomas Armijo	Charlie B. Stine	Andre Flore
11	Joy Franklin	Justine Vargas	John Toth	Gregory Reese	Tim Q. Lowery	Doris Howe
12	John I. Jimenez	Maria Pilon	Lucille T. Coward	Jean Schwab	Lauren Rosa	Anna Goodv
13	Denise N. Page	Christopher R. Drake	Linda Sanders	Sarah Alonso	Paul L. Marks	Delia Ware
14	Jennifer Schoonmaker	Michael Borg	Leon Gibson	Donald Dehaven	Hattie Herrera	Donna M. Fc
15	William Mckinstry	Gerald Trujillo	Stephen J. Guajardo	Santos H. Purdie	William Hartzler	Lawrence O
16	Lucille H. Pack	Angel C. Lemos	Velma Fincher	Jay Brown	Beth Martin	Diane Aceve
17	Jennifer Machen	Gregory Davis	Armando U. Taylor	Douglas Snipes	Evette Jeffords	James B. Me
18	Dana Wilson	Jason Palmieri	Randy D. Phillips	Wanda Bergerson	Angela Mitchell	Daniel P. Mi
19	Karen Pierce	Ray Z. Everett	Evelyn Mcdaniel	Ted Mccarthy	Ida Wyse	Kristen Brov
20	Gordon Weaver	Pasquale Valenzuela	Kira Dalton	Sherri N. Kittrell	Rebecca Morgan	Michael Joh
21	Corey Alvarez	Lois Patin	John Popp	Beverly Deloach	Hope Holston	Leah R. Rod
22	William Young	Ashley Silvestri	Frankie Higby	Suzanne Witt	Anita I. Loughran	Angela Dick
23	Joe Ewert	Kurt K. Aultman	John Torres	Mary Starks	Joe Mcray	Alma Crand

AltRow Checkerboard Groups4 AllData **SameFirstLetter** VariableCriteria

Figure 19-22: Names that begin with the letter entered in cell A1 are highlighted.

Identifying Cells That Meet a Numeric Criteria

The example in this section is similar to the previous example, but it involves values. The range A5:P32 uses the following conditional formatting formula:

```
=COUNTIF(A5,$A$1)=1
```

This formula takes advantage of the fact that the COUNTIF function can handle criteria that are entered in a cell. Figure 19-23 shows the worksheet when cell A1 contains the text >90.

	A	B	C	D	E	F	G	H	I	J
1	>90	<--- Enter a condition								
2										
3										
4										
5	41	9	-16	2	85	-57	43	56	1	74
6	-75	66	38	-35	-17	-13	15	39	13	39
7	-90	48	0	-7	14	12	-18	-96	-33	21
8	-21	6	-18	83	69	-50	47	77	90	-11
9	96	-84	-3	73	79	-61	12	88	89	-7
10	-92	80	51	3	-98	-48	85	-85	-73	-35
11	25	7	-69	71	-55	36	12	-13	-34	13
12	-6	-23	8	-88	52	55	51	66	-79	-46
13	12	70	-38	38	-35	40	-94	96	23	-99
14	20	89	14	-65	92	96	-27	40	-72	-23
15	-80	-54	17	91	-77	-31	-18	-75	69	-43
16	-21	-25	-34	69	-29	84	88	-20	93	-62
17	79	52	-37	63	-9	-73	37	24	46	40
18	-41	41	72	-64	-96	-71	57	-62	-56	-54
19	-48	71	75	-32	59	-44	-74	-12	50	-61
20	61	-100	59	94	-27	-1	-78	80	-87	-41
21	-86	-78	-2	61	89	-51	62	87	41	84
22	86	75	-2	74	-58	37	13	-99	92	63
23	-14	58	-100	24	-91	-34	80	-50	69	86
24	21	-54	-32	-46	49	70	-78	30	83	12

Groups4 / AllData / SameFirstLetter / **VariableCriteria**

Figure 19-23: Cells that meet the criteria entered in cell A1 are highlighted.

USING CUSTOM FUNCTIONS IN CONDITIONAL FORMATTING FORMULAS

Excel's conditional formatting feature is very versatile. If it's not versatile enough, you can create your own formulas to define the conditions (as I explained in the previous sections). And if custom formulas still aren't versatile enough, you can create custom VBA function and use those in a conditional formatting formula.

This section provides three examples of VBA functions used in conditional formatting formulas.

CROSS REF

Part VI provides an overview of VBA, with specific information about creating custom worksheet functions.

ON THE CD

The companion CD-ROM contains all the examples in this section. The file is named conditional formatting with VBA function.xlsm.

Part V

Identifying Formula Cells

Oddly, Excel does not have a function that determines whether a cell contains a formula. When Excel lacks a feature, you often can overcome the limitation by using VBA. The following custom VBA function uses the VBA `HasFormula` property. The function, which is entered into a VBA module, returns TRUE if the cell (specified as its argument) contains a formula; otherwise, it returns FALSE.

```
Function ISFORMULACELL(cell) As Boolean
    ISFORMULACELL = cell.HasFormula
End Function
```

After you enter this function into a VBA module, you can use the function in your worksheet formulas. For example, the following formula returns TRUE if cell A1 contains a formula:

```
=ISFORMULACELL(A1)
```

And you also can use this function in a conditional formatting formula. The worksheet in Figure 19-24, for example, uses conditional formatting to highlight all cells that contain a formula.

	A	B	C	D	E
1		**Last Year**	**This Year**	**Difference**	
2	Jan	143	155	12	
3	Feb	155	188	33	
4	Mar	133	122	-11	
5	Q1	431	465	34	
6	Apr	160	178	18	
7	May	187	203	16	
8	Jun	199	221	22	
9	Q2	546	602	56	
10	Jul	201	273	72	
11	Aug	177	212	35	
12	Sep	191	198	7	
13	Q3	569	683	114	
14	Oct	244	255	11	
15	Nov	199	188	-11	
16	Dec	211	233	22	
17	Q4	654	676	22	
18	Total	2200	2426	226	
19					
20					

| ◄ ◄ ► ► | Formulas | Dates | InvalidData |

Figure 19-24: Using a custom VBA function to apply conditional formatting to cells that contain a formula.

NOTE

Another way to identify formula cells is to use the Home⇨Editing⇨Find & Select⇨Go To Special command, which displays the Go To Special dialog box. Choose the Formulas option and click OK to select all cells that contain a formula.

Identifying Date Cells

Excel also lacks a function to determine whether a cell contains a date. The following VBA function, which uses the VBA IsDate function, overcomes this limitation. The custom HASDATE function returns TRUE if the cell contains a date.

```
Function HASDATE(cell) As Boolean
    HASDATE = IsDate(cell)
End Function
```

The following conditional formatting formula applies formatting to cell A1 if it contains a date and the month is June:

```
=AND(HASDATE(A1),MONTH(A1)=6)
```

The following conditional formatting formula applies formatting to cell A1 if it contains a date and the date falls on a weekend:

```
=AND(HASDATE(A1),OR(WEEKDAY(A1)=7,WEEKDAY(A1)=1))
```

Identifying Invalid Data

You might have a situation in which the data entered must adhere to some very specific rules, and you'd like to apply special formatting if the data entered is not valid. You might have part numbers that consist of seven characters: four uppercase alphabetic characters, followed by a hyphen, and then a two-digit number — for example, ADSS-09 or DYUU-43.

You can write a conditional formatting formula to determine whether part numbers adhere to this structure, but the formula is very complex. The following formula, for example, returns TRUE only if the value in A1 meets the part number rules specified:

```
=AND(LEN(A1)=7,AND(LEFT(A1)>="A",LEFT(A1)<="Z"),
AND(MID(A1,2,1)>="A",MID(A1,2,1)<="Z"),AND(MID(A1,3,1)>="A",
MID(A1,3,1)<="Z"),AND(MID(A1,4,1)>="A",MID(A1,4,1)<="Z"),
MID(A1,5,1)="-",AND(VALUE(MID(A1,6,2))>=0,
VALUE(MID(A1,6,2))<=99))
```

For a simpler approach, write a custom VBA worksheet function. The VBA Like operator makes this sort of comparison relatively easy. The following VBA function procedure returns TRUE if its argument does not correspond to the part number rules outlined previously:

```
Function INVALIDPART(n) As Boolean
    If n Like "[A-Z][A-Z][A-Z][A-Z]-##" Then
        INVALIDPART = False
```

Part V

```
    Else
        INVALIDPART = True
    End If
End Function
```

After defining this function in a VBA module, you can enter the following conditional formatting formula to apply special formatting if cell A1 contains an invalid part number:

```
=INVALIDPART(A1)
```

Figure 19-25 shows a range that uses the custom INVALIDPART function in a conditional formatting formula. Cells that contain invalid part numbers have a colored background.

In many cases, you can simply take advantage of Excel's data validation feature, which is described next.

	A	B
1	AFDD-98	
2	*afdd-98*	
3	*PKJJ-YT*	
4	TRYP-74	
5	TRYP-09	
6	TRYP-10	
7	*RFGG98*	
8	PRFF-00	
9	MOKJ-78	
10	ADSF-71	
11	*KBR4-998*	
12	KLRR-90	
13	AGGT-91	
14	*KBTR=71*	
15		
16		
17		

Formulas / Dates

Figure 19-25: Using conditional formatting to highlight cells with invalid entries.

Data Validation

Excel's data validation feature is similar in many respects to the conditional formatting feature. This feature enables you to set up certain rules that dictate what you can enter into a cell. For example, you may want to limit data entry to whole numbers between 1 and 12. If the user makes an invalid entry, you can display a custom message, such as the one shown in Figure 19-26.

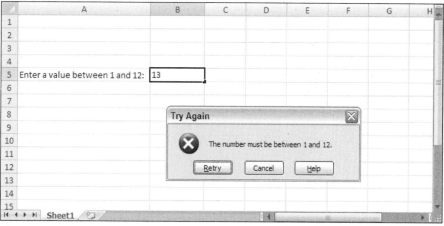

Figure 19-26: Displaying a message when the user makes an invalid entry.

As with the conditional formatting feature, you can use a logical formula to specify your data validation criteria.

Excel 2007 has lots of new conditional formatting features, but the data validation feature has not changed at all.

CAUTION

The data validation feature suffers from a potentially serious problem: If the user copies a cell and pastes it to a cell that contains data validation, the data validation rules are deleted. Consequently, the cell then accepts any type of data.

Specifying Validation Criteria

To specify the type of data allowable in a cell or range, follow these steps:

1. Select the cell or range.

2. Choose Data⇨Data Tools⇨Data Validation. Excel displays its Data Validation dialog box.

3. Click the Settings tab (see Figure 19-27).

4. Choose an option from the drop-down box labeled Allow. The contents of the Data Validation dialog box will change, and display controls based on your choice. To specify a formula, select Custom.

5. Specify the conditions by using the displayed controls. Your selection in Step 4 determines what other controls you can access.

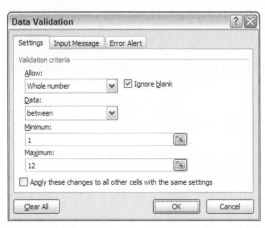

Figure 19-27: The Settings tab of the Data Validation dialog box.

6. (Optional) Click the Input Message tab and specify which message to display when a user selects the cell. You can use this optional step to tell the user what type of data is expected. If this step is omitted, no message will appear when the user selects the cell.

7. (Optional) Click the Error Alert tab and specify which error message to display when a user makes an invalid entry. The selection for Style determines what choices users have when they make invalid entries. To prevent an invalid entry, choose Stop. If this step is omitted, a standard message will appear if the user makes an invalid entry.

8. Click OK.

After you've performed these steps, the cell or range contains the validation criteria you specified.

Types of Validation Criteria You Can Apply

The Settings tab of the Data Validation dialog box enables you to specify a wide variety of data validation criteria. The following options are available in the Allow drop-down box. Keep in mind that the other controls in the Settings tab vary, depending on your choice in the Allow drop-down box.

- **Any Value:** Selecting this option removes any existing data validation. Note, however, that the input message (if any) still displays if the check box is checked in the Input Message tab.

- **Whole Number:** The user must enter a whole number. You specify a valid range of whole numbers by using the Data drop-down list. For example, you can specify that the entry must be a whole number greater than or equal to 100.

- **Decimal:** The user must enter a number. You specify a valid range of numbers by using the Data drop-down list. For example, you can specify that the entry must be greater than or equal to 0 and less than or equal to 1.

- **List:** The user must choose from a list of entries you provide. This option is very useful, and I discuss it in detail later in this chapter (see "Creating a Drop-Down List").

- **Date:** The user must enter a date. You specify a valid date range by using the Data drop-down list. For example, you can specify that the entered data must be greater than or equal to January 1, 2007, and less than or equal to December 31, 2007.

- **Time:** The user must enter a time. You specify a valid time range by using the Data drop-down list. For example, you can specify that the entered data must be greater than 12:00 p.m.

- **Text Length:** The length of the data (number of characters) is limited. You specify a valid length by using the Data drop-down list. For example, you can specify that the length of the entered data be 1 (a single alphanumeric character).

- **Custom:** To use this option, you must supply a logical formula that determines the validity of the user's entry. (A logical formula returns either TRUE or FALSE.) You can enter the formula directly into the Formula control (which appears when you select the Custom option), or you can specify a cell reference that contains a formula. This chapter contains examples of useful formulas.

The Settings tab of the Data Validation dialog box contains two other check boxes:

- **Ignore Blank:** If checked, blank entries are allowed.

- **Apply These Changes to All Other Cells with the Same Settings:** If checked, the changes you make apply to all other cells that contain the original data validation criteria.

It's important to understand that even with data validation in effect, the user can enter invalid data. If the Style setting in the Error Alert tab of the Data Validation dialog box is set to anything except Stop, invalid data *can* be entered. Also, remember that data validation does not apply to the calculated results of formulas. In other words, if the cell contains a formula, applying conditional formatting to that cell will have no effect.

Tip

The Data⇨Data Tools⇨Data Validation drop-down control contains an item named Circle Invalid Data. When you click this item, circles appear around cells that contain incorrect entries. If you correct an invalid entry, the circle disappears. To get rid of the circles, choose Data⇨Data Tools⇨Data Validation⇨Clear Validation Circles. In Figure 19-28, invalid entries are defined as values that are greater than 100.

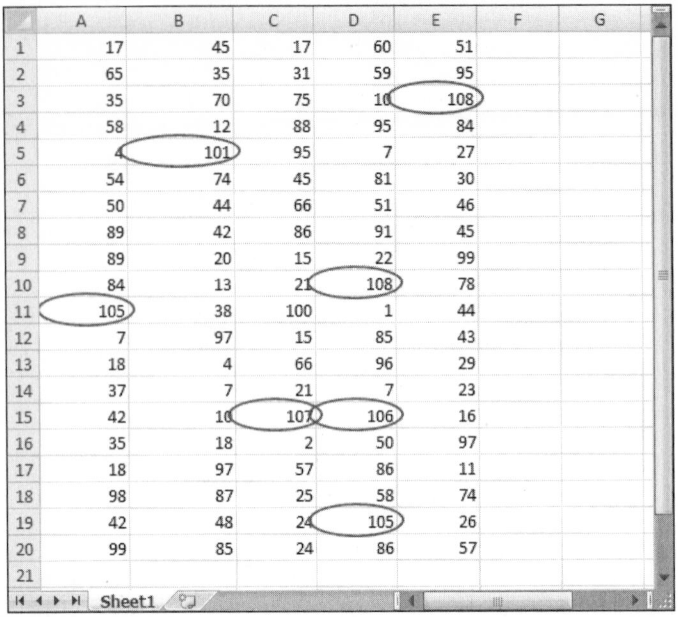

	A	B	C	D	E	F	G
1	17	45	17	60	51		
2	65	35	31	59	95		
3	35	70	75	10	108		
4	58	12	88	95	84		
5	4	101	95	7	27		
6	54	74	45	81	30		
7	50	44	66	51	46		
8	89	42	86	91	45		
9	89	20	15	22	99		
10	84	13	21	108	78		
11	105	38	100	1	44		
12	7	97	15	85	43		
13	18	4	66	96	29		
14	37	7	21	7	23		
15	42	16	107	106	16		
16	35	18	2	50	97		
17	18	97	57	86	11		
18	98	87	25	58	74		
19	42	48	24	105	26		
20	99	85	24	86	57		
21							

Sheet1

Figure 19-28: Excel can draw circles around invalid entries (in this case, cells that contain values greater than 100).

Creating a Drop-Down List

Perhaps one of the most common uses of data validation is to create a drop-down list in a cell. Figure 19-29 shows an example that uses the month names in A1:A12 as the list source.

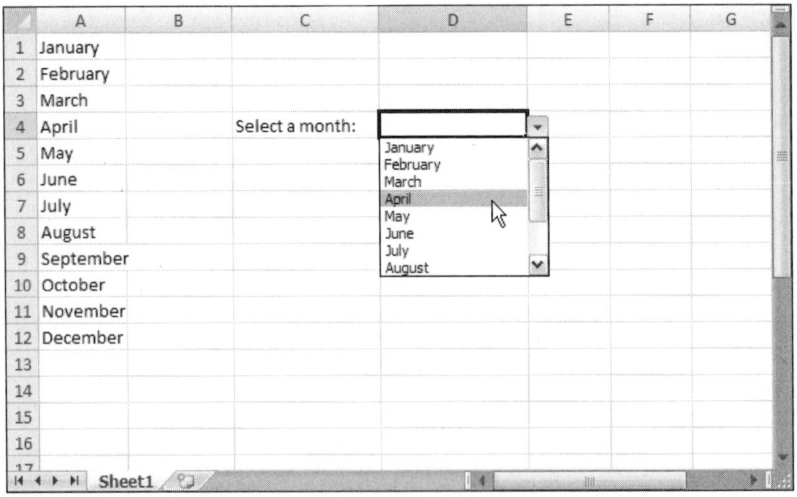

	A	B	C	D	E	F	G
1	January						
2	February						
3	March						
4	April		Select a month:				
5	May			January			
6	June			February			
7	July			March			
8	August			April			
9	September			May			
10	October			June			
11	November			July			
12	December			August			
13							
14							
15							
16							
17							

Sheet1

Figure 19-29: This drop-down list was created using data validation.

To create a drop-down list in a cell

1. Enter the list items into a single-row or single-column range. These items are the ones that appear in the drop-down list.

2. Select the cell that will contain the drop-down list and access the Data Validation dialog box.

3. In the Settings tab, select the List option and specify the range that contains the list using the Source control.

4. Make sure that the In-Cell Dropdown check box is checked.

5. Set any other Data Validation options as desired.

After performing these steps, the cell displays a drop-down arrow when it's activated. Click the arrow and choose an item from the list that appears.

TIP

If you have a short list, you can enter the items directly into the Source control in the Settings tab of the Data Validation dialog box. (This control appears when you choose the List option in the Allow drop-down list.) Just separate each item with list separator specified in your regional settings; use a comma if you use the U.S. regional settings.

TIP

If you specify a range for a list, the range must be on the same sheet. If your list is in a range on a different worksheet, you can provide a name for the range and then use the name as your list source (preceded by an equal sign). For example, if the list is on a different sheet in a range named MyList, enter the following:

```
=MyList
```

Using Formulas for Data Validation Rules

For simple data validation, the data validation feature is quite straightforward and easy to use, but the real power of this feature becomes apparent when you use data validation formulas.

NOTE

The formula that you specify must be a logical formula that returns either TRUE or FALSE. If the formula evaluates to TRUE, the data is considered valid and remains in the cell. If the formula evaluates to FALSE, a message box appears that displays the message specified in the Error Alert tab of the Data Validation dialog box.

Part V

You specify a formula in the Data Validation dialog box by selecting the Custom option in the Allow drop-down list on the Settings tab. You can enter the formula directly into the Formula control, or you can enter a reference to a cell that contains a formula. Note that the Formula control appears in the Settings tab of the Data Validation dialog box only when the Custom option is selected.

If the formula that you enter contains a cell reference, that reference will be considered to be a relative reference, based on the active cell in the selected range. This works exactly the same as using a formula for conditional formatting. (See "Creating Formula-Based Rules," earlier in this chapter.)

USING DATA VALIDATION FORMULAS TO ACCEPT ONLY SPECIFIC ENTRIES

Each of the following data validation examples uses a formula entered directly into the Formula control in the Data Validation dialog box. You can set up these formulas to accept only text, a certain value, nonduplicate entries, or text that begins with a specific letter.

ON THE CD

All the examples in this section are available on the companion CD-ROM. The filename is `data validation examples.xlsx`.

Accepting Text Only

Excel has a Data Validation option to limit the length of text entered into a cell, but it doesn't have an option to force text (rather than a number) into a cell. To force a cell or range to accept only text (no values), use the following data validation formula:

```
=ISTEXT(A1)
```

This formula assumes that the active cell in the selected range is cell A1.

Using Custom Worksheet Functions in Data Validation Formulas

Earlier in this chapter, I describe how to use custom VBA functions for custom formatting. (See "Using Custom Functions in Conditional Formatting Formulas.") For some reason, Excel does not permit you to use a custom VBA function in a data validation formula. If you attempt to do so, you get the following (erroneous) error message: `A named range you specified cannot be found`.

To bypass this limitation, you can use the custom function in a cell formula and then specify a data validation formula that refers to that cell.

Accepting a Larger Value Than the Previous Cell

The following data validation formula allows the user to enter a value only if it's greater than the value in the cell directly above it:

```
=A2>A1
```

This formula assumes that A2 is the active cell in the selected range. Note that you can't use this formula for a cell in row 1.

Accepting Nonduplicate Entries Only

The following data validation formula does not permit the user to make a duplicate entry in the range A1:C20:

```
=COUNTIF($A$1:$C$20,A1)=1
```

This formula assumes that A1 is the active cell in the selected range. Note that the first argument for COUNTIF is an absolute reference. The second argument is a relative reference, and it adjusts for each cell in the validation range. Figure 19-30 shows these validation criteria in effect, using a custom error alert message. The user is attempting to enter 17 into cell B6.

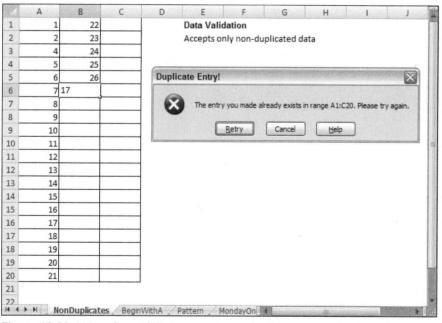

Figure 19-30: Using data validation to prevent duplicate entries in a range.

Accepting Text That Begins with a Specific Character

The following data validation formula demonstrates how to check for a specific character. In this case, the formula ensures that the user's entry is a text string that begins with the letter A (either upper- or lowercase).

```
=LEFT(A1)="a"
```

This formula assumes that the active cell in the selected range is cell A1.

The following formula is a variation of the preceding validation formula. In this case, the formula ensures that the entry begins with the letter A and contains exactly five characters.

```
=COUNTIF(A1,"A????")=1
```

Accepting Only a Date That's a Monday

The following data validation formula ensures that the cell entry is a date and also that the date is a Monday:

```
=WEEKDAY(A1)=2
```

This formula assumes that the active cell in the selected range is cell A1. It uses the WEEKDAY function, which returns 1 for Sunday, 2 for Monday, and so on.

Accepting Only Values That Don't Exceed a Total

Figure 19-31 shows a simple budget worksheet, with the budget item amounts in the range B1:B6. The total budget is in cell E5, and the user is attempting to enter a value in cell B4 that would cause the total to exceed the budget. The following data validation formula ensures that the sum of the budget items does not exceed the budget:

```
=SUM($B$1:$B$6)<=$E$5
```

Figure 19-31: Using data validation to ensure that the sum of a range does not exceed a certain value.

Chapter 20

Creating Megaformulas

IN THIS CHAPTER

◆ What is a megaformula, and why would you want to use such a thing?

◆ How to create a megaformula

◆ Examples of megaformulas

◆ Pros and cons of using megaformulas

This chapter describes a useful technique that lets you combine several formulas into a single formula — what I call a *megaformula*. This technique can eliminate intermediate formulas and may even speed up recalculation. The downside, as you'll see, is that the resulting formula is virtually incomprehensible and may be impossible to edit.

What Is a Megaformula?

Often, a worksheet may require intermediate formulas to produce a desired result. In other words, a formula may depend on other formulas, which in turn depend on other formulas. After you get all these formulas working correctly, you often can eliminate the intermediate formulas and create a single (and more complex) formula. For lack of a better term, I call such a formula a *megaformula*.

What are the advantages of employing megaformulas? They use fewer cells (less clutter), and recalculation may be faster. And, you can impress people in the know with your formula-building abilities. The disadvantages? The formula probably will be impossible to decipher or modify, even by the person who created it.

NOTE

I used the techniques described in this chapter to create many of the complex formulas presented elsewhere in this book.

Creating a Megaformula: A Simple Example

Creating a megaformula basically involves copying formula text and pasting it into another formula. I start with a relatively simple example. Examine the spreadsheet shown in Figure 20-1. This sheet uses formulas to calculate mortgage loan information.

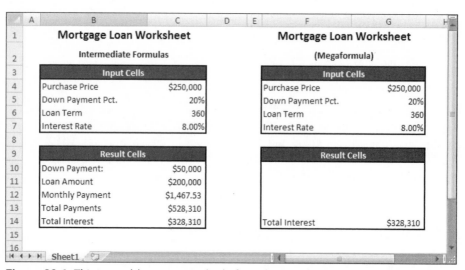

Figure 20-1: This spreadsheet uses multiple formulas to calculate mortgage loan information.

ON THE CD

This workbook, named `total interest.xlsx`, is available on the companion CD-ROM.

The Result Cells section of the worksheet uses information entered into the Input Cells section and contains the formulas shown in Table 20-1.

TABLE 20-1   FORMULAS USED TO CALCULATE TOTAL INTEREST

Cell	Formula	What It Does
C10	=C4*C5	Calculates the down payment amount
C11	=C4-C10	Calculates the loan amount
C12	=PMT(C7/12,C6,-C11)	Calculates the monthly payment
C13	=C12*C6	Calculates the total payments
C14	=C13-C11	Calculates the total interest

Suppose you're really interested in the total interest paid (cell C14). You could, of course, simply hide the rows that contain the extraneous information. However, it's also possible to create a single formula that does the work of several intermediary formulas.

 NOTE

This example is for illustration only. The CUMIPMT function provides a more direct way to calculate total interest on a loan.

The formula that calculates total interest depends on the formulas in cells C11 and C13 (which are the direct precedent cells). In addition, the formula in cell C13 depends on the formula in cell C12. And cell C12, in turn, depends on cell C11. Therefore, calculating the total interest uses five formulas. The steps that follow describe how to create a single formula to calculate total interest so that you can eliminate the intermediate formulas. C14 contains the following formula:

```
=C13-C11
```

The steps that follow describe how to convert this formula into a megaformula:

1. Substitute the formula contained in cell C13 for the reference to cell C13. Before doing this, add parentheses around the formula in C13. (Without the parentheses, the calculations occur in the wrong order.) Now the formula in C14 is

    ```
    =(C12*C6)-C11
    ```

2. Substitute the formula contained in cell C12 for the reference to cell C12. Now the formula in C14 is

    ```
    =(PMT(C7/12,C6,-C11)*C6)-C11
    ```

3. Substitute the formula contained in cell C11 for the two references to cell C11. Before copying the formula, you need to insert parentheses around it. Now the formula in C14 is

    ```
    =(PMT(C7/12,C6,-(C4-C10))*C6)-(C4-C10)
    ```

Copying Text from a Formula

Creating megaformulas involves copying formula text and then replacing a cell reference with the copied text. To copy the contents of a formula, activate the cell and press F2. Then select the formula text (without the equal sign) by pressing Shift+ Home, followed by Shift+→. Then press Ctrl+C to copy the selected text to the Clipboard. Press Esc to cancel cell editing. Then, activate the cell that contains the megaformula and press F2. Use the arrow keys, and hold down Shift to select the cell reference you want to replace. Finally, press Ctrl+V to replace the selected text with the clipboard contents.

In some cases, you need to insert parentheses around the copied formula text to make the formula calculate correctly. If the formula returns a different result after you paste the formula text, press Ctrl+Z to undo the paste. Insert parentheses around the formula you want to copy and paste it into the megaformula—it should then calculate correctly.

4. Substitute the formula contained in C10 for the two references to cell C10. Before copying the formula, insert parentheses around it. After you've done so, the formula in C14 is

```
=(PMT(C7/12,C6,-(C4-(C4*C5))))*C6)-(C4-(C4*C5))
```

At this point, the formula contains references only to input cells. You can safely delete the formulas in C10:C13. The single megaformula now does the work previously performed by the intermediary formulas.

Unless you're a world-class Excel formula wizard, it's quite unlikely that you could arrive at that formula without first creating intermediate formulas.

Creating a megaformula essentially involves substituting formula text for cell references in a formula. You perform substitutions until the megaformula contains no references to formula cells. At each step along the way, you can check your work by ensuring that the formula continues to display the same result. In the previous example, a few of the steps required parentheses around the copied formula in order to ensure the correct order of calculation.

Megaformula Examples

This section contains three additional examples of megaformulas. These examples provide a thorough introduction to applying the megaformula technique for streamlining a variety of tasks, including cleaning up a list of names by removing middle names and initials, returning the position of the last space character in a string, determining whether a credit card number is valid, and generating a list of random names.

Using a Megaformula to Remove Middle Names

Consider a worksheet with a column of names, like the one shown in Figure 20-2. Suppose you have a worksheet with thousands of such names, and you need to remove all the middle names and middle initials from the names. Editing the cells manually would take hours, and you're not up to writing a VBA macro, so that leaves using a formula-based solution. Notice that not all the names have a middle name or a middle initial, which makes the task a bit trickier. Although this is not a difficult task, it normally involves several intermediate formulas.

	A
1	Robert E. Lee
2	Jim Jones
3	R. L Burnside
4	Michael J. Hammer
5	Timothy Franklin
6	T. Henry Jackson
7	Frank J Thomas
8	Mary Richards Helton
9	Tom A. Smith
10	

Figure 20-2: The goal is to remove the middle name or middle initial from each name.

Figure 20-3 shows the results of the more conventional solution, which requires six intermediate formulas, as shown in Table 20-2. The names are in column A; column H displays the end result. Columns B–G hold the intermediate formulas.

ON THE CD

You can access the workbook for removing middle names and initials on the companion CD-ROM. The filename is `no middle names.xlsx`.

	A	B	C	D	E	F	G	H
1	Robert E. Lee	Robert E. Lee	7	10	10	Robert	Lee	Robert Lee
2	Jim Jones	Jim Jones	4	#VALUE!	4	Jim	Jones	Jim Jones
3	R. L Burnside	R. L Burnside	3	5	5	R.	Burnside	R. Burnside
4	Michael J. Hammer	Michael J. Hammer	8	11	11	Michael	Hammer	Michael Hammer
5	Timothy Franklin	Timothy Franklin	8	#VALUE!	8	Timothy	Franklin	Timothy Franklin
6	T. Henry Jackson	T. Henry Jackson	3	9	9	T.	Jackson	T. Jackson
7	Frank J Thomas	Frank J Thomas	6	8	8	Frank	Thomas	Frank Thomas
8	Mary Richards Helton	Mary Richards Helton	5	14	14	Mary	Helton	Mary Helton
9	Tom A. Smith	Tom A. Smith	4	7	7	Tom	Smith	Tom Smith
10								

Figure 20-3: Removing the middle names and initials requires six intermediate formulas.

Part V

TABLE 20-2 INTERMEDIATE FORMULAS IN THE FIRST ROW OF SHEET1 IN FIGURE 20-3

Cell	Intermediate Formula	What It Does
B1	=TRIM(A1)	Removes excess spaces
C1	=FIND(" ",B1)	Locates the first space
D1	=FIND(" ",B1,C1+1)	Locates the second space, if any
E1	=IFERROR(D1,C1)	Uses the first space if no second space exists
F1	=LEFT(B1,C1-1)	Extracts the first name
G1	=RIGHT(B1,LEN(B1)-E1)	Extracts the last name
H1	=F1&" "&G1	Concatenates the two names

Note that cell E1 uses the IFERROR function, which is available only in Excel 2007. For compatibility with earlier versions, use this formula:

```
=IF(ISERROR(D1),C1,D1)
```

NOTE

Notice that the result isn't perfect. For example, it will not work if the cell contains only one name (for example, Enya). And, this method also fails if a name has two middle names (such as John Jacob Robert Smith). That occurs because the formula simply searches for the second space character in the name. In this example, the megaformula *returns John Robert Smith.* Later in this chapter, I present an array formula method to identify the last space character in a string.

With a bit of work, you can eliminate all the intermediate formulas and replace them with a single megaformula. You do so by creating all the intermediate formulas and then editing the final result formula (in this case, the formula in column H) by replacing each cell reference with a copy of the formula in the cell referred to. Fortunately, you can use the clipboard to copy and paste. (See the sidebar, "Copying Text from a Formula," earlier in this chapter.) Keep repeating this process until cell H1 contains nothing but references to cell A1. You end up with the following megaformula in one cell:

```
=LEFT(TRIM(A1),FIND(" ",TRIM(A1))-1)&" "&RIGHT
(TRIM(A1),LEN(TRIM(A1))-IFERROR(FIND(" ",TRIM(A1),
FIND(" ",TRIM(A1))+1),FIND(" ",TRIM(A1))))
```

When you're satisfied that the megaformula works, you can delete the columns that hold the intermediate formulas because they are no longer used.

THE STEP-BY-STEP PROCEDURE

If you're still not clear about this process, take a look at the step-by-step procedure:

1. Examine the formula in H1. This formula contains two cell references (F1 and G1):

   ```
   =F1&" "&G1
   ```

2. Activate cell G1 and copy the contents of the formula (without the equal sign) to the Clipboard.

3. Activate cell H1 and replace the reference to cell G1 with the Clipboard contents. Now cell H1 contains the following formula:

   ```
   =F1&" "&RIGHT(B1,LEN(B1)-E1)
   ```

4. Activate cell F1 and copy the contents of the formula (without the equal sign) to the Clipboard.

5. Activate cell H1 and replace the reference to cell F1 with the Clipboard contents. Now the formula in cell H1 is as follows:

   ```
   =LEFT(B1,C1-1)&" "&RIGHT(B1,LEN(B1)-E1)
   ```

6. Now cell H1 contains references to three cells (B1, C1, and E1). The formulas in those cells will replace each of the three references.

7. Replace the reference to cell E1 with the formula in E1. The result is

   ```
   =LEFT(B1,C1-1)&" "&RIGHT(B1,LEN(B1)-IFERROR(D1,C1))
   ```

8. Replace the reference to cell D1 with the formula in D1. The formula now looks like this:

   ```
   =LEFT(B1,C1-1)&" "&RIGHT(B1,LEN(B1)-IFERROR
   (FIND(" ",B1,C1+1),C1))
   ```

9. The formula has three references to cell C1. Replace all three of those references to cell C1 with the formula contained in cell C1. The formula in cell H1 is as follows:

   ```
   =LEFT(B1,FIND(" ",B1)-1)&" "&RIGHT(B1,LEN(B1)-IFERROR
   (FIND(" ",B1,FIND(" ",B1)+1),FIND(" ",B1)))
   ```

10. Finally, replace the seven references to cell B1 with the formula in cell B1. The result is

    ```
    =LEFT(TRIM(A1),FIND(" ",TRIM(A1))-1)&" "&RIGHT
    (TRIM(A1),LEN(TRIM(A1))-IFERROR(FIND(" ",TRIM(A1),
    FIND(" ",TRIM(A1))+1),FIND(" ",TRIM(A1))))
    ```

Notice that the formula in cell H1 now contains references only to cell A1. The megaformula is complete, and it performs exactly the same tasks as all the intermediate formulas (which you can now delete).

This megaformula uses the Excel 2007 IFERROR function. A comparable formula that's compatible with previous versions is

```
=LEFT(TRIM(A1),FIND(" ",TRIM(A1),1)-1)&" "&RIGHT
(TRIM(A1),LEN(TRIM(A1))-IF(ISERROR(FIND(" ",TRIM(A1),
FIND(" ",TRIM(A1),1)+1)),FIND(" ",TRIM(A1),1),FIND(" ",TRIM
(A1),FIND(" ",TRIM(A1),1)+1)))
```

Interestingly, the formula that uses IFERROR contains 52 fewer characters.

COMPARING SPEED AND EFFICIENCY

Because a megaformula is so complex, you may think that using one slows down recalculation. Actually, that's not the case. As a test, I created a workbook that used the megaformula 150,000 times. Then I created another workbook that used six intermediate formulas to compute the 150,000 results. I compared the results in terms of calculation time and file size; see Table 20-3.

TABLE 20-3 COMPARING INTERMEDIATE FORMULAS AND MEGAFORMULA

Method	Recalculation Time (Seconds)	File Size
Intermediate formulas	6.3	11.1MB
Megaformula	4.2	2.6MB

Of course, the actual results will vary depending on processor speed and the amount of memory installed.

As you can see, using a megaformula in this case resulted in faster recalculations as well as a *much* smaller workbook.

 ON THE CD

The two test workbooks I used are available on the companion CD-ROM. The filenames are `time test intermediate.xlsx` and `time test megaformula.xlsx`. To perform your own time tests, change the name in cell A1 and start your stopwatch (your cell phone probably has one). Keep your eye on the status bar, which indicates when the calculation is finished.

Using a Megaformula to Return a String's Last Space Character Position

As previously noted, the "remove middle name" example presented earlier contains a flaw: To identify the last name, the formula searches for the second space character. A better solution is to search for the *last* space character. Unfortunately, Excel doesn't provide any simple way to locate the position of the first occurrence of a character from the *end* of a string. The example in this section solves that problem and describes a way to determine the position of the first occurrence of a specific character going backward from the end of a text string.

CROSS REF

This technique involves arrays, so you might want to review the material in Part IV to familiarize yourself with this topic.

This example describes how to create a megaformula that returns the character position of the last *space character* in a string. You can, of course, modify the formula to work with any other character.

CREATING THE INTERMEDIATE FORMULAS

The general plan is to create an array of characters in the string but in reverse order. After that array is created, you can use the MATCH function to locate the first space character in the array.

Refer to Figure 20-4, which shows the results of the intermediate formulas. Cell A1 contains an arbitrary name, which happens to comprise 12 characters. The range B1:B12 contains the following array formula:

```
{=ROW(INDIRECT("1:"&LEN(A1)))}
```

	A	B	C	D	E	F	G
1	Jim E. Brown	1	12	n		6	7
2		2	11	w			
3		3	10	o			
4		4	9	r			
5		5	8	B			
6		6	7				
7		7	6	.			
8		8	5	E			
9	.	9	4				
10		10	3	m			
11		11	2	i			
12		12	1	J			
13							
14							

Sheet1 / Sheet2

Figure 20-4: These intermediate formulas will eventually be converted to a single megaformula.

ON THE CD

This example, named `position of last space.xlsx`, is available on the companion CD-ROM.

You enter this multicell array formula into the entire B1:B12 range by selecting the range, typing the formula, and pressing Ctrl+Shift+Enter. Don't type the curly brackets. Excel adds the curly brackets to indicate an array formula. This formula returns an array of 12 consecutive integers.

The range C1:C12 contains the following array formula:

```
{=LEN(A1)+1-B1:B12}
```

This formula essentially reverses the integers generated in column B.

The range D1:D12 contains the following array formula:

```
{=MID(A1,C1:C12,1)}
```

This formula uses the MID function to extract the individual characters in cell A1. The MID function uses the array in C1:C12 as its second argument. The result is an array of the name's characters in reverse order.

The formula in cell E1 is as follows:

```
=MATCH(" ",D1:D12,0)
```

This formula, which is *not* an array formula, uses the MATCH function to return the position of the first space character in the range D1:D12. In the example shown in Figure 20-4, the formula returns 6, which means that the first space character is six characters from the end of the text in A1.

The formula in cell F1 is

```
=LEN(A1)+1-E1
```

This formula returns the character position of the last space in the string.

You may wonder how all of these formulas can possibly be combined into a single formula. Keep reading for the answer.

CREATING THE MEGAFORMULA

At this point, cell F1 contains the result you're looking for. The challenge is consolidating all of those intermediate formulas into a single formula. The goal is to produce a formula that contains only references to cell A1. These steps will get you to that goal:

1. The formula in cell F1 contains a reference to cell E1. Replace that reference with the text of the formula in cell E1. As a result, the formula in cell F1 becomes

   ```
   =LEN(A1)+1-MATCH(" ",D1:D12,0)
   ```

2. Now the formula contains a reference to D1:D12. This range contains a single array formula. Replacing the reference to D1:D12 with the array formula results in the following array formula in cell F1:

```
{=LEN(A1)+1-MATCH(" ",MID(A1,C1:C12,1),0)}
```

NOTE

Because an array formula replaced the reference in cell F1, you now must enter the formula in F1 as an array formula (enter by pressing Ctrl+Shift+Enter).

3. Now the formula in cell F1 contains a reference to C1:C12, which also contains an array formula. Replace the reference to C1:C12 with the array formula in C1:C12 to get this array formula in cell F1:

```
{=LEN(A1)+1-MATCH(" ",MID(A1,LEN(A1)+1-B1:B12,1),0)}
```

4. Next, replace the reference to B1:B12 with the array formula in B1:B12. The result is

```
{=LEN(A1)+1-MATCH(" ",MID(A1,LEN(A1)+1-ROW(INDIRECT
("1:"&LEN(A1))),1),0)}
```

Now the array formula in cell F1 refers only to cell A1, which is exactly what you want. The megaformula does the job, and you can delete all the intermediate formulas.

NOTE

Although you use a 12-digit value and arrays stored in 12-row ranges to create the formula, the final formula does not use any of these range references. Consequently, the megaformula works with a value of any length.

PUTTING THE MEGAFORMULA TO WORK

Figure 20-5 shows a worksheet with names in column A. Column B contains the megaformula developed in the previous section. Column C contains a formula that extracts the characters beginning after the last space, which represents the last name of the name in column A.

Cell C1, for example, contains this formula:

```
=RIGHT(A1,LEN(A1)-B1)
```

If you like, you can eliminate the formulas in column B and create a specialized formula that returns the last name. To do so, substitute the formula in B1 for the reference to B1 in the formula. The result is the following array formula:

```
{=RIGHT(A1,LEN(A1)-(LEN(A1)+1-MATCH(" ",MID(A1,LEN(A1)+
1-ROW(INDIRECT("1:"&LEN(A1))),1),0))))}
```

Part V

	A	B	C	D
1	Paula M. Smith	9	Smith	
2	Michael Alan Jones	13	Jones	
3	Mike Helton	5	Helton	
4	Tom Alvin Jacobs	10	Jacobs	
5	John Jacob Robert Smith	18	Smith	
6	Mr. Hank R. Franklin	12	Franklin	
7	James Jackson Jr.	14	Jr.	
8	Jill M. Horneg	8	Horneg	
9	Rodger K. Moore	10	Moore	
10	Andy R. Maxwell	8	Maxwell	
11	Michelle Theresa Hunt	17	Hunt	
12				

Sheet1 Sheet2

Figure 20-5: Column B contains a megaformula that returns the character position of the last space of the name in column A.

NOTE

You must insert parentheses around the formula text copied from cell B1. Without the parentheses, the formula does not evaluate correctly.

Using a Megaformula to Determine the Validity of a Credit Card Number

Many people are not aware that you can determine the validity of a credit card number by using a relatively complex algorithm to analyze the digits of the number. In addition, you can determine the type of credit card by examining the initial digits and the length of the number. Table 20-4 shows information about four major credit cards.

TABLE 20-4 INFORMATION ABOUT FOUR MAJOR CREDIT CARDS

Credit Card	Prefix Digits	Total Digits
MasterCard	51–55	16
Visa	4	13 or 16
American Express	34 or 37	15
Discover	6011	16

NOTE

Validity, as used here, means whether the credit card number itself is a valid number as determined by the following steps. This technique, of course, cannot determine whether the number represents an actual credit card account.

You can test the validity of a credit card account number by processing its checksum digits. All account numbers used in major credit cards use a Mod 10 check-digit algorithm. The general process is as follows:

1. Add leading zeros to the account number to make the total number of digits equal 16.

2. Beginning with the first digit, double the value of alternate digits of the account number. If the result is a two-digit number, add the two digits together.

3. Add the eight values generated in Step 2 to the sum of the skipped digits of the original number.

4. If the sum obtained in Step 3 is evenly divisible by 10, the number is a valid credit card number.

The example in this section describes a megaformula that determines whether a credit card number is a valid number.

THE BASIC FORMULAS

Figure 20-6 shows a worksheet set up to analyze a credit card number and determine its validity. This workbook uses quite a few formulas to make the determination.

	A	B	C	D	E	F	G
1				Credit Card Number:		4384842201065	*INVALID*
2						0004384842201065	
3							
4	Digit Number	Digit	Digit Multiplier	Equals	Sum of the digits		
5	1	0	2	0	0		
6	2	0	1	0	0		
7	3	0	2	0	0		
8	4	4	1	4	4		
9	5	3	2	6	6		
10	6	8	1	8	8		
11	7	4	2	8	8		
12	8	8	1	8	8		
13	9	4	2	8	8		
14	10	2	1	2	2		
15	11	2	2	4	4		
16	12	0	1	0	0		
17	13	1	2	2	2		
18	14	0	1	0	0		
19	15	6	2	12	3		
20	16	5	1	5	5		
21					58		
22							

Multiple formulas   Multiple array formulas   Megafor

Figure 20-6: The formulas in this worksheet determine the validity of a credit card number.

ON THE CD

You can access the credit card number validation workbook on the companion CD-ROM. The file is named `credit card validation.xlsx`.

In this worksheet, the credit card number is entered in cell F1, with no spaces or hyphens. The formula in cell F2 follows. This formula appends leading zeros, if necessary, to make the card number exactly 16 digits long. The other formulas use the string in cell F2.

```
=REPT("0",16-LEN(F1))&F1
```

⚠ **CAUTION**

When entering a credit card number that contains more than 15 digits, you must be careful that Excel does not round the number to 15 digits. You can precede the number with an apostrophe or preformat the cell as Text (using Home⇨Number⇨Number Format⇨Text).

Column A contains a series of integers from 1–16, each representing the digit positions of the credit card.

Column B contains formulas that extract each digit from cell F2. For example, the formula in cell B5 is as follows:

```
=MID($F$2,A5,1)
```

Column C contains the multipliers for each digit: alternating 2s and 1s.

Column D contains formulas that multiply the digit in column B by the multiplier in column C. For example, the formula in cell D5 is

```
=B5*C5
```

Column E contains formulas that sum the digits displayed in column D. A single digit value in column D is returned directly. For two-digit values, the sum of the digits is displayed in Column E. For example, if column D displays 12, the formula in column E returns 3: that is, 1 + 2. The formula that accomplishes this is as follows:

```
=INT((D5/10)+MOD((D5),10))
```

Cell E21 contains a simple SUM formula to add the values in column E:

```
=SUM(E5:E20)
```

The formula in cell G1, which follows, calculates the remainder when cell E21 is divided by 10. If the remainder is 0, the card number is valid, and the formula displays *VALID*. Otherwise, the formula displays *INVALID*.

```
=IF(MOD(E21,10)=0,"VALID","INVALID")
```

CONVERT TO ARRAY FORMULAS

The megaformula that performs all of these calculations will be an array formula because the intermediary formulas occupy multiple rows.

First, you need to convert all the formulas to array formulas. Note that columns A and C consist of values, not formulas. To use the values in a megaformula, they must be generated by formulas — more specifically, array formulas.

Enter the following array formula into the range A5:A20. This array formula returns a series of 16 consecutive integers:

```
{=ROW(INDIRECT("1:16"))}
```

1. For column B, select B5:B20 and enter the following array formula, which extracts the digits from the credit card number:

   ```
   {=MID($F$2,A5:A20,1)}
   ```

2. Next, column C requires an array formula that generates alternating values of 2 and 1. Such a formula, entered into the range C5:C20, is shown here:

   ```
   {=(MOD(ROW(INDIRECT("1:16")),2)+1)}
   ```

3. For column D, select D5:D20 and enter the following array formula:

   ```
   {=B5:B20*C5:C20}
   ```

4. Finally, select E5:E20 and enter this array formula:

   ```
   {=INT((D5:D20/10)+MOD((D5:D20),10))}
   ```

Now the worksheet contains five columns of 16 rows, but only five actual formulas (which are multicell array formulas).

BUILD THE MEGAFORMULA

To create the megaformula for this task, start with cell G1, which is the cell that has the final result. The original formula in G1 is

```
=IF(MOD(E21,10)=0,"VALID","INVALID")
```

1. First, replace the reference to cell E21 with the formula in E21. Doing so results in the following formula in cell G1:

   ```
   =IF(MOD(SUM(E5:E20),10)=0,"VALID","INVALID")
   ```

2. Next, replace the reference to E5:E20 with the array formula contained in that range. Now the formula becomes an array formula, so you must enter it by pressing Ctrl+Shift+Enter. After the replacement, the formula in G1 is as follows:

   ```
   {=IF(MOD(SUM(INT((D5:D20/10)+MOD((D5:D20),10))),10)=0,
   "VALID","INVALID")}
   ```

3. Replace the two references to range D5:D20 with the array formula contained in D5:20. Doing so results in the following array formula in cell G1:

```
{=IF(MOD(SUM(INT((B5:B20*C5:C20/10)+MOD((B5:B20*C5:C20),
10))),10)=0,"VALID","INVALID")}
```

4. Next, replace the references to cell C5:C20 with the array formula in C5:C20. Note that you must have a set of parentheses around the copied formula text. The result is as follows:

```
{=IF(MOD(SUM(INT((B5:B20*(MOD(ROW(INDIRECT("1:16")),
2)+1)/10)+MOD((B5:B20*(MOD(ROW(INDIRECT("1:16")),2)+1)),
10))),10)=0,"VALID","INVALID")}
```

5. Replacing the references to B5:B20 with the array formula contained in B5:B20 yields the following:

```
{=IF(MOD(SUM(INT((MID($F$2,A5:A20,1)*(MOD(ROW(INDIRECT
("1:16")),2)+1)/10)+MOD((MID($F$2,A5:A20,1)*(MOD(ROW
(INDIRECT("1:16")),2)+1)),10))),10)
=0,"VALID","INVALID")}
```

6. Substitute the array formula in range A5:A20 for the references to that range. The resulting array formula is as follows:

```
{=IF(MOD(SUM(INT((MID($F$2,ROW(INDIRECT("1:16")),1)*(MOD(ROW
(INDIRECT("1:16")),2)+1)/10)+MOD((MID($F$2,ROW(INDIRECT
("1:16")),1)*(MOD(ROW(INDIRECT("1:16")),2)+1)),10))),10)=0,
"VALID","INVALID")}
```

7. Finally, substitute the formula in cell F2 for the two references to cell F2. After making the substitutions, the formula is as follows:

```
{=IF(MOD(SUM(INT((MID(REPT("0",16-LEN(F1))&F1,
ROW(INDIRECT("1:16")),1)*(MOD(ROW(INDIRECT("1:16")),2)+1)/
10)+MOD((MID(REPT("0",16-EN(F1))&F1,ROW(INDIRECT("1:16")),
1)*(MOD(ROW(INDIRECT("1:16")),2)+1)),10))),10)=0,"VALID",
"INVALID")}
```

You can delete the now superfluous intermediate formulas. The final megaformula, a mere 229 characters in length, does the work of 51 intermediary formulas!

Generating Random Names

The final example is a useful application that generates random names. It uses three name lists, compiled by the U.S. Census Bureau: 4,275 female first names; 1,219 male first names; and 18,839 last names. The names are sorted by frequency of occurrence. The megaformula selects random names such that more frequently occurring names have a higher probability of being selected. Therefore, if you create a list of random names, they will appear to be somewhat realistic. (Common names will appear more often than uncommon names.)

Figure 20-7 shows the workbook. Cells B7 and B8 contains values that determine the probability that the random name is a male as well as the probability that the random name contains a middle initial. The randomly generated names begin in cell A11.

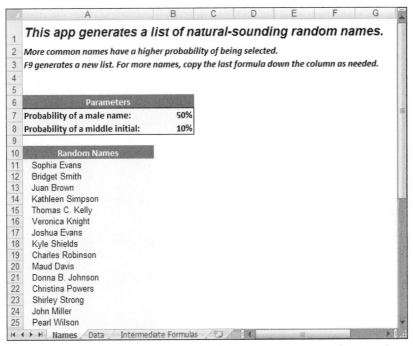

Figure 20-7: This workbook uses a megaformula to generate realistic random names.

ON THE CD

This workbook, named `name generator.xlsx`, is available on the companion CD-ROM.

The megaformula is as follows (the workbook uses several names):

```
=IF(RAND()<=PctMale,INDEX(MaleNames,MATCH(RAND(),
MaleProbability,-1)),INDEX(FemaleNames,MATCH(RAND(),
FemaleProbability,-1)))&IF(RAND()<=PctMiddle," "&
INDEX(MiddleInitials,MATCH(RAND(),MiddleProbability,-1))&
".","")&" "&INDEX(LastNames,MATCH(RAND(),LastProbability,-1))
```

I don't list the intermediate formulas here, but you can examine them by opening the file on the CD-ROM.

Part V

The Pros and Cons of Megaformulas

If you followed the examples in this chapter, you probably realize that the main advantage of creating a megaformula is to eliminate intermediate formulas. Doing so can streamline your worksheet, reduce the size of your workbook files, and even result in faster recalculations.

The downside? Creating a megaformula does, of course, require some additional time and effort. And, as you've undoubtedly noticed, a megaformula is virtually impossible for anyone (even the author) to figure out. If you decide to use megaformulas, take extra care to ensure that the intermediate formulas are performing correctly before you start building a megaformula. Even better, keep a single copy of the intermediate formulas somewhere in case you discover an error or need to make a change.

Chapter 21

Tools and Methods for Debugging Formulas

IN THIS CHAPTER

◆ What is formula debugging?

◆ How to identify and correct common formula errors

◆ A description of Excel's auditing tools

Errors happen. And when you create Excel formulas, errors happen very frequently. This chapter describes common formula errors and also discusses tools and methods that you can use to help create formulas that work as they are intended to work.

Formula Debugging?

The term *debugging* refers to the process of identifying and correcting errors in a computer program. Strictly speaking, an Excel formula is not a computer program. Formulas, however, are subject to the same types of problems that occur in a computer program. If you create a formula that does not work as it should, you need to identify and correct the problem.

The ultimate goal in developing a spreadsheet solution is to generate accurate results. For simple worksheets, this is not difficult, and you can usually tell whether the results are correct. But as your worksheets grow in size or complexity, ensuring accuracy becomes more difficult.

581

Research on Spreadsheet Errors

Using a spreadsheet can be hazardous to your company's bottom line. It's tempting to simply assume that your spreadsheet produces accurate results. If you use the results of a spreadsheet to make a major decision, it's especially important to make sure that the formulas return accurate and meaningful results.

Researchers have conducted quite a few studies that deal with spreadsheet errors. Generally, these studies have found that between 20 and 40 percent of all spreadsheets contain some type of error. If this type of research interests you, I urge you to check out the Spreadsheet Research (SSR) Web site maintained by Raymond Panko of the University of Hawaii. The URL is

```
http://panko.cba.hawaii.edu/ssr/
```

Making a change in a worksheet — even a relatively minor change — may produce a ripple effect that introduces errors in other cells. For example, accidentally entering a value into a cell that previously held a formula is all too easy to do. This simple error can have a major impact on other formulas, and you may not discover the problem until long after you made the change — or you may *never* discover the problem.

Formula Problems and Solutions

Formula errors tend to fall into one of the following general categories:

- **Syntax errors:** You have a problem with the syntax of a formula. For example, a formula may have mismatched parentheses, or a function may not have the correct number of arguments.

- **Logical errors:** A formula does not return an error, but it contains a logical flaw that causes it to return an incorrect result.

- **Incorrect reference errors:** The logic of the formula is correct, but the formula uses an incorrect cell reference. As a simple example, the range reference in a SUM formula may not include all the data that you want to sum.

- **Semantic errors.** An example of a semantic error is a function name that is spelled incorrectly. Excel attempts to interpret the misspelled function as a name and displays the #NAME? error.

- **Circular references:** A circular reference occurs when a formula refers to its own cell, either directly or indirectly. Circular references are useful in a few cases, but most of the time, a circular reference indicates a problem.

- **Array formula entry error:** When entering (or editing) an array formula, you must press Ctrl+Shft+Enter to enter the formula. If you fail to do so, Excel does not recognize the formula as an array formula. The formula may return an error (if you're lucky) or an incorrect result (if you're not lucky).

- **Incomplete calculation errors:** The formulas simply aren't calculated fully. Microsoft has acknowledged problems with Excel's calculation engine in some versions of Excel. To ensure that your formulas are fully calculated, press Ctrl+Alt+F9.

Syntax errors are usually the easiest to identify and correct. In most cases, you will know when your formula contains a syntax error. For example, Excel won't permit you to enter a formula with mismatched parentheses. Other syntax errors also usually result in an error display in the cell.

The remainder of this section describes some common formula problems and offers advice on identifying and correcting them.

Mismatched Parentheses

In a formula, every left parenthesis must have a corresponding right parenthesis. If your formula has mismatched parentheses, Excel usually won't permit you to enter it. An exception to this rule involves a simple formula that uses a function. For example, if you enter the following formula (which is missing a closing parenthesis), Excel accepts the formula and provides the missing parenthesis:

```
=SUM(A1:A500
```

A formula may have an equal number of left and right parentheses, but the parentheses may not match properly. For example, consider the following formula, which converts a text string such that the first character is uppercase and the remaining characters are lowercase. This formula has five pairs of parentheses, and they match properly.

```
=UPPER(LEFT(A1))&RIGHT(LOWER(A1),LEN(A1)-1)
```

The following formula also has five pairs of parentheses, but they are mismatched. The result displays a syntactically correct formula that simply returns the wrong result.

```
=UPPER(LEFT(A1)&RIGHT(LOWER(A1),LEN(A1)-1))
```

Often, parentheses that are in the wrong location will result in a syntax error, which is usually a message that tells you that you entered too many or too few arguments for a function.

TIP

Excel can help you out with mismatched parentheses. When you edit a formula, use the arrow keys to move the cursor to a parenthesis and pause. Excel displays it (and its matching parenthesis) in bold for about one second. In addition, nested parentheses appear in a different color.

Using Formula AutoCorrect

When you enter a formula that has a syntax error, Excel attempts to determine the problem and offers a suggested correction. The accompanying figure shows an example of a proposed correction.

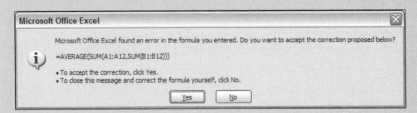

Exercise caution when accepting corrections for your formulas from Excel because it does not always guess correctly. For example, I entered the following formula (which has mismatched parentheses):

`=AVERAGE(SUM(A1:A12,SUM(B1:B12))`

Excel then proposed the following correction to the formula:

`=AVERAGE(SUM(A1:A12,SUM(B1:B12)))`

You may be tempted to accept the suggestion without even thinking. In this case, the proposed formula is syntactically correct—but not what I intended. The correct formula is as follows:

`=AVERAGE(SUM(A1:A12),SUM(B1:B12))`

Cells Are Filled with Hash Marks

A cell displays a series of hash marks (#) for one of two reasons:

- The column is not wide enough to accommodate the formatted numeric value. To correct it, you can make the column wider or use a different number format.

- The cell contains a formula that returns an invalid date or time. For example, Excel does not support dates prior to 1900 or the use of negative time values. Attempting to display either of these will result in a cell filled with hash marks. Widening the column won't fix it.

Blank Cells Are Not Blank

Some Excel users have discovered that by pressing the spacebar, the contents of a cell seem to erase. Actually, pressing the spacebar inserts an invisible space character, which is not the same as erasing the cell.

For example, the following formula returns the number of nonempty cells in range A1:A10. If you "erase" any of these cells by using the spacebar, these cells are included in the count, and the formula returns an incorrect result:

```
=COUNTA(A1:A10)
```

If your formula does not ignore blank cells the way that it should, check to make sure that the blank cells are really blank cells. One way to do this is to use the Go To Special dialog box. (Choose Home⇨Editing⇨Find & Select⇨Go To Special.) If you choose the Blanks option in the Go To Special dialog box, Excel selects all blank cells so you can spot cells that appear to be empty but are not.

Extra Space Characters

If you have formulas that rely on comparing text, be careful that your text doesn't contain additional space characters. Adding an extra space character is particularly common when data has been imported from another source.

Excel automatically removes trailing spaces from values that you enter, but trailing spaces in text entries are not deleted. It's impossible to tell just by looking at a cell whether text contains one or more trailing space characters.

Formulas Returning an Error

A formula may return any of the following error values:

- #DIV/0!
- #N/A
- #NAME?
- #NULL!
- #NUM!
- #REF!
- #VALUE!

The following sections summarize possible problems that may cause these errors.

TIP

Excel allows you to choose how error values are printed. To access this feature, choose Page Layout⇨Page Setup⇨Print Titles. In the Sheet tab of the Page Setup dialog box, you can choose to print cell error values as displayed (the default), or as blank cells, dashes, or #N/A.

Part V

Tracing Error Values

Often, an error in one cell is the result of an error in a *precedent cell* (a cell that is used by the formula). To help track down the source of an error value in a cell, select the cell and choose Formulas⇨Formula Auditing⇨Error Checking⇨Trace Error. Excel draws arrows to indicate the error source.

After you identify the error, use Formulas⇨Formula Auditing⇨Error Checking⇨Remove Errors to get rid of the arrow display.

#DIV/0! ERRORS

Division by zero is not a valid operation. If you create a formula that attempts to divide by zero, Excel displays its familiar #DIV/0! error value.

Because Excel considers a blank cell to be zero, you also get this error if your formula divides by a missing value. This problem is common when you create formulas for data that you haven't entered yet, as shown in Figure 21-1. The formula in cell D2, which was copied to the cells below it, is as follows:

```
=(C2-B2)/C2
```

	A	B	C	D	E	F
1	Month	Last Year	This Year	Change		
2	January	175	188	6.9%		
3	February	156	166	6.0%		
4	March	198	175	-13.1%		
5	April	144	187	23.0%		
6	May	132	149	11.4%		
7	June	198		#DIV/0!		
8	July	202		#DIV/0!		
9	August	184		#DIV/0!		
10	September	140		#DIV/0!		
11	October	198		#DIV/0!		
12	November	232		#DIV/0!		
13	December	255		#DIV/0!		
14						

Figure 21-1: #DIV/0! errors occur when the data in column C is missing.

This formula calculates the percent change between the values in columns B and C. Data is not available for months beyond May, so the formula returns a #DIV/0! error.

To avoid the error display, you can use an IF function to check for a blank cell in column C:

```
=IF(C2=0,"",(C2-B2)/C2)
```

This formula displays an empty string if cell C2 is blank or contains 0; otherwise, it displays the calculated value.

Another approach is to use the new IFERROR function to check for *any* error condition. The following formula, for example, displays an empty string if the formula results in any type of error:

```
=IFERROR((C2-B2)/C2,"")
```

For versions prior to Excel 2007, use this formula.

```
=IF(ISERROR((C2-B2)/C2),"",(C2-B2)/C2)
```

#N/A ERRORS

The #N/A error occurs if any cell referenced by a formula displays #N/A.

NOTE

Some users like to enter =NA() or #N/A explicitly for missing data (that is, Not Available). This method makes it perfectly clear that the data is not available and hasn't been deleted accidentally.

The #N/A error also occurs when a lookup function (HLOOKUP, LOOKUP, MATCH, or VLOOKUP) can't find a match.

#NAME? ERRORS

The #NAME? error occurs under these conditions:

- The formula contains an undefined range or cell name.

- The formula contains text that Excel *interprets* as an undefined name. A misspelled function name, for example, generates a #NAME? error.

- The formula uses a worksheet function that's defined in an add-in, and the add-in is not installed.

NOTE

Excel has a bit of a problem with range names. If you delete a name for a cell or range and the name is used in a formula, the formula continues to use the name even though it's no longer defined. As a result, the formula displays #NAME?. You may expect Excel to automatically convert the names to their corresponding cell references, but this does not happen. In fact, Excel does not even provide a way to convert the names used in a formula to the equivalent cell references!

Part V

#NULL! ERRORS

The #NULL! error occurs when a formula attempts to use the intersection of two ranges that don't actually intersect. Excel's intersection operator is a space. The following formula, for example, returns #NULL! because the two ranges have no cells in common:

```
=SUM(B5:B14 A16:F16)
```

The following formula does not return #NULL! but instead displays the contents of cell B9 — which represents the intersection of the two ranges.

```
=SUM(B5:B14 A9:F9)
```

#NUM! ERRORS

A formula returns a #NUM! error if any of the following occurs:

- You pass a non-numeric argument to a function when a numeric argument is expected.

- You pass an invalid argument to a function. For example, this formula returns #NUM!:

  ```
  =SQRT(-1)
  ```

- A function that uses iteration can't calculate a result. Examples of functions that use iteration are IRR and RATE.

- A formula returns a value that is too large or too small. Excel supports values between −1E-307 and 1E+307.

#REF! ERRORS

The #REF! error occurs when a formula uses an invalid cell reference. This error can occur in the following situations:

- You delete a cell that is referenced by the formula. For example, the following formula displays a #REF! error if row 1, column A, or column B is deleted.

  ```
  =A1/B1
  ```

- You copy a formula to a location that invalidates the relative cell references. For example, if you copy the following formula from cell A2 to cell A1, the formula returns #REF! because it attempts to refer to a nonexistent cell.

  ```
  =A1-1
  ```

- You cut a cell (using Home⇨Clipboard⇨Cut, or by pressing Ctrl+X) and then paste it to a cell that's referenced by a formula. The formula will display #REF!.

Pay Attention to the Colors

When you edit a cell that contains a formula, Excel color-codes the cell and range references in the formula. Excel also outlines the cells and ranges used in the formula by using corresponding colors. Therefore, you can see at a glance the cells that are used in the formula.

You also can manipulate the colored outline to change the cell or range reference. To change the references that are used in the formula, drag the outline's border or *fill handle* (at the lower-right corner of the outline). Using this technique is often easier than editing the formula.

#VALUE! ERRORS

The #VALUE! error is very common and can occur under the following conditions:

- An argument for a function is of an incorrect data type or the formula attempts to perform an operation using incorrect data. For example, a formula that adds a value to a text string returns the #VALUE! error.

- A function's argument is a range when it should be a single value.

- A custom worksheet function is not calculated. With some versions of Excel, inserting or moving a sheet may cause this error. You can use Ctrl+Alt+F9 to force a recalculation.

- A custom worksheet function attempts to perform an operation that is not valid. For example, custom functions cannot modify the Excel environment or make changes to other cells.

- You forget to press Ctrl+Shift+Enter when entering an array formula.

Absolute/Relative Reference Problems

As I describe in Chapter 2, a cell reference can be relative (for example, A1), absolute (for example, $A$1), or mixed (for example, $A1 or A$1). The type of cell reference that you use in a formula is relevant only if the formula will be copied to other cells.

A common problem is to use a relative reference when you should use an absolute reference. As shown in Figure 21-2, cell C1 contains a tax rate, which is used in the formulas in column C. The formula in cell C4 is as follows:

```
=B4+(B4*$C$1)
```

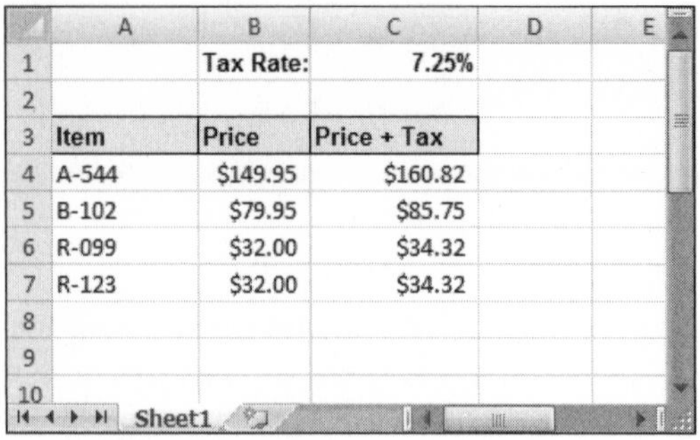

	A	B	C	D	E
1		Tax Rate:	7.25%		
2					
3	Item	Price	Price + Tax		
4	A-544	$149.95	$160.82		
5	B-102	$79.95	$85.75		
6	R-099	$32.00	$34.32		
7	R-123	$32.00	$34.32		
8					
9					
10					

Figure 21-2: Formulas in the range C4:C6 use an absolute reference to cell C1.

Notice that the reference to cell C1 is an absolute reference. When the formula is copied to other cells in column C, the formula continues to refer to cell C1. If the reference to cell C1 were a relative reference, the copied formulas would return an incorrect result.

Operator Precedence Problems

Excel has some straightforward rules about the order in which mathematical operations are performed in a formula. In Table 21-1, operations with a lower precedence number are performed before operations with a higher precedence number. This table, for example, shows that multiplication has a higher precedence than addition. Therefore, multiplication is performed first.

TABLE 21-1 OPERATOR PRECEDENCE IN EXCEL FORMULAS

Symbol	Operator	Precedence
–	Negation	1
%	Percent	2
^	Exponentiation	3
* and /	Multiplication and division	4
+ and –	Addition and subtraction	5
&	Text concatenation	6
=, <, >, and <>	Comparison	7

When in doubt (or when you simply need to clarify your intentions), use parentheses to ensure that operations are performed in the correct order. For example, the following formula multiplies A1 by A2, and then adds 1 to the result. The multiplication is performed first because it has a higher order of precedence.

```
=1+A1*A2
```

The following is a clearer version of this formula. The parentheses aren't necessary — but in this case, the order of operations is perfectly obvious.

```
=1+(A1*A2)
```

Notice that the negation operator symbol is exactly the same as the subtraction operator symbol. This, as you may expect, can cause some confusion. Consider these two formulas:

```
=-3^2
=0-3^2
```

The first formula, as expected, returns 9. The second formula, however, returns –9. Squaring a number always produces a positive result, so how is it that Excel can return the –9 result?

In the first formula, the minus sign is a negation operator and has the highest precedence. However, in the second formula, the minus sign is a subtraction operator, which has a lower precedence than the exponentiation operator. Therefore, the value 3 is squared, and the result is subtracted from zero, producing a negative result.

 NOTE

Excel is a bit unusual in interpreting the negation operator. Other spreadsheet products (for example, Lotus 1-2-3 and Quattro Pro) return –9 for both formulas. In addition, Excel's VBA language also returns –9 for these expressions.

Using parentheses, as shown in the following formula, causes Excel to interpret the operator as a minus sign rather than a negation operator. This formula returns 9.

```
=-(3^2)
```

Formulas Are Not Calculated

If you use custom worksheet functions written in VBA, you may find that formulas that use these functions fail to get recalculated and may display incorrect results. To force a single formula to be recalculated, select the cell, press F2, and then press Enter. To force a recalculation of all formulas, press Ctrl+Alt+F9.

Actual versus Displayed Values

You may encounter a situation in which values in a range don't appear to add up properly. For example, Figure 21-3 shows a worksheet with the following formula entered into each cell in the range B2:B4:

```
=1/3
```

	A	B	C	D	E
1					
2					
3		0.333			
4		0.333			
5		0.333			
6		1.000			
7					
8					

Sheet1

Figure 21-3: A simple demonstration of numbers that appear to add up incorrectly.

Cell B5 contains the following formula:

```
=SUM(B2:B4)
```

All the cells are formatted to display with three decimal places. As you can see, the formula in cell B5 appears to display an incorrect result. (You may expect it to display 0.999.) The formula, of course, *does* return the correct result. The formula uses the *actual* values in the range B2:B4, not the displayed values.

You can instruct Excel to use the displayed values by checking the Set Precision as Displayed check box on the Advanced tab of the Excel Options dialog box. (Choose Office⇨ Excel Options to display this dialog box.) This setting applies to the active workbook.

CAUTION

Use the Set Precision as Displayed option with caution, and make sure you understand how it works. This setting also affects normal values (nonformulas) that have been entered into cells. For example, if a cell contains the value 4.68 and is displayed with no decimal places (that is, 5), checking the Set Precision as Displayed check box converts 4.68 to 5.00. This change is permanent, and you can't restore the original value if you later clear the Set Precision as Displayed check box. A better approach is to use Excel's ROUND function to round the values to the desired number of decimal places (see Chapter 10). I've used Excel for many years, and I've never had a need to use the Set Precision as Displayed option.

Floating-Point Number Errors

Computers, by their very nature, don't have infinite precision. Excel stores numbers in binary format by using 8 bytes, which can handle numbers with 15-digit accuracy. Some numbers can't be expressed precisely by using 8 bytes, so the number stores as an approximation.

To demonstrate how this limited precision may cause problems, enter the following formula into cell A1:

```
=(5.1-5.2)+1
```

The result should be 0.9. However, if you format the cell to display 15 decimal places, you'll discover that Excel calculates the formula with a result of 0.899999999999999. This small error occurs because the operation in parentheses is performed first, and this intermediate result stores in binary format by using an approximation. The formula then adds 1 to this value, and the approximation error is propagated to the final result.

In many cases, this type of error does not present a problem. However, if you need to test the result of that formula by using a logical operator, it *may* present a problem. For example, the following formula (which assumes that the previous formula is in cell A1) returns FALSE:

```
=A1=.9
```

One solution to this type of error is to use Excel's ROUND function. The following formula, for example, returns TRUE because the comparison is made by using the value in A1 rounded to one decimal place.

```
=ROUND(A1,1)=0.9
```

Here's another example of a "precision" problem. Try entering the following formula:

```
=(1.333-1.233)-(1.334-1.234)
```

This formula should return 0, but it actually returns $-2.220446E-16$ (a number very close to zero).

If that formula were in cell A1, the following formula would return Not Zero.

```
=IF(A1=0,"Zero","Not Zero")
```

One way to handle these very-close-to-zero rounding errors is to use a formula like this:

```
=IF(ABS(A1)<1E-6,"Zero","Not Zero")
```

This formula uses the less-than operator to compare the absolute value of the number with a very small number. This formula would return Zero.

Phantom Link Errors

You may open a workbook and see a message like the one shown in Figure 21-4. This message sometimes appears even when a workbook contains no linked formulas.

Figure 21-4: Excel's way of asking whether you want to update links in a workbook.

First, try using Office⇨Prepare⇨Edit Links To Files to display the Edit Links dialog box. Then select each link and click Break Link. If that doesn't solve the problem, this phantom link may be caused by an erroneous name. Choose Formulas⇨Defined Names⇨Name Manager, and scroll through the list of names. If you see a name that refers to #REF!, delete the name. The Name Manager dialog box has a Filter button that lets you filter the names. For example, you can filter the lists to display only the names with errors.

CROSS REF

These phantom links may be created when you copy a worksheet that contains names. See Chapter 3 for more information about names.

Logical Value Errors

As you know, you can enter TRUE or FALSE into a cell to represent logical True or logical False. Although these values seem straightforward enough, Excel is inconsistent about how it treats TRUE and FALSE.

Figure 21-5 Shows a worksheet with three logical values in A1:A3 as well as three formulas that sum these logical values in A5:A6. As you see, these formulas return three different answers!

	A	B	C	D	E
1	TRUE				
2	TRUE				
3	FALSE				
4					
5	2	=A1+A2+A3			
6	0	=SUM(A1:A3)			
7	-2	=VBASUM(A1:A3)			
8					
9					
10					

Figure 21-5: This worksheet demonstrates an inconsistency when summing logical values.

The formula in cell A5 uses the addition operator. The sum of these three cells is 2. The conclusion: Excel treats TRUE as 1, and FALSE as 0.

But wait! The formula in cell A6 uses Excel's SUM function. In this case, the sum of these three cells is 0. In other words, the SUM function ignores logical values. However, it's possible to force these logical values to be treated as values by the SUM function by using an array formula. Enter the following formula using Ctrl+Shift+Enter, and it returns 2.

```
=SUM(A1:A3*1)
```

To add to the confusion, the SUM function *does* return the correct answer if the logical values are passed as literal arguments. The following formula returns 2:

```
=SUM(TRUE,TRUE,FALSE)
```

Although the VBA macro language is tightly integrated with Excel, sometimes it appears that the two applications don't understand each other. I created a simple VBA function that adds the values in a range. The function (which follows), returns –2!

```
Function VBASUM(rng)
    Dim cell As Range
    VBASUM = 0
    For Each cell In rng
        VBASUM = VBASUM + cell.Value
    Next cell
End Function
```

VBA considers True to be –1, and False to be 0.

The conclusion is that you need to be aware of Excel's inconsistencies and also be careful when summing a range that contains logical values.

Circular Reference Errors

A *circular reference* is a formula that contains a reference to the cell that contains the formula. The reference may be direct or indirect. For help tracking down a circular reference, see the following section, "Excel's Auditing Tools."

CROSS REF

As described in Chapter 16, you may encounter some situations in which you create an intentional circular reference.

Excel's Auditing Tools

Excel includes a number of tools that can help you track down formula errors. The following sections describe the auditing tools built into Excel.

Identifying Cells of a Particular Type

The Go To Special dialog box is a handy tool that enables you to locate cells of a particular type. To display this dialog box, choose Home⇨Editing⇨Find & Select⇨Go To Special, which displays the Go To Special dialog box, as shown in Figure 21-6.

Figure 21-6: The Go To Special dialog box.

NOTE

If you select a multicell range before displaying the Go To Special dialog box, the command operates only within the selected cells. If a single cell is selected, the command operates on the entire worksheet.

You can use the Go To Special dialog box to select cells of a certain type, which can often help you identify errors. For example, if you choose the Formulas option, Excel selects all the cells that contain a formula. If you zoom the worksheet out to a small size, you can get a good idea of the worksheet's organization (see Figure 21-7).

TIP

Selecting the formula cells may also help you to spot a common error—a formula that has been replaced accidentally with a value. If you find a cell that's not selected amid a group of selected formula cells, chances are good that the cell previously contained a formula that has been replaced by a value.

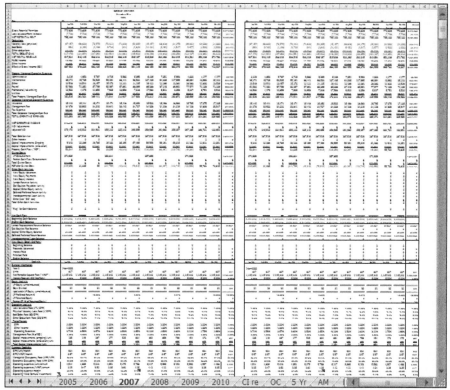

Figure 21-7: Zooming out and selecting all formula cells can give you a good overview of how the worksheet is designed.

Viewing Formulas

You can become familiar with an unfamiliar workbook by displaying the formulas rather than the results of the formulas. To toggle the display of formulas, choose Formulas⇨Formula Auditing⇨Show Formulas. You may want to create a second window for the workbook before issuing this command. This way, you can see the formulas in one window and the results of the formula in the other window. Choose View⇨Window⇨New Window to open a new window.

TIP

You can also use Ctrl+` (the accent grave key, usually located above the Tab key) to toggle between Formula view and Normal view.

Figure 21-8 shows an example of a worksheet displayed in two windows. The window on the top shows Normal view (formula results), and the window on the bottom displays the formulas. The View⇨Window⇨View Side by Side command, which allows synchronized scrolling, is also useful for viewing two windows.

Third-Party Auditing Tools

Several third-party auditing tools for Excel are available, including my Power Utility Pak. If you're interested in finding out about such tools, try searching the Web.

When Formula view is in effect, Excel highlights the cells that are used by the formula in the active cell. In Figure 21-7, for example, the active cell is C11. The cells used by this formula are highlighted in both windows.

commission calc.xls:1 [Compatibility Mode]

	A	B	C	D	E	F	G	H
1	Commission Rate	5.50%	Normal commission rate					
2	Sales Goal	15%	Improvement from prior month					
3	Bonus Rate	6.50%	Paid if Sales Goal is attained					
4								
5	Sales Rep	Last Month	This Month	Change	Pct. Change	Met Goal?	Commission	
6	Murray	101,233	108,444	7,211	7.1%	TRUE	7,049	
7	Knuckles	120,933	108,434	-12,499	-10.3%	FALSE	5,964	
8	Lefty	139,832	165,901	26,069	18.6%	TRUE	10,784	
9	Lucky	98,323	100,083	1,760	1.8%	FALSE	5,505	
10	Scarface	78,322	79,923	1,601	2.0%	FALSE	4,396	
11	Total	538,643	562,785	24,142	4.5%		33,697	
12								
13	Average Commission Rate:		5.99%					

H ◄ ► H   Sheet1

commission calc.xls:2 [Compatibility Mode]

	B	C	D	E	F	
1	0.055	Normal commission				
2	0.15	Improvement from p				
3	0.065	Paid if Sales Goal is a				
4						
5	Last Month	This Month	Change	Pct. Change	Met Goal?	
6	101233	108444	=C6-B6	=D6/B6	=E6>=$B$3	=IF(F6
7	120933	108434	=C7-B7	=D7/B7	=E7>=$B$3	=IF(F7
8	139832	165901	=C8-B8	=D8/B8	=E8>=$B$3	=IF(F8
9	98323	100083	=C9-B9	=D9/B9	=E9>=$B$3	=IF(F9
10	78322	79923	=C10-B10	=D10/B10	=E10>=$B$3	=IF(F1
11	=SUM(B6:B10)	=SUM(C6:C10)	=SUM(D6:D10)	=D11/B11		=SUM
12						

H ◄ ► H   Sheet1

Figure 21-8: Displaying formulas (bottom window) and their results (top window).

Tracing Cell Relationships

To understand how to trace cell relationships, you need to familiarize yourself with the following two concepts:

- **Cell precedents:** Applicable only to cells that contain a formula, a formula cell's precedents are all the cells that contribute to the formula's result. A *direct precedent* is a cell that you use directly in the formula. An *indirect precedent* is a cell that is not used directly in the formula but is instead used by a cell that you refer to in the formula.

- **Cell dependents:** These are formula cells that depend on a particular cell. A cell's dependents consist of all formula cells that use the cell. Again, the formula cell can be a direct dependent or an indirect dependent.

Identifying cell precedents for a formula cell often sheds light on why the formula is not working correctly. Conversely, knowing which formula cells depend on a particular cell is also helpful. For example, if you're about to delete a formula, you may want to check whether it has any dependents.

IDENTIFYING PRECEDENTS

You can identify cells used by a formula in the active cell in a number of ways:

- **Press F2.** The cells that are used directly by the formula are outlined in color, and the color corresponds to the cell reference in the formula. This technique is limited to identifying cells on the same sheet as the formula.

- **Display the Go To Special dialog box** (choose Home⇨Editing⇨Find & Select⇨Go To Special). Select the Precedents option and then select either Direct Only (for direct precedents only) or All Levels (for direct and indirect precedents). Click OK, and Excel selects the precedent cells for the formula. This technique is limited to identifying cells on the same sheet as the formula.

- **Press Ctrl+[** to select all direct precedent cells on the active sheet.

- **Press Ctrl+Shift+{** to select all precedent cells (direct and indirect) on the active sheet.

- **Choose Formulas⇨Formula Auditing⇨Trace Precedents.** Excel will draw arrows to indicate the cell's precedents. Click this button multiple times to see additional levels of precedents. Choose Formulas⇨Formula Auditing⇨Remove Arrows to hide the arrows. Figure 21-9 shows a worksheet with precedent arrows drawn to indicate the precedents for the formula in cell C13.

Part V

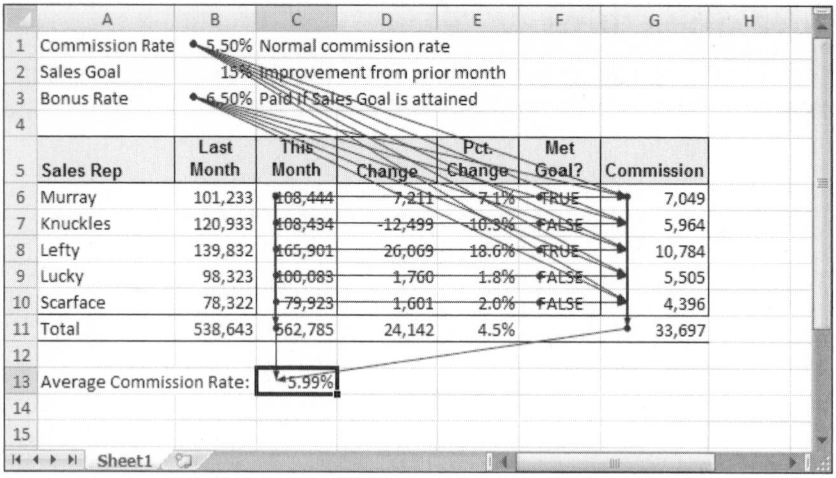

Figure 21-9: This worksheet displays lines that indicate cell precedents for the formula in cell C13.

IDENTIFYING DEPENDENTS

You can identify formula cells that use a particular cell in a number of ways:

- **Display the Go To Special dialog box.** Select the Dependents option and then select either Direct Only (for direct dependents only) or All Levels (for direct and indirect dependents). Click OK. Excel selects the cells that depend on the active cell. This technique is limited to identifying cells on the active sheet only.

- **Press Ctrl+]** to select all direct dependent cells on the active sheet.

- **Press Ctrl+Shift+]** to select all dependent cells (direct and indirect) on the active sheet.

- **Choose Formulas⇨Formula Auditing⇨Trace Dependents.** Excel will draw arrows to indicate the cell's dependents. Click this button multiple times to see additional levels of dependents. Choose Formulas⇨Formula Auditing⇨Remove Arrows to hide the arrows.

Tracing Error Values

If a formula displays an error value, Excel can help you identify the cell that is causing that error value. An error in one cell is often the result of an error in a precedent cell. Activate a cell that contains an error value and choose Formulas⇨Formula Auditing⇨Error Checking⇨Trace Error. Excel draws arrows to indicate the error source.

Fixing Circular Reference Errors

If you accidentally create a circular reference formula, Excel displays a warning message, displays Circular Reference (with the cell address) in the status bar, and draws arrows on the worksheet to help you identify the problem. If you can't figure out the source of the problem, use Formulas⇨Formula Auditing⇨Error Checking⇨Circular References. This command displays a list of all cells that are involved in the circular references. Start by selecting the first cell listed and then work your way down the list until you figure out the problem.

Using Background Error Checking

Some people may find it helpful to take advantage of Excel's automatic error-checking feature. This feature is enabled or disabled by using the check box labeled Enable Background Error Checking, in the Formulas tab in the Excel Options dialog box shown in Figure 21-10. In addition, you can specify which types of errors to check for by using the check boxes in the Error Checking Rules section.

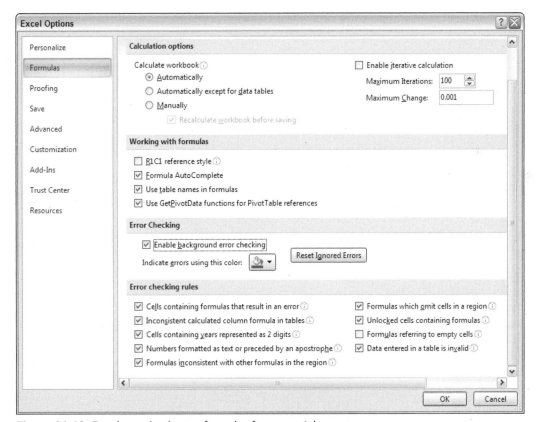

Figure 21-10: Excel can check your formulas for potential errors.

When error checking is turned on, Excel continually evaluates your worksheet, including its formulas. If a potential error is identified, Excel places a small triangle in the upper-left corner of the cell. When the cell is activated, a Smart Tag appears. Clicking this Smart Tag provides you with options. Figure 21-11 shows the options that appear when you click the Smart Tag in a cell that contains a #DIV/0! error. The options vary, depending on the type of error.

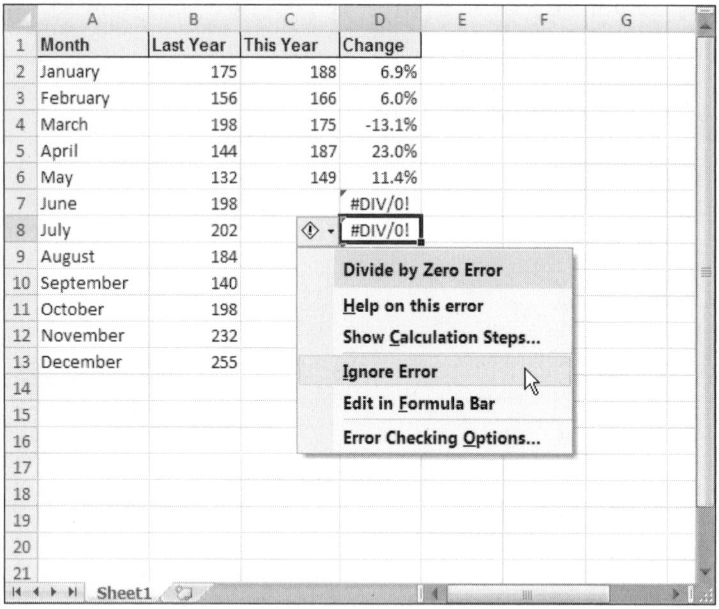

Figure 21-11: Clicking an error Smart Tag gives you a list of options.

In many cases, you will choose to ignore an error by selecting the Ignore Error option. Selecting this option eliminates the cell from subsequent error checks. However, all previously ignored errors can be reset so that they appear again. (Use the Reset Ignored Errors button in the Formulas tab of the Excel Options dialog box.)

You can choose Formulas⇨Formula Auditing⇨Error Checking to display a dialog box that describes each potential error cell in sequence, much like using a spell-checking command. This command is available even if you disable background error checking. Figure 21-12 shows the Error Checking dialog box. Note that this dialog box is *modeless,* so you can still access your worksheet when the Error Checking dialog box is displayed.

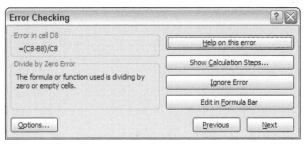

Figure 21-12: Using the Error Checking dialog box to cycle through potential errors identified by Excel.

 CAUTION

It's important to understand that the error-checking feature is not perfect. In fact, it's not even close to perfect. In other words, you can't assume that you have an error-free work-sheet simply because Excel does not identify any potential errors! Also, be aware that this error checking feature won't catch a very common type of error — that of overwriting a formula cell with a value.

Using Excel's Formula Evaluator

Excel's Formula Evaluator enables you to see the various parts of a nested formula evaluated in the order that the formula is calculated.

To use the Formula Evaluator, select the cell that contains the formula and choose Formula➪Formula Auditing➪Evaluate Formula to display the Evaluate Formula dialog box, as shown in Figure 21-13.

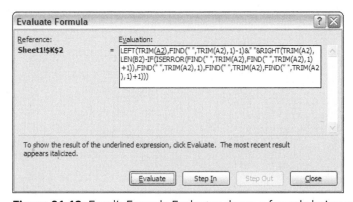

Figure 21-13: Excel's Formula Evaluator shows a formula being calculated one step at a time.

Part V

Click the Evaluate button to show the result of calculating the expressions within the formula. Each click of the button performs another calculation. This feature may seem a bit complicated at first, but if you spend some time working with it, you'll understand how it works and see the value.

Excel provides another way to evaluate a part of a formula:

1. Select the cell that contains the formula.

2. Press F2 to get into cell edit mode.

3. Use your mouse to highlight the portion of the formula that you want to evaluate. Or, press Shift and use the arrow keys.

4. Press F9.

The highlighted portion of the formula displays the calculated result. You can evaluate other parts of the formula or press Esc to cancel and return your formula to its previous state.

CAUTION

Be careful when using this technique because if you press Enter (rather than Esc), the formula will be modified to use the calculated values.

Part VI

Developing Custom Worksheet Functions

Chapter 22

Introducing VBA

IN THIS CHAPTER

♦ An introduction to Visual Basic for Applications (Excel's programming language)

♦ How to use the Visual Basic Editor

♦ How to work in the code windows of the Visual Basic Editor

This chapter introduces you to Visual Basic for Applications (VBA). VBA is Excel's programming language, and it is used to create custom worksheet functions. Before you can create custom functions by using VBA, you need to have some basic background knowledge of VBA as well as some familiarity with the Visual Basic Editor.

About VBA

VBA is best thought of as Microsoft's common application scripting language. VBA is included with most Office 2007 applications, and it's also available in applications from other vendors. In Excel, VBA has two primary uses:

• Automating spreadsheet tasks

• Creating custom functions that you can use in your worksheet formulas

NOTE

Excel also includes another way of creating custom functions by using the XLM macro language. XLM is pretty much obsolete, but it is still supported for compatibility purposes. This book completely ignores the XLM language and focuses on VBA. By the way, the XLM macro language has absolutely nothing to with XML, which is a mark-up language for storing structured data.

VBA is a complex topic — far too complex to be covered completely in this book. Because this book deals with formulas, I hone in on one important (and useful) aspect of VBA — creating custom worksheet functions. You can use a custom worksheet function (sometimes known as a *user-defined function*) in formulas.

 NOTE

If your goal is to become a VBA expert, this book nudges you in that direction, but it does not get you to your final destination. You may want to check out another book of mine: *Excel 2007 Power Programming with VBA* (Wiley). That book covers all aspects of VBA programming for Excel.

Displaying the Developer Tab

If you plan to work with VBA macros, you'll want to make sure that the Developer tab is displayed in Excel. To display this tab

1. Choose Office⇨Excel Options.

2. In the Excel Options dialog box, select Popular.

3. Place a checkmark next to Show Developer tab in the Ribbon.

Figure 22-1 shows how the Ribbon looks when the Developer tab is selected.

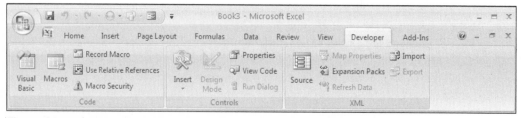

Figure 22-1: The Developer tab, which is not displayed by default, contains commands that are useful for VBA users.

About Macro Security

Macro security was a key priority in developing Excel 2007. The reason is that macros are powerful — so powerful that they can do serious damage to your computer. The macro security features in Excel 2007 were created to help prevent macro-related problems.

Figure 22-2 shows the Macro Settings section of the Trust Center dialog box. To display this dialog box, choose Developer⇨Macro Security.

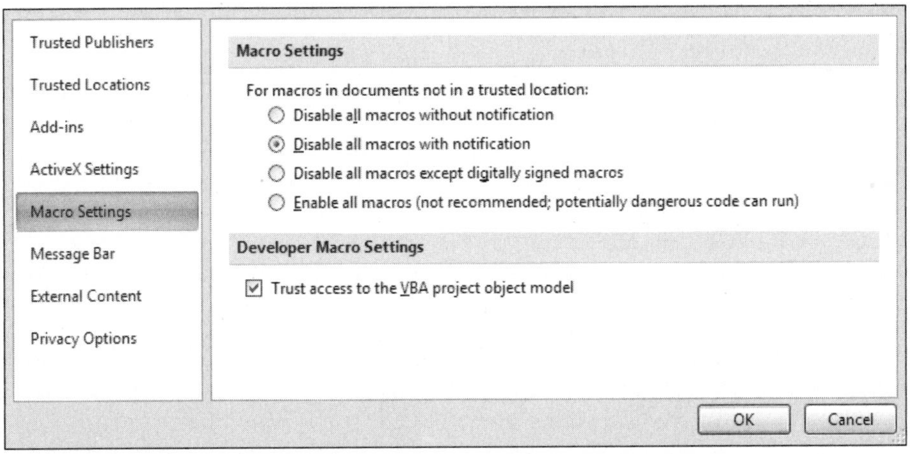

Figure 22-2: The Macro Settings section of the Trust Center dialog box.

By default, Excel uses the Disable All Macros with Notification option. With this setting in effect, if you open a workbook that contains VBA macros (and the file is not digitally "signed" or is from an untrusted location), Excel displays a Security Warning above the Formula bar. (See Figure 22-3.) If you are certain that the workbook comes from a trusted source and the macros are safe, click the Options button, which displays a dialog box in which you can enable the macros in the workbook.

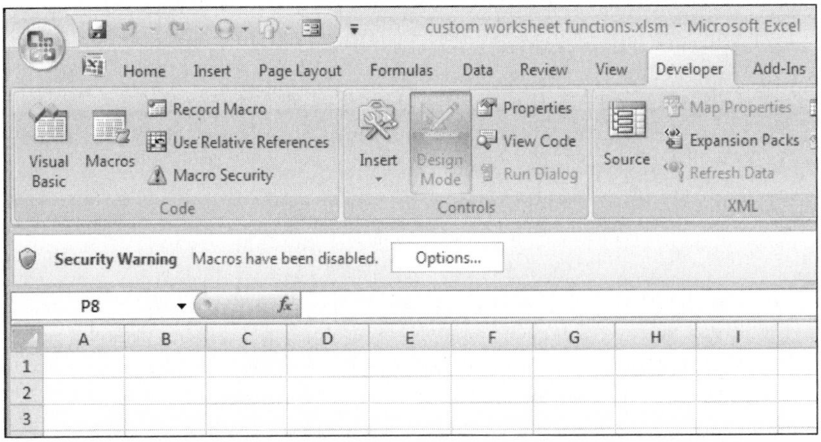

Figure 22-3: Excel's Security Warning that the file contains macros.

NOTE

If the VBA window is open when you open a workbook that contains macros, Excel does not display the Security Warning in the workbook. Rather, it displays the dialog box shown in Figure 22-4. You can use this dialog box to enable or disable the macros.

Figure 22-4: You see this warning when the VBA window is open and a workbook contains macros.

Perhaps the best way to handle macro security is to designate one or more folders as trusted locations. All workbooks in a trusted location are opened without a macro warning. You designate trusted folders in the Trusted Locations section of the Trust Center dialog box.

Saving Workbooks That Contain Macros

If you store one or more VBA macros in a workbook, the file must be saved with macros enabled. This is a file with an XLSM extension (or XLAM extension if it's an add-in). This file format is not the default format, so you need to make sure that you save the file with the correct extension.

For example, assume that you create a new workbook containing one or more macros. The first time you save the workbook, the file format defaults to XLSX, which is a file format that cannot contain macros. Unless you change the file format to XLSM, Excel displays the warning shown in Figure 22-5. You need to click No, and then choose Excel Macro-Enabled Workbook (*.xlsm) from the Save as Type drop-down.

CAUTION

Be careful because Excel makes it *very* easy to accidentally delete all your macros with a single button click. If you accidentally click Yes instead of No, Excel deletes the macros from the saved workbook. The macros are still available in the copy that you're working on, however. So if you catch your mistake, it's still not too late to resave the workbook with an XLSM extension.

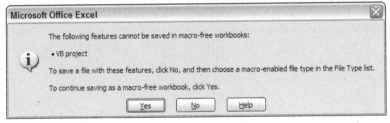

Figure 22-5: Excel warns you if your workbook contains macros and you attempt to save it in a non-macro file format.

Introducing the Visual Basic Editor

Before you can begin creating custom functions, you need to become familiar with the Visual Basic Editor, or VB Editor for short. The VB Editor enables you to work with *VBA modules*, which are containers for your VBA code.

Activating the VB Editor

When you work in Excel, you can switch to the VB Editor by using either of the following techniques:

- Press Alt+F11.
- Choose Developer⇨Code⇨Visual Basic.

Figure 22-6 shows the VB Editor. Chances are that your VB Editor window won't look exactly like the window shown in the figure. This window is highly customizable. You can hide windows, change their sizes, "dock" them, rearrange them, and so on.

The VB Editor Components

The VB Editor consists of a number of components. I briefly describe some of the key components in the following sections.

NOTE

Excel 2007 got a major facelift, but the VB Editor looks exactly as it did in the previous version. The VB Editor still uses a menu and toolbar interface rather than a Ribbon interface.

Part VI

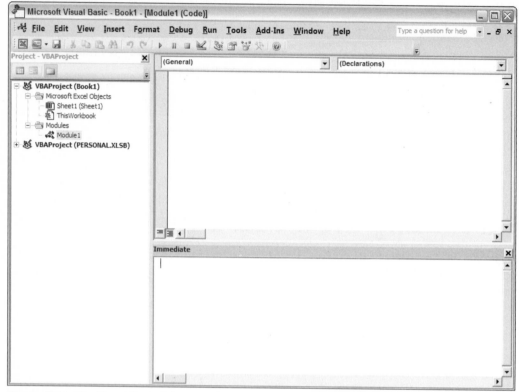

Figure 22-6: The Visual Basic Editor window.

MENU BAR

The VB Editor menu bar is like the menu bar for most Windows applications. It contains commands that you use to work with the various components in the VB Editor. The VB Editor also features shortcut menus. Right-click virtually anything in a VB Editor window to get a shortcut menu of common commands.

TOOLBARS

The standard toolbar, directly under the menu bar by default, is one of six VB Editor toolbars that are available. You can customize toolbars, move them around, dock them, display additional toolbars, and so forth.

PROJECT WINDOW

The Project window displays a tree diagram that consists of every workbook that's currently open in Excel (including add-ins and hidden workbooks). In the VB Editor, each workbook is known as a *project*. I discuss the Project window in more detail in the upcoming section, "Using the Project Window." If the Project window is not visible, press Ctrl+R.

CODE WINDOW

A code window contains VBA code. Just about every item in a project has an associated code window. To view a code window for an object, either double-click the object in the Project window, or select the item and then click the View Code button at the top of the Project window.

For example, to view the code window for the Sheet1 object for a particular workbook, double-click Sheet1 in the Project window. Unless you've added some VBA code, the code window will be empty. I discuss code windows later on in this chapter (see "Using Code Windows").

PROPERTIES WINDOW

The Properties window contains a list of all properties for the selected object. Use this window to examine and change properties. You can use the F4 shortcut key to display the Properties window.

IMMEDIATE WINDOW

The Immediate window is most useful for executing VBA statements directly, testing statements, and debugging your code. This window may or may not be visible. If the Immediate window is not visible, press Ctrl+G. To close the Immediate window, click the Close button on its title bar.

Using the Project Window

When you work in the VB Editor, each Excel workbook and add-in that's currently open is considered a project. You can think of a project as a collection of objects arranged as an outline. You can expand a project by clicking the plus sign (+) at the left of the project's name in the Project window. To contract a project, click the minus sign (–) to the left of a project's name. Figure 22-7 shows the Project window with two projects listed.

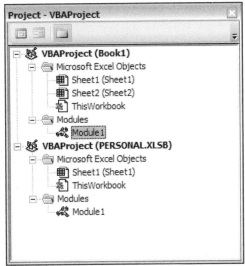

Figure 22-7: A Project window with two projects listed.

If you try to expand a project that is password protected, you are prompted to enter the password.

Every project expands to show at least one node called *Microsoft Excel Objects.* This node expands to show an item for each worksheet and chart sheet in the workbook (each sheet is considered an object), and another object called ThisWorkbook (which represents the Workbook object). If the project has any VBA modules, the project listing also shows a Modules node with the modules listed there. A project may also contain a node called Forms (which contains UserForm objects) and a node called Class Modules (which contain Class Module objects). This book focuses exclusively on standard VBA modules and does not cover the objects contained in the Microsoft Excel Objects node, UserForms node, or Class Modules node.

 NOTE

A project may have another node called References. This node contains a list of all references that are used by the project. References are added or removed by using the Tools⇨References command. Unlike other items listed in the Project window, Reference items don't have an associated code module.

RENAMING A PROJECT

By default, all projects are named VBAProject. In the Project window, the workbook name appears (in parentheses) next to the project name. For example, a project may appear as follows:

```
VBAProject (budget.xlsm)
```

You may prefer to change the name of your project to a more descriptive name. To do so, follow these steps:

1. Select the project in the Project window.

2. Make sure that the Properties window is displayed (press F4 if it's not displayed).

3. Use the Properties window to change the name from VBAProject to something else.

After making the change, the Project window displays the new name.

ADDING A NEW VBA MODULE

A new Excel workbook does not have any VBA modules. To add a VBA module to a project, select the project's name in the Project window and choose Insert⇨Module.

⚠️ **CAUTION**

When you create custom worksheet functions, they *must* reside in a standard VBA module and not in a code window for a Sheet object (for example, Sheet1) or the ThisWorkbook object. If the code for your custom function does not reside in a VBA module, it won't work. Putting VBA code in the wrong place is perhaps the most common error made by users who are learning to write custom worksheet functions.

RENAMING A MODULE

VBA modules have default names, such as Module1, Module2, and so on. To rename a VBA module, select it in the Project window, and then change the Name property by using the Properties window. (A VBA module has only one property — Name.) If the Properties window is not visible, press F4 to display it. Figure 22-8 shows a VBA module that is being renamed to modFunctions.

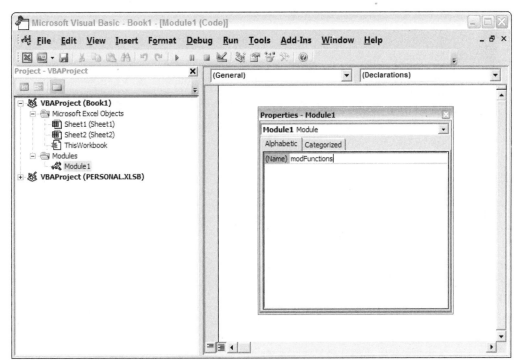

Figure 22-8: Use the Properties window to change the name of a VBA module.

Removing a VBA Module

If you want to remove a VBA module from a project, select the module's name in the Project window and choose File⇨Remove *xxx* (where *xxx* is the name of the module). You are asked whether you want to export the module before removing it. Exporting a module makes a backup file of the module's contents. You can import an exported module into any other project.

Using Code Windows

With the exception of Reference objects, each object in a project has an associated code window. To summarize, these objects can be

- The workbook itself (the item named ThisWorkbook in the Project window)

- A worksheet or chart sheet in a workbook (for example, Sheet1 or Chart1 in the Project window)

- A VBA module (a module that contains general VBA code, including the code for custom worksheet functions)

- A UserForm (a module that contains code for a custom dialog box)

- A Class module (a special type of module that enables you to create new object classes)

- A Reference (a list of references inserted by using the Tools⇨References command)

 Note

This book focuses exclusively on VBA modules, also known as standard modules, which is where custom worksheet functions are stored.

Minimizing and Maximizing Windows

At any given time, the VB Editor may have lots of code windows. Figure 22-9 shows an example.

Code windows are much like worksheet windows in Excel. You can minimize them, maximize them, hide them, rearrange them, and so on. Most people find that it's much easier to maximize the code window that they're working on. Sometimes, however, you may want to have two or more code windows visible. For example, you may want to compare the code in two modules or copy code from one module to another.

Minimizing a code window gets it out of the way. You also can click the Close button in a code window's title bar to close the window completely. To open it again, just double-click the appropriate object in the Project window.

You can't close a workbook from the VB Editor. You must reactivate Excel and close it from there.

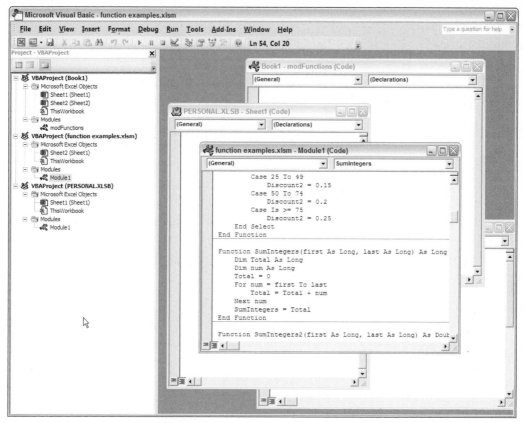

Figure 22-9: Code window overload.

STORING VBA CODE

In general, a module can hold three types of code:

- **Sub procedures:** A *procedure* is a set of instructions that performs some action. For example, you may have a Sub procedure that combines various parts of a workbook into a concise report.

- **Function procedures:** A *function* is a set of instructions that returns a single value or an array. You can use Function procedures in worksheet formulas.

- **Declarations:** A *declaration* is information about a variable that you provide to VBA. For example, you can declare the data type for variables that you plan to use. Declarations go at the top of the module.

A single VBA module can store any number of procedures and declarations.

NOTE

This book focuses exclusively on `Function` procedures, which are the only type of procedure that you can use in worksheet formulas.

Entering VBA Code

This section describes the various ways of entering VBA code in a code window. For `Function` procedures, the code window will always be a VBA module. You can add code to a VBA module in three ways:

- Use your keyboard to type it.

- Use the Excel macro-recorder feature to record your actions and convert them into VBA code.

- Copy the code from another module and paste it into the module that you are working on.

ENTERING CODE MANUALLY

Sometimes, the most direct route is the best one. Type the code by using your keyboard. Entering and editing text in a VBA module works just as you expect. You can select text and copy it, or cut and paste it to another location.

Use the Tab key to indent the lines that logically belong together — for example, the conditional statements between an `If` and an `End If` statement. Indentation is not necessary, but it makes the code easier to read.

A single instruction in VBA can be as long as you want. For the sake of readability, however, you may want to break a lengthy instruction into two or more lines. To do so, end the line with a space followed by an underscore character, and then press Enter and continue the instruction on the following line. The following code, for example, is a single statement split over three lines.

```
If IsNumeric(MyCell) Then _
        Result = "Number" Else _
        Result = "Non-Number"
```

Notice that I indented the last two lines of this statement. Doing this is optional, but it helps to clarify the fact that these three lines make up a single statement.

After you enter an instruction, the VB Editor performs the following actions to improve readability:

- It inserts spaces between operators. If you enter **Ans=1+2** (without any spaces), for example, VBA converts it to

  ```
  Ans = 1 + 2
  ```

- The VB Editor adjusts the case of the letters for keywords, properties, and methods. If you enter the following text

  ```
  user=application.username
  ```

  VBA converts it to

  ```
  user = Application.UserName
  ```

- Because variable names are not case sensitive, the VB Editor adjusts the names of all variables with the same letters so that their case matches the case of letters that you most recently typed. For example, if you first specify a variable as `myvalue` (all lower-case) and then enter the variable as `MyValue` (mixed case), VBA changes all other occurrences of the variable to `MyValue`. An exception to this occurs if you declare the variable with `Dim` or a similar statement; in this case, the variable name always appears as it was declared.

- The VB Editor scans the instruction for syntax errors. If it finds an error, it changes the color of the line and may display a message describing the problem. You can set various options for the VB Editor in the Options dialog box (accessible by choosing Tools➪ Options).

TIP

Like Excel, the VB Editor has multiple levels of Undo and Redo. Therefore, if you find that you mistakenly deleted an instruction, you can click the Undo button (or press Ctrl+Z) repeatedly until the instruction returns. After undoing the action, you can choose Edit➪ Redo Delete (or click the Redo Delete toolbar button) to redo previously undone changes.

USING THE MACRO RECORDER

Another way to get code into a VBA module is to record your actions by using the Excel macro recorder. No matter how hard you try, you cannot record a `Function` procedure (the type of procedure that is used for a custom worksheet function). All recorded macros are `Sub` procedures. Using the macro recorder *can* help you to identify various properties that you can use in your custom functions. For example, turn on the macro recorder to record your actions while you change the username. Follow these steps in Excel:

1. Choose Developer➪Code➪Record Macro.

2. In the Record Macro dialog box, accept the default settings and click OK to begin recording. The Record Macro button's caption changes to Stop Recording.

3. Choose Excel Options➪Popular.

4. Under the Personalize Your Copy of Microsoft Office heading, change the name in the User Name box.

5. Click OK to close the Excel Options dialog box.

6. Choose Developer⇨Code⇨Stop Recording.

7. Press Alt+F11 to activate the VB Editor.

8. In the Project window, select the project that corresponds to your workbook.

9. Double-click the VBA module that contains your recorded code. Generally, this will be the module with the highest number (for example, Module3).

You'll find a VBA procedure that looks something like this:

```
Sub Macro1()
'
' Macro1 Macro
'


'
    Application.UserName = "Robert Smith"
End Sub
```

Note that this is a `Sub` procedure, not a `Function` procedure. In other words, you can't use this procedure in a worksheet formula. If you examine the code, however, you'll see a reference to the `UserName` property. You can use this information when creating a `Function` procedure. For example, the following `Function` procedure uses the `UserName` property. This function, when used in a worksheet formula, returns the name of the user.

```
Function USER()
    USER = Application.UserName
End Function
```

You can consult the VBA Help system to identify various properties, but using the macro recorder is often more efficient if you don't know exactly what you're looking for. After you identify what you need, you can check the Help system for details.

 NOTE

You can use the Excel Options dialog box to change the UserName property back to what it was. Or, you can make the change by using VBA. Just edit the code in the recorded macro (replace the name quotes with the original user name). Then, move the cursor anywhere within the `Macro1` procedure and choose Run⇨Run Sub/UserForm (or press F5) to execute the macro. Executing the macro changes the `UserName` property.

COPYING VBA CODE

This section has covered entering code directly and recording your actions to generate VBA code. The final method of getting code into a VBA module is to copy it from another module. For example, you may have written a custom function for one project that would also be useful in your current project. Rather than re-enter the code, you can open the workbook, activate the module, and use the normal Clipboard copy-and-paste procedures to copy it into your current VBA module.

You also can copy VBA code from other sources. For example, you may find a listing on a Web page or in a newsgroup. In such a case, you can select the text in your browser (or newsreader), copy it to the Clipboard, and then paste it into a module.

Saving Your Project

As with any application, you should save your work frequently while working in the VB Editor. To do so, use the Save *xxxx* command (where *xxxx* is the name of the active workbook), press Ctrl+S, or click the Save button on the standard toolbar.

 NOTE
When you save your project, you actually save your Excel workbook. By the same token, if you save your workbook in Excel, you also save the changes made in the workbook's VB project.

The VB Editor does not have a Save As command. To save your project with a different name, activate Excel and use Excel's Save As command.

Chapter **23**

Function Procedure Basics

Previous chapters in this book examined Excel's worksheet functions and how you can use them to build more complex formulas. These functions provide a great deal of flexibility when creating formulas. However, you may encounter situations that call for custom functions. This chapter discusses the reasons why you may want to use custom functions, how you can create a VBA Function procedure, and methods for testing and debugging them.

Why Create Custom Functions?

You are, of course, familiar with Excel's worksheet functions — even novices know how to use the most common worksheet functions, such as SUM, AVERAGE, and IF. Excel 2007 includes 340 predefined worksheet functions — everything from ABS to ZTEST.

You can use Visual Basic for Applications (VBA) to create additional worksheet functions, which are known as *custom functions* or *user-defined functions* (UDFs). With all the functions that are available in Excel and VBA, you may wonder why you would ever need to create new functions. The answer: to simplify your work and give your formulas more power.

For example, you can create a custom function that can significantly shorten your formulas. Shorter formulas are more readable and easier to work with. However, it's important to understand that custom functions in your formulas are usually much slower than built-in functions. On a fast system, though, the speed difference often goes unnoticed.

The process of creating a custom function is not difficult. In fact, many people (this author included) *enjoy* creating custom functions. This book provides you with the information that you need to create your own functions. In this and subsequent chapters, you'll find many custom function examples that you can adapt for your own use.

An Introductory VBA Function Example

Without further ado, I'll show you a simple VBA `Function` procedure. This function, named USER, does not accept any arguments. When used in a worksheet formula, this function simply displays the user's name in uppercase characters. To create this function, follow these steps:

1. Start with a new workbook. (This is not really necessary, but keep it simple for right now.)

2. Press Alt+F11 to activate the VB Editor.

3. Click your workbook's name in the Project window. If the Project window is not visible, press Ctrl+R to display it.

4. Choose Insert➪Module to add a VBA module to the project.

5. Type the following code in the code window:

```
Function USER()
'    Returns the user's name
     USER = Application.UserName
     USER = UCase(USER)
End Function
```

Figure 23-1 shows how the function looks in a code window.

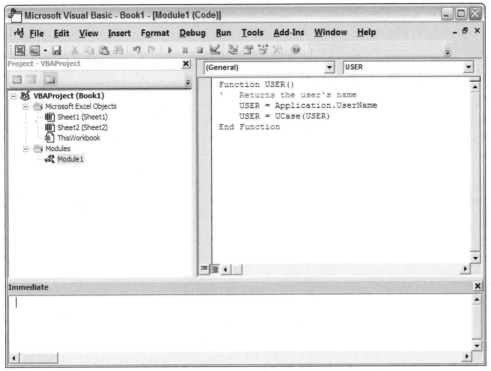

Figure 23-1: A simple VBA function displayed in a code window.

To try out the USER function, activate Excel (press Alt+F11) and enter the following formula into any cell in the workbook:

```
=USER()
```

If you entered the VBA code correctly, the `Function` procedure executes, and your name displays (in uppercase characters) in the cell.

NOTE

If your formula returns an error, make sure that the VBA code for the USER function is in a VBA module (and not a module for a Sheet or ThisWorkbook object). Also, make sure that the module is in the project associated with the workbook into which you enter the formula.

When Excel calculates your worksheet, it encounters the USER custom function. Each instruction in the function is evaluated, and the result is returned to your worksheet. You can use this function any number of times in any number of cells.

You'll find that this custom function works just like any other worksheet function. You can insert it into a formula by using the Insert Function dialog box, and it will also appear in the Formula AutoComplete drop-down as you type it in a cell. In the Insert Function dialog box, custom functions appear in the User Defined category. As with any other function, you can use it in a more complex formula. For example, try this.

What Custom Worksheet Functions Can't Do

As you develop custom worksheet functions, you should understand a key point. A `Function` procedure used in a worksheet formula must be *passive:* In other words, it can't change things in the worksheet.

You may be tempted to try to write a custom worksheet function that changes the formatting of a cell. For example, you may want to edit the USER function (presented in this section) so that the name displays in a different color. Try as you might, a function such as this is impossible to write—everybody tries this, and no one succeeds. No matter what you do, the function always returns an error because the code attempts to change something on the worksheet. Remember that a function can return only a value. It can't perform actions with objects.

```
="Hello "&USER()
```

Or use this formula to display the number of characters in your name:

```
=LEN(USER())
```

If you don't like the fact that your name is in uppercase, edit the procedure as follows:

```
Function USER()
'    Returns the user's name
     USER = Application.UserName
End Function
```

After editing the function, reactivate Excel and press F9 to recalculate. Any cell that uses the USER function displays a different result.

About Function Procedures

In this section, I discuss some of the technical details that apply to `Function` procedures. These are general guidelines for declaring functions, naming functions, using custom functions in formulas, and using arguments in custom functions.

Declaring a Function

The official syntax for declaring a function is as follows:

```
[Public | Private][Static] Function name ([arglist]) [As type]
    [statements]
    [name = expression]
```

```
    [Exit Function]
    [statements]
    [name = expression]
End Function
```

The following list describes the elements in a `Function` procedure declaration:

- `Public`: Indicates that the function is accessible to all other procedures in all other modules in the workbook (optional).

- `Private`: Indicates that the function is accessible only to other procedures in the same module (optional). If you use the `Private` keyword, your functions won't appear in the Insert Function dialog box and will not be shown in the Formula AutoComplete drop-down.

- `Static`: Indicates that the values of variables declared in the function are preserved between calls (optional).

- `Function`: Indicates the beginning of a `Function` procedure (required).

- *Name:* Can be any valid variable name. When the function finishes, the result of the function is the value assigned to the function's name (required).

- *Arglist:* Is a list of one or more variables that represent arguments passed to the function. The arguments are enclosed in parentheses. Use a comma to separate arguments. (Arguments are optional.)

- *Type:* Is the data type returned by the function (optional).

- *Statements:* Are valid VBA statements (optional).

- `Exit Function`: Is a statement that causes an immediate exit from the function (optional).

- `End Function`: Is a keyword that indicates the end of the function (required).

Choosing a Name for Your Function

Each function must have a unique name, and function names must adhere to a few rules:

- **You can use alphabetic characters, numbers, and some punctuation characters.** However, the first character must be alphabetic.

- **You can use any combination of uppercase and lowercase letters.**

- **You can't use a name that looks like a worksheet cell's address** (such as J21). Actually, you *can* use such a name for a function although doing so can cause unexpected results.

- **You can use mixed case.** VBA does not distinguish between cases. To make a function name more readable, you can use `InterestRate` rather than `interestrate`.

- **You can't use spaces or periods.** To make function names more readable, you can use the underscore character (`Interest_Rate`).

- **You can't embed the following characters in a function's name: #, $, %, &, or !.** These are type declaration characters that have a special meaning in VBA.

- **You can use a function name with as many as 255 characters.** However, shorter names are usually more readable and easier to work with.

Using Functions in Formulas

Using a custom VBA function in a worksheet formula is like using a built-in worksheet function except that you must ensure that Excel can locate the Function procedure. If the Function procedure is in the same workbook as the formula, you don't have to do anything special. If it's in a different workbook, you may have to tell Excel where to find it. You can do so in three ways:

- **Precede the function's name with a file reference.** For example, if you want to use a function called CountNames that's defined in a workbook named Myfuncs.xlsm, you can use a formula like the following:

  ```
  =Myfuncs.xlsm!CountNames(A1:A1000)
  ```

  If you insert the function with the Insert Function dialog box, the workbook reference is inserted automatically.

- **Set up a reference to the workbook.** You do this with the VB Editor's Tools⇨References command (see Figure 23-2). If the function is defined in a referenced workbook, you don't need to use the worksheet name. Even when the dependent workbook is assigned as a reference, the Insert Function dialog box continues to insert the workbook reference (even though it's not necessary).

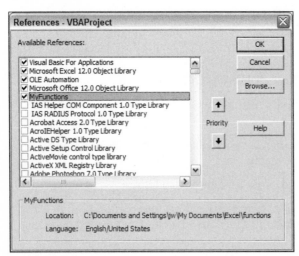

Figure 23-2: Use the References dialog box to create a reference to a project that contains a custom VBA function.

TIP

By default, all projects are named VBAProject—and that's the name that appears in the Available References list in the References dialog box. To make sure that you select the correct project in the References dialog box, keep your eye on the bottom of the dialog box, which shows the workbook name for the selected item. Better yet, change the name of the project to be more descriptive. To change the name, select the project, press F4 to display the Properties window, and then change the Name property to something other than VBAProject. It's best to use a unique name because Excel will not let you create two references with the same name.

- **Create an add-in.** When you create an add-in from a workbook that has `Function` procedures, you don't need to use the file reference when you use one of the functions in a formula; however, the add-in must be installed. I discuss add-ins later in this chapter (see "Creating Add-Ins").

NOTE

None of these three methods will cause the function name to appear in the Formula AutoComplete drop-down. Formula AutoComplete works only when the formula is entered into the workbook that contains the custom function. This is a known bug in the initial release of Excel 2007, and the problem may be corrected in an update.

Using Function Arguments

Custom functions, like Excel's built-in functions, vary in their use of arguments. Keep the following points in mind regarding VBA `Function` procedure arguments:

- A function can have no argument.

- A function can have a fixed number of required arguments (from 1 to 60).

- A function can have a combination of required and optional arguments.

- A function can have a special optional argument called a paramarray, which allows a function to have an indefinite number of arguments.

CROSS REF

See Chapter 25 for examples of functions that use various types of arguments.

All cells and ranges that are used by a function should be passed as arguments. In other words, a `Function` procedure should never contain direct references to cells or ranges.

Part VI

Using the Insert Function Dialog Box

Excel's Insert Function dialog box is a handy tool that enables you to choose a particular worksheet function from a list of available functions. The Insert Function dialog box also displays a list of your custom worksheet functions and prompts you for the function's arguments.

 NOTE

Custom Function procedures defined with the `Private` keyword don't appear in the Insert Function dialog box. This option is useful if you create functions that are intended to be used by other VBA procedures rather than in a formula.

By default, custom functions are listed under the User Defined category, but you can have them appear under a different category. You also can add some text that describes the function.

Adding a Function Description

When you select one of Excel's built-in functions in the Insert Function dialog box, a brief description of the function appears (see Figure 23-3). You may want to provide such a description for the custom functions that you create.

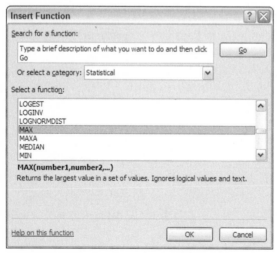

Figure 23-3: Excel's Insert Function dialog box displays a brief description of the selected function.

 NOTE

If you don't provide a description for your custom function, the Insert Function dialog box displays the following text: `No help available`.

The following steps describe how to provide a description for a custom function:

1. Create your function in the VB Editor.

2. Activate Excel and choose Developer⇨Code⇨Macros (or press Alt+F8). The Macro dialog box lists available Sub procedures but not functions.

3. Type the name of your function in the Macro Name box. Make sure that you spell it correctly.

4. Click the Options button to display the Macro Options dialog box. If the Options button is not enabled, you probably spelled the function's name incorrectly.

5. Enter the function description in the Description box (see Figure 23-4). The Shortcut key field is irrelevant for functions.

Figure 23-4: Provide a function description in the Macro Options dialog box.

6. Click OK and then click Cancel.

NOTE

When you use the Insert Function dialog box to enter a function, the Function Arguments dialog displays after you click OK. For built-in functions, the Function Arguments dialog displays a description for each of the function's arguments. Unfortunately, providing argument descriptions for your custom functions is not possible.

Specifying a Function Category

Oddly, Excel does not provide a direct way to assign a custom function to a particular function category. If you want your custom function to appear in a function category other than User Defined, you need to execute some VBA code in order to do so.

For example, assume that you've created a custom function named COMMISSION, and you'd like this function to appear in the Financial category (that is, Category 1) in the Insert Function dialog box. To accomplish this, you need to execute the following VBA statement:

```
Application.MacroOptions Macro:="COMMISSION", Category:=1
```

One way to execute this statement is to use the Immediate window in the VB Editor. Figure 23-5 shows an example. Just type the statement and press Enter. Then save the workbook, and the category assignment is also stored in the workbook. Therefore, this statement needs to be executed only one time. In other words, it is not necessary to assign the function to a new category every time the workbook is opened.

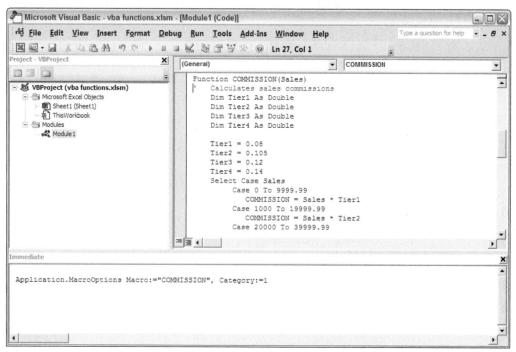

Figure 23-5: Executing a VBA statement that assigns a function to a particular function category.

Alternatively, you can create a Sub procedure and then execute the procedure.

```
Sub AssignToFunctionCategory()
    Application.MacroOptions Macro:="COMMISSION", Category:=1
End Sub
```

After you've executed the procedure, you can delete it.

You will, of course, substitute the actual name of your function, and you can specify a different function category. The AssignToFunctionCategory procedure can contain any number of statements — one for each of your functions.

Table 23-1 lists the function category numbers that you can use. Notice that a few of these categories (10–13) normally don't display in the Insert Function dialog box. If you assign your function to one of these categories, the category then appears.

TABLE 23-1   FUNCTION CATEGORIES

Category Number	Category Name
0	All (no specific category)
1	Financial
2	Date & Time
3	Math & Trig
4	Statistical
5	Lookup & Reference
6	Database
7	Text
8	Logical
9	Information
10	Commands
11	Customizing
12	Macro Control
13	DDE/External
14	User Defined
15	Engineering

Testing and Debugging Your Functions

Naturally, testing and debugging your custom function is an important step that you must take to ensure that it carries out the calculation that you intend. This section describes some debugging techniques that you may find helpful.

NOTE

If you're new to programming, the information in this section will make a lot more sense after you're familiar with the material in Chapter 22.

VBA code that you write can contain three general types of errors:

- **Syntax errors:** An error in writing the statement — for example, a misspelled keyword, a missing operator, or mismatched parentheses. The VB Editor lets you know about syntax errors by displaying a pop-up error box. You can't use the function until you correct all syntax errors.

- **Runtime errors:** Errors that occur as the function executes. For example, attempting to perform a mathematical operation on a string variable generates a runtime error. Unless you spot it beforehand, you won't be aware of a runtime error until it occurs.

- **Logical errors:** Code that runs but simply returns the wrong result.

 TIP

To force the code in a VBA module to be checked for syntax errors, choose Debug↝ Compile *xxx* (where *xxx* is the name of your project). Executing this command highlights the first syntax error, if any exists. Correct the error and issue the command again until you find all of the errors.

An error in code is sometimes called a *bug.* The process of locating and correcting such an error is *debugging.*

When you test a `Function` procedure by using a formula in a worksheet, runtime errors can be difficult to locate because (unlike syntax errors) they don't appear in a pop-up error box. If a runtime error occurs, the formula that uses the function simply returns an error value (#VALUE!). This section describes several approaches to debugging custom functions.

 TIP

While you're testing and debugging a custom function, it's a good idea to use the function in only one formula in the worksheet. If you use the function in more than one formula, the code is executed for each formula, which will get annoying very quickly!

Using the VBA MsgBox Statement

The `MsgBox` statement, when used in your VBA code, displays a pop-up dialog box. You can use `MsgBox` statements at strategic locations within your code to monitor the value of specific variables. The following example is a `Function` procedure that should reverse a text string passed as its argument. For example, passing `Hello` as the argument should return olleH. If you try to use this function in a formula, however, you will see that it does not work — it contains a logical error:

```
Function REVERSETEXT(text) As String
'   Returns its argument, reversed
    TextLen = Len(text)
    For i = TextLen To 1 Step -1
        REVERSETEXT = Mid(text, i, 1) & REVERSETEXT
    Next i
End Function
```

You can insert a temporary MsgBox statement to help you figure out the source of the problem. Here's the function again, with the MsgBox statement inserted within the loop:

```
Function REVERSETEXT(text) As String
'   Returns its argument, reversed
    TextLen = Len(text)
    For i = TextLen To 1 Step -1
        REVERSETEXT = Mid(text, i, 1) & REVERSETEXT
        MsgBox REVERSETEXT
    Next i
End Function
```

When this function is evaluated, a pop-up message box appears, once for each time through the loop. The message box shows the current value of REVERSETEXT. In other words, this technique enables you to monitor the results as the function is executed. Figure 23-6 shows an example.

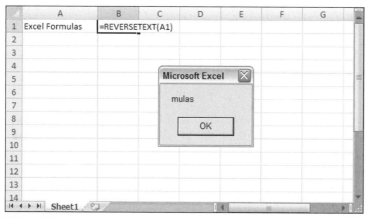

Figure 23-6: Use a MsgBox statement to monitor the value of a variable as a Function procedure executes.

Part VI

The information displayed in the series of message boxes shows that the text string is being built within the loop, but the new text is being added to the beginning of the string, not the end. The corrected assignment statement is

```
REVERSETEXT = REVERSETEXT & Mid(text, i, 1)
```

When the function is working properly, make sure that you remove all the MsgBox statements. They get very annoying.

TIP

If you get tired of seeing the message boxes, you can halt the code by pressing Ctrl+Break.

To display more than one variable in a message box, you need to concatenate the variables and insert a space character between each variable. The following statement, for example, displays the value of three variables (x, y, and z) in a message box:

```
MsgBox x & " " & y & " " & z
```

If you omit the blank space, you can't distinguish the separate values.

Alternatively, you can separate the variable with vbNewLine, which is a constant that inserts a line break. When you execute the following statement, x, y, and z each appear on a separate line in the message box.

```
MsgBox x & vbNewLine & y & vbNewLine & z
```

Using Debug.Print Statements in Your Code

If you find that using MsgBox statements is too intrusive, another option is to insert some temporary code that writes values directly to VB Editor Immediate window. (See the sidebar, "Using the Immediate Window.") You use the Debug.Print statement to write the values of selected variables.

For example, if you want to monitor a value inside a loop, use a routine like the following:

```
Function VOWELCOUNT(r)
    Count = 0
    For i = 1 To Len(r)
        Ch = UCase(Mid(r, i, 1))
        If Ch Like "[AEIOU]" Then
            Count = Count + 1
            Debug.Print Ch, i
        End If
    Next i
    VOWELCOUNT = Count
```

```
End Function
```

In this case, the value of two variables (Ch and i) print to the Immediate window whenever the Debug.Print statement is encountered. Figure 23-7 shows the result when the function has an argument of California.

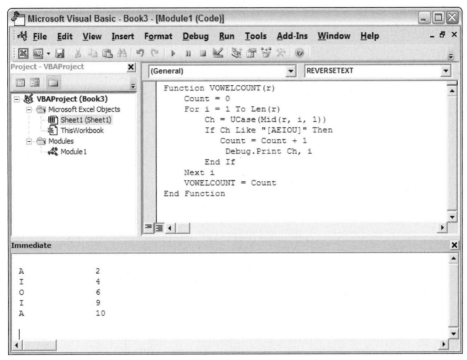

Figure 23-7: Using the VB Editor Immediate window to display results while a function is running.

When your function is debugged, make sure that you remove the Debug.Print statements.

Calling the Function from a Sub Procedure

Another way to test a Function procedure is to call the function from a Sub procedure. To do this, simply add a temporary Sub procedure to the module and insert a statement that calls your function. This is particularly useful because runtime errors display as they occur.

The following Function procedure contains an error (a runtime error). As I noted previously, the runtime errors don't display when testing a function by using a worksheet formula. Rather, the function simply returns an error (#VALUE!).

Using the Immediate Window

The VB Editor Immediate window can be helpful when debugging code. To activate the Immediate window, choose View⇨Immediate Window (or press Ctrl+G).

You can type VBA statements in the Immediate window and see the result immediately. For example, type the following code in the Immediate window and press Enter:

```
Print Sqr(1156)
```

The VB Editor prints the result of this square root operation (34). To save a few keystrokes, you can use a single question mark (?) in place of the `Print` keyword.

The Immediate window is particularly useful for debugging runtime errors when VBA is in break mode. For example, you can use the Immediate window to check the current value for variables, or to check the data type of a variable.

Errors often occur because data is of the wrong type. The following statement, for example, displays the data type of a variable named `Counter` (which you probably think is an `Integer` variable).

```
? TypeName(Counter)
```

If you discover that `Counter` is of a data type other than `Integer`, you may have solved your problem.

You can execute multiple statements in the Immediate window if you separate them with a colon. This line contains three statements:

```
x=12: y=13 : ? x+y
```

Most, but not all, statements can be executed in this way.

```
Function REVERSETEXT(text) As String
'    Returns its argument, reversed
    TextLen = Len(text)
    For i = TextLen To 1 Step -1
        REVERSETEXT = REVERSETEXT And Mid(text, i, 1)
    Next i
End Function
```

To help identify the source of the runtime error, insert the following `Sub` procedure:

```
Sub Test()
    x = REVERSETEXT("Hello")
    MsgBox x
End Sub
```

This `Sub` procedure simply calls the `REVERSETEXT` function and assigns the result to a variable named `x`. The `MsgBox` statement displays the result.

You can execute the Sub procedure directly from the VB Editor. Simply move the cursor anywhere within the procedure and choose Run➪Run Sub/UserForm (or just press F5). When you execute the Test procedure, you see the error message that is shown in Figure 23-8.

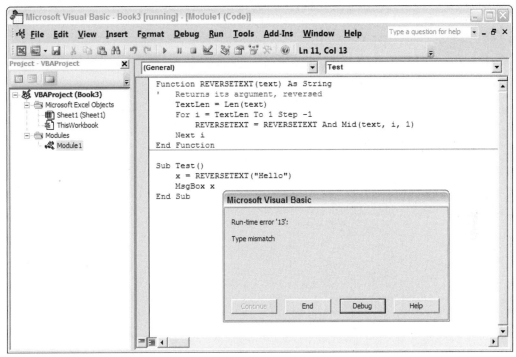

Figure 23-8: A runtime error identified by VBA.

Click the Debug button, and the VB Editor highlights the statement causing the problem (see Figure 23-9). The error message does not tell you how to correct the error, but it does narrow your choices. After you've identified the statement that's causing the error, you can examine it more closely, or you can use the Immediate window (see the sidebar, "Using the Immediate Window") to help locate the exact problem.

In this case, the problem is the use of the And operator instead of the concatenation operator (&). The correct statement is as follows:

```
REVERSETEXT = REVERSETEXT & Mid(text, i, 1)
```

NOTE

When you click the Debug button, the procedure is still running—it's just halted and is in break mode. After you make the correction, press F5 to continue execution, press F8 to continue execution on a line-by-line basis, or click the Reset button to halt execution.

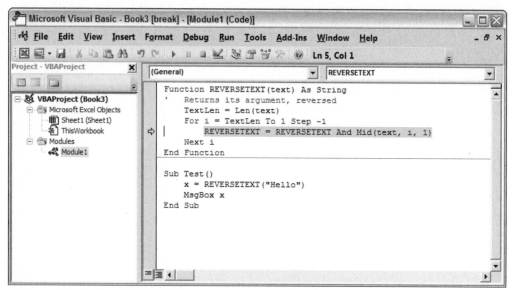

Figure 23-9: The highlighted statement has generated a runtime error.

Setting a Breakpoint in the Function

Another debugging option is to set a breakpoint in your code. Execution pauses when VBA encounters a breakpoint. You can then use the Immediate window to check the values of your variables, or you can use F8 to step through your code line by line.

To set a breakpoint, move the cursor to the statement at which you want to pause execution and choose Debug⇨Toggle Breakpoint. Alternatively, you can press F9, or you can click the vertical bar to the left of the code window. Any of these actions highlights the statement to remind you that a breakpoint is in effect (you also see a dot in the code window margin). You can set any number of breakpoints in your code. To remove a breakpoint, move the cursor to the statement and press F9. Figure 23-10 shows a `Function` procedure that contains a breakpoint.

TIP

To remove all the breakpoints in all of the open projects, choose Debug⇨Clear All Breakpoints, or press Control+Shift+F9.

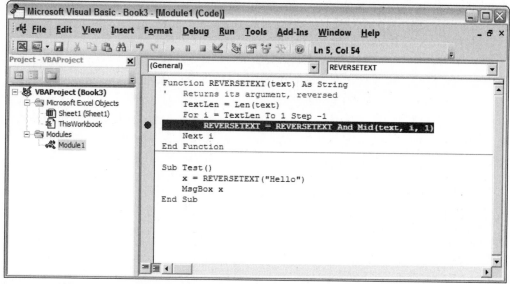

```
Microsoft Visual Basic - Book3 - [Module1 (Code)]

File   Edit   View   Insert   Format   Debug   Run   Tools   Add-Ins   Window   Help    _ & x
                                                              Ln 5, Col 54

Project - VBAProject          x    (General)                    REVERSETEXT

                                   Function REVERSETEXT(text) As String
   VBAProject (Book3)              '    Returns its argument, reversed
     Microsoft Excel Objects           TextLen = Len(text)
         Sheet1 (Sheet1)               For i = TextLen To 1 Step -1
         ThisWorkbook                      REVERSETEXT = REVERSETEXT And Mid(text, i, 1)
     Modules                            Next i
         Module1                    End Function

                                   Sub Test()
                                       x = REVERSETEXT("Hello")
                                       MsgBox x
                                   End Sub
```

Figure 23-10: The highlighted statement contains a breakpoint.

Creating Add-Ins

If you create some custom functions that you use frequently, you may want to store these functions in an add-in file. A primary advantage to this is that you can use the functions in formulas in any workbook without a filename qualifier.

Assume that you have a custom function named ZAPSPACES and that it's stored in Myfuncs.xlsm. To use this function in a formula in a workbook other than Myfuncs.xlsm, you need to enter the following formula:

```
=Myfuncs.xlsm!ZAPSPACES(A1:C12)
```

If you create an add-in from Myfuncs.xlsm and the add-in is loaded, you can omit the file reference and enter a formula like the following:

```
=ZAPSPACES(A1:C12)
```

Creating an add-in from a workbook is simple. The following steps describe how to create an add-in from a normal workbook file:

1. Develop your functions, and make sure that they work properly.

2. Activate the VB Editor and select the workbook in the Project window. Choose Tools⇨ *xxx* Properties and click the Protection tab (where *xxx* corresponds to the name of your project). Select the Lock Project for Viewing checkbox and enter a password (twice). Click OK.

You need to do this step only if you want to prevent others from viewing or modifying your macros or custom dialog boxes.

3. Reactivate Excel. Choose Office⇨Prepare⇨Properties, and Excel displays its Document Properties panel above the Formula bar. Enter a brief, descriptive title in the Title field and a longer description in the Comments field.

This step is not required, but it makes the add-in easier to use by displaying descriptive text in the Add-Ins dialog box.

4. Choose Office⇨Save As⇨Other Formats.

5. In the Save As dialog box, select Excel Add-In (*.xlam) from the Save as Type drop-down list (see Figure 23-11).

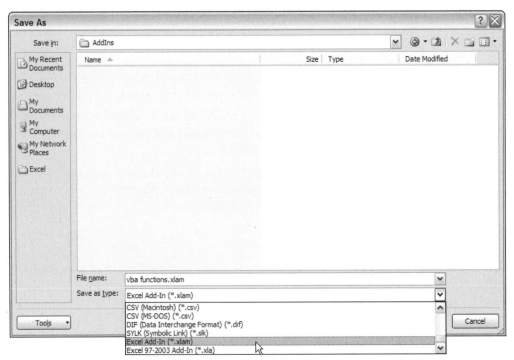

Figure 23-11: Saving a workbook as an add-in.

A Few Words about Passwords

Microsoft has never promoted Excel as a product that creates applications with secure source code. The password feature provided in Excel is sufficient to prevent casual users from accessing parts of your application that you want to keep hidden. However, the truth is that several password-cracking utilities are available. The security features in Excel 2002 and later are much better than those in previous versions, but it's possible that these can also be cracked. If you must absolutely be sure that no one ever sees your code or formulas, Excel is not your best choice as a development platform.

6. If you don't want to store the add-in in the default directory, select a different directory.

7. Click Save. A copy of the workbook is saved (with an .xlam extension), and the original macro-enabled workbook (.xlsm) remains open.

 CAUTION

When you use functions that are stored in an add-in, Excel creates a link to that add-in file. Therefore, if you distribute your workbook to someone else, they must also have a copy of the linked add-in. Furthermore, the add-in must be stored in the exact same directory because the links are stored with complete path references. As a result, the recipient of your workbook may need to use the Data⇨Connections⇨Edit Links command to change the source of the linked add-in.

After you create your add-in, you can install it by using the standard procedure:

1. Choose Office⇨Excel Options⇨Add-Ins.

2. Select Excel Add-ins from the Manage box.

3. Click Go, to show the Add-Ins dialog box.

4. Click the Browse button in the Add-Ins dialog box.

5. Locate your *.xlam file.

Chapter 24

VBA Programming Concepts

This chapter discusses some of the key language elements and programming concepts in VBA. If you've used other programming languages, much of this information may sound familiar. VBA has a few unique wrinkles, however, so even experienced programmers may find some new information.

This chapter does not even come close to being a comprehensive guide to VBA. Motivated readers will consult the Help system and make use of Internet resources or other books for additional information.

ON THE CD

Many of the code examples in this chapter are on the companion CD-ROM. The file is named function examples.xlsm.

An Introductory Example Function Procedure

To get the ball rolling, I'll begin with an example Function procedure. This function, named REMOVESPACES, accepts a single argument and returns that argument without any spaces. For example, the following formula uses the REMOVESPACES function and returns ThisIsATest.

```
=REMOVESPACES("This Is A Test")
```

To create this function, insert a VBA module into a project, and then enter the following Function procedure into the code window of the module:

```
Function REMOVESPACES(cell) As String
'    Removes all spaces from cell
    Dim CellLength As Integer
    Dim Temp As String
    Dim Characters As String
    Dim i As Integer
    CellLength = Len(cell)
    Temp = ""
    For i = 1 To CellLength
        Character = Mid(cell, i, 1)
        If Character <> Chr(32) Then Temp = Temp & Character
    Next i
    REMOVESPACES = Temp
End Function
```

Look closely at this function's code line by line:

- The first line of the function is called the function's *declaration line.* Notice that the procedure starts with the keyword Function, followed by the name of the function (REMOVESPACES). This function uses only one argument (cell); the argument name is enclosed in parentheses. As String defines the data type of the function's return value. The As part of the function declaration is optional.

- The second line is simply a comment (optional) that describes what the function does. The initial apostrophe designates this line as a comment.

- The next four lines use the Dim keyword to declare the four variables used in the procedure: CellLength, Temp, Character, and i. Declaring a variable is not necessary, but (as you'll see later) it's an excellent practice.

- The procedure's next line assigns a value to a variable named `CellLength`. This statement uses the VBA `Len` function to determine the length of the contents of the argument (`cell`).

- The next statement creates a variable named `Temp` and assigns it an empty string.

- The next four statements make up a `For-Next` loop. The statements between the `For` statement and the `Next` statement are executed a number of times; the value of `CellLength` determines the number of times. For example, assume the cell passed as the argument contains the text `Bob Smith`. The statements within the loop would execute nine times, one time for each character in the string.

- Within the loop, the `Character` variable holds a single character that is extracted using the VBA `Mid` function (which works just like Excel's MID function). The `If` statement determines whether the character is not a space. (The VBA `Chr` function is equivalent to Excel's CHAR function, and an argument of `32` represents a space character.) If the character is not a space, the character is appended to the string stored in the `Temp` variable (using an ampersand, the concatenation operator). If the character is a space, the `Temp` variable is unchanged, and the next character is processed. If you prefer, you can replace this statement with the following:

```
If Character <> " " Then Temp = Temp & Character
```

- When the loop finishes, the `Temp` variable holds all the characters that were originally passed to the function in the cell argument, except for the spaces.

- The string contained in the `Temp` variable is assigned to the function's name. This string is the value that the function returns.

- The `Function` procedure ends with an `End Function` statement.

The REMOVESPACES procedure uses some common VBA language elements, including

- A `Function` declaration statement
- A comment (the line preceded by the apostrophe)
- Variable declarations
- Three assignment statements
- Three built-in VBA functions (`Len`, `Mid`, and `Chr`)
- A looping structure (`For-Next`)
- An `If-Then` structure
- String concatenation (using the `&` operator)

Not bad for a first effort, eh? The remainder of this chapter provides more information on these (and many other) programming concepts.

NOTE

The REMOVESPACES function listed here is for instructional purposes only. You can accomplish the same effect by using the Excel SUBSTITUTE function, which is much more efficient than using a custom VBA function. The following formula, for example, removes all space characters from the text in cell A1:

```
=SUBSTITUTE(A1," ","")
```

Using Comments in Your Code

A *comment* is descriptive text embedded within your code. VBA completely ignores the text of a comment. It's a good idea to use comments liberally to describe what you do because the purpose of a particular VBA instruction is not always obvious.

You can use a complete line for your comment, or you can insert a comment after an instruction on the same line. A comment is indicated by an apostrophe. VBA ignores any text that follows an apostrophe up until the end of the line. An exception occurs when an apostrophe is contained within quotation marks. For example, the following statement does not contain a comment, even though it has an apostrophe:

```
Result = "That doesn't compute"
```

The following example shows a VBA Function procedure with three comments:

```
Function MYFUNC()
'   This function does nothing of value
    x = 0    'x represents nothingness
'   Return the result
    MYFUNC = x
End Function
```

When developing a function, you may want to test it without including a particular statement or group of statements. Instead of deleting the statement, simply convert it to a comment by inserting an apostrophe at the beginning. VBA then ignores the statement(s) when the routine is executed. To convert the comment back to a statement, delete the apostrophe.

 TIP

The VB Editor Edit toolbar contains two very useful buttons. Select a group of instructions and then use the Comment Block button to convert the instructions to comments. The Uncomment Block button converts a group of comments back to instructions. If the Edit toolbar is not visible, choose View⇨Toolbars⇨Edit.

Using Variables, Data Types, and Constants

A *variable* is a named storage location in your computer's memory. Variables can accommodate a wide variety of *data types* — from simple Boolean values (TRUE or FALSE) to large, double-precision values (see the following section). You assign a value to a variable by using the assignment operator, which is an equal sign.

The following are some examples of assignment statements that use various types of variables. The variable names are to the left of the equal sign. Each statement assigns the value to the right of the equal sign to the variable on the left.

```
x = 1
InterestRate = 0.075
LoanPayoffAmount = 243089
DataEntered = False
x = x + 1
MyNum = YourNum * 1.25
HallOfFamer = "Trevor Hoffman"
DateStarted = #3/14/2007#
```

VBA has many *reserved words,* which are words that you can't use for variable or procedure names. If you attempt to use one of these words, you get an error message. For example, although the reserved word Next (which is used in a For-Next loop) may make a very descriptive variable name, the following instruction generates a syntax error:

```
Next = 132
```

Unfortunately, sometimes syntax error messages aren't descriptive. The preceding instruction generates the error Compile error: Expected: variable in Excel 2007. (Earlier versions of Excel may produce a different error.) So if an assignment statement produces an error that does not seem to make sense, check the Help system to make sure that your variable name does not have a special use in VBA.

Defining Data Types

VBA makes life easy for programmers because it can automatically handle all the details involved in dealing with data. *Data type* refers to how data is stored in memory — as integers, logical values, strings, and so on.

Although VBA can take care of data typing automatically, it does so at a cost — namely, slower execution and less efficient use of memory. If you want optimal speed for your functions, you need to be familiar with data types. Generally, it's best to use the data type that uses the smallest number of bytes yet still is able to handle all of the data that will be assigned to it. When VBA works with data, execution speed is a function of the number of bytes that VBA has at its disposal. In other words, the fewer bytes used by data, the faster VBA can access and manipulate the data. Table 24-1 lists VBA's assortment of built-in data types.

TABLE 24-1   VBA DATA TYPES

Data Type	Bytes Used	Range of Values
Byte	1 byte	0 to 255
Boolean	2 bytes	TRUE or FALSE
Integer	2 bytes	–32,768 to 32,767
Long	4 bytes	–2,147,483,648 to 2,147,483,647
Single	4 bytes	–3.402823E38 to –1.401298E–45 (for negative values); 1.401298E–45 to 3.402823E38 (for positive values)
Double	8 bytes	–1.79769313486231E308 to –4.94065645841247E–324 (negative values); 4.94065645841247E–324 to 1.79769313486232E308 (positive values)
Currency	8 bytes	–922,337,203,685,477.5808 to 922,337,203,685,477.5807
Decimal	14 bytes	+/–79,228,162,514,264,337,593,543,950,335 with no decimal point; +/–7.9228162514264337593543950335 with 28 places to the right of the decimal
Date	8 bytes	January 1, 0100 to December 31, 9999
Object	4 bytes	Any object reference
String (variable length)	10 bytes + string length	0 to approximately 2 billion
String (fixed length)	Length of string	1 to approximately 65,400
Variant (with numbers)	16 bytes	Any numeric value up to the range of a double data type
Variant (with characters)	22 bytes + string length	0 to approximately 2 billion

Declaring Variables

Before you use a variable in a procedure, you may want to *declare* it. Declaring a variable tells VBA its name and data type. Declaring variables provides two main benefits:

- **Your procedures run faster and use memory more efficiently.** The default data type — `Variant` — causes VBA to repeatedly perform time-consuming checks and reserve more memory than necessary. If VBA knows the data type for a variable, it does not have to investigate; it can reserve just enough memory to store the data.

- **If you use an** `Option Explicit` **statement at the top of your module, you avoid problems resulting from misspelled variable names.** Suppose that you use an undeclared variable named `CurrentRate`. At some point in your procedure, however, you insert the statement `CurentRate = .075`. This misspelled variable name, which is very difficult to spot, will likely cause your function to return an incorrect result. See the nearby sidebar, "Forcing Yourself to Declare All Variables."

You declare a variable by using the `Dim` keyword. For example, the following statement declares a variable named `Count` to be an integer.

```
Dim Count As Integer
```

You also can declare several variables with a single `Dim` statement. For example

```
Dim x As Integer, y As Integer, z As Integer
Dim First As Long, Last As Double
```

CAUTION

Unlike some languages, VBA does not permit you to declare a group of variables to be a particular data type by separating the variables with commas. For example, the following statement — although valid — does *not* declare all the variables as integers:

```
Dim i, j, k As Integer
```

In the preceding statement, only `k` is declared to be an integer. To declare all variables as integers, use this statement:

```
Dim i As Integer, j As Integer, k As Integer
```

If you don't declare the data type for a variable that you use, VBA uses the default data type — `Variant`. Data stored as a variant acts like a chameleon: It changes type depending on what you do with it. The following procedure demonstrates how a variable can assume different data types:

```
Function VARIANT_DEMO()
    MyVar = "123"
    MyVar = MyVar / 2
    MyVar = "Answer: " & MyVar
    VARIANT_DEMO = MyVar
End Function
```

Forcing Yourself to Declare All Variables

To force yourself to declare all the variables that you use, include the following as the first instruction in your VBA module:

```
Option Explicit
```

This statement causes your procedure to stop whenever VBA encounters an undeclared variable name. VBA issues an error message (Compile error: Variable not defined), and you must declare the variable before you can proceed.

To ensure that the Option Explicit statement appears in every new VBA module, enable the Require Variable Declaration option on the Editor tab of the VB Editor Options dialog box. To display this dialog box, choose Tools↪Options.

In the VARIANT_DEMO Function procedure, MyVar starts out as a three-character text string that looks like a number. Then this string is divided by two, and MyVar becomes a numeric data type. Next, MyVar is appended to a string, converting MyVar back to a string. The function returns the final string: Answer: 61.5.

NOTE

You'll notice that I don't follow my own advice in this chapter. In many of the subsequent function listings in this chapter, I don't declare the variables used. I omitted the variable declarations to keep the code simple so you can focus on the concept being discussed. In the code examples on the companion CD-ROM, I always declare the variables.

Using Constants

A variable's value may — and often does — change while a procedure is executing. That's why it's called a *variable*. Sometimes, you need to refer to a named value or string that never changes: in other words, a *constant*.

You declare a constant by using the Const statement. Here are some examples:

```
Const NumQuarters as Integer = 4
Const Rate = .0725, Period = 12
Const CompanyName as String = "Acme Snapholytes"
```

The second statement declares two constants with a single statement, but it does not declare a data type. Consequently, the two constants are variants. Because a constant never changes its value, you normally want to declare your constants as a specific data type. The *scope* of a constant depends on where it is declared within your module:

- To make a constant available within a single procedure only, declare it after the `Sub` or `Function` statement to make it a local constant.

- To make a constant available to all procedures in a module, declare it before the first procedure in the module.

- To make a constant available to all modules in the workbook, use the `Public` keyword and declare the constant before the first procedure in a module. The following statement creates a constant that is valid in all VBA modules in the workbook:

```
Public AppName As String = "Budget Tools"
```

NOTE

If you attempt to change the value of a constant in a VBA procedure, you get an error — as you would expect. A constant is a constant, not a variable.

Using constants throughout your code in place of hard-coded values or strings is an excellent programming practice. For example, if your procedure needs to refer to a specific value (such as an interest rate) several times, it's better to declare the value as a constant and use the constant's name rather than its value in your expressions. This technique makes your code more readable and makes it easier to change should the need arise — you have to change only one instruction rather than several.

VBA and Excel define many constants that you can use in your code without declaring them. For example, the following statement uses a constant named `vbInformation`:

```
MsgBox "Hello", vbInformation
```

The `vbInformation` constant has a value of 64, but it's not important that you know that. If you use the Excel macro recorder to record you actions, you'll find many other constants in the recorded code.

Using Strings

Like Excel, VBA can manipulate both numbers and text (strings). VBA supports two types of strings:

- **Fixed-length strings** are declared with a specified number of characters. The maximum length is 65,535 characters.

- **Variable-length strings** theoretically can hold up to 2 billion characters.

Each character in a string takes 1 byte of storage. When you declare a string variable with a `Dim` statement, you can specify the maximum length if you know it (that is, a fixed-length string), or you can let VBA handle it dynamically (a variable-length string). In some cases, working with fixed-length strings may be slightly more efficient in terms of memory usage.

In the following example, the `MyString` variable is declared to be a string with a fixed length of 50 characters. `YourString` is also declared as a string but with an unspecified length.

```
Dim MyString As String * 50
Dim YourString As String
```

Using Dates

You can use a string variable to store a date, of course, but then you can't perform date calculations using the variable. Using the `Date` data type is a better way to work with dates.

A variable defined as a `Date` uses 8 bytes of storage and can hold dates ranging from January 1, 0100, to December 31, 9999. That's a span of nearly 10,000 years — more than enough for even the most aggressive financial forecast! The `Date` data type is also useful for storing time-related data. In VBA, you specify dates and times by enclosing them between two pound signs (#).

 NOTE

The range of dates that VBA can handle is much larger than Excel's own date range, which begins with January 1, 1900. Therefore, be careful that you don't attempt to use a date in a worksheet that lies outside of Excel's acceptable date range.

Here are some examples of declaring variables and constants as `Date` data types:

```
Dim Today As Date
Dim StartTime As Date
Const FirstDay As Date = #1/15/2007#
Const Noon = #12:00:00#
```

 NOTE

Date variables display dates according to your system's short date format, and times appear according to your system's time format (either 12 or 24 hours). You can modify these system settings by using the Regional Settings option in the Windows Control Panel.

Using Assignment Expressions

An *assignment expression* is a VBA instruction that evaluates an expression and assigns the result to a variable or an object. An *expression* is a combination of keywords, operators, variables, and constants that yields a string, number, or object. An expression can perform a calculation, manipulate characters, or test data.

If you know how to create formulas in Excel, you'll have no trouble creating expressions in VBA. With a worksheet formula, Excel displays the result in a cell. Similarly, you can assign a VBA expression to a variable or use it as a property value.

VBA uses the equal sign (=) as its assignment operator. Note the following examples of assignment statements. (The expressions are to the right of the equal sign.)

```
x = 1
x = x + 1
x = (y * 2) / (z * 2)
MultiSheets = True
```

Expressions often use functions. These can be VBA's built-in functions, Excel's worksheet functions, or custom functions that you develop in VBA. I discuss VBA's built-in functions later in this chapter.

Operators play a major role in VBA. Familiar operators describe mathematical operations, including addition (+), multiplication (*), division (/), subtraction (–), exponentiation (^), and string concatenation (&). Less familiar operators are the backslash (\) that's used in integer division and also the Mod operator that's used in modulo arithmetic. The Mod operator returns the remainder of one integer divided by another. For example, the following expression returns 2:

```
17 Mod 3
```

You may be familiar with the Excel MOD function. Note that in VBA, Mod is an operator, not a function.

VBA also supports the same comparative operators used in Excel formulas: Equal to (=), greater than (>), less than (<), greater than or equal to (>=), less than or equal to (<=), and not equal to (<>). Additionally, VBA provides a full set of logical operators, as shown in Table 24-2. Refer to the online help for additional information and examples of these operators.

TABLE 24-2   VBA LOGICAL OPERATORS

Operator	What It Does
Not	Performs a logical negation on an expression
And	Performs a logical conjunction on two expressions
Or	Performs a logical disjunction on two expressions
Xor	Performs a logical exclusion on two expressions
Eqv	Performs a logical equivalence on two expressions
Imp	Performs a logical implication on two expressions

The order of precedence for operators in VBA exactly matches that in Excel. Of course, you can add parentheses to change the natural order of precedence.

Using Arrays

An *array* is a group of elements of the same type that have a common name; you refer to a specific element in the array by using the array name and an index number. For example, you may define an array of 12 string variables so that each variable corresponds to the name of a different month. If you name the array MonthNames, you can refer to the first element of the array as MonthNames(0), the second element as MonthNames(1), and so on, up to MonthNames(11).

Declaring an Array

You declare an array with a Dim or Public statement just as you declare a regular variable. You also can specify the number of elements in the array. You do so by specifying the first index number, the keyword To, and the last index number — all inside parentheses. For example, here's how to declare an array comprising exactly 100 integers:

```
Dim MyArray(1 To 100) As Integer
```

When you declare an array, you need to specify only the upper index, in which case VBA (by default) assumes that 0 is the lower index. Therefore, the following two statements have the same effect:

```
Dim MyArray(0 to 100) As Integer
Dim MyArray(100) As Integer
```

In both cases, the array consists of 101 elements.

If you want VBA to assume that 1 is the lower index for all arrays that declare only the upper index, include the following statement before any procedures in your module:

```
Option Base 1
```

If this statement is present, the following two statements have the same effect (both declare an array with 100 elements):

```
Dim MyArray(1 to 100) As Integer
Dim MyArray(100) As Integer
```

Declaring Multidimensional Arrays

The array examples in the preceding section are one-dimensional arrays. VBA arrays can have up to 60 dimensions although it's rare to need more than 3 dimensions (a 3-D array). The following statement declares a 100-integer array with two dimensions (2-D):

```
Dim MyArray(1 To 10, 1 To 10) As Integer
```

You can think of the preceding array as occupying a 10 x 10 matrix. To refer to a specific element in a 2-D array, you need to specify two index numbers. For example, here's how you can assign a value to an element in the preceding array:

```
MyArray(3, 4) = 125
```

A *dynamic array* does not have a preset number of elements. You declare a dynamic array with a blank set of parentheses:

```
Dim MyArray() As Integer
```

Before you can use a dynamic array in your code, however, you must use the ReDim statement to tell VBA how many elements are in the array (or ReDim Preserve if you want to keep the existing values in the array). You can use the ReDim statement any number of times, changing the array's size as often as you like.

Arrays crop up later in this chapter in the sections that discuss looping.

Using Built-In VBA Functions

VBA has a variety of built-in functions that simplify calculations and operations. Many of VBA's functions are similar (or identical) to Excel's worksheet functions. For example, the VBA function UCase, which converts a string argument to uppercase, is equivalent to the Excel worksheet function UPPER.

TIP

To display a list of VBA functions while writing your code, type **VBA** followed by a period (.). The VB Editor displays a list of all functions and constants (see Figure 24-1). If this does not work for you, make sure that you select the Auto List Members option. Choose Tools⇨Options and click the Editor tab. In addition to functions, the displayed list also includes built-in constants. The VBA functions are all described in the online help. To view Help, just move the cursor over a function name and press F1.

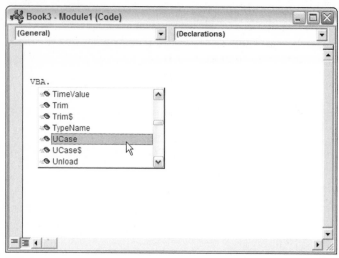

Figure 24-1: Displaying a list of VBA functions in the VB Editor.

Here's a statement that calculates the square root of a variable by using VBA's Sqr function and then assigns the result to a variable named *x*:

```
x = Sqr(MyValue)
```

Having knowledge of VBA's functions can save you lots of work. For example, consider the REMOVESPACES Function procedure presented at the beginning of this chapter. That function uses a For-Next loop to examine each character in a string and builds a new string. A much simpler (and more efficient) version of that Function procedure uses the VBA Replace function. The following is a rewritten version of the Function procedure:

```
Function REMOVESPACES2(cell) As String
'   Removes all spaces from cell
    REMOVESPACES2 = Replace(cell, " ", "")
End Function
```

You can use many (but not all) of Excel's worksheet functions in your VBA code. To use a worksheet function in a VBA statement, just precede the function name with WorksheetFunction and a period.

The following code demonstrates how to use an Excel worksheet function in a VBA statement. Excel's infrequently used ROMAN function converts a decimal number into a Roman numeral.

```
DecValue = 2007
RomanValue = WorksheetFunction.Roman(DecValue)
```

The variable `RomanValue` contains the string `MMVII`. Fans of old movies are often dismayed when they learn that Excel does not have a function to convert a Roman numeral to its decimal equivalent. You can, of course, create such a function using VBA. Are you up for a challenge?

It's important to understand that you can't use worksheet functions that have an equivalent VBA function. For example, VBA can't access Excel's SQRT worksheet function because VBA has its own version of that function: `Sqr`. Therefore, the following statement generates an error:

```
x = WorksheetFunction.SQRT(123)    'error
```

Controlling Execution

Some VBA procedures start at the top and progress line by line to the bottom. Often, however, you need to control the flow of your routines by skipping over some statements, executing some statements multiple times, and testing conditions to determine what the routine does next.

This section discusses several ways of controlling the execution of your VBA procedures:

- `If-Then` constructs
- `Select Case` constructs
- `For-Next` loops
- `Do While` loops
- `Do Until` loops
- `On Error` statements

The If-Then Construct

Perhaps the most commonly used instruction grouping in VBA is the `If-Then` construct. This instruction is one way to endow your applications with decision-making capability. The basic syntax of the `If-Then` construct is as follows:

```
If condition Then true_instructions [Else false_instructions]
```

The `If-Then` construct executes one or more statements conditionally. The `Else` clause is optional. If included, it enables you to execute one or more instructions when the condition that you test is not true.

The following `Function` procedure demonstrates an `If-Then` structure without an `Else` clause. The example deals with time. VBA uses the same date-and-time serial number system as Excel. The time of day is expressed as a fractional value — for example, noon is represented as .5. The VBA Time function returns a value that represents the time of day, as reported by the system clock. In the following example, the function starts out by assigning an empty string to GreetMe. The If-Then statement checks the time of day. If the time is before noon, the Then part of the statement executes, and the function returns Good Morning.

```
Function GreetMe()
    GreetMe = ""
    If Time < 0.5 Then GreetMe= "Good Morning"
End Function
```

The following function uses two If-Then statements. It displays either Good Morning or Good Afternoon:

```
Function GreetMe()
    If Time < 0.5 Then GreetMe = "Good Morning"
    If Time >= 0.5 Then GreetMe = "Good Afternoon"
End Function
```

Notice that the second If-Then statement uses >= (greater than or equal to). This covers the extremely remote chance that the time is precisely 12:00 noon when the function is executed.

Another approach is to use the Else clause of the If-Then construct:

```
Function GreetMe()
    If Time < 0.5 Then GreetMe = "Good Morning" Else _
        GreetMe = "Good Afternoon"
End Function
```

Notice that the preceding example uses the line continuation sequence (a space followed by an underscore); If-Then-Else is actually a single statement.

The following is another example that uses the If-Then construct. This Function procedure calculates a discount based on a quantity (assumed to be an integer value). It accepts one argument (quantity) and returns the appropriate discount based on that value.

```
Function Discount(quantity)
    If quantity <= 5 Then Discount = 0
    If quantity >= 6 Then Discount = 0.1
    If quantity >= 25 Then Discount = 0.15
    If quantity >= 50 Then Discount = 0.2
    If quantity >= 75 Then Discount = 0.25
End Function
```

Notice that each If-Then statement in this procedure is always executed, and the value for Discount can change as the function is executed. The final value, however, is the desired value.

The preceding examples all used a single statement for the Then clause of the If-Then construct. However, you often need to execute multiple statements if a condition is TRUE. You can still use the If-Then construct, but you need to use an End If statement to signal the end of the statements that make up the Then clause. Here's an example that executes two statements if the If clause is TRUE:

```
If x > 0 Then
    y = 2
    z = 3
End If
```

You can also use multiple statements for an If-Then-Else construct. Here's an example that executes two statements if the If clause is TRUE, and two other statements if the If clause is not TRUE:

```
If x > 0 Then
    y = 2
    z = 3
Else
    y = -2
    z = -3
End If
```

The Select Case Construct

The Select Case construct is useful for choosing among three or more options. This construct also works with two options and is a good alternative to using If-Then-Else. The syntax for Select Case is as follows:

```
Select Case testexpression
    [Case expressionlist-n
        [instructions-n]]
    [Case Else
        [default_instructions]]
End Select
```

The following example of a Select Case construct shows another way to code the GreetMe examples presented in the preceding section:

```
Function GreetMe()
    Select Case Time
        Case Is < 0.5
            GreetMe = "Good Morning"
        Case 0.5 To 0.75
            GreetMe = "Good Afternoon"
        Case Else
```

```
        GreetMe = "Good Evening"
    End Select
End Function
```

And here's a rewritten version of the `Discount` function from the previous section, this time using a `Select Case` construct:

```
Function Discount2(quantity)
    Select Case quantity
        Case Is <= 5
            Discount2 = 0
        Case 6 To 24
            Discount2 = 0.1
        Case 25 To 49
            Discount2 = 0.15
        Case 50 To 74
            Discount2 = 0.2
        Case Is >= 75
            Discount2 = 0.25
    End Select
End Function
```

Any number of instructions can be written below each `Case` statement; they all execute if that case evaluates to TRUE.

Looping Blocks of Instructions

Looping is the process of repeating a block of VBA instructions within a procedure. You may know the number of times to loop, or it may be determined by the values of variables in your program. VBA offers a number of looping constructs:

- `For-Next` loops
- `Do While` loops
- `Do Until` loops

FOR-NEXT LOOPS

The following is the syntax for a `For-Next` loop:

```
For counter = start To end [Step stepval]
    [instructions]
    [Exit For]
    [instructions]
Next [counter]
```

The following listing is an example of a `For-Next` loop that does not use the optional `Step` value or the optional `Exit For` statement. This function accepts two arguments and returns the sum of all integers between (and including) the arguments:

```
Function SumIntegers(first, last)
    total = 0
    For num = first To last
        total = total + num
    Next num
    SumIntegers = total
End Function
```

The following formula, for example, returns 55 — the sum of all integers from 1 to 10:

```
=SumIntegers(1,10)
```

In this example, `num` (the loop counter variable) starts out with the same value as the first variable, and increases by 1 each time the loop repeats. The loop ends when num is equal to the last variable. The total variable simply accumulates the various values of num as it changes during the looping.

 CAUTION

When you use `For-Next` loops, you should understand that the loop counter is a normal variable — it is not a special type of variable. As a result, you can change the value of the loop counter within the block of code executed between the `For` and `Next` statements. This is, however, a *very bad* practice and can cause problems. In fact, you should take special precautions to ensure that your code does not change the loop counter.

You also can use a `Step` value to skip some values in the loop. Here's the same function rewritten to sum *every other* integer between the first and last arguments:

```
Function SumIntegers2(first, last)
    total = 0
    For num = first To last Step 2
        total = total + num
    Next num
    SumIntegers2 = Total
End Function
```

The following formula returns 25, which is the sum of 1, 3, 5, 7, and 9:

```
=SumIntegers2(1,10)
```

`For-Next` loops can also include one or more `Exit For` statements within the loop. When this statement is encountered, the loop terminates immediately, as the following example demonstrates.

```
Function RowOfLargest(c)
    NumRows = Rows.Count
    MaxVal = WorksheetFunction.Max(Columns(c))
    For r = 1 To NumRows
        If Cells(r, c) = MaxVal Then
            RowOfLargest = r
            Exit For
        End If
    Next r
End Function
```

The RowOfLargest function accepts a column number (1–16,384) for its argument and returns the row number of the largest value in that column. It starts by getting a count of the number of rows in the worksheet. (This varies, depending on the version of Excel.) This number is assigned to the NumRows variable. The maximum value in the column is calculated by using the Excel MAX function, and this value is assigned to the MaxVal variable.

The For-Next loop checks each cell in the column. When the cell equal to MaxVal is found, the row number (variable r, the loop counter) is assigned to the function's name, and the Exit For statement ends the procedure. Without the Exit For statement, the loop continues to check all cells in the column — which can take quite a long time!

The previous examples use relatively simple loops. But you can have any number of statements in the loop, and you can even nest For-Next loops inside other For-Next loops. The following is VBA code that uses nested For-Next loops to initialize a 10 x 10 x 10 array with the value –1. When the three loops finish executing, each of the 1,000 elements in MyArray contains –1.

```
Dim MyArray(1 to 10, 1 to 10, 1 to 10)
For i = 1 To 10
    For j = 1 To 10
        For k = 1 To 10
            MyArray(i, j, k) = -1
        Next k
    Next j
Next i
```

Do While Loops

A Do While loop is another type of looping structure available in VBA. Unlike a For-Next loop, a Do While loop executes while a specified condition is met. A Do While loop can have one of two syntaxes:

```
Do [While condition]
    [instructions]
    [Exit Do]
    [instructions]
```

```
Loop
```

or

```
Do
    [instructions]
    [Exit Do]
    [instructions]
Loop [While condition]
```

As you can see, VBA enables you to put the While condition at the beginning or the end of the loop. The difference between these two syntaxes involves the point in time when the condition is evaluated. In the first syntax, the contents of the loop may never be executed: That is, if the condition is met as soon as the Do statement is executed. In the second syntax, the contents of the loop are always executed at least one time.

The following example is the RowOfLargest function presented in the previous section, rewritten to use a Do While loop (using the first syntax):

```
Function RowOfLargest2(c)
    NumRows = Rows.Count
    MaxVal = Application.Max(Columns(c))
    r = 1
    Do While Cells(r, c) <> MaxVal
        r = r + 1
    Loop
    RowOfLargest2 = r
End Function
```

The variable r starts out with a value of 1 and increments within the Do While loop. The looping continues as long as the cell being evaluated is not equal to MaxVal. When the cell is equal to MaxVal, the loop ends, and the function is assigned the value of r. Notice that if the maximum value is in row 1, the looping does not occur.

The following procedure uses the second Do While loop syntax. The loop always executes at least once.

```
Function RowOfLargest(c)
    MaxVal = Application.Max(Columns(c))
    r = 0
    Do
        r = r + 1
    Loop While Cells(r, c) <> MaxVal
    RowOfLargest = r
End Function
```

Do While loops can also contain one or more Exit Do statements. When an Exit Do statement is encountered, the loop ends immediately.

Do Until Loops

The Do Until loop structure closely resembles the Do While structure. The difference is evident only when the condition is tested. In a Do While loop, the loop executes *while* the condition is true. In a Do Until loop, the loop executes *until* the condition is true. Do Until also has two syntaxes:

```
Do [Until condition]
    [instructions]
    [Exit Do]
    [instructions]
Loop
```

or

```
Do
    [instructions]
    [Exit Do]
    [instructions]
Loop [Until condition]
```

The following example demonstrates the first syntax of the Do Until loop. This example makes the code a bit clearer because it avoids the negative comparison required in the Do While example.

```
Function RowOfLargest4(c)
    NumRows = Rows.Count
    MaxVal = Application.Max(Columns(c))
    r = 1
    Do Until Cells(r, c) = MaxVal
        r = r + 1
    Loop
    RowOfLargest4 = r
End Function
```

Finally, the following function is the same procedure but is rewritten to use the second syntax of the Do Until loop:

```
Function RowOfLargest5(c)
    NumRows = Rows.Count
    MaxVal = Application.Max(Columns(c))
    r = 0
    Do
        r = r + 1
    Loop Until Cells(r, c) = MaxVal
    RowOfLargest5 = r
End Function
```

The On Error Statement

Undoubtedly, you've used one of Excel's worksheet functions in a formula and discovered that the formula returns an error value (for example, #VALUE!). A formula can return an error value in a number of situations, including these:

- You omitted one or more required argument(s).

- An argument was not the correct data type (for example, text instead of a value).

- An argument is outside of a valid numeric range (division by zero, for example).

In many cases, you can ignore error handling within your functions. If the user does not provide the proper number of arguments, the function simply returns an error value. It's up to the user to figure out the problem. In fact, this is how Excel's worksheet functions handle errors.

In other cases, you want your code to know if errors occurred and then do something about them. Excel's On Error statement enables you to identify and handle errors.

To simply ignore an error, use the following statement:

```
On Error Resume Next
```

If you use this statement, you can determine whether an error occurs by checking the Number property of the Err object. If this property is equal to zero, an error did not occur. If Err.Number is equal to anything else, an error *did* occur.

The following example is a function that returns the name of a cell or range. If the cell or range does not have a name, an error occurs, and the formula that uses the function returns a #VALUE! error.

```
Function RANGENAME(rng)
    RANGENAME = rng.Name.Name
End Function
```

The following list shows an improved version of the function. The On Error Resume Next statement causes VBA to ignore the error. The If Err statement checks whether an error occurs. If so, the function returns an empty string.

```
Function RANGENAME(rng)
    On Error Resume Next
    RANGENAME = rng.Name.Name
    If Err.Number <> 0 Then RANGENAME = ""
End Function
```

The following statement instructs VBA to watch for errors; and if an error occurs, continues executing at a different named location — in this case, a statement labeled ErrHandler.

```
On Error GoTo ErrHandler
```

The following `Function` procedure demonstrates this statement. The `DIVIDETWO` function accepts two arguments (num1 and num2) and returns the result of num1 divided by num2.

```
Function DIVIDETWO(num1, num2)
    On Error GoTo ErrHandler
    DIVIDETWO = num1 / num2
    Exit Function
ErrHandler:
    DIVIDETWO = "ERROR"
End Function
```

The `On Error GoTo` statement instructs VBA to jump to the statement labeled `ErrHandler` if an error occurs. As a result, the function returns a string (ERROR) if any type of error occurs while the function is executing. Note the use of the `Exit Function` statement. Without this statement, the code continues executing, and the error handling code *always* executes. In other words, the function always returns ERROR.

It's important to understand that the `DIVIDETWO` function is *non-standard* in its approach. Returning an error message string when an error occurs (ERROR) is not how Excel functions work. Excel functions return an actual error value.

CROSS REF

Chapter 25 contains several examples of the `On Error` statement, including an example that demonstrates how to return an actual error value from a function.

Using Ranges

Many of the custom functions that you develop will work with the data contained in a cell or in a range of cells. Recognize that a range can be a single cell or a group of cells. This section describes some key concepts to make this task easier. The information in this section is intended to be practical, rather than comprehensive. If you want more details, consult the online help.

CROSS REF

Chapter 25 contains many practical examples of functions that use ranges. Studying these examples helps to clarify the information in this section.

The For Each-Next Construct

Your `Function` procedures often need to loop through a range of cells. For example, you may write a function that accepts a range as an argument. Your code needs to examine each cell in the range and do something. The `For Each-Next` construct is very useful for this sort of thing. The syntax of the `For Each-Next` construct is

```
For Each element In group
    [instructions]
    [Exit For]
    [instructions]
Next [element]
```

The following `Function` procedure accepts a range argument and returns the sum of the squared values in the range:

```
Function SUMOFSQUARES(rng as Range)
    Dim total as Double
    Dim cell as Range
    total = 0
    For Each cell In rng
        total = total + cell ^ 2
    Next cell
    SUMOFSQUARES = total
End Function
```

The following is a worksheet formula that uses the `SumOfSquares` function:

```
=SumOfSquares(A1:C100)
```

In this case, the function's argument is a range that consists of 300 cells.

 NOTE

In the preceding example, `cell` and `rng` are both variable names. There's nothing special about either name; you can replace them with any valid variable name.

Referencing a Range

VBA code can reference a range in a number of different ways:

- Using the `Range` property
- Using the `Cells` property
- Using the `Offset` property

THE RANGE PROPERTY

You can use the Range property to refer to a range directly by using a cell address or name. The following example assigns the value in cell A1 to a variable named Init. In this case, the statement accesses the range's Value property.

```
Init = Range("A1").Value
```

In addition to the Value property, VBA enables you to access a number of other properties of a range. For example, the following statement counts the number of cells in a range and assigns the value to the Cnt variable:

```
Cnt = Range("A1:C300").Count
```

The Range property is also useful for referencing a single cell in a multicell range. For example, you may create a function that is supposed to accept a single-cell argument. If the user specifies a multicell range as the argument, you can use the Range property to extract the upper-left cell in the range. The following example uses the Range property (with an argument of "A1") to return the value in the upper-left cell of the range represented by the cell argument.

```
Function Square(cell as Range)
    CellValue = cell.Range("A1").Value
    Square = CellValue ^ 2
End Function
```

Assume that the user enters the following formula:

```
=Square(C5:C12)
```

The Square function works with the upper-left cell in C5:C12 (which is C5) and returns the value squared.

 NOTE

Many Excel worksheet functions work in this way. For example, if you specify a multicell range as the first argument for the LEFT function, Excel uses the upper-left cell in the range. However, Excel is not consistent. If you specify a multicell range as the argument for the SQRT function, Excel returns an error.

THE CELLS PROPERTY

Another way to reference a range is to use the Cells property. The Cells property accepts two arguments (a row number and a column number), and returns a single cell. The following statement assigns the value in cell A1 to a variable named FirstCell:

```
FirstCell = Cells(1, 1).Value
```

The following statement returns the upper-left cell in the range C5:C12:

```
UpperLeft = Range("C5:C12").Cells(1,1)
```

TIP

If you use the Cells property without an argument, it returns a range that consists of all cells on the worksheet. In the following example, the TotalCells variable contains the total number of cells in the worksheet.

```
TotalCells = Cells.Count
```

The following statement uses the Excel COUNTA function to determine the number of non-empty cells in the worksheet:

```
NonEmpty =WorksheetFunction.COUNTA(Cells)
```

THE OFFSET PROPERTY

The Offset property (like the Range and Cells properties) also returns a Range object. The Offset property is used in conjunction with a range. It takes two arguments that correspond to the relative position from the upper-left cell of the specified Range object. The arguments can be positive (down or right), negative (up or left), or zero. The following example returns the value one cell below cell A1 (that is, cell A2) and assigns it to a variable named NextCell:

```
NextCell = Range("A1").Offset(1,0).Value
```

The following Function procedure accepts a single-cell argument and returns the sum of the eight cells that surround it:

```
Function SumSurroundingCells(cell)
    Dim Total As Double
    Dim r As Integer, c As Integer
    Total = 0
    For r = -1 To 1
        For c = -1 To 1
            Total = Total + cell.Offset(r, c)
        Next c
    Next r
    SumSurroundingCells = Total - cell
End Function
```

This function uses a nested For-Next loop. So, when the r loop counter is -1, the c loop counter goes from -1 to 1. Nine cells are summed, including the argument cell, which is Offset(0, 0). The final statement subtracts the value of the argument cell from the total.

The function returns an error if the argument does not have eight surrounding cells (for example, if it's in row 1 or column 1).

To better understand how the nested loop works, following are nine statements that perform exactly the same calculation:

```
Total = Total + cell.Offset(-1, -1) ' upper left
Total = Total + cell.Offset(-1, 0) 'left
Total = Total + cell.Offset(-1, 1) 'upper right
Total = Total + cell.Offset(0, -1) 'above
Total = Total + cell.Offset(0, 0) 'the cell itself
Total = Total + cell.Offset(0, 1) 'right
Total = Total + cell.Offset(1, -1) 'lower left
Total = Total + cell.Offset(1, 0) 'below
Total = Total + cell.Offset(1, 1) 'lower right
```

Some Useful Properties of Ranges

Previous sections in this chapter give you examples that used the Value property for a range. VBA gives you access to many additional range properties. Some of the more useful properties for function writers are briefly described in the following sections. For complete information on a particular property, refer to Excel's online help.

THE FORMULA PROPERTY

The Formula property returns the formula (as a string) contained in a cell. If you try to access the Formula property for a range that consists of more than one cell, you get an error. If the cell does not have a formula, this property returns a string, which is the cell's value as it appears in the formula bar. The following function simply displays the formula for the upper-left cell in a range:

```
Function CELLFORMULA(cell)
    CELLFORMULA = cell.Range("A1").Formula
End Function
```

You can use the HasFormula property to determine whether a cell has a formula.

THE ADDRESS PROPERTY

The Address property returns the address of a range as a string. By default, it returns the address as an absolute reference (for example, $A$1:$C$12). The following function, which is not all that useful, returns the address of a range:

```
Function RANGEADDRESS(rng)
    RANGEADDRESS = rng.Address
End Function
```

For example, the following formula returns the string $A$1:$C$3:

```
=RANGEADDRESS(A1:C3)
```

The formula below returns the address of a range named MyRange:

```
=RANGEADDRESS(MyRange)
```

THE COUNT PROPERTY

The Count property returns the number of cells in a range. The following function uses the Count property:

```
Function CELLCOUNT(rng)
    CELLCOUNT = rng.Count
End Function
```

The following formula returns 9:

```
=CELLCOUNT(A1:C3)
```

CAUTION
The Count property of a Range object is not the same as the COUNT worksheet function. The Count property returns the number of cells in the range, including empty cells and cells with any kind of data. The COUNT worksheet function returns the number of cells in the range that contain numeric data.

NEW
Excel 2007 worksheets contain over 17 billion cells compared with a mere 17 million in previous versions. Because of this dramatic increase, the Count property—which returns a Long—may return an error if there are more than 2,147,483,647 cells to be counted. You can use the new CountLarge property instead of Count to be safe, but beware that CountLarge will not work in older versions of Excel. In the CELLCOUNT function, the following statement will handle any size range (including all cells on a worksheet):

```
    CELLCOUNT = rng.CountLarge
```

THE PARENT PROPERTY

The Parent property returns an object that corresponds to an object's *container* object. For a Range object, the Parent property returns a Worksheet object (the worksheet that contains the range).

The following function uses the `Parent` property and returns the name of the worksheet of the range passed as an argument:

```
Function SHEETNAME(rng)
    SHEETNAME = rng.Parent.Name
End Function
```

The following formula, for example, returns the string `Sheet1`:

```
=SHEETNAME(Sheet1!A16)
```

THE NAME PROPERTY

The `Name` property returns a `Name` object for a cell or range. To get the actual cell or range name, you need to access the `Name` property of the `Name` object. If the cell or range does not have a name, the `Name` property returns an error.

The following `Function` procedure displays the name of a range or cell passed as its argument. If the range or cell does not have a name, the function returns an empty string. Note the use of `On Error Resume Next`. This handles situations in which the range does not have a name.

```
Function RANGENAME(rng)
    On Error Resume Next
    RANGENAME = rng.Name.Name
    If Err.Number <> 0 Then RANGENAME = ""
End Function
```

THE NUMBERFORMAT PROPERTY

The `NumberFormat` property returns the number format (as a string) assigned to a cell or range. The following function simply displays the number format for the upper-left cell in a range:

```
Function NUMBERFORMAT(cell)
    NUMBERFORMAT = cell.Range("A1").NumberFormat
End Function
```

THE FONT PROPERTY

The `Font` property returns a `Font` object for a range or cell. To actually do anything with this `Font` object, you need to access its properties. For example, a `Font` object has properties such as `Bold`, `Italic`, `Name`, `Color`, and so on. The following function returns TRUE if the upper-left cell of its argument is formatted as bold:

```
Function ISBOLD(cell)
    ISBOLD = cell.Range("A1").Font.Bold
End Function
```

TIP

A cell's background color is not part of the `Font` object; it's stored in the `Interior` object. This function returns `True` if the upper-left cell of its argument is colored red (`vbRed` is a built-in constant):

```
Function ISREDBKGRD(cell)
    ISREDBKGRD = cell.Range("A1").Interior.Color = vbRed
End Function
```

THE COLUMNS AND ROWS PROPERTIES

The `Columns` and `Rows` properties work with columns or rows in a range. For example, the following function returns the number of columns in a range by accessing the `Count` property:

```
Function COLUMNCOUNT(rng)
    COLUMNCOUNT = rng.Columns.Count
End Function
```

THE ENTIREROW AND ENTIRECOLUMN PROPERTIES

The `EntireRow` and `EntireColumn` properties enable you to work with an entire row or column for a particular cell. The following function accepts a single cell argument and then uses the `EntireColumn` property to get a range consisting of the cell's entire column. It then uses the Excel COUNTA function to return the number of nonempty cells in the column.

```
Function NONEMPTYCELLSINCOLUMN(cell)
    NONEMPTYCELLSINCOLUMN = WorksheetFunction.CountA(cell.EntireColumn)
End Function
```

You cannot use this function in a formula that's in the same column as the cell argument. Doing so will generate a circular reference.

THE HIDDEN PROPERTY

The `Hidden` property is used with rows or columns. It returns TRUE if the row or column is hidden. If you try to access this property for a range that does not consist of an entire row or column, you get an error. The following function accepts a single cell argument and returns TRUE if either the cell's row or the cell's column is hidden:

```
Function CELLISHIDDEN(cell)
    If cell.EntireRow.Hidden Or cell.EntireColumn.Hidden Then
        CELLISHIDDEN = True
    Else
        CELLISHIDDEN = False
    End If
End Function
```

Part VI

You can also write this function without using an If-Then-Else construct. In the following function, the expression to the right of the equal sign returns either TRUE or FALSE — and this value is assigned returned by the function:

```
Function CELLISHIDDEN(cell)
    CELLISHIDDEN = cell.EntireRow.Hidden Or _
       cell.EntireColumn.Hidden
End Function
```

The Set Keyword

An important concept in VBA is the ability to create a new Range object and assign it to a variable — more specifically, an *object variable*. You do so by using the Set keyword. The following statement creates an object variable named MyRange:

```
Set MyRange = Range("A1:A10")
```

After the statement executes, you can use the MyRange variable in your code in place of the actual range reference. Examples in subsequent sections help to clarify this concept.

NOTE

Creating a Range object is not the same as creating a named range. In other words, you can't use the name of a Range object in your formulas.

The Intersect Function

The Intersect function returns a range that consists of the intersection of two other ranges. For example, consider the two ranges selected in Figure 24-2. These ranges, D3:D10 and B5:F5, contain one cell in common (D5). In other words, D5 is the intersection of D3:D10 and B5:F5.

The following Function procedure accepts two range arguments and returns the count of the number of cells that the ranges have in common:

```
Function CELLSINCOMMON(rng1, rng2)
    Dim CommonCells As Range
    On Error Resume Next
    Set CommonCells = Intersect(rng1, rng2)
    If Err.Number = 0 Then
        CELLSINCOMMON = CommonCells.CountLarge
    Else
        CELLSINCOMMON = 0
    End If
End Function
```

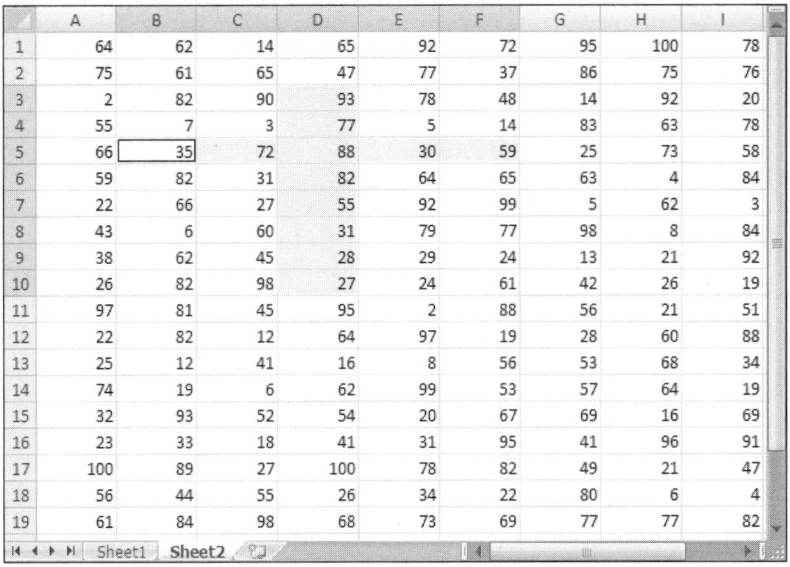

	A	B	C	D	E	F	G	H	I
1	64	62	14	65	92	72	95	100	78
2	75	61	65	47	77	37	86	75	76
3	2	82	90	93	78	48	14	92	20
4	55	7	3	77	5	14	83	63	78
5	66	35	72	88	30	59	25	73	58
6	59	82	31	82	64	65	63	4	84
7	22	66	27	55	92	99	5	62	3
8	43	6	60	31	79	77	98	8	84
9	38	62	45	28	29	24	13	21	92
10	26	82	98	27	24	61	42	26	19
11	97	81	45	95	2	88	56	21	51
12	22	82	12	64	97	19	28	60	88
13	25	12	41	16	8	56	53	68	34
14	74	19	6	62	99	53	57	64	19
15	32	93	52	54	20	67	69	16	69
16	23	33	18	41	31	95	41	96	91
17	100	89	27	100	78	82	49	21	47
18	56	44	55	26	34	22	80	6	4
19	61	84	98	68	73	69	77	77	82

◄ ◄ ► ► | Sheet1   Sheet2

Figure 24-2: Use the `Intersect` function to work with the intersection of two ranges.

The CELLSINCOMMON function uses the `Intersect` function to create a range object named `CommonCells`. Note the use of `On Error Resume Next`. This statement is necessary because the `Intersect` function returns an error if the ranges have no cells in common. If the error occurs, it is ignored. The final statement checks the `Number` property of the `Err` object. If it is 0, no error occurs, and the function returns the value of the `CountLarge` property for the `CommonCells` object. If an error does occur, `Err.Number` has a value other than 0, and the function returns 0.

The Union Function

The `Union` function combines two or more ranges into a single range. The following statement uses the `Union` function to create a range object that consists of the first and third columns of a worksheet:

```
Set TwoCols = Union(Range("A:A"), Range("C:C"))
```

The `Union` function takes between 2 and 30 arguments.

The UsedRange Property

The `UsedRange` property returns a `Range` object that represents the used range of the worksheet. Press Ctrl+End to activate the lower-right cell of the used range. The `UsedRange` property can be *very useful* in making your functions more efficient.

Consider the following `Function` procedure. This function accepts a range argument and returns the number of formula cells in the range.

```
Function FORMULACOUNT(rng)
    cnt = 0
    For Each cell In rng
        If cell.HasFormula Then cnt = cnt + 1
    Next cell
    FORMULACOUNT = cnt
End Function
```

In many cases, the preceding function works just fine. But what if the user enters a formula like this one?

```
=FORMULACOUNT(A:C)
```

The three-column argument consists of 3,145,728 cells. With an argument that consists of one or more entire columns, the function does not work well because it loops through every cell in the range, even those that are well beyond the area of the sheet that's actually used. The following function is rewritten to make it more efficient:

```
Function FORMULACOUNT(rng)

    cnt = 0
    Set WorkRange = Intersect(rng, rng.Parent.UsedRange)
    For Each cell In WorkRange
        If cell.HasFormula Then cnt = cnt + 1
    Next cell
    FORMULACOUNT = cnt
End Function
```

This function creates a Range object variable named WorkRange that consists of the intersection of the range passed as an argument and the used range of the worksheet. In other words, WorkRange consists of a subset of the range argument that only includes cells in the used range of the worksheet.

Chapter **25**

VBA Custom Function Examples

IN THIS CHAPTER

- ◆ Simple custom function examples
- ◆ A custom function to determine a cell's data type
- ◆ A custom function to make a single worksheet function act like multiple functions
- ◆ A custom function for generating random numbers and selecting cells at random
- ◆ Custom functions for calculating sales commissions
- ◆ Custom functions for manipulating text
- ◆ Custom functions for counting and summing cells
- ◆ Custom functions that deal with dates
- ◆ A custom function example for returning the last nonempty cell in a column or row
- ◆ Custom functions that work with multiple worksheets
- ◆ Advanced custom function techniques

This chapter is jam-packed with a wide variety of useful (or potentially useful) VBA custom worksheet functions. You can use many of the functions as they are written. You may need to modify other functions to meet your particular needs. For maximum speed and efficiency, these Function procedures declare all variables that are used.

Simple Functions

The functions in this section are relatively simple, but they can be very useful. Most of them are based on the fact that VBA can obtain useful information that's not normally available for use in a formula. For example, your VBA code can access a cell's HasFormula property to determine whether a cell contains a formula. Oddly, Excel does not have a built-in worksheet function that tells you this.

ON THE CD

The companion CD-ROM contains the workbook simple functions.xlsm that includes all the functions in this section.

Does a Cell Contain a Formula?

The following CELLHASFORMULA function accepts a single-cell argument and returns TRUE if the cell has a formula:

```
Function CELLHASFORMULA(cell As Range) As Boolean
'    Returns TRUE if cell has a formula
    CELLHASFORMULA = cell.Range("A1").HasFormula
End Function
```

If a multicell range argument is passed to the function, the function works with the upper-left cell in the range.

Returning a Cell's Formula

The following CELLFORMULA function returns the formula for a cell as a string. If the cell does not have a formula, it returns an empty string.

```
Function CELLFORMULA(cell As Range) As String
'    Returns the formula in cell, or an
'    empty string if cell has no formula
    Dim UpperLeft As Range
    Set UpperLeft = cell.Range("A1")
    If UpperLeft.HasFormula Then
        CELLFORMULA = UpperLeft.Formula
    Else
```

```
        CELLFORMULA = ""
    End If
End Function
```

This function creates a `Range` object variable named `UpperLeft`. This variable represents the upper-left cell in the argument that is passed to the function.

Is the Cell Hidden?

The following `CELLISHIDDEN` function accepts a single cell argument and returns TRUE if the cell is hidden. It is considered a hidden cell if either its row or its column is hidden.

```
Function CELLISHIDDEN(cell As Range) As Boolean
'   Returns TRUE if cell is hidden
    Dim UpperLeft As Range
    Set UpperLeft = cell.Range("A1")
    CELLISHIDDEN = UpperLeft.EntireRow.Hidden Or _
        UpperLeft.EntireColumn.Hidden
End Function
```

Returning a Worksheet Name

The following `SHEETNAME` function accepts a single argument (a range) and returns the name of the worksheet that contains the range. It uses the `Parent` property of the `Range` object. The `Parent` property returns an object — the object that contains the `Range` object.

```
Function SHEETNAME(rng As Range) As String
'   Returns the sheet name for rng
    SHEETNAME = rng.Parent.Name
End Function
```

Using the Functions in This Chapter

If you see a function listed in this chapter that you find useful, you can use it in your own workbook. All the `Function` procedures in this chapter are available on the companion CD-ROM. Just open the appropriate workbook (see Appendix D for a description of the files), activate the VB Editor, and copy and paste the function listing to a VBA module in your workbook. If you prefer, you can collect a number of functions and create an add-in (see Chapter 23 for details).

It's impossible to anticipate every function that you'll ever need. However, the examples in this chapter cover a wide variety of topics, so it's likely that you can locate an appropriate function and adapt the code for your own use.

The following function is a variation on this theme. It does not use an argument; rather, it relies on the fact that a function can determine the cell from which it was called by using `Application.Caller`.

```
Function SHEETNAME2() As String
'    Returns the sheet name of the cell that
'    contains the function
     SHEETNAME2 = Application.Caller.Parent.Name
End Function
```

In this function, `Application.Caller` returns a `Range` object that corresponds to the cell that contains the function. For example, suppose that you have the following formula in cell A1:

```
=SHEETNAME2()
```

When the `SHEETNAME2` function is executed, `Application.Caller` returns a `Range` object corresponding to the cell that contains the function. The `Parent` property returns the `Worksheet` object, and the `Name` property returns the name of the worksheet.

Returning a Workbook Name

The next function, `WORKBOOKNAME`, returns the name of the workbook. Notice that it uses the `Parent` property twice. The first `Parent` property returns a `Worksheet` object, the second `Parent` property returns a `Workbook` object, and the `Name` property returns the name of the workbook.

```
Function WORKBOOKNAME() As String
'    Returns the workbook name of the cell
'    that contains the function
     WORKBOOKNAME = Application.Caller.Parent.Parent.Name
End Function
```

Returning the Application's Name

The following function, although not very useful, carries this discussion of object parents to the next logical level by accessing the `Parent` property three times. This function returns the name of the `Application` object, which is always the string *Microsoft Excel*.

```
Function APPNAME() As String
'    Returns the application name of the cell
'    that contains the function
     APPNAME = Application.Caller.Parent.Parent.Parent.Name
End Function
```

Understanding Object Parents

Objects in Excel are arranged in a hierarchy. At the top of the hierarchy is the `Application` object (Excel itself). Excel contains other objects; these objects contain other objects, and so on. The following hierarchy depicts how a `Range` object fits into this scheme:

`Application` object (Excel)

`Workbook` object

`Worksheet` object

`Range` object

In the lingo of object-oriented programming (OOP), a `Range` object's parent is the `Worksheet` object that contains it. A `Worksheet` object's parent is the workbook that contains the worksheet. And a `Workbook` object's parent is the `Application` object. Armed with this knowledge, you can make use of the `Parent` property to create a few useful functions.

Returning Excel's Version Number

The following function returns Excel's version number. For example, if you use Excel 2007, it returns the text string *12.0.*

```
Function EXCELVERSION() as String
'   Returns Excel's version number
    EXCELVERSION = Application.Version
End Function
```

Note that the EXCELVERSION function returns a string, not a value. The following function returns TRUE if the application is Excel 97 or later (Excel 97 is version 8). This function uses the VBA `Val` function to convert the text string to a value:

```
Function EXCEL97ORLATER() As Boolean
    EXCEL97ORLATER = Val(Application.Version) >= 8
End Function
```

Returning Cell Formatting Information

This section contains a number of custom functions that return information about a cell's formatting. These functions are useful if you need to sort data based on formatting (for example, sorting all bold cells together).

CAUTION

The functions in this section use the following statement:

```
Application.Volatile True
```

This statement causes the function to be reevaluated when the workbook is calculated. You'll find, however, that these functions don't always return the correct value. This is because changing cell formatting, for example, does not trigger Excel's recalculation engine. To force a global recalculation (and update all the custom functions), press Ctrl+Alt+F9.

The following function returns TRUE if its single-cell argument has bold formatting:

```
Function ISBOLD(cell As Range) As Boolean
'    Returns TRUE if cell is bold
    Application.Volatile True
    ISBOLD = cell.Range("A1").Font.Bold
End Function
```

The following function returns TRUE if its single-cell argument has italic formatting:

```
Function ISITALIC(cell As Range) As Boolean
'    Returns TRUE if cell is italic
    Application.Volatile True
    ISITALIC = cell.Range("A1").Font.Italic
End Function
```

Both of the preceding functions have a slight flaw: They return an error (#VALUE!) if the cell has mixed formatting. For example, it's possible that only some characters in the cell are bold.

The following function returns TRUE only if all the characters in the cell are bold. If the Bold property of the Font object returns Null (indicating mixed formatting), the If statement will generate an error, and the function name will never be set to True. The function name was previously set to False, so that's the value returned by the function.

```
Function ALLBOLD(cell As Range) As Boolean
'    Returns TRUE if all characters in cell are bold
    Dim UpperLeft As Range
    Application.Volatile True
    Set UpperLeft = cell.Range("A1")
    ALLBOLD = False
    If UpperLeft.Font.Bold Then ALLBOLD = True
End Function
```

The following FILLCOLOR function returns an integer that corresponds to the color index of the cell's interior (the cell's fill color). If the cell's interior is not filled, the function returns –4142. The ColorIndex property ranges from 0 to 56.

```
Function FILLCOLOR(cell As Range) As Long
'    Returns a long integer corresponding to
'    cell's interior color
     Application.Volatile True
     FILLCOLOR = cell.Range("A1").Interior.ColorIndex
End Function
```

 NOTE
If a cell is part of a table that uses a style, the `FILLCOLOR` function does not return the correct color.

The following function returns the number format string for a cell:

```
Function NUMBERFORMAT(cell As Range) As String
'    Returns a string that represents
'    the cell's number format
     Application.Volatile True
     NUMBERFORMAT = cell.Range("A1").NumberFormat
End Function
```

If the cell uses the default number format, the function returns the string *General*.

Determining a Cell's Data Type

Excel provides a number of built-in functions that can help determine the type of data contained in a cell. These include ISTEXT, ISLOGICAL, and ISERROR. In addition, VBA includes functions such as ISEMPTY, ISDATE, and ISNUMERIC.

The following function accepts a range argument and returns a string (*Blank, Text, Logical, Error, Date, Time,* or *Value*) that describes the data type of the upper-left cell in the range:

```
Function CELLTYPE(cell As Range) As String
'    Returns the cell type of the upper-left
'    cell in a range
     Dim UpperLeft As Range
     Application.Volatile True
     Set UpperLeft = cell.Range("A1")
     Select Case True
         Case UpperLeft.NumberFormat = "@"
             CELLTYPE = "Text"
         Case IsEmpty(UpperLeft.Value)
             CELLTYPE = "Blank"
```

```
        Case WorksheetFunction.IsText(UpperLeft.Value)
            CELLTYPE = "Text"
        Case WorksheetFunction.IsLogical(UpperLeft.Value)
            CELLTYPE = "Logical"
        Case WorksheetFunction.IsErr(UpperLeft.Value)
            CELLTYPE = "Error"
        Case IsDate(UpperLeft.Value)
            CELLTYPE = "Date"
        Case InStr(1, UpperLeft.Text, ":") <> 0
            CELLTYPE = "Time"
        Case IsNumeric(UpperLeft.Value)
            CELLTYPE = "Value"
    End Select
End Function
```

Figure 25-1 shows the CELLTYPE function in use. Column B contains formulas that use the CELLTYPE function with an argument from column A. For example, cell B1 contains the following formula:

```
=CELLTYPE(A1)
```

	A	B	C	D
1	1	Value	*A simple value*	
2	8.6	Value	*Formula that returns a value*	
3	Budget Sheet	Text	*Simple text*	
4	FALSE	Logical	*Logical formula*	
5	TRUE	Logical	*Logical value*	
6	#DIV/0!	Error	*Formula error*	
7	10/1/2006	Text	*Formula that returns a date*	
8	4:00 PM	Time	*A time*	
9	143	Text	*Value preceded by apostrophe*	
10	434	Text	*Cell formatted as Text*	
11	A1:C4	Text	*Text with a colon*	
12		Blank	*Empty cell*	
13		Text	*Cell with a single space*	
14		Text	*Cell with an empty string (single apostrophe)*	
15				
16				

Sheet1

Figure 25-1: The CELLTYPE function returns a string that describes the contents of a cell.

ON THE CD

The workbook celltype function.xlsm that demonstrates the CELLTYPE function is available on the companion CD-ROM.

A Multifunctional Function

This section demonstrates a technique that may be helpful in some situations — the technique of making a single worksheet function act like multiple functions. The following VBA function, named STATFUNCTION, takes two arguments — the range (rng) and the operation (op). Depending on the value of op, the function returns a value computed by using any
of the following worksheet functions: AVERAGE, COUNT, MAX, MEDIAN, MIN, MODE, STDEV, SUM, or VAR. For example, you can use this function in your worksheet:

```
=STATFUNCTION(B1:B24,A24)
```

The result of the formula depends on the contents of cell A24, which should be a string, such as *Average*, *Count*, *Max*, and so on. You can adapt this technique for other types of functions.

```
Function STATFUNCTION(rng As Variant, op As String) As Variant
    Select Case UCase(op)
        Case "SUM"
            STATFUNCTION = Application.Sum(rng)
        Case "AVERAGE"
            STATFUNCTION = Application.Average(rng)
        Case "MEDIAN"
            STATFUNCTION = Application.Median(rng)
        Case "MODE"
            STATFUNCTION = Application.Mode(rng)
        Case "COUNT"
            STATFUNCTION = Application.Count(rng)
        Case "MAX"
            STATFUNCTION = Application.Max(rng)
        Case "MIN"
            STATFUNCTION = Application.Min(rng)
        Case "VAR"
            STATFUNCTION = Application.Var(rng)
        Case "STDEV"
            STATFUNCTION = Application.StDev(rng)
        Case Else
            STATFUNCTION = CVErr(xlErrNA)
    End Select
End Function
```

Figure 25-2 shows the STATFUNCTION function that is used in conjunction with a drop-down list generated by Excel's Data⇨Data Tools⇨Data Validation command. The formula in cell C14 is as follows:

```
=STATFUNCTION(C1:C12,B14)
```

⊿	A	B	C	D	E	F
1		Observation 1	135.52			
2		Observation 2	244.09			
3		Observation 3	187.33			
4		Observation 4	209.00			
5		Observation 5	200.91			
6		Observation 6	189.23			
7		Observation 7	198.22			
8		Observation 8	231.78			
9		Observation 9	189.14			
10		Observation 10	221.15			
11		Observation 11	189.05			
12		Observation 12	198.22			
13						
14		Max	244.09	<-- STATFUNCTION		
15		Average				
16		Median				
		Mode				
17		Count				
18		Max				
		Min				
19		Var				
20		StDev				
21						

Sheet1

Figure 25-2: Selecting an operation from the list displays the result in cell C14.

ON THE CD

The workbook, `statfunction function.xlsm`, shown in Figure 25-2, is available on the companion CD-ROM.

The following STATFUNCTION2 function is a much simpler approach that works exactly like the STATFUNCTION function. It uses the Evaluate method to evaluate an expression.

```
Function STATFUNCTION2(rng As Range, op As String) As Double
    STATFUNCTION2 = Evaluate(Op & "(" & _
        rng.Address(external:=True) & ")")
End Function
```

For example, assume that the rng argument is C1:C12 and also that the op argument is the string *SUM*. The expression that is used as an argument for the Evaluate method is

```
SUM(C1:C12)
```

The Evaluate method evaluates its argument and returns the result. In addition to being much shorter, a benefit of this version of STATFUNCTION is that it's not necessary to list all the possible functions.

Worksheet Function Data Types

You may have noticed some differences in the data types used for functions and arguments so far. For instance, in STATFUNCTION, the variable rng was declared as a Variant, while the same variable was declared as a Range in STATFUNCTION2. Also, the former's return value was declared as a Variant, while the latter's is a Double data type.

Data types are two-edged swords. They can be used to limit the type of data that can be passed, or returned from, a function, but they can also reduce the flexibility of the function. Using Variant data types maximizes flexibility but slows execution speed.

One of the possible return values of STATFUNCTION is an error, in the Case Else section of the Select Case statement. That means that the function can return a Double data type or an Error. The most restrictive data type that can hold both an Error and a Double is a Variant (which can hold anything), so the function is typed as a Variant. On the other hand, STATFUNCTION2 does not have any provision for returning an error, so it's typed as the more restrictive Double data type. Numeric data in cells is treated as a Double even if it looks like an Integer.

The rng arguments are also typed differently. In STATFUNCTION2, the Address property of the Range object is used. Because of this, you *must* pass a Range to the function, or it will return an error. However, there is nothing in STATFUNCTION that forces rng to be a Range. By declaring rng as a Variant, the user has flexibility to provide inputs in other ways. Excel will happily try to convert whatever it's given into something it can use. If it can't convert it, the result will surely be an error. A user can enter the following formula:

```
=STATFUNCTION({123.45,643,893.22},"Min")
```

Neither argument is a cell reference, but Excel doesn't mind. It can find the minimum of an array constant as easily as a range of values. It works the other way too, as in the case of the second argument. If a cell reference is supplied, Excel will try to convert it to a String and will have no problem doing so.

In general, you should endeavor to use the most restrictive data types possible for your situation while providing for the most user flexibility.

Generating Random Numbers

This section presents two functions that deal with random numbers. One generates random numbers that don't change. The other selects a cell at random from a range.

Generating Random Numbers That Don't Change

You can use the Excel RAND function to quickly fill a range of cells with random values. But, as you may have discovered, the RAND function generates a new random number whenever the worksheet is recalculated. If you prefer to generate random numbers that don't change with each recalculation, use the following STATICRAND Function procedure:

```
Function STATICRAND() As Double
'    Returns a random number that doesn't
'    change when recalculated
     STATICRAND = Rnd
End Function
```

The STATICRAND function uses the VBA Rnd function, which, like Excel's RAND function, returns a random number between 0 and 1. When you use STATICRAND, however, the random numbers don't change when the sheet is calculated.

Controlling Function Recalculation

When you use a custom function in a worksheet formula, when is it recalculated?

Custom functions behave like Excel's built-in worksheet functions. Normally, a custom function is recalculated only when it needs to be recalculated — that is, when you modify any of a function's arguments — but you can force functions to recalculate more frequently. Adding the following statement to a Function procedure makes the function recalculate whenever any cell changes:

```
Application.Volatile True
```

The Volatile method of the Application object has one argument (either True or False). Marking a Function procedure as "volatile" forces the function to be calculated whenever calculation occurs in *any* cell in the worksheet.

For example, the custom STATICRAND function presented in this chapter can be changed to emulate the Excel RAND() function by using the Volatile method, as follows:

```
Function NONSTATICRAND()
'    Returns a random number that
'    changes when the sheet is recalculated
     Application.Volatile True
     NONSTATICRAND = Rnd
End Function
```

Using the False argument of the Volatile method causes the function to be recalculated only when one or more of its arguments change (if a function has no arguments, this method has no effect). By default, all functions work as if they include an Application.Volatile False statement.

NOTE

Pressing F9 does not generate new values from the STATICRAND function, but pressing Ctrl+Alt+F9 (Excel's "global recalc" key combination) does.

Following is another version of the function that returns a random integer within a specified range of values. This function is essentially a "wrapper" for Excel's RANDBETWEEN function.

```
Function STATICRANDBETWEEN(lo As Long, hi As Long) As Long
'    Returns a random integer that doesn't
'    change when recalculated
     STATICRANDBETWEEN = WorksheetFunction.RandBetween(lo, hi)
End Function
```

For example, if you want to generate a random integer between 1 and 1000, you can use a formula such as

```
=STATICRANDBETWEEN(1,1000)
```

Selecting a Cell at Random

The following function, named DRAWONE, randomly chooses one cell from an input range and returns the cell's contents:

```
Function DRAWONE(rng As Variant) As Double
'    Chooses one cell at random from a range
     DRAWONE = rng(Int((rng.Count) * Rnd + 1))
End Function
```

If you use this function, you'll find that it is not recalculated when the worksheet is calculated. In other words, the function is not a volatile function. (For more information about controlling recalculation, see the nearby sidebar, "Controlling Function Recalculation." You can make the function volatile by adding the following statement:

```
Application.Volatile True
```

After doing so, the DRAWONE function displays a new random cell value whenever the sheet is calculated.

A more general function, one that accepts array constants as well as ranges, is shown here:

```
Function DRAWONE2(rng As Variant) As Variant
'    Chooses one value at random from an array
     Dim ArrayLen As Long

     If TypeName(rng) = "Range" Then
```

```
        DRAWONE2 = rng(Int((rng.Count) * Rnd + 1)).Value
    Else
        ArrayLen = UBound(rng) - LBound(rng) + 1
        DRAWONE2 = rng(Int(ArrayLen * Rnd + 1))
    End If
End Function
```

This function uses the VBA built-in `TypeName` function to determine whether the argument passed is a `Range`. If not, it's assumed to be an array. Following is a formula that uses the `DRAWONE2` function. This formula returns a text string that corresponds to a suit in a deck of cards:

```
=DRAWONE2({"Clubs","Hearts","Diamonds","Spades"})
```

Following is a formula that has the same result, written using Excel's built-in functions:

```
=CHOOSE(RANDBETWEEN(1,3),"Clubs","Hearts","Diamonds","Spades")
```

I present two additional functions that deal with randomization later in this chapter (see "Advanced Function Techniques").

Calculating Sales Commissions

Sales managers often need to calculate the commissions earned by their sales forces. The calculations in the function example presented here are based on a sliding scale: Employees who sell more earn a higher commission rate (see Table 25-1). For example, a salesperson with sales between $10,000 and $19,999 qualifies for a commission rate of 10.5 percent.

TABLE 25-1   COMMISSION RATES FOR MONTHLY SALES

Monthly Sales	Commission Rate
Less than $10,000	8.0%
$10,000 to $19,999	10.5%
$20,000 to $39,999	12.0%
$40,000 or more	14.0%

You can calculate commissions for various sales amounts entered into a worksheet in several ways. You can use a complex formula with nested `IF` functions, such as the following:

```
=IF(A1<0,0,IF(A1<10000,A1*0.08,
IF(A1<20000,A1*0.105,
IF(A1<40000,A1*0.12,A1*0.14))))
```

This may not be the best approach for a couple of reasons. First, the formula is overly complex, thus making it difficult to understand. Second, the values are hard-coded into the formula, thus making the formula difficult to modify.

A better approach is to use a lookup table function to compute the commissions. For example:

```
=VLOOKUP(A1,Table,2)*A1
```

Using VLOOKUP is a good alternative, but it may not work if the commission structure is more complex. (See the next subsection for more information.) Yet another approach is to create a custom function.

A Function for a Simple Commission Structure

The following COMMISSION function accepts a single argument (Sales) and computes the commission amount:

```
Function COMMISSION(Sales As Double) As Double
'    Calculates sales commissions
    Const Tier1 As Double = 0.08
    Const Tier2 As Double = 0.105
    Const Tier3 As Double = 0.12
    Const Tier4 As Double = 0.14
    Select Case Sales
        Case Is >= 40000
            COMMISSION = Sales * Tier4
        Case Is >= 20000
            COMMISSION = Sales * Tier3
        Case Is >= 10000
            COMMISSION = Sales * Tier2
        Case Is < 10000
            COMMISSION = Sales * Tier1
    End Select
End Function
```

The following worksheet formula, for example, returns 3,000 (the sales amount — 25,000 — qualifies for a commission rate of 12 percent):

```
=COMMISSION(25000)
```

This function is very easy to understand and maintain. It uses constants to store the commission rates as well as a Select Case structure to determine which commission rate to use.

NOTE

When a Select Case structure is evaluated, program control exits the Select Case structure when the first true Case is encountered.

A Function for a More Complex Commission Structure

If the commission structure is more complex, you may need to use additional arguments for your COMMISSION function. Imagine that the aforementioned sales manager implements a new policy to help reduce turnover: The total commission paid increases by 1 percent for each year that a salesperson stays with the company.

The following is a modified COMMISSION function (named COMMISSION2). This function now takes two arguments: the monthly sales (Sales) and the number of years employed (Years).

```
Function COMMISSION2(Sales As Double, Years As Long) As Double
'    Calculates sales commissions based on
'    years in service
    Const Tier1 As Double = 0.08
    Const Tier2 As Double = 0.105
    Const Tier3 As Double = 0.12
    Const Tier4 As Double = 0.14
    Select Case Sales
        Case Is >= 40000
            COMMISSION2 = Sales * Tier4
        Case Is >= 20000
            COMMISSION2 = Sales * Tier3
        Case Is >= 10000
            COMMISSION2 = Sales * Tier2
        Case Is < 10000
            COMMISSION2 = Sales * Tier1
    End Select
    COMMISSION2 = COMMISSION2 + (COMMISSION2 * Years / 100)
End Function
```

Figure 25-3 shows the COMMISSION2 function in use. The formula in cell D2 is

```
=COMMISSION2(B2,C2)
```

 ON THE CD

The workbook, commission function.xlsm, shown in Figure 25-3, is available on the companion CD-ROM.

	A	B	C	D	E
1	Sales Rep	Amount Sold	Years Employed	Commission	
2	Adams, Robert	5,010.54	1	404.85	
3	Baker, Sheila	9,833.91	0	786.71	
4	Clarke, Edward	12,500.32	2	1,338.78	
5	Davis, Don	35,988.22	3	4,448.14	
6	Elfin, Bill	41,822.99	3	6,030.88	
7	Franklin, Ben	8,090.32	1	653.70	
8	Gomez, Chris	11,098.32	2	1,188.63	
9	Harley, Mary	48,745.23	5	7,165.55	
10					

Figure 25-3: Calculating sales commissions based on sales amount and years employed.

Text Manipulation Functions

Text strings can be manipulated with functions in a variety of ways, including reversing the display of a text string, scrambling the characters in a text string, or extracting specific characters from a text string. This section offers a number of function examples that manipulate text strings.

ON THE CD

The companion CD-ROM contains a workbook named `text manipulation functions.xlsm` that demonstrates all the functions in this section.

Reversing a String

The following REVERSETEXT function returns the text in a cell backward:

```
Function REVERSETEXT(text As String) As String
'    Returns its argument, reversed
     REVERSETEXT = StrReverse(text)
End Function
```

This function simply uses the VBA StrReverse function. The following formula, for example, returns tfosorciM:

```
=REVERSETEXT("Microsoft")
```

Scrambling Text

The following function returns the contents of its argument with the characters randomized. For example, using *Microsoft* as the argument may return *oficMorts,* or some other random permutation.

```
Function SCRAMBLE(text As Variant) As String
'    Scrambles its string argument
    Dim TextLen As Long
    Dim i As Long
    Dim RandPos As Long
    Dim Temp As String
    Dim Char As String * 1
    If TypeName(text) = "Range" Then
        Temp = text.Range("A1").text
    ElseIf IsArray(text) Then
        Temp = text(LBound(text))
    Else
        Temp = text
    End If
    TextLen = Len(Temp)
    For i = 1 To TextLen
        Char = Mid(Temp, i, 1)
        RandPos = WorksheetFunction.RandBetween(1, TextLen)
        Mid(Temp, i, 1) = Mid(Temp, RandPos, 1)
        Mid(Temp, RandPos, 1) = Char
    Next i
    SCRAMBLE = Temp
End Function
```

This function loops through each character and then swaps it with another character in a randomly selected position.

You may be wondering about the use of Mid. Note that when Mid is used on the right side of an assignment statement, it is a function. However, when Mid is used on the left side of the assignment statement, it is a statement. Consult the Help system for more information about Mid.

Returning an Acronym

The ACRONYM function returns the first letter (in uppercase) of each word in its argument. For example, the following formula returns *IBM:*

```
=ACRONYM("International Business Machines")
```

The listing for the ACRONYM Function procedure follows:

```
Function ACRONYM(text As String) As String
'    Returns an acronym for text
    Dim TextLen As Long
    Dim i As Long
    text = Application.Trim(text)
    TextLen = Len(text)
    ACRONYM = Left(text, 1)
    For i = 2 To TextLen
        If Mid(text, i, 1) = " " Then
            ACRONYM = ACRONYM & Mid(text, i + 1, 1)
        End If
    Next i
    ACRONYM = UCase(ACRONYM)
End Function
```

This function uses the Excel TRIM function to remove any extra spaces from the argument. The first character in the argument is always the first character in the result. The For-Next loop examines each character. If the character is a space, the character *after* the space is appended to the result. Finally, the result converts to uppercase by using the VBA UCase function.

Does the Text Match a Pattern?

The following function returns TRUE if a string matches a pattern composed of text and wildcard characters. The ISLIKE function is remarkably simple, and is essentially a wrapper for the useful VBA Like operator.

```
Function ISLIKE(text As String, pattern As String) As Boolean
'    Returns true if the first argument is like the second
    ISLIKE = text Like pattern
End Function
```

The supported wildcard characters are as follows:

?	Matches any single character
*	Matches zero or more characters
#	Matches any single digit (0–9)
[*list*]	Matches any single character in the list
[!*list*]	Matches any single character not in the list

The following formula returns TRUE because the question mark (?) matches any single character. If the first argument were "Unit12", the function would return FALSE.

```
=ISLIKE("Unit1","Unit?")
```

The function also works with values. The following formula, for example, returns TRUE if cell A1 contains a value that begins with 1 and has exactly three numeric digits:

```
=ISLIKE(A1,"1##")
```

The following formula returns TRUE because the first argument is a single character contained in the list of characters specified in the second argument:

```
=ISLIKE("a","[aeiou]")
```

If the character list begins with an exclamation point (!),the comparison is made with characters *not* in the list. For example, the following formula returns TRUE because the first argument is a single character that does not appear in the second argument's list:

```
=ISLIKE("g","[!aeiou]")
```

To match one of the special characters from the table above, put that character in brackets. This formula returns TRUE because the pattern is looking for three consecutive question marks. The question marks in the pattern are in brackets so they no longer represent any single character:

```
=ISLIKE("???","[?][?][?]")
```

The Like operator is very versatile. For complete information about the VBA Like operator, consult the Help system.

Does a Cell Contain Text?

A number of Excel's worksheet functions are at times unreliable when dealing with text in a cell. For example, the ISTEXT function returns FALSE if its argument is a number that's formatted as Text. The following CELLHASTEXT function returns TRUE if the cell argument contains text or contains a value formatted as Text:

```
Function CELLHASTEXT(cell As Range) As Boolean
'    Returns TRUE if cell contains a string
'    or cell is formatted as Text
    Dim UpperLeft as Range
    CELLHASTEXT = False
    Set UpperLeft = cell.Range("A1")
    If UpperLeft.NumberFormat = "@" Then
        CELLHASTEXT = True
        Exit Function
```

```
        End If
        If Not IsNumeric(UpperLeft.Value) Then
            CELLHASTEXT = True
            Exit Function
        End If
End Function
```

The following formula returns TRUE if cell A1 contains a text string or if the cell is formatted as Text:

```
=CELLHASTEXT(A1)
```

Extracting the *n*th Element from a String

The EXTRACTELEMENT function is a custom worksheet function that extracts an element from a text string based on a specified separator character. Assume that cell A1 contains the following text:

```
123-456-789-9133-8844
```

For example, the following formula returns the string *9133*, which is the fourth element in the string. The string uses a hyphen (-) as the separator.

```
=EXTRACTELEMENT(A1,4,"-")
```

The EXTRACTELEMENT function uses three arguments:

- Txt: The text string from which you're extracting. This can be a literal string or a cell reference.

- n: An integer that represents the element to extract.

- Separator: A single character used as the separator.

 NOTE

If you specify a space as the Separator character, multiple spaces are treated as a single space (almost always what you want). If n exceeds the number of elements in the string, the function returns an empty string.

The VBA code for the EXTRACTELEMENT function follows:

```
Function EXTRACTELEMENT(Txt As String, n As Long,
    Separator As String) As String
'   Returns the nth element of a text string, where the
'   elements are separated by a specified separator character
```

```
     Dim AllElements As Variant
     AllElements = Split(Txt, Separator)
     EXTRACTELEMENT = AllElements(n - 1)
End Function
```

This function uses the VBA Split function, which returns a variant array that contains each element of the text string. This array begins with 0 (not 1), so using n-1 references the desired element.

Spelling Out a Number

The SPELLDOLLARS function returns a number spelled out in text — as on a check. For example, the following formula returns the string *One hundred twenty-three and 45/100 dollars:*

```
=SPELLDOLLARS(123.45)
```

Figure 25-4 shows some additional examples of the SPELLDOLLARS function. Column C contains formulas that use the function. For example, the formula in C1 is

```
=SPELLDOLLARS(A1)
```

Note that negative numbers are spelled out and enclosed in parentheses.

	A	B	C	D	E	F	G	H	I	J	K
1	32		Thirty-Two and 00/100 Dollars								
2	37.56		Thirty-Seven and 56/100 Dollars								
3	-32		(Thirty-Two and 00/100 Dollars)								
4	-26.44		(Twenty-Six and 44/100 Dollars)								
5	-4		(Four and 00/100 Dollars)								
6	1.87341		One and 87/100 Dollars								
7	1.56		One and 56/100 Dollars								
8	1		One and 00/100 Dollars								
9	6.56		Six and 56/100 Dollars								
10	12.12		Twelve and 12/100 Dollars								
11	1000000		One Million and 00/100 Dollars								
12	10000000000		Ten Billion and 00/100 Dollars								
13	1111111111		One Billion One Hundred Eleven Million One Hundred Eleven Thousand One Hundred Eleven and 00/100 Dollars								
14											

H ◀ ▶ H   Sheet1

Figure 25-4: Examples of the SPELLDOLLARS function.

 ON THE CD

The SPELLDOLLARS function is too lengthy to list here, but you can view the complete listing in spelldollars function.xlsm on the companion CD-ROM.

Counting Functions

Chapter 7 contains many formula examples to count cells based on various criteria. If you can't arrive at a formula-based solution for a counting problem, then you can probably create a custom function. This section contains three functions that perform counting.

 ON THE CD

The companion CD-ROM contains the workbook `counting functions.xlsm` that demonstrates the functions in this section.

Counting Pattern-Matched Cells

The COUNTIF function accepts limited wildcard characters in its criteria: the question mark and the asterisk, to be specific. If you need more robust pattern matching, you can use the LIKE operator in a custom function.

```
Function COUNTLIKE(rng As Range, pattern As String) As Long
'    Count the cells in a range that match a pattern
     Dim cell As Range
     Dim cnt As Long
     For Each cell In rng.Cells
         If cell.Text Like pattern Then cnt = cnt + 1
     Next cell
     COUNTLIKE = cnt
End Function
```

The following formula counts the number of cells in G4:J15 that do not contain the letter *e*:

```
=COUNTLIKE(G4:J15,"?[!e]*")
```

Counting Sheets in a Workbook

The following COUNTSHEETS function accepts no arguments and returns the number of sheets in the workbook from where it's called:

```
Function COUNTSHEETS() As Long
     COUNTSHEETS = Application.Caller.Parent.Parent.Sheets.Count
End Function
```

This function uses `Application.Caller` to get the range where the formula was entered. Then it uses two `Parent` properties to go to the sheet and the workbook. Once at the workbook level, the `Count` property of the `Sheets` property is returned.

Counting Words in a Range

The WORDCOUNT function accepts a range argument and returns the number of words in that range:

```
Function WORDCOUNT(rng As Range) As Long
'    Count the words in a range of cells
    Dim cell As Range
    Dim WdCnt As Long
    For Each cell In rng.Cells
        If WorksheetFunction.IsText(cell.Value) Then
            WdCnt = WdCnt + (Len(cell.Text) - _
                Len(Replace(cell.Text, " ", ""))) + 1
        End If
    Next cell
    WORDCOUNT = WdCnt
End Function
```

Looping through the cells in the supplied range, the ISTEXT worksheet function is used to determine whether the cell has text. If it does, the number of spaces are counted and added to the total. Then one more space is added because a sentence with three spaces has four words. Spaces are counted by comparing the length of the text string with the length after the spaces have been removed with the VBA Replace function.

Counting Colors

The COUNTREDS function accepts a range argument and returns the number of cells whose font is red.

```
Function COUNTREDS(rng As Range) As Long
'    Count cells whose font color is red
    Dim cell As Range
    For Each cell In rng.Cells
        If cell.Font.Color = vbRed Then COUNTREDS = COUNTREDS + 1
    Next cell
End Function
```

The Color property of each cell's Font object is compared with vbRed, which is a built-in constant whose intrinsic value is the same as Excel's value for the color red. This function is very specialized. However, a more general function — one in which the color to be counted is supplied as an argument — could be written.

NOTE

Although this section deals with counting, many of the functions can easily be converted into summing functions. The COUNTREDS function, for example, could be changed to SUMREDS with only a slight change to the loop:

```
SUMREDS = SUMREDS + cell.Value
```

Date Functions

Chapter 6 presents a number of useful Excel functions and formulas for calculating dates, times, and time periods by manipulating date and time serial values. This section presents additional functions that deal with dates.

ON THE CD

The companion CD-ROM contains a workbook, `date functions.xlsm`, that demonstrates the functions presented in this section.

Calculating the Next Monday

The following NEXTMONDAY function accepts a date argument and returns the date of the following Monday:

```
Function NEXTMONDAY(d As Date) As Date
    NEXTMONDAY = d + 8 - WeekDay(d, vbMonday)
End Function
```

This function uses the VBA WeekDay function, which returns an integer that represents the day of the week for a date (1 = Sunday, 2 = Monday, and so on). It also uses a predefined constant, vbMonday.

The following formula returns 12/31/2007, which is the first Monday after Christmas Day, 2007 (which is a Tuesday):

```
=NEXTMONDAY(DATE(2006,12,25))
```

NOTE

The function returns a date serial number. You will need to change the number format of the cell to display this serial number as an actual date.

If the argument passed to the NEXTMONDAY function is a Monday, the function will return the *following* Monday. If you prefer the function to return the same Monday, use this modified version:

```
Function NEXTMONDAY2(d As Date) As Date
    If WeekDay(d) = 2 Then
        NEXTMONDAY2 = d
    Else
        NEXTMONDAY2 = d + 8 - WeekDay(d, vbMonday)
    End If
End Function
```

Calculating the Next Day of the Week

The following NEXTDAY function is a variation on the NEXTMONDAY function. This function accepts two arguments: A date and an integer between 1 and 7 that represents a day of the week (1 = Sunday, 2 = Monday, and so on). The NEXTDAY function returns the date for the next specified day of the week.

```
Function NEXTDAY(d As Date, day As Integer) As Variant
'   Returns the next specified day
'   Make sure day is between 1 and 7
    If day < 1 Or day > 7 Then
        NEXTDAY = CVErr(xlErrNA)
    Else
        NEXTDAY = d + 8 - WeekDay(d, day)
    End If
End Function
```

The NEXTDAY function uses an If statement to ensure that the day argument is valid (that is, between 1 and 7). If the day argument is not valid, the function returns #N/A. Because the function can return a value other than a date, it is declared as type Variant.

Which Week of the Month?

The following MONTHWEEK function returns an integer that corresponds to the week of the month for a date:

```
Function MONTHWEEK(d As Date) As Variant
'   Returns the week of the month for a date
    Dim FirstDay As Integer

'   Check for valid date argument
    If Not IsDate(d) Then
        MONTHWEEK = CVErr(xlErrNA)
```

```
        Exit Function
    End If

'   Get first day of the month
    FirstDay = WeekDay(DateSerial(Year(d), Month(d), 1))

'   Calculate the week number
    MONTHWEEK = Application.RoundUp((FirstDay + day(d) - 1) / 7, 0)
End Function
```

Working with Dates Before 1900

Many users are surprised to discover that Excel can't work with dates prior to the year 1900. To correct this deficiency, I created a series of extended date functions. These functions enable you to work with dates in the years 0100 through 9999.

The extended date functions are

- **XDATE(y,m,d,fmt):** Returns a date for a given year, month, and day. As an option, you can provide a date formatting string.

- **XDATEADD(xdate1,days,fmt):** Adds a specified number of days to a date. As an option, you can provide a date formatting string.

- **XDATEDIF(xdate1,xdate2):** Returns the number of days between two dates.

- **XDATEYEARDIF(xdate1,xdate2):** Returns the number of full years between two dates (useful for calculating ages).

- **XDATEYEAR(xdate1):** Returns the year of a date.

- **XDATEMONTH(xdate1):** Returns the month of a date.

- **XDATEDAY(xdate1):** Returns the day of a date.

- **XDATEDOW(xdate1):** Returns the day of the week of a date (as an integer between 1 and 7).

Figure 25-5 shows a workbook that uses a few of these functions.

ON THE CD

These functions are available on the companion CD-ROM, in a file named `extended date functions.xlsm`. The CD also contains a Word file (`extended data functions help.docx`) that describes these functions.

	A	B	C	D	E	F	G	H
5								
6	President	Year	Month	Day	XDATE	XDATEDIF	XDATEYEARDIF	XDATEDOW
7	George Washington	1732	22	1	10/1/1733	99,711	273	Thursday
8	John Adams	1735	30	10	6/10/1737	98,363	269	Monday
9	Thomas Jefferson	1743	13	4	1/4/1744	95,964	262	Saturday
10	James Madison	1751	16	3	4/3/1752	92,952	254	Monday
11	James Monroe	1758	28	4	4/4/1760	90,029	246	Friday
12	John Quincy Adams	1767	11	7	11/7/1767	87,256	238	Saturday
13	Andrew Jackson	1767	15	3	3/3/1768	87,139	238	Thursday
14	Martin Van Buren	1782	5	12	5/12/1782	81,956	224	Sunday
15	William Henry Harrison	1773	9	2	9/2/1773	85,130	233	Thursday
16	John Tyler	1790	29	3	5/3/1792	78,312	214	Thursday
17	James K. Polk	1795	2	11	2/11/1795	77,298	211	Wednesday
18	Zachary Taylor	1784	24	11	12/11/1785	80,647	220	Sunday
19	Millard Fillmore	1800	7	1	7/1/1800	75,332	206	Tuesday
20	Franklin Pierce	1804	23	11	11/11/1805	73,373	200	Monday
21	James Buchanan	1791	23	4	11/4/1792	78,127	213	Sunday
22	Abraham Lincoln	1809	12	2	12/2/1809	71,891	196	Saturday
23	Andrew Johnson	1808	29	12	5/12/1810	71,730	196	Saturday

H ◀ ▶ H Sheet1

Figure 25-5: Examples of the extended date function.

CAUTION

The extended date functions don't make any adjustments for changes made to the calendar in 1582. Consequently, working with dates prior to October 15, 1582, may not yield correct results.

Returning the Last Nonempty Cell in a Column or Row

This section presents two useful functions: LASTINCOLUMN, which returns the contents of the last nonempty cell in a column, and LASTINROW, which returns the contents of the last nonempty cell in a row. Chapter 15 presents array formulas for this task, but you may prefer to use a custom function.

ON THE CD

The companion CD-ROM contains last nonempty cell.xlsm, a workbook that demonstrates the functions presented in this section.

Each of these functions accepts a range as its single argument. The range argument can be a column reference (for LASTINCOLUMN) or a row reference (for LASTINROW). If the supplied argument is not a complete column or row reference (such as 3:3 or D:D), the function uses the column or row of the upper-left cell in the range. For example, the following formula returns the contents of the last nonempty cell in column B:

```
=LASTINCOLUMN(B5)
```

The following formula returns the contents of the last nonempty cell in row 7:

```
=LASTINROW(C7:D9)
```

The LASTINCOLUMN Function

The following is the LASTINCOLUMN function:

```
Function LASTINCOLUMN(rng As Range) As Variant
'    Returns the contents of the last non-empty cell in a column
    Dim LastCell As Range
    Application.Volatile
    With rng.Parent
        With .Cells(.Rows.Count, rng.Column)
            If Not IsEmpty(.Value) Then
                LASTINCOLUMN = .Value
            ElseIf IsEmpty(.End(xlUp).Value) Then
                LASTINCOLUMN = ""
            Else
                LASTINCOLUMN = .End(xlUp).Value
            End If
        End With
    End With
End Function
```

Notice the references to the Parent of the range. This is done in order to make the function work with arguments that refer to a different worksheet or workbook.

The LASTINROW Function

The following is the LASTINROW function:

```
Function LASTINROW(rng As Range) As Variant
'    Returns the contents of the last non-empty cell in a row
    Application.Volatile
    With rng.Parent
        With .Cells(rng.Row, .Columns.Count)
            If Not IsEmpty(.Value) Then
                LASTINROW = .Value
            ElseIf IsEmpty(.End(xlToLeft).Value) Then
                LASTINROW = ""
            Else
                LASTINROW = .End(xlToLeft).Value
            End If
```

```
        End With
    End With
End Function
```

CROSS REF

In Chapter 15, I describe array formulas that return the last cell in a column or row.

Multisheet Functions

You may need to create a function that works with data contained in more than one worksheet within a workbook. This section contains two VBA functions that enable you to work with data across multiple sheets, including a function that overcomes an Excel limitation when copying formulas to other sheets.

ON THE CD

The companion CD-ROM contains the workbook `multisheet functions.xlsm` that demonstrates the multisheet functions presented in this section.

Returning the Maximum Value Across All Worksheets

If you need to determine the maximum value in a cell (for example, B1) across a number of worksheets, use a formula like this one:

```
=MAX(Sheet1:Sheet4!B1)
```

This formula returns the maximum value in cell B1 for Sheet1, Sheet4, and all of the sheets in between. But what if you add a new sheet (Sheet5) after Sheet4? Your formula does not adjust automatically, so you need to edit it to include the new sheet reference:

```
=MAX(Sheet1:Sheet5!B1)
```

The following function accepts a single-cell argument and returns the maximum value in that cell across all worksheets in the workbook. For example, the following formula returns the maximum value in cell B1 for all sheets in the workbook:

```
=MAXALLSHEETS(B1)
```

If you add a new sheet, you don't need to edit the formula.

```
Function MAXALLSHEETS(cell as Range) As Variant
    Dim MaxVal As Double
    Dim Addr As String
```

```
    Dim Wksht As Object
    Application.Volatile
    Addr = cell.Range("A1").Address
    MaxVal = -9.9E+307
    For Each Wksht In cell.Parent.Parent.Worksheets
        If Not Wksht.Name = cell.Parent.Name Or _
          Not Addr = Application.Caller.Address Then
            If IsNumeric(Wksht.Range(Addr)) Then
                If Wksht.Range(Addr) > MaxVal Then _
                    MaxVal = Wksht.Range(Addr).Value
            End If
        End If
    Next Wksht
    If MaxVal = -9.9E+307 Then MaxVal = CVErr(xlErrValue)
    MAXALLSHEETS = MaxVal
End Function
```

The `For Each` statement uses the following expression to access the workbook:

```
cell.Parent.Parent.Worksheets
```

The parent of the cell is a worksheet, and the parent of the worksheet is the workbook. Therefore, the `For Each-Next` loop cycles among all worksheets in the workbook. The first `If` statement inside the loop checks whether the cell being checked is the cell that contains the function. If so, that cell is ignored to avoid a circular reference error.

 NOTE

You can easily modify the `MAXALLSHEETS` function to perform other cross-worksheet calculations: Minimum, Average, Sum, and so on.

The SHEETOFFSET Function

A recurring complaint about Excel (including Excel 2007) is its poor support for relative sheet references. For example, suppose that you have a multisheet workbook, and you enter a formula like the following on Sheet2:

```
=Sheet1!A1+1
```

This formula works fine. However, if you copy the formula to the next sheet (Sheet3), the formula continues to refer to Sheet1. Or if you insert a sheet between Sheet1 and Sheet2, the formula continues to refer to Sheet1, when most likely, you want it to refer to the newly inserted sheet. In fact, you can't create formulas that refer to worksheets in a relative manner. However, you can use the SHEETOFFSET function to overcome this limitation.

Following is a VBA Function procedure named SHEETOFFSET:

```
Function SHEETOFFSET(Offset As Long, Optional cell As Variant)
'    Returns cell contents at Ref, in sheet offset
    Dim WksIndex As Long, WksNum As Long
    Dim wks As Worksheet
    Application.Volatile
    If IsMissing(cell) Then Set cell = Application.Caller
    WksNum = 1
    For Each wks In Application.Caller.Parent.Parent.Worksheets
        If Application.Caller.Parent.Name = wks.Name Then
            SHEETOFFSET = Worksheets(WksNum + Offset)_
                .Range(cell(1).Address).Value
            Exit Function
        Else
            WksNum = WksNum + 1
        End If
    Next wks
End Function
```

The SHEETOFFSET function accepts two arguments:

- offset: The sheet offset, which can be positive, negative, or 0.
- cell: (Optional) A single-cell reference. If this argument is omitted, the function will use the same cell reference as the cell that contains the formula.

For more information about optional arguments, see the section, "Using Optional Arguments," later in this chapter.

The following formula returns the value in cell A1 of the sheet before the sheet that contains the formula:

```
=SHEETOFFSET(-1,A1)
```

The following formula returns the value in cell A1 of the sheet after the sheet that contains the formula:

```
=SHEETOFFSET(1,A1)
```

Advanced Function Techniques

In this section, I explore some even more advanced functions. The examples in this section demonstrate some special techniques that you can use with your custom functions.

Returning an Error Value

In some cases, you may want your custom function to return a particular error value. Consider the simple REVERSETEXT function, which I presented earlier in this chapter:

```
Function REVERSETEXT(text As String) As String
'    Returns its argument, reversed
     REVERSETEXT = StrReverse(text)
End Function
```

This function reverses the contents of its single-cell argument (which can be text or a value). If the argument is a multicell range, the function returns #VALUE!

Assume that you want this function to work only with strings. If the argument does not contain a string, you want the function to return an error value (#N/A). You may be tempted to simply assign a string that looks like an Excel formula error value. For example:

```
REVERSETEXT = "#N/A"
```

Although the string *looks* like an error value, it is not treated as such by other formulas that may reference it. To return a *real* error value from a function, use the VBA CVErr function, which converts an error number to a real error.

Fortunately, VBA has built-in constants for the errors that you want to return from a custom function. These constants are listed here:

- xlErrDiv0
- xlErrNA
- xlErrName
- xlErrNull
- xlErrNum
- xlErrRef
- xlErrValue

The following is the revised REVERSETEXT function:

```
Function REVERSETEXT(text As Variant) As Variant
'    Returns its argument, reversed
     If WorksheetFunction.ISNONTEXT(text) Then
         REVERSETEXT = CVErr(xlErrNA)
     Else
         REVERSETEXT = StrReverse(text)
     End If
End Function
```

First, change the argument from a String data type to a Variant. If the argument's data type is String, Excel will try to convert whatever it gets (for example, number, Boolean value) to a String and will usually succeed. Next, the Excel ISNONTEXT function is used to determine whether the argument is not a text string. If the argument is not a text string, the function returns the #N/A error. Otherwise, it returns the characters in reverse order.

NOTE

The data type for the return value of the original REVERSETEXT function was String because the function always returned a text string. In this revised version, the function is declared as a variant because it can now return something other than a string.

Returning an Array from a Function

Most functions that you develop with VBA return a single value. It's possible, however, to write a function that returns multiple values in an array.

CROSS REF

Part III deals with arrays and array formulas. Specifically, these chapters provide examples of a single formula that returns multiple values in separate cells. As you'll see, you can also create custom functions that return arrays.

VBA includes a useful function called Array. The Array function returns a variant that contains an array. It's important to understand that the array returned is not the same as a normal array composed of elements of the variant type. In other words, a variant array is not the same as an array of variants.

If you're familiar with using array formulas in Excel, you have a head start understanding the VBA Array function. You enter an array formula into a cell by pressing Ctrl+Shift+Enter. Excel inserts brackets around the formula to indicate that it's an array formula. See Chapter 15 for more details on array formulas.

NOTE

The lower bound of an array created by using the Array function is, by default, 0. However, the lower bound can be changed if you use an Option Base statement.

The following MONTHNAMES function demonstrates how to return an array from a Function procedure:

```
Function MONTHNAMES() As Variant
    MONTHNAMES = Array( _
        "Jan", "Feb", "Mar", "Apr", _
```

```
        "May", "Jun", "Jul", "Aug", _
        "Sep", "Oct", "Nov", "Dec")
End Function
```

Figure 25-6 shows a worksheet that uses the MONTHNAMES function. You enter the function by selecting A4:L4 and then entering the following formula:

```
{=MONTHNAMES()}
```

Figure 25-6: The MONTHNAMES function entered as an array formula.

NOTE

As with any array formula, you must press Ctrl+Shift+Enter to enter the formula. Don't enter the brackets — Excel inserts the brackets for you.

The MONTHNAMES function, as written, returns a horizontal array in a single row. To display the array in a vertical range in a single column (as in A7:A18 in Figure 25-5), select the range and enter the following formula:

```
{=TRANSPOSE(MONTHNAMES())}
```

Alternatively, you can modify the function to do the transposition. The following function uses the Excel TRANSPOSE function to return a vertical array:

```
Function VMONTHNAMES() As Variant
    VMONTHNAMES = Application.Transpose(Array( _
        "Jan", "Feb", "Mar", "Apr", _
        "May", "Jun", "Jul", "Aug", _
        "Sep", "Oct", "Nov", "Dec"))
End Function
```

ON THE CD

The workbook monthnames.xlsm that demonstrates MONTHNAMES and VMONTHNAMES is available on the companion CD-ROM.

Part VI

Returning an Array of Nonduplicated Random Integers

The RANDOMINTEGERS function returns an array of nonduplicated integers. This function is intended for use in a multicell array formula. Figure 25-7 shows a worksheet that uses the following formula in the range A3:D12:

```
{=RANDOMINTEGERS()}
```

	A	B	C	D	E	F
1						
2						
3	2	4	6	7		
4	8	10	11	15		
5	16	17	18	19		
6	21	23	24	25		
7	31	32	35	36		
8	38	39	14	5		
9	9	26	27	28		
10	29	30	3	1		
11	33	34	12	20		
12	37	13	22	40		
13						
14						

Sheet1

Figure 25-7: An array formula generates nonduplicated consecutive integers, arranged randomly.

This formula was entered into the entire range by using Ctrl+Shift+Enter. The formula returns an array of nonduplicated integers, arranged randomly. Because 40 cells contain the formula, the integers range from 1 to 40. The following is the code for RANDOMINTEGERS:

```
Function RANDOMINTEGERS()
    Dim FuncRange As Range

    Dim V() As Integer, ValArray() As Integer
    Dim CellCount As Double
    Dim i As Integer, j As Integer
    Dim r As Integer, c As Integer
    Dim Temp1 As Variant, Temp2 As Variant
    Dim RCount As Integer, CCount As Integer
    Randomize
'   Create Range object
    Set FuncRange = Application.Caller

'   Return an error if FuncRange is too large
    CellCount = FuncRange.Count
    If CellCount > 1000 Then
        RANDOMINTEGERS = CVErr(xlErrNA)
```

```
            Exit Function
        End If

    '   Assign variables
        RCount = FuncRange.Rows.Count
        CCount = FuncRange.Columns.Count
        ReDim V(1 To RCount, 1 To CCount)
        ReDim ValArray(1 To 2, 1 To CellCount)

    '   Fill array with random numbers
    '   and consecutive integers
        For i = 1 To CellCount
            ValArray(1, i) = Rnd
            ValArray(2, i) = i
        Next i

    '   Sort ValArray by the random number dimension
        For i = 1 To CellCount
            For j = i + 1 To CellCount
                If ValArray(1, i) > ValArray(1, j) Then
                    Temp1 = ValArray(1, j)
                    Temp2 = ValArray(2, j)
                    ValArray(1, j) = ValArray(1, i)
                    ValArray(2, j) = ValArray(2, i)
                    ValArray(1, i) = Temp1
                    ValArray(2, i) = Temp2
                End If
            Next j
        Next i

    '   Put the randomized values into the V array
        i = 0
        For r = 1 To RCount
            For c = 1 To CCount
                i = i + 1
                V(r, c) = ValArray(2, i)
            Next c
        Next r
        RANDOMINTEGERS = V
    End Function
```

ON THE CD

The workbook random integers function.xlsm containing the RANDOMINTEGERS function is available on the companion CD-ROM.

Randomizing a Range

The following RANGERANDOMIZE function accepts a range argument and returns an array that consists of the input range in random order:

```
Function RANGERANDOMIZE(rng)
    Dim V() As Variant, ValArray() As Variant
    Dim CellCount As Double
    Dim i As Integer, j As Integer
    Dim r As Integer, c As Integer
    Dim Temp1 As Variant, Temp2 As Variant
    Dim RCount As Integer, CCount As Integer
    Randomize

'   Return an error if rng is too large
    CellCount = rng.Count
    If CellCount > 1000 Then
        RANGERANDOMIZE = CVErr(xlErrNA)
        Exit Function
    End If

'   Assign variables
    RCount = rng.Rows.Count
    CCount = rng.Columns.Count
    ReDim V(1 To RCount, 1 To CCount)
    ReDim ValArray(1 To 2, 1 To CellCount)

'   Fill ValArray with random numbers
'   and values from rng
    For i = 1 To CellCount
        ValArray(1, i) = Rnd
        ValArray(2, i) = rng(i)
    Next i

'   Sort ValArray by the random number dimension
    For i = 1 To CellCount
        For j = i + 1 To CellCount
            If ValArray(1, i) > ValArray(1, j) Then
                Temp1 = ValArray(1, j)
                Temp2 = ValArray(2, j)
                ValArray(1, j) = ValArray(1, i)
                ValArray(2, j) = ValArray(2, i)
                ValArray(1, i) = Temp1
                ValArray(2, i) = Temp2
            End If
```

```
        Next j
    Next i

'   Put the randomized values into the V array
    i = 0
    For r = 1 To RCount
        For c = 1 To CCount
            i = i + 1
            V(r, c) = ValArray(2, i)
        Next c
    Next r
    RANGERANDOMIZE = V
End Function
```

The code closely resembles the code for the RANDOMINTEGERS function. Figure 25-8 shows the function in use. The following array formula, which is in C2:C11, returns the contents of A2:A11 in a random order:

```
{=RANGERANDOMIZE(A2:A11)}
```

	A	B	C	D	E	F	G
13							
14		Original			Randomized		
15		A	N		B	J	
16		B	O		Z	U	
17		C	P		V	O	
18		D	Q		S	F	
19		E	R		Q	P	
20		F	S		I	H	
21		G	T		G	Y	
22		H	U		W	N	
23		I	V		L	X	
24		J	W		D	R	
25		K	X		M	E	
26		L	Y		C	T	
27		M	Z		K	A	
28							

I◄ ◄ ► ►I   Sheet1

Figure 25-8: The RANGERANDOMIZE function returns the contents of a range, but in a randomized order.

ON THE CD

The workbook range randomize function.xlsm, which contains the RANGERANDOMIZE function, is available on the companion CD-ROM.

Using Optional Arguments

Many of the built-in Excel worksheet functions use optional arguments. For example, the LEFT function returns characters from the left side of a string. Its official syntax is as follows:

LEFT(text, *num_chars*)

The first argument is required, but the second is optional. If you omit the optional argument, Excel assumes a value of 1.

Custom functions that you develop in VBA can also have optional arguments. You specify an optional argument by preceding the argument's name with the keyword `Optional`. The following is a simple function that returns the user's name:

```
Function USER()
    USER = Application.UserName
End Function
```

Suppose that in some cases, you want the user's name to be returned in uppercase letters. The following function uses an optional argument:

```
Function USER(Optional UpperCase As Variant) As String
    If IsMissing(UpperCase) Then UpperCase = False
    If UpperCase = True Then
        USER = Ucase(Application.UserName)
    Else
        USER = Application.UserName
    End If
End Function
```

NOTE

If you need to determine whether an optional argument was passed to a function, you must declare the optional argument as a variant data type. Then you can use the IsMissing function within the procedure, as demonstrated in this example.

If the argument is FALSE or omitted, the user's name is returned without any changes. If the argument is TRUE, the user's name converts to uppercase (using the VBA `Ucase` function) before it is returned. Notice that the first statement in the procedure uses the VBA `IsMissing` function to determine whether the argument was supplied. If the argument is missing, the statement sets the `UpperCase` variable to FALSE (the default value).

Optional arguments also allow you to specify a default value in the declaration, rather than testing it with the IsMissing function. The preceding function can be rewritten in this alternate syntax as

```
Function USER(Optional UpperCase As Boolean = False) As String
    If UpperCase = True Then
        USER = UCase(Application.UserName)
    Else
        USER = Application.UserName
    End If
End Function
```

If no argument is supplied, UpperCase is automatically assigned a value of False. This has the advantage of allowing you type the argument appropriately instead of with the generic Variant data type. If you use this method, however, there is no way to tell whether the user omitted the argument or supplied the default argument.

All the following formulas are valid in either syntax (and the first two have the same effect):

```
=USER()
=USER(False)
=USER(True)
```

Using an Indefinite Number of Arguments

Some of the Excel worksheet functions take an indefinite number of arguments. A familiar example is the SUM function, which has the following syntax:

```
SUM(number1,number2...)
```

The first argument is required, but you can have as many as 254 additional arguments. Here's an example of a formula that uses the SUM function with four range arguments:

```
=SUM(A1:A5,C1:C5,E1:E5,G1:G5)
```

You can mix and match the argument types. For example, the following example uses three arguments — a range, followed by a value, and finally an expression:

```
=SUM(A1:A5,12,24*3)
```

You can create function procedures that have an indefinite number of arguments. The trick is to use an array as the last (or only) argument, preceded by the keyword ParamArray.

Part VI

NOTE

ParamArray can apply only to the last argument in the procedure. It is always a variant data type, and it is always an optional argument (although you don't use the Optional keyword).

A SIMPLE EXAMPLE OF INDEFINITE ARGUMENTS

The following is a Function procedure that can have any number of single-value arguments. It simply returns the sum of the arguments.

```
Function SIMPLESUM(ParamArray arglist() As Variant) As Double
    Dim arg as Variant
    For Each arg In arglist
        SIMPLESUM = SIMPLESUM + arg
    Next arg
End Function
```

The following formula returns the sum of the single-cell arguments:

```
=SIMPLESUM(A1,A5,12)
```

The most serious limitation of the SIMPLESUM function is that it does not handle multicell ranges. This improved version does:

```
Function SIMPLESUM(ParamArray arglist() As Variant) As Double
    Dim arg as Variant
    Dim cell as Range
    For Each arg In arglist
        If TypeName(arg) = "Range" Then
            For Each cell In arg
                SIMPLESUM = SIMPLESUM + cell.Value
            Next cell
        Else
            SIMPLESUM = SIMPLESUM + arg
        End If
    Next arg
End Function
```

This function checks each entry in the Arglist array. If the entry is a range, then the code uses a For Each-Next loop to sum the cells in the range.

Even this improved version is certainly no substitute for the Excel SUM function. Try it out by using various types of arguments, and you'll see that it fails unless each argument is a value or a range reference. Also, if an argument consists of an entire column, you'll find that the function is *very* slow because it evaluates every cell — even the empty ones.

EMULATING THE EXCEL SUM FUNCTION

This section presents a Function procedure called MYSUM. Unlike the SIMPLESUM function listed in the previous section, MYSUM emulates the Excel SUM function perfectly.

Before you look at the code for the MYSUM function, take a minute to think about the Excel SUM function. This very versatile function can have any number of arguments (even missing arguments), and the arguments can be numerical values, cells, ranges, text representations of numbers, logical values, and even embedded functions. For example, consider the following formula:

```
=SUM(A1,5,"6",,TRUE,SQRT(4),B1:B5,{1,3,5})
```

This formula — which is a valid formula — contains all the following types of arguments, listed here in the order of their presentation:

- A single cell reference (A1)

- A literal value (5)

- A string that looks like a value ("6")

- A missing argument

- A logical value (TRUE)

- An expression that uses another function (SQRT)

- A range reference (B1:B5)

- An array ({1,3,5})

The following is the listing for the MYSUM function that handles all these argument types:

```
Function MySum(ParamArray args() As Variant) As Variant
' Emulates Excel's SUM function

' Variable declarations
    Dim i As Variant
    Dim TempRange As Range, cell As Range
    Dim ECode As String
    Dim m, n
    MySum = 0

' Process each argument
    For i = 0 To UBound(args)
'   Skip missing arguments
        If Not IsMissing(args(i)) Then
'       What type of argument is it?
            Select Case TypeName(args(i))
                Case "Range"
```

```
      ' Create temp range to handle full row or column ranges
        Set TempRange = Intersect(args(i).Parent.UsedRange, args(i))
        For Each cell In TempRange
          If IsError(cell) Then
            MySum = cell ' return the error
            Exit Function
          End If
          If cell = True Or cell = False Then
            MySum = MySum + 0
          Else
            If IsNumeric(cell) Or IsDate(cell) Then _
               MySum = MySum + cell
            End If
          Next cell
        Case "Variant()"
           n = args(i)
           For m = LBound(n) To UBound(n)
              MySum = MySum(MySum, n(m)) 'recursive call
           Next m
        Case "Null"  'ignore it
        Case "Error" 'return the error
          MySum = args(i)
          Exit Function
        Case "Boolean"
          ' Check for literal TRUE and compensate
          If args(i) = "True" Then MySum = MySum + 1
        Case "Date"
          MySum = MySum + args(i)
        Case Else
          MySum = MySum + args(i)
      End Select
    End If
  Next i
End Function
```

ON THE CD

The workbook `mysum function.xlsm` containing the `MYSUM` function is available on the companion CD-ROM.

As you study the code for `MYSUM`, keep the following points in mind:

- Missing arguments (determined by the `IsMissing` function) are simply ignored.

- The procedure uses the VBA `TypeName` function to determine the type of argument (`Range`, `Error`, or something else). Each argument type is handled differently.

- For a range argument, the function loops through each cell in the range and adds its value to a running total.

- The data type for the function is `Variant` because the function needs to return an error if any of its arguments is an error value.

- If an argument contains an error (for example, #DIV0!), the MYSUM function simply returns the error — just like the Excel SUM function.

- The Excel SUM function considers a text string to have a value of 0 unless it appears as a literal argument (that is, as an actual value, not a variable). Therefore, MYSUM adds the cell's value only if it can be evaluated as a number (VBA's `IsNumeric` function is used for this).

- Dealing with Boolean arguments is tricky. For MYSUM to emulate SUM exactly, it needs to test for a literal TRUE in the argument list and compensate for the difference (that is, add 2 to −1 to get 1).

- For range arguments, the function uses the `Intersect` method to create a temporary range that consists of the intersection of the range and the sheet's used range. This handles cases in which a range argument consists of a complete row or column, which would take forever to evaluate.

You may be curious about the relative speeds of SUM and MYSUM. MYSUM, of course, is much slower, but just how much slower depends on the speed of your system and the formulas themselves. On my system, a worksheet with 1,000 SUM formulas recalculated instantly. After I replaced the SUM functions with MYSUM functions, it took about 12 seconds. MYSUM may be improved a bit, but it can never come close to SUM's speed.

By the way, I hope you understand that the point of this example is not to create a new SUM function. Rather, it demonstrates how to create custom worksheet functions that look and work like those built into Excel.

Part VII

Appendixes

Appendix A

Excel Function Reference

This appendix contains a complete listing of the Excel worksheet functions. The functions are arranged alphabetically in tables by categories used by the Insert Function dialog box.

For more information about a particular function, including its arguments, select the function in the Insert Function dialog box and click Help on This Function.

ON THE CD

A workbook that contains this information is available on the companion CD-ROM. The filename is `worksheet functions.xlsx`. The workbook also contains hyperlinks to the specific help for each function.

TABLE A-1   CUBE CATEGORY FUNCTIONS

Function	What It Does
CUBEKPIMEMBER*	Returns a key performance indicator name, property, and measure; and displays the name and property in the cell
CUBEMEMBER*	Returns a member or tuple in a cube hierarchy

continued

TABLE A-1 CUBE CATEGORY FUNCTIONS (continued)

Function	What It Does
CUBEMEMBERPROPERTY*	Returns the value of a member property in the cube
CUBERANKEDMEMBER*	Returns the nth, or ranked, member in a set
CUBESET*	Defines a calculated set of members or tuples by sending a set expression to the cube on the server
CUBESETCOUNT*	Returns the number of items in a set
CUBEVALUE*	Returns an aggregated value from a cube

*Indicates a new function in Excel 2007

TABLE A-2 DATABASE CATEGORY FUNCTIONS

Function	What It Does
DAVERAGE	Averages the values in a column of a list or database that match conditions you specify
DCOUNT	Counts the cells that contain numbers in a column of a list or database that match conditions you specify
DCOUNTA	Counts the nonblank cells in a column of a list or database that match conditions you specify
DGET	Extracts a single value from a column of a list or database that matches conditions you specify
DMAX	Returns the largest number in a column of a list or database that matches conditions you specify
DMIN	Returns the smallest number in a column of a list or database that matches conditions you specify
DPRODUCT	Multiplies the values in a column of a list or database that match conditions you specify
DSTDEV	Estimates the standard deviation of a population based on a sample by using the numbers in a column of a list or database that match conditions you specify
DSTDEVP	Calculates the standard deviation of a population based on the entire population, using the numbers in a column of a list or database that match conditions you specify
DSUM	Adds the numbers in a column of a list or database that match conditions you specify

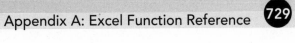

Function	What It Does
DVAR	Estimates the variance of a population based on a sample by using the numbers in a column of a list or database that match conditions you specify
DVARP	Calculates the variance of a population based on the entire population by using the numbers in a column of a list or database that match conditions you specify

Part VII

TABLE A-3   DATE & TIME CATEGORY FUNCTIONS

Function	What It Does
DATE	Returns the serial number of a particular date
DATEVALUE	Converts a date in the form of text to a serial number
DAY	Converts a serial number to a day of the month
DAYS360	Calculates the number of days between two dates, based on a 360-day year
EDATE	Returns the serial number of the date that is the indicated number of months before or after the start date
EOMONTH	Returns the serial number of the last day of the month before or after a specified number of months
HOUR	Converts a serial number to an hour
MINUTE	Converts a serial number to a minute
MONTH	Converts a serial number to a month
NETWORKDAYS	Returns the number of whole workdays between two dates
NOW	Returns the serial number of the current date and time
SECOND	Converts a serial number to a second
TIME	Returns the serial number of a particular time
TIMEVALUE	Converts a time in the form of text to a serial number
TODAY	Returns the serial number of today's date
WEEKDAY	Converts a serial number to a day of the week
WEEKNUM	Returns the week number in the year

continued

TABLE A-3   DATE & TIME CATEGORY FUNCTIONS (continued)

Function	What It Does
WORKDAY	Returns the serial number of the date before or after a specified number of work days
YEAR	Converts a serial number to a year
YEARFRAC	Returns the year fraction representing the number of whole days between start_date and end_date

TABLE A-4   ENGINEERING CATEGORY FUNCTIONS

Function	What It Does
BESSELI	Returns the modified Bessel function In(x)
BESSELJ	Returns the Bessel function Jn(x)
BESSELK	Returns the modified Bessel function Kn(x)
BESSELY	Returns the Bessel function Yn(x)
BIN2DEC	Converts a binary number to decimal
BIN2HEX	Converts a binary number to hexadecimal
BIN2OCT	Converts a binary number to octal
COMPLEX	Converts real and imaginary coefficients into a complex number
CONVERT	Converts a number from one measurement system to another
DEC2BIN	Converts a decimal number to binary
DEC2HEX	Converts a decimal number to hexadecimal
DEC2OCT	Converts a decimal number to octal
DELTA	Tests whether two values are equal
ERF	Returns the error function
ERFC	Returns the complementary error function
GESTEP	Tests whether a number is greater than a threshold value
HEX2BIN	Converts a hexadecimal number to binary
HEX2DEC	Converts a hexadecimal number to decimal
HEX2OCT	Converts a hexadecimal number to octal

Function	What It Does
IMABS	Returns the absolute value (modulus) of a complex number
IMAGINARY	Returns the imaginary coefficient of a complex number
IMARGUMENT	Returns the argument *theta*, an angle expressed in radians
IMCONJUGATE	Returns the complex conjugate of a complex number
IMCOS	Returns the cosine of a complex number
IMDIV	Returns the quotient of two complex numbers
IMEXP	Returns the exponential of a complex number
IMLN	Returns the natural logarithm of a complex number
IMLOG10	Returns the base 10 logarithm of a complex number
IMLOG2	Returns the base 2 logarithm of a complex number
IMPOWER	Returns a complex number raised to an integer power
IMPRODUCT	Returns the product of complex numbers
IMREAL	Returns the real coefficient of a complex number
IMSIN	Returns the sine of a complex number
IMSQRT	Returns the square root of a complex number
IMSUB	Returns the difference of two complex numbers
IMSUM	Returns the sum of complex numbers
OCT2BIN	Converts an octal number to binary
OCT2DEC	Converts an octal number to decimal
OCT2HEX	Converts an octal number to hexadecimal

TABLE A-5   FINANCIAL CATEGORY FUNCTIONS

Function	What It Does
ACCRINT	Returns the accrued interest for a security that pays periodic interest.
ACCRINTM	Returns the accrued interest for a security that pays interest at maturity.
AMORDEGRC	Returns the depreciation for each accounting period.

continued

TABLE A-5   FINANCIAL CATEGORY FUNCTIONS (continued)

Function	What It Does
AMORLINC	Returns the depreciation for each accounting period. (The depreciation coefficient depends on the life of the assets.)
COUPDAYBS	Returns the number of days from the beginning of the coupon period to the settlement date.
COUPDAYS	Returns the number of days in the coupon period that contains the settlement date.
COUPDAYSNC	Returns the number of days from the settlement date to the next coupon date.
COUPNCD	Returns the next coupon date after the settlement date.
COUPNUM	Returns the number of coupons payable between the settlement date and maturity date.
COUPPCD	Returns the previous coupon date before the settlement date.
CUMIPMT	Returns the cumulative interest paid between two periods.
CUMPRINC	Returns the cumulative principal paid on a loan between two periods.
DB	Returns the depreciation of an asset for a specified period, using the fixed-declining-balance method.
DDB	Returns the depreciation of an asset for a specified period, using the double-declining-balance method or some other method that you specify.
DISC	Returns the discount rate for a security.
DOLLARDE	Converts a dollar price, expressed as a fraction, into a dollar price, expressed as a decimal number.
DOLLARFR	Converts a dollar price, expressed as a decimal number, into a dollar price, expressed as a fraction.
DURATION	Returns the annual duration of a security with periodic interest payments.
EFFECT	Returns the effective annual interest rate.
FV	Returns the future value of an investment.
FVSCHEDULE	Returns the future value of an initial principal after applying a series of compound interest rates.
INTRATE	Returns the interest rate for a fully invested security.
IPMT	Returns the interest payment for an investment for a given period.

Function	What It Does
IRR	Returns the internal rate of return for a series of cash flows.
ISPMT	Returns the interest associated with a specific loan payment.
MDURATION	Returns the Macauley-modified duration for a security with an assumed par value of $100.
MIRR	Returns the internal rate of return where positive and negative cash flows are financed at different rates.
NOMINAL	Returns the annual nominal interest rate.
NPER	Returns the number of periods for an investment.
NPV	Returns the net present value of an investment based on a series of periodic cash flows and a discount rate.
ODDFPRICE	Returns the price per $100 face value of a security with an odd first period.
ODDFYIELD	Returns the yield of a security with an odd first period.
ODDLPRICE	Returns the price per $100 face value of a security with an odd last period.
ODDLYIELD	Returns the yield of a security with an odd last period.
PMT	Returns the periodic payment for an annuity.
PPMT	Returns the payment on the principal for an investment for a given period.
PRICE	Returns the price per $100 face value of a security that pays periodic interest.
PRICEDISC	Returns the price per $100 face value of a discounted security.
PRICEMAT	Returns the price per $100 face value of a security that pays interest at maturity.
PV	Returns the present value of an investment.
RATE	Returns the interest rate per period of an annuity.
RECEIVED	Returns the amount received at maturity for a fully invested security.
SLN	Returns the straight-line depreciation of an asset for one period.
SYD	Returns the sum-of-years' digits depreciation of an asset for a specified period.
TBILLEQ	Returns the bond-equivalent yield for a Treasury bill.

continued

TABLE A-5   FINANCIAL CATEGORY FUNCTIONS (continued)

Function	What It Does
TBILLPRICE	Returns the price per $100 face value for a Treasury bill.
TBILLYIELD	Returns the yield for a Treasury bill.
VDB	Returns the depreciation of an asset for a specified or partial period using a declining-balance method.
XIRR	Returns the internal rate of return for a schedule of cash flows that is not necessarily periodic.
XNPV	Returns the net present value for a schedule of cash flows that is not necessarily periodic.
YIELD	Returns the yield on a security that pays periodic interest.
YIELDDISC	Returns the annual yield for a discounted security: for example, a Treasury bill.
YIELDMAT	Returns the annual yield of a security that pays interest at maturity.

TABLE A-6   INFORMATION CATEGORY FUNCTIONS

Function	What It Does
CELL	Returns information about the formatting, location, or contents of a cell
ERROR.TYPE	Returns a number corresponding to an error type
INFO	Returns information about the current operating environment
ISBLANK	Returns TRUE if the value is blank
ISERR	Returns TRUE if the value is any error value except #N/A
ISERROR	Returns TRUE if the value is any error value
ISEVEN	Returns TRUE if the number is even
ISLOGICAL	Returns TRUE if the value is a logical value
ISNA	Returns TRUE if the value is the #N/A error value
ISNONTEXT	Returns TRUE if the value is not text
ISNUMBER	Returns TRUE if the value is a number
ISODD	Returns TRUE if the number is odd
ISREF	Returns TRUE if the value is a reference

Function	What It Does
ISTEXT	Returns TRUE if the value is text
N	Returns a value converted to a number
NA	Returns the error value #N/A
TYPE	Returns a number indicating the data type of a value

TABLE A-7 LOGICAL CATEGORY FUNCTIONS

Function	What It Does
AND	Returns TRUE if all its arguments are TRUE
FALSE	Returns the logical value FALSE
IF	Specifies a logical test to perform
IFERROR*	Returns a different result if the first argument evaluates to an error
NOT	Reverses the logic of its argument
OR	Returns TRUE if any argument is TRUE
TRUE	Returns the logical value TRUE

*Indicates a new function in Excel 2007

TABLE A-8 LOOKUP & REFERENCE CATEGORY FUNCTIONS

Function	What It Does
ADDRESS	Returns a reference as text to a single cell in a worksheet
AREAS	Returns the number of areas in a reference
CHOOSE	Chooses a value from a list of values
COLUMN	Returns the column number of a reference
COLUMNS	Returns the number of columns in a reference
GETPIVOTDATA	Returns data stored in a pivot table

continued

TABLE A-8 LOOKUP & REFERENCE CATEGORY FUNCTIONS (continued)

Function	What It Does
HLOOKUP	Searches for a value in the top column of a table and then returns a value in the same column from a row you specify in the table
HYPERLINK	Creates a shortcut that opens a document on your hard drive, a server, or the Internet
INDEX	Uses an index to choose a value from a reference or array
INDIRECT	Returns a reference indicated by a text value
LOOKUP	Returns a value either from a one-row or one-column range or from an array
MATCH	Returns the relative position of an item in an array
OFFSET	Returns a reference offset from a given reference
ROW	Returns the row number of a reference
ROWS	Returns the number of rows in a reference
RTD	Returns real-time data from a program that supports COM automation
TRANSPOSE	Returns the transpose of an array
VLOOKUP	Searches for a value in the leftmost column of a table and then returns a value in the same row from a column you specify in the table

TABLE A-9 MATH & TRIG CATEGORY FUNCTIONS

Function	What It Does
ABS	Returns the absolute value of a number
ACOS	Returns the arccosine of a number
ACOSH	Returns the inverse hyperbolic cosine of a number
ASIN	Returns the arcsine of a number
ASINH	Returns the inverse hyperbolic sine of a number
ATAN	Returns the arctangent of a number
ATAN2	Returns the arctangent from x and y coordinates
ATANH	Returns the inverse hyperbolic tangent of a number

Function	What It Does
CEILING	Rounds a number to the nearest integer or to the nearest multiple of significance
COMBIN	Returns the number of combinations for a given number of objects
COS	Returns the cosine of a number
COSH	Returns the hyperbolic cosine of a number
DEGREES	Converts radians to degrees
EVEN	Rounds a number up to the nearest even integer
EXP	Returns e raised to the power of a given number
FACT	Returns the factorial of a number
FACTDOUBLE	Returns the double factorial of a number
FLOOR	Rounds a number down, toward 0
GCD	Returns the greatest common divisor
INT	Rounds a number down to the nearest integer
LCM	Returns the least common multiple
LN	Returns the natural logarithm of a number
LOG	Returns the logarithm of a number to a specified base
LOG10	Returns the base 10 logarithm of a number
MDETERM	Returns the matrix determinant of an array
MINVERSE	Returns the matrix inverse of an array
MMULT	Returns the matrix product of two arrays
MOD	Returns the remainder from division
MROUND	Returns a number rounded to the desired multiple
MULTINOMIAL	Returns the multinomial of a set of numbers
ODD	Rounds a number up to the nearest odd integer
PI	Returns the value of pi
POWER	Returns the result of a number raised to a power
PRODUCT	Multiplies its arguments
QUOTIENT	Returns the integer portion of a division
RADIANS	Converts degrees to radians

continued

TABLE A-9   MATH & TRIG CATEGORY FUNCTIONS *(continued)*

Function	What It Does
RAND	Returns a random number between 0 and 1
RANDBETWEEN	Returns a random number between the numbers that you specify
ROMAN	Converts an Arabic numeral to Roman, as text
ROUND	Rounds a number to a specified number of digits
ROUNDDOWN	Rounds a number down, toward 0
ROUNDUP	Rounds a number up, away from 0
SERIESSUM	Returns the sum of a power series based on the formula
SIGN	Returns the sign of a number
SIN	Returns the sine of the given angle
SINH	Returns the hyperbolic sine of a number
SQRT	Returns a positive square root
SQRTPI	Returns the square root of pi
SUBTOTAL	Returns a subtotal in a list or database
SUM	Adds its arguments
SUMIF	Adds the cells specified by a given criteria
SUMIFS*	Adds the cells specified by a multiple criteria
SUMPRODUCT	Returns the sum of the products of corresponding array components
SUMSQ	Returns the sum of the squares of the arguments
SUMX2MY2	Returns the sum of the difference of squares of corresponding values in two arrays
SUMX2PY2	Returns the sum of the sum of squares of corresponding values in two arrays
SUMXMY2	Returns the sum of squares of differences of corresponding values in two arrays
TAN	Returns the tangent of a number
TANH	Returns the hyperbolic tangent of a number
TRUNC	Truncates a number (when you specify the precision of the truncation)

Indicates a new function in Excel 2007

TABLE A-10   STATISTICAL CATEGORY FUNCTIONS

Function	What It Does
AVEDEV	Returns the average of the absolute deviations of data points from their mean
AVERAGE	Returns the average of its arguments
AVERAGEA	Returns the average of its arguments and includes evaluation of text and logical values
AVERAGEIF*	Returns the average for the cells specified by a given criterion
AVERAGEIFS*	Returns the average for the cells specified by multiple criteria
BETADIST	Returns the cumulative beta probability density function
BETAINV	Returns the inverse of the cumulative beta probability density function
BINOMDIST	Returns the individual term binomial distribution probability
CHIDIST	Returns the one-tailed probability of the chi-squared distribution
CHIINV	Returns the inverse of the one-tailed probability of the chi-squared distribution
CHITEST	Returns the test for independence
CONFIDENCE	Returns the confidence interval for a population mean
CORREL	Returns the correlation coefficient between two data sets
COUNT	Counts how many numbers are in the list of arguments
COUNTA	Counts how many values are in the list of arguments
COUNTBLANK	Counts the number of blank cells in the argument range
COUNTIF	Counts the number of cells that meet the criteria you specify in the argument
COUNTIFS*	Counts the number of cells that meet multiple criteria
COVAR	Returns *covariance*, the average of the products of paired deviations
CRITBINOM	Returns the smallest value for which the cumulative binomial distribution is less than or equal to a criterion value
DEVSQ	Returns the sum of squares of deviations
EXPONDIST	Returns the exponential distribution
FDIST	Returns the F probability distribution

continued

TABLE A-10 STATISTICAL CATEGORY FUNCTIONS *(continued)*

Function	What It Does
FINV	Returns the inverse of the F probability distribution
FISHER	Returns the Fisher transformation
FISHERINV	Returns the inverse of the Fisher transformation
FORECAST	Returns a value along a linear trend
FREQUENCY	Returns a frequency distribution as a vertical array
FTEST	Returns the result of an F-Test
GAMMADIST	Returns the gamma distribution
GAMMAINV	Returns the inverse of the gamma cumulative distribution
GAMMALN	Returns the natural logarithm of the gamma function, G(x)
GEOMEAN	Returns the geometric mean
GROWTH	Returns values along an exponential trend
HARMEAN	Returns the harmonic mean
HYPGEOMDIST	Returns the hypergeometric distribution
INTERCEPT	Returns the intercept of the linear regression line
KURT	Returns the kurtosis of a data set
LARGE	Returns the kth largest value in a data set
LINEST	Returns the parameters of a linear trend
LOGEST	Returns the parameters of an exponential trend
LOGINV	Returns the inverse of the lognormal distribution
LOGNORMDIST	Returns the cumulative lognormal distribution
MAX	Returns the maximum value in a list of arguments, ignoring logical values and text
MAXA	Returns the maximum value in a list of arguments, including logical values and text
MEDIAN	Returns the median of the given numbers
MIN	Returns the minimum value in a list of arguments, ignoring logical values and text
MINA	Returns the minimum value in a list of arguments, including logical values and text

Function	What It Does
MODE	Returns the most common value in a data set
NEGBINOMDIST	Returns the negative binomial distribution
NORMDIST	Returns the normal cumulative distribution
NORMINV	Returns the inverse of the normal cumulative distribution
NORMSDIST	Returns the standard normal cumulative distribution
NORMSINV	Returns the inverse of the standard normal cumulative distribution
PEARSON	Returns the Pearson product moment correlation coefficient
PERCENTILE	Returns the kth percentile of values in a range
PERCENTRANK	Returns the percentage rank of a value in a data set
PERMUT	Returns the number of permutations for a given number of objects
POISSON	Returns the Poisson distribution
PROB	Returns the probability that values in a range are between two limits
QUARTILE	Returns the quartile of a data set
RANK	Returns the rank of a number in a list of numbers
RSQ	Returns the square of the Pearson product moment correlation coefficient
SKEW	Returns the skewness of a distribution
SLOPE	Returns the slope of the linear regression line
SMALL	Returns the kth smallest value in a data set
STANDARDIZE	Returns a normalized value
STDEV	Estimates standard deviation based on a sample, ignoring text and logical values
STDEVA	Estimates standard deviation based on a sample, including text and logical values
STDEVP	Calculates standard deviation based on the entire population, ignoring text and logical values
STDEVPA	Calculates standard deviation based on the entire population, including text and logical values
STEYX	Returns the standard error of the predicted y-value for each x in the regression

continued

TABLE A-10   STATISTICAL CATEGORY FUNCTIONS *(continued)*

Function	What It Does
TDIST	Returns the student's t-distribution
TINV	Returns the inverse of the student's t-distribution
TREND	Returns values along a linear trend
TRIMMEAN	Returns the mean of the interior of a data set
TTEST	Returns the probability associated with a student's t-Test
VAR	Estimates variance based on a sample, ignoring logical values and text
VARA	Estimates variance based on a sample, including logical values and text
VARP	Calculates variance based on the entire population, ignoring logical values and text
VARPA	Calculates variance based on the entire population, including logical values and text
WEIBULL	Returns the Weibull distribution
ZTEST	Returns the two-tailed P-value of a z-test

Indicates a new function in Excel 2007

TABLE A-11   TEXT CATEGORY FUNCTIONS

Function	What It Does
BAHTTEXT	Converts a number to Baht text
CHAR	Returns the character specified by the code number
CLEAN	Removes all nonprintable characters from text
CODE	Returns a numeric code for the first character in a text string
CONCATENATE	Joins several text items into one text item
DOLLAR	Converts a number to text, using currency format
EXACT	Checks whether two text values are identical
FIND	Finds one text value within another (case sensitive)
FIXED	Formats a number as text with a fixed number of decimals
LEFT	Returns the leftmost characters from a text value

Part VII

Function	What It Does
LEN	Returns the number of characters in a text string
LOWER	Converts text to lowercase
MID	Returns a specific number of characters from a text string, starting at the position you specify
PROPER	Capitalizes the first letter in each word of a text value
REPLACE	Replaces characters within text
REPT	Repeats text a given number of times
RIGHT	Returns the rightmost characters from a text value
SEARCH	Finds one text value within another (not case sensitive)
SUBSTITUTE	Substitutes new text for old text in a text string
T	Returns the text referred to by value
TEXT	Formats a number and converts it to text
TRIM	Removes excess spaces from text
UPPER	Converts text to uppercase
VALUE	Converts a text argument to a number

Appendix B

Using Custom Number Formats

Although Excel provides a good variety of built-in number formats, you may find that none of these suits your needs. This appendix describes how to create custom number formats and provides many examples.

About Number Formatting

By default, all cells use the General number format. This is basically a "what you type is what you get" format. If the cell is not wide enough to show the entire number, the General format rounds numbers with decimals and uses scientific notation for large numbers. In many cases, you may want to format a cell with something other than the General number format.

The key thing to remember about number formatting is that it affects only how a value is displayed. The actual number remains intact, and any formulas that use a formatted number use the actual number.

NOTE

An exception to this rule occurs if you specify the Precision as Displayed option on the Calculation tab of the Options dialog box. If that option is in effect, formulas will use the values that are actually displayed in the cells. In general, using this option is not a good idea because it changes the underlying values in your worksheet.

One more thing to keep in mind: If you use Excel's Find and Replace dialog box (displayed by choosing Home⇨Editing⇨Find & Select⇨Find, characters that are displayed a result of number formatting (for example, a currency symbol) are not searchable.

Automatic Number Formatting

Excel is smart enough to perform some formatting for you automatically. For example, if you enter **12.3%** into a cell, Excel knows that you want to use a percentage format and applies it automatically. If you use commas to separate thousands (such as 123,456), Excel applies comma formatting for you. And if you precede your value with a currency symbol, Excel formats the cell for currency.

NOTE

You have an option when it comes to entering values into cells formatted as a percentage. Access the Excel Options and click the Advanced tab. If the check box labeled Enable Automatic Percent Entry is checked (the default setting), you can simply enter a normal value into a cell formatted to display as a percent (for example, enter **12.5** for 12.5%). If this check box isn't checked, you must enter the value as a decimal (for example, **.125** for 12.5%).

Excel automatically applies a built-in number format to a cell based on the following criteria:

- If a number contains a slash (/), it may be converted to a date format or a fraction format.

- If a number contains a hyphen (-), it may be converted to a date format.

- If a number contains a colon (:), or is followed by a space and the letter A or P, it may be converted to a time format.

- If a number contains the letter E (in either uppercase or lowercase), it may be converted to scientific notation or exponential format.

TIP

To avoid automatic number formatting when you enter a value, pre-format the cell with the desired number format or precede your entry with an apostrophe. (The apostrophe makes the entry text, so number formatting is not applied to the cell.)

Formatting Numbers by Using the Ribbon

The Number group on the Home tab of the Ribbon contains several controls that enable you to apply common number formats quickly. The Number Format drop-down control gives you quick access to 11 common number formats. In addition, the Number group contains some button. When you click one of these buttons, the selected cells take on the specified number format. Table B-1 summarizes the formats that these buttons perform in the U.S. English version of Excel.

NOTE

Some of these buttons actually apply predefined styles to the selected cells. Access Excel's styles by using the style gallery, in the Styles group of the Home tab.

TABLE B-1 NUMBER-FORMATTING BUTTONS ON THE RIBBON

Button Name	Formatting Applied
Accounting Number Format	Adds a dollar sign to the left, separates thousands with a comma, and displays the value with two digits to the right of the decimal point. This is a drop-down control, so you can select other common currency symbols.
Percent Style	Displays the value as a percentage, with no decimal places.
Comma Style	Separates thousands with a comma and displays the value with two digits to the right of the decimal place.
Increase Decimal	Increases the number of digits to the right of the decimal point by one.
Decrease Decimal	Decreases the number of digits to the right of the decimal point by one.

Using Shortcut Keys to Format Numbers

Another way to apply number formatting is to use shortcut keys. Table B-2 summarizes the shortcut key combinations that you can use to apply common number formatting to the selected cells or range.

TABLE B-2 NUMBER-FORMATTING KEYBOARD SHORTCUTS

Key Combination	Formatting Applied
Ctrl+Shift+~	General number format (that is, unformatted values).
Ctrl+Shift+$	Currency format with two decimal places. (Negative numbers appear in parentheses.)

continued

TABLE B-2   NUMBER-FORMATTING KEYBOARD SHORTCUTS *(continued)*

Key Combination	Formatting Applied
Ctrl+Shift+%	Percentage format with no decimal places.
Ctrl+Shift+^	Scientific notation number format with two decimal places.
Ctrl+Shift+#	Date format with the day, month, and year.
Ctrl+Shift+@	Time format with the hour, minute, and AM or PM.
Ctrl+Shift+!	Two decimal places, thousands separator, and a hyphen for negative values.

Using the Format Cells Dialog Box to Format Numbers

For maximum control of number formatting, use the Number tab of the Format Cells dialog box. You can access this dialog box in any of several ways:

- Click the dialog box selector in the Home⇨Number group.
- Choose Home⇨Number⇨Number Format⇨More Number Formats.
- Press Ctrl+1.

The Number tab of the Format Cells dialog box contains 12 categories of number formats from which to choose. When you select a category from the list box, the right side of the dialog box changes to display appropriate options.

Following is a list of the number-format categories along with some general comments:

- **General:** The default format; it displays numbers as integers, decimals, or in scientific notation if the value is too wide to fit into the cell.

- **Number:** Enables you to specify the number of decimal places, whether to use your system thousands separator (for example, a comma) to separate thousands, and how to display negative numbers.

- **Currency:** Enables you to specify the number of decimal places, to choose a currency symbol, and to display negative numbers. This format always uses the system thousands separator symbol (for example, a comma) to separate thousands.

- **Accounting:** Differs from the Currency format in that the currency symbols always line up vertically, regardless of the number of digits displayed in the value.

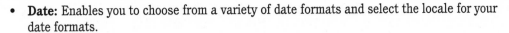

- **Date:** Enables you to choose from a variety of date formats and select the locale for your date formats.

- **Time:** Enables you to choose from a number of time formats and select the locale for your time formats.

- **Percentage:** Enables you to choose the number of decimal places; always displays a percent sign.

- **Fraction:** Enables you to choose from among nine fraction formats.

- **Scientific:** Displays numbers in exponential notation (with an E): 2.00E+05 = 200,000. 2.05E+05 = 205,000. You can choose the number of decimal places to display to the left of E.

- **Text:** When applied to a value, causes Excel to treat the value as text (even if it looks like a value). This feature is useful for such items as numerical part numbers and credit card numbers.

- **Special:** Contains additional number formats. The list varies, depending on the Locale you choose. For the English (United States) locale, the formatting options are Zip Code, Zip Code +4, Phone Number, and Social Security Number.

- **Custom:** Enables you to define custom number formats not included in any of the other categories.

NOTE

If the cell displays a series of hash marks after you apply a number format (such as ########), it usually means that the column isn't wide enough to display the value by using the number format that you selected. Either make the column wider (by dragging the right border of the column header) or change the number format. A series of hash marks also can mean that the cell contains an invalid date or time.

Creating a Custom Number Format

The Custom category on the Number tab of the Format Cells dialog box (see Figure B-1) enables you to create number formats not included in any of the other categories. Excel gives you a great deal of flexibility in creating custom number formats.

TIP

Custom number formats are stored with the workbook in which they are defined. To make the custom format available in a different workbook, you can just copy a cell that uses the custom format to the other workbook.

Figure B-1: The Number tab of the Format Cells dialog box.

You construct a number format by specifying a series of codes as a *number format string*. You enter this code sequence in the Type field after you select the Custom category on the Number tab of the Format Cells dialog box. Here's an example of a simple number format code:

`0.000`

This code consists of placeholders and a decimal point; it tells Excel to display the value with three digits to the right of the decimal place. Here's another example:

`00000`

This custom number format has five placeholders and displays the value with five digits (no decimal point). This format is good to use when the cell holds a five-digit ZIP code. (In fact, this is the code actually used by the Zip Code format in the Special category.) When you format the cell with this number format and then enter a ZIP code, such as 06604 (Bridgeport, CT), the value is displayed with the leading zero. If you enter this number into a cell with the General number format, it displays 6604 (no leading zero).

Scroll through the list of number formats in the Custom category of the Format Cells dialog box to see many more examples. In many cases, you can use one of these codes as a starting point, and you'll need to customize it only slightly.

ON THE CD

The companion CD-ROM contains a workbook with many custom number format examples. The file is named `number formats.xlsx`.

Parts of a Number Format String

A custom format string can have up to four sections, which enables you to specify different format codes for positive numbers, negative numbers, zero values, and text. You do so by separating the codes with a semicolon. The codes are arranged in the following order:

`Positive format; Negative format; Zero format; Text format`

If you don't use all four sections of a format string, Excel interprets the format string as follows:

- **If you use only one section:** The format string applies to all types of entries.
- **If you use two sections:** The first section applies to positive values and zeros, and the second section applies to negative values.
- **If you use three sections:** The first section applies to positive values, the second section applies to negative values, and the third section applies to zeros.
- **If you use all four sections:** The last section applies to text stored in the cell.

The following is an example of a custom number format that specifies a different format for each of these types:

`[Green]General;[Red]General;[Black]General;[Blue]General`

This custom number format example takes advantage of the fact that colors have special codes. A cell formatted with this custom number format displays its contents in a different color, depending on the value. When a cell is formatted with this custom number format, a positive number is green, a negative number is red, a zero is black, and text is blue.

CROSS REF

If you want to apply cell formatting automatically (such as text or background color) based on the cell's contents, a much better solution is to use Excel's Conditional Formatting feature. Chapter 19 covers conditional formatting.

Pre-formatting Cells

Usually, you'll apply number formats to cells that already contain values. You also can format cells with a specific number format *before* you make an entry. Then, when you enter information, it takes on the format that you specified. You can pre-format specific cells, entire rows or columns, or even the entire worksheet.

Rather than pre-format an entire worksheet, however, you can change the number format for the Normal style. (Unless you specify otherwise, all cells use the Normal style.) Change the Normal style by displaying the Style gallery (choose Home⇨Styles). Right-click the Normal style icon and then choose Modify to display the Style dialog box. In the Style dialog box, click the Format button and then choose the new number format that you want to use for the Normal style.

Custom Number Format Codes

Table B-3 lists the formatting codes available for custom formats, along with brief descriptions.

TABLE B-3   CODES USED TO CREATE CUSTOM NUMBER FORMATS

Code	Comments
General	Displays the number in General format.
#	Digit placeholder. Displays only significant digits, and does not display insignificant zeros.
0 (zero)	Digit placeholder. Displays insignificant zeros if a number has fewer digits than there are zeros in the format.
?	Digit placeholder. Adds spaces for insignificant zeros on either side of the decimal point so that decimal points align when formatted with a fixed-width font. You can also use ? for fractions that have varying numbers of digits.
.	Decimal point.
%	Percentage.
,	Thousands separator.
E- E+ e- e+	Scientific notation

Code	Comments
$ - + / ( ) : space	Displays this character.
\	Displays the next character in the format.
*	Repeats the next character, to fill the column width.
_ (underscore)	Leaves a space equal to the width of the next character.
"text"	Displays the text inside the double quotation marks.
@	Text placeholder.
[color]	Displays the characters in the color specified. Can be any of the following text strings (not case sensitive): Black, Blue, Cyan, Green, Magenta, Red, White, or Yellow.
[Color n]	Displays the corresponding color in the color palette, where n is a number from 0 to 56.
[condition value]	Enables you to set your own criterion for each section of a number format.

Table B-4 lists the codes used to create custom formats for dates and times.

Where Did Those Number Formats Come From?

Excel may create custom number formats without you realizing it. When you use the Increase Decimal or Decrease Decimal button on the Home⇨Number group of the Ribbon (or in the Mini Toolbar), Excel creates new custom number formats, which appear on the Number tab of the Format Cells dialog box. For example, if you click the Increase Decimal button five times, the following custom number formats are created:

```
0.0
0.000
0.0000
0.000000
```

A format string for two decimal places is not created because that format string is built in.

TABLE B-4   CODES USED IN CREATING CUSTOM FORMATS FOR DATES AND TIMES

Code	Comments
m	Displays the month as a number without leading zeros (1–12).
mm	Displays the month as a number with leading zeros (01–12).
mmm	Displays the month as an abbreviation (Jan–Dec).
mmmm	Displays the month as a full name (January–December).
mmmmm	Displays the first letter of the month (J–D).
d	Displays the day as a number without leading zeros (1–31).
dd	Displays the day as a number with leading zeros (01–31).
ddd	Displays the day as an abbreviation (Sun–Sat).
dddd	Displays the day as a full name (Sunday–Saturday).
yy or yyyy	Displays the year as a two-digit number (00–99) or as a four-digit number (1900–9999).
h or hh	Displays the hour as a number without leading zeros (0–23) or as a number with leading zeros (00–23).
m or mm	Displays the minute as a number without leading zeros (0–59) or as a number with leading zeros (00–59).
s or ss	Displays the second as a number without leading zeros (0–59) or as a number with leading zeros (00–59).
[ ]	Displays hours greater than 24 or minutes or seconds greater than 60.
AM/PM	Displays the hour using a 12-hour clock. If no AM/PM indicator is used, the hour uses a 24-hour clock.

Custom Number Format Examples

The remainder of this appendix consists of useful examples of custom number formats. You can use most of these format codes as-is. Others may require slight modification to meet your needs.

Scaling Values

You can use a custom number format to scale a number. For example, if you work with very large numbers, you may want to display the numbers in thousands (that is, displaying 1,000,000 as 1,000). The actual number, of course, will be used in calculations that involve that cell. The formatting affects only how it is displayed.

DISPLAYING VALUES IN THOUSANDS

The following format string displays values without the last three digits to the left of the decimal place, and no decimal places. In other words, the value appears as if it's divided by 1,000 and rounded to no decimal places.

```
#,###,
```

A variation of this format string follows. A value with this number format appears as if it's divided by 1,000 and rounded to two decimal places.

```
#,###.00,
```

Table B-5 shows examples of these number formats.

TABLE B-5   EXAMPLES OF DISPLAYING VALUES IN THOUSANDS

Value	Number Format	Display
123456	#,###,	123
1234565	#,###,	1,235
–323434	#,###,	–323
123123.123	#,###,	123
499	#,###,	(blank)
500	#,###,	1
123456	#,###.00,	123.46
1234565	#,###.00,	1,234.57
–323434	#,###.00,	–323.43
123123.123	#,###.00,	123.12
499	#,###.00,	.50
500	#,###.00,	.50

DISPLAYING VALUES IN HUNDREDS

The following format string displays values in hundreds, with two decimal places. A value with this number format appears as if it's divided by 100 and rounded to two decimal places.

```
0"."00
```

Table B-6 shows examples of these number formats.

TABLE B-6   EXAMPLES OF DISPLAYING VALUES IN HUNDREDS

Value	Number Format	Display
546	0"."00	5.46
100	0"."00	1.00
9890	0"."00	98.90
500	0"."00	5.00
–500	0"."00	–5.00
0	0"."00	0.00

DISPLAYING VALUES IN MILLIONS

The following format string displays values in millions, with no decimal places. A value with this number appears as if it's divided by 1,000,000, and rounded to no decimal places.

```
#,###,,
```

A variation of this format string follows. A value with this number appears as if it's divided by 1,000,000, and rounded to two decimal places.

```
#,###.00,,
```

Another variation follows. This adds the letter M to the end of the value.

```
#,###,,M
```

The following format string is a bit more complex. It adds the letter M to the end of the value — and also displays negative values in parentheses as well as displaying zeros.

```
#,###.0,,"M"_);(#,###.0,,"M)";0.0"M"_)
```

Table B-7 shows examples of these format strings.

TABLE B-7   EXAMPLES OF DISPLAYING VALUES IN MILLIONS

Value	Number Format	Display
123456789	#,###,,	123
1.23457E+11	#,###,,	123,457
1000000	#,###,,	1
5000000	#,###,,	5
–5000000	#,###,,	–5
0	#,###,,	(blank)
123456789	#,###.00,,	123.46
1.23457E+11	#,###.00,,	123,457.00
1000000	#,###.00,,	1.00
5000000	#,###.00,,	5.00
–5000000	#,###.00,,	–5.00
0	#,###.00,,	.00
123456789	#,###,,"M"	123M
1.23457E+11	#,###,,"M"	123,457M
1000000	#,###,,"M"	1M
5000000	#,###,,"M"	5M
–5000000	#,###,,"M"	–5M
0	#,###,,"M"	M
123456789	#,###.0,,"M"_);(#,###.0,,"M)";0.0"M"_)	123.5M
1.23457E+11	#,###.0,,"M"_);(#,###.0,,"M)";0.0"M"_)	123,456.8M
1000000	#,###.0,,"M"_);(#,###.0,,"M)";0.0"M"_)	1.0M
5000000	#,###.0,,"M"_);(#,###.0,,"M)";0.0"M"_)	5.0M
–5000000	#,###.0,,"M"_);(#,###.0,,"M)";0.0"M"_)	(5.0M)
0	#,###.0,,"M"_);(#,###.0,,"M)";0.0"M"_)	0.0M

ADDING ZEROS TO A VALUE

The following format string displays a value with three additional zeros and no decimal places. A value with this number format appears as if it's rounded to no decimal places and then multiplied by 1,000.

```
#",000"
```

Examples of this format string, plus a variation that adds six zeros, are shown in Table B-8.

TABLE B-8   EXAMPLES OF DISPLAYING A VALUE WITH EXTRA ZEROS

Value	Number Format	Display
1	#",000"	1,000
1.5	#",000"	2,000
43	#",000"	43,000
–54	#",000"	–54,000
5.5	#",000"	6,000
0.5	#",000,000"	1,000,000
0	#",000,000"	,000,000
1	#",000,000"	1,000,000
1.5	#",000,000"	2,000,000
43	#",000,000"	43,000,000
–54	#",000,000"	–54,000,000
5.5	#",000,000"	6,000,000
0.5	#",000,000"	1,000,000

Hiding Zeros

In the following format string, the third element of the string is empty, which causes zero value cells to display as blank:

```
General;-General;
```

This format string uses the General format for positive and negative values. You can, of course, substitute any other format codes for the positive and negative parts of the format string.

Displaying Leading Zeros

To display leading zeros, create a custom number format that uses the 0 character. For example, if you want all numbers to display with ten digits, use the number format string that follows. Values with fewer than ten digits will display with leading zeros.

```
0000000000
```

You also can force all numbers to display with a fixed number of leading zeros. The format string that follows, for example, prepends three zeros to each number:

```
"000"#
```

In the following example, the format string uses the repeat character code (an asterisk) to apply enough leading zeros to fill the entire width of the cell:

```
*00
```

Displaying Fractions

Excel supports quite a few built-in fraction number formats. (Select the Fraction category from the Number tab of the Format Cells dialog box.) For example, to display the value .125 as a fraction with 8 as the denominator, select As Eighths (4/8) from the Type list.

You can use a custom format string to create other fractional formats. For example, the following format string displays a value in 50ths:

```
# ??/50
```

The following format string displays a value in terms of fractional dollars. For example, the value 154.87 is displayed as 154 and 87/100 Dollars.

```
0 "and "??/100 "Dollars"
```

The following example displays the value in sixteenths, with an appended double quotation mark. This format string is useful when you deal with inches (for example, $\frac{3}{16}$").

```
# ??/16\"
```

Displaying N/A for Text

The following number format string uses General formatting for all cell entries except text. Text entries appear as N/A.

```
0.0;0.0;0.0;"N/A"
```

You can, of course, modify the format string to display specific formats for values. The following variation displays values with one decimal place:

```
0.0;0.0;0.0;"N/A"
```

Displaying Text in Quotes

The following format string displays numbers normally but surrounds text with double quotation marks:

```
General;General;General;\"@\"
```

Repeating A Cell Entry

The following number format is perhaps best suited as an April Fool's gag played on an office mate. It displays the contents of the cell three times. For example, if the cell contains the text Budget, the cell displays Budget Budget Budget. If the cell contains the number 12, it displays as 12 12 12.

```
@ @ @
```

Displaying a Negative Sign on the Right

The following format string displays negative values with the negative sign to the right of the number. Positive values have an additional space on the right, so both positive and negative numbers align properly on the right.

```
0.00_-;0.00-
```

> ### Testing Custom Number Formats
>
> When you create a custom number format, don't overlook the Sample box in the Number tab of the Format Cells dialog box. This box displays the value in the active cell using the format string in the Type box.
>
> It's a good idea to test your custom number formats by using the following data: a positive value, a negative value, a zero value, and text. Often, creating a custom number format takes several attempts. Each time you edit a format string, it is added to the list. When you finally get the correct format string, access the Format Cells dialog box one more time and delete your previous attempts.

To make the negative numbers more prominent, you can add a color code to the negative part of the number format string:

```
0.00_-;[Red]0.00-
```

Conditional Number Formatting

Conditional formatting refers to formatting that is applied based on the contents of a cell. Excel's Conditional Formatting feature provides the most efficient way to perform conditional formatting of numbers, but you also can use custom number formats.

NOTE

A conditional number formatting string is limited to three conditions: Two of them are explicit, and the third one is implied (that is, everything else). The conditions are enclosed in square brackets and must be simple numeric comparisons.

The following format string displays different text (no value), depending on the value in the cell. This format string essentially separates the numbers into three groups: less than or equal to 4, greater than or equal to 8, and other.

```
[<=4]"Low"* 0;[>=8]"High"* 0;"Medium"* 0
```

The following number format is useful for telephone numbers. Values greater than 9999999 (that is, numbers with area codes) are displayed as (xxx) xxx-xxxx. Other values (numbers without area codes) are displayed as xxx-xxxx.

```
[>9999999](000) 000-0000;000-0000
```

For U.S. ZIP codes, you might want to use the format string that follows. This displays ZIP codes using five digits. But if the number is greater than 99999, it uses the ZIP-plus-four format (xxxxx-xxxx).

```
[>99999]00000-0000;00000
```

Coloring Values

Custom number format strings can display the cell contents in various colors. The following format string, for example, displays positive numbers in red, negative numbers in green, zero values in black, and text in blue:

```
[Red]General;[Green]-General;[Black]General;[Blue]General
```

Following is another example of a format string that uses colors. Positive values are displayed normally; negative numbers and text cause Error! to be displayed in red.

```
General;[Red]"Error!";0;[Red]"Error!"
```

Using the following format string, values that are less than 2 are displayed in red. Values greater than 4 are displayed in green. Everything else (text, or values between 2 and 4) displays in black.

```
[Red][<2]General;[Green][>4]General;[Black]General
```

As seen in the preceding examples, Excel recognizes color names such as [Red] and [Blue]. It also can use other colors from the color palette, indexed by a number. The following format string, for example, displays the cell contents using the sixteenth color in the color palette:

```
[Color16]General
```

 NOTE

Excel's conditional formatting is a much better way to color text in a cell based on the cell's value.

Formatting Dates and Times

When you enter a date into a cell, Excel formats the date using the system short date format. You can change this format using the Windows Control Panel (Regional and Language Options).

Excel provides many useful built-in date and time formats. Table B-9 shows some other custom date and time formats that you may find useful. The first column of the table shows the date/time serial number.

TABLE B-9   USEFUL CUSTOM DATE AND TIME FORMATS

Value	Number Format	Display
39264	mmmm d, yyyy (dddd)	July 1, 2007 (Sunday)
39264	"It's" dddd!	It's Sunday!
39264	dddd, mm/dd/yyyy	Sunday, 07/01/2007
39264	"Month: "mmm	Month: July
39264	General (m/d/yyyy)	39264 (7/1/2007)

Value	Number Format	Display
0.345	h "Hours"	8 Hours
0.345	h:mm o'clock	8:16 o'clock
0.345	h:mm a/p"m"	8:16 am
0.78	h:mm a/p".m."	6:43 p.m.

CROSS REF

See Chapter 6 for more information about Excel's date and time serial number system.

Displaying Text with Numbers

The ability to display text with a value is one of the most useful benefits of using a custom number format. To add text, just create the number format string as usual (or use a built-in number format as a starting point) and put the text within quotation marks. The following number format string, for example, displays a value with the text (US Dollars) added to the end:

```
#,##0.00 "(US Dollars)"
```

Here's another example that displays text before the number:

```
"Average: "0.00
```

If you use the preceding number format, you'll find that the negative sign appears before the text for negative values. To display number signs properly, use this variation:

```
"Average: "0.00;"Average: "-0.00
```

The following format string displays a value with the words Dollars and Cents. For example, the number 123.45 displays as 123 Dollars and .45 Cents.

```
0 "Dollars and" .00 "Cents"
```

Displaying a Zero with Dashes

The following number format string displays zero values as a series of dashes:

```
#,##0.0;-###0.0;------
```

Formatting Numbers Using the TEXT Function

Excel's TEXT function accepts a number format string as its second argument. For example, the following formula displays the contents of cell A1 using a custom number format that displays a fraction:

```
=TEXT(A1,"# ??/50")
```

However, not all formatting codes work when used in this manner. For example, colors and repeating characters are ignored. The following formula does not display the contents of cell A1 in red:

```
=TEXT(A1,"[Red]General")
```

You can, of course, create lots of variations. For example, you can replace the six hyphens with any of the following:

```
<0>
-0-
~~
"<NULL>"
"[NULL]"
```

 NOTE

When using angle brackets or square brackets, you must place them within quotation marks.

Using Special Symbols

Your number format strings can use special symbols, such as the copyright symbol, degree symbol, and so on.

The easiest way to use insert a symbol into a number format string is to enter it into a cell. Copy the character and then paste it into your custom number format string (using Ctrl+V). Use the Insert⇨Text⇨Symbol command, which displays the Insert Symbol dialog box, to enter a special character into a cell.

Suppressing Certain Types of Entries

You can use number formatting to hide certain types of entries. For example, the following format string displays text but not values:

```
;;
```

Displaying a Number Format String in a Cell

Excel doesn't have a worksheet function that displays the number format for a specified cell. You can, however, create your own function using VBA. Insert the following function procedure into a VBA module:

```
Function NumberFormat(cell) As String
'   Returns the number format string for a cell
    Application.Volatile True
    NumberFormat = cell.Range("A1").NumberFormat
End Function
```

Then you can create a formula such as the following:

```
=NumberFormat(C4)
```

This formula returns the number format for cell C4. If you change a number format, use Ctrl+Alt+F9 to force the function to be reevaluated.

This function can be useful in formulas that calculate a conditional sum. For example, you can create a formula that sums only the cells that use a particular number format. See Chapter 7 for information about computing conditional sums.

This format string displays values (with one decimal place) but not text or zeros:

```
0.0;-0.0;;
```

This format string displays everything except zeros (values display with one decimal place):

```
0.0;-0.0;;@
```

You can use the following format string to completely hide the contents of a cell:

```
;;;
```

Note that when the cell is activated, however, the cell's contents are visible on the formula bar.

Cross Ref

Refer to Part VI for more information about creating custom worksheet functions using VBA.

Filling a Cell with a Repeating Character

The asterisk (*) symbol specifies a repeating character in a number format string. The repeating character completely fills the cell, and adjusts if the column width changes. The following format string, for example, displays the contents of a cell padded on the right with dashes:

```
General*-;-General*-;General*-;General*-
```

Displaying Leading Dots

The following custom number format is a variation on the accounting format. Using this number format displays the dollar sign on the left and the value on the right. The space in between is filled with dots.

```
_($*.#,##0.00_);_($*.(#,##0.00);_($* "-"??_);_(@_)
```

Appendix C

Additional Excel Resources

If I've done my job, the information provided in this book will be very useful to you. The book, however, cannot cover every conceivable topic. Therefore, I've compiled a list of additional resources that you may find helpful. I classify these resources into four categories: the Excel Help system, Microsoft technical support, Internet newsgroups, and Internet Web sites.

The Excel Help System

Some users tend to forget about an excellent source of information that's readily available: the Excel Help system. This Help information is available by clicking the question mark icon in the upper-right corner of Excel's window. Or, just press F1. Either of these methods displays Excel Help in a new window. Then, type your search query and click Search.

TIP

The Search button is a drop-down control that lets you specify what and where to search.

The Excel Help system isn't perfect; it often provides only superficial help and ignores some topics altogether. But, if you're stuck, a quick search of the Help system may be worth a try.

Microsoft Technical Support

Technical support is the common term for assistance provided by a software vendor. In this case, I'm talking about assistance that comes directly from Microsoft. Microsoft technical support is available in several different forms.

Support Options

The Microsoft support options are constantly changing. To find out what options are available (both free and fee-based), go to: `http://support.microsoft.com`

Microsoft Knowledge Base

Perhaps your best bet for solving a problem may be the Microsoft Knowledge Base, which is the primary Microsoft product information source. It's an extensive, searchable database that consists of tens of thousands of detailed articles containing technical information, bug lists, fix lists, and more.

You have free and unlimited access to the Knowledge Base via the Internet. To access the Knowledge Base, use the following URL and then click Search the Knowledge Base: `http://support.microsoft.com/search`

Microsoft Excel Home Page

The official home page of Excel is at: `http://www.microsoft.com/office/excel`

This site contains a variety of material, such as tips, templates, answers to questions, training materials, and links to companion products.

Microsoft Office Home Page

For information about Office 2007 (including Excel), try this site: `http://office.microsoft.com`

You'll find product updates, add-ins, examples, and lots of other useful information.

NOTE

As you know, the Internet is a dynamic entity that changes rapidly. Web sites are often reorganized, so a particular URL listed in this appendix may not be available when you try to access it.

Internet Newsgroups

Usenet is an Internet service that provides access to several thousand special interest groups that enable you to communicate with people who share common interests. A newsgroup works like a public bulletin board. You can post a message or questions, and (usually) others reply to your message.

Thousands of newsgroups cover virtually every topic you can think of (and many that you haven't thought of). Typically, questions posed on a newsgroup are answered within 24 hours — assuming, of course, that you ask the questions in a manner that makes others want to reply.

Accessing Newsgroups by Using a Newsreader

You can use newsreader software to access the Usenet newsgroups. Many such programs are available, but probably already have one installed: Microsoft Outlook Express, which is installed with Internet Explorer.

Microsoft maintains an extensive list of newsgroups, including quite a few devoted to Excel. If your ISP doesn't carry the Microsoft newsgroups, you can access them directly from the Microsoft news server. (In fact, that's the preferred method.) You need to configure your newsreader software (not your Web browser) to access the Microsoft news server at this address: `msnews.microsoft.com`

Accessing Newsgroups by Using a Web Browser

As an alternative to using newsreader software, you can read and post to the Microsoft newsgroups directly from your Web browser. This option is often significantly slower than using standard newsgroup software and is best suited for situations in which newsgroup access is prohibited by network policies.

- Access thousands of newsgroups at Google Groups. The URL is

  `http://groups.google.com`

- Access the Microsoft newsgroups (including Excel newsgroups) from this URL:

  `www.microsoft.com/communities/newsgroups/default.mspx`

Table C-1 lists the most popular English-language Excel newsgroups found on the Microsoft news server (and also available at Google Groups).

TABLE C-1   POPULAR EXCEL-RELATED NEWSGROUPS

Newsgroup	Topic
`microsoft.public.excel`	General Excel topics
`microsoft.public.excel.charting`	Building charts with Excel
`microsoft.public.excel.interopoledde`	OLE, DDE, and other cross-application issues
`microsoft.public.excel.macintosh`	Excel issues on the Macintosh operating system
`microsoft.public.excel.misc`	General topics that don't fit one of the other categories
`microsoft.public.excel.newusers`	Help for newcomers to Excel
`microsoft.public.excel.printing`	Printing with Excel
`microsoft.public.excel.programming`	Programming Excel with VBA macros
`microsoft.public.excel.templates`	Spreadsheet Solutions templates and other XLT files
`microsoft.public.excel.worksheet.functions`	Worksheet functions

Searching Newsgroups

The fastest way to find a quick answer to a question is to search the past newsgroup postings. Often, searching past newsgroup postings is an excellent alternative to posting a question to the newsgroup because you can get the answer immediately. Unless your question is very obscure, there's an excellent chance that your question has already been asked and answered. The best source for searching newsgroup postings is Google Groups, at the following Web address: `http://groups.google.com`

How does searching work? Suppose that you have a problem identifying unique values in a range of cells. You can perform a search using the following keywords: `Excel`, `Range`, and `Unique`. The Google search engine probably will find dozens of newsgroup postings that deal with these topics.

If the number of results is too large, refine your search by adding search terms. Sifting through the messages may take a while, but you have an excellent chance of finding an answer to your question. In fact, I estimate that at least 90 percent of the questions posted in the Excel newsgroups can be answered by searching Google.

A Dozen Tips for Posting to a Newsgroup

If you're new to online newsgroups, here are some pointers:

1. Conduct a search upfront to make sure that your question has not already been answered.

2. Make the subject line descriptive. Postings with a subject line such as *Help me!* and *Another Question* is less likely to be answered than postings with a more specific subject, such as *Sizing a Chart's Plot Area*.

3. Specify the Excel version that you use. In many cases, the answer to your question depends on your version of Excel.

4. For best results, ask only one question per message.

5. Make your question as specific as possible.

6. Keep your question brief and to the point but provide enough information so that someone can answer it adequately.

7. Indicate what you've done to try to answer your own question.

8. Post in the appropriate newsgroup, and don't cross-post to other groups unless the question applies to multiple groups.

9. Don't type in all uppercase or all lowercase; check your grammar and spelling.

10. Don't include a file attachment.

11. Avoid posting in HTML format. Plain text is the preferred format.

12. If you request an e-mail reply in addition to a newsgroup reply, don't use an anti-spam e-mail address that requires the responder to modify your address. Why cause extra work for someone doing you a favor?

Web Sites

The World Wide Web (WWW) has dozens of excellent sites devoted to Excel. I list a few of my favorites here.

The Spreadsheet Page

This is my own Web site, which contains files to download, developer tips, instructions for accessing Excel Easter eggs, spreadsheet jokes, an extensive list of links to other Excel sites, and information about my books. The URL is: http://www.j-walk.com/ss

Daily Dose of Excel

This is a frequently updated Weblog created by Dick Kusleika, with about a dozen contributors (including me). It covers a variety of topics, and readers can leave comments. The URL is: `http://dailydoseofexcel.com`

Jon Peltier's Excel Page

Those who frequent the microsoft.public.excel.charting newsgroup are familiar with Jon Peltier. Jon has an uncanny ability to solve practically any chart-related problem. His Web site contains many Excel tips and an extensive collection of charting examples. The URL is: `http://peltiertech.com/Excel`

Pearson Software Consulting

This site, maintained by Chip Pearson, contains dozens of useful examples of VBA and clever formula techniques. The URL is: `www.cpearson.com/excel.htm`

Stephen Bullen's Excel Page

Stephen's Web site contains some fascinating examples of Excel code, including a section titled "They Said It Couldn't Be Done." The URL is: `www.bmsltd.co.uk/excel`

David McRitchie's Excel Pages

David's site is jam-packed with useful Excel information and is updated frequently. The URL is: `www.mvps.org/dmcritchie/excel/excel.htm`

Mr. Excel

Mr. Excel, also known as Bill Jelen, maintains an extensive site devoted to Excel. The site also features a message board. The URL is: `www.mrexcel.com`

Appendix D

What's on the CD-ROM

This appendix provides you with information on the contents of the CD that accompanies this book. For the latest and greatest information, please refer to the ReadMe file located at the root of the CD.

This appendix provides information on the following topics:

- System Requirements
- Using the CD
- Files and software on the CD
- Troubleshooting

System Requirements

Make sure that your computer meets the minimum system requirements listed in this section. If your computer doesn't match up to most of these requirements, you may have a problem using the contents of the CD.

- Windows Vista, Windows XP, or Windows 2000. Microsoft Office 2007 only works with these operating systems.
- A PC with a fast processor running at 500 MHz or faster (800 MHz for Windows Vista).

- At least 256MB of total RAM installed on your computer (512MB RAM for Windows Vista). For best performance, we recommend a minimum of 512MB for all versions of Windows.

- A CD-ROM drive.

Using the CD

To install the items from the CD to your hard drive, follow these steps:

1. Insert the CD into your computer's CD-ROM drive.

   A window appears displaying the License Agreement.

2. Press Accept to continue.

Files and Software on the CD

The following sections provide more details about the software and other materials available on the CD.

Example files for Excel 2007 Formulas

Most of the chapters in this book refer to workbook files that are available on the CD-ROM. Each chapter has its own subdirectory on the CD. For example, you can find the files for Chapter 5 in the following directory:

```
examples\chapter 05
```

The files are all Excel 2007 workbook files that have either of the following extensions:

- XLSX: An Excel workbook file

- XLSM: An Excel workbook file that contains VBA macros

When you open an XLSM file, Excel may display a Security Warning, and tells you that macros have been disabled. To enable macros, click the Options button in the Security Warning panel, and then select the option labeled Enable This Content.

Because the files on this CD are from a trusted source, you may want to copy the files to your hard drive, and then designate the folder as a trusted location. To do so, follow these steps:

1. Open an Explorer window, and select the CD-ROM drive that contains the companion CD-ROM.

2. Right-click the folder that corresponds to the root folder for the samples files, and select Copy from the shortcut menu.

3. Activate the folder on your hard drive where you'd like to copy the files. Right-click the directory, and choose Paste from the shortcut menu.

The CD-ROM files will be copied to a subfolder in the folder you specified in Step 3. To designate this new folder as a trusted location:

1. Start Excel and choose Office➪Excel Options to display the Excel Options dialog box.

2. In the Excel Options dialog box, click the Trust Center tab.

3. Click the Trust Center Settings button.

4. In the Trust Center dialog box, click the Trusted Locations tab.

5. Click the Add New Location button to display the Microsoft Office Trusted Location dialog box.

6. In the Microsoft Office Trusted Location dialog box, click the Browse button, and locate the folder the contains the files copied from the CD-ROM.

7. Make sure you select the option labeled Subfolders Of This Location Are Also Trusted.

After performing these steps, when you open XLSM files from this location, the macros are enabled and you don't see the security warning.

Following is a list of the chapter example workbooks with a brief description of each. Note that not all chapters have example files.

Chapter 1

- `worksheet controls.xlsx` — Demonstrates that use of controls placed directly on a worksheet.

Chapter 5

- `character set.xlsm` — Displays the characters in any font installed on your system.

- `text formula examples.xlsx` — Contains examples of formulas that work with text.

- `text histogram.xlsx` — Demonstrates how to create a simple histogram directly in a range.

Chapter 6

- `day of the week count.xlsx` — Demonstrates how to count the occurrences of a day of the week.

- `gmt conversion.xlsx` — Demonstrates how to convert times between time zones.

- `holidays.xlsx` — Contains formulas to calculate the dates of various U.S. holidays.

- `jogging log.xlsx` — Demonstrates how to work with time values that do not represent a time of day.

- `ordinal dates.xlsx` — Demonstrates a formula to express a date as an ordinal number.

- `time sheet.xlsm` — Calculates a weekly time sheet.

- `work days.xlsx` — Demonstrates the NETWORKDAYS function.

Chapter 7

- `adjustable bins.xlsx` — Demonstrates formula that create adjustable bins for a frequency distribution.

- `basic counting.xlsx` — Demonstrates some basic counting formulas.

- `conditional summing.xlsx` — Demonstrates various ways to calculate conditional sums.

- `count unique.xlsx` — Demonstrates how to count unique (nonduplicated) entries in a range.

- `counting text in a range.xlsx` — Contains various formulas that count occurrences of specific text.

- `cumulative sum.xlsx` — Demonstrates how to display a cumulative sum a values.

- `frequency distribution.xlsx` — Demonstrates three ways to create a frequency distribution.

- `multiple criteria counting.xlsx` — Demonstrates formulas that perform multiple criteria counting.

Chapter 8

- `basic lookup examples.xlsx` — Contains examples of lookup formulas.

- `specialized lookup examples.xlsx` — Contains examples of specialized lookup formulas.

Chapter 9

- database formulas.xlsx — Demonstrates database functions.
- nested subtotals.xlsx — Demonstrates how to create nested subtotals.
- real estate database.xlsx — Contains a table of real estate listings, used to demonstrate advanced filtering.
- real estate table.xlsx — Contains a table of real estate listings, used to demonstrate sorting and filtering.
- table formulas.xlsx — Demonstrate how to use structured references to data within a table.

Chapter 10

- simultaneous equations.xlsx — Demonstrates how to solve simultaneous equations using matrix functions.
- solve right triangle.xlsm — Demonstrates how to solve right triangles.
- unit conversion tables.xlsx — Contains conversion factors for a variety of measurement units.

Chapter 11

- basic financial formulas.xlsx — Demonstrates various financial functions: PV, FV, PMT, RATE, and NPER.
- bond calculations.xlsx — Demonstrates the PRICE and YIELD functions.
- extending basic functions.xlsx — Demonstrates how to combine various financial functions.
- payment components.xlsx — Demonstrates the IPMT and PPMT functions.
- rate conversion.xlsx — Demonstrates the EFFECT and NOMINAL functions.

Chapter 12

- depreciation.xlsx — Demonstrates the depreciation functions.
- fvschedule.xlsx — Demonstrates the FVSCHEDULE function.
- internal rate of return.xlsx — Demonstrates the IRR function.
- irregular cash flows.xlsx — Demonstrates the XMPV and XIRR functions.

- `multiple irr.xlsx` — Demonstrates the MIRR function.
- `net present value.xlsx` — Demonstrates the NPV function.

Chapter 13

- `amortization.xlsx` — Contains a simple loan amortization schedule.
- `financial statements.xlsx` — Contains several types of financial statements.
- `indices.xlsx` — Demonstrates how to create indices.
- `loan data tables.xlsx` — Demonstrates a one-way and a two-way data table.

Chapter 15

- `array formula calendar.xlsx` — Demonstrates how to display a calendar using a single multi-cell array formula.
- `logical functions.xlsx` — Demonstrates some inconsistencies with logical functions.
- `multi-cell array formulas.xlsx` — Demonstrates various multi-cell array formulas.
- `single-cell array formulas.xlsx` — Demonstrates various single-cell array formulas.

Chapter 16

- `iterative chart animation.xlsx` — Contains an example of an animated chart based on an intentional circular reference.
- `net profit (circular).xlsm` — Demonstrates an intentional circular reference.
- `net profit (not circular).xlsx` — Demonstrates an alternative to using a curricular reference formula.
- `recursive equations.xlsx` — Demonstrates how to solve recursive equations by using an intentional circular reference.
- `simultaneous equations.xlsx` — Demonstrates how to solve simultaneous equations by using an intentional circular reference.
- `unique random integers.xlsx` — Demonstrates how to generate a list of unique random integers by using an intentional circular reference.

CHAPTER 17

- `box plot.xlsx` — Demonstrates how to create a box plot.
- `chart from combo box.xlsx` — Demonstrates how to display a chart series by selecting the data from a combo box.
- `clock chart.xlsm` — Displays a fully functional analog clock, created with an XY chart.
- `comparative histogram.xlsx` — Demonstrates how to create a comparative histogram.
- `conditional colors.xlsx` — Demonstrates how to create a column chart with colors that depend on the value of each data point.
- `function plot 2D.xlsx` — Plots functions with one variable.
- `function plot 3D.xlsm` — Plots functions with two variables.
- `gantt chart.xlsx` — Demonstrates how to create a Gantt chart.
- `gauge chart.xlsx` — Demonstrates how to create a gauge chart.
- `hypocycloid - animated.xlsm` — Plots an animated hypocycloid curve.
- `hypocycloid chart.xlsx` — Plots a hypocycloid curve.
- `linear trendline.xlsx` — Demonstrates linear trendlines.
- `nonlinear trendlines.xlsx` — Demonstrates nonlinear trendlines.
- `plot circles.xlsx` — Demonstrates how to plot a circle using an XY chart.
- `plot every nth data point.xlsx` — Demonstrates how to plot every nth value in a chart.
- `plot last n data points.xlsx` — Demonstrates how to plot the most recent n values in a chart.
- `thermometer chart.xlsx` — Demonstrates how to create a thermometer chart.

CHAPTER 18

- `bank accounts.xlsx` — The bank account pivot table examples.
- `calculated fields and items.xlsx` — The pivot table calculated fields and items example.
- `county data.xlsx` — A pivot table example.
- `employee list.xlsx` — The pivot table grouping example.
- `hourly readings.xlsx` — The pivot table grouping by time example.
- `income and expense.xlsx` — The pivot table referencing example.

- `music list.xlsx` — The pivot table report example.
- `sales by date.xlsx` — The pivot table grouping by date example.
- `test scores.xlsx` — The pivot table frequency distribution example.

CHAPTER 19

- `conditional formatting examples.xlsx` — Demonstrates formatting examples.
- `conditional formatting formulas.xlsx` — Demonstrates conditional formatting formulas.
- `conditional formatting with VBA functions.xlsm` — Demonstrates conditional formatting using VBA functions.
- `daily staffing level.xlsx` — Demonstrates a conditional formatting color scale.
- `data bars examples.xlsx` — Demonstrates conditional formatting data bars.
- `data validation examples.xlsx` — Contains data validation examples.
- `extreme color scale.xlsx` — Demonstrates a conditional formatting color scale.
- `icon set examples.xlsx` — Demonstrates conditional formatting icon sets.

CHAPTER 20

- `credit card validation.xlsx` — Contains a megaformula to determine if a numbers is a valid credit card number.
- `name generator.xlsx` — Contains a megaformula to generate random names.
- `no middle name.xlsx` — Contains a megaformula to remove middle names from full names.
- `position of last space.xlsx` — Contains a megaformula to determine the position of the last space character in a text string.
- `time test intermediate.xlsx` — Uses intermediate formulas to remove middle names from full names.
- `time test megaformula.xlsx` — Uses megaformulas to remove middle names from full names.
- `total interest.xlsx` — Demonstrates a simple megaformula.

CHAPTER 24

- `function examples.xlsm` — Contains VBA function examples.

CHAPTER 25

- `celltype function.xlsm` — Contains a VBA function that describes the contents of a cell.

- `commission function.xlsm` — Contains a VBA function to calculate sales commission.

- `counting functions.xlsm` — Contains VBA functions that perform counting.

- `date functions.xlsm` — Contains VBA functions that work with dates.

- `extended data functions help.docx` — A Word document that describes the functions in extended date functions.xlsm.

- `extended date functions.xlsm` — Contains a VBA functions that work with pre-1900 dates.

- `last nonempty cell.xlsm` — Contains VBA functions that return the last non-empty cell in a row or column.

- `monthnames.xlsm` — Contains a VBA function that returns an array.

- `multisheet functions.xlsm` — Contains a VBA function designed to work across multiple worksheets.

- `mysum function.xlsm` — Contains a VBA function that emulates Excel's SUM function.

- `random integers function.xlsm` — Contains a VBA function that returns an array of nonduplicated random integers.

- `range randomize function.xlsm` — Contains a VBA function that returns an array randomized cells.

- `simple functions.xlsm` — Contains simple VBA function examples.

- `spelldollars function.xlsm` — Contains a VBA function that spells out a numerical value.

- `statfunction function.xlsm` — Contains a VBA function that returns a variety of statistical calculations.

- `text manipulation functions.xlsm` — Contains VBA functions that manipulate text.

eBook version of *Excel 2007 Formulas*

The complete text of the book you hold in your hands is provided on the CD in Adobe's Portable Document Format (PDF). You can read and quickly search the content of this PDF file by using Adobe's Acrobat Reader, also included on the CD.

Troubleshooting

If you have difficulty installing or using any of the materials on the companion CD, try the following solutions:

- **Turn off any antivirus software that you may have running.** Installers sometimes mimic virus activity and can make your computer incorrectly believe that it is being infected by a virus. (Be sure to turn the antivirus software back on later.)

- **Close all running programs.** The more programs you're running, the less memory is available to other programs. Installers also typically update files and programs; if you keep other programs running, installation may not work properly.

- **Reference the ReadMe:** Please refer to the ReadMe file located at the root of the CD-ROM for the latest product information at the time of publication.

If you still have trouble with the CD, please call the Customer Care phone number: 800-762-2974. Outside the United States, call 1-317-572-3994. You can also contact Customer Service via the Web at http://support.wiley.com. Wiley Publishing, Inc., will provide technical support only for installation and other general quality-control items; for technical support on an application, consult the program's vendor.

Index

Symbols & Numbers

continued

Wiley Publishing, Inc.
End-User License Agreement

READ THIS. You should carefully read these terms and conditions before opening the software packet(s) included with this book "Book". This is a license agreement "Agreement" between you and Wiley Publishing, Inc. "WPI". By opening the accompanying software packet(s), you acknowledge that you have read and accept the following terms and conditions. If you do not agree and do not want to be bound by such terms and conditions, promptly return the Book and the unopened software packet(s) to the place you obtained them for a full refund.

1. **License Grant.** WPI grants to you (either an individual or entity) a nonexclusive license to use one copy of the enclosed software program(s) (collectively, the "Software") solely for your own personal or business purposes on a single computer (whether a standard computer or a workstation component of a multi-user network). The Software is in use on a computer when it is loaded into temporary memory (RAM) or installed into permanent memory (hard disk, CD-ROM, or other storage device). WPI reserves all rights not expressly granted herein.

2. **Ownership.** WPI is the owner of all right, title, and interest, including copyright, in and to the compilation of the Software recorded on the physical packet included with this Book "Software Media". Copyright to the individual programs recorded on the Software Media is owned by the author or other authorized copyright owner of each program. Ownership of the Software and all proprietary rights relating thereto remain with WPI and its licensers.

3. **Restrictions on Use and Transfer.**

   (a) You may only (i) make one copy of the Software for backup or archival purposes, or (ii) transfer the Software to a single hard disk, provided that you keep the original for backup or archival purposes. You may not (i) rent or lease the Software, (ii) copy or reproduce the Software through a LAN or other network system or through any computer subscriber system or bulletin-board system, or (iii) modify, adapt, or create derivative works based on the Software.

   (b) You may not reverse engineer, decompile, or disassemble the Software. You may transfer the Software and user documentation on a permanent basis, provided that the transferee agrees to accept the terms and conditions of this Agreement and you retain no copies. If the Software is an update or has been updated, any transfer must include the most recent update and all prior versions.

4. **Restrictions on Use of Individual Programs.** You must follow the individual requirements and restrictions detailed for each individual program in the "About the CD" appendix of this Book or on the Software Media. These limitations are also contained in the individual license agreements recorded on the Software Media. These limitations may include a requirement that after using the program for a specified period of time, the user must pay a registration fee or discontinue use. By opening the Software packet(s), you agree to abide by the licenses and restrictions for these individual programs that are detailed in the "About the CD" appendix and/or on the Software Media. None of the material on this Software Media or listed in this Book may ever be redistributed, in original or modified form, for commercial purposes.

5. Limited Warranty.

(a) WPI warrants that the Software and Software Media are free from defects in materials and workmanship under normal use for a period of sixty (60) days from the date of purchase of this Book. If WPI receives notification within the warranty period of defects in materials or workmanship, WPI will replace the defective Software Media.

(b) WPI AND THE AUTHOR(S) OF THE BOOK DISCLAIM ALL OTHER WARRANTIES, EXPRESS OR IMPLIED, INCLUDING WITHOUT LIMITATION IMPLIED WARRANTIES OF MERCHANTABILITY AND FITNESS FOR A PARTICULAR PURPOSE, WITH RESPECT TO THE SOFTWARE, THE PROGRAMS, THE SOURCE CODE CONTAINED THEREIN, AND/OR THE TECHNIQUES DESCRIBED IN THIS BOOK. WPI DOES NOT WARRANT THAT THE FUNCTIONS CONTAINED IN THE SOFTWARE WILL MEET YOUR REQUIREMENTS OR THAT THE OPERATION OF THE SOFTWARE WILL BE ERROR FREE.

(c) This limited warranty gives you specific legal rights, and you may have other rights that vary from jurisdiction to jurisdiction.

6. Remedies.

(a) WPI's entire liability and your exclusive remedy for defects in materials and workmanship shall be limited to replacement of the Software Media, which may be returned to WPI with a copy of your receipt at the following address: Software Media Fulfillment Department, Attn.: *Excel 2007 Formulas,* Wiley Publishing, Inc., 10475 Crosspoint Blvd., Indianapolis, IN 46256, or call 1-800-762-2974. Please allow four to six weeks for delivery. This Limited Warranty is void if failure of the Software Media has resulted from accident, abuse, or misapplication. Any replacement Software Media will be warranted for the remainder of the original warranty period or thirty (30) days, whichever is longer.

(b) In no event shall WPI or the author be liable for any damages whatsoever (including without limitation damages for loss of business profits, business interruption, loss of business information, or any other pecuniary loss) arising from the use of or inability to use the Book or the Software, even if WPI has been advised of the possibility of such damages.

(c) Because some jurisdictions do not allow the exclusion or limitation of liability for consequential or incidental damages, the above limitation or exclusion may not apply to you.

7. U.S. Government Restricted Rights.
Use, duplication, or disclosure of the Software for or on behalf of the United States of America, its agencies and/or instrumentalities "U.S. Government" is subject to restrictions as stated in paragraph (c)(1)(ii) of the Rights in Technical Data and Computer Software clause of DFARS 252.227-7013, or subparagraphs (c) (1) and (2) of the Commercial Computer Software - Restricted Rights clause at FAR 52.227-19, and in similar clauses in the NASA FAR supplement, as applicable.

8. General.
This Agreement constitutes the entire understanding of the parties and revokes and supersedes all prior agreements, oral or written, between them and may not be modified or amended except in a writing signed by both parties hereto that specifically refers to this Agreement. This Agreement shall take precedence over any other documents that may be in conflict herewith. If any one or more provisions contained in this Agreement are held by any court or tribunal to be invalid, illegal, or otherwise unenforceable, each and every other provision shall remain in full force and effect.

Special Offer... Save $30.00!

Power Utility Pak v7

"The Excel tools Microsoft forgot"

A $39.95 value. Yours for only $9.95.

PRO-QUALITY TOOLS

PUP v7 is a handy collection of 60 general purpose Excel utilities, plus 50 new worksheet functions. Download a trial version from the URL at the bottom of this page. If you like it, use this coupon and save $30 on the licensed version.

VBA SOURCE CODE IS AVAILABLE

You can also get the complete VBA source files for only $20.00 more. Learn how the utilities and functions were written, and pick up useful tips and programming techniques in the process. This is a must for all VBA programmers.

PUP v7 is compatible only with Excel 2007. For earlier versions of Excel, use PUP v6.